lonely

West Africa

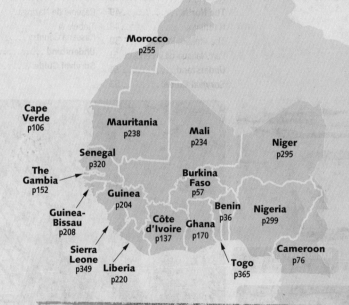

Morocco
p255

Cape Verde
p106

Mauritania
p238

Mali
p234

Niger
p295

Senegal
p320

The Gambia
p152

Burkina Faso
p57

Guinea
p204

Benin
p36

Nigeria
p299

Guinea-Bissau
p208

Côte d'Ivoire
p137

Ghana
p170

Sierra Leone
p349

Liberia
p220

Togo
p365

Cameroon
p76

THIS EDITION WRITTEN AND RESEARCHED BY

Anthony Ham,
Jean-Bernard Carillet, Paul Clammer, Emilie Filou, Nana Luckham,
Tom Masters, Anja Mutić, Caroline Sieg, Kate Thomas,
Vanessa Wruble

PLAN YOUR TRIP

ON THE ROAD

MAURITANIA P238

TAFI ATOME, GHANA P182

BOBO-DIOULASSO, BURKINA FASO P64

SIERPINSKI JACQUES / HEMIS.FR / GETTY IMAGES ©

MAX MILLIGAN / GETTY IMAGES ©

ANTHONY HAM / GETTY IMAGES ©

Contents

ON THE ROAD

CHRISTIAN ASLUND / GETTY IMAGES ©

DAKAR, SENEGAL P321

Contents

SPECIAL FEATURES

Culture & Daily Life

Welcome to West Africa

West Africa has cachet and soul. Home to African landscapes of our imaginations and inhabited by an astonishing diversity of traditional peoples, this is Africa as it once was.

African Landscapes

From the Sahara to tropical rain forests, from volcanic outcrops to stony depressions in the desert's heart, West Africa is an extraordinary sweep of iconic African terrain. Sand dunes of the Sahara yield to the Sahel where human settlements sit on the edge of eternity. A few latitude lines to the south, savannah and woodland take over, building to a crescendo of primeval forest crowding the coast and its pristine beaches. Through it all runs one of Africa's longest rivers, the Niger.

A Musical Soundtrack

West Africa's musical tradition is one of incredible depth and richness. Youssou N'Dour, Tinariwen and other musicians may have been 'discovered' in recent decades, but the region's music is so much more than mere performance. The *griots* of ancient African empires – Mali's master *kora* player Toumani Diabaté is a 71st generation *griot* – bestowed upon West Africa's musicians the gift of storytelling as much as the power to entertain. They do both exceptionally well and their ability to make you dance or learn something new about the region may just rank among your most memorable travel experiences.

African Peoples

The mosaic of peoples who inhabit West Africa is one of the region's most beguiling characteristics. The sheer number of peoples who call the region home will take your breath away. Drawing in a little nearer, you'll discover that traditions survive in West Africa like nowhere else on the continent, revealing themselves in fabulous festivals, irresistible music and the mysterious world of masks and secret societies. These are peoples whose histories are epic and whose daily struggles are similarly so. West Africa is in-your-face, full-volume Lagos or the quiet solitude of an indigo-clad nomad – not to mention everything in between.

Secret Wildlife

You wouldn't come to West Africa in search of an East African–style safari. If you did, you'd be disappointed. And yet there's more to West Africa's wildlife than initially meets the eye. If you look in the right places, there are elephants and primate species in abundance, and big cats stalk the undergrowth. Throw in pygmy hippos and some of the world's best birdwatching and it becomes clear that West Africa is greatly underrated as a wildlife-watching destination. And unlike in East or Southern Africa, you're likely to have whatever you find all to yourself.

Why I Love West Africa

By Anthony Ham

On my first journey into West Africa, I felt like I was visiting another planet, and I loved it. It was the cooling sand beneath my feet as I shared a campfire with Tuareg nomads in the Sahara, or a dawn glimpse of paradise at a bend in the river deep in the Cameroonian rainforest. It was dancing the night away in the bars of Bamako or Dakar, or the silence of the Sahelian night. And no matter how many times I return, I never lose that sense of having wandered into some kind of otherworldly African fairytale.

For more about our authors, see page 520

West Africa

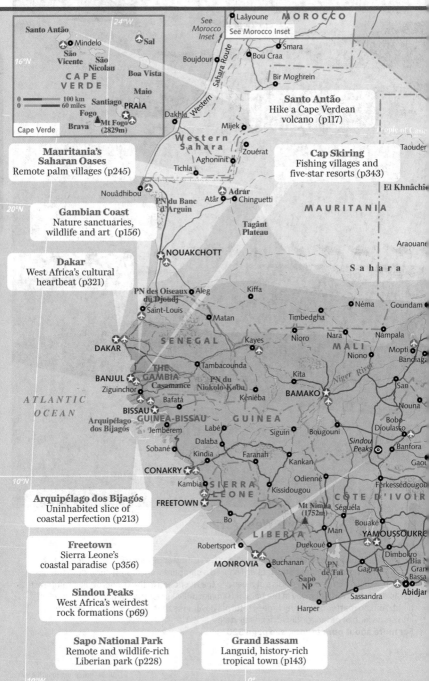

Santo Antão
Santo Antão
Mindelo
São Vicente
São Nicolau
CAPE VERDE
Sal
Boa Vista
Maio
Santiago **PRAIA**
Fogo
Mt Fogo (2829m)
Brava
Cape Verde

0 — 100 km
0 — 60 miles

Santo Antão
Hike a Cape Verdean volcano (p117)

Mauritania's Saharan Oases
Remote palm villages (p245)

Gambian Coast
Nature sanctuaries, wildlife and art (p156)

Dakar
West Africa's cultural heartbeat (p321)

Cap Skiring
Fishing villages and five-star resorts (p343)

Laâyoune MOROCCO
See Morocco Inset
Boujdour Bou Craa Smara
Bir Moghrein
Dakhla
Mijek
Western Sahara
Zouérat
Aghoninit
Tichla
Nouâdhibou Atâr Adrar Chinguetti
PN du Banc d'Arguin
Tagânt Plateau
MAURITANIA
El Khnâchîe
Araouane
NOUAKCHOTT
Sahara
PN des Oiseaux du Djoudj Aleg Kiffa Néma Goundam
Saint-Louis Matan Timbedgha
Nioro Nara Nampala
SENEGAL Kayes Niono MALI Mopti Bandiag
DAKAR Tambacounda Kita San Nouna
BANJUL THE GAMBIA Casamance PN du Niokolo-Koba BAMAKO Bobo-Dioulasso
Ziguinchor Bafatá Kéniéba Banfora
BISSAU GUINEA-BISSAU GUINEA Sindou Peaks Gaot
Arquipélago dos Bijagós Jemberem Labé Siguiri Bougouni
Sobané Dalaba Faranah Kankan Odienné CÔTE D'IVOIR
Kindia Kissidougou Ferkessédougou
CONAKRY Kambia SIERRA LEONE Mt Nimba (1752m) Séguéla Bouaké YAMOUSSOUKRE
FREETOWN Bo Man Dimbokro
LIBERIA Robertsport Duekoué Bia N Gran Bassa
MONROVIA Buchanan Gagnoa Abidjan
Sapo NP PN de Taï
Sassandra
Harper

ATLANTIC OCEAN

Tropic of Canc
Taouder
Niger River

Arquipélago dos Bijagós
Uninhabited slice of coastal perfection (p213)

Freetown
Sierra Leone's coastal paradise (p356)

Sindou Peaks
West Africa's weirdest rock formations (p69)

Sapo National Park
Remote and wildlife-rich Liberian park (p228)

Grand Bassam
Languid, history-rich tropical town (p143)

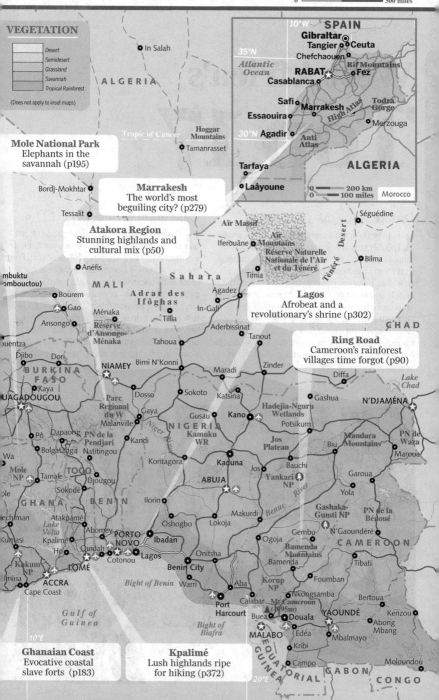

VEGETATION

- Desert
- Semidesert
- Grassland
- Savannah
- Tropical Rainforest

(Does not apply to inset maps)

Mole National Park
Elephants in the savannah (p195)

Marrakesh
The world's most beguiling city? (p279)

Atakora Region
Stunning highlands and cultural mix (p50)

Lagos
Afrobeat and a revolutionary's shrine (p302)

Ring Road
Cameroon's rainforest villages time forgot (p90)

Ghanaian Coast
Evocative coastal slave forts (p183)

Kpalimé
Lush highlands ripe for hiking (p372)

Map labels (main map):
In Salah, ALGERIA, Tropic of Cancer, Hoggar Mountains, Tamanrasset, Bordj-Mokhtar, Tessalit, Aïr Massif, Iferouâne, Aïr Mountains, Réserve Naturelle Nationale de l'Aïr et du Ténéré, Timia, Séguédine, Ténéré Desert, Bilma, Anéfis, Sahara, MALI, Adrar des Ifôghas, Agadez, In-Gall, ...mbuktu (...ombouctou), Bourem, Gao, Ménaka, Ansongo, Réserve d'Ansongo-Ménaka, Tahoua, Aderbissinat, Tanout, CHAD, ...uentza, Djibo, Dori, BURKINA FASO, Kaya, NIAMEY, Birni N'Konni, Maradi, Zinder, Diffa, Gashua, Lake Chad, N'DJAMÉNA, UAGADOUGOU, Dosso, Sokoto, Katsina, Kano, Hadejia-Nguru Wetlands, Potsikum, Mandara Mountains, PN de Waza, Maroua, Pô, Dapaong, Parc Regional du W, Gaya, Gusau, NIGERIA, Kamuku WR, Jos Plateau, Biu, Bolgatanga, PN de la Pendjari, Malanville, Kandi, Niger, Wa, Natitingou, Kontagora, Kaduna, Jos, Bauchi, Yankari NP, Garoua, Mole NP, Tamale, Djougou, ABUJA, Yola, TOGO, Sokodé, BENIN, Ilorin, Makurdi, Benue River, Gashaka-Gumti NP, PN de la Bénoué, N'Gaoundéré, GHANA, ...echiman, Atakpamé, Lake Volta, Abomey, PORTO NOVO, Oshogbo, Lokoja, Ogoja, Gembu, Bamenda Mountains, CAMEROON, Tibati, ...umasi, Kpalimé, Ho, Ouidah, Cotonou, Ibadan, Onitsha, Bamenda, Fomban, Kakum NP, ...lmina, LOMÉ, Lagos, Benin City, Korup NP, Nkongsamba, Bertoua, ACCRA, Cape Coast, Bight of Benin, Warri, Aba, Calabar, Mt Cameroon (4095m), Douala, Kenzou, Gulf of Guinea, Port Harcourt, Buea, Abong Mbang, MALABO, Edéa, Mbalmayo, YAOUNDÉ, Bight of Biafra, EQUATORIAL GUINEA, Kribi, Moloundou, GABON, Campo, CONGO

Inset map (Morocco):
SPAIN, Gibraltar, Tangier, Ceuta, Chefchaouen, Rif Mountains, Atlantic Ocean, RABAT, Casablanca, Fez, Safi, Marrakesh, High Atlas, Todra Gorge, Essaouira, Merzouga, Agadir, Anti Atlas, ALGERIA, Tarfaya, Laâyoune, Morocco

Scale bars: 0–500 km / 0–300 miles; 0–200 km / 0–100 miles

West Africa's
Top 17

Dakar, Senegal

1 Hit West Africa's trendiest nightlife venues (p329) and swing your hips to *mbalax*, the mix of Cuban beats and traditional drumming that forms the heart and soul of the Senegalese music scene. Relax with a lazy day at the beach and feast on fresh-off-the-boat seafood, or explore the workshops of Senegal's most promising artists at the Village des Arts (p321). Finally, climb up one of Dakar's 'breasts' (p325) to contemplate the controversial, socialist-style African Renaissance monument and take in sweeping views across the city. Below: Drummers and dancer, Dakar

Casamance, Senegal

2 Take a *pirogue* (traditional canoe) from busy fishing village Elinkine over to Île de Karabane (p343). Visit this 19th century French trading station's Breton-style church, complete with ancient pews, or sip palm wine on its peaceful beaches. Venture out on a fishing or kayaking expedition from Cap Skiring (p343), followed by a dose of live music and dancing barefoot with abandon under a star-filled sky, before checking into a room with a view of the waves gently lapping at the sand.

Wildlife & Art, Gambian Coast

3 Gambia's Atlantic Coast (p156) is peppered with oodles of flashy resorts, but if you look a little further you'll also encounter superb nature sanctuaries like Bijilo Forest Park, where you can observe monkeys, monitor lizards and over 100 bird species; and the Kachikally Crocodile Pool, where you can discover why crocodiles are considered sacred. Pick up a new painting to grace your wall at home and discuss the local modern-art scene with painters and sculptors at the African Living Art Centre.

Below: Hand-painted textile, The Gambia

Beaches of Freetown, Sierra Leone

4 Freetown's long peninsula is lined with sun-drenched beaches (p356) that you'll find hard to leave. Begin with the famous River No 2 – the home of fresh barracuda and breeze-blown nights – and when high tide hits, boat across to Tokeh Sands, probably the most spectacular of them all. Sussex Beach and John Obey Beach both offer special – yet wildly different – dining experiences, while Whale Bay and Black Johnson Beach will take you off that beaten track.

SETH LAZAR / ALAMY ©

MAX MILLIGAN / GETTY IMAGES ©

Saharan Oases, Mauritania

5 Mauritania's Adrar region (p245) is where the Sahara desert gets serious – rocky escarpments and grand canyons give way to an ocean of sand, dotted with palm-fringed oases. Start at the gateway town of Atâr and head into the heart of the desert by 4WD or camel, making sure to take in the remote caravan towns of Chinguetti, Ouadâne and Terjît, part of the ancient network of trade and cultural exchange that stitched the desert together from Timbuktu in the south to Marrakesh in the north. Above: Terjît

Ring Road, Cameroon

6 Deep in Cameroon's Anglophone northwest, the so-called Ring Road (p90) is a grassland area of unparalleled natural beauty, boasting rushing rivers, soaring hilltops, lush forests and small, tradition-al *fondoms* (kingdoms ruled by traditional chiefs known as *fons*) where foreigners are rarely seen. The area is great for hiking, though it's best explored with your own wheels, as local public transport is extremely in-frequent. Be aware that the 'ring road' itself is most of the time little more than a dirt track – don't attempt it in the rainy season! Top right: Fon's Palace, Bafut

Ghana's Slave Forts

7 No matter how well versed you are with the history of the slave trade, nothing can prepare you for the experience of visit-ing Ghana's slave forts. Standing in the damp dun-geons or being shut in the pitch-black punishment cells will chill your blood, and the wreaths and mes-sages left by those whose forebears went through the ordeal are poignant. Cape Coast Castle (p183) and St George's Castle (p186) are the two largest and best-preserved forts, but there are many smaller ones along the coast, too, which tell the same sorry tale. Above: St George's Castle

SETH LAZAR / ALAMY ©

Kpalimé, Togo

8 Itchy feet? Consider exploring the Kpalimé area (p372), which offers lots of hiking opportunities amid stunning scenery. With its lush forested hills, numerous waterfalls and profusion of butterflies, it is a walking heaven, and most walks are suitable for all levels of fitness. Tackle Mt Agou (986m) or Mt Klouto (710m) with a knowledgeable local guide, who'll give you the lowdown on local fauna and flora and show you the highlights.

Sindou Peaks, Burkina Faso

9 Nature's work of art, the otherworldly rock formations of Sindou Peaks (p69) are a sight to behold. Cast against the darkening sky of a brewing storm or the lush paddy fields of the plains below, they are one of Burkina's great signature landscapes. Trekking is the best way to explore this natural wonder, although there will be plenty of wonderful photo opportunities on the drive there. Local guides organise sunset breakfasts at a particularly scenic spot, an experience that will likely be the highlight of your trip. Top right: Gecko

Hiking in Santo Antão, Cape Verde

10 From long lonely walks through lush valleys to strenuous treks along craggy peaks and remote ravines, the dramatic island of Santo Antão (p117) is a hiker's paradise. Set aside at least three full days; first tackle its classic hikes, like the sharp descent along the cobbled path from the Cova crater to Paúl valley, and then set out to explore the island's uncharted western section. Get a good map, stock up on local advice and hire a guide for the more demanding treks. Above: Seafront path near Fontainhas

Marrakesh, Morocco

11 Marrakesh has been Morocco's top draw for several centuries now, and it's easy to see why. There's a heady mix of Arab and Berber culture here, and at the heart of its traditional medina is the Djemaa el-Fna (p279) – a square full of vibrant street entertainers, food vendors and snake charmers every night of the year. Its winding alleys (and carpet sellers) could divert you for weeks, while its gardens and international restaurants can recharge your batteries. Below: People praying in the medina

Mole National Park, Ghana

12 West Africa is no match for East and Southern Africa's national parks but it does have more wildlife than many imagine. Mole (p195) is a prime example of this stunning diversity: antelopes, warthogs, elephants, monkeys, crocodiles and thousands of birds are just some of the animals you'll be able to see, and all at a fraction of the cost of a 'traditional' safari. The park's hotel even has a pool, perfect to while away the midday hours between morning walking safaris and afternoon wildlife drives. Bottom: Olive baboons

Atakora Region, Benin

13 Northwestern Benin is dominated by the rugged landscapes of the Atakora mountains (p50). There's a lot to love about this area: the captivating culture and traditions of the animist Betama-ribé people, the eye-catching architecture of the *tata somba* houses (round-tiered huts), and utterly beautiful hills that offer plenty of breathtaking panoramas. It's still a secretive world with a peculiar appeal, and it begs exploration. You can base yourself in Natitingou (p49) or, even better, stay in villages. Below: An Atakoran village

New Afrika Shrine, Nigeria

14 With steamy dancers, Afrobeat, and revolutionary politics, there's nothing like the New Afrika Shrine (p304) in Lagos. Literally a shrine, this night club is dedicated to the legacy of Africa's musical genius, the founder of Afrobeat, the oft-imprisoned revolutionary, and Nigeria's conscience, Fela Anikulapo Kuti. He never stopped fighting the powers of imperialism, colonialism and racism with music as his weapon. Now his sons perform with a force and style of their own, blowing minds politically and musically. Bottom: Kuti's dancers

AURORA PHOTOS / ALAMY ©

TRAVELINK / GETTY IMAGES ©

Arquipélago dos Bijagós, Guinea-Bissau

15 Like Atlantis or Treasure Island, the Bijagós (p213) is such a magical archipelago that you may wonder if it's fictional. Its 88 islands fall away from the mainland in a constellation that would take light years to navigate. With two or three weeks, you can explore a tiny percentage of the archipelago, starting in Ilha de Bubaque or Bolama. From there, you might head to Ilha de Orango to spot the salty sea hippos, or throw your luggage into a speedboat and make for the luxury lodges on Ilha de Kere or Rubane. Above: Canhabaque island

Sapo National Park, Liberia

16 For years, Liberia's Sapo National Park (p228) – baked between skinny red roads and clandestine gold mines – was off-limits to travellers. Now its towering trees, rare flora and unusual inhabitants – like the secretive pygmy hippo – are ready to be discovered. But that doesn't mean a trip to Sapo is easy. Prepare to tackle Liberia's bumpiest roads on the 12-hour drive there, where you'll have to bed down beneath the stars, until plans to build an ecolodge come to fruition. Top right: Jalay's Town, the gateway to Sapo National Park

Grand Bassam, Côte d'Ivoire

17 Arty Grand Bassam (p143) is everything its neighbour Abidjan is not: gentle, quiet and unassuming. Yet it's teeming with creative endeavours, from local street-art initiatives to wild horseback rides on golden sands. It makes an easy weekend trip from the economic capital – only 40 minutes away by car, you'll have plenty of time to take in the old French architecture, art market and cosy terrace restaurants.

Need to Know

For more information, see Survival Guide (p449)

Currency
West African CFA franc (eight countries), nine other currencies

Language
French, English, hundreds of local languages

Money
ATMs widespread; Visa widely used, MasterCard less so

Visas
Vary between countries, but best arranged before departure

Mobile Phone
Local SIM cards widely available; European and Australian phones work, others should be set to roaming

Time
All on GMT/UTC except Cape Verde (one hour behind), and Benin, Cameroon, Niger and Nigeria (all one hour ahead)

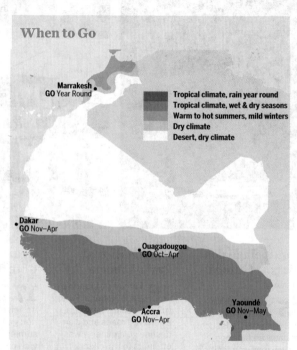

When to Go

Marrakesh
GO Year Round

Tropical climate, rain year round
Tropical climate, wet & dry seasons
Warm to hot summers, mild winters
Dry climate
Desert, dry climate

Dakar
GO Nov–Apr

Ouagadougou
GO Oct–Apr

Accra
GO Nov–Apr

Yaoundé
GO Nov–May

High Season
(Nov–Mar)

➡ Generally cooler temperatures and dry weather make getting around easy

➡ Atlantic coast beaches packed with European sunbathers December to March

➡ December and January prime time for trekking

Shoulder
(Apr–May)

➡ Temperatures begin to rise across the Sahel

➡ May can be unbearably hot in the Sahara

➡ Rains can arrive in May and humidity very high along the coast

Low Season
(Jun–Oct)

➡ High humidity and heavy rains in coastal countries and many roads impassable

➡ Many wildlife reserves closed to visitors and tracks impassable

➡ Extreme temperatures in the Sahara and Sahel

Useful Websites

Lonely Planet (www.lonely planet.com) Destination information, hotel bookings, traveller forum and more.

Ecowas (www.ecowas.int) The official site of the Economic Community of West African States (Ecowas) with a few useful links.

Sahara Overland (www.sahara-overland.com) The best practical guide for travellers to the Sahara, with useful forums, route information and book reviews.

Travel Africa (www.travel africamag.com) Excellent print magazine on Africa; articles on West Africa thinly scattered.

Africa Geographic (www .africageographic.com) Nature-focused Africa mag with good wildlife and birdwatching.

Important Numbers

To dial listings in this book from outside the region, dial your international access code (☑00), each country's country code, then the area code (if applicable), then the number. To dial international numbers from Cape Verde dial ☑0 and from Nigeria dial ☑009.

Currencies

Benin, Burkina Faso, Cameroon, Côte d'Ivoire, Guinea-Bissau, Mali, Niger, Senegal and Togo (West African Franc; CFA)

Cape Verde (escudo; CVE)

The Gambia (dalasi; D)

Ghana (cedi; C)

Guinea (Guinean franc; GF)

Liberia (Liberian dollar; L$)

Mauritania (ouguiya; UM)

Nigeria (naira; N)

Sierra Leone (Leone; Le)

Daily Costs

Budget: less than US$40

➡ If you're staying in the most basic accommodation, eating only local food and getting around on local transport, count on spending a minimum of US$20 per day, although US$25 to US$35 is more manageable.

Midrange: US$40–$80

➡ Those looking for more comfort and preferring to eat in reasonable restaurants could get by on US$40, but US$70 is a more reasonable budget.

Top End: more than US$80

➡ At the upper end, the sky's the limit. Top-end hotels start at around US$80 and car rental averages at least US$100 per day and sometimes more, plus petrol.

Opening Hours

The following are a guide only with great variation across the region.

Banks 8am-noon or 1pm Monday to Thursday and Saturday (Muslim countries) or 9am-3pm Monday to Friday and 9am-noon Saturday elsewhere

Restaurants noon-3pm and 6.30-11pm

Shops 8am-noon and 3-5pm Monday to Friday, 8am-noon Saturday or 9am-5pm or 6pm Monday to Saturday; in Muslim areas, markets are quiet on Friday, and busier on Sunday

Arriving in West Africa

Murtala Mohammed International Airport (Lagos; p306) No public transport from international terminal; licensed airport taxis (N4000) can be booked from arrivals hall; get local to meet you.

Mohammed V International Airport (Casablanca; p292) Trains run 6am to midnight (Dh35, 35 minutes) to Casa Voyageurs; taxi to/from city centre (Dh250; 30 to 60 minutes)

Léopold Sédar Senghor International Airport (Dakar; p347) No public transport; taxis outside arrivals hall cost CFA4000 to city centre.

Getting Around

Air Major capitals are reasonably well connected by flights within West Africa; other smaller capitals may require inconvenient connections. Royal Air Maroc connects most major cities with Casablanca.

Bus & Bush Taxi Often the only option in rural areas, bush taxis in varying stages of disrepair leave when full; buses connect major cities with those of neighbouring countries.

Car Reasonable road infrastructure connects major cities; roads deteriorate elsewhere, and are sometimes impassable after rains; car rental prices comparable to Europe.

Train Trains operate in Benin, Burkina Faso, Cameroon, Côte d'Ivoire, Ghana, Mali, Mauritania, Nigeria, Senegal and Togo. International services connect Dakar and Bamako, and, depending on the security situation, Ouagadougou and Abidjan.

For much more on getting around, see p467

If You Like...

Wildlife

West Africa is an underrated wildlife destination and its little-known national parks host more African megafauna than they do tourists. They can be difficult to reach, but worth it for sheer isolation.

Mole National Park, Ghana Almost 100 mammal species, savannah and good for elephants. (p195)

Parc National de la Pendjari, Benin Big cats and elephants in one of West Africa's best parks. (p51)

Parc National de Niokolo-Koba, Senegal Elephants, lions, crocs and hippos with river tours and an accessible waterhole. (p340)

Kakum National Park, Ghana Rich birdlife, a canopy walk but better if you venture deeper. (p186)

Parc National de Waza, Cameroon Elephants, giraffes and lions in Cameroon's most accessible park. (p99)

Ebodjé & Parc National de Campo-Ma'an, Cameroon Sea turtles and nascent ecotourism projects. (p95)

Tiwai Island, Sierra Leone Rare pygmy hippos, 11 primate species in Sierra Leone's showcase sanctuary. (p359)

Réserve de Nazinga, Burkina Faso Some of the best elephant-watching in West Africa (p70)

Beaches

From Morocco to Cameroon, the West African coast includes some of the continent's most pristine stretches of sand. Whether you opt for a popular resort or a palm-fringed beach all your own, it's all here.

Ebodjé, Cameroon Less known than nearby Kribi but postcard-perfect with ecotourism possibilities. (p95)

Akwidaa, Ghana Wonderfully long stretch of white sand with a fine tropical hinterland. (p189)

Busua, Ghana Backpackers and volunteers, great surf and fishing villages are an irresistible combination. (p188)

Arquipélago dos Bijagós, Guinea-Bissau A prime candidate for paradise undiscovered with islands, mangroves and turquoise waters. (p213)

Robertsport, Liberia A cult classic for surfers and a world-class beach destination in waiting. (p227)

Freetown Peninsula, Sierra Leone Fabulous Freetown beaches with whale-watching a possibility. (p356)

Maio, Cape Verde Typically pretty Cape Verde beach but usually with more untramelled sand than elsewhere. (p128)

Cap Skiring, Senegal First-class, all-inclusive beach resort. (p343)

Untouched Landscapes

West Africa's wilderness areas rank among Africa's best-kept secrets, including extraordinary seas of Saharan sand, the offshore archipelagos of Guinea-Bissau and rainforests from Sierra Leone to Cameroon.

Erg Chigaga, Morocco One of the most beautiful set of sand dunes in the Sahara. (p286)

Arquipélago dos Bijagós, Guinea-Bissau One of the world's most spectacular chains of offshore islands, with endangered wildlife. (p213)

Sindou Peaks, Burkina Faso Rock formations that could just be the prettiest place in the Sahel. (p69)

Outamba-Kilimi National Park, Sierra Leone Remote savannah with dense rainforest. (p359)

Siné-Saloum Delta, Senegal Splendid network of mangroves best explored in a wooden canoe. (p334)

Sapo National Park, Liberia Primary rainforest rich in wildlife

and far from well-trodden trails. (p228)

Parc National de Campo-Ma'an, Cameroon A precursor to the vast rain forests of Central Africa. (p95)

Slavery's Tragic Story

A visit to the sites where West Africa's slaves left the continent's shores for the last time is one of the region's most poignant experiences. It's an extraordinary, evocative story.

Cape Coast Castle, Ghana Grim former slave cells and fascinating guided tours. (p183)

St George's Castle, Elmina, Ghana Ire dungeons, punishment cells and a Door of No Return. (p186)

National Museum, Ghana An evocative scene-setting exhibition as you head for the coastal forts and castles. (p175)

Île de Gorée, Senegal Maison des Esclaves, a grim former holding centre for slaves. (p333)

Ouidah, Benin A well-marked Route des Esclaves and a moving 'Point of No Return' memorial. (p45)

Jufureh & James Island, The Gambia Slaving museum, fort and the origins of Alex Haley's *Roots*. (p165)

Bunce Island, Sierra Leone A major shipping port for slaves; nearby Freetown was founded as a refuge for ex-slaves. (p358)

West African Music

West Africa moves to one of the most alluring beats on the planet, from soulful Cape Verdean mornas to

(Above) A band with traditional instruments, Banjul (p154), The Gambia
(Below) Surfers in Robertsport (p227), Liberia

frenetic Ghanian and Nigerian Highlife.

+233, Accra, Ghana One of the region's best venues with live acts from all over the continent turning up. (p179)

Bobo-Dioulasso, Burkina Faso This languid Burkina town is the epicentre of the country's music industry. Try Le Samanké, Les Bambous or Le Bois d'Ebène. (p64)

Mognori, Ghana Traditional drumming and dance performances in Ghana's north with an emphasis on participation. (p195)

Dakar, Senegal Get down and groove to Senegal's *mbalax*, a blend of Cuban sounds and traditional drum beats. Try Just 4 U. (p321)

Mindelo, Cape Verde A wonderful mix of Portuguese melancholy with sultry Cape Verdean sounds. (p112)

Moroccan Festivals Don't miss the Fez Festival of World Sacred Music and Essaouira's Gnaoua & World Music Festival (both in June). (p290)

Unesco World Heritage Sites

Tracking down even some of West Africa's more than 40 Unesco World Heritage Sites can provide an evocative focal point for your exploration of the region; check online for the full list.

Fez and Marrakesh, Morocco North Africa's finest medinas and the essence of Morocco's charm. (p273 and p279)

Royal palaces of Abomey, Benin Fabulous bas reliefs, tapestries and a museum mark ancient Dahomey. (p48)

Saint-Louis, Senegal Decaying colonial architecture. (p337)

Ashanti traditional buildings, Kumasi, Ghana The heartland of one of West Africa's most enlightened precolonial civilisations. (p189)

Koutammakou, Togo Homeland of the Batammariba, with picturesque mountain scenery and unusual architecture. (p375)

Old Saharan towns, Mauritania The *ksour* (fortified strongholds) of Ouadâne, Chinguetti and Oualâta are among the Sahara's prettiest towns. (p245)

Osun Sacred Forest & Groves, Nigeria At once tranquil oasis and centre of Yoruban spirituality; a potent combination. (p310)

Volubilis, Morocco West Africa's largest and best-preserved city of Roman ruins. (p279)

Hiking

From the mountains of Morocco to the soul-filled hikes south of the Sahara, these trails take you deep into an extraordinary human and natural landscape.

Atlas Mountains, Morocco High-altitude trekking through the land of the Berbers in Jebel Toubkal and the southern gorges. (p284)

Sindou Peaks, Burkina Faso Otherworldly rock formations and intriguing cultural backdrop in Burkina's southwest. (p69)

Kpalimé, Togo Outstanding hiking amid lush, forested hills in the heart of coffee country. (p372)

Mt Cameroon Two- to three-day hike to the summit of West Africa's highest peak. (p87)

Mandara Mountains, Cameroon Extraordinary postvolcanic landscapes and timeless villages along the trails. (p99)

Santo Antão, Cape Verde Spectacular canyons, cloud-soaked peaks and vertigo-inspiring drops. (p117)

Amedzofe, Ghana Fabulous, little-known trails with a waterfall in Ghana's east. (p182)

Architecture

The breadth of architectural styles on offer in West Africa is astounding – mud-brick mosques, painted houses, stilt villages, colonial-era forts and serpentine medinas are just the start.

Fez el-Bali, Morocco Soaring mosques and exquisitely decorated *medersas* in a tangle of medieval lanes. (p273)

Aït Benhaddou, Morocco Arguably the finest kasbah in North Africa and a favourite of filmmakers the world over. (p285)

Grande Mosquée, Bobo-Dioulasso, Burkina Faso One of West Africa's most beautiful mud-built mosques. (p64)

Tiébélé, Burkina Faso Stunningly decorated painted traditional windowless homes of the Gourounsi people. (p71)

Koutammakou, Togo Fortified mud-brick homes that resemble castles in northern Togo. (p375)

Ganvié, Benin Fishing villages consisting largely of bamboo huts built high on stilts above Lake Nokoué. (p44)

Cape Coast Castle, Ghana Part of a chain of coastal, colonial-era forts steeped in history. (p183)

Ring Road and Foumban, Cameroon Traditional Ring Road thatched villages and Foumban's muscular royal palace. (p90)

Yaoundé, Cameroon A surfeit of fine 1960s and 1970s modernist African structures. (p77)

Month by Month

TOP EVENTS

Mardi Gras, March

Fespaco film festival, February/March

Fêtes des Masques, February

Voodoo Festival, January

Festival of World Sacred Music, June/July

January

January is the height of West Africa's high season, with cooler, dry weather and a host of fine festivals; one downside can be the early arrival of the dust-laden harmattan winds late in the month.

 Voodoo Festival

Held on 10 January across Benin; the celebrations in the voodoo heartland around Ouidah are the largest and most exuberant.

Festival Sur Le Niger

Mali's premier music festival (www.festivalsegou.org) draws a cast of world-renowned local and international musicians to the Niger riverbank in Ségou in late January or early February.

Race to the Summit

In late January/early February Cameroonian and international athletes gather for the Race of Hope to the summit of Mt Cameroon, West Africa's highest peak.

February

February is high season and accommodation should be booked well in advance. The relatively cool, dry weather makes for good hiking and it's the last month where you would sensibly head into the Sahel or Sahara.

Carnival

West Africa's former Portuguese colonies celebrate Carnival (also spelled Carnaval) with infectious zeal. Bissau – with its Latin-style street festival with masks, parties and parades – or Cape Verde are the places to be, while Porto Novo in Benin also gets into the spirit. It's sometimes in January, sometimes March.

Fêtes des Masques

Held in the villages around Man in western Côte d'Ivoire, the region's most significant mask festival brings together a great variety of masks and dances from the area.

Fespaco

Africa's premier film festival (www.fespaco-bf.net) is held in February and/or March in Ouagadougou in Burkina Faso in odd years. Cinemas across the city screen African films with a prestigious awards ceremony.

Argungu Fishing Festival

This fantastic fishing and culture festival takes place on the banks of the Sokoto River in Nigeria's north. It's celebrated with traditional music performances, sports and a massive regional market.

March

March can be a bit hit or miss, although it's still generally considered high season. Temperatures are warming up, the harmattan winds are usually blowing but at least one festival is worth sticking around for.

Mardi Gras

Cape Verde can feel like Rio during the Mardi Gras, which takes place 40 days before Easter. It's a sexy, spectacular carnival-type celebration with street parades, especially in Mindelo.

April

By now, much of the Sahel and Sahara are too hot for comfort and the harmattan is a staple throughout the month. The humidity along the coast and hinterland is starting to get uncomfortable.

Jazz à Ouaga

An established fixture on West Africa's musical circuit, this fine festival (www.jazz-ouaga.org) traverses jazz, Afrobeat, soul and blues with some respected regional names in attendance.

Midnight Hijinks

Côte d'Ivoire's Fête du Dipri, held in Gomon, 100km northwest of Abidjan, sees naked women and children carry out midnight rites to rid the village of evil incantations.

May

Unbearably hot in the Sahara, unbearably humid elsewhere – it's invariably a relief when the rains arrive. Few festivals enliven the month, but Dakar hosts a notable exception.

Art Biennale

In even years, in May or sometimes June, Dakar hosts the Dak'Art Biennale, which is easily West Africa's premier arts festival. In addition to the main exhibitions, there's some fabulous fringe stuff happening.

Saint-Louis Jazz Festival

Hands-down the most internationally renowned festival in West Africa, attracting major performers to this sexy, Unesco Heritage–designated colonial town.

Gambian Roots

The biannual Roots International Festival (www.rootsgambia.gm) celebrates the culture of the Gambia and its slaving history with music workshops, carnival parades and performances by local ethnic groups in late May and early June.

June

There are few reasons to visit the region at this time with the rains well and truly underway. The exception is Morocco, which starts to see the annual influx of summer visitors from Europe. Ramadan will take place in June in 2014 and 2015.

Gnaoua & World Music Festival

Held on the third weekend in June in Essaouira, this four-day musical extravaganza (www.festival-gnaoua.net/en) features international, national and local performers as well as a series of art exhibitions.

Festival of World Sacred Music

World-renowned festival (www.fesfestival.com) that is based on the pluralism of Moroccan Sufism and has in recent years attracted international stars such as Patti Smith, Youssou N'Dour and Salif Keita. It

sometimes spills over into July.

July

Rain is heavy south of the Sahara, but the festivals are aimed at a local audience. In Morocco, Europeans flood the country and accommodation prices can be high and availability low.

Harvest Festival

On the first Tuesday in July, Elmina (Ghana) hosts the colourful Bakatue Festival, a joyous harvest thanksgiving feast. One of its highlights is watching the priest in the harbour waters casting a net to lift a ban on fishing in the lagoon.

Fire Festival

In the heat of Tamale in Ghana, the Dagomba Fire Festival commemorates the local legend whereby a chief was overjoyed to find his missing son asleep under a tree. Angry that the tree had hidden his son, he punished it by having it burnt.

Wrestling Festival

In Togo's north, watch out for Evala, the coming-of-age and wrestling festival in the Kabyé region around Kara.

August

Europeans flock to Morocco and Cape Verde; for the latter you'd generally need to book months in advance. Elsewhere, the rains and humidity make this a difficult time for travelling.

Cape Verde Music

Every August, Mindelo's Festival de Música in Cape Verde attracts musicians of all styles from around the islands and way beyond. It's wonderful fun with a three-day extravaganza of singing, dancing and partying.

Panafest

Ghana's Cape Coast hosts the biennial Pan-African Historical Theatre Festival (Panafest; www.panafest ghana.org) with a focus on African contemporary and traditional arts, including music, dance, fashion and theatre. Its centrepiece is a moving candlelit emancipation ceremony to honour African slaves.

Osun Festival

With nary a tourist in sight, the Osun Festival takes place in Oshogbo, 86km northeast of Ibadan in Nigeria, on the last Friday in August. It has music, dancing and sacrifices, and is a highlight of the Yoruba cultural and spiritual year.

September

The rains should be easing off and minor roads across the region may soon be passable once again, although this can vary from region to region. It's a lovely time to visit Morocco, with smaller crowds and milder temperatures.

Cape Coast Carnival

Cape Coast's Fetu Afahye Festival is a raucous celebration on the first Saturday of September. The main ritual event is the slaughter of a cow for the gods.

La Cure Salée

Niger's world-famous annual celebration by Fula herders features a male beauty contest and camel races, near In-Gall. It usually occurs in the first half of September, but like most Saharan festivals it depends on the prevailing security situation.

Kano Durbar & Tabaski

West Africa's most colourful Tabaski celebrations are those in Kano where there are cavalry processions and high ceremony. Tabaski, which takes place 69 days after Ramadan, is widely celebrated in Muslim areas, especially Niger and Cameroon.

Ashanti Festivals

Coinciding with the yam harvest season, the Adae Kese Festival in Ghana celebrates the glorious Ashanti past and involves ritual purifications of the ancestral burial shrines.

October

October can be a good month for travelling in the region – clear, post-rain skies make for good visibility and the high-season crowds have yet to arrive. Temperatures can be decidedly chilly in Morocco, especially in the High Atlas.

Artisans in Ouagadougou

In even-numbered years Ouagadougou hosts the Salon International de l'Artisanat de Ouagadougou (www.siao.bf), which attracts artisans and vendors from all over the continent.

November

High season has just begun but the beginning of the month can be surprisingly quiet. Night-time temperatures in desert regions can drop close to zero, while there's a chill in the air, too, in Morocco's north.

Grand Bassam Carnival

Close to Abidjan in Côte d'Ivoire, Grand Bassam hosts the Fête de l'Abissa (www.abissafestivale.com) in October or November. Over the course of a week, the N'Zima people honour their dead and publicly exorcise evil spirits with big street parties and men dressed in drag.

December

High season is very much underway south of the Sahara, and you should make accommodation bookings months in advance; beach areas are particularly busy with sun-starved Europeans. Weather mild and dry.

Igue Festival

Also called the Ewere Festival, this colourful seven-day festival in Benin City, Nigeria, in the first half of the month, showcases traditional dances, mock battles and a procession to the palace to reaffirm local loyalty to the *oba* (king).

Itineraries

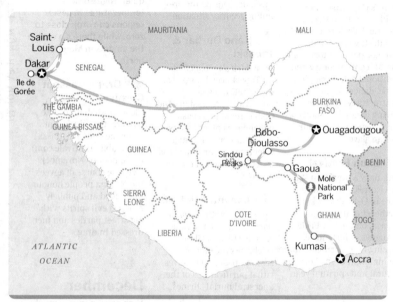

 Best of the West

If you're wondering why Francophone Africa gets under the skin, begin in cosmopolitan **Dakar** (p321), in particular visiting the outstanding **Musée Théodore Monod** (p321) by day then diving into the city's vibrant nightlife after dark. After excursions to the World Heritage–listed architecture of **Saint-Louis** (p337) and offshore to tranquil **Île de Gorée** (p333), fly to **Ouagadougou** (p60) in Burkina Faso. One of West Africa's more agreeable cities, Ouaga has excellent places to stay and eat as well as a happening cultural scene. Take a bus to languid **Bobo-Dioulasso** (p64) and then continue on to the otherworldly **Sindou Peaks** (p69), one of West Africa's most remarkable landscapes. Travel through **Gaoua** (p69) in the heart of Lobi Country then cross the border into northern Ghana and enjoy some of West Africa's best wildlife-watching at **Mole National Park** (p195). Depending on how long you linger, there should be just enough time to stop off in **Kumasi** (p189) to absorb a little Ashanti culture en route to buzzing **Accra** (p171).

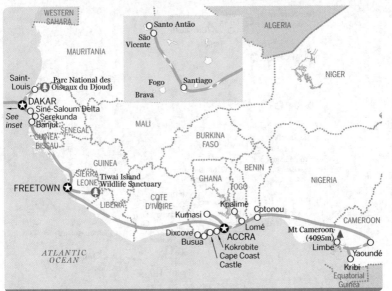

 Atlantic Odyssey

From the arid coastlines of the northwest to the palm-fringed tropics of Cameroon, West Africa's coastline has it all. Senegal's capital **Dakar** (p321), with its African sophistication and role as regional air hub, serves both as a starting point and a base for the first part of your journey. To the north, **Saint-Louis** (p337) is like stepping back into precolonial Africa. Other Senegalese excursions include enjoying some of Africa's best birdwatching in the **Parc National des Oiseaux du Djoudj** (p340) and drifting through the **Siné-Saloum Delta** (p334). From Dakar, fly to the Cape Verde islands with their soulful musical soundtrack, unspoiled beaches, mountainous interior and laid-back locals; **Santiago** (p107), **São Vicente** (p111) and **Santo Antão** (p117) are particularly beautiful. Returning to Dakar, head south to The Gambia, which may be small, but its beaches, especially those around **Serekunda** (p156), make a good (English-speaking) rest stop for taking time out from the African road. From **Banjul** (p154), consider flying to **Freetown** (p350) in Sierra Leone – the nearby beaches are beautiful and utterly undeveloped. Attractions such as **Tiwai Island Wildlife Sanctuary** (p359) with its fabulous wildlife concentrations should not be missed.

You could continue along the coast through Liberia and Côte d'Ivoire, but most travellers fly over them to agreeable **Accra** (p171) in Ghana. From there excursions to the old coastal forts, **Cape Coast Castle** (p183) and stunning beaches at **Kokrobite** (p183), **Busua** (p188) and **Dixcove** (p188) never disappoint. Don't fail to detour north to **Kumasi** (p189) in the Ashanti heartland. There's plenty of onward transport to the fascinating markets and fine museum of **Lomé** (p367), and don't miss an inland hiking detour around **Kpalimé** (p372). Not far away is Benin, with Ouidah, the evocative former slaving port and home of voodoo, the history-rich town of Abomey and the stilt-villages of Ganvié. **Cotonou** (p38) has all the steamy appeal of the tropics; from here fly to **Yaoundé** (p77) in Cameroon, which has a distinctive Central African feel. **Limbe** (p87) has distinctive black-sand beaches and sits in the shadow of **Mt Cameroon** (p87), West Africa's highest peak. **Kribi** (p93), an idyllic tropical beach, is the perfect place to laze on the sand and consider just how far you've travelled.

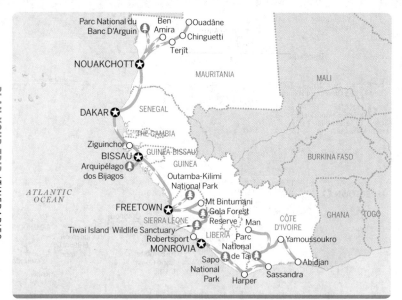

Unknown West Africa

The westernmost extremity of Africa's bulge has, until recently, been off-limits to travellers. But while peace has come, the same can't be said for tourists – you could have these destinations all to yourself. Begin in **Nouakchott** (p239), the dry-as-dust capital of Mauritania. The Mauritanian Sahara is one of the safest corners of the world's largest desert and the three oases – **Chinguetti** (p247), **Terjît** (p246) and **Ouadâne** (p247)– are everything you dreamed the Sahara would be. **Ben Amira** (p246) and the birdwatcher's paradise of **Parc National du Banc D'Arguin** (p245) are other worthy detours. Across the border in Senegal, pass through **Dakar** (p321) to catch the ferry to **Ziguinchor** (p341), capital of Casamance, home to fine beaches, labyrinthine river systems and lush forests. Guinea-Bissau has a village-like capital, **Bissau** (p209). The **Arquipélago dos Bijagos** (p213) is isolated, rich in wildlife and like nowhere else on the coast – it could just be West Africa's most pristine slice of paradise.

Continuing along the coast, pass through Guinea en route to Sierra Leone. After lingering in **Freetown** (p350) and the nearby beaches, head inland to remote **Mt Bintumani** (p358) and the unknown gems of **Outamba-Kilimi National Park** (p359) – which will call to mind Graham Greene's 1930s exploration of inland Sierra Leone – and **Gola Forest Reserve** (p360). On your way to Liberia, stop at **Tiwai Island Wildlife Sanctuary** (p359). Liberia is slowly emerging from the shadows and is well worth exploring – begin in **Monrovia** (p221) and don't miss **Sapo National Park** (p228), **Robertsport** (p227) and **Harper** (p228). By now, you've almost fallen completely off the travel map but it's easy to rejoin the trail – from Harper, it's a short hop across the border into Côte d'Ivoire and **Sassandra** (p146), a glorious fishing village with great beaches. Security permitting, head north to the rainforests of the **Parc National de Taï** (p147), then on to **Man** (p147) in the heart of Dan country. From there, head for **Yamoussoukro** (p146) and its improbable basilica, then on to **Abidjan** (p138), the still-sophisticated one-time 'Paris of Africa'.

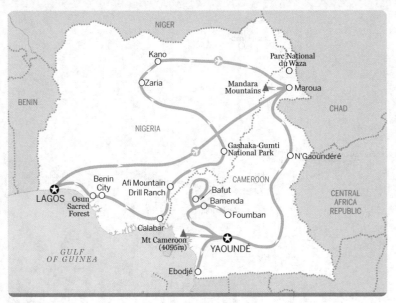

8 WEEKS Nigeria & Cameroon

Nigeria is one of those destinations that suffers from bad press, although it must be said that most of the horror stories are told by those who've never set foot in the country. **Lagos** (p302) may be in-your-face, high-volume and logistically confronting, but it's also Africa's most energetic city, awash with pulsating nightlife, clamorous markets and a terrific museum. **Osun Sacred Forest** (p310), in Okumu Sanctuary, and the Oba's Palace in **Benin City** (p310) are worthwhile stopovers as you head across the south en route to **Calabar** (p310), which is likeable for its old colonial buildings, fish market and lovely setting. Close to Calabar, don't miss **Afi Mountain Drill Ranch** (p311), the focus of an outstanding primate project, and then continue northeast to the remote but terrific **Gashaka-Gumti National Park** (p314) for some of Nigeria's best wildlife-watching. On your way north, check the security situation and if all's well stop off in **Zaria**, then on to **Kano** (p313), West Africa's oldest city and one of the Sahel's most significant cultural centres.

From Kano or (if you've been forced to backtrack) from Lagos, fly to **Maroua** (p97), a pleasant base for exploring the weird-and-wonderful landscapes of the **Mandara Mountains** (p99) and **Parc National du Waza** (p99), one of West Africa's finest wildlife parks. From **N'Gaoundéré** (p95) you can either head deep into the utterly un-touristed rainforests of the southeast, which offer a verdant taste of Central Africa, or take the train through the country's heart, all the way to **Yaoundé** (p77), the country's steamy capital set amid lush green hills. After longish detours to see the sea turtles at **Ebodjé** (p95) and to climb **Mt Cameroon** (p87), West Africa's highest peak, head for **Bamenda** (p90) which serves as a gateway to the villages of the **Ring Road** (p90), a deeply traditional area of Cameroon that feels untouched by time; **Bafut** (p92) is one of our favourite villages in the region. Later, head for **Foumban** (p92) for a slice of tradi-tional West Africa.

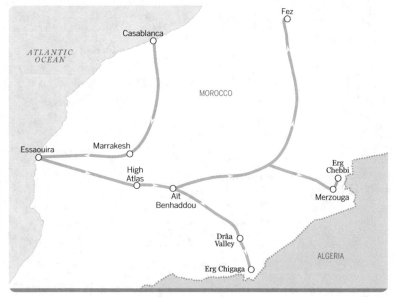

 The Heart of Morocco

Casablanca (p266) is one of the most convenient air gateways to West Africa. Before you take one of the Royal Air Maroc flights that fan out across West Africa, spend a couple of weeks exploring Morocco. From Casablanca, make tracks for **Marrakesh** (p279), one of the great African cities where the nightly spectacle in the Djemaa el-Fna is one of world travel's greatest experiences. **Essaouira** (p267) on the coast is the charming evocation of some bohemian fairytale, and it serves as a launch pad for a journey into the **High Atlas** (p279), home of the Berbers and West Africa's most beautiful mountain range with numerous hiking opportunities. **Aït Benhaddou** (p285) is a glorious mudbrick fortress village, while away to the south, the **Drâa Valley** (p285), **Erg Chebbi** (p286), **Erg Chigaga** (p286) and **Merzouga** (p286) are simply magnificent places to experience the Sahara. From Merzouga it's a long ride (though utterly worth it) to the ancient imperial city of **Fez** (p273), home to West and North Africa's finest medina.

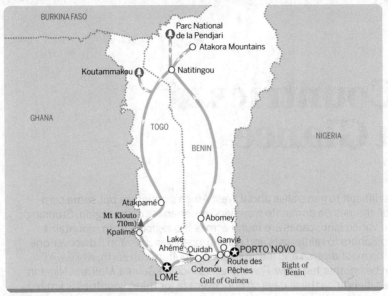

Benin & Togo

Sassy and steamy, **Cotonou** (p38) is one of West Africa's most underrated cities. It's also a good base for excursions to **Ganvié** (p44) and the beaches of the **Route Des Pêches** (p43). **Porto Novo** (p43) is Cotonou's tranquil alter ego, with superb architecture, good museums and a palpable tropical languor. Travelling north, **Abomey** (p48) is the one-time site of the ancient civilisation of Dahomey. Make for **Natitingou** (p49), gateway to the spectacular **Atakora Mountains** (p50) and wildlife-rich **Parc National de la Pendjari** (p51).

Across the border in northern Togo, **Koutammakou** (p375) is one of West Africa's least-known treasures, with remote clay-and-straw fortresses set amid stunning scenery. On your way south, you'll pass through some striking mountain and forest landscapes. **Atakpamé** (p373), **Mt Klouto** (p372) and **Kpalimé** (p372) are all worth sampling as you make your way to the fascinating melting pot of **Lomé** (p367), Togo's capital. On your way back to Cotonou, visit the powerful voodoo strongholds of **Lake Ahémé** (p47) and **Ouidah** (p45).

Countries at a Glance

It's difficult to generalise about West Africa's countries but some common themes do dominate travellers' experiences of the region. Stunning and varied landscapes are found across the region – from mountains and Sahara to rainforests and palm-fringed beaches. You'll discover one of the most diverse and intriguing mix of cultures on earth, while wildlife can be another big draw. Few travellers include Guinea, Mali and Niger in their itineraries these days so our coverage for these countries is limited.

Benin

Culture
Beaches
Wildlife

For culture buffs, Benin will impress with its Afro-Brazilian heritage, voodoo traditions, stilt villages around Lake Nohoué and Somba culture. The palm-fringed coastline will wow beach hounds, while the Parc National de la Pendjari is a wildlife-lovers' magnet.

p36

Burkina Faso

Culture
Landscapes
Peoples

Burkina Faso is a dream destination in Africa: the food is good, the music fabulous, the landscapes stunning and the people delightful. Despite this wealth of assets, it remains relatively low-key, which makes it all the more attractive.

p57

Cameroon

Culture
Scenery
Beaches

With West Africa's highest peak, the glorious landscape of the Ring Road and some of Africa's most accessible traditional cultures, Cameroon is for scenery and culture lovers. Kribi and Limbe also vie for the title of best beach in the country.

p76

Cape Verde

Landscapes
Beaches
Music

A set of spectacular Atlantic islands, Cape Verde is a world of its own, away from the African mainland yet very much a part of it. Come for dramatic hikes through mountains, forests and volcanoes, miles of pristine sand beaches and the islands' soulful music.

p106

Côte d'Ivoire

Culture
Beaches
Landscapes

Speed through the sleek, scraper-lined arteries of Abidjan, stopping for a bite of *poisson braise* and local beer. See the fabled crocs that guard Yamassoukrou. Explore some of West Africa's last remaining rain forest, before lazing on the blonde sands of Assinie.

p137

The Gambia

Birdwatching
Landscapes
Beaches

Beyond the glittering resort towns begging you to unwind and stare at your toes for days, the Gambia offers nature reserves and decadent ecolodges where you'll see new bird life every day and fall asleep in a jungle hammock built for two.

p152

Ghana

History
Wildlife
Peoples

West Africa's rising star is the most exciting place to be in Africa right now: the economy is taking off and the energy is palpable. There is a plethora of attractions, from hiking to partying, wildlife viewing to cultural tours.

p170

Guinea-Bissau

Islands
Wildlife
Landscapes

West Africa's roughest gem, Guinea-Bissau is a place you don't yet know you've been dreaming of. It's that place where you can experience scarlet sunsets, sip cool juice infused with magic, knock back oysters sweet as the sea and weave between hippo-inhabited islands.

p208

Liberia

Culture
Landscapes
Music

Better known for its long civil war than its cashmere sands and swathes of rainforest, Liberia is at last ready to show its face to travellers. Against a soundtrack of birdsong, discover its pretty ecolodges, secret surf spots and haunting architecture.

p220

Mauritania

**National Parks
Desert
Birdwatching**

Mauritania is a country of big horizons – leave Nouakchott, the dusty capital, to revel in the wide vistas of the true Saharan oases of the Adrar region, and the bird-rich Banc d'Arguin and Diawling national parks.

p238

Morocco

**National Parks
Desert
Culture**

Morocco tries to have it all and makes a good job of succeeding. The ancient medina cities of Fez and Marrakesh, camel trips on the edge of the Sahara, and trekking in the High Atlas mountains – it's all here.

p255

Nigeria

**Culture
Landscapes
Peoples**

Nigeria is West Africa's cultural powerhouse, a brash, sassy, complicated melting pot of fascinating peoples arrayed across a land that spans the full range of African landscapes, from the sultry rainforests of the south to the semideserts of the north.

p299

Senegal

**National Parks
Culture
Birdwatching**

From snazzy, sophisticated Dakar and its endless live music and urban grit to the Unesco-designated colonial architecture of sultry Saint-Louis to the water gently lapping while you float though the Siné-Saloum Delta, Senegal captivates from beginning to end.

p320

Sierra Leone

**Food
Wildlife
Landscapes**

Peel back the mountainous curtains of Sierra Leone and slip into its soft blue waters, populated by colourful fish and glittering phosphorescence. This place has it all, from chimpanzees to sea turtles, from spicy chop to lobster suppers, velvety beaches to rocky peaks.

p349

Togo

**Hiking
Rural Landscapes
Beaches**

Togo may well be one of the most secretive countries in West Africa. Very few travellers know that its beaches are thick with white sand and its rugged interior is rife with hiking opportunities. It's also easy to arrange a village stay and learn about local culture.

p365

On the Road

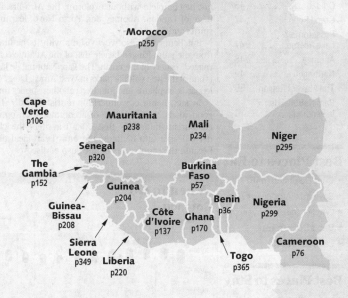

Benin

POP 9.6 MILLION

Best Places to Eat

➡ Chez Delphano (p48)

➡ Saveurs d'Afrique (p47)

➡ L'Atelier (p39)

➡ Bab's Dock (p43)

➡ La Brèche (p50)

Best Places to Stay

➡ La Guesthouse (p38)

➡ Maison Rouge (p38)

➡ Auberge Le Jardin Secret – Chez Pascal (p46)

➡ Pendjari Lodge (p51)

➡ Hôtel Chez Théo (p48)

Why Go?

The birthplace of voodoo and a pivotal platform of the slave trade for nearly three centuries, Benin is steeped in a rich and complex history still very much in evidence across the country.

A visit to this small, club-shaped nation could therefore not be complete without exploring the Afro-Brazilian heritage of Ouidah, Abomey and Porto Novo, learning about spirits and fetishes.

But Benin will also wow visitors with its natural beauty, from the palm-fringed beach idyll of the Atlantic coast to the rugged scenery of the north. The Parc National de la Pendjari is one of the best wildlife parks in West Africa. Lions, cheetahs, leopards, elephants and hundreds of other species thrive here.

In fact, Benin is wonderfully tourist friendly. There are good roads, a wide range of accommodation options and ecotourism initiatives that offer travellers the chance to delve deeper into Beninese life. Now is an ideal time to go because the country sits on the cusp of discovery.

When to Go
Cotonou

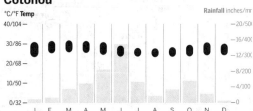

Nov–Feb Warm and dry weather. Prime wildlife watching. Harmattan can produce hazy skies.

Mar–May The hottest period, after the harmattan lifts. Clear skies and some rain in the south.

Jun–Oct Usually downright wet and humid; a dry spell mid-July to mid-September in the south.

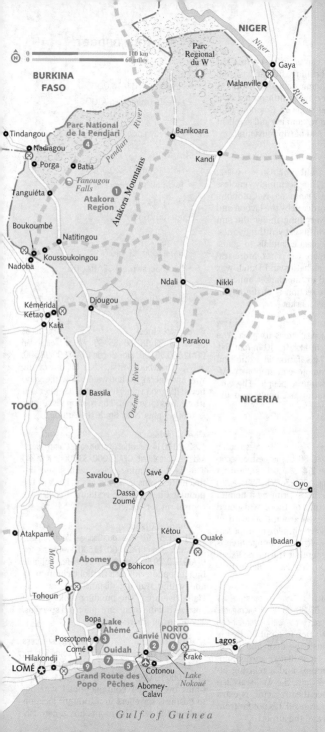

Benin Highlights

1 Exploring the rugged landscapes of the **Atakora Region** (p50) and be awed by the intriguing Somba country.

2 Spending a night at the lacustrine stilt village of **Ganvié** (p44).

3 Learning traditional fishing techniques on the shores of **Lake Ahémé** (p47).

4 Spotting lions, cheetahs, elephants and more in **Parc National de la Pendjari** (p51), West Africa's best wildlife park.

5 Spending an afternoon chilling out at **Route des Pêches** (p43), blessed with endless beaches.

6 Discovering **Porto Novo** (p43), Benin's mellow capital, with its Afro-Brazilian heritage.

7 Checking out **Ouidah** (p45), once a capital of the slave trade and now the centre of voodoo worship.

8 Visiting the ruined palaces of the kings of Dahomey in **Abomey** (p48).

9 Putting your bags down at lovely **Grand Popo** (p47) and relaxing on Benin's beautiful, palm-fringed coast.

COTONOU

POP 890,000

Cotonou is Benin's capital in everything but name: a vibrant, bustling, full-on city, and very much the economic engine of Benin. As a first port of call, it can be a little overwhelming, but life can be sweet in Cotonou, with good nightlife, great restaurants and excellent shopping (ideal for end-of-trip souvenirs).

◉ Sights

Grand Marché de Dantokpa   MARKET

(north of Jonquet) The seemingly endless Grand Marché du Dantokpa is Cotonou's throbbing heart, bordered by the lagoon and Blvd St Michel. Everything under the sun can be purchased in its labyrinthine lanes, from fish to soap, plastic sandals to goats, pirated DVDs to spare car parts. More traditional fare, such as batiks and Dutch wax cloth, can be found in the market building. The fetish market section is at the northern end of the larger market.

Fondation Zinsou   GALLERY

(☑ 21 30 99 92; www.fondationzinsou.org; Haie Vive District; ⊗ 8.30am-7pm Mon-Fri, 10am-7pm Sat, 2-7pm Sun) FREE This fantastic exhibition space seeks to promote contemporary African art among Beninese people. The chic boutique sells beautiful art books and the cafe offers wi-fi access.

🛏 Sleeping

★ La Guesthouse   GUESTHOUSE $

(☑ 67 34 64 77, 99 36 80 09; laguesthousecotonou@gmail.com; Rue 214, Sikécodji; s/d without bathroom incl breakfast CFA8500/12,500; P �) This adorable guesthouse, run by a helpful French couple, is one of those whispered secrets that are passed around by word of mouth. The rooms are simple yet impeccably clean and the welcoming lounge area is a good place to meet other travellers. Excellent meals (CFA4500) are also available. Brilliant value.

Ancrage de l'Océan   GUESTHOUSE $

(☑ 90 04 58 17, 97 07 38 95; www.ancragedelocean.com; Fidjirossé; r with fan/air-con CFA10,500/15,500;) Don't be put off by the concrete facade; push the door and you're in another reality – a seductive garden, no-frills, but spruce rooms and a relaxing atmosphere. Edouard Coffi, the well-travelled owner and a former theatre actor, is extra nice. Meals can be arranged. It's not far from the Rte des Pêches and the airport.

Qualimax Hotel   HOTEL $$

(☑ 21 38 23 18, 66 85 99 77; s/d with fan CFA12,500/15,500, with air-con CFA14,500/18,500;) Drawbacks first: it's a bit out of the way and there's no hot water. Now the good news: it's good value, it's secure, it's quiet and it's clean as all get out. The rooftop restaurant is another plus. Near Stade de l'Amitié.

Chez Clarisse   GUESTHOUSE $$

(☑ 21 30 60 14; clarishot@yahoo.com; Camp Guézo; s/d incl breakfast CFA28,000/33,000;) This is a charming place, with seven immaculate rooms in a villa at the back of the popular Chez Clarisse restaurant (p39). It's central yet very quiet.

Le Chant d'Oiseau   HOTEL $$

(☑ 21 30 57 51; Rue du Collège Père Aupiais; s/d with fan CFA12,000/19,500, with air-con CFA19,500/29,500;) A safe, reliable budget option run by a Catholic community and within walking distance of the lively Haie Vive area. The building looks a little austere, but the rooms are quiet and spacious. There's an on-site restaurant.

Maison Rouge   BOUTIQUE HOTEL $$$

(☑ 21 30 09 01; www.maison-rouge-cotonou.com; off Blvd de la Marina; s CFA65,000-100,000, d CFA76,000-111,000; P) A quiet, sometimes overlooked boutique hotel catering to business travellers in a tranquil location close to the sea. The rooms are generously sized and tastefully designed, and the communal areas are expertly decorated with arts and crafts. Other perks include a soothing plant-filled garden, a gym, a pool and a panoramic terrace with sea views. Evening meals are available by request. Rates include breakfast.

Hôtel du Lac   HOTEL $$$
(☑21 33 19 19; www.hoteldulac-benin.com; r CFA41,000-45,000; P✷@☎☲) A good-value choice on a breezy spot at the edge of the lagoon. Though the rooms show some signs of wear and tear, they are sunny, spacious and clean, and most have water views. The restaurant has a great panoramic terrace and the large swimming pool is popular at the weekend.

Azalai Hotel de la Plage   HOTEL $$$
(www.azalaihotels.com; Blvd de la Marina; s CFA105,000-135,000,dCFA115,000-145,000;P✷@ ☎☲) The ultramodern rooms at this waterfront hotel are arguably the best in the city – especially those with sea views – with sleek bathrooms and attractive decor. The list of facilities is prolific, with a restaurant, a bar, a swimming pool, a business centre and tennis courts. Rates include breakfast.

Novotel Orisha & Ibis Cotonou   HOTEL $$$
(☑21 30 56 69; www.accorhotels.com; Blvd de la Marina; Novotel r CFA95,000, Ibis s/d CFA60,000/66,000; P✷@☎☲) The Accor chain has two hotels on the same property. Both lack charm, but rooms are spotless and well equipped. If you want water views, opt for the Novotel Orisha. The beautiful swimming pool is a great perk.

✗ Eating

Most places to stay have an on-site restaurant.

★Maman Aimé   OPEN-AIR RESTAURANT $
(☑97 64 16 49; off Pl de Bulgarie; mains CFA1200; ☺11.30am-10pm daily) This is a super atmospheric Beninese *maquis* (rustic open-air restaurant) with little more than a few wooden benches and tables under a corrugated-iron roof. Here you'll get a blob of *pâte* (starch staple, often made from millet, corn, plantains, manioc or yams) and a ladle of sauce for next to nothin'. And yes, you'll eat with your fingers. There's no signboard; it's in a *von* (alleyway) off Pl de Bulgarie.

Chez Maman Bénin   AFRICAN $
(☑21 32 33 38; Rue 201A; meals CFA1000-3000; ☺11.30am-11pm daily) This long-standing no-frills canteen off Blvd St Michel has a large selection of West African dishes scooped from steaming pots. There's no decor except for a couple of blaring TVs showing the latest football action.

Maquis du Port   AFRICAN $$
(☑21 31 14 15; Blvd de la Marina; mains CFA2000-6000; ☺lunch & dinner daily) Great-value local food. More an upmarket African eatery than a *maquis*, this hugely popular venture serves a good mix of local classics like *ndole* (a stew made of leaves and nuts), salads, braised fish and meat stews. It's in a multistorey building overlooking the fishing harbour.

Pili Pili   AFRICAN $$
(☑21 31 29 32; Zongo; mains CFA2500-5000; ☺lunch & dinner daily) This well-run eatery rates equally highly with Beninese and expats for its amazing West African food. Prices are very reasonable and the jugs of freshly squeezed pineapple juice at lunchtime are a refreshing godsend.

Chez Clarisse   FRENCH $$
(☑21 30 60 14; Camp Guézo; mains CFA3000-4500; ☺breakfast, lunch & dinner daily) This small French restaurant, in a pretty residential area next to the US embassy, is a perennial favourite that churns out excellent French specialities as well as pancakes and sandwiches.

Hai King   CHINESE $$
(☑97 98 53 63; Carrefour de Cadjéhoun; mains CFA2500-5500; ☺lunch & dinner daily) One of Cotonou's older Chinese restaurants, this has an atmospheric covered roof terrace overlooking the bustling Carrefour de Cadjéhoun, a row of red lanterns, a comprehensive menu and a complement of Chinese expat clientele – always a good sign.

★L'Atelier   FRENCH $$$
(☑21 30 17 04; Cadjéhoun; mains CFA6000-12,000; ☺lunch & dinner Mon-Sat) Considered by some connoisseurs to be one of the most refined restaurants in town, with excellent French and fusion cuisine, and an ambience that's as optimal for business lunches as it is for a romantic evening out.

Les Trois Mousquetaires   FRENCH $$$
(☑21 31 61 22; Ave Dodds; mains CFA6000-12,000; ☺lunch & dinner Mon-Sat) This fine establishment serves delicate French cuisine and features an extensive wine list. The old colonial dining room is the perfect setting for a sophisticated evening.

Cotonou

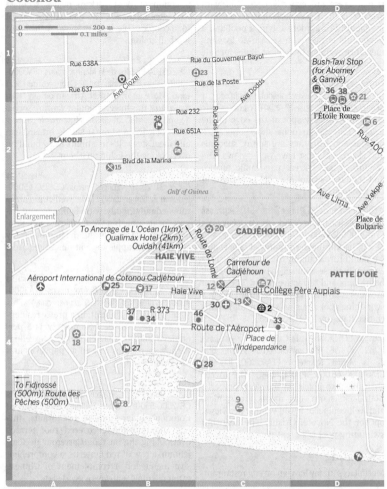

0 ——— 200 m
0 ——— 0.1 miles

Rue 638A

Rue 637

Ave Clozel

PLAKODJI

Rue du Gouverneur Bayol
23
Rue de la Poste

Ave Dodds

Rue 232

29

Rue 651A

4

Rue des Hindous

Blvd de la Marina

15

Gulf of Guinea

Bush-Taxi Stop
(for Abomey
& Ganvié)
36 38
21
Place de
l'Étoile Rouge
6

Rue 400

Ave Lima

Ave Yekpe

Place de
Bulgarie

Enlargement

To Ancrage de L'Océan (1km);
Qualimax Hotel (2km);
Ouidah (41km)

20   CADJÉHOUN

Route de Lomé

HAIE VIVE

Carrefour de
Cadjéhoun

PATTE D'OIE

Aéroport International de Cotonou Cadjéhoun

25   17   Haie Vive   12   Rue du Collège Père Aupiais   7

37   R 373   30   13   2
18   34   46
Route de l'Aéroport   33

Place de
l'Indépendance

27   28

To Fidjrossé
(500m); Route des
Pêches (500m)

8   9

7

🍷 Drinking & Nightlife

Haie Vive is a lively, safe area by night, with many of the city's best bars and restaurants. There are also plenty of unpretentious bars and *buvettes* (small cafes that double as drinking places) in the Jonquet area and around Stade de l'Amitié.

★ Jammin Bar   BAR

(☑97 64 82 74; Fidjirossé; ☺6pm-late Thu-Sat) This hip, convivial bar with an open-air terrace is a great spot to swill a beer or two before hitting the clubs. The crowd ranges from expats to well-heeled locals. Also serves good food.

Le Livingstone   BAR

(☑21 30 27 58; Haie Vive; ☺11am-late daily) One of the most atmospheric spots for a drink is the terrace of this pub in Haie Vive. There's also a tempting menu (meals CFA3400 to CFA6200), and darts.

The Sanctuary   MUSIC

(Haie Vive; ☺6pm-late Thu-Sat) This cool den hosts gigs from local bands, with an emphasis on rock 'n' blues. There's no cover charge, but a beer costs CFA3000.

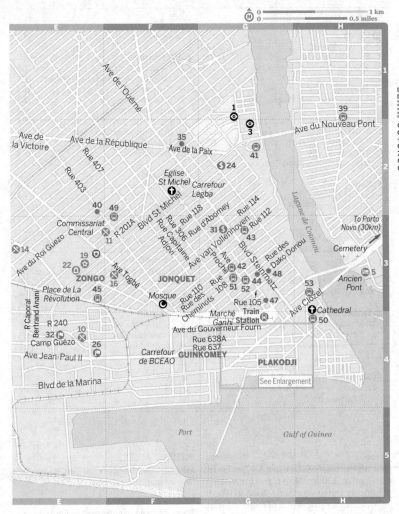

Yes Papa
MUSIC

(leyespapa.blogspot.fr; Sikécodji; ⊘9pm-late Thu-Sat) This venture is famed for the quality of its live music sessions featuring reggae, jazz and African sounds. Near Pl de l'Étoile Rouge.

Makoomba
CLUB

(Rte de l'Aéroport; ⊘from 10pm daily) A pulsating club near the airport. It plays African and Western tunes and doesn't really kick off before 1am.

New York, New York
CLUB

(Blvd St Michel; ⊘daily) This Cotonou institution has been around for yonks and isn't showing signs of slowing down. If you want to rub shoulders with hip-gyrating Beninese dancing to African tunes, this is the place.

🛍 Shopping

Centre de Promotion de l'Artisanat
HANDICRAFTS

(Blvd St Michel; ⊘9am-7pm) Here you'll find woodcarvings, bronzes, batiks, leather goods, jewellery and appliqué banners.

Cotonou

Woodin   CLOTHING
(Rue des Hindous; ⊙ 8.30am-1pm & 4-7pm Tue-Fri, 9am-1pm Sat, 3.30-7pm Mon) If you are looking for quality Dutch wax fabric, head to Woodin, where *demi-pièces* (6m of material) start at CFA15,000.

❶ Information

DANGERS & ANNOYANCES
The biggest danger in Cotonou is the traffic – the 80,000 reckless *zemi-johns* (taxi-motos) in particular. They're unavoidable, however, so always make sure that the driver agrees to drive slowly *(aller doucement)* before hopping on.

The Jonquet, the beach and the port area all have their fair share of undesirables: don't walk alone at night and watch your bag at traffic lights if you're on a *zem.*

INTERNET ACCESS
Ave Clozel, Blvd Steinmetz and Rue des Cheminots have the most internet cafes.

MEDICAL SERVICES
There are numerous pharmacies around town.
Polyclinique les Cocotiers (☑ 21 30 14 20; Rue 373, Cadjéhoun) A private clinic at Carrefour de Cadjéhoun; also has a dentist.

MONEY
All banks change cash. There are plenty of ATMs in Cotonou, most of which accept Visa.
Banque Atlantique (Blvd St Michel; ⊙ 8am-5pm Mon-Fri, 9am-12.30pm Sat) Has a MasterCard and Visa ATM, but it was not functioning at the time of research.

Trinity Forex (Bureau de Change Forex Bureau; ☑ 21 31 79 38; Ave van Vollenhoven; ⊙ 8am-6.30pm Mon-Fri, to 2pm Sat) Changes US dollars, euros, Swiss francs and British pounds.

ℹ Getting There & Away

BUSH TAXI & BUS

Cotonou has a confusingly large number of stations for minibuses, buses and bush taxis. It's easiest to ask a taxi or a *zemi-john* to take you to the right one.

Gare Jonquet (Rue des Cheminots), just west of Blvd Steinmetz, services western destinations such as Grand Popo (CFA4000, two hours).

Bush taxis for Porto Novo (CFA500 to CFA700, 45 minutes) leave from **Gare du Dantokpa** (Ave de la Paix) at the new bridge; those to Calavi-Kpota (for Ganvié; CFA500, 25 minutes), Ouidah (CFA1000) and Abomey (CFA3000, two hours) leave north of Stade de l'Amitié. **Gare Missébo** (Ave van Vollenhoven) services Abomey (CFA2500).

For more-distant destinations, such as Natitingou, take the bus. The most reliable companies at the time of writing were **ATT** (☑ 95 95 34 18; Pl de l'Étoile Rouge) and **Confort Lines** (Pl de l'Étoile Rouge). Both have daily services for Natitingou (CFA8500).

There are also international services.

ℹ Getting Around

TO/FROM THE AIRPORT

The international airport is on the western fringe of town. A private taxi from the city centre to the airport costs around CFA3000, although drivers will demand double this amount *from* the airport. Zemi-johns will be happy to load you and your luggage for much less.

TAXI

A *zemi-john* will whiz you around town for CFA100 to CFA500, depending on the distance.

Fares in shared taxis are CFA150 to CFA400.

AROUND COTONOU

Route des Pêches

West of Cotonou, past the airport and all the way to Ouidah, is the sandy Rte des Pêches, a land of seemingly endless beaches and fishing villages, a world away from the big-smoke mayhem.

As you leave Cotonou behind, the suburb gives way to thatched huts and palm groves. Many expats and Beninese families rent little *paillotes* (huts) for the weekend around here. For those just passing by, there are many popular bars and restaurants along the route.

🛏 Sleeping & Eating

Tichani GUESTHOUSE **$**

(☑ 96 66 80 08, 97 88 65 60; www.tichani.com; off Rte des Pêches; r with fan/air-con incl breakfast 10,000/15,000; 🛜) This well-run guesthouse scores high points with its location – it's only 300m away from the beach in a peaceful area. The five sun-soaked rooms are neat and tidy, the flower-filled garden is a great spot to decompress and the views of the sea from the rooftop terrace are nothing short of charming. Meals can be arranged (from CFA3000).

★ **Bab's Dock** EUROPEAN, BAR **$$$**

(☑ 97 97 01 00; off Rte des Pêches; mains CFA3000-7000; ⏱ 10am-7pm Sat, Sun & bank holidays) The hidden gem near the Rte des Pêches is this secluded retreat on the edge of the lagoon. Almost everything is made of local wood – the tables, the bar, the deck. You can swim in the shallow (but somewhat murky) waters of the lagoon, canoe and even sail or just relax in a hammock. Food is European in style but local in production. Bab's Dock is 11km from Cotonou. A secure car park is signposted from the route; from there, a boat takes you to the restaurant through thick mangrove. There's an admission fee (CFA2500) for the day, which covers the car park and boat trip.

Wado SEAFOOD **$$**

(☑ 97 68 53 18; Rte des Pêches; mains CFA3700-3900, seafood platters CFA25,000; ⏱ lunch & dinner Sat & Sun) This eatery overlooking the beach has garnered high praise for its ultra-fresh fish and seafood platters.

THE SOUTH

Benin's south is an enticing but intriguing mix of heavenly shores and momentous history.

Porto Novo

POP 270,00

Nestling on the shores of Lake Nokoué, Porto Novo is Benin's unlikely capital. Its leafy streets, wonderful colonial architecture, unperturbed pace and interesting museums are in striking contrast to full-on Cotonou.

WORTH A TRIP

GANVIÉ

The main attraction near Cotonou (and one of Benin's highlights) is Ganvié, where 30,000 Tofinu people live in bamboo huts on stilts several kilometres out on Lake Nokoué. They live almost exclusively from fishing.

Despite the fact that the town has become a tourist magnet, it's a terrific place to explore and sample village life. Tip: rather than signing up for a tour, it's not a bad idea to overnight in Ganvié – thus you'll soak up the atmosphere and get a better understanding of the environment and traditional life of the community. Ganvié has a handful of guesthouses, including the friendly **Chez M** (📞 95 42 04 68, 97 37 22 71; hotelcarre-fourchezm@hotmail.fr; Ganvié; s CFA8500, d CFA10,500-12,500), which offers 22 rooms with bathrooms, standing fans and mosquito nets. The setting is lovely – the dining room overlooks the main stream and the floating market, right in the middle of the village. Meals (CFA4500) are available on request and various tours can be organised. Transfers from Calavi-Kpota cost CFA7500 return and must be booked in advance.

To get there, get a taxi from Pl de l'Étoile Rouge or Stade de l'Amitié to Calavi-Kpota (CFA500, 25 minutes). The embarkation point is 800m downhill (take a *zem*). If you opt for a tour, head to the **official counter** (🕘 9am-5pm). Return fares to Ganvié in a regular/motorised *pirogue* are CFA6050/7050 per person, CFA4050/5050 each for two to four people. Prices include a circuit of the village with stop-offs. The trip takes about 2½ hours. You can also hire a guide.

The Portuguese named the city after Porto when they established a slave-trading post here in the 16th century.

⊙ Sights

Centre Songhai
GARDENS
(📞 20 24 68 81; www.songhai.org; Rte de Pobè; guided tours CFA500; 🕘 guided tours at 8.30am, 10.30am, noon, 3.30pm & 5pm Mon-Sat) The Centre Songhai is a major research, teaching and production centre in sustainable farming. There are one-hour **guided tours** to visit the plantations and workshops. You can also buy the centre's produce – anything from fresh quail eggs to biscuits and preserves. Songhai is about 1km north of town. Every *zem* knows where it is.

Musée Ethnographique de Porto Novo
MUSEUM
(📞 20 21 25 54; Ave 6; admission CFA1000; 🕘 9am-6pm, closed 1 May & 1 Jan) Housed in a pretty colonial building, this museum is well worth a gander. The top floor is organised thematically around birth, life and death, with everything from costumes to carved drums. Downstairs there's an impressive display of ceremonial masks.

Musée Honmé
MUSEUM
(📞 20 21 35 66; Rue Toffa; admission CFA1000; 🕘 9am-6pm, to 5pm Sat & Sun) This establishment is housed in the walled compound of King Toffa, who signed the first treaty with

the French in 1863. The site hasn't been well maintained and you'll need some imagination to make something out of the bare chambers, but François, the guide, puts on a good show.

Musée da Silva
MUSEUM
(📞 20 21 50 71; Ave Liotard; admission CFA2000; 🕘 9am-6pm) This wonderfully eclectic museum is housed in a beautiful 1870 Afro-Brazilian house.

🛏 Sleeping & Eating

Centre Songhai
HOTEL $
(📞 20 24 68 81; www.songhai.org; Rte de Pobè; r with fan CFA5500-7500, with air-con CFA12,500-15,500, ste CFA30,000-50,000; 🅿 ❄ @ 🛜) Built to accommodate its numerous visitors, the 70 rooms at Centre Songhai are spartan but clean. Fan rooms have a shower cubicle but shared toilets; the more-expensive air-con rooms have a private bathroom (with hot water) but are still very good value. The centre has two good restaurants: a cheap African *maquis* (mains CFA1200) and a more upmarket restaurant (mains CFA2500 to CFA3500). There's also an internet cafe (CFA250 per hour).

Le Palais
BUNGALOW $$
(📞 20 21 40 90; www.cthlepalais.com; Blvd Lagunaire; bungalows CFA30,000-41,800; 🅿 ❄ 🛜) Poised on the edge of the lagoon, this is an unexpected oasis: well-furnished, comfy bungalows with all mod cons, neat garden,

good views and a restaurant-bar. Service is a bit lackadaisical, though.

Java Promo
AFRICAN, FRENCH $

(☎ 66 96 68 78; Pl du Gouvernement; meals CFA1000-3500; ☺ breakfast, lunch & dinner daily) No one seems to remember a time before Java Promo. Hidden behind the aquamarine shutters of a crumbling colonial building and shielded from the sun by a big *paillote*, this is a popular haunt for an omelette at brekkie or rustic European meals for lunch.

JPN
AFRICAN $

(mains CFA1500-2500; ☺ breakfast, lunch & dinner daily; 🛜) Here the setting is the real draw, with an Eden-like garden replete with big trees, which puts you in the mood for a cold beer or a braised chicken as soon as you sit down. Free wi-fi. It's inside the Jardin des Plantes et de la Nature, right in the centre of town.

ℹ Information

Porto Novo has several banks with Visa ATMs and internet cafes.

Tourist Office (☎ 97 02 52 29; www.porto-novo.org; Pl Bayol; ☺ 9am-1pm & 3-6pm Mon-Fri) Has a few brochures and can help with finding guides. Near the cathedral.

ℹ Getting There & Away

Plenty of minibuses and bush taxis leave for Cotonou (minibus/bush taxi CFA500/800, 45 minutes) from Carrefour Catchi and in front of Ouando mosque. To Abomey from Porto Novo is CFA3500. ATT buses that ply the Cotonou–Natitingou route also stop in front of Ouando mosque (CFA7500 for Natitingou).

For Nigeria, you can get a taxi to the border point in Kraké (CFA800, 30 minutes), but you'll have to change there to go on to Lagos.

Ouidah

POP 87,200

Some 42km west of Cotonou is Ouidah, a relaxed, relatively prosperous town and a must-see for anyone interested in voodoo or Benin's history of slavery. From the 17th to the late 19th century, captured countrymen from across West Africa left Ouidah for the Americas.

When voodoo has finished working its magic on you, there are sweeping expanses of golden-sand beaches to laze upon.

⊙ Sights

Route des Esclaves
MEMORIAL

Once sold, slaves were taken from the fort to the beach down the 4km Rte des Esclaves. Lining the sandy track now are fetishes and monuments, such as the Monument of Repentance and the Tree of Forgetfulness. There is a poignant memorial on the beach, the **Point of No Return**, with bas-relief depicting slaves in chains. It's such a beautiful spot that it's hard to fathom that 12 million people were deported from this very shore.

Musée d'Histoire de Ouidah
MUSEUM

(☎ 21 34 10 21; www.museeouidah.org; Rue van Vollenhoven; admission CFA1000; ☺ 8am-12.30pm & 3-5pm Mon-Fri, 9am-5pm Sat & Sun) Ouidah's main site is its Musée d'Histoire de Ouidah, housed in the beautiful Fortaleza São João

---

WORTH A TRIP

ADJARA

Adjara, 9km northeast of Porto Novo on a back road to Nigeria, is a wonderful detour from Porto Novo. It's famous for its market, one of the most colourful in Benin. Held every fourth day, it's stocked with fetishes, *grigri* charms, unique blue and white tie-dyed cloth, some of the best pottery in Benin, *tamtams* and other musical instruments. You'll also see blacksmiths at work. Culture buffs will make a beeline for the small **Musée d'Adjara** (☎ 97 60 07 95; admission CFA1000; ☺ 9am-6pm daily), which has a good display of African masks. The curator, Noël Agossou, will be happy to show you Adjara's highlights (CFA5000) and can also organise *pirogue* trips on a nearby river.

No visit to Adjara would be complete without having lunch at **Chez Houssou** (mains CFA1000; ☺ lunch daily). This unpretentious *maquis*, with no more than a couple of wooden benches, is famous for one thing and one thing only: *porc grillé sauce sang* (grilled pork cooked in a blood sauce). Houssou cuts morsels of pork, puts them in a mud-brick oven, and then serves them on a small plate – it can't get more authentic than that.

From Porto Novo, a *zem* ride shouldn't cost more than CFA900.

VOODOO DAY

Vodou (voodoo) got its current name in Haiti and Cuba, where the religions arrived with Fon and Ewe slaves from the Dahomey Kingdom and mixed with Catholicism. It means 'the hidden' or 'the mystery'. Traditional priests are consulted for their power to communicate with particular spirits and seek intercession with them. This communication is achieved through spirit possession and ritual that often involves a gift or 'sacrifice' of palm wine, chickens or goats.

Voodoo was formally recognised as a religion by the Beninese authorities in February 1996. Since then, 10 January, Voodoo Day, has been a bank holiday, with celebrations all over the country. Those in Ouidah, voodoo's historic centre, are among the best and most colourful, with endless singing, dancing, beating of drums and drinking.

Batista, a Portuguese fort built in 1721. It retraces the town's slave-trading history and explores the links between Benin, Brazil and the Caribbean.

Python Temple RELIGIOUS
(off Rue F Colombani; admission CFA1000, photos CFA5000; ☺9am-6.30pm) Those interested in voodoo could visit the python temple, home to some 60 sleepy pythons. The guide explains some of the beliefs and ceremonies associated with the temple.

🛌 Sleeping & Eating

For a tasty meal, a hotel is your best bet. Otherwise, Rue F Colombani is peppered with food stalls and small *maquis*.

★**Auberge Le Jardin Secret –**
Chez Pascal GUESTHOUSE $
(☑96 66 90 14; www.lejardinsecretouidah.net; near Radio Kpassé; r CFA10,000; ℙ) An atmosphere of dreamlike tranquillity wafts over this well-organised guesthouse tucked away in a side *von* in a tranquil neighbourhood. The neatly tended garden has places to lounge, the six rooms, though not luxurious, are crisp and spruce, and there's an on-site restaurant (meals from CFA3500). Everything was built using natural materials. Bike rent-

al is available. It's run by a Frenchman who travelled around West Africa by moped.

Le Jardin Brésilien Auberge de
la Diaspora HOTEL $$
(☑94 56 96 73; www.bda2.com; Porte du Non Retour; r CFA8000-30,000; ℙ❄🛜🏊) Just off the beach near the Point of No Return, rooms here occupy two characterless, muscular buildings. Opt for the air-con rooms, which are spacious and meticulously clean. Avoid the fan rooms, which are overpriced and furnace-like. Also available is a cluster of modern, well-appointed bungalows. The real draws are the large pool and the restaurant (mains CFA4500 to CFA6500) slap bang on the beach.

Casa Del Papa RESORT $$$
(☑95 95 39 04; www.casadelpapa.com; Ouidah Plage; d incl breakfast CFA47,000-68,000; ℙ❄🏊) Squeezed between the ocean and the lagoon, Casa Del Papa is the closest thing to an exclusive resort you'll find on the coast. It features a host of facilities and amenities, including three pools, a volleyball court, two bars and a restaurant overlooking the beach. There are numerous activities on offer as well as excursions across the lagoon and to nearby villages. The hotel is 7km beyond the Point of No Return.

Côté Pêche SEAFOOD $$
(☑96 82 27 03, 97 46 43 79; Rte des Esclaves; mains CFA2500-3500; ☺breakfast, lunch & dinner daily) Fish lovers, you'll find nirvana here: Côté Pêche has a wide assortment of fish delivered daily from the harbour, including barracuda and grouper. The menu also features meat dishes, pasta, salads and sandwiches. The owners have three rooms for rent (CFA6000). It's at the beginning of Rte des Esclaves.

🛈 Information

There are several internet cafes in town but only one bank (UBA) with an ATM (Visa only).
Tourist Office (☑21 19 35 11, 97 87 80 93; ouidah_tourisme@yahoo.fr; ☺8.30am-6.30pm daily) Has various brochures and can arrange cultural tours. Ask for Modeste Zinsou. Near the post office.

🛈 Getting There & Away

From Carrefour Gbena, north of town, you can catch shared taxis to Cotonou (CFA1000, one hour), Grand Popo (CFA1500, one hour) and the Hilakondji border (CFA1500, 1½ hours).

Grand Popo

POP 10,000

Grand Popo is a wonderful spot to spend a few tranquil days. The village has plenty going on at the weekend when Cotonou residents come to decompress.

◉ Sights & Activities

On the main road through the village, **Villa Karo** (☑ 94 20 31 20; www.villakaro.org; ☺ gallery 8am-noon & 4-6pm Mon-Fri, 8-11am Sat) has a small gallery with great exhibitions.

Run by two local guides, **GG Tours** (☑ 95 85 74 40) organises excursions on the Mono River or to the Bouche du Roy, where the river meets the ocean. Trips on the river last about two hours (CFA5000 per person). Trips to the Bouche du Roy cost CFA45,000 as you need a motorised boat; boats fit up to eight people and the trip lasts about six hours.

🛏 Sleeping & Eating

★ **Saveurs d'Afrique**   BUNGALOW $
(☑ 97 89 28 19, 66 69 69 80; www.saveursdafrique. net; bungalows CFA15,500; ℗) Looking for a night at some place extra-special? Make a beeline for this lovely property, the pride and joy of affable Mathieu Yélomé, a young Beninese chef. The six units borrow from African traditional designs and are embellished with various artistic touches. Food is a big thing here; the range of daily specials (around CFA4500) on offer – mostly French-influenced dishes prepared with local ingredients – is well priced and filled with subtle flavours. Near the beach.

Lion Bar   GUESTHOUSE $
(☑ 95 42 05 17; kabla_gildas@yahoo.fr; campsites per person CFA1500, r without bathroom CFA5000) Down a track from the main street, you'll easily find this reggae land by following Bob Marley's languorous beats. It's the hideout of choice for Cotonou's expat beatniks and oozes peace and love: cocktails flow at all hours of the day and night, rooms are spartan yet funky and the shared facilities surprisingly clean. Daily specials cost CFA2500. It's right on the beach and you're free to pitch your tent.

Auberge Victor's Place   CAMPGROUND $
(☑ 97 04 91 02; campsites per person CFA1000, bungalows without bathroom s/d CFA5500/7500; ℗) Victor's Place boasts a spiffing beach frontage in a green location. Pitch your tent on the grassy plot or choose one of the three slightly threadbare bungalows. The real draws are the cool atmosphere and the wicked cocktails prepared by Victor, a friendly Rasta. You can hire a tent if you don't have your own. Overall, it's very simple, but there's plenty of heart.

Awalé Plage   RESORT $$
(☑ 22 43 01 17; www.hotel-benin-awaleplage.com; Rte du Togo; campsites CFA6000, bungalows with fan/air-con CFA20,500/25,500; ℗ ✳ ⏚ ☒) A great place to recharge the batteries, Awalé Plage's most notable features are its beachfront setting, its beautiful gardens awash with tropical trees, its large swimming pool and its well-maintained bungalows. There is an excellent beach bar and the on-site restaurant (mains CFA2000 to CFA6500) prepares delectable French-inspired dishes with a tropical twist. It's also a good bargain for campers.

❶ Getting There & Away

From Cotonou, take a bush taxi from Gare Jonquet, Stade de l'Amitié or Pl de l'Étoile Rouge (CFA2500, two hours) and have it drop you off at the Grand Popo junction on the main coastal highway, 20km east of the Togo border crossing at Hilakondji. The beach and village are 3.5km off the main road and are easily accessible via *zemi-john* (CFA250).

Possotomé & Lake Ahémé

The fertile shores of Lake Ahémé are a wonderful place to spend a few days, particularly around Possotomé, the area's biggest village. It's even possible to swim in the lake.

Various trips and excursions are offered by local tour operators, including **Eco-Bénin** (www.ecobenin.org). Learn traditional fishing techniques, meet craftspeople at work or go on a fascinating two-hour botanic journey to hear about local plants and their medicinal properties. There are half a dozen thematic circuits to choose from (from two hours to day trips, CFA3500 to CFA12,000), all run by delightful local guides.

🛏 Sleeping & Eating

Gîte de Possotomé   GUESTHOUSE $
(☑ 94 38 80 34, 67 19 58 37; www.ecobenin.org; s without bathroom CFA4500-6000, d CFA7000-8500, s/d with bathroom CFA9500/12,500; ℗ ⏚) Embedded in a manicured tropical garden, this well-run venture has eight impeccable rooms with salubrious bathrooms. It's not on the lakeshore, but the congenial atmosphere

more than makes up for this. The ethos here is laid-back, ecological and activity-oriented – various tours can be arranged.

Camping de Possotomé – Chez Préfet
CAMPGROUND $

(☎ 95 35 86 53; campsites per person CFA3000; P) How does watching the sun rise over Lake Ahémé sound? This campsite, on an idyllic spot on the sandy lakeshore, is basic (bucket showers and toilets) but very atmospheric. Prefet, the cook, will whisk up African wonders for sustenance (meals CFA3500).

Hôtel Chez Théo
RESORT $$

(☎ 95 05 53 15, 96 44 47 88; www.chez-theo.com; r CFA15,000-20,000, bungalows CFA30,000; P ❋ 🛜) In a stunning lakeside location, Chez Théo is guaranteed to help you switch to 'relax' mode. A path through a garden bursting with all sorts of exotic trees leads to a great bar-restaurant (mains from CFA3500) on a stilt platform with cracking views. Rooms are far from fancy but are kept scrupulously clean. Four bungalows, including two overwater units, were being built at the time of research. All kinds of tours can be organised.

ⓘ Getting There & Away

Taxis that ply the Cotonou–Hilakondji (or Comé) route will generally drop you off at the Comé turn-off (CFA2000), from where the only option to Possotomé is a *zemi-john* (CFA1000).

Abomey
POP 125,000

If you're looking to immerse yourself in ancient Beninese history, one of the best places to start is Abomey. The name is mythical, and not without reason: Abomey, 144km northwest of Cotonou, was the capital of the fierce Dahomey Kingdom and a force colonial powers had to reckon with for centuries. Its winding lanes dotted with palaces and temples, Abomey is shrouded with a palpable historical aura and filled with character.

ⓞ Sights

Musée Historique d'Abomey
MUSEUM

(☎ 22 50 03 14; www.epa-prema.net/abomey; admission CFA2500; ⓞ 9am-4.30pm) Abomey's main and seriously impressive attraction (and a World Heritage Site), this sprawling museum is housed in two palaces, those of the ancient kings Ghézo and Glélé. The museum displays royal thrones and tapestries, human skulls that were once used as musical instruments,

THE ROUTE OF KINGS

The tourist office runs excellent cultural tours focusing on Abomey's rich architectural heritage. They last about two hours and cost CFA3000 per person (not including *zem* rental). There are some 10 sites to be seen, all of which have an air of faded majesty about their crumbling walls. Highlights include Palais Akaba, Place de Goho, Palais Ghézo, Palais de Glélé, Temple Hwemu, Temple Zéwa and Palais Agonglo – the best kept of Abomey's nine palaces.

fetish items and Ghézo's throne, mounted on four real skulls of vanquished enemies.

The admission fee includes a guide (only French is spoken), who will take about an hour to show you around the courtyards, ceremonial rooms and burial chambers. The tour finishes at the Centre des Artisans, where you can buy appliqué banners.

🛏 Sleeping & Eating

A La Lune – Chez Monique
GUESTHOUSE $

(☎ 22 50 01 68; north of Rond-Point de la Préfecture; r CFA7500-8500; P) You'll love the exotic garden, complete with antelopes, crocodiles, tortoises, monkeys, flower bushes and huge wood carvings. Accommodation-wise, it's a bit less overwhelming, with no-frills, yet spacious, rooms. The on-site restaurant is average; opt for a contemplative drink in the garden instead.

Auberge d'Abomey
GUESTHOUSE $$

(☎ 95 82 80 28, 97 89 87 25; www.hotels-benin. com; Rond-Point de la Préfecture; s/d with fan CFA12,500/14,000, with air-con CFA17,000/20,000; ❋) This reliable option off the main roundabout is a small, rustic hotel with a colonial feel and just a handful of spare rooms. It gets high marks from travellers for its relaxing garden full of mango trees and its on-site restaurant (mains from CFA2500). Various excursions can be organised.

★ Chez Delphano
OPEN-AIR RESTAURANT $

(☎ 93 64 02 40; mains CFA800-1900; ⓞ breakfast, lunch & dinner daily) This delightful *maquis* is a winner. Marguerite prepares exquisite Beninese cuisine in a jovial atmosphere. She also prepares *crêpes* in the morning, with freshly ground coffee and a mountain of fruit. Yum! Chez Delphano is north of Rond-Point de la Préfecture.

ℹ️ Information

You'll find banks and internet cafes in Bohicon, 9km east of Abomey.

Tourist Office (📞95 79 09 45, 94 14 67 30; Office du Tourisme d'Abomey; ⏱9am-1pm & 3-6pm Mon-Fri, 9am-4pm Sat) Has some interesting brochures and can provide information about Abomey's main sights. It also keeps a list of accredited guides (some of whom speak English) and can arrange guided tours. Ask for Gabin Djimassé, the knowledgeable director. It's near the Rond-Point de la Préfecture.

ℹ️ Getting There & Away

Plenty of bush taxis depart from Cotonou (CFA3000, three hours), sometimes with a connection at Bohicon. *Zemi-johns* (CFA800) frequently run between Abomey and Bohicon.

ATT and Confort Lines buses (between Cotonou and Natitingou) stop in Bohicon on the way.

THE NORTH

Northern Benin's arid, mountainous landscape is a world away from the south's beaches and lagoons but all the more attractive for it. It's all about the natural heritage, with one fantastic wildlife park and a mountain range. It is also ethnically more diverse than the south, and Islam is the main religion.

Natitingou

POP 75,600

Affectionately known as Nati, Natitingou is the most vibrant town in northern Benin and is a fabulous base for excursions to the nearby Atakora Mountains and the Parc National de la Pendjari.

🔆 Sights

Musée Régional de Natitingou   MUSEUM
(📞23 02 00 53; Rte Inter-État; admission CFA1000; ⏱8am-12.30pm & 3.30-6.30pm Mon-Fri, 9am-noon & 4-6pm Sat & Sun) Housed in a colonial building built by slaves at the beginning of the 20th century, this museum gives an overview of life in Somba communities. The exhibition includes various musical instruments, jewellery, crowns and artefacts. Most interesting is the habitat room, which has models of the different types of *tata somba* (Somba houses).

🛏️ Sleeping & Eating

Hôtel Bellevue   BUNGALOW $
(📞90 92 33 69, 23 82 13 36; myriamsare13@hotmail.com; s/d with fan from CFA7500/8500, with air-con from CFA14,500/17,000; 🅿✳@🛜) Set in a rambling garden, the Bellevue is a charming collection of sweet bungalows and *paillotes*. Myriam, the formidable owner, runs a tight ship and rooms are simple yet spotless, as is the food in the restaurant (much of which comes from her vegie garden). Your host also makes jewellery, for sale at the reception. She had plans to retire at the time of writing.

Palais Somba   BUNGALOW $
(📞96 27 29 51; s/d with fan CFA6500/8500, with air-con CFA12,500/16,500; ✳) 'Palace' might be pushing it a bit, but this venture is something special, blending African touches with European levels of comfort. All the bungalows, which are arranged around a leafy compound, are embellished with paintings made by a local artist. The garden is compact but easily one of the nicest in Nati. There's an on-site restaurant, with a limited selection of simple dishes. It's in a quiet area.

Hôtel de Bourgogne   HOTEL $$
(📞23 82 22 40, 97 90 97 38; www.natitingou.org/bourgogne; Rte Inter-État; r with fan CFA14,000-18,000, with air-con from CFA18,000-25,000; 🅿✳🛜) This efficiently run hotel is a safe bet. Although not the height of luxury, rooms are colourful, comfy, spacious and serviceable, with modern, clean beds, and the restaurant has a reputation for fine food, with an emphasis on meat dishes (mains from

---

THE SOMBA

Commonly referred to as the Somba, the Betamaribé people are concentrated to the southwest of Natitingou in the plains of Boukoumbé on the Togo border. What's most fascinating about the Betamaribé is their *tata somba* houses – fort-like huts with clay turrets and thatched spires. The ground floor of a house is mostly reserved for livestock. A stepladder leads from the kitchen to the roof terrace, where there are sleeping quarters and grain stores.

The Betamaribé's principal religion is animism – as seen in the rags and bottles they hang from the trees. Once famous for their nudity, they began wearing clothes in the 1970s.

CFA4800). Hot water is available in the more expensive rooms. One downside: the hotel is not shielded from the noise of the main road.

La Brèche
AFRICAN $$

(☑96 90 07 66; mains CFA1700-3000; ☺lunch & dinner daily) Highly original is this appealing eatery set in a *tata somba* house with superb views of Nati and the Atakora Mountains. Book ahead for the house specialities: *canard au tchouk* (duck cooked in *tchoukoutou* – sorghum beer – sauce) and *lapin au sodabe* (rabbit cooked in *sodabe* – moonshine – sauce). And be sure to try the delicious *salade peule* (tomatoes with local cheese).

ℹ Information

Internet cafes are easy to find around town. Ecobank, at the main junction, changes cash and has one ATM (Visa only).

For information about tours and excursions in the wider area, including the Atakora and the Parc National de la Pendjari, ask at your hotel or contact the Natitingou-based Bénin Aventure (p56), a highly recommended company run by excellent local guides.

ℹ Getting There & Away

From the *gare routière* in the centre, bush taxis and minibuses go to Tanguiéta (CFA1500, one hour), from where you can find services to the border with Burkina Faso and Ouagadougou (there aren't any direct services to Burkina Faso from Natitingou). For Koussoukoingou and Boukoumbé, it's easier to get there by *zem* (about CFA300).

Bus services linking Nati and Cotonou (CFA8500, eight hours) include ATT and Confort Lines and leave from the *gare routière* south

---

WORTH A TRIP

KOTA FALLS

Fancy a refreshing dip? Consider heading to the Kota Falls (admission CFA300), 15km southeast of Natitingou, off the main highway. You can swim in the pool at the bottom of the falls or just sit down and read in the cool shade of the undergrowth. Pure bliss! Hire a *zem* (CFA5000 per day) to get there. Take note that it's possible to overnight near the falls – there's a cluster of surprisingly well-maintained bungalows (room CFA10,500).

---

of town. Services leave at 7am; book ahead or arrive early on the day.

The Atakora Region

About 30km west of Nati is the mountain village of Koussoukoingou (also known as Koussou-Kovangou), famous for its stunning location and breathtaking views of the Atakora range. Further west, 43km southwest of Natitingou, on the Togo border, Boukombé is the capital of Somba country, at the heart of the Atakora Mountains. The drive there is stunning, bumping along a red *piste* (rough track) past corn fields and huge baobab trees. Boukombé has a lively market every four days, when *tchoukoutou* (sorghum beer) gingerly flows.

◎ Sights & Activities

Ecotourism association Perle de l'Atakora (Pearl of the Atakora; ☑97 44 28 61; www.ecobenin.org/koussoukoingou) offers guided walks around Koussoukoingou (CFA2500 to CFA3500 for 2½ to 3½ hours) taking in local sights such as the famous *tata* houses (fort-like huts with clay turrets and thatched spires). You can arrange to spend the night at a *tata* (CFA6000 per person including breakfast and dinner).

🛏 Sleeping & Eating

Ecolodge La Perle de l'Atakora GUESTHOUSE $

(☑67 46 78 01, 97 35 02 86; www.ecobenin.org; Koussoukoingou; r without bathroom CFA8000; P) We can't think of a better place for immersion in local culture. This modernish *tata* house features five rooms that are tidy, functional and well priced, and a well-scrubbed ablutions block. Hearty meals too. It's run by Ecobenin, which offers high-quality ecotours in the area. Bikes are also available.

Tata Touristique
Koubetti Victor
GUESTHOUSE $

(☑94 68 75 49, 97 35 29 24; www.tatabenin.wordpress.com; Boukombé; r without bathroom CFA5000; P 🛜) This is a wonderfully laid-back Boukombé haven, with a leafy courtyard, a chilled-out ambience and tasty meals. Rooms occupy a large *tata* house. It's basic but clean and high on character. Joséphine and her daughter Valérie can organise village visits, cultural tours and dance classes. Pick-ups from Natitingou can also be arranged.

ℹ Getting There & Away

It's best to get to the Atakora with your own transport, but a few bush taxis do ply the dusty trail between Nati, Koussoukoingou and Boukoumbé (CFA2000, two hours), where you can cross into Togo. Otherwise, *zemi-johns* (about CFA5000, three hours) will take you, but be prepared for a dusty and tiring ride.

Parc National de la Pendjari

Amid the majestic landscape of the Atakora's rugged cliffs and wooded savannah live lions, cheetahs, leopards, elephants, baboons, hippos, myriad birds and countless antelopes. The 275,000-hectare **Parc National de la Pendjari** (Pendjari National Park; www.pendjari.net; per person CFA10,000, per vehicle CFA3000; ⊙6am-5pm), the main entrance of which is 100km north of Natitingou, is one of the best in West Africa. The best viewing time is near the end of the dry season, when animals start to hover around waterholes.

To maximise your chances of seeing animals, go for an accredited guide (graded as 'A' or 'B'). The list of accredited guides can be found on the park's website, at park entrances and in Nati's better hotels. It costs CFA10,000 for a 'A' guide and CFA8000 for a 'B' guide.

The main entrances to Pendjari are roughly 100km north of Natitingou, in Porga (near the border with Burkina Faso) and Batia (41km northeast of Tanguiéta, on a good track).

On the park's periphery, some 11km before Batia in Tanougou, you can take a dip in the lovely natural pools at the bottom of the **Tanougou Falls** (admission CFA1000).

🛏 Sleeping & Eating

Many visitors stay in Natitingou and make excursions from there, but you'll have a better chance of seeing animals if you stay at the park itself.

★**Pendjari Lodge** LODGE $$
(☑in France 336 68 42 73 43; www.pendjari-lodge.com; tents CFA31,000; ⊙Nov-Jul; P🐾) A lovely place in a beautiful setting on a small hill (views!), Pendjari Lodge mixes old-style safari ambience with nouveau bush chic. It sports a handful of luxury, semipermanent tents and a large dining area and lounge with wooden decks overlooking a valley. One quibble: the menu (mains from CFA4000) is

ℹ CROSSING INTO TOGO

If you cross into Togo from Boukombé, make sure you get your passport stamped at the *gendarmerie* (police station) at Boukoumbé as there is no border checkpoint.

a bit limited. No phone network, but wi-fi is available.

Hôtel de la Pendjari HOTEL $$
(☑23 82 11 24; www.hoteltatasomba.com; r with fan/air-con CFA21,000/26,000, bungalows without bathroom CFA15,000; ⊙Dec-May; P🌬🐾) Although it's starting to fray around the edges, this establishment offers spacious, utilitarian rooms with good bedding, and its location at the heart of the park is hard to beat. If you're watching your money, opt for the spartan bungalows. Electricity runs for a few hours a day only. There's an on-site restaurant (meals CFA6000), but service can be absent-minded.

ℹ Getting There & Away

Travellers without vehicles could try to team up with other parties at hotels in Natitingou. Most guides based in Natitingou can also organise vehicle rentals, and some of them have their own 4WDs. **Bénin Aventure** rents out 4WD vehicles for CFA75,000 per day (for up to four people), including a chauffeur guide (rated 'A' by the park) and fuel.

UNDERSTAND BENIN

Benin Today

The country is one of the more stable in the region, although things are not all that rosy. The current president, Yayi Boni, former head of the West African Development Bank, beat Adrien Houngbédji in a run-off in 2006. In his campaign, which he based around the slogan of 'change', he pledged to fight corruption and revive the country's economy.

It hasn't, however, been plain sailing: despite Boni's party winning a majority of seats in the parliamentary elections of 2007 and a number of local seats in the 2008 municipal elections, reforms have come about more slowly than hoped. Yayi Boni was re-elected in March 2011. In theory, the constitution limits presidents to two terms in office, but opposition parties fear that Boni may try to reform the constitution in order to stand for a third mandate in 2016.

History

More than 350 years ago the area now known as Benin was split into numerous principalities. Akaba of Abomey conquered his neighbouring ruler Dan and called the new kingdom Dan-Homey, later shortened to Dahomey by French colonisers. By 1727, Dahomey spread from Abomey down to Ouidah and Cotonou and into parts of modern Togo. The kingdoms of Nikki, Djougou and Parakou were still powerful in the north, as was the Kingdom of Toffa in Porto-Novo.

Each king pledged to leave his successor more land than he inherited, achieved by waging war with his neighbours. They grew rich by selling slaves to the European traders, notably the Portuguese, who established trading posts in Porto Novo, Ouidah and along the coast. For more than a century, an average of 10,000 slaves per year were shipped to the Americas. Southern Dahomey was dubbed the Slave Coast.

Following colonisation by the French, great progress was made in education, and many Dahomeyans were employed as government advisers throughout French West Africa.

Independence & Le Folklore

When Dahomey became independent in 1960, other former French colonies started deporting their Dahomeyan populations. Back home without work, they were the root of a highly unstable political situation. Three years after independence, following the example of neighbouring Togo, the Dahomeyan military staged a coup.

During the next decade Dahomey saw four military coups, nine changes of government and five changes of constitution: what the Dahomeyans called, in jest, *le folklore*.

Revolution

In 1972 a group of officers led by Lieutenant Colonel Mathieu Kérékou seized power in a coup, then embraced Marxist-Leninist ideology and aligned the country with superpowers such as China. To emphasise the break from the past, Kérékou changed the flag and renamed the country Benin. He informed his people of the change by radio on 13 November 1975.

The government established Marxist infrastructure, which included implementing collective farms. However, the economy became a shambles, and there were ethnic tensions between the president, a Natitingou-born northerner, and the Yoruba population in the south. There were six attempted coups in one year alone.

In December 1989, as a condition of French financial support, Kérékou ditched Marxism and held a conference to draft a new constitution. The delegates engineered a coup, forming a new cabinet under Nicéphore Soglo.

Soglo won the first free multiparty elections, held in March 1991, but his autocracy, nepotism and austere economic measures – following the devaluation of the CFA franc – came under fire. Kérékou was voted back into power in March 1996. Kérékou's second and final five-year term in office finished with the presidential elections in March 2006, bringing an end to his 33 years at the top.

People of Benin

There is an array of different ethnic groups within Benin's narrow borders, although three of them account for nearly 60% of the population: Fon, Adja and Yoruba. The Fon and Yoruba both migrated from Nigeria and occupy the southern and mideastern zones of Benin.

The Bariba and the Betamaribé, who make up 9% and 8% of the population respectively, live in the northern half of the country and have traditionally been very protective of their cultures and distant towards southern people.

The nomadic Fula (also called Fulani or Peul), found widely across West Africa, live primarily in the north and constitute 6% of the population.

Despite the underlying tensions between the southern and northern regions, the various groups live in relative harmony and have intermarried.

Religion

Some 40% of the population is Christian and 25% Muslim, but most people practise voodoo, whatever their religion. The practice mixed with Catholicism in the Americas, where the Dahomeyan slaves took it and from where their Afro-Brazilian descendants brought it back. Christian missionaries also won over Dahomeyans by fusing their creed with voodoo.

The Arts

Under the Dahomeyan kings, richly coloured appliqué banners were used to depict the rulers' past and present glories. With their bright, cloth-cut figures, the banners are still being made, particularly in Abomey.

Benin has a substantial Afro-Brazilian architectural heritage, best preserved in Porto Novo and Ouidah – there are plenty of hidden gems to seek out in the streets. The Lake Nokoué stilt villages, especially Ganvié, and the *tata somba* houses around Natitingou are remarkable examples of traditional architecture.

The *cire perdue* (lost wax) method used to make the famous Benin bronzes originates from Benin City, which lies in present-day Nigeria. However, the method spread west and the figures can be bought throughout Benin itself.

If you're into music, you'll love Angélique Kidjo, a major international star and Benin's most famous recording artist. Born in Ouidah in 1960 to a choreographer and a musician with Portuguese and English ancestry, Kidjo is a world musician in the true, boundary-busting sense of the phrase. Her music is inspired by the links between Africa and Latin America and the fusion of cultures. Check out www.kidjo.com for more information about her career. Other well-known Beninese artists include Gnonnas Pedro, Nel Oliver and Yelouassi Adolphe, and the bands Orchestre Poly-Rythmo and Disc Afrique.

Food & Drink

Beninese grub is unquestionably among the best in West Africa and is very similar to Togolese food, the main differences being the names: *fufu* is generally called *igname pilé*, and *djenkoumé* is called *pâte rouge*, for example. In southern Benin, fish is a highlight of local cuisine. It's usually barracuda, dorado or grouper, and is usually served grilled or fried.

The local beer, La Béninoise, is a passable drop. Mineral water and fruit juices are sold in all major towns. The adventurous could try the millet-based brew *tchoukoutou* or *sodabe* (moonshine).

Environment

Sandwiched between Nigeria and Togo, Benin is 700km long and 120km across in the south, widening to about 300km in the north. Most of the coastal plain is a sand bar that blocks the seaward flow of several rivers. As a result, there are lagoons a few kilometres inland all along the coast, which is being eroded by the strong ocean currents. Inland is a densely forested plateau and, in the far northwest, the Atakora Mountains.

Wildlife thrives in Parc National de la Pendjari, with elephants and several feline species.

Deforestation and desertification are major issues because of the logging of valuable wood, such as teak.

SURVIVAL GUIDE

ⓘ Directory A–Z

ACCOMMODATION

Benin has accommodation to suit every budget – from beach resorts to guesthouses. Swanky hotels are confined to Cotonou and, to a lesser extent, Ouidah and Natitingou. Most have restaurants and bars, and offer wi-fi service and have air-con.

EMBASSIES & CONSULATES

The following offices are all in Cotonou.

British Community Liaison Officer (☑ 21 30 32 65; www.fco.gov.uk; Haie Vive) Officially, British nationals must deal with the British Deputy High Commission in Lagos (Nigeria). However, the Community Liaison Officer for the British community in Benin, based at the English International School, can be of some help.

French Embassy (☑ 21 36 55 33; www.ambafrance-bj.org; Ave Jean-Paul II)

German Embassy (☑ 21 31 29 67; www.cotonou.diplo.de; Ave Jean-Paul II)

Ghanaian Embassy (☑ 21 30 07 46; off Blvd de la Marina)

Nigerian Embassy (☑ 21 31 56 65; Blvd de la Marina)

Nigerien Embassy (☑ 21 31 56 65; off Blvd de la Marina)

US Embassy (☑ 21 30 06 50; cotonou.usembassy.gov; Rue Caporal Bernard Anani)

FOOD & DRINK

For more information on the gastronomy of Benin, see p53.

INTERNET ACCESS

➡ In towns and cities, complimentary wi-fi is available in almost every midrange and top-end hotel.

➡ Internet cafes are plentiful in towns and cities. Rates are CFA300 per hour. Connection speeds vary from pretty good to acceptable.

MONEY

➡ The currency in Benin is the West African CFA franc.

➡ The best foreign currency to carry is euros, easily exchanged at any bank, hotel or bureau de change.

➡ Travellers cheques cannot be exchanged in Benin.

➡ There are numerous Visa ATMs in every city; the only bank to accept MasterCard is Banque Atlantique (in Cotonou only), though its MasterCard ATMs were not functioning at the time of research.

➡ Credit cards are accepted at some upmarket hotels and shops. Some places levy a commission of about 5% for credit-card payment.

OPENING HOURS

Banks Open 8am to 12.30pm and 3pm to 6.30pm Monday to Friday, plus 9am to 1pm Saturday. Some banks are open through lunchtime.

Bars Normally serve from late morning until the last customers leave (late); nightclubs generally go from 10pm into the wee hours.

Restaurants Lunch is usually from 11.30am to 2.30pm, dinner 6.30pm to 10.30pm.

Shops & Businesses Open 8am to noon and 3pm to 7pm Monday to Saturday.

PUBLIC HOLIDAYS

Benin celebrates Muslim holidays.
New Year's Day 1 January
Vodoun 10 January
Easter Monday March/April
Labour Day 1 May
Ascension Thursday May
Pentecost Monday May
Independence Day 1 August
Assumption 15 August
Armed Forces Day 26 October
All Saints' Day 1 November
Christmas 25 December

SAFE TRAVEL

Cotonou has its fair share of traffic accidents and muggings, so be careful. In Ouidah, avoid

---

PRACTICALITIES

Electricity Supply is 220V and plugs are of the European two-round-pin variety. Network cuts are frequent.
Newspapers Cotonou's daily newspapers include *La Nation* and *Le Matinal*.
Radio The state-owned ORTB broadcasts on the radio in French and local languages.
Languages Include French, Fon, Yoruba, Dendi, Aja and Bariba. More than 50 languages are spoken in total.

---

the roads to and along the coast at any time of day.

Children, and sometimes also adults, will shout '*Yovo! Yovo!*' (meaning 'white person') ad nauseam. It's normally harmless, but tiresome.

The beaches along the coast are not safe for swimming because of strong currents. Stick to hotel swimming pools or the lagoon.

TELEPHONE

➡ Benin's country code is 229.

➡ Phone numbers have eight digits. Landline numbers start with 21, mobile numbers with 9 or 6.

➡ Mobile-phone coverage is excellent and fairly cheap. Local networks include Moov and MTN.

➡ Depending on which mobile network you use at home, your phone may or may not work while in Cotonou – ask your mobile network provider. You can also bring your phone and buy a local SIM card (CFA1000). Top-up vouchers are readily available.

VISAS

Visas are required for all travellers except nationals of the Economic Community of West African States (Ecowas).

Local authorities have had a couple of U-turns on visa policies in recent years. At the time of writing, visas were not obtainable at the border or upon arrival at the airport. Be sure to get your visa from a Beninese embassy before travelling. Allow €50 for a one-month single-entry visa.

Note that at the time of research the Visa des Pays de l'Entente was not available in Benin.

Visas for Onward Travel

The following embassies deliver visas:

Burkina Faso No diplomatic representation in Benin – contact the French consulate.

Niger The embassy in Cotonou issues 30-day visas. They cost CFA22,500 and you'll need two photos. Allow three to four working days. You cannot get visas at the border.

Nigeria The Nigerian embassy only issues transit visas to travellers with a Nigerian embassy in their home country (there is no need to contact the embassy in your home country beforehand). You need two photos, along with photocopies of your passport and, if you have one, your ticket for onward travel from Nigeria. Fees vary according to nationality. Visas are normally issued on the same day.

Togo Seven-day visas (CFA10,000) are issued at the border. If crossing the border at Nadoba (coming from Boukombé), head to Kara where the Direction Régionale de la Documentation Nationale issues 30-day multiple-entry visas (CFA10,000, four photos).

WOMEN TRAVELLERS

Beninese men can be sleazy and women travellers will get a lot of unwanted attention. Particularly unnerving are military and other officials using their power to get more of your company than is strictly necessary. Always stay polite but firm and make sure you have a good 'husband story'.

ⓘ Getting There & Away

You will need a yellow-fever vaccination certificate to come to Benin.

AIR

The **Aéroport International de Cotonou Cadjéhoun** (www.aeroport-cotonou.com) is Benin's main gateway.

The main international carriers are **Air France** (www.airfrance.com; Rte de l'Aéroport), **Royal Air Maroc** (☑ 21 30 86 04; www.royalairmaroc.com; Rte de l'Aéroport), **Brussels Airlines** (☑ 21 30 16 82; www.brusselsairlines.com; Rte de l'Aéroport) and **Ethiopian Airlines** (☑ 21 32 71 61; www.flyethiopian.com; Rue 403), which offer direct flights to France, Morocco, Belgium and Ethiopia respectively, and connecting flights to the rest of the world.

Other major airlines include **Asky** (☑ 21 32 54 18; www.flyasky.com; Ave de la Paix), which flies to major capitals in West and Central Africa via Lomé; **South African Airways** (www.flysaa.com; Ave Steinmetz), which flies to Johannesburg (South Africa); **Kenya Airways** (☑ 21 31 63 71; www.kenya-airways.com; Ave Steinmetz), which flies to Nairobi (Kenya) and Ouagadougou (Burkina Faso); **Air Burkina** (www.air-burkina.com; Rte de l'Aéroport), which serves Ouagadougou (Burkina Faso) and Abidjan (Côte d'Ivoire); and **Senegal Airlines** (☑ 21 31 76 51; www.senegalairlines.aero; Ave Steinmetz), which flies to Dakar (Senegal) and Abidjan (Côte d'Ivoire). All airlines have offices in Cotonou.

LAND

Burkina Faso

From Tanguiéta in north western Benin, you can find bush taxis to Nadiagou, on the Burkina side of the border north or Porga, from where you can find services to Ouagadougou. There's also a daily bus from Tanguiéta to Ouagadougou.

TCV (☑ 97 60 39 68; Rue 108) and **TSR** (☑ 97 88 17 94; Rue Proche) run bus services three times a week between Cotonou and Bobo Dioulasso via Ouagadougou (CFA18,000, 18 hours).

Niger

From Malanville in northeastern Benin, a *zemijohn* or shared taxi can take you across the Niger River to Gaya in Niger.

From Cotonou, **Rimbo-RTV** (☑ 95 23 24 82; Zongo) has daily services to Niamey (CFA22,000, 18 hours).

Nigeria

ABC Transport (☑ 66 56 45 15; Stade de l'Amitié) and **Cross Country International** (☑ 66 99 92 41; Ave du Nouveau Pont) both operate a daily Lagos–Accra bus service, which stops in Cotonou (CFA11,000 to CFA12,500, four hours). Add another CFA5000 for the *convoyeur* (the middleman who'll handle and facilitate formalities at the border).

There are no direct taxis to Lagos from Porto Novo, so you'll have to change at the Kraké–Seme border (CFA800, 30 minutes). Make sure you have some naira to pay for your journey on the other side.

Togo

Cotonou and Lomé are connected by frequent bush taxis (CFA5000, three hours), which regularly leave the Gare Jonquet in Cotonou for Lomé. Alternatively, pick up a taxi to the border point at Hilakondji and grab another taxi on the Togolese side of the border.

Various bus companies, including **STIF** (☑ 97 98 11 80; off Ave Clozel), **STC** (☑ 21 32 66 69; off Rue 303) and **UTB** (☑ 95 42 71 20; Ave Clozel), also regularly plough the Cotonou–Lomé–Accra–Abidjan route (CFA5000 for Lomé, four hours).

Other crossings are at Kétao–Ouaké, on the Kara–Djougou road, and between Nadoba in Togo and Boukombé in Benin along a good track. The latter crossing takes you through spectacular countryside but has little public transport except on Wednesday, Nadoba market day.

ⓘ Getting Around

BUSH TAXI

Bush taxis, generally beaten-up old vehicles, cover outlying communities that large buses don't serve but also run between major towns and cities. There is sometimes a surcharge for luggage. Most leave from the *gares routières*; morning is the best time to find them.

BUS

➡ Buses are the most reliable and comfortable way to get around, especially between cities in southern Benin and Natitingou to the north.

➡ ATT and Confort Lines buses are better maintained and more reliable than those of other companies. They also have air-con.

➡ Buses almost always operate with guaranteed seating and fixed departure times; arrive early or book the day before to ensure you have a seat on your preferred service.

CAR & MOTORCYCLE

➡ Roads are in relatively good condition throughout Benin except the Cotonou–Bohicon road, which is appalling. It's scheduled to be resurfaced though.

➡ Hiring a car with a driver is a good option if you're short on time. Travel agencies and tour operators in Cotonou can organise 4WD rental for about 50,000 per day (with driver). For a regular vehicle, you'll pay about CFA20,000 per day. Fuel is extra.

➡ If you're driving, you need an International Driving Permit.

➡ A litre of petrol cost around CFA600 at the time of research. Petrol stations are easy to find throughout the country.

ZEMI-JOHNS

The omnipresence of *zems* (*zemi-johns;* motorbike taxis) has translated into the near disap-

pearance of car taxis for short journeys. While they are by far the fastest and most convenient way of getting around, they are dangerous: most drive like lunatics and helmets are not available.

Zem drivers wear numbered yellow shirts in Cotonou (various colours in other towns). Hail them just as you would a taxi, and be sure to agree on a price before the journey. The typical fare costs from CFA150 to CFA250 for trips within a town. They are also an easy way to get to remote villages where public transport is infrequent.

TOURS

For tours around Benin and further afield, the following companies are recommended and can arrange English-speaking guides.

Bénin Aventure (☑ 97 50 23 74, 23 02 00 17; www.beninaventure.com; Hôtel de Bourgogne, Rte Inter-État) Organises guided, tailor-made trips around Benin in chauffeur-driven 4WDs.

Eco-Bénin (www.ecobenin.org) This small Beninese NGO promoting sustainable tourism runs activities in three sites across the country: Possotomé and Lake Ahémé, Koussoukoingou in the Somba country and Tanougou next to the Parc National de la Pendjari. The basis of its activities is guided tours exploring the culture and heritage of the area. It also organises vehicle rentals.

Double Sens (www.doublesens.fr) Another reputable tour operator with a strong ethic. Can arrange all kinds of tours, including village stays.

Burkina Faso

POP 17 MILLION

Best Places to Eat

➡ La Canne d'Or (p65)

➡ Le Calypso (p68)

➡ Maquis Aboussouan (p61)

➡ Le Verdoyant (p61)

➡ Le Saint-Germain (p65)

Best Places to Stay

➡ Villa Bobo (p64)

➡ Le Pavillon Vert (p60)

➡ Le Calypso (p68)

➡ Les Jardins de Koulouba (p60)

➡ Campement de l'Éléphant (p71)

Why Go?

Burkina may not have many big-ticket attractions, yet it invariably wins the hearts of travellers for the warmth of its welcome. The Burkinabé are disarmingly charming and easygoing, and wherever you go you'll be greeted with a memorable *bonne arrivée* (welcome).

The country's other big draws are its enchanting landscapes – from atmospheric Sahelian plains, to rolling savannah and surprising geology – and the lively cultural scene. Ouagadougou and Bobo-Dioulasso, Burkina's two largest and gloriously named cities, are famous for their musical traditions and beautiful handicrafts. Throw in Fespaco, Africa's premier film festival, held in the capital every odd-numbered year, and there's enough to engage your mind and senses for a couple of weeks or so.

Tourism infrastructure is fairly limited, but there is a handful of gems, especially in Ouaga, Bobo and Banfora, as well as family-run, simple *campements* (guesthouses) in more remote areas.

When to Go
Ouagadougou

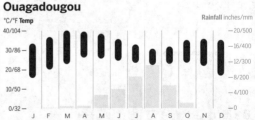

| Jan–Feb Perfect wildlife-viewing time; dusty harmattan winds can produce hazy skies. | Apr–Sep Hot season (Apr/May) best avoided; rainy season (Jun–Sep) can be challenging for transport. | Oct–Dec A lovely time of year, with green landscapes and pleasant temperatures. |

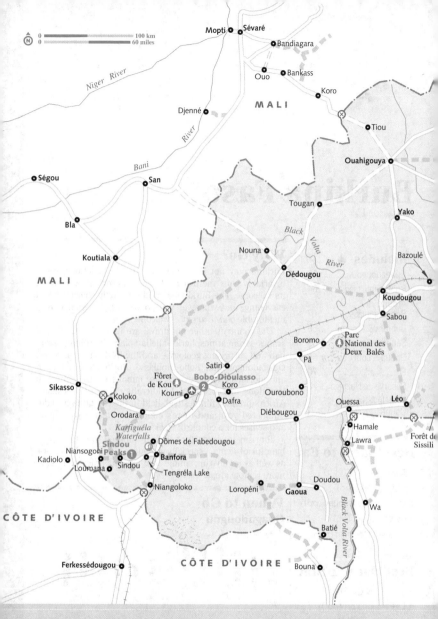

Burkina Faso Highlights

① Wander amid other-worldly rock formations and Burkina's lush landscapes at the **Sindou Peaks** (p69)

② Sip a few beers to the sound of Bobo-Dioulasso's fantastic **live music scene** (p66)

③ Come face to face with elephants at **Réserve de Nazinga** (p70)

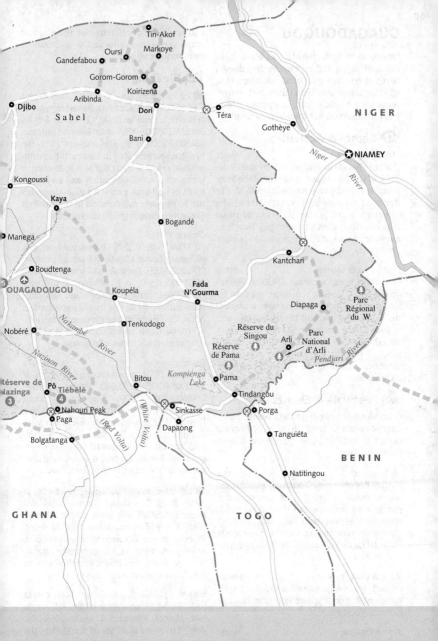

OUAGADOUGOU

POP 1.4 MILLION

Ouaga, as it's affectionately dubbed, lacks standout sights and its architecture doesn't have much to turn your head, but it thrives as an eclectic arts hub, with dance and concert venues, live bands, theatre companies, a busy festival schedule and beautiful handicrafts.

Sights & Activities

Moro-Naba Palace PALACE

(Ave Moro-Naba) On Fridays at 7am the Moro-Naba of Ouagadougou – emperor of the Mossi and the most powerful traditional chief in Burkina Faso – presides over the Moro-Naba ceremony at the palace. It's a formal ritual that lasts only about 15 minutes. Travellers are welcome to attend, but photos are not permitted.

Musée de la Musique MUSEUM

(Ave d'Oubritenga; admission CFA1000; ⏲9am-noon & 3-6pm Tue-Sat) You don't need to be into music to enjoy this excellent museum: the Burkinabé live and breathe music and a visit to the museum serves as a great introduction to Burkinabé culture. At the time of writing, the museum was about to relocate to shiny new premises on Ave d'Oubritenga.

Festivals & Events

Ouagadougou has one of the liveliest calendars of events in West Africa, with Fespaco definitely justifying you tailor your trip to match its dates.

★ **Fespaco** FILM

(Festival Pan-Africain du Cinéma de Ouagadougou; www.fespaco.bf; ⏲Feb-Mar of odd-numbered years) Going strong since 1969, this world-renowned festival, held biennially, sees African films competing for the prestigious Étalon d'Or de Yennenga – Fespaco's equivalent of the Oscars.

Rock à Ouaga MUSIC

(⏲Mar) A low-key festival featuring Burkina's most happening musicians, with international guest stars.

Jazz à Ouaga MUSIC

(www.jazz-ouaga.org; ⏲Apr-May) This is a well-established music festival that brings out the Afrobeat, soul and blues influence in jazz.

SIAO ARTS & CRAFTS

(Salon International de l'Artisanat de Ouagadougou; www.siao.bf; ⏲Oct of even-numbered years) Biennial trade fair of reference for the arts and crafts sector in Africa and a godsend for gem-hunting visitors.

Sleeping

★ **Le Pavillon Vert** BACKPACKERS $

(☎50 31 06 11; www.hotel-pavillonvert.com; Ave de la Liberté; s/d with fan CFA12,500/13,500, with air-con CFA17,000/18,000, with fan & without bathroom CFA8000/8500; ❄📶) The stalwart 'PV' is the best backpackers spot in Ouaga. It has competitive prices, a lively bar and restaurant, a gorgeous plant-filled garden and an assortment of well-kept rooms for all budgets. It's run by the same management as the excellent Couleurs d'Afrique (p63) travel agency.

Case d'Hôtes B&B $

(☎78 00 86 16, 50 31 03 61; www.case-hotes.com; off Ave de la Liberté; s/d with fan & without bathroom CFA10,000/13,500, with air-con & without bathroom CFA14,500/17,500; ❄📶) Expect firm beds, crisp linen, artistic touches and spic-and-span bathrooms at this friendly guesthouse. Alain, the French owner, prepares great, jovial evening meals, which are served in a shady courtyard. Rates include breakfast.

Cocooning GUESTHOUSE $

(☎50 34 28 14; www.cocooning-faso.com; s/d/tr CFA8000/10,000/15,000, without bathroom CFA6500/8000/12,000) Cocooning's great selling point is its delightful owner, Dalila, a French-Algerian woman who fell in love with Burkina and never left. She runs an NGO to help destitute families and it is her welcome, grace and knowledge that make staying here special rather than the utilitarian rooms.

★ **Les Jardins de Koulouba** GUESTHOUSE $$

(☎50 30 25 81; www.jardins-koulouba.fr; r with air-con CFA25,000, with fan & without bathroom CFA15,000; 📶🏊) Considering its chic decor, spacious rooms, fantastic location, pool and, as its name suggests, rather wonderful garden and patio, this lovely guesthouse wins the *palme d'or* for best value in Ouaga.

Villa Yiri Suma GUESTHOUSE $$

(☎50 30 54 82; www.yirisuma.com; 428 Ave du Petit Maurice Yameogo; d CFA21,000-28,000; ❄📶) Yiri Suma is all about art. Lucien, the owner, is passionate about African art and likes nothing better than to share his passion with guests. The villa regularly houses exhibitions and cultural events, and the five spotless rooms enjoy their own contemporary decor and unique works.

Chez Giuliana
GUESTHOUSE **$$**

(☑50 36 33 97; www.chezgiuliana.com; Rue Lamine Gueye, Quartier 1200 Logements; s/d CFA19,500/23,000, without bathroom CFA15,000/19,000; ❀⬚) This bustling Italian guesthouse is a perennial favourite among aid workers: the welcome is as colourful as the rooms and the roof terrace is simply awesome for sundowners. It's about 3km outside the centre, near the Maternité Sainte Camille. Rates include breakfast.

Auberge Le Karité Bleu
B&B **$$$**

(☑50 36 90 46; www.karitebleu.com; 214 Blvd de l'Onatel, Zone du Bois; d CFA30,000-43,000; ❀⬚) In a residential neighbourhood, this adorable B&B offers eight spiffy rooms decorated according to different African styles (Dogon, Berber, Ashanti etc). The gorgeous terrace and Jacuzzi are lovely perks. It's about 2km west of the city centre. Prices include breakfast.

Hôtel Les Palmiers
HOTEL **$$$**

(☑50 33 33 30; www.hotellespalmiers.net; Rue Joseph Badoua; d CFA32,000-41,000; ❀⬚⛱) Les Palmiers is an oasis blending African touches with European levels of comfort. The rooms are arranged around a leafy compound and embellished with local decorations. The garden, pool and terrace provide the finishing touches.

✗ Eating

Marina Market
MARKET **$**

(Ave Yennenga; ⊘8am-9pm Mon-Sat, 9am-8pm Sun) Great selection of groceries and long opening hours.

★Maquis Aboussouan
AFRICAN **$$**

(☑50 34 27 20; Rue Simon Compaoré; mains CFA2500-5000; ⊘11am-11pm Tue-Sun; ❀) This upmarket *maquis* is the place to enjoy Burkinabé staples such as *poulet kedjenou* (slow-cooked chicken with peppers and tomatoes) or *attiéké* (grated cassava).

★Le Verdoyant
PIZZERIA **$$**

(☑50 31 54 07; Ave Dimdolobsom; mains CFA4000-6000; ⊘noon-2.30pm & 6.30-11pm Thu-Tue) A favourite haunt of expats, the ultracentral Le Verdoyant is famous for its pasta, wood-fired pizzas and ice creams. Note that the mosquitoes are ferocious at night.

Kfête
CAFE **$$**

(Institut Français, Ave de la Nation; mains CFA2000-5000; ⊘9am-6pm; ⬚) The Institut Français' gorgeous restaurant is a lovely spot for lunch: sit in colourful raffia chairs under the modern *paillote* (straw awning) and tuck into bursting baguettes, juicy crêpes, or just sip a coffee to the sound of *chanson française*.

Cappuccino
EUROPEAN **$$**

(Ave Kwame N'Krumah; mains CFA2000-6000; ⊘6am-1am; ❀⬚) Long opening hours and a large menu catering to all tastes and all budgets (anything from pastries to copious salads and pizzas) make this brasserie one of Ouaga's popular eateries.

L'Eau Vive
FRENCH **$$**

(Rue de l'Hôtel de Ville; mains CFA2000-7000; ⊘noon-2.30pm & 7-10pm; ❀) This Ouagadougou institution is run by an order of nuns and promises an air-conditioned haven from the clamour outside; there's also a garden dining area out the back. 'Ave Maria' is sung at 9.30pm every night.

Espace Gondwana
FUSION **$$$**

(☑50 36 11 24; www.africartisanat.com; Rue du Dr Balla Moussa Traoré, Zone du Bois; mains CFA4000-9000; ⊘6-11pm; ❀⬚) Espace Gondwana sports sensational decor, with four dining rooms richly adorned with masks and traditional furniture. The food impresses, too, with an imaginative menu that runs the gamut from frogs' legs and fish dishes to grilled meats and salads.

🍷 Drinking & Entertainment

Maquis dancing (simple open-air bars with blaring sound systems) are scattered all around Ouaga, but the most happening area is Gounghin, west of the centre.

★Bar K
BAR

(Koulougou; ⊘noon-2am) Bar K is all about its vast roof terrace: order a cold beer or cocktail, sink into one of the sofas and enjoy the music under a canopy of stars and fairy lights.

De Niro
BAR

(off Ave Houari Boumedienne; ⊘5pm-midnight Thu-Tue) This jazz bar is a gem: the music is great, the decor original (with fab photos, posters and two beautiful pool tables), the terrace breezy and the service super friendly.

Institut Français
PERFORMING ARTS

(Ave de la Nation) The French cultural centre has one of the best line-ups of Burkinabé

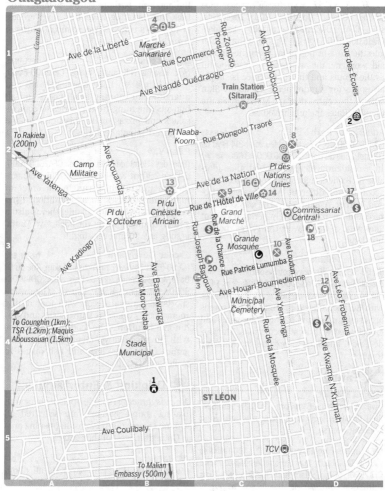

and West African musicians, theatre directors and visual artists.

Zaka
LIVE MUSIC

(⊙10am-late) A pleasant watering hole by day and live-music venue by night (especially traditional music), with bands every night from 8pm.

🔒 Shopping

Nuances
SOUVENIRS

(☑50 31 72 74; Ave Yennenga; ⊙8.30am-12.30pm & 3.30-7pm Mon-Sat, 10am-noon Sun) A gorgeous boutique, with a combination of

eclectic African art, textiles, clothing and carvings.

Nimba Art
JEWELLERY

(www.nimbaart.com; Ave de la Liberté; ⊙8am-7pm) A great boutique specialising in jewellery but also stocking woodcarvings and other souvenirs.

Village Artisanal de Ouaga
SOUVENIRS

(☑50 37 14 83; Blvd Tengsoba, known as Blvd Circulaire; ⊙7am-7pm) A government-run cooperative with a wide range of crafts, ideal for souvenir shopping without the hard sell.

Ouagadougou

⊙ Sights
1 Moro-Naba Palace	B4
2 Musée de la Musique	D2

🛏 Sleeping
3 Hôtel Les Palmiers	C3
4 Le Pavillon Vert	B1
5 Les Jardins de Koulouba	E3
6 Villa Yiri Suma	E3

🍴 Eating
7 Cappuccino	D4
Kfête	(see 13)
8 Le Verdoyant	D2
9 L'Eau Vive	C2
10 Marina Market	C3

🍷 Drinking & Nightlife
11 Bar K	E3
12 De Niro	D3

🎭 Entertainment
13 Institut Français	B2
14 Zaka	C2

🛍 Shopping
15 Nimba Art	B1
16 Nuances	C2

ℹ Information
17 Canadian Embassy	D3
18 Dutch Embassy	D3
19 French Embassy	E2
20 German Embassy	C3
21 Ghanaian Embassy	E1
22 Ivorian Embassy	F2

ℹ Transport
L'Agence Tourisme	(see 3)

ℹ Information

Ouagadougou is one of the safer cities in the region, but avoid walking alone at night. Bag snatching is a problem: don't carry valuables.

There are numerous banks around town, most with ATM.

Centre Médical International (📞70 20 00 00, 50 30 66 07; Rue Nazi Boni; ⊙24hr)

Commissariat Central (📞17; Ave Loudun)

Couleurs d'Afrique (www.couleurs-afrique. com; Ave de l'Olympisme, Gounghin) Run by Frenchman Guillaume Adeline, this well-established operator offers circuits in Burkina and neighbouring countries. Highly recommended.

Cyberposte (off Ave de la Nation; per hour CFA500; ⊙8am-8pm Mon-Sat) Also offers printing and scanning services.

L'Agence Tourisme (www.agence-tourisme. com; Rue Joseph Badoua, Hôtel les Palmiers, Burkina Faso) Excellent tour operator, with many years' experience in Burkina and West Africa.

Visa extension (Service des Passeports; Ave Kadiogo; ⊙8-11.30am & 3-5pm Mon-Fri) Visa extensions (two photos, CFA39,000 for six months) and Visa de l'Entente (p74). Both services take 72 hours.

ℹ Getting There & Away

Buses leave from the bus companies' depots. Every taxi knows where to find them. Routes include:

➡ **Bobo Dioulasso** (CFA7000, five hours, seven daily; operated by TCV, Rakiéta)

➡ **Banfora** (CFA8500, 6½ hours, six daily; operated by TCV, Rakiéta)

➡ **Gaoua** (CFA7000, four hours, five daily; operated by TSR, STAFF)

➡ **Pô** (CFA2500, 2½ hours, four daily; operated by Rakiéta)

For international services, see p75.

❶ Getting Around

The taxi ride to the Aéroport International de Ouagadougou from the centre costs about CFA3000.

Shared taxis (beaten-up old green cars) cost a flat CFA300; flag them anywhere in town. They tend to follow set routes, often to/from the Grand Marché. Chartered taxis will cost a minimum of CFA1500; negotiate before you set off.

A good alternative if you happen to be in a street without much traffic or would like to be picked up at a certain time or place is **Allo Taxi** (☎ 50 34 34 35). Taxis must be booked and they run on the meter. They are more expensive than green taxis.

THE SOUTHWEST

Southwestern Burkina Faso ticks all the right boxes, with a heady mix of natural and cultural sights vying for your attention.

Bobo-Dioulasso

POP 490,000

Bobo, as it's widely known, may be Burkina Faso's second-largest city, but it has a small-town charm and its tree-lined streets exude a languid, semi-tropical atmosphere that makes it a favourite rest stop for travellers.

You'll have plenty to do during the day in and around the city, but save some energy for night-time to enjoy Bobo's thriving music scene and excellent restaurants.

❍ Sights

Grande Mosquée   MOSQUE
(admission CFA1000) Built in 1893, the Grande Mosquée is an outstanding example of Sahel-style mud architecture, with conical towers and wooden struts (which both support the structure and act as scaffolding during replastering). Visits take you inside the building and onto the roof terrace, where you'll get a different perspective of the towers.

Kibidwé   NEIGHBOURHOOD
(admission CFA1000) Bobo's historical centre is a thriving neighbourhood. Little has changed over the centuries in terms of organisation: Muslims, *griots* (traditional caste of musicians or praise singers), blacksmiths and 'nobles' (farmers) still live in their respective quarters but happily trade services and drink at the same *chopolo* (millet beer) bars.

Guided tours are not official, but are unavoidable in practice – allow CFA2000 to CFA3000. They offer a great insight into local life, although the compulsory craft-shop stops are tedious.

**Musée Communal
Sogossira Sanon**   MUSEUM
(Place de la Nation; admission CFA1000; ☒ 9am-12.30pm & 3-5.30pm Tue-Sat) A small museum that showcases masks, statues and ceremonial dress from all over Burkina Faso. There are full-scale examples of traditional buildings inside the grounds.

🛏 Sleeping

Campement Le Pacha   HOTEL $
(☎ 76 61 16 01; lepachabo@yahoo.fr; Rue Malherbe; d with air-con CFA15,000, with fan & without bathroom CFA9500; ❄) For a Franco-Swiss venture, the unadorned rooms are a tad disappointing, but there's an attractive courtyard and a great garden restaurant famed for its wood-fired pizzas. Location is ace, too.

Villa Rose   GUESTHOUSE $
(☎ 70 63 54 88, 20 98 54 16; www.villarosebobodioulasso.com; Koko; s/d with fan CFA9000/10,000, with air-con CFA15,000/17,000; ❄ 🛜) This lovely guesthouse run by a Dutch-Burkinabé couple, Franca and Moctar, was about to move to a new location in the leafy neighbourhood of Koko, east of the centre, at the time of our visit. Thankfully, the friendly welcome will stay the same.

★ **Villa Bobo**   B&B $$
(☎ 70 53 78 17, 20 98 20 03; www.villabobo.com; Koko; s/d/tr with fan CFA12,000/15,000/17,000, with air-con CFA17,000/20,000/22,000; ❄ 🛜 ⛱) With its four zealously maintained rooms, prim bathrooms, atmospheric verandah, colourful garden and pool, Villa Bobo is a delight. Xavier, the French owner, speaks English and can arrange excursions in the area.

Entente Hôtel HOTEL **$$**

(☎ 20 97 12 05; sopresbobo@yahoo.fr; Rue du Commerce; s/d with fan CFA9300/12,600 s/d/tr with air-con CFA12,300/20,600/27,900; ❄ 🛜) One of the few central establishments in Bobo, L'Entente has clean, tidy rooms. The fan rooms are rather small for the price, but there is plenty of space to hang out in the pleasant courtyard.

Les 2 Palmiers HOTEL **$$$**

(☎ 20 97 27 59; www.hotelles2palmiers.com; off Rue Malherbe; d CFA34,500-39,500; ❄ 🛜) In a quiet street, this excellent option gets an A-plus for its spotless rooms embellished with African knick-knacks. The on-site restaurant is hailed as one of the best in Bobo.

🍴 Eating

As well as restaurants, there are lots of *maquis* in the centre that serve inexpensive food. Les Bambous (p66) also serves excellent pizzas.

Mandé AFRICAN **$**

(Ave de la Révolution; mains CFA1000-4000; ⏱7am-3pm & 6-11pm; 🛜) With an open-air terrace, great prices and a wide-ranging menu specialising in African dishes, Mandé is an excellent deal. If you just eat *riz sauce* (rice with sauce) or couscous and drink tamarind juice, you'll be well fed for around CFA1500.

**Boulangerie Pâtisserie La
Bonne Miche** BAKERY **$**

(Ave Ouédraogo; ⏱6am-7pm) Excellent bread and pastries.

FÊTE DES MASQUES

In the Bobo-Dioulasso region, whenever there's a major funeral, it's accompanied by a late-night *fête des masques* (festival of masks).

Masked men dance to an orchestra of flutelike instruments and narrow drums beaten with curved canes. Each dancer, representing a different spirit, performs in turn, leaping, waving sticks and looking for evil spirits that might prevent the deceased from going to paradise.

As the celebrations go on, dancers become increasingly wild, performing acrobatic feats and waving their heads backwards and forwards until they catch someone and strike them. The victim, however, must not complain.

ℹ SET YOUR BUDGET

Budget
➡ Hotel room CFA10,000
➡ *Riz sauce* in a *maquis* CFA1000
➡ Brakina CFA650
➡ Shared taxi ride CFA300

Midrange
➡ Hotel room CFA18,000
➡ Pizza CFA4000
➡ Drink in a bar CFA1500
➡ Moped rental, per day CFA4000

Top End
➡ Hotel room CFA30,000
➡ Two-course meal CFA8000
➡ Glass of wine CFA3000
➡ 4WD with driver, per day CFA60,000

Marina Market SUPERMARKET **$**

(Ave de la République; ⏱8am-1pm & 3.30-9pm Mon-Sat, 9am-1pm Sun) Great range of grocery items, ideal for stocking up ahead of picnics and bus journeys.

L'Eau Vive FRENCH **$$**

(Rue Delafosse; mains CFA2500-6000; ⏱noon-2.30pm & 6.30-10pm Mon-Sat) L'Eau Vive offers imaginative French cooking and a varied menu. It's the sister venue of the restaurant of the same name in Ouagadougou, and is also run by nuns.

⭐ La Canne d'Or FRENCH **$$$**

(☎ 20 98 15 96; Ave Philippe Zinda Kaboré; mains CFA4000-6000; ⏱11.30am-2.30pm & 6.30-10pm Tue-Sun) This villa-style eatery, with its African decor and riot of fairy lights, serves French fare with an African twist. House faves include frogs' legs and a great grill selection (kebabs, steak, Nile perch etc). Service is stellar.

⭐ Le Saint-Germain FRENCH **$$$**

(Ave du Gouverneur Clozel; mains CFA6000-10,000; ⏱noon-3pm & 6.30-11pm; 🛜) Bobo's gourmet address is wrapped around an exotic garden and art gallery. The restaurant serves delicious spiced-up French cuisine; it also has one of the finest wine cellars in Burkina. All this class comes at a price: expect to pay an eye-watering CFA15,000 to CFA20,000 per person.

Bobo-Dioulasso

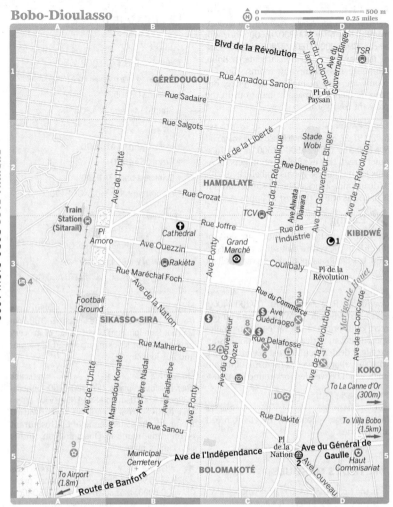

🍷 Drinking & Entertainment

Drinking in Bobo goes hand in hand with music, whether live or in the form of dancing. Admission (CFA500) is sometimes charged for live-music events. There is dancing at most *maquis* on Friday and Saturday nights, and from 4pm onwards on Sundays (known as *matinée*).

⭐ Le Samanké
LIVE MUSIC

(Koko; ⏰10am-late) Bobo's best live-music venue, with an excellent sound system, a big stage, a fab garden and a fantastic program of Burkinabé and African artists (music mostly but also dance and theatre).

Tharkay
CLUB

(Koko; ⏰11am-late) Come and shake your stuff to *coupé-décalé* (Ivorian beats) and other Afro-beats at the funky Tharkay. The Sunday *matinée* is particularly popular.

Les Bambous
LIVE MUSIC

(Ave du Gouverneur Binger; ⏰6.30pm-late Tue-Sun) One of Bobo's long-standing music venues, with concerts every night. It also serves excellent pizzas (CFA3000 to CFA4000).

Bobo-Dioulasso

Le Bois d'Ébène　　　　　　　　LIVE MUSIC
(Ave de l'Unité; ⊙ noon-late) One of the best venues in town for live music. Concerts Thursday to Sunday.

🛍 Shopping

★**Gafreh**　　　　　　　　　　ACCESSORIES
(www.gafreh.org; Rue Delafosse; ⊙ 7am-7pm Mon-Sat) This brilliant initiative, a women's cooperative, recycles the millions of black sachets handed out with purchases across Burkina into chic handbags, wallets and other accessories.

Galerie Le Saint Germain　　ARTS & CRAFTS
(Ave du Gouverneur Clozel; ⊙ 9am-7pm) This swish gallery showcases fantastic works by Burkinabé and other West African artists, including furniture and decorative objects.

🛈 Getting There & Away

Buses leave from the companies' depots. Routes include:
➡ **Ouaga** (CFA7000, five hours, seven daily; operated by TCV, Rakiéta)
➡ **Banfora** (CFA1500, 1½ hours, eight daily; operated by TCV, Rakiéta)
➡ **Gaoua** (CFA5000, 2½ hours, two daily; operated by TSR)
For international services, see p75.

🛈 Getting Around

Standard taxi fare is CFA300 for a shared cab ride in town.
　Ismael Sawadogo (🖉 76 45 85 71) is a delightful and very reliable taxi driver (he is also a professional storyteller). He can arrange anything from early-morning pick-ups for bus services to day trips around Bobo.

Around Bobo-Dioulasso

The area around Bobo is rich in day trips, many of which are scenic excursions. Pack a picnic.

Kou & Koumi

About 18km west of Bobo-Dioulasso, the 115-hectare **Forêt de Kou** (admission CFA1000) is an unexpected gem: the reserve includes three completely different ecosystems – tropical rainforest, teak plantation and wooded savannah – that visitors can explore through a small network of paths. The rainforest in particular is delightful, remaining blissfully cool even during the midday heat.

A couple of kilometres before the forest, you'll pass a small drinking shack and a bathing area referred to as **La Guinguette** (admission CFA500). It's popular at weekends but generally quiet during the week.

Six kilometres south of Kou along a well-maintained dirt track, the village of **Koumi** (admission CFA1000, guiding fee CFA1000), on the Bobo-Orodara road, is well-known for its ochre adobe houses. Villagers run informative tours taking in animist beliefs, architecture and local life.

La Mare aux Poissons Sacrés & Koro

The sacred fish pond of **Dafra**, around 6km southeast of Bobo, is an important animist site: local people come here to solicit spirits by sacrificing chickens and feeding them to the fish. It is a fairly grisly sight, with chicken bones and feathers everywhere; the 30-minute walk from the nearest parking spot to the pond is truly stunning, however, with arresting rock formations and gorgeous savannah landscapes. A taxi there and back from Bobo-Dioulasso will cost around CFA10,000 (the track is atrocious).

You can easily follow on from Dafra to the village of **Koro** (admission CFA1000), 13km east of Bobo, off the main Ouagadougou road. Perched on the hillside, its houses – built amid rock formations – are unique in the area, and there are fine panoramic views over the countryside from the top of the village.

Banfora & Around

Banfora

POP 76,000

Banfora is a sleepy town in one of the most beautiful areas in Burkina Faso. It has delightful accommodation and eating options and therefore makes an ideal base for exploring the lush surrounding countryside. The town itself has a lively Sunday market, with plenty of goods from nearby Côte d'Ivoire.

🛏 Sleeping & Eating

⭐ Le Calypso   LODGE $
(☑70 74 14 83, 20 91 02 29; famille_houitte@yahoo.fr; Rte de Bobo-Dioulasso; r with fan/air-con CFA9500/16,000; ✳🛜) Le Calypso's lovely rooms combine traditional adobe architecture with modern comforts and impeccable cleanliness. The huts are arranged around a beautiful garden. It's about 1km outside of town on the road to Bobo.

Hôtel La Canne à Sucre   HOTEL $$
(☑20 91 01 07; www.banfora.com; off Rue de la Poste; d with fan from CFA7500, with air-con from CFA18,900, 4-bed apt CFA49,000; ✳🛜🏊) Beautiful rooms are kitted out with African woodcarvings and cloth and the leafy garden feels like heaven after a tiring day. The apartments are ideal for groups and have exclusive use of the pool.

The restaurant is the fanciest in town, perfect for a treat (mains CFA3000 to CFA5000).

⭐ Le Calypso   EUROPEAN, AFRICAN $$
(☑20 91 02 29; off Rue de la Poste; mains around CFA3000; ⊙11.30am-11pm; 🛜) Run by the same jovial Franco-Burkinabé family as Le Calypso hotel, this popular restaurant is a wonderful place for tasty slow-cooked fish, marinated steak and pizzas. The homemade juices are highly recommended.

McDonald   BURGERS $$
(off Rue de la Préfecture; mains CFA1500-3000; ⊙11am-10pm Thu-Tue) This cool den off the main drag boasts an inviting covered terrace. It churns out a good range of satisfying dishes, including its famous *hamburger frites* (burger with fries).

🍷 Drinking & Entertainment

Le Mistral   BAR
(⊙11am-midnight) The outdoor terrace bar is open every night and is a relaxed place for a beer, but what really draws the crowds to this place is the indoor (air-con) nightclub open Friday, Saturday and Sunday nights (CFA500; doors open at 9pm). The bar is located southeast of town on one of the new sealed roads.

ℹ Information

Banque Atlantique (Rte de la Côte d'Ivoire)
Ecobank (Rte de la Côte d'Ivoire)

ℹ Getting There & Away

Rakiéta (Rue de la Poste) and **TCV** (Rue de la Poste) have regular departures for Bobo-Dioulasso (CFA1500, 1½ hours, eight daily) and Ouaga (CFA8500, 6½ hours, six daily), and one daily service each to Bouaké in Côte d'Ivoire (CFA11,500, 10 hours).

The road to Gaoua is in bad condition and only serviced by *taxi-brousse* (bush taxi; CFA5000, four to five hours). Pick them up at the **Gare Routière** (bus station; Rte de Bobo-Dioulasso). Otherwise go by bus via Bobo.

Around Banfora

Just 7km west of Banfora, Tengréla Lake (admission CFA2000) is home to a variety of bird life and, if you're lucky, you'll see hippos (especially from January to April). The admission price includes a *pirogue* (traditional canoe) trip. Want to laze a few days away in the area? Park your backpack at Campement Farafina (☑76 45 75 15, 78 17 25 04; soloisa6@hotmail.com; Tengréla; r without bathroom CFA4000), a five-minute walk from the lake: facilities are very basic (bucket shower, mud huts without fan), but the owner, Solo, is an adept musician and a fantastic host.

Some 11km northwest of Banfora, the Karfiguéla Waterfalls (Cascades de Karfiguéla; admission CFA1000) are reached through a magnificent avenue of mango trees. You can take a dip in the lovely natural pools on the upper part of the waterfalls. About 3km north, off the N2 road to Bobo, the Dômes de Fabedougou (admission CFA1000), limestone formations sculpted over millennia by water and erosion into quirky domelike shapes, are another arresting sight.

On the road to the Dômes, the sugar factory Société Nouvelle Sucrière de la Comoé (Sosuco; ☑20 91 81 11; www.sn-sosuco.com;

off Rte de Bobo-Dioulasso; admission free) is one of Burkina's more unusual sights. It produces 35,000 tonnes of sugar a year from 4000 hectares of sugar cane. You can visit the factory and attend the spectacular sugar-cane fires from November to April. Ring the factory for details of the visits or ask your hotel.

You'll need wheels to explore the area; if you don't have your own, charter a taxi for the day. Taxi driver Hema Dounbia (76 40 44 47) comes warmly recommended.

Sénoufo Country

Sindou Peaks

One of Burkina Faso's most spectacular landscapes, the Sindou Peaks (Pics de Sindou; admission CFA1000, includes 45min guided walk) are a narrow, craggy chain featuring a fantastic array of tortuous cones sculpted by the elements.

Located about 50km west of Banfora, this geological fantasyland is ideal for hiking. Coming from Banfora, the main gateway is about 1km before the entrance to Sindou town. There's a little booth staffed by guides from the local tourism cooperative Association Djiguiya (76 08 46 60; www.djiguiya.org). Run by the brilliant Tiémoko Ouattara, it promotes responsible travel and offers a range of services to travellers: anything from half-day walks to multiday treks in Sénoufo country with sunrise breakfast in the peaks, moped and cycling tours, cultural activities and homestays.

The association runs the friendly Campement Soutrala (76 08 46 60; Sindou; r without bathroom CFA4000) in Sindou. Facilities are spartan (bucket showers, no electricity) and meals must be ordered two hours in advance (mains CFA800 to CFA2000), but it's a good base if you'd like to spend time in the area rather than visit on a day trip from Banfora.

There is a handful of taxis-brousses plying the dirt road (slated to be surfaced in 2013) between Sindou and Banfora every day. Consider chartering a taxi for the day (CFA25,000) to make it more expedient.

Niansogoni

Well off the beaten path – Niansogoni is 37km southwest of Sindou, near the border with Mali – this tiny settlement is a terrific place to experience local life. The scenery is gorgeous, with a series of limestone hills, cliffs and escarpmentlike formations that loom on the horizon. From Niansogoni, you can walk to an old village nestled in an alcove of the escarpment, where you can see old granaries and dwellings. The village dates back to the 14th century and was abandoned in 1980.

From Sindou, it's a long way along a dirt track to Niansogoni (no public transport). But the reward is sweet. The Campement de Niansogoni (76 48 06 59; traorichard@yahoo.fr; Niansogoni; r without bathroom CFA4000) offers simple yet well-maintained huts with thatched roofs in a glorious setting. Meals (and cold beer!) are available (CFA2000). The owner, Richard Traoré, is passionate about the region and can arrange all kinds of excursions.

Gaoua & Lobi Country

The small town of Gaoua (population 25,100) is a good base for exploring Lobi country, an area that's culturally distinct (see p70).

There are a couple of ATMs (Visa only) in town. For internet, head to the women-run Association Pour la Promotion Féminine de Gaoua (Gaoua; per hr CFA500; 7.30am-8pm Mon-Sat) in the centre. It also sells local handicrafts such as shea-butter soap and creams, pottery and textiles (the shop is open 7.30am to 12.30pm and 3pm to 6pm Monday to Friday).

◎ Sights

There's a vibrant Sunday market, but the town's unique selling point is its excellent ethnological museum, Musée de Poni (www.musee-gaoua.gov.bf; Gaoua; admission CFA2000; 8am-12.30pm & 3-6pm Tue-Sun). There are full-scale reproductions of a Lobi and a Gan compound as well as a wide range of photographs and artefacts. The guides really know their stuff too; Loukmane Savadogo (76 93 12 55) is particularly recommended.

🛏 Sleeping & Eating

Maison Madeleine Père GUESTHOUSE $
(20 90 03 26; Gaoua; s/d CFA6000/8000) Run by nuns, this quiet establishment in a monastery southwest of the city centre has impeccable rooms in pretty grounds. The biggest downside is that it doesn't serve meals. To find it, ask in the centre: most people know it.

Hôtel Hala HOTEL **$$**
(☑20 90 01 21; www.hotelhala.com; Gaoua; s/d with fan CFA12,500/15,000, with air-con CFA23,000/27,500; ❈ ☎) This is, all told, Gaoua's best option: service is glacial and the rooms are nothing to write home about, but the compound is very pleasant, it has a handy location between town and the bus station, and the wi-fi works. It also has the only decent restaurant in town, serving grilled meat and a few Lebanese specials (mains CFA2000 to CFA3000).

Le Flamboyant AFRICAN **$**
(Gaoua; mains CFA800-2000; ⊙10am-10pm) One of the town's better *maquis,* right in the centre of town; expect the usual rice or *tô* (millet or sorghum-based *pâte*) with sauce.

❶ Getting There & Around

The *gare routière* is 2km out of town. You'll find bus services to Bobo-Dioulasso (CFA5000, 2½ hours, two to three daily) and Ouagadougou (CFA7000, five daily, four hours). Direct services to Banfora are by *taxi-brousse* only (CFA5000, four hours); it's best to go to Bobo and find onward connections.

To get around Lobi country, charter a taxi in Gaoua (starting around CFA25,000, depending on how far you want to go).

THE SOUTH

The beauty of southern Burkina is a highlight of any Burkina itinerary; this area is also one of the most accessible. The gateway town of Pô is just a couple of hours from Ouaga (and 20 minutes from the Ghanaian border).

Pô
24,300

There isn't much of interest for travellers in Pô, but it makes a useful halt on journeys between Ouaga and southern sights or Ghana.

If you need to spend the night, the friendly **Hôtel Tiandora** (☑70 74 63 67, 50 40 34 39; r with fan/air-con CFA5000/7500; ❈) has acceptable rooms at very reasonable prices. For sustenance, *maquis* **La Pyramide** (mains CFA500-2000; ⊙11am-10pm) on the main street is an institution, with regal service and delicious daily specials (grilled chicken, couscous, macaroni etc).

Ecobank (⊙7.30am-5.30pm Mon-Fri, 8am-1pm Sat) on the main drag has an ATM (Visa). Rakiéta runs four buses a day to and from Ouaga (CFA2500, 2½ hours).

Réserve de Nazinga

This 97,000-hectare wildlife **reserve** (☑50 41 36 17; admission CFA10,000, vehicle entry CFA1000, guiding fees CFA5000; ⊙6am-6pm), about 40km southwest of Pô near the Ghanaian border, has become a highlight on many a wildlife lover's itinerary. The park has antelopes, monkeys, warthogs, crocodiles and plenty of birds, but elephants are the stars of the show. The best times to see them are December to April, although the chances of sightings are pretty good year-round.

There are some good accommodation options in Nazinga. At the heart of the reserve, **Ranch de Nazinga** (☑50 41 36 17; nazinga-ranch@yahoo.fr; Réserve de Nazinga; r CFA10,000, bungalows CFA16,000) has an exceptional location right by the reserve's biggest watering

---

LOBI TRADITIONS

Lobi traditions are some of the best preserved in West Africa. For travellers, the most obvious is the architecture of rural Lobi homes. The mudbrick compounds are rectangular and walls only have small slits for windows, for defensive purposes. In the old days, polygamous men built a bedroom for each of their wives.

The Lobi are also known for their cultural rituals. For example, the *dyoro* initiation rites, which take place every seven years, are still widely observed. As part of this important rite of passage, young men and women are tested on their stamina and skills; they also learn about sexual mores, the clan's history and the dos and don'ts of their culture.

Your best bet to explore Lobi heritage is to hire a guide in Gaoua (ask at Hôtel Hala). Visits will take in villages such as **Sansana** and **Doudou**, where you can admire different architectural styles and crafts (pottery, basket weaving, sculpture). Doudou is famed for its artisanal gold-mining, which is the prerogative of women, and its market (every five days).

hole. Accommodation is a little lacklustre, but the restaurant churns out tasty meals (mains CFA3000 to CFA4000) and the setting is unrivalled with animals regularly roaming among the bungalows.

Those in search of something a little more sophisticated should opt for Campement de l'Éléphant (☑70 70 17 34 34; www.nahourisafari.com; Réserve de Nazinga; d/f CFA25,000/35,000; ☉Nov-May; ❋☎), right on the edge of the reserve. Rooms are spacious and clean, but it is the pool that's the real draw, perfect to while away the hours between wildlife drives. The restaurant also gets the thumbs up from travellers for its impeccable French cuisine.

You will need your own vehicle to access the reserve and go on wildlife drives. The travel agencies in Ouagadougou (p63) are your best bet.

Tiébélé & Kassena Country

Set in the heart of the green and low-lying Kassena country, Tiébélé, 40km east of Pô on a dirt track, is famous for its *sukhala*, colourful windowless traditional houses. Decorated by women, who work with guinea-fowl feathers, in geometrical patterns of red, black and white, the houses offer an antidote to the monochrome mudbrick villages found elsewhere in Burkina Faso.

Association Pour le Développement de Tiébélé (☑70 02 78 26; www.tiebele-developpement.org; Tiébélé) is the best organisation to contact for local guides, be it to tour Kassena houses, visit local markets or organise treks in the area.

◉ Sights & Activities

Cour Royale   ARCHITECTURE
(Tiébélé; admission CFA2000; ☉8am-5.30pm) More than 450 people live in Tiébélé's royal court, a large compound of typical *sukhalas*. Children live with their grandparents in eight-shaped huts, couples in rectangular huts and single people in square ones. Painting is generally done in February or March, after the harvest. Each drawing (geometrical or illustrative) has a meaning (fertility, afterlife, wisdom etc).

Nahouri Peak   HIKING
(admission CFA1000, local guide CFA500) This cone-shape karst is the tallest structure for miles around and the steep climb to its summit guarantees 360 degrees of uninterrupted savannah views. Guides from the Association pour le Développement de Tiébélé can organise sunrise and sunset climbs, a good option both for wow factor and clement temperatures.

🛏 Sleeping & Eating

Auberge Kunkolo   GUESTHOUSE $
(☑76 53 44 55, 50 36 97 38; Tiébélé; d with fan & without bathroom CFA5000) This lovely guesthouse, with its impeccable Kassena-style huts and beautiful garden, is the best place to stay in the area. It's just 200m from the chief's compound in Tiébélé. Meals are also served.

ℹ Getting There & Around

There is one direct bus from Ouaga (bus station Ouagainter) to Tiébélé (and back) on Tuesdays, Fridays and Sundays (CFA3000, 3½ hours).

If you don't have your own vehicle, you can easily rent mopeds in Tiébélé for CFA4000 to CFA6000 per day.

UNDERSTAND BURKINA FASO

Burkina Faso Today

Burkina Faso stands out as a beacon of stability in a region rocked by insecurity. Despite widespread riots in 2011, the country managed to steer itself back on course and held peaceful municipal and legislative elections in December 2012. There are still rumblings about the state of the country – Burkina ranks 181st out of 187 countries on the UN's Human Development Index – and a president who has been in power for 25 years, but Burkinabés mostly just want to get on with things.

The economy has been steadily growing over the past decade, averaging more than 5% per year between 2000 and 2010. It remains overly reliant on cotton export, however, and a recent gold rush – which has seen a huge increase in illegal mining – has increased the country's exposure to market fluctuations. Socially, Burkina's biggest challenges are to improve access to education (the child literacy rate remains under 30%) and address chronic food insecurity.

THE SAHEL

Northern Burkina Faso is dominated by the desolate confines of the Sahel. It's certainly inhospitable at most times of the year, but it also features stupendously colourful markets, fascinating local cultures and traditions, and landscapes that are much less monotonous than you might imagine.

The deteriorating security situation in neighbouring Mali has severely affected tourism in the Sahel; more than 30,000 Malian refugees have settled in the area, leading the Burkinabé authorities and foreign governments to advise against travel to the region. It was unclear at the time of writing when the situation would improve, so check the latest travel advice before you set off.

History

The Mossi & the French

Little is known about Burkina Faso's early history, though archaelogical finds suggest the country was populated as far back as the Stone Age. Its modern history starts with the Mossi peoples (now almost half of Burkina Faso's population), who moved westward from settlements near the Niger River in the 13th century; they founded their first kingdom in what is now Ouagadougou. Three more Mossi states were subsequently established in other parts of the country, all paying homage to Ouagadougou, the strongest. The government of each of the Mossi states was highly organised, with ministers, courts and a cavalry known for its devastating attacks against the Muslim empires in Mali.

During the Scramble for Africa in the second half of the 19th century, the French exploited rivalries between the different Mossi kingdoms and established their sway over the region. At first the former Mossi states were assimilated into the Colonie du Haut Sénégal-Niger. Then, in 1919, the area was hived off for administrative expedience as a separate colony, Haute Volta (Upper Volta).

Independence & Thomas Sankara

World War II brought about profound changes in France's relationship with its colonies. The Mossi, like numerous other people in Africa, started challenging the colonial hegemony. The Upper Volta became a state in 1947, and in 1956 France agreed to give its colonies their own governments, with independence quickly following in 1960.

Following independence, dreams of freedom and prosperity quickly evaporated. Between 1960 and 1983, the country experienced six coups and counter-coups and the economy stagnated. Then, in 1983, Captain Thomas Sankara, an ambitious young leftwing military star, seized power.

Over the next four years 'Thom Sank' (as he was popularly known) recast the country. He changed its name to Burkina Faso (meaning 'Land of the Incorruptible'), restructured the economy to promote self-reliance in rural areas and tackled corruption with rare zeal. He was ahead of his time, promoting women's rights and standing up against Western paradigms on aid and development. But his authoritarian grip on power and his intolerance of those who didn't share his ideals were to be his downfall: in late 1987 a group of junior officers seized power and Sankara was killed.

The Compaoré Years

The new junta was headed by Captain Blaise Compaoré, Sankara's former friend and co-revolutionary. In late 1991 Compaoré was elected president. But as sole candidate, with low turnout and with the assassination of Clément Ouédraogo, the leading opposition figure, a couple of weeks later, his legitimacy remained weak.

In a bid to mark a clear break with Sankara, Compaoré immediately orchestrated a U-turn on the economy, overturning nationalisations and bringing the country back into the IMF fold. He has since been re-elected three times, in 1998, 2005 and 2010, each time with more than 80% of the vote. He is one of Africa's last 'big men' (long-serving, authoritarian leaders) and his democratic credentials will be tested in 2015: a 2000 constitutional amendment stipulates that a president may only run for two terms, although Compaoré craftily only introduced it after his victory in 2005.

People of Burkina Faso

Burkina Faso, which occupies an area about half the size of France, is extremely diverse, with its 17 million people scattered among some 60 ethnic groups. The largest of these is the Mossi, who are primarily concentrated in the central plateau area. Important groups in the south include the Bobo, Senoufo, Lobi and Gourounsi. In the Sahel areas of the north are the Hausa, Fulani, Bella and Tuareg. Around 75% of Burkinabés live in rural areas.

Religion

An old joke goes that 50% of Burkinabés are Muslim, 50% Christian and 100% animist. The figures for Islam and Christianity are about 60% and 23%, respectively, in reality, but most people do retain traditional beliefs.

The Arts

Burkina Faso has a vibrant contemporary arts and crafts scene (painting, sculpture, wood-carvings, bronze and brass work, and textiles). Artists' works are exhibited in Ouagadougou's galleries, cultural centres and collective workshops. And there's no shortage of artisans' stalls and craft shops, selling masks and leatherwork, in Ouagadougou and Bobo-Dioulasso.

The Burkinabés live and breathe music. It is the mainstay of traditional celebrations with *djembe* (drum), *balafon* (a kind of xylophone) and flutes the main instruments. Modern musicians draw on traditional influences from home and the rest of the continent, especially Mali, Congo and Côte d'Ivoire, as well as Jamaican reggae, jazz, rock and rap. You'll find numerous bars in Ouga and Bobo offering live music several nights a week.

Burkina Faso also has a thriving film industry that receives considerable stimulation from the biennial Fespaco film festival. Two Burkinabé film-makers who have won prizes and developed international reputations are Idrissa Ouédraogo, who won the 1990 Grand Prix at Cannes for *Tilä*, and Gaston Kaboré, whose film *Buud Yam* was the 1997 winner of the Étalon d'Or.

Food & Drink

Burkinabé food is largely influenced by Senegalese and Côte d'Ivoire cuisines. Sauces, especially *arachide* (groundnut) or *graine* (a hot sauce made with oil-palm nuts), are the mainstay and are always served with a starch – usually rice (it's called *riz sauce* or *riz gras*) or the Burkinabé staple, *tô*, a millet- or sorghum-based *pâte* (a pounded, doughlike substance). The Ivorian *attiéké* (grated cassava), *aloco* (plantain fried with chilli in palm oil) and *kedjenou* (simmered chicken or fish with vegetables) are also commonly found.

Grilled dishes of chicken, mutton, beef, guinea fowl, fish (especially Nile perch, known locally as *capitaine*) and agouti (a large rodent) also feature on the menu. In the Sahel, couscous (semolina grains) is widely available.

Castel, Flag, Brakina, Beaufort and So.b.bra are popular and palatable lagers. More adventurous – and potent – is *dolo* (millet beer). Locally produced juices include *bissap* (hibiscus), *gingembre* (ginger), tamarind and mango; soft drinks are available everywhere, too.

Environment

Landlocked Burkina Faso's terrain ranges from the harsh desert and semidesert of the north to the woodland and savannah of the green southwest. Around Banfora rainfall is heavier, and forests thrive alongside irrigated sugar-cane and rice fields; it's here that most of Burkina Faso's meagre 13% of arable land is found. The country's dominant feature, however, is the vast central laterite plateau of the Sahel, where hardy trees and bushes thrive.

Burkina's former name, Haute Volta (Upper Volta), referred to its three major rivers – the Black, White and Red Voltas, known today as the Mouhoun, Nakambé and Nazinon Rivers. All flow south into the world's second-largest artificial lake, Lake Volta, in Ghana.

SURVIVAL GUIDE

ℹ Directory A–Z

ACCOMMODATION

Ouagadougou, Bobo and Banfora have a good range of accommodation, including charming B&Bs. In more remote areas, *campements* (basic mud huts with bucket showers and no electricity) are usually the only option but can be very atmospheric.

PRACTICALITIES

➡ **Electricity** Supply is 220V and plugs are of the European two-round-pin variety.

➡ **Languages** French, Moré, Fulfudé and Dioula.

➡ **Newspapers & Magazines** International versions of French- and (a few) English-language publications are available in Ouagadougou and Bobo-Dioulasso.

➡ **Radio** BBC World Service is on 99.2FM in Ouagadougou. For a French-language service, tune in to RFI, 94FM.

EMBASSIES & CONSULATES

The following embassies are based in Ouagadougou. British citizens should contact the British High Commission (p200) in Accra, Ghana.

Beninese Embassy (☑50 38 49 96; 401 Rue Bagen Nini, near Ouagainter)

Canadian Embassy (☑50 31 18 94; www.canadainternational.gc.ca/burkinafaso; 316 Ave du Professeur Joseph Ki Zerbo) Also offers diplomatic help to Australian citizens.

Dutch Embassy (☑50 30 61 34; http://burkinafaso.nlambassade.org; 415 Ave Kwame N'Krumah)

French Embassy (☑50 49 66 66; www.ambafrance-bf.org; Ave du Trésor)

German Embassy (☑50 30 67 31; www.ouagadougou.diplo.de; Rue Joseph Badoua)

Ghanaian Embassy (☑50 30 76 35; embagna@fasonet.bf; Ave d'Oubritenga; ⊘8am-2pm)

Ivorian Embassy (☑50 31 82 28; cnr Ave Raoul Follereau & Blvd du Burkina Faso)

US Embassy (☑50 49 53 00; http://ouagadougou.usembassy.gov; Ouaga 2000)

INTERNET ACCESS

➡ Wi-fi is available in most midrange and top-end establishments in towns and cities.

➡ Internet cafes are plentiful in towns and cities (the post office is usually a good bet) but nonexistent in more remote areas.

MONEY

➡ The currency in Burkina Faso is the West African CFA franc.

➡ The best foreign currency to carry is euros, easily exchanged at any bank, hotel or bureau de change.

➡ Travellers cheques cannot be exchanged in Burkina.

➡ There are numerous Visa ATMs in every city; the only bank to accept MasterCard is Banque Atlantique (in Ouaga, Bobo and Banfora only).

➡ Payments by credit card are rarely accepted and subject to a 5% surcharge.

OPENING HOURS

Banks Typically open 8am to 11am and 3.30pm to 5pm Monday to Friday.

Bars Normally serve from late morning until the last customers leave (late); nightclubs generally open from 9pm into the wee hours.

Restaurants Lunch 11.30am to 2.30pm; dinner 6.30pm to 10.30pm.

Shops and businesses Usually 8am to noon and 3pm to 6pm Monday to Friday, and 9am to 1pm Saturday.

PUBLIC HOLIDAYS

Burkina Faso also celebrates Islamic holidays, whose dates change every year.

New Year's Day 1 January

Revolution Day 3 January

Women's Day 8 March

Easter Monday March/April

Labour Day 1 May

Ascension Day 40 days after Easter

National Day 5 August

Assumption 15 August

All Saints' Day 1 November

Republic Day 11 December

Christmas Day 25 December

SAFE TRAVEL

Burkina Faso is one of the safest countries in West Africa. Crime isn't unknown, particularly around big markets and *gares routières*, but it's usually confined to petty theft and pickpocketing.

TELEPHONE

➡ Burkina's country code is 226.

➡ Landline numbers start with 5, mobile numbers with 7.

➡ Mobile-phone coverage is excellent and cheap. Local networks include Telmob, Airtel and Telecel. International texts cost from CFA50 and calls from CFA75 per minute with pay-as-you-go credit (CFA500 for a SIM card).

VISAS

➡ Everyone except Ecowas nationals needs a visa.

➡ One-month visas are available at border crossings and the airport for CFA10,000 (bring two photos), but visa policies can change, so it is strongly recommended you get your visa from a Burkinabé embassy before travelling; allow €35/45 for a three-month single/multiple-entry visa.

Visas for Onward Travel

The Visa de l'Entente, valid in Côte d'Ivoire, Niger, Togo and Benin, is available at the Service des Passeports (p63) in Ouagadougou; bring two photos, your passport and CFA25,000. It takes 72 hours to process.

If you're only visiting a single country, the following embassies deliver visas:

Benin A three-month, single-entry visa costs CFA15,000. You need two photos and photocopies of your passport.

Côte d'Ivoire A three-month, single-entry visa costs €100 and requires one photo and a hotel confirmation. Check www.snedai.ci for details.

Ghana Three-month visas are issued within 48 hours for CFA17,500 and require four photos.

ⓘ Getting There & Away

You will need a yellow-fever vaccination certificate to come to Burkina.

AIR

➡ The tiny Aéroport International de Ouagadougou is Burkina's main gateway.

➡ The main international carriers are **Air France** (www.airfrance.com) and **Royal Air Maroc** (www.royalairmaroc.com), which offer direct flights to France and Morocco and connecting flights to the rest of the world.

➡ **Air Burkina** (www.air-burkina.com), the national carrier, flies to Paris (France) as well as regional destinations including Accra (Ghana), Abidjan (Côte d'Ivoire), Bamako (Mali), Cotonou (Benin), Dakar (Senegal) and Lomé (Togo).

LAND

Burkina's land borders are open from 6am to 6pm. Crossings are generally hassle-free. The main border points are:

➡ Niangoloko for Côte d'Ivoire
➡ Tanguiéta for Benin
➡ Paga for Ghana
➡ Sinkasse for Togo
➡ Kantchari for Niger
➡ Koloko or Tiou for Mali

There are plenty of international bus services from Ouaga and Bobo. Routes include:

➡ **Kumasi, Ghana** (CFA10,000, 11 hours, one daily; operated by TCV)
➡ **Bamako, Mali** (CFA17,000, 17 hours, one daily; operated by TCV)
➡ **Bouaké & Abidjan, Côte d'Ivoire** (CFA17,000 & CFA27,000, 20 hours & 36 hours, one daily; operated by TCV, Rakiéta)
➡ **Cotonou, Benin** (CFA18,000, 24 hours, two weekly; operated by TCV, TSR)
➡ **Lomé, Togo** (CFA18,000, 24 hours, two weekly; operated by TCV, TSR)
➡ **Lagos, Nigeria** (CFA38,000, 36 hours, one weekly; operated by TCV)

ⓘ Getting Around

BUS

➡ Buses are the most reliable and comfortable way to get around.

➡ TCV and Rakiéta buses are better maintained and more reliable than those of other companies. They also have air-con.

➡ Buses almost always operate with guaranteed seating and fixed departure times; arrive early or book the day before to ensure you have a seat on your preferred service.

BUSH TAXI

➡ Bush taxis (taxis-brousses), generally beaten-up old vehicles, cover outlying communities that large buses don't serve.

➡ Most leave from the gares routières; morning is the best time to find them.

CAR & MOTORCYCLE

➡ Travel agencies in Ouagadougou can organise 4WD rental for about CFA60,000 per day (with driver).

➡ In rural areas, mopeds are ideal on unsealed roads and readily available for CFA4000 per day (not including fuel).

Cameroon

POP 20.1 MILLION

Best Places to Eat

➡ La Fourchette (p86)

➡ Vegetarian Carnivore (p100)

➡ La Plazza (p97)

➡ La Paillote (p81)

Best Places to Stay

➡ Foyer du Marin (p83)

➡ Bird Watchers' Club (p89)

➡ Relais de la Porte Mayo (p97)

➡ Hotel Ilomba (p94)

Why Go?

Cameroon is Africa's throbbing heart, a crazed, sultry mosaic of active volcanoes, white-sand beaches, thick rainforest and magnificent parched landscapes broken up by the bizarre rock formations of the Sahel. With both Francophone and Anglophone regions, not to mention some 230 local languages, the country is a vast ethnic and linguistic jigsaw, yet one that, in contrast to so many of its neighbours, enjoys a great deal of stability.

With good infrastructure (think decent roads and functioning trains), travel is a lot easier here than in many parts of Africa. Still, you'll miss none of those indicators that you're in the middle of this fascinating continent: everyone seems to be carrying something on their heads, *makossa* music sets the rhythm, the street smells like roasting plantains and African bliss is just a piece of grilled fish and a sweating beer away.

When to Go
Yaoundé

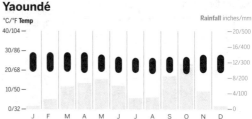

Nov–Feb It's dry but not too hot, though you can usually expect a harmattan haze.

Feb Join athletes running to the summit of Mt Cameroon in the Race of Hope.

Oct Cameroon's biggest festival, Tabaski, takes place, most impressively in Foumban.

YAOUNDÉ

POP 1.8 MILLION

Let's be brutally honest: West Africa is famous for many things, but pleasant cities – especially capitals – are not among them. Then Yaoundé comes along: green and spread over seven hills, though not exactly a garden city, it's planned, thoughtfully laid out and self-contained. While it is nowhere near as vibrant (or chaotic) as its coastal rival Douala, it enjoys a temperate climate, relatively clean and well-maintained streets and even boasts a host of 1970s government buildings in various exuberant styles that will keep architecture fans happy. Located in the centre of the country, Yaoundé makes a fine stop for getting a visa or before heading off into the rest of Cameroon.

🔾 Sights & Activities

Musée d'Art Camerounais   MUSEUM
(Quartier Fébé; admission CFA1500; ⏱ 3-6pm Thu, Sat & Sun) At the Benedictine monastery on Mt Fébé, north of the city centre, the Musée d'Art Camerounais has an impressive collection of masks, bronze- and woodwork and other examples of Cameroonian art. The chapel is also worth a look.

Mvog-Betsi Zoo   ZOO
(Mvog-Betsi; admission CFA2000, camera CFA5000; ⏱ 9am-6pm) This is one of the better zoos in West Africa, co-run by the **Cameroon Wildlife Aid Fund** (www.cwaf.org), with a sizeable collection of native primates, rescued from poachers and the bushmeat trade.

🛏 Sleeping

Ideal Hotel   HOTEL $
(Map p80; ☎ 2266 9537, 2220 9852; idealhotel72@yahoo.fr; Carrefour Nlongkak; r CFA8000-10,000, apt CFA15,000; ℗) Rooms here are decent enough for the low price, though there's no hot water and rooms are fan cooled. Balconies in some make up for a general lack of light (plus you get Yaoundé smog for free). If you're visa hunting, this is well located for embassies.

Foyer International de l'Église Presbytérienne   HOSTEL $
(Map p80; ☎ 9985 2376; off Rue Joseph Essono Balla; tents/dm/s/d CFA2000/5000/8000/10,000; ℗) This 100-year-old building has two fairly uninviting private rooms and two eight-bed dorms, all of which share the same very basic bathrooms. Campers can set up their own

---

ℹ SET YOUR BUDGET

Budget
➡ Hotel room CFA5000
➡ Two-course dinner CFA2000
➡ Coffee CFA500
➡ Local bus ride CFA1000

Midrange
➡ Hotel room CFA20,000
➡ Two-course dinner CFA6000
➡ Coffee CFA1000
➡ Short taxi ride CFA2000

Top End
➡ Hotel room CFA40,000
➡ Two-course dinner CFA10,000
➡ Coffee CFA1000
➡ Long taxi ride CFA5000

---

tents in the garden. From the main road, walk to the right of the water towers, and it's in the second brick house on your left.

Tou'ngou Hotel   HOTEL $$
(☎ 2220 1026; www.toungouhotel.com; Rue Onembele Nkou; s/d/ste incl breakfast CFA20,000/30,000/45,000; ℗❄🛜) One of Yaoundé's better-value midrange hotels, the Tou'ngou is a smart and popular option. Staff can seem a little indifferent, but the rooms are comfortable and clean, the location is central and there's a good restaurant. It's best to book ahead.

Prestige Hotel   HOTEL $$
(Map p80; ☎ 2222 6055, 2222 6039; www.groupprestigehotel.com; Ave Charles Atangana; ❄🛜) This sprawling and rather raucous hotel has good-value rooms and is handily located for buses to Douala. Rooms are on the small side, but they're clean and secure, with many enjoying balconies. There's a popular bar and restaurant on the site too, but also lots of traffic noise.

El Panaden Hotel   HOTEL $$
(Map p82; ☎ 9858 7419; elpanaden@yahoo.fr; Pl de l'Indépendance; r CFA15,500-30,000; ❄) This is an old travellers' favourite, with a good wanderer vibe going around. The generously sized and spotless rooms often come with balconies. A renovation was ongoing at the time of our last visit, and so prices may go up when it's complete.

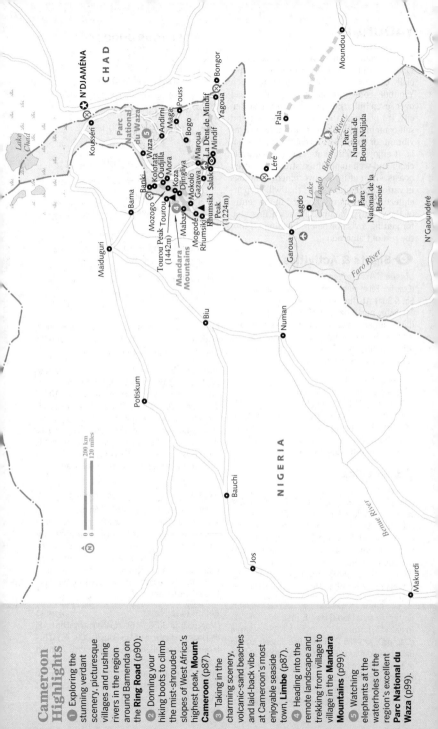

Cameroon Highlights

1 Exploring the stunning verdant scenery, picturesque villages and rushing rivers in the region around Bamenda on the **Ring Road** (p90).

2 Donning your hiking boots to climb the mist-shrouded slopes of West Africa's highest peak, **Mount Cameroon** (p87).

3 Taking in the charming scenery, volcanic-sand beaches and laid-back vibe at Cameroon's most enjoyable seaside town, **Limbe** (p87).

4 Heading into the remote landscape and trekking from village to village in the **Mandara Mountains** (p99).

5 Watching elephants at the waterholes of the region's excellent **Parc National du Waza** (p99).

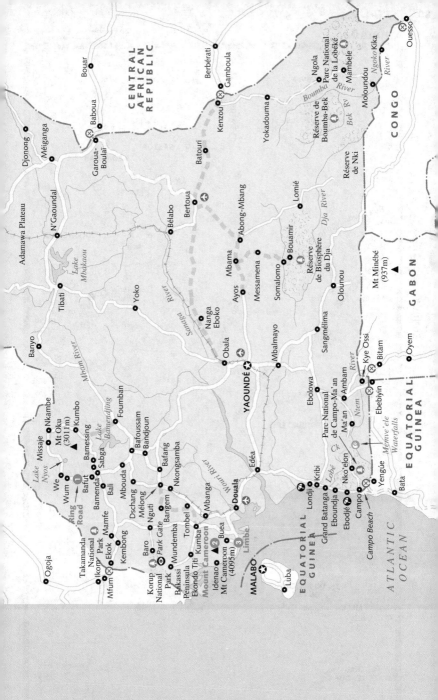

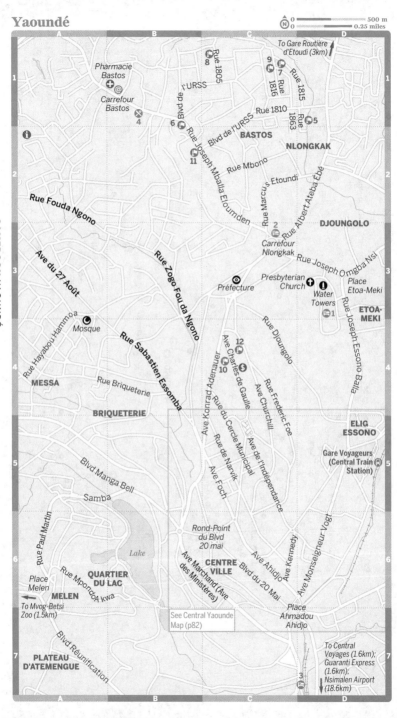

Yaoundé

Sleeping

⊗ Eating

ℹ Information

Merina Hotel HOTEL $$$

(Map p82; 📋 2222 2131; hotelmerina@cameroun-plus.com; Ave Ahidjo; s & d CFA37,000-42,000; P ✳ 🛜 🌊) Located right in the heart of the city, the smart Merina has a fancy orchid-strewn lobby, modern and comfortable rooms and good service. Other perks include a free airport-shuttle service and a small pool.

✗ Eating

Around Carrefours Bastos and Nlongkak you can find grills serving *brochettes* (kebabs) throughout the day. On Pl de l'Indépendance, there are women grilling delicious fish, served with chilli or peanut sauce from CFA1000.

Le Sintra INTERNATIONAL $

(Map p82; Ave Kennedy; dishes CFA3000-5000; ⊗6am-11pm Mon-Sat) A friendly welcome, a whiff of colonial atmosphere and a terrace made for people-watching in the heart of Yaoundé, La Sintra does a full breakfast menu, Italian and Cameroonian cuisine as well as delicious French dishes such as *crevettes à la provençale* (shrimps cooked in garlic).

Istanbul TURKISH $

(Map p80; Rue Joseph Mballa Eloumden; mains CFA4500; ⊗8am-11pm) Fresh and well-prepared Turkish food is served up at this smart terrace restaurant (with an even smarter inside dining room complete with white tablecloths and silver service). Take away is available.

Patisserie Select Plus BAKERY $

(Map p82; Ave Monseigneur Vogt; baked goods CFA200-1500; ⊗breakfast, lunch & dinner) This excellent bakery sells a delicious line of freshly baked croissants, *beignets* (pastries) and sandwiches. Other treats include pizzas, burgers and coffee to go.

★La Paillote CHINESE $$

(Rue Joseph Essono Balla; mains CFA3500-6000; ⊗noon-2pm & 7-10pm) This stylish Chinese restaurant has a charming shaded terrace and a smart dining room inside, both of which attract a loyal crowd of expats. The dishes are delicious and service is good.

🍷 Drinking & Nightlife

The best bars are in Carrefours Bastos and Nlongkak, most with open-air seating facing the street – great for people-watching. Solo female travellers might find the atmosphere uneasy in some bars once the sun dips.

ℹ Information

DANGERS & ANNOYANCES

Yaoundé is more relaxed than Douala, but muggings happen. Daytime is generally fine, but take taxis at night and be particularly wary around the Marché Central and tourist hotels.

INTERNET ACCESS

Your best bet is the smarter hotels and restaurants for a wireless connection.

Espresso House (Carrefour Bastos; ⊗9am-11pm) Offers wi-fi for CFA1500 per hour.

MEDICAL SERVICES

Pharmacie Bastos (📋220 6555; Carrefour Bastos) Well-stocked pharmacy.

Polyclinique André Fouda (📋222 6612) For medical emergencies; in Elig-Essono, southeast of Carrefour Nlongkak.

MONEY

There are ATMs at most of the major banks. As always in Cameroon, travellers cheques are problematic to change in banks – try the banks around the cathedral.

Bicec Bank (Map p82; Ave Ahidjo) Has an ATM.

SCB (Map p82; near Pl Ahmadou Ahidjo) Money exchange and ATM.

POST

Central Post Office (Map p82; Pl Ahmadou Ahidjo; ⊗7.30am-3.30pm Mon-Fri, to noon Sat)

Central Yaoundé

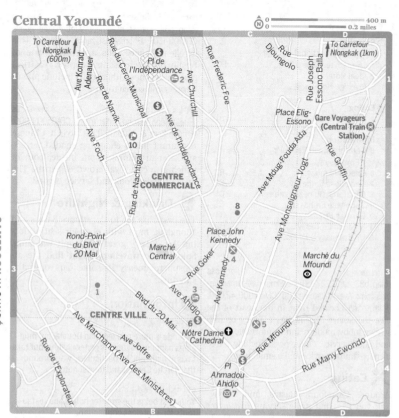

Central Yaoundé

🟢 Activities, Courses & Tours
1 Safar Tours A3

🛏 Sleeping
2 El Panaden Hotel B1
3 Merina Hotel... B3

🍴 Eating
4 Le Sintra C3
5 Patisserie Select Plus.......................... C4

ℹ Information
6 Bicec Bank B4
7 Central Post Office C4
8 Ministry of Immigration C2
9 SCB.. C4
10 US Embassy.. B2

ℹ Getting There & Away

AIR

Yaoundé has an international airport, although far more international services go to and from Douala. Internal flights with Camair-Co connect Yaoundé to Douala (CFA31,100, 45 minutes), Garoua (CFA108,700, three hours) and Maroua (CFA121,100, three hours).

BUS

There are buses between Yaoundé and all major cities in Cameroon. Buses leave from their companies' offices, spread out on the outskirts of town. For Douala (CFA3000 to CFA6000, three to four hours), **Central Voyages** (Mvog-Mbi) and **Guaranti Express** (Quartier Nsam) are recommended. Guaranti Express is also recommended for Limbe (CFA5000, five hours), Bamenda (CFA5000, six hours), Bafoussam (CFA2500, three hours) and Kumba (CFA4000, four hours).

Otherwise, all agency and nonagency buses for Kribi, Bertoua, Batouri, Ebolowa, Limbe and

Buea depart from Blvd de l'Ocam, about 3km south of Pl Ahmadou Ahidjo (direct taxi drivers to Agences de Mvan).

Transport to Bafoussam, Bamenda and points north departs from Gare Routière d'Etoudi, 5km north of Centre Ville.

TRAIN

The most popular and convenient way to travel north from Yaoundé is by train, which runs all the way to N'Gaoundéré. Trains depart daily at 6.15pm and are scheduled to arrive in N'Gaoundéré at 6.30am the next day, although in practice delays on the line are common.

For seating, there's a choice of comfortable 1st-class couchettes (sleeping compartments; per person four-/two-bed cabin CFA25,000/28,000), 1st-class airline-style seats (CFA17,000) and crowded 2nd-class benches (CFA10,000). Seats in 1st and 2nd class are in open wagons, with no way to secure your bag. Even in couchettes, be alert for thieves.

The train has a restaurant car where you can buy passable meals (breakfast/dinner CFA1000/2500). If you're in 1st class, someone will come and take your order and deliver it to you. At every station stop, people will offer street food at the windows.

There are also two daily services between Yaoundé and Douala (1st/2nd class CFA6000/3000), though these are used much less frequently, as buses are cheaper, faster and more convenient.

❶ Getting Around

Shared taxis and *moto-taxis* (motorbike taxis) are the only public-transport option. Fares are CFA200 per place for short- to medium-length rides. A private taxi to Nsimalen airport from central Yaoundé should cost CFA4000 to CFA6000 (40 minutes).

WESTERN CAMEROON

Imagine Africa: wormy red tracks and vegetation so intensely green you can almost taste the colour. This image comes alive in Western Cameroon. The country's economic heart intermittently beats in Douala, and from here it's a short hop to the haze and laze of beach towns like Limbe and the savannah-carpeted slopes of the Mountain of Thunder – Mt Cameroon. In the Anglophone northwest you can slip between sunburnt green hills while exploring a patchwork of secret societies, traditional chiefdoms and some of the country's best arts and crafts, particularly the wooden masks that are so often associated with Africa.

Douala

POP 2 MILLION

Sticky, icky and frenetic, Douala isn't as bad as some say, but it's not likely to be your first choice for a honeymoon, either. By any measure but political power this is Cameroon's main city: its primary air hub, biggest port and leading business centre, and the result is a chaotic hodgepodge. There are few charms, but you can set your finger here to gauge Cameroon's pulse.

⊙ Sights

Espace Doual'art   MUSEUM
(Pl du Gouvernement; ⊙ 9am-7pm Mon-Sat) **FREE**
Well worth dropping into if you're nearby, this contemporary-art space hosts changing displays of work from all over Cameroon and the rest of Africa. There's a little cafe here too, and it's a good place to gauge the city's small art scene.

🛏 Sleeping

Centre d'Accueil Missionaire   HOSTEL $
(☑ 7707 1283, 3342 2797; aprocure@yahoo.fr; Rue Franqueville; s CFA10,000, without shower CFA8000, d/tr CFA14,000/18,000; 🅿 ❄ 🛜 🛂) Praise be to this Catholic mission, with its clean if basic rooms, pleasant verandah and lovely pool. A convenient laundry service and an excellent location seal the deal.

★ Foyer du Marin   GUESTHOUSE $$
(☑ 9991 5448, 3342 2794; www.seemanns mission.org; Rue Gallieni; s/d/apt CFA22,000/ 25,000/30,000; 🅿 ❄ @ 🛂) Definitely the best-value accommodation in Douala, the German Seaman's Mission is a literal oasis of tranquillity in the city centre. It's set in a gorgeous garden with a pool and terrific views towards the port, the rooms are comfortable and spacious and the restaurant serves up delicious poolside food all day long. The only complaint is the management's attitude towards tourists, who are generally made to feel like they're there under sufferance: the wireless password is only given to regular guests and front-desk staff can seem frosty. Book ahead.

Hotel Beausejour Mirabel   HOTEL $$
(☑ 9978 9725, 3300 5996; resahotelbsejour@ gmail.com; Rue Joffre; r from CFA30,000; ❄ 🛜) Centrally located and with very friendly staff, the Beausejour was once quite a smart place, as evidenced by its impressive facade and former rooftop pool. It's fallen on less

Douala

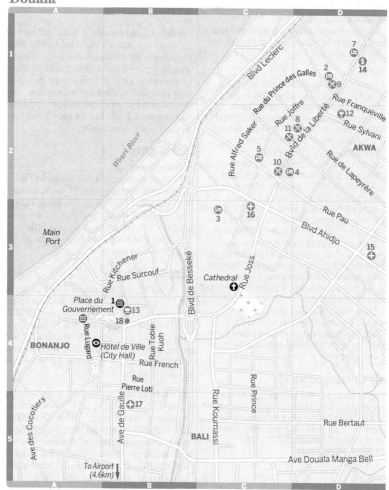

glamorous times, but the rooms have balconies and are clean and spacious, while downstairs there's wi-fi and a good on-site restaurant, making it one of Douala's best midrange options.

Hotel Majestic
HOTEL **$$**

(☑9767 1332, 3342 8734; ngatcherv1@yahoo.fr; Blvd de la Liberté; r from CFA25,000; ❋🛜) You can expect quite a bit of noise at this otherwise excellent-value hotel; as well as the traffic on Douala's main avenue outside, there's an incredibly loud music shop downstairs blaring out pop music all day. That said, rooms are clean and comfortable, each coming with fridge, TV and decent modern bathroom.

Hotel Hila
HOTEL **$$**

(☑9975 0082; Blvd de l'Unité; s CFA17,000-20,000, d CFA25,000; ❋) Ideally located for the Yaoundé bus agencies, the Hila sits on a very busy road, so get a room at the back if you can. Rooms are a decent size and clean, if rather sterile. Many have balconies, all have hot water, and there's even a mosque on the 2nd floor.

CAMEROON DOUALA

Hotel Akwa Palace
LUXURY HOTEL **$$$**

(☎ 3343 3916, 3342 2675; www.hotel-akwa-palace.com; Blvd de la Liberté; r CFA120,000-180,000; P❋@☎☒) If money's not a concern then this is still the best choice in town, if for nothing else than its superb location in the heart of things. Rooms are plush and stylish, staff helpful, and the vast and normally empty swimming pool in the back garden is the best place to forget the chaos outside.

✕ Eating

There are plenty of good restaurants along Blvd de la Liberté.

Delices
BAKERY **$**

(Blvd de la Liberté; pastries from CFA500; ☉7am-10pm, to 3pm Sun) A great early-morning stop for pastries and a shot of coffee, this Douala institution has a good selection of baked goods as well as more filling toasted sandwiches.

Méditerranée Restaurant
MEDITERRANEAN **$$**

(☎ 3342 3069; Blvd de la Liberté; mains CFA3000-6000; ☉8am-midnight) With an open terrace but still cleverly sheltered from the busy road, the Méditerranée is a perennially popular spot for expats to soak up the city. The menu is a good mix of Greek, Italian and Lebanese dishes, including wood-fired pizzas and changing daily specials.

Saga African Restaurant
AFRICAN **$$**

(Blvd de la Liberté; mains CFA4000-7000; ☉noon-11pm) Atmospheric and upmarket, the Saga offers an interesting mix of African dishes with some local classics, such as *ndole* (sauce made with bitter leaves similar to spinach and flavoured with smoked fish), plus pizza,

Chinese and pasta dishes. It's nicely decked out, with an open-air area at the front and a cool glass-fronted dining room behind.

Foyer du Marin EUROPEAN **$$**
(Rue Gallieni; mains CFA4000-8000; ☺8am-10pm) It's worth making a diversion for the nightly poolside grill at this hotel; great kebabs, steaks, chicken, seafood dishes and juicy German sausage are all well prepared and served up by the friendly staff. This is also a great drinking spot.

★**La Fourchette** INTERNATIONAL **$$$**
(☑3343 2611; Rue Franqueville; mains CFA7000-18,000; ☺10am-11pm Mon-Sat) An incredibly smart and tasteful option, La Fourchette's menu is out of this world if you're used to the more normal Cameroonian choice of chicken or fish. Here you'll find steak tartare, grilled zebu fillet, goat's cheese ravioli and stuffed crab, with prices to match. Service is charmingly formal, you should dress to impress and booking ahead is a good idea.

🍸 Drinking & Nightlife

Douala has a lively nightlife scene, though much of it can be inaccessible to visitors without local contacts. The areas of Bonapriso, Bonanjo and Akwa contain the most bars and clubs.

Café des Palabres CAFE
(Pl du Gouvernement; ☺7.30am-11pm Mon-Sat; ☎) Housed inside a 1905 colonial German residence, this charming cafe on Bonanjo's main square has a great garden terrace perfect for an evening drink, as well as a cool interior with a full menu and an intellectual/alternative vibe. Literary types might like to know that this is the building identified as 'la Pagode' in Céline's *Journey to the End of the Night*.

American Graffiti BAR
(Rue Sylvani; ☎) Pool bar, retro-diner and generally cool hang-out, this is the place to go drinking with a friendly and cool selection of Doualan youth. Try the delicious burgers, or your hand at pool on one of the two tables while downing a cool beer.

ℹ️ Information

DANGERS & ANNOYANCES

Muggings happen: if you'd rather be safe than sorry, it's recommended to take a taxi after dark. Leave valuables in a safe place, and be extra careful around nightspots.

MEDICAL SERVICES

Pharmacie du Centre (Blvd de la Liberté)
Pharmacie de Douala (Blvd Ahidjo)
Polyclinique Bonanjo (☑3342 7936, 3342 9910, emergencies 3342 1780; www.clibo.com; Ave de Gaulle) For medical emergencies.

MONEY

For changing money, try the banks along Blvd de la Liberté or Rue Joss; most have ATMs. Underneath the arcade next to the Hôtel Akwa Palace you'll find the best rates and tax-free exchange on the streets – but watch yourself.

POST

Central Post Office (Rue Joss)

ℹ️ Getting There & Away

Douala has an international airport with links to cities in Cameroon, around the region and to Europe.

Buses to Yaoundé (CFA3000 to CFA6000, three to four hours) depart from agency offices along Blvd de l'Unité throughout the day. For buses to Kribi (CFA2000, three hours) use Centrale Voyages on Blvd Ahidjo.

For other destinations, use the sprawling Gare Routière Bonabéri, 6km north of the city centre. Routes include Limbe (CFA2000, 1½ hours), Bamenda (CFA4500, seven hours), Bafoussam (CFA3500, five hours) and Foumban (CFA3500, six hours).

ℹ️ Getting Around

The main ways of getting around are shared taxis and *moto-taxi*, of which there are thousands; they are cheaper than taxis (CFA100 to CFA200 per short ride). Charter taxis from central Douala to Bonabéri generally charge CFA3000. A taxi to the airport costs CFA3000.

Buea

Basically built into the side of Mt Cameroon, Buea (pronounced boy-ah) has a hill station's coolness, especially compared to sticky Limbe. If you're going up the mountain, you're inevitably coming here.

Conveniently, **Express Exchange** (Molyko Rd) will exchange euros, US dollars and travellers cheques.

🛏️ Sleeping

Presbyterian Mission GUESTHOUSE **$**
(☑3332 2336; Market Rd; campsites CFA1000, s/d CFA4000/6000, without bathroom CFA3000/5000; Ⓟ) This church mission is set in attractive gardens and has comfy and

spotless rooms. There's a tidy communal sitting room and cooking facilities. It's up the hill from the police station.

Paramount Hotel HOTEL **$**
(✆3332 2341, 3332 2074; Molyko Rd; s/d/tr CFA7000/9000/11,000; **P**) The Paramount Hotel is one of the better places to sleep in Buea. The pretty rooms come with TV and are a nice respite from the mountain. To get here turn left off the main road and continue some way up the hill and you'll find the hotel on your right.

Hiking Mount Cameroon

Most hikes to the summit of West Africa's highest peak take two or three days, but it's no stroll in the park. The difficulty stems not only from its height (4095m), but from the fact that you start from near sea level, making a big change in altitude in a relatively short distance. November to April is the main climbing season, and although it's possible to climb the mountain year-round, you won't get much in the way of views during the rainy season. Warm clothes and waterproofs are a must. A popular ascent is a two-night, three-day hike via the Mann Spring route and descending via the Guinness Route.

Hikes are arranged in Buea through the **Mt Cameroon Ecotourism Organisation** (✆332 2038; mountceo@yahoo.uk; Buea Market; ⊙8am-5pm Mon-Fri, 7am-noon Sat & Sun). The organisation works closely with the 12 villages around the mountain, employing many villagers as guides and porters. All hikers pay a flat 'stakeholder fee' of CFA3000, which goes into a village development fund and is used for community projects, such as improving electricity and water supply. The organisation's office also has a small shop selling locally produced handicrafts.

Guides, well versed in the local flora and fauna, cost CFA6000 per day (maximum five hikers per guide); porters cost CFA5000. Establish a comfortable pace for yourself; some guides have a tendency – conscious or not – of rushing up the mountain. Equipment can be hired on a daily basis in Buea.

Limbe

Limbe is a charming place, blessed with a fabulous natural position between the rainforest-swathed foothills of Mt Cameroon and the dramatic Atlantic coastline. Popular with both foreign and Cameroonian tourists, this is a great spot to chill out on the beach for a few days before heading on elsewhere.

◉ Sights & Activities

Limbe Wildlife Centre ZOO
(www.limbewildlife.org; admission CFA3000; ⊙9am-4.30pm) Many zoos in Africa are depressing places, but the Limbe Wildlife Centre is a shining exception. Jointly run by the Ministry of the Environment and the primate charity Pandrillus, it contains rescued chimpanzees, gorillas, drills and other primates, all housed in large enclosures, with lots of interesting information about local conservation issues. Staff are well informed, and are heavily involved in community education.

Botanical Gardens GARDENS
(admission CFA2000, camera CFA2000; ⊙8am-6pm) The second-oldest botanical gardens in Africa are the home of, among others, cinnamon, nutmeg, mango, ancient cycads and an unnamed tree locals describe as 'African Viagra'. There's a small visitor centre and an area with Commonwealth War Graves. Guides (CFA1000) aren't required but are recommended as labelling is minimal. Bring bug spray.

Beaches BEACH
The best of Limbe's beaches are north of town and known by their distance from Limbe. Mile 6 and Mile 11 beaches are popular, but our favourite is at the village of Batoké at Mile 8, from where the lava flows of one of Mt Cameroon's eruptions are still visible.

Bimbia Rainforest & Mangrove Trail WALKING
(✆7733 7014; bbcnaturetrail@yahoo.com) Located about an hour south of Limbe and running through the only coastal lowland rainforest remaining between Douala and Limbe. An experienced guide will take you on day tours through some rather lovely submerged woods, birdwatching areas and old slave-trading sites. You'll have to pay CFA5000 for the local development fee, which goes towards the village of Bimbia and mangrove preservation, CFA3000 for a guide, and CFA15,000 for a *taxi brousse* (bush taxi) from Limbe,

Limbe

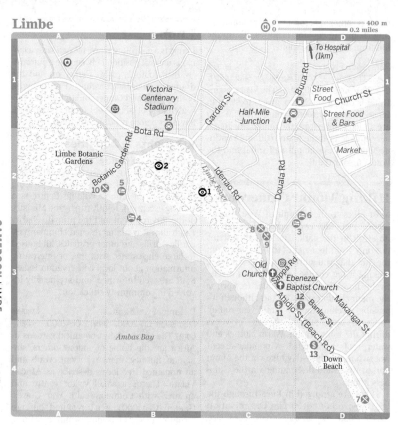

0 ——— 400 m
0 ——— 0.2 miles

Limbe

◎ Sights
1 Botanical Gardens C2
2 Limbe Botanic Gardens
  Visitors Centre B2

🛏 Sleeping
3 Bay Hotel D2
4 Bird Watchers' Club B2
5 Miramare Gardens
  Resort B2
6 Victoria Guest House D2

⊗ Eating
7 Grilled Fish Stalls D4

8 Le Moulin C3
9 Mt Cameroon Bakery C3
10 The Hot Spot A2

ℹ Information
11 Bicec Bank C3
12 Fako Tourist Board D3
13 SGBC Bank D4

ℹ Transport
14 Shared Taxis to Mile 4 Motor
  Park & Douala.....................................C1
15 Shared Taxis to Western
  Beaches B1

making this a trip best done in a group. To arrange tours talk to the guys who hang around the botanic gardens, arrange a trip through the Fako Tourist Board (p89) or contact Bimbia Rainforest and Mangrove Trail.

🛏 Sleeping

Victoria Guest House GUESTHOUSE **$**
(📞 2281 6245; off Makangal St; r CFA9000, with air-con CFA12,000-16,000; 🅿 ❄) The best-value budget place in town, the Victoria has clean

Labels on map:
- To Hospital (1km)
- Buua Rd
- Street Food
- Church St
- Victoria Centenary Stadium
- Garden St
- Half-Mile Junction
- Street Food & Bars
- Bota Rd
- Market
- Botanic Garden Rd
- Limbe Botanic Gardens
- Idenao Rd
- Douala Rd
- Limbe River
- Old Church
- Ebenezer Baptist Church
- Makangal St
- Ahidjo St (Beach Rd)
- Banley St
- Ambas Bay
- Down Beach

CAMEROON LIMBE

and well-maintained rooms on the hill above Limbe's main restaurant strip: follow the path up behind the King William Hotel. Nearly all rooms have air-con, but there are a couple of cheaper fan-cooled variants.

Bay Hotel
HOTEL $

(☑ 7467 8084; off Makangal St; s/d/ste from CFA6000/10,000/15,000) If you're on a very tight budget then the Bay offers big, rather damp fan-cooled rooms with tiny bathrooms that, in some cases at least, come with wide verandahs. Unfortunately, they also tend to pick up the noise of the party people in the nearby bars.

★ Bird Watchers' Club
GUESTHOUSE $$

(☑ 9683 8188, 7573 4086; Limbe Botanical Gardens; r CFA15,000; P ❈) This charmingly secluded spot on a rocky promontory overlooks the sea. With just two rooms it's a good idea to call ahead and book. You'll be rewarded with spacious accommodation with double beds and mosquito nets and a great restaurant with superb sea views.

Hotel Seme Beach
RESORT $$

(☑ 9496 5751, 7793 4552; www.semebeach.com; Mile 11, Rte d'Idenau, Bakingili; r incl breakfast CFA25,000-35,000, ste incl breakfast CFA50,000-100,000; P ❈ 🛜 ⛱) Not in Limbe itself, but 18km beyond along the coast, this is a good choice if you want to enjoy the beach and some creature comforts. The location is gorgeous, with full frontage onto the beach and views of Equatorial Guinea rising in the distance, while touches such as a freshwater swimming pool and a spa make for great relaxation. Service can be on the surly side, but otherwise this is a highly recommended place.

Miramare Gardens Resort
HOTEL $$

(☑ 3333 2941, 3332 2332; miramare.breeze@facebook.com; Botanic Garden Rd; incl breakfast campsites CFA5000, s/d CFA15,000/20,000; P ❈ 🛜 ⛱) While this place has certainly seen better days, its location on a wave-kissed cliff backed by screaming jungle is unbeatable. Accommodation is in cute, if rather dark, boukarous (self-contained huts) that abut a restaurant and a decent-sized, though rather green, swimming pool. Book ahead, as this place remains Limbe's most popular choice.

✖ Eating

The Hot Spot
INTERNATIONAL $

(Limbe Botanical Gardens; mains CFA3000-4000; ⊘ 7.30am-11pm) With hands down the best location in town, overlooking the dramatic coastline and the Park Hotel Miramar, this place offers a fairly standard selection of meat grills, shrimps, fish and chicken dishes. The friendly staff, outdoor seating and views make it, though. On the dirt road to the hotels through the gardens take the middle path after the bridge.

Le Moulin
INTERNATIONAL $

(Idenao Rd; mains CFA2000-3000; ⊘ 10am-10pm) Right on the roundabout in the thick of things, Le Moulin is the best eating option in the town centre. The menu encompasses ndole, chicken and beef dishes served up with fresh vegetables, plantains or rice. Service is friendly.

Mt Cameroon Bakery
BAKERY $

(Idenao Rd; pastries from CFA500; ⊘ 6am-11pm) Limbe's best spot for breakfast if your hotel doesn't serve it. Here you'll find life's essentials such as fresh-baked pastries and coffee.

Grilled Fish Stalls
SEAFOOD $

(Down Beach; dishes from CFA1000; ⊘ 7am-10pm) You'll find this cluster of open-air grills with attached seating where the fishing boats haul up on the beach. Soak up your beer with something from the sea that was probably happily unaware it would be your dinner a few minutes before you ordered it.

ℹ Information

The **Fako Tourist Board** (☑ 3333 2861; Banley St; ⊘ 7.30am-5pm Mon-Sat) can arrange local tours, hotels and bookings with the Mt Cameroon Ecotourism Organisation. Internet access is available at **Computer World** (Banley St; per hr CFA300; ⊘ closed Sun). Ahidjo St has several ATMs.

ℹ Getting There & Away

The main motor park is Mile 4, about 6km out of town. Minibuses and taxis brousses leave approximately hourly to Buea (CFA800, 25 minutes) and Douala (CFA1500, 70 minutes). From Mile 2, there are buses to Yaoundé (CFA5000, five hours).

Ferries (☑ 9998 9491, info 7727 6211) travel every Monday and Thursday from Limbe to Calabar in Nigeria (1st/2nd class CFA35,000/45,000, four hours), departing at 2am and returning on Tuesday and Friday at 7am. Take your own food and water.

Ferries weren't going to Malabo in Equatorial Guinea at the time of research, although a new ferry service was being discussed in late 2012.

CAMEROON LIMBE

Bamenda

The capital of Northwest Province is a dusty sprawl that tumbles down a hill at an altitude of more than 1000m; you'll see some impressive views of the town as you descend the hill coming from Douala. With a decent range of hotels and restaurants, it's a good jumping-off point for exploring the Ring Road circuit. It's also a centre of political opposition to President Biya.

🛏 Sleeping

Baptist Mission Resthouse   GUESTHOUSE $
(☑7545 8339; Finance Junction; dm/s/d CFA4000/9000/13,000, apt CFA50,000; Ⓟ 🛜) This compound on the main road into the town centre has a bunch of well-maintained rooms, all fan cooled and with mosquito nets and hot water, though some are a little on the small side and rather mildewy. There's a communal kitchen and it's secure and welcoming.

International Hotel   HOTEL $
(☑7606 7018; off Commercial Ave; s/d CFA10,000/12,000; ❄) Right in the middle of town and convenient for buses, this budget place charges extra for hot water and air-con. Rooms are modern and clean and have decent bathrooms as well as balconies offering sweeping views over, er, 'scenic' Bamenda.

Ex-Serviceman's Rest House   GUESTHOUSE $
(☑7727 6375; Hotel Rd; r CFA5000) This compound is intended for ex-soldiers, but if rooms are available they'll be happily rented out to travellers on a tight budget; expect very basic digs with running water. It's a decent deal, but solo female travellers may feel uncomfortable.

Hotel Mondial   HOTEL $$
(☑7793 8378; off Hotel Rd; s/d/ste CFA14,500/16,000/22,000; Ⓟ) Definitely one of Bamenda's smarter choices, the Mondial is a little more modern than its equivalents elsewhere, though bathrooms are in a poor state and the swimming pool sits forlorn and empty. The otherwise comfortable rooms come with hot water, balconies and satellite TV.

🍴 Eating

Dreamland Restaurant   AFRICAN $
(Commercial Ave; mains CFA1500-3500; ⊙7am-11pm) Dreamland doesn't look like much

Bamenda

🛏 Sleeping
1 Baptist Mission Resthouse D1
2 Ex-Serviceman's Rest House C2
3 Hotel Mondial C2
4 International Hotel B1

🍴 Eating
5 CTT Restaurant & Handicrafts
    Cooperative D1
6 Dreamland Restaurant B1
7 Super Class Restaurant D1

ℹ Information
8 Express Exchange B1
9 SGBC Bank B2
10 Tourist Office B1

ℹ Transport
11 Bali Motor Park (Transport to
    Bali & Mamfe) A3
12 Nkwen Motor Park D1
13 Ntarikon Motor Park A1
14 Vatican Express & Agency Bus
    Offices to Bafoussam &
    Points South B1

from the outside, but inside it's a well set out establishment with a large menu. There's a daily lunchtime buffet (CFA3500 per person) and a choice of grills, salads, fish and soups the rest of the time.

Super Class Restaurant   AFRICAN $
(near Finance Junction; mains CFA3000; ⊙7.30am-8pm) This cute little shack with red tablecloths and friendly service serves up simple Cameroonian fare such as fried chicken and plantains or meat grills with rice.

CTT Restaurant &
Handicrafts Cooperative   AFRICAN $$
(near Finance Junction, Upstation; mains CFA1000-9000; ⊙8am-9pm) The food here is a standard blend of Cameroonian and slightly better Western fare. The real drawcard is the surrounds, specifically a workshop of regional handicrafts, a shop with a superb collection of handcrafted souvenirs and great views of Bamenda below.

ℹ Information

The **tourist office** (☑336 1395) can provide basic maps and dates of local festivals. **Express Exchange** (City Chemist's Roundabout) changes travellers cheques as well as US dollars. **SGBC Bank** (Commercial Ave) has an ATM.

Bamenda

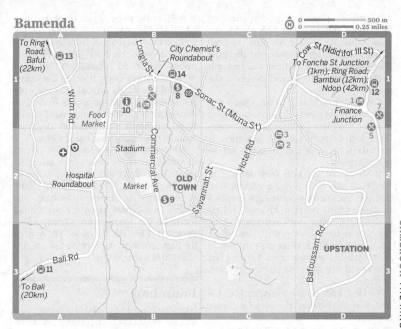

ℹ Getting There & Away

Most agency offices for destinations to the south are on Sonac St. Destinations include Yaoundé (CFA5000, six hours), Douala (CFA4500, seven hours) and Bafoussam (CFA1500, 90 minutes). Nkwen Motor Park has transport to the eastern stretch of the Ring Road, including Ndop (CFA1200, 90 minutes) and Kumbo (CFA3000, five hours). The west Ring Road is served by Ntarikon Motor Park, which runs minibuses to Wum (CFA3000, six hours). Shared taxis to the further motor parks shouldn't cost you any more than CFA150.

The Ring Road

The northwest highlands bear the pretty name 'Grassfields', an appellation too pleasant to really capture the look of this landscape. These aren't gentle fields; they're green and yellow valleys, tall grass, red earth and sharp mountains. Clouds of mist rise with wood smoke and dung smoke that mark the location of villages speckled on this deceptively inviting – but hard and rugged – terrain.

The 367km Ring Road runs a circle around the Grassfields, and if it were in better shape, it'd be one of Cameroon's great scenic drives. In fairness, it still can't be missed – but get your butt ready for some bumpy, red-earth roads. The pay-off? Mountains dolloped with lakes, cattle loping into the hills and one of the greatest concentrations of *fondoms* (traditional kingdoms) in Cameroon. Tourism is DIY here, with public transport extremely slow, crowded and irregular and very basic sleeping options in the few actual towns on the road. But a visit here is all about the journey itself: driving through tiny villages and enjoying the extraordinary and ever-changing scenery along the route.

Hiking, cycling and camping are all options, but always ask the permission of the local chief, and bring some gifts (whisky is a good idea). If you plan to drive this incredibly challenging road, hire a 4x4 and don't even think about it in the rainy season.

Transport links are reasonable but not particularly frequent, with minibuses usually leaving very early in the morning. Roads are poor throughout. Kumbo is the Ring Road's largest town, but apart from there, there's little infrastructure and nowhere to change money (stock up on CFA before leaving Bamenda). There are basic hotels in Ndop, Kumbo, Nkambe and Wum.

Starting from Bamenda and heading east, you pass Sabga Hill, which rises powerfully above Ndop, then Bamessing, with a handicraft centre and pottery workshop.

After that you reach Kumbo, dominated by its Catholic cathedral and *fon's* (traditional chief's) palace. It's a good place to base yourself, with a nice market and the Ring Road's best hotels. From there you go north to Nkambe, then Missaje and the end of the road.

The road from Missaje to We is just a dirt track and in the rainy season you won't find it. Some travellers continue on foot, sometimes with help from Fulani herdsmen. It can take a couple of days to get to We, so bring supplies.

If you make the hike from Missaje to We, you'll pass Lake Nyos, a volcanic lake that was the site of a natural-gas eruption in 1986, which resulted in around 1700 deaths. Continuing south you reach Wum, the biggest town on the west side of the Ring Road. South of Wum the road passes the Metchum Falls, where most shared-taxi drivers will stop to let you take a quick peek or photo.

The last town on the Ring Road (or the first, if you're heading clockwise) is Bafut, traditionally the strongest of the kingdoms in this region. The fon's palace (admission CFA1000, camera CFA1500, museum CFA2000) is a highlight of the Ring Road and includes a tour of the compound where the *fon's* large family lives.

Bafoussam

There's initially little to love about Bafoussam. The Bamiléké stronghold seems haphazardly built on agriculture money and a refined sense of chaos. But despite its heavy traffic and uninspiring appearance, the town is super friendly and has one of the best traditional palaces in the country. Make sure you check out the huge chefferie (Chief's Compound; www.museumcam.org; admission CFA2000; ⊙10am-5pm), about 15km south at Bandjoun.

Good value, with a decent bar to boot, the rooms at Hotel Federal (☑3344 1309; Rte de Foumban; r CFA10,000-12,000, with air-con CFA16,000) are neat and tidy. Although located in a blocky bomb-shelter chic building, the rooms in Hotel du Centre (☑7512 4025, 3344 2079; Carrefour Total; r CFA12,000-15,000) are open and fresh, many come with a balcony, and the toilets – bless them – have seats. It's well located (as the name suggests) and a useful landmark. For far better midrange accommodation head to Hotel Altitel (☑3344 5111; www.hotelaltitel.net; r CFA23,000-33,000;

P ❄ 🛜) or the more distant Hotel Le Saré (☑9944 5059, 3344 2599; r CFA15,000-28,000), both on the road towards Bamenda.

Boulangerie La Paix (Rte de Foumban; pastries from CFA150; ⊙8am-10pm) sells good bread and sticky sweet treats in the morning, and is a handy general food shop the rest of the day. Supermarché le Point (Ave de la République), at the opposite end of Rue de Marché, fulfils the same function. The usual fish and meat stalls come out at night.

Minibuses to Foumban (CFA800 to CFA1000, one hour) depart from near Carrefour Total, along with shared taxis. Agencies to Yaoundé (CFA2500 to CFA3000, three hours) and Douala (CFA4000, five hours) have offices along the main road south of the town centre. Transport to Bamenda (CFA1500, 1½ hours) leaves from the Bamenda road, north of the town centre (CFA150 in a shared taxi).

Foumban

Foumban has a deep tradition of homegrown arts and the traditional monarchy centred on a sultan, who resides in a palace. The town is plopped architecturally and conceptually between West and North Africa, as if the Sahel and its sharp music, bright robes and Islam – this is the city with most Muslims in the south – were slowly creeping into the eastern corner of West Province.

There's a slow internet cafe east of the market. CPAC bank (south of the market) may change euros if you're lucky, but it's best to change money in Bafoussam.

⦿ Sights

The Grand Marché is a warren of narrow stalls and alleys, which are great fun to explore; the paths eventually lead to where the Grande Mosquée faces the palace.

Palais Royal   PALACE
(Rue du Palais; admission CFA2000, camera CFA2000; ⊙9am-6pm) The must-see attraction of Foumban is the sultan's palace, currently home to the 19th sultan of the Bamoun dynasty. It has a fascinating and well-organised museum containing previous sultans' possessions and great historical insight into the region – assuming you know French. You'll find the palace opposite the market and main mosque, the minaret of which can be climbed as part of the palace tour.

Village des Artisans
ARTS CENTRE

(Rue des Artisans) South of town, the Village des Artisans seems to produce more handicrafts than the rest of Cameroon combined.

Musée des Arts et Traditions Bamoun
MUSEUM

(admission CFA1000; ⊙9am-5pm) Close to the Village des Artisans, this museum houses a private collection of art and historical artefacts.

✽✽ Festivals & Events

Every year at Tabaski, the Islamic holiday of Eid al-Adha, Foumban attracts thousands of pilgrims for an extraordinary blend of Muslim and traditional Bamoun ceremonies.

It all starts before sunrise with the call to prayer blasting from loudspeakers at the mosque. Thousands of men and boys, dressed in their finest, climb the hill to the Sacred Mountain and kneel in prayer. Around dawn the imam arrives, followed by the sultan in his white Cadillac. There are sunrise prayers, a sermon from the imam and a blessing from the sultan (on Eid al-Adha this is when the sheep is sacrificed). The sultan then gets on his horse surrounded by warriors in full regalia, and everyone follows him in an enormous parade to the palace, while the women and girls, so far absent from the proceedings, line the streets dressed all in white and ululate as the sultan passes.

After the parade there's a rest, and then horses race through town. There's another break until it gets dark, when the drumming and dancing start in front of the Palais Royal. Meanwhile (this is still Cameroon, after all) people pack the bars and clubs, and when these are full they set up speakers on the streets for heavy drinking and dancing until the sun comes up.

🛏 Sleeping & Eating

Bars, beer and grilled meat are abundant. Happy days.

Hotel Complexe Adi
HOTEL $

(✆7607 9507, 9953 5515; Rue de l'Hotel Beau Regarde; r CFA6000) Look for the giant voodoo statue of a man studded by nails to find Adi's entrance. While the rooms here are clean, they're smallish and very basic (just a bed and a small bathroom), and the bar downstairs gets pretty loud. If there are no rooms available here, try the similar Hotel Beau Regard across the road.

★ Hotel Pekassa de Karché
HOTEL $$

(✆3348 2935; hotelpekassadekarche@yahoo.fr; Rte de Bafoussam; s/d without air-con CFA10,000/ 15,000, d with air-con & balcony CFA25,000, ste CFA40,000; P ✲ @) This brand-new hotel is by far the best choice in Foumban. Just 200m from the royal palace, it makes for a pleasant change from the norm in Cameroonian hotels: smart, clean rooms with relatively tasteful decor, friendly staff and good security. There's a good on-site restaurant (mains CFA2500 to CFA4000) too.

Rifam Hotel
HOTEL $$

(✆3348 2878; Rte de Bafoussam; r CFA10,000-25,000; P) Near the bus-agency offices, this hotel is one of Foumban's plushest. There's a big choice of rooms at various different prices, all of which have been recently repainted. There's also hot water, a TV set and plenty of space in each. A good restaurant downstairs makes up for the location, some way from the town centre.

ℹ Getting There & Away

There are a few direct buses to Yaoundé (CFA3500, five hours) and Douala (CFA3500, six hours); otherwise head for Bafoussam (CFA800 to CFA1000, one hour) and change there. Bus-agency offices are on the west side of town, about 3km from the Grande Marché (CFA150 in a shared taxi).

Transport between Foumban and Kumbo (CFA3000, around six hours) runs year-round, with journey times varying according to the rains. Although the road is very, very poor, it's easily one of the most beautiful in the country, skirting along the edge of the spectacular Mbam Massif.

SOUTHERN CAMEROON

Southern Cameroon is largely taken up by thick jungle, and there are few large towns or other population centres here. However, the coastline here is by far Cameroon's best: head to Kribi for great scenery and a relaxed vibe, and continue further down the coast to indulge in a spot of beach exploration and ecotourism in Parc National de Campo-Ma'an.

Kribi

Kribi is home to Cameroon's best beaches: the sand is fine, the water crystal clear, fresh fish is on the menu and cold beer on tap; there are times when Africa hugs you.

Most of Kribi's hotels, usually with their own beachfronts, start at the southern end of town, but camping isn't advised. The **Chutes de la Lobé**, 8km south of town (*moto-taxi* CFA500), are an impressive set of waterfalls that empty directly into the sea – it's a beautiful sight.

🛏 Sleeping

Kribi's main business is tourism and there's plenty of choice in where to stay. If you're visiting in the rainy season, ask for a discount.

Hotel Panoramique   HOTEL $
(☑2346 1773, 9694 2575; hotel panoramique@ yahoo.fr; Rue du Marché; r CFA6000-15,000; ✳) This semi-sprawling compound feels like a down-at-heel villa evolved into low-rent flophouse. Some rooms are good value, but at the cheapest end you're in an ugly annexe with the dust and roaches.

★ Hotel Ilomba   HOTEL $$
(☑9991 2923; www.hotelilomba.com; Rte de Campo; r CFA40,000, ste CFA120,000; P✳@🛜🏊) Some way out of Kribi, this is the loveliest hotel in the area. Rooms are in *boukarous* and all well furnished and tastefully decorated. It's also just a short walk to the Chutes de la Lobé and right on a beautiful stretch of beach, so it's a great place to base yourself for true relaxation.

New Hotel Coco Beach   HOTEL $$
(☑9999 8790, 3346 1584; off Rte de Campo; r without/with sea view CFA20,000/30,000; P✳🏊) There's not much new about the New Hotel Coco Beach, indeed its rooms have certainly seen better days, but they're clean and comfortable and some of them have fantastic sea views. The beach is just below the hotel and you can have breakfast as the waves splash just a short wander away – magic.

Les Gîtes de Kribi   GUESTHOUSE $$
(☑7508 0845; www.kribiholidays.com; Rte de Campo; r CFA20,000, gîtes CFA45,000; P✳🛜🏊) Ideal for families, the *gîtes* (self-contained cottages) here are of varying sizes, but all are well equipped and have their own small kitchens. There are also normal rooms in the main building for those not *en famille*. Across the road there's a charming beach restaurant that serves up fresh fish in high season.

Auberge du Phare   GUESTHOUSE $$$
(☑7564 0464; www.pharedekribi.cm; off Rte de Campo; r CFA28,000-50,000; P✳🛜🏊) Right on the seafront, this great place has classy

blonde-wood accents, navy-blue sheets and nautical embellishments that give rooms some character, while the peeling courtyard, crystal pool and thatched bar are tropically indulgent.

🍴 Eating

All of the beach hotels have restaurants, and these are the nicest dining options in Kribi. Expect to pay from CFA3000 per meal; seafood obviously features heavily.

Fish Market   SEAFOOD $
(meals from CFA1000; ⊙10am-5pm Wed & Sat) This market at the marina grills the day's catch over coals. From crab and lobster to massive barracuda, you'd be hard-pressed to find a better and tastier selection of seafood anywhere in Cameroon.

Fish & Meat Stands   FAST FOOD $
(meals from CFA1000; ⊙10am-late) On Carrefour Kingué you'll find plenty of fish and meat stands lined up in front of the bars.

ℹ Getting There & Away

Bus agencies have offices on Rue du Marché in the town centre. Nonagency transport leaves from the main *gare routière* (bus station). Buses for Douala (CFA1800 to CFA2000, three hours) leave throughout the day, along with transport to Campo (CFA2000, three hours) and Yaoundé (CFA3000, 3½ hours).

Ebolowa

Ebolowa, capital of Ntem district, is a bustling place and a possible stopping point en route between Yaoundé and Equatorial Guinea or Gabon. Its main attraction is the artificial **Municipal Lake** in the centre of town.

The best accommodation is at **Hotel Porte Jaune** (☑2228 4339; Rte de Yaoundé; r CFA10,000-12,000) in the town centre, with some cheaper *auberges* (hostels) near the main roundabout, including **Hotel Âne Rouge** (☑2228 3438; Pl Ans 2000; r CFA5000).

During the dry season there's at least one vehicle daily along the rough road between Ebolowa and Kribi. There are also many buses daily to Yaoundé (CFA3000, three hours). Several vehicles depart in the morning for Ambam (CFA1000, one hour), from where you can find transport towards Ebebiyin (Equatorial Guinea) or Bitam (Gabon).

Campo & Ebodjé

Campo is the last town before the Equatorial Guinea border. Taking the road here is half the attraction – it's a hard but rewarding slog through immense rainforest past pygmy villages with views out to the ocean and fire-spouting petrol platforms shimmering in the west.

For travellers, Campo mainly serves as a jumping-off point for visiting Parc National de Campo Ma'an as well as the community-tourism project in nearby Ebodjé. There's scruffy accommodation, simple meals and very friendly faces at **Auberge Bon Course** (☑ 7451 1883; r CFA5000) at Bon Course Supermarché at the main junction in Campo.

Parc National de Campo-Ma'an, comprising 2608 sq km, protects rainforest, many plants and various animals, including buffalo, elephants and mandrills. The park is being developed by WWF as an ecotourism destination, with newly constructed canopy walks and river trips available.

Ebodjé, a small fishing village 25km north of Campo, is home to a **sea turtle conservation project** and ecotourism site run by **KUDU Cameroun** (☑ 3348 1648, 9622 0829). Visitors are taken out at night to spot egg-laying turtles, although there's no guarantee you'll see any – some tour groups encounter none, some as many as six. Even if you don't see any turtles, the beach is gorgeous, pristine and better than anything in Kribi.

The cost of a turtle walk (around CFA12,000 per person) includes accommodation in a local home, village development fee, meal and tour. A portion of fees help locals, many of whom have been trained as guides, and for between CFA5000 and CFA10,000 you can arrange trips up local rivers or cultural nights with traditional dancing and singing. Remember to bring your own water or filter, mosquito net and sleeping sheets.

There are daily minibuses between Campo and Kribi (CFA1500), which also stop at Ebodjé. *Moto-taxis* to Campo Beach (for Equatorial Guinea) cost CFA500. Taxis to Ebodjé from Campo cost CFA500. *Moto-taxis* to Ebodjé cost around CFA2000.

NORTHERN CAMEROON

The north of Cameroon is the fringe of the world's greatest dry zone. This is the Sahel, a red and ochre and yellow and brown rolling sea of dust, dirt and strange, utterly beautiful hills and pinnacles of rock, crisscrossed by the dry wind, the thin strides of Fulani people and the broad steps of their long-horned cattle.

N'Gaoundéré

N'Gaoundéré is the terminus of the railway line and beginning of the great bus and truck routes to the far north and Chad. The sense of adventure imparted upon reaching the Sahel is helped by the sight of government soldiers – there's a major training facility nearby – striding through the desert lanes with AK-47s strapped to their backs and extra banana clips taped to the stocks of their guns.

Some areas of N'Gaoundéré have a bad reputation for safety at night, including the area around the stadium and north of the cathedral. If in doubt, take a *moto-taxi*.

◎ Sights

Palais du Lamido   PALACE
(admission CFA2000, guide CFA1000, camera CFA1000; ⊙ 9am-5pm) To enter the Palais du Lamido, the palace of the local Muslim ruler, you pass between three pillars stuffed with the remains of individuals who were buried alive to consecrate the site of the royal residence. One of Cameroon's more macabre foyers, yes, which leads into a complex of low-slung, heavily thatched roundhouses whose aesthetic feels more West African than Islamic. Some rooms are underwhelming, but if you come on a Friday or (especially) Sunday, when nobles pay their respects and thin, gorgeous desert music settles over the nearby square dominated by the Grande Mosquée, there's a palpable sense of being... well, somewhere else. Beware of black-painted areas within the compound – these sections are reserved for the *lamido*.

🛏 Sleeping

Nice Hotel   HOTEL $
(☑ 7550 7523, 2225 1013; Rte de Garoua; r from CFA10,000; ℗) With spacious rooms, a peaceful, leafy setting, long cool corridors and TV in all rooms, the Nice is just that, and about as good as midrange options get in town, and surprisingly cheap. It's a very quick *moto-taxi* ride from the station.

Auberge de la Gare   GUESTHOUSE $
(☑ 9980 3680, 2225 2217; r CFA8500; ℗) This pleasant enough spot in a N'Gaoundéré backstreet offers easy access to bus agencies

N'Gaoundéré

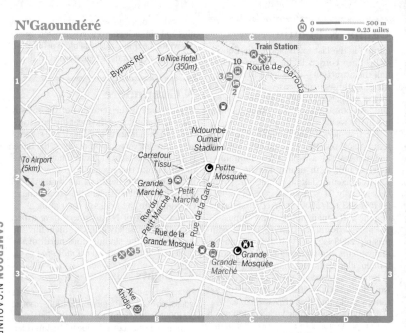

Train Station

Route de Garoua

Ndoumbe Oumar Stadium

Carrefour Tissu

Grande Marché

Petite Mosquée

Petit Marché

Rue du Petit Marché

Rue de la Gare

Rue de la Grande Mosquée

Grande Marché

Grande Mosquée

To Nice Hotel (350m)

Bypass Rd

To Airport (5km)

Ave Ahidjo

N'Gaoundéré

and the train station. Rooms are tidy and simple, some with hot water, making it a good budget option There's a cute outdoor bar-restaurant with a thatched roof here too.

Hotel Pousada Style   HOTEL $
(☑ 9985 4454, 2225 1703; r CFA5000-9000; ℗) A basic but friendly resthouse a short walk from the Catholic cathedral, the Pousada Style is divided into two wings. The one

around the back is a little cheaper with smaller rooms, while those at the front are better, though still quite basic. All have mosquito nets, TV and bathrooms. Take a *moto-taxi* late at night in this area.

★ **Adamaoua Hotel**   HOTEL $$
(☑ 9901 7566, 2225 1255; adamaouahotel@yahoo.fr; Rue de la Gare; r CFA15,000-25,000; ℗ 🛜) This brand-new hotel is easily the best option in town: a short stroll from the station and next to the main bus companies, its sparkling fan-cooled modern rooms all have hot water, cable TV and plenty of African art on the lurid pink walls. Staff are friendly, there's a good on-site restaurant and even (yes, really!) wi-fi in the lobby.

✗ Eating

The best street food is easily found at the row of shops, stalls and bars opposite the train station – worth the detour even if you don't have a train to catch.

The main market is the Petit Marché; the Grand Marché only sells vegetables.

Le Verger   AFRICAN $
(Rue de la Grande Mosquée; mains CFA1500-3000; ⊙ 6am-10pm) Tucked away in a courtyard off the main drag (look for the small sign), this green-painted restaurant serves up a range

of local dishes as well as the chicken and fish mains you find everywhere else. There's breezy outdoor seating as well as a more formal dining room with white tablecloths. Staff are charming.

★**La Plazza** INTERNATIONAL $$
(Rue de la Grande Mosquée; mains from CFA3000-7000; ⊙10am-2pm & 7-11pm) Something of a N'Gaoundéré institution, this place has live music nightly and cold draught beer from the thatched bar. The Lebanese and pasta dishes are excellent, but don't miss the perennially popular Sunday buffet from noon (CFA6000). It's a little tricky to find as it's not on the street itself, but in a courtyard. Look for Ecobank and go through the gates to one side.

ℹ Getting There & Away

The airport, 5km outside the town, was being rebuilt at the time of research, so your only option for reaching N'Gaoundéré at present is overland.

The train station is at the eastern end of town. Trains to Yaoundé leave daily at around 7pm (CFA28,000 in 1st-class couchette, 12 hours), and you can reserve your seat a day in advance.

By bus, Touristique Express and Alliance Voyages are the best, with several buses daily to Garoua (CFA3500, five hours) and Maroua (CFA6000, eight hours). Kawtal Voyages operates a battered Garoua-Boulaï (CFA4000, 12 hours) service most days from the *gare routière* by the Grande Mosquée. Think twice before attempting this during the rains. Equally strenuous is the appalling road south to Foumban, run by Alliance Voyages (CFA11,000, around 15 hours).

Garoua

Garoua is a pleasant enough spot to spend the night or wait for a vehicle transfer, which is the extent of most people's plans here. You may need to make a stopover if you're overlanding into Chad; pay a visit to the Chadian consulate (☏2227 3128) for visas, a far better place to get a visa than the embassy in Yaoundé.

Near the port, **Auberge Hiala Village** (☏2227 2407; Rue Cicai; r CFA5000-8000; ℗❄) has decent self-contained rooms, with a good bar and restaurant. **Super Restaurant** (Rte de Maroua; mains from CFA1000) is a breezy place, with decent food and juices.

Several bus agencies run daily to Maroua (CFA2500, 2½ hours), and N'Gaoundéré (CFA3500, five hours), while Camair.Co flies to Yaoundé and Douala.

Maroua

Red and brown streets of sand run like dry riverbeds between rounded beige buildings while a cast of Fulani and Chadians in robes of sky blue, electric purple and blood red populate the chaos. This is Maroua, Cameroon's northernmost major town and its best base for exploring the extreme North Province, particularly the Mandara Mountains, as well as a good place to plan border crossings into Nigeria and Chad.

☞ Tours

Maroua has numerous tour operators that can arrange hiking in the Mandara Mountains and visits to Parc National du Waza.

Fagus Voyages GUIDED TOURS
(☏9986 1871, 9616 6070; www.fagusvoyages.ch) Swiss-owned company offering safaris to nearby national parks.

Jean-Luc Sini GUIDED TOURS
(☏7143 8603, 9985 5328; sinijeanluc@yahoo.fr) Runs sightseeing and trekking tours to the villages of the Mandara Mountains.

Safari Kirdi GUIDED TOURS
(☏9976 8395, 7764 4831) English-speaking Mr Dabala can arrange drivers, guides and safaris to the Mandara Mountains and national parks.

⌓ Sleeping

Relais Ferngo GUESTHOUSE $
(☏9452 8488, 2229 2153; off Blvd de Diarenga; r CFA6000; ℗❄) By far the best budget choice in town: sleep in spacious, whitewashed *boukarous* in the shade of willowy neem trees and shower in the alfresco but walled-off bathrooms. There's a busy bar at the back and guides offering tours often hang out here.

Residence Walya GUESTHOUSE $
(☏9991 6523, 2229 2026; residencewalya@yahoo.fr; off Blvd de Diarenga; r CFA12,000; ❄@☎) This recently opened guesthouse in a pristine courtyard off a sandy side street offers excellent, bright and clean rooms. There's no hot water, but it's well located and friendly.

★**Relais de la Porte Mayo** HOTEL $$
(☏9950 0149, 2229 2692; Pont Rouge; s/d/apt CFA15,000/18,00/19,500; ℗❄@) Streets ahead of anywhere else in town, it's frankly amazing that a place like this exists in a town like Maroua. French run, the Porte Mayo has bundles

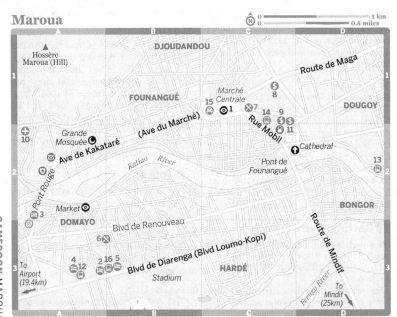

Maroua

of charm with its relaxed, modern-amenities-but-you're-still-in-the-Sahel kinda vibe, with roomy *boukarous,* an excellent restaurant-bar and friendly staff. A true oasis in the middle of dusty Maroua. Internet is by cable only.

Hotel Le Sahel   HOTEL **$$**
(☑ 2215 3901, 2229 2960; Blvd de Diarenga; r CFA15,000-25,000, ste 50,000; P ❄ @ 🛜) The cheapest rooms here will get you fairly dark and forlorn cells at the back of this otherwise impressive property, but they're still decent value and allow you the perks of the hotel such as the pool, courtyard bar and wi-fi. The rooms in the main building are far better, with balconies and both light and space in most.

✕ Eating & Drinking

Maroua doesn't have many eating options, but there are plenty of bars, the liveliest of which are strung along Blvd de Renouveau. Several stalls on Blvd de Renouveau offer *brochettes* and grilled fish.

Restaurant Le Baobab   AFRICAN **$**
(dishes CFA2000-4000; ⏱ 7am-11pm) This pleasant spot by the main market has outdoor seating under a thatched roof, a friendly atmosphere and good food, including a nightly buffet. Check what's available – the lunchtime menu can be limited.

Relais de la Porte Mayo FRENCH **$$**
(dishes CFA4000-8000; ☺ 7am-11pm) For upscale dining, this is Maroua's best option, popular with the local French community. The restaurant has great French options, including a good-value daily set meal. Tables are scattered around outside in the charming garden.

ℹ Information

If your hotel doesn't have wi-fi try **Braouz** (internet per hr CFA750).

For medical emergencies, try Meskine Hospital, southwest of town off the Garoua road.

Maroua's banks can be reluctant to change even cash euros. If the main banks won't help, try CCA Bureau de Change next to SGBC bank. The latter also has an ATM, as does **Bicec Bank** (Rte de Maga).

ℹ Getting There & Away

Flights with Camair.Co connect Maroua with Douala via Yaoundé (CFA115,000 to both cities) three times a week. The airport is 20km south of town along the Garoua road (CFA3000 in a chartered taxi, if you can find one).

Touristique Express and Alliance Voyages have several daily buses to Garoua (CFA2500, 2½ hours) and N'Gaoundéré (CFA6000, eight hours). You can book tickets for the N'Gaoundéré–Yaoundé train here at the same time. Several other bus agencies operate along the N'Gaoundéré route, with depots on the same road; Star Express in the town centre is also good.

Plentiful transport to Mokolo (CFA1000, 1½ hours) and less frequently to Rhumsiki (CFA2000, around three hours) departs from Carrefour Parrah in Djarangol at the southern end of town.

Transport to Kousséri for the Chad border (CFA3500, five hours) departs from the *gare routière* on Maroua's eastern edge. Minibuses to Banki for the Nigerian border (CFA2000, two hours) also depart from here.

Mandara Mountains

Basalt cliffs dot a volcanic plain, dust storms conceived on the Nigerian border sweep out of the sunset onto thorn trees, red rock cairns and herds of brindle cattle...and frankly, you wouldn't be half surprised to see a cowboy or a dragon or both pass across this awesome, evocative landscape. The Mandara Mountains run west from Maroua to the Nigerian border and have become very popular – justifiably so – with Africa hikers.

The villages that dot these ranges are as captivating as the vistas they are built on, including **Rhumsiki**, with its striking mountain scenery; **Djingliya** and **Koza**, set against steep terraced hillsides; **Tourou**, known for the calabash hats worn by local women; and **Maga**, with its domed houses made entirely of clay. **Mora** has a particularly notable weekly market. Hiking between villages is one of the best ways to appreciate the scenery and culture alike.

Rhumsiki is the main entrance point for visitors to the Mandara Mountains, and is the one place where there's a tangible feel of a tourist scene (although in Cameroon this is a relative term).

There's accommodation in Rhumsiki, Mokolo, Mora, Waza, Maga and a few other villages, but otherwise no infrastructure. If you're travelling independently, allow plenty of time and plan to be self-sufficient with food and water. Local minibuses usually set off around 6am. *Moto-taxis* are sometimes the only option for getting around.

For those with limited time, travel agencies in Maroua can organise visits, although it's just as easy to arrange things on the spot in Rhumsiki or Mokolo, which will ensure that more of the money you spend is pumped directly into the local economy. Expect to pay around CFA9000 per day, including guide, simple meals and accommodation.

Parc National du Waza

The most accessible of Cameroon's national parks, **Parc National du Waza** (admission CFA5000, vehicle CFA2000, camera CFA2000; ☺ 6am-6pm 15 November-15 May) is also the best for viewing wildlife. While it can't compare with East African parks, you're likely to see elephants, hippos, giraffes, antelopes and – with luck – lions. Late March to April is the best time for viewing, as the animals congregate at water holes before the rains. Waza is also notable for its particularly rich birdlife. The park is closed during the rainy season.

A guide (CFA5000) is obligatory in each vehicle. Walking isn't permitted.

The park entrance is signposted and about 400m off the main highway. Unless you have your own vehicle, the best way to visit is to hire a vehicle in Maroua (about CFA30,000 per day plus petrol). A 4WD vehicle is recommended.

Accessing the park by public transport is difficult; any bus between Maroua and Kousséri should be able to drop you off at the park turn-off, but after that you'll be reliant

EATING WELL IN RHUMSIKI

In Rhumsiki make a beeline for **Vegetarian Carnivore** (mains CFA2500), at the entrance to the village. Here you'll be met by friendly, English-speaking Kodji, who runs one of Cameroon's most innovative and charming restaurants. All the produce comes from Rhumsiki (much of it from the kitchen garden behind the outdoor eating area) and is prepared to order whenever guests come. The freshly made bread is the restaurant's calling card, and the Cameroonian vegetable pizza is superb. As its name suggests, both carnivores and vegetarians are well catered for, and if you're tired, you can even take a nap in one of the hammocks strung up in the garden, or take a room (CFA2500) for the night.

on hitching a lift into the park itself, which is likely to involve a long wait.

🛏 Sleeping

Waza can easily be done as a day trip from Maroua if you start early (bring a packed lunch). Otherwise, there are a few places to stay near the park entrance.

There's (very) basic accommodation in Waza village, just north of the park entrance.

Centre d'Accueil de Waza   LODGE $
(☑ 2229 2207; campsites per person CFA3000, r CFA8000) This simple place at the park entrance has accommodation in no-frills two-person *boukarous* with shared bathroom facilities. Meals can be arranged (CFA2000) and there is a small kitchen.

Campement de Waza   LODGE $$
(☑ 2229 1646, in Maroua 2229 1646, in Waza 7765 7717; r CFA18,000; ❈) Perched on a hill amid smooth boulders are these *boukarous,* with views that stretch out to the scrub plains and some lizards thrown in gratis. The huts are comfy, staff helpful and the on-site restaurant good for sinking a beer post lion-spotting.

EASTERN CAMEROON

Cameroon's remote east is wild and untamed. Seldom visited by travellers, it's very much a destination for those with plenty of time and the stamina to back up an appetite for adventure. There's little infrastructure and travel throughout is slow and rugged, with dense green forest and red laterite earth roads. The rainforest national parks are the main attraction, along with routes into the Central African Republic and Congo.

Bertoua

The capital of East Province, Bertoua is a genuine boomtown, born of logging and mining. Here you'll find all the facilities lacking elsewhere in the region, including banks and sealed roads.

The town's best hotel is **Hotel Mansa** (☑ 2224 1650; Mokolo II; r CFA25,000-35,000; ❈ ❈), which comes complete with an artificial lake, satellite TV and a tennis court. It's definitely worth a splurge if you've been lost in the forest.

Buses to Yaoundé (CFA5000, seven hours), Bélabo (for the train; CFA1000, one hour) and Garoua-Boulaï leave from the *gare routière* near the market.

Garoua-Boulaï

If you're looking for a rough African frontier town, Garoua-Boulaï is it. On the Central African Republic border, it's a place of bars, trucks and prostitutes. The *auberges* aren't recommended, so try the **Mission Catholique** (dm for a donation, r about CFA5000) instead.

There's a bus to N'Gaoundéré (CFA4000, 12 hours, one daily) during the dry season and year-round service to Bertoua; both roads are just tolerable. The Central African Republic border crossing is on the edge of Garoua-Boulaï next to the motor park.

UNDERSTAND CAMEROON

Cameroon Today

Having re-elected presidential strongman Paul Biya in a contentious yet, broadly speaking, free election in 2011, Cameroon has sealed its reputation as a stable and peaceful country.

For most people though, corruption remains Cameroon's major issue. For example, the paperwork for opening a business can take an extremely long time to process, and many people feel that paying bribes is the only way to get government services. The international anticorruption organisation, Transparency International, consistently ranks Cameroon among the world's most corrupt countries. Until this is addressed and genuine political openness permitted, Cameroon will inevitably continue to limp along.

Yet the most spoken about person in the country is none other than the first lady, Chantal Biya, who has taken on the mantle of an African Princess Diana. Her love of haute couture, her famous 'banana' haircut and high-profile charity work mean she is a staple in the national press.

History

Parts of what is now Cameroon were divided and ceded between European countries throughout the colonial era until the modern boundaries were established in 1961, creating a part-Anglophone, part-Francophone nation.

Prawns for Starters

Portuguese explorers first sailed up the Wouri River in 1472, and named it Rio dos Camarões (River of Prawns). Soon after, Fulani pastoral nomads from what is now Nigeria began to migrate overland from the north, forcing the indigenous forest peoples southwards. The Fulani migration took on added urgency in the early 17th century as they fled Dutch, Portuguese and British slave-traders.

British influence was curtailed in 1884 when Germany signed a treaty with the chiefdoms of Douala and central Bamiléké Plateau. After WWI the German protectorate of Kamerun was carved up between France and Great Britain.

Local revolts in French-controlled Cameroon in the 1950s were suppressed, but the momentum throughout Africa for throwing off the shackles of colonial rule soon took hold. Self-government was granted in French Cameroon in 1958, quickly followed by independence on 1 January 1960.

Wily Ahidjo

Ahmadou Ahidjo, leader of one of the independence parties, became president of the newly independent state, a position he was to hold until his resignation in 1982. Ahidjo ensured his longevity through the cultivation of expedient alliances, brutal repression and wily regional favouritism.

In October 1961 a UN-sponsored referendum in British-mandated northwestern Cameroon split the country in two, with the area around Bamenda opting to join the federal state of Cameroon and the remainder joining Nigeria. In June 1972 the federal structure of two Cameroons was replaced by the centralised United Republic of Cameroon – a move that is resented to this day by Anglophone Cameroonians, who feel they have become second-class citizens.

The Biya Era

In 1982 Ahidjo's hand-picked successor, Paul Biya, distanced himself from his former mentor, but adopted many of Ahidjo's repressive measures, clamping down hard on calls for multiparty democracy. Diversions such as the national football team's stunning performance in the 1990 World Cup bought him time, but Biya was forced eventually to legalise 25 opposition parties. The first multiparty elections in 25 years were held in 1992 and saw the Cameroonian Democratic People's Movement, led by Biya, hang on to power with the support of minority parties. International observers alleged widespread vote-rigging and intimidation; such allegations were repeated in elections in 1999, 2004 and, most recently, 2011.

Culture

It's hard to pigeonhole more than 280 distinct ethnolinguistic groups divided by colonial languages, Christianity and Islam and an urban-rural split into one identity. The Cameroonian psyche is, ultimately, anything and everything African – diversity is the key.

There's a distinct cultural and political gap between the Francophone and Anglophone parts of Cameroon, albeit one felt predominantly by the Anglophone minority, who complain of discrimination in education (most universities lecture in French only) and in the workplace.

A few characteristics do seem shared across Cameroon's divides. Traditional social structures dominate life. Local chiefs (known as *fon* in the west or *lamido* in the north) wield considerable influence, and when travelling in places that don't receive many tourists, it's polite to announce your presence.

CAMEROON HISTORY

Many Cameroonians demonstrate a half-laconic, half-angry sense of frustration with the way their country is run. Many are aware that while Cameroon is doing well compared with its neighbours, it could be immeasurably better off if corruption didn't curtail so much potential. Mixed in with this frustration is a resignation ('such is life'), expressed as serenity in good times, but simmering rage in bad times.

Meanwhile, the arrival of Chinese immigrants in great numbers – especially visible in Yaoundé and Douala – is bringing an even richer dash of multiculturalism to this already incredibly multiethnic society.

Arts & Crafts

Cameroon has produced a few of the region's most celebrated artists: in literature, Mongo Beti deals with the legacies of colonialism; musically, Manu Dibango is the country's brightest star.

Woodcarving makes up a significant proportion of traditional arts and crafts. The northwestern highlands are known for their carved masks. These are often representations of animals, and it's believed that the wearers of the masks can transform themselves and take on the animal's characteristics and powers. Cameroon also has some highly detailed bronze- and brasswork, particularly in Tikar areas north and east of Foumban. The areas around Bali and Bamessing (both near Bamenda), and Foumban, are rich in high-quality clay, and some of Cameroon's finest ceramic work originates here.

Sport

Cameroon exploded onto the world's sporting consciousness at the 1990 World Cup when the national football team, the Indomitable Lions, became the first African side to reach the quarter-finals. Football is truly the national obsession. Every other Cameroonian male seems to own a copy of the team's strip; go into any bar and there'll be a match playing on the TV. When Cameroon narrowly failed to qualify for the 2006 World Cup, the country's grief was almost tangible. In contrast, when Cameroon qualified for the 2010 World Cup, the nation exploded into wild celebration. This qualification marked the sixth time Cameroon had entered the tournament, setting a record for any African nation.

Food & Drink

Cameroonian cuisine is more functional than flavourful. The staple dish is some variety of peppery sauce served with starch – usually rice, pasta or *fufu* (mashed yam, corn, plantain or couscous). One of the most popular sauces is *ndole,* made with bitter leaves similar to spinach and flavoured with smoked fish.

Grilled meat and fish are eaten in huge quantities. Beer is incredibly popular and widely available, even in the Muslim north.

A street snack of fish or *brochettes* (kebabs) will rarely cost more than CFA1500. In sit-down restaurants and business hotels outside of the major cities, expect to pay around CFA5000 to CFA7000 for a full meal; that can climb to CFA10,000 or more in Yaoundé and Douala.

Environment

Cameroon is geographically diverse. The south is a low-lying coastal plain covered by swaths of equatorial rainforest extending east towards the Congo Basin. Heading north, the sparsely populated Adamawa Plateau divides the country in two. To the plateau's north, the country begins to dry out into a rolling landscape dotted with rocky escarpments that are fringed to the west by the barren Mandara Mountains. That range represents the northern extent of a volcanic chain that forms a natural border with Nigeria down to the Atlantic coast, often punctuated with stunning crater lakes. One active volcano remains in Mt Cameroon, at 4095m the highest peak in West Africa.

There is a range of wildlife, although more exotic species are in remote areas. Lions prowl in Parc National du Waza in the north, and elephants stomp through the southern and eastern jungles. Of note are several rare primate species, including the Cross River gorilla, mainland drill, chimpanzees and Preuss' red colobus.

Bushmeat has traditionally been big business in Cameroon. While there have been crackdowns on the trade both here and abroad (African expats are some of the main consumers of bushmeat), it has not been entirely stamped out.

SURVIVAL GUIDE

ℹ Directory A–Z

ACCOMMODATION

Cameroon has a decent range of accommodation options, from simple *auberges* (hostels) and dorm beds in religious missions to luxury hotels. Expect to pay around CFA15,000 for a decent single room with bathroom and fan. Most hotels quote prices per room – genuine single and twin rooms are the exception rather than the norm.

In Cameroon, budget accommodation costs up to CFA15,000 for a double room, midrange from CFA15,000 to CFA30,000 and top end from CFA30,000. Rather than seasonal rates, most hotels in Kribi and Limbe generally charge more during holidays and weekends.

ACTIVITIES

Hiking is a big drawcard in Cameroon. The two most popular hiking regions are Mt Cameroon near the coast and the Mandara Mountains in the north. The Ring Road near Bamenda also offers great hiking possibilities, but you'll need to be self-sufficient here.

BUSINESS HOURS

Banks From 7.30am or 8am to 3.30pm Monday to Friday.

Businesses From 7.30am or 8am until 6pm or 6.30pm Monday to Friday, generally with a one-to two-hour break sometime between noon and 3pm. Most are also open from 8am to 1pm (sometimes later) on Saturday.

Government offices From 7.30am to 3.30pm Monday to Friday.

EMBASSIES & CONSULATES

A number of embassies and consulates are located in Yaoundé. Australians and New Zealanders should contact the Canadian High Commission in case of an emergency.

Canadian Embassy (☑ 2223 2311; Ave de l'Indépendance, Immeuble STC-TOM, Pl de l'Hôtel de Ville)

Central African Republic Embassy (Map p80; ☑ 2220 5155; Rue 1863, Bastos)

Chadian Embassy (Map p80; ☑ 2221 0624; Rue Joseph Mballa Eloumden, Bastos)

Congolese Embassy (Map p80; ☑ 2223 2458; Rue 1815, Bastos)

Equatorial Guinean Embassy (Map p80; ☑ 2221 0884; Rue 1805, Bastos)

French Embassy (☑ 2222 7900; Rue Joseph Atemengué, near Pl de la Réunification)

Gabonese Embassy (Map p80; ☑ 2220 2966; Rue 1816, Bastos)

German Embassy (Map p80; ☑ 2221 7292; Ave Charles de Gaulle, Centre Ville)

PRACTICALITIES

➡ **Electricity** Supply is 220V and plugs are of the European two-round-pin variety.

➡ **Languages** French throughout the country, English in the northwest and some 280 local languages.

➡ **Newspapers** The *Cameroon Tribune* is the government-owned bilingual daily. The thrice-weekly *Le Messager* (in French) is the main independent newspaper.

➡ **Radio & TV** Most broadcast programming is government run and in French, through Cameroon Radio-TV Corporation (CRTV). TVs at top-end hotels often have CNN or French news stations.

Nigerian Embassy (Map p80; ☑ 2223 4551; Rue Joseph Mballa Eloumden, Bastos)

UK Embassy (Map p80; ☑ 2222 0545; Ave Churchill, Centre Ville)

US Embassy (Map p82; ☑ 2220 1500; Ave Rosa Parks, Centre Ville)

EMERGENCIES

The number for all emergencies is ☑ 112, but it really only applies in big cities.

FESTIVALS & EVENTS

The biggest festival celebrated in Cameroon is Tabaski (p93), with most festivities taking place in Foumban.

Each February Cameroonian and international athletes gather for the **Race of Hope** to the summit of Mt Cameroon, attracting large crowds of spectators. Considerably faster than the leisurely hike most people opt for, winners usually finish in a staggering 4½ hours for men and 5½ hours for women. For more information contact Fako Tourist Board (p89) in Limbe or the **Fédération Camerounaise d'Athlétisme** (☑ 2222 4744) in Yaoundé.

INTERNET ACCESS

Internet access can be found in any town of a reasonable size. Connections range from decent to awful, and costs average CFA300 to CFA600 per hour.

MONEY

The unit of currency is the Central African Franc (CFA), which is pegged to the West African Franc. Cash is king in Cameroon, especially in remote regions where it's the only way to pay – bring plenty of euros. Banks regularly refuse to change travellers cheques, and charge around 5% commission when they do. Moneychangers on the street in Douala and Yaoundé will change money at good rates and without taxes or commission, but there's always an element of risk to such transactions.

Most towns now have at least one ATM, which is always tied to the Visa network. Banks won't generally offer cash advances on credit cards. If you get stuck, Western Union has branches throughout Cameroon for international money transfers.

Express Exchange moneychangers change travellers cheques and US dollars; there are branches in many towns across the country.

POST

International post is fairly reliable for letters, but international couriers should be preferred for packages – there are branches in all large towns.

PUBLIC HOLIDAYS

New Year's Day 1 January
Youth Day 11 February
Easter March/April
Labour Day 1 May
National Day 20 May
Assumption Day 15 August
Christmas Day 25 December

Islamic holidays are also observed throughout Cameroon; dates change yearly for these.

SAFE TRAVEL

The major cities, Douala and Yaoundé, both have reputations for petty crime, especially in the crowded central areas. The roads pose a greater risk, with plenty of badly maintained vehicles driven at punishing speeds.

Scams and official corruption are a way of life in Cameroon; keep your guard up and maintain a sense of humour. It's theoretically a legal requirement to carry your passport with you at all times. In practice the police rarely target travellers, however.

TELEPHONE

All Cameroonian telephone numbers have eight digits. Mobile numbers begin with 7, 8 or 9. There are no city area codes in Cameroon – all landline numbers begin with a 2 or 3. It's quite easy to buy a SIM card for an unlocked mobile phone to make local calls. MTN and Orange are the main national networks.

VISAS

Visas are required for all travellers and must be bought prior to arrival in the country. At Cameroonian embassies in neighbouring countries, visas are issued quickly for around US$60. Applications in Europe and the US will require a confirmed flight ticket, a hotel reservation and proof of funds for the trip (a copy of a recent bank statement should suffice).

Visa Extensions

You can obtain visa extensions at the **Ministry of Immigration** (Map p82; ☑ 222 2413; Ave Mdug-Fouda Ada) in Yaoundé, where one photo plus CFA15,000 is required.

Visas for Onward Travel

Visas available in Yaoundé for neighbouring African countries include the following:

Central African Republic A one-month visa costs FA55,000 and takes 48 hours to process.

Chad The embassy in Yaoundé is unhelpful and generally only issues visas to residents. The Garoua consulate is a far better place to try (CFA50,000).

Congo A 15-day visa costs CFA50,000, three months costs CFA100,000. An invitation is required and processing takes 48 hours.

Equatorial Guinea Does not generally issue visas to nonresidents or people with an Equatorial Guinea embassy in their home country.

Gabon A one-month visa costs CFA50,000; unlike at many Gabonese embassies, a hotel reservation is not required here.

Nigeria In Yaoundé a one-month visa costs CFA45,000 to CFA60,000 and takes 48 hours to process, and you'll need an invitation.

ⓘ Getting There & Away

AIR

Both Yaoundé and Douala have international airports linking Cameroon to major cities in Africa and Europe. The national carrier of Cameroon is **Camair-Co** (www.camair-co.cm), which flies to Libreville, N'Djaména, Malabo, Brazzaville, Lagos, Cotonou, Kinshasa and Paris. There is a departure tax of CFA10,000 payable on all international flights.

LAND

Neighbouring countries' borders are open, but the border with Congo is sometimes closed, so check in advance.

Central African Republic

The standard, if rough, route is via Garoua-Boulaï, which straddles the border, and on to Bangui (via Bouar). An alternative is to travel to Kenzou, south of Batouri.

Chad

Travellers head to Kousséri in the north for the border near N'Djaména. Minibuses go to Kousséri from Maroua; some border officials have been known to rip travellers off.

Congo

This border is as remote as you can get, but possible to reach if it's the dry season. From Yokadouma, travel south to Sokamba, where you can catch a ferry (large enough for 4WDs) or *pirogue* (traditional canoe) across the Ngoko River to the Congolese port of Ouesso. From there, head for Pokola and the logging road to Brazzaville. If you come this way, consider visting Congo's Parc National Nouabalé-N'doki, one of the best parks in Central Africa, and relatively convenient to access from here.

Equatorial Guinea & Gabon

The main border crossings into Equatorial Guinea and Gabon are a few kilometres from each other, and are accessible from Ambam. The road splits here, with the easterly route heading for Bitam and Libreville (Gabon) and the westerly route heading for Ebebiyin and Bata (Equatorial Guinea).

The Cameroon–Equatorial Guinea border at Campo is normally closed.

Nigeria

The main crossing points are Ekok, west of Mamfe, where you cross to Mfum for shared taxis to Calabar (treacherous in the rainy season), and at Banki in the extreme north for crossings to Maiduguri.

SEA
Nigeria

A twice-weekly ferry sails from Limbe to Calabar on Monday and Thursday, and in the opposite direction every Tuesday and Friday. Boats are dangerous and not recommended.

🛈 Getting Around

AIR

Internal flights are operated by Camair-Co and connect Douala and Yaoundé to Maroua and Garoua. The hop between Yaoundé and Douala costs around CFA30,000 one way; from either city to Maroua or Garoua they will cost around CFA125,000 one way.

BUS

Agences de voyages (agency buses) run along all major and many minor routes in Cameroon. Prices are low and fixed, and on some bus lines you can even reserve a seat. From Yaoundé to Douala it costs anywhere between CFA3000 and CFA6000, depending on the class of bus you take: so called 'VIP' services have air-conditioning and aren't quite so cramped. However, some drivers are extremely reckless, and bus accidents occur all too frequently. *Taxis brousses* (bush taxis) are also popular, especially to some more remote destinations.

CAR

Driving in Cameroon is perfectly feasible, with decent roads and no police harassment. You can hire cars in all large towns, but there's more choice in Douala and Yaoundé. Car hire is very expensive, however, partly because you'll need a 4x4 for most itineraries, and this becomes essential in the rainy season. A couple of outfits in Douala include **Location Auto Joss** (☑ 9984 4404, 3342 8619; locationauto.joss@gmail. com; Rue Score, Bonapriso), and **Avis** (☑ 2230 2627) in the Hotel Akwa Palace.

TRAIN

Cameroon's rail system (Camrail) operates three main lines: Yaoundé to N'Gaoundéré, Yaoundé to Douala, and Douala to Kumba. In practice, only the first is of interest to travellers, as it's the main way to get between the southern and northern halves of the country.

Cape Verde

⏱ 238 / POP 491,683

Best Places to Eat

➡ La Bodeguita de Mindelo (p115)

➡ Calheta por Sol (p118)

➡ Cafe Criolo (p125)

Best Places to Stay

➡ Casa Colonial (p114)

➡ Migrante (p127)

➡ Casa Cavoquinho (p119)

Why Go?

Set sail with the Saharan trade winds and rock and roll across stormy Atlantic seas for days. Then, just before you're halfway to Brazil, an island rises into view. You have reached Cape Verde, an arrow-shaped archipelago that is the region's most Westernised country, where the people are richer and better educated than almost anywhere on the continent.

Though it may appear as a set of flyspecks poking out of the eastern Atlantic, this 10-island archipelago packs a punch. On Santo Antão, craggy peaks hide piercing green valleys of flowers and sugar cane, ideal for epic hikes. São Vicente is home to the cultural capital of the islands, Mindelo, which throbs with bars and music clubs. On Boa Vista, Sal and Maio, wispy white dunes merge with indigo-blue seas on unspoiled beaches of soft sand. Throw in the constant beat of music that Cape Verde is famed for and the renowned *morabeza* (Creole for hospitality) of its people and you'll see why many have come – and never left.

When to Go
Praia

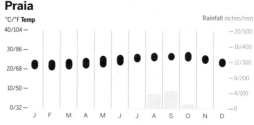

Aug–Oct During the so-called rainy, but very hot, season, weeks can go by without a downpour.

Dec–Apr Strong winds blow in dust all the way from the Sahara and make it the best time for surfing.

Jun–Oct Turtle-watching season (February to May is whale-watching time).

SANTIAGO

POP 249,529

Santiago, the largest member of the archipelago and the first to be settled, has a little bit of all the other islands. It has the sandy beaches, the desert plains, the verdant valleys and the mountainous interior as well as the capital, Praia. All this makes it a worthy stop on your Cape Verdean rambles.

Getting There & Away

AIR

Praia's airport is, together with Sal's, the main air hub for the islands. There are daily flights to Boa Vista, Fogo (São Filipe), Sal and São Vicente (Mindelo), two weekly to Maio and four weekly (via Sal or São Vicente) to São Nicolau.

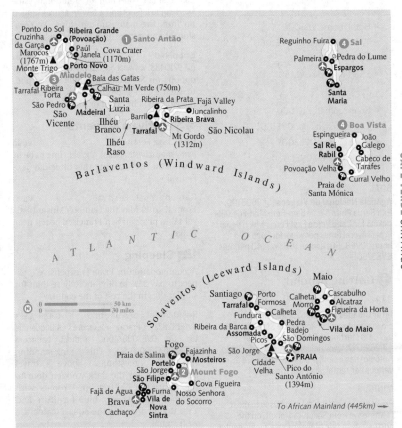

Cape Verde Highlights

❶ Hiking the misty pine-clad ridges, the sheer canyons and the verdant valleys of Cape Verde's most spectacular island, **Santo Antão** (p117).

❷ Admiring the views from the summit of the country's only active volcano, stunning, cinder-clad, 2829m-high **Mount Fogo** (p121).

❸ Swinging hips, elaborate costumes and dirty dancing; Mindelo's celebration is a sexy and colourful **Mardi Gras** (p113).

❹ Riding the giant waves of **Sal** (p124) and **Boa Vista** (p126), two fine destinations for windsurfing.

❺ Listening to musicians wave loved ones goodbye with a *morna* (mournful song) in smoky back-room bars dedicated to **traditional music**.

CAPE VERDE SANTIAGO

ℹ SET YOUR BUDGET

Budget
→ Hotel room CVE3500
→ Lunchtime special CVE400
→ Coffee CVE50
→ Local bus ride CVE100

Midrange
→ Hotel room CVE6000
→ Two-course dinner CVE1000
→ Beer in bar CVE120
→ Short taxi ride CVE150

Top End
→ Hotel room CVE10,000
→ Two-course dinner CVE1800
→ Glass of wine CVE300
→ Car and driver CVE8000

BOAT

Agência Nacional de Viagens (☑ 2603100; Rua Serpa Pinto 58; ☺ 8am-6pm Mon-Fri) sells tickets for Cabo Verde Fast Ferry, which departs Praia several times per week for Fogo (3½ hours, CVE3350) and on to Brava (40 minutes, CVE3750).

ℹ Getting Around

CAR

Inter Cidades (☑ 2612525; www.inter cidadesrentacar.cv; Achada de Santo António) has cars starting at €45 per day. **Delcar** (☑ 2623717; www.delcar.cv; Achada de Santo António) has a similar service. There are also various car-rental offices at the airport.

MINIBUS

Private *aluguer* (for hire) minibuses to most towns leave from Sucupira Market, on the northwestern side of Platô, Praia's town centre.

Praia

POP 131,602

Cape Verde's capital and largest city, Praia, has the sprawling suburbs of any developing city. In the centre, standing on a large fortresslike plateau (hence the name Platô) and overlooking the ocean, is an attractive old quarter with enough to keep you happily occupied for a day.

⊙ Sights & Activities

During your ambles around the multihued streets of the old Platô quarter, be sure to spend some time ferreting around the small food **market**.

Museu Etnográfico de Praia　　　MUSEUM
(☑ 2618421; Av 5 de Julho; admission CVE100; ☺ 8am-6pm Mon-Fri) This one-room museum has a small collection of traditional Cape Verdean artefacts and a few treasures hauled up from the many sunken ships. An occasional temporary exhibit focuses on a theme.

CaboNed　　　HIKING, SAFARIS
(☑ 9210488; www.caboned.com) Great day-trip options on Santiago, including hikes, photo safaris and explorations of the island's interior. Book by email or phone.

✦✦ Festivals & Events

Kriol Jazz Festival　　　MUSIC
(www.krioljazzfestival.com) A great time to be in town is in April, during this three-day jazz festival.

Gamboa Music Festival　　　MUSIC
From 17 to 19 May the Gamboa Music Festival takes place on San Francisco beach near Praia.

🛏 Sleeping

Accommodation in Praia is expensive – expect to pay 25% to 30% more here than for similar digs in the rest of the country.

Residencial Sol Atlántico　　　GUESTHOUSE $
(☑ 2612872; Praça Alexandre Albuquérque 13; s/d CVE3000/4000, without bathroom CVE2300/3300; ✴) This long-standing *residencial* (guesthouse) above a travel agency (look for the dark wooden door to the right) has old-fashioned rooms with starched white sheets, blue furniture and TVs. Rooms fronting the square catch the wi-fi signal.

Residencial Paraíso　　　GUESTHOUSE $
(☑ 2613539; Rua Serpa Pinto 625; s/d CVE3500/4000) At the leafy northern end of Platô, this well-run guesthouse has blindingly white rooms, piping-hot water and a decent breakfast. It is the most low-key and quiet option in Platô.

Hotel Santa Maria　　　HOTEL $$
(☑ 2614337; www.girassol.cv; Rua Serpa Pinto 35; s/d CVE4770/5936; ✴) The positioning of

this sky-blue hotel, right in the heart of all the action, is tops. The cheaper rooms are clean and well-equipped, if a little dark, and make for a decent Praia base. The new, pricier, lighter units (singles/doubles CVE5936/6996) overlook the front street. There are laundry service, tours around the island and airport transfers on request.

Hotel Oásis Atlântico Praiamar   HOTEL $$$
(🖉2608440; www.oasisatlantico.com; Prainha; s/d from CVE13,900/17,400; 🅿✳@🛜⛱) On a breezy bluff pointing out to sea is this glossy Praia address. Though similar to a business-class hotels around the world, the spacious rooms are comfortable with a touch of class. Some come with garden views; others overlook the ocean.

✕ Eating
The food scene in Praia is surprisingly limited, and pricey to boot.

Pão Quente de Cabo Verde   BAKERY $
(🕑6am-10pm daily) For the best pastries in town, head to this busy place. You can eat in or take your delicately wrapped treat away with you. There's another branch in Achada Santo António.

Esplanada Morabeza   CAFETERIA $
(Praça Alexandre Albuquérque; mains CVE750; 🕑8am-midnight daily) Right on the plaza, in a white modern structure with alfresco covered seating, this spot is a great place to grab a bite and see the action. The menu ranges from sandwiches, pastas, crepes and pizzas to daily-changing mains.

A Grelha   SEAFOOD $$
(🖉2626083; Rua Cidade Funchal, Achada Santo António; mains CVE1000; 🕑5pm-midnight Mon-Sat) Locals flock to this simple Portuguese-run restaurant for the amazing grilled tuna belly *(barriga de atum),* skewered and served with potatoes on a wraparound terrace. Reserve ahead; it gets busy.

Gamboa   SEAFOOD $$
(🖉2612826; Rua 19 de Maio, Chã d'Areia; mains CVE1200; 🕑noon-3pm & 7-11pm) This seafront spot with a large pink interior is where locals come for a good meal paired with eager service. The extensive menu features lots of fish and shellfish. Located on the road to Prainha, in Chã d'Areia.

Kapa   INTERNATIONAL $$$
(Quebra-Canela; mains CVE1350; 🕑6pm-2am Tue-Sun) Upscale beachfront spot with a loungy outdoor area and a varied menu of international and local favourites. The night to come is Thursday, when there's live music. Friday and Saturday are lively too, as the upstairs pub gets packed.

🍷 Drinking & Nightlife
The best of nightlife and live music in Praia happens in hidden little bars that aren't easy to find without a local. Platô has surprisingly little night-time action.

The big night of the week in Praia is Thursday, known locally as *sextinha,* or little Friday.

Kebra Cabana   BAR
(Quebra-Canela beach; 🕑2pm-2am Mon-Fri, 10am-2am Sat & Sun) Cool beach bar with a hipster crowd, loungy tunes, live music on Friday nights and good food to boot.

Café Palkus   CAFE
(Amilcar Cabral 17A; 🕑closed Sun) Praia's most bohemian cafe-bar, on Platô's main square, with an inner patio that hosts dance, theatre and music performances on weekends, and film nights on Monday.

Alkimist   BAR
(Rua da Prainha) Just up from Quebra-Canela beach, Alkimist is a low-key, popular hang-out.

Snack Bar Serenata   LIVE MUSIC
(Rua Capela 30; 🕑4pm-midnight Tue-Thu & Sun, 6pm-3am Fri & Sat) Lively hang-out in a small leafy courtyard in Achada Santo António, where locals drink beers and *grogue* (a sugar cane spirit) and snack on inexpensive food to the sounds of *morna* and *coladeira* peformed on a small stage.

Quintal da Música   LIVE MUSIC
(🖉2611679; Av Amilcar Cabral; 🕑8am-midnight Mon-Sat) For the best of local music, head to this Platô bar-restaurant which showcases live acts every night except Sunday. Traditional sounds abound, from *morna* and *coladeira* to *batuko* and *funaná.* Reserve ahead.

ℹ Orientation
Around Platô, the town tumbles onto the land below; to the east are Achada Grande and the port, and to the southwest is the more affluent

Praia

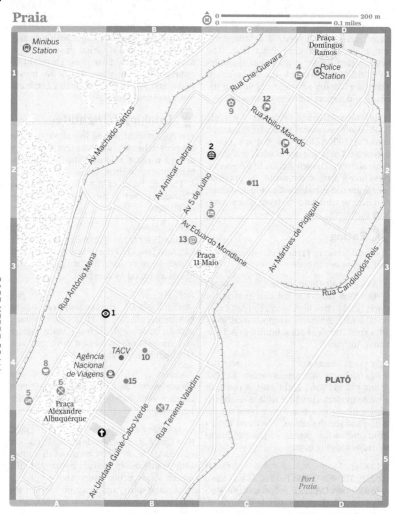

residential area of Achada Santo António, home to the parliament building and some embassies. Due south of Platô is the beachfront area known as Prainha and further away is the beach of Quebra-Canela, with several restaurants and bars.

ℹ Information

There are ATMs throughout the city, especially around Praça Alexandre Albuquérque.

The main post office is three blocks east of this square.

There's no official tourist office as such; you're best off talking to a private travel agency.

Internet cafes are scarce, but the two main squares in Platô (Praça Alexandre Albuquérque and Praça 11 Maio) have free wi-fi.

Girassol Tours (☑ 2614178; www.girassol. cv; Rua Serpo Pinto 47; ⊙ 8am-6pm Mon-Fri, to noon Sat) Travel agency that sells plane tickets and offers tours of Santiago and car rental.

Sofia Café (Praça 11 Maio 31; per hr CVE200; ⊙ 7am-11pm daily) A cafe-restaurant in Platô, with a handful of computer terminals.

Praia

ℹ Getting Around

It is best to move around Praia by taxi at night, no matter what the distance, as crime has been on the rise, especially in Achada Santo António.

TO/FROM THE AIRPORT

A taxi from the airport to Platô (5km) costs around CVE800. There's no regular bus service.

BUS

Small Transcor buses connect Platô with all sections of the city; short journeys cost from CVE70. Destinations are marked on the windshields.

TAXI

Cream-coloured taxis are plentiful, inexpensive and easy to spot – you can go from Platô to Achada Santo António, for example, for about CVE200. Note that fares go up after 8pm. You can rent a taxi for the day for around CVE7000.

Cidade Velha

Dramatically situated on the sea, 15km from Praia, Cidade Velha (literally 'Old City') gained Unesco World Heritage status in 2009 as the first European settlement in the tropics. Founded in 1462 as Ribeira Grande, the city became wealthy as a station for the transatlantic slave trade. Raids by pirates – including a particularly destructive visit by Sir Francis Drake in 1585 – eventually forced the Portuguese to move shop to Praia.

Remains from its heyday include the ruins of the cathedral, constructed in 1693, and the pillory on the town square where enslaved captives were chained up and displayed. Most impressive is the town's position between the sea and the mouth of a canyon that, thanks to irrigation, remains green even in the driest months. For sweeping views, take the curving trail up to the dramatic cliff-side fort built in 1593, Fortaleza Real de São Filipe (CVE500; ◉8am-6pm daily). Also worth a look is São Francisco monastery and church (CVE500; ◉8am-6pm daily), reachable along a marked trail that leads up from the lush valley.

There are several cafes and restaurants around the main square. Try Tereru di Kultura (mains CVE1100; ◉9am-9pm Mon, Wed-Fri & Sun, to 10pm Sat) for its lovely oceanfront terrace. The more local and downhome Penedinho (mains CVE800) next door bustles with action.

There's a tourist info point (◉9am-noon & 3-5pm) along the coastal road, up from the main square, in a little white house with yellow windows.

Buses from Praia (CVE80, 30 minutes) leave from Sucupira Market and return regularly until 7pm. Taxis charge about CVE3500 for a return trip, including up to two hours to visit the sites.

SÃO VICENTE

POP 76,107

Small, stark and undulating, São Vicente on its own would be fairly forgettable were it not for the beautiful Mediterranean town of Mindelo, Cape Verde's prettiest city and home to one of Africa's most raucous festivals.

If you do need a break from the city, Mt Verde (750m), the island's highest peak and only touch of green, is an easy day's hike. There are also some windy but fine beaches at Baía das Gatas, Calhau and Salamansa.

CAPE VERDE CIDADE VELHA

OTHER SANTIAGO HIGHLIGHTS

It's worth spending a day or two exploring Santiago's fertile mountainous interior and the pristine coastline away from Praia. The mountain village of **Rui Vaz** near the town of São Domingos is a picturesque base for hikes into surrounding mountains. It's home to the hilltop **Quinta da Montanha** (☑2685002; quintamontanha@cvtelecom.cv; s/d CVE4200/5200, weekend buffet CVE1500 (for guests, CVE1200); @🛜), which has live traditional music at Sunday lunch. Country town **Assomada** features a bustling African **market** on Wednesday and Friday.

Parque Natural Serra da Malagueta covers dramatic, tumbling ridges outside of Praia. Spectacular and fairly well-signposted walking trails weave up and down valleys and through hamlets; you might encounter an elusive vervet monkey.

With a small white-sand beach and cooling breezes, **Tarrafal** is a favourite getaway from Praia, some 70km to the southeast. The town has a hibiscus-lined main square. If you take the popular walk to the **lighthouse** it's best to go with a trustworthy local guide, as muggings have been reported. To stay overnight, there's **Tarrafal Residence** (☑2662060; tarrafalresidence@gmail.com; Ribeira do Coquiero; s CVE3300-3500, d CVE4000-4500), with contemporary and colourful rooms. For wood-fired pizzas and good fish dishes, head to French-run **Alto Mira** (mains CVE750; ☺6.30-10pm).

Minibuses from Praia depart from Sucupira Market for Rui Vaz, Assomada and Tarrafal (CVE500); service is most frequent early in the morning and returns in the afternoon. You can hire a taxi for the day or book a tour with an agency in Praia.

Other highlights hide in Santiago's interior. **Porto Madeira** (www.portomadeira.org) is a creative community that was converted into an artists' retreat by local cultural activist Misá. It's possible to visit for the day or overnight in basic accommodation (doubles with breakfast CVE2000). Make contact ahead via the website.

Misá also 'opened up' a long-isolated community of *rabelados*, descendants of runaway slaves who in the 1940s refused the Catholic missionaries and have remained isolated in Santiago's highlands. Outsiders can visit the community of **Espinho Branco**, and see the studio with colourful artwork made by the villagers (you're highly encouraged to buy something) and even spend the night in the village (CVE1500 per couple, with breakfast). Make arrangements via www.portomadeira.org.

ⓘ Getting There & Away

AIR

TACV (☑2321524; www.flytacv.com) has one to two flights daily to and from Praia, one daily to Sal and two weekly to São Nicolau. **TAP** (www.flytap.com) has two weekly flights to/from Lisbon. Taxis to and from the Cesária Évora Airport cost CVE900.

BOAT

Ferries connect Mindelo with daily boats to neighbouring Santo Antão. For service to other islands, including Praia, Sal and São Nicolau, check at the ferry port, a short walk from downtown; note that departures are sporadic and crossings long.

ⓘ Getting Around

The most convenient way around the island is by taxi from Mindelo, including trips to Monte Verde (CVE1100), Calhau (CVE1000), Baía das Gatas (CVE900) and Salamansa (CVE850). Alternatively, there are *aluguers* to Baía das Gatas and Calhau that leave from near Praça Estrela in Mindelo. Both cost around CVE150 each way. Note that service is irregular on weekdays and can involve long waits.

Mindelo

Set around a moon-shaped port and ringed by barren mountains, Mindelo is Cape Verde's answer to the Riviera, complete with cobblestone streets, candy-coloured colonial buildings and yachts bobbing in a peaceful harbour. Around a bend is the country's deepest industrial port, which in the late 19th century was a key coaling station for British ships and remains the source of the city's relative prosperity.

Mindelo has long been the country's cultural centre, producing more than its share of poets and musicians, including the late Cesária Évora, and it's still a fine place to hear *morna* while downing some *grogue*.

Savvy locals, plus a steady flow of travellers, support a number of cool bistros and bars.

Sights & Activities

Mindelo is a city to savour, taste and experience. Its colonial heart is centred on Rua da Libertad d'Africa, also known as Rua de Lisboa, which runs from the oceanfront to **Palácio de Presidente**, a pink colonial confection that now serves as the island's supreme court.

Heading about 1km north via the coastal road, Avenida Marginal, you'll reach **Prainha Laginha**, the pleasant town beach. It may be ringed by industrial-looking silos, but its waters are clean and crystal clear.

Centro Cultural
do Mindelo   CULTURAL BUILDING
(⊙9am-9pm Mon-Thu, 9am-12.30pm Fri, 10am-9pm Sat, 5-9pm Sun) `FREE` Inside the old customs house, the cultural centre houses changing exhibitions of local arts and culture and has a great little shop selling local crafts, music and books.

Fish Market   MARKET
The city's photogenic fish market lies just beyond Torre de Belém, with a jetty right behind it where fishermen unload their daily catch.

Mercado Municipal   MARKET
The restored two-storey food market from 1784 is a great place to see colourfully dressed vendors hawking local produce and medicinal herbs.

Pont d'Agua   MARINA
With its modern glass and concrete constructions, this swank new complex looks and feels more like the south of France than Cape Verde. Dotted with palm trees, it has an upscale restaurant, a swimming pool, shops and a spa. It's a nice spot for a sunset drink at **Cafe Kriola** (⊙8am-11pm daily), which offers a great upfront view of the harbour.

Torre de Belém   MONUMENT
Jutting out into the harbour is the fortress-like Torre de Belém – a Disney World version of the 15th-century tower that guards Lisbon's port.

Sabura Adventures   ADVENTURE TOURS
(☑9775681; www.sabura-adventures.com) Tour agency with wide-ranging offerings like culinary and dance workshops, water sports, trekking, horseback riding and off-road adventures.

Festivals & Events

During the Creole Carnival and Baía das Gatas Festival finding accommodation or aeroplane seats is virtually impossible. Book way ahead.

Creole Carnival   CARNIVAL
In February, Mindelo puts on the sexiest Mardi Gras this side of Río, Creole Carnival, with colourful street parades. See the box for further information.

Baía das Gatas Festival   MUSIC
Every August, the Baía das Gatas Festival attracts musicians of all styles from around the islands and beyond. Held at the Baía das Gatas over the August full moon, it's a three-day extravaganza of singing, dancing and partying.

CAPE VERDE MINDELO

MINDELO'S MARDI GRAS

There's nothing like Mindelo's Mardi Gras (usually in February) anywhere else in Africa. Taking the best African beats and mixing it up with a healthy dose of Latin style and Brazilian sex appeal, the result is one sultry, raunchy party you'll never forget. Preparations begin several months in advance and on Sunday you can see the various groups practising for the procession. The saucy costumes, however, are worn only on Mardi Gras Tuesday. The weekend just prior to this sees a number of lesser processions and street parties, while on the Monday afternoon the whole city goes crazy as a huge street party takes place and people dress up in 'lesser costumes'. The Tuesday itself is a much more organised affair and after the procession has wound around the city a couple of times everyone seems to magically disappear.

If you want to be a part of it, plan accordingly, as all flights and accommodation are booked up way in advance. If you can't make it to Mindelo then head to São Nicolau, which puts on a fabulous and utterly nontouristy affair around the same time. Fogo puts on a pretty good show as well.

Mindelo

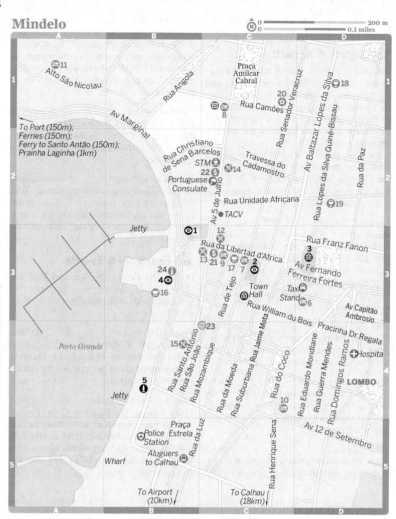

Mindelact Festival   THEATRE
During September; brings theatre to the streets, squares and cultural centres of Mindelo.

🛌 Sleeping

Residencial Chez Loutcha   GUESTHOUSE **$**
(☑2321636; www.chezloutchacv.com; Rua do Coco; s from CVE2400, d CVE3800-4850; ❄) A decent base camp, but take a look at a couple of rooms as some are a bit cramped, dark and without air-con. The restaurant serves simple traditional dishes (mains CVE800), with live music on Wednesday and Friday.

★**Casa Colonial**   GUESTHOUSE **$$**
(☑9995350; www.casacolonial.info; Rua 24 de Setembro; s/d CVE6050/7150; 🛜🏊) Boutique British-owned guesthouse on a quiet street and inside a beautifully restored colonial building with a fresh green coat of paint and white wooden shutters. Rooms have period details and fans; only one (of five) has a private bathroom. Perks include a small patio with a plunge pool where breakfast is served, and free wi-fi.

Mindelo

Cosy guesthouse with rooms piled around a sunny, glass-roofed courtyard. In-room amenities include safes, air-con and free wi-fi. Snag one of the rooms overlooking the quieter back part of the building.

MindelHotel
HOTEL $$

(☎2328885; www.mindelhotel.cv; Av 5 de Julho; s/d CVE7500/8500; P❄@📶) This big blue hotel on the main square has decent if unexciting rooms and is a good midrange option. The lack of character is mitigated with good service, a great buffet breakfast, free wi-fi and complimentary airport transfers.

✕ Eating

Chave d'Ouro
SEAFOOD $

(Ave 5 de Julho; mains CVE600; ⊙noon-3pm & 7-11pm) This old-fashioned 2nd-floor restaurant hasn't changed in decades. Daily specials are a steal (CVE400) and sides of veggies particularly generous (a rarity in Cape Verde). There's live music at Sunday dinner in summer.

Bella Napoli
PIZZERIA $

(☎9766524; Ribeira Bote; pizzas CVE400-650; ⊙dinner only) Catch a taxi to the low-income Ribeira Bote neighbourhood for Mindelo's best pizza, inside the basement of a family home. This word-of-mouth pizzeria run by an Italian from Naples has colourful wall decorations, good Montepulciano red and a familial vibe. Reserve ahead. Tell the driver to look for Polivalente in Ribeira Bote and don't get out until you're at the door.

La Pergola
CAFETERIA $

(Alliance Française, Rua Santo António; mains CVE650; ⊙8am-7pm Mon-Fri, to 2pm Sat) This cosy cafe, under a straw roof inside the courtyard of the Alliance Française, serves good-value lunch specials as well as a range of cakes and pastries.

★ La Bodeguita de Mindelo
CARIBBEAN $$

(end of Travessa do Cadamostro, Alto Miramar; mains CVE900; ⊙noon-3pm & 7pm-midnight) Cool little *bodega* (wine bar) with a series of small low-lit rooms, graffitied walls and excellent Caribbean fare prepared by the owner from Guadeloupe. Daily specials are written out on a board; don't miss the bruschetta. Wash it all down with *pela rob* (a speciality drink with ginger, *grogue* and orange juice). Take Rua Camões from the main square (Praça Amilcar Cabral) all the way up to the end, a 10-minute walk. The cool Mindelo crowd kicks off the night around 10pm here, before moving on.

Residencial Jenny
GUESTHOUSE $$

(☎2328969; www.jenny-mindelo.com; Alto São Nicolau; s/d from CVE3800/4500; ❄@) Set on a hill above the ferry dock, this modern digs in an orange building has standard rooms overlooking the inner patio, and pricier rooms (singles/doubles CVE5600/6500) with balconies with harbour views. Air-con and internet access cost extra.

Hotel Gaudi
HOTEL $$

(☎2318954; www.hotelgaudimindelo.com; Rua Senador Veracruz 210; s/d CVE3960/5940; 📶) Good, central option with small and cramped but neat and cosy rooms (and two apartments) equipped with TV, fridge and fans. The downstairs restaurant has live music every night and happy hour on Friday. Note that noise is part of the package.

Mindelo Residencial
GUESTHOUSE $$

(☎2300863; m.residencial@gmail.com; Rua São João; s CVE4770-6360, d CVE6360-7950; ❄@📶)

Pica-Pau

SEAFOOD **$$**

(2328207; Rua Santo António 42; mains CVE600; ⊘ 11am-2pm & 6-10pm Mon-Sat, 6-10pm Sun) You know you must be doing something right when your customers start scrawling messages of appreciation all over the walls. Specialising in seafood, especially lobster and shellfish, this tiny restaurant is a treat. Book ahead.

O Cocktail

INTERNATIONAL **$$**

(2327275; Av 5 de Julho; mains CVE800; ⊘ 8am-midnight) Open-air terrace restaurant perched above the street, with a wideranging menu, from pizzas and burgers to grilled mains and some vegetarian options. It has live-music acts on weekends at 8.30pm (book ahead).

Drinking & Nightlife

Evening breezes bring people out into the streets, and they inevitably head for Praça Amilcar Cabral (also called Praça Nova), where they sit on plastic chairs in the popular *quiosque* cafes under spreading acacia trees. For daytime coffee or an evening beer, try the tiny and adorable **Café Lisboa** (Rua da Libertad d'Africa; ⊘ 7.30am-11pm).

★ Jazzy Bird

BAR

(Av Baltazar Lopes da Silva; ⊘ closed Sun) Known to locals as Vou, after the friendly owner, this cool little basement bar plastered with old jazz posters attracts an older crowd. Big-name local musicians play jazz late on Friday night.

ZeroPointArt

WINE BAR

(www.zeropointart.org; Rua Unidade Africana 62; ⊘ 6pm-midnight Mon & Wed-Fri, 8pm-2am Sat, 8pm-midnight Sun) Gallery space downstairs and a chilled wine bar upstairs, with lots of contempo artwork, dark ambient lighting and cool music. A good place for a low-key night out, over wine and tapas-style snacks.

Syrius

CLUB

(cnr of Rua Camões & Senador Veracruz; admission from CVE200) Just around the corner from Praça Amilcar Cabral, under Porto Grande Hotel, Syrius is the city's perennially fashionable but often empty disco.

Information

The city centre has several banks with ATMs. There's free wi-fi on Praça Amilcar Cabral, although with finnicky signal.

Banco Comercial do Atlântico (Rua da Libertad d'Africa)

Caixa Económica (Av 5 de Julho)

Mindelo Phone (⊘ 8am-10pm Mon-Sat, 10am-2.30pm & 5.30-9pm Sun) Phones, printing, scanning and internet (CVE100 for one hour, CVE40 for 15 minutes).

Tourist Info (9110016; www.cabocontact. com; ⊘ 9am-7pm Mon-Sat, 10am-3pm Sun) This kiosk near the harbour offers comprehensive info on attractions on São Vicente and beyond, and books a variety of activities, excursions and tours. You can also book accommodation, cars and ferry tickets and store luggage (CVE200 per piece).

Getting Around

Official taxis are generally safe and easy to find in Mindelo. In the city centre, expect to pay CVE150 for a ride; it's CVE170 to suburbs. After 8pm, the fare goes up by CVE30.

Around Mindelo

Few people venture beyond Mindelo's city streets, but there are a couple of worthwhile sites on the island. For panoramic views of Mindelo, all of São Vicente as well as Santo Antão and Santa Luzia, head to **Mount Verde** (750m), São Vicente's highest peak, and hope for a clear day.

Some of the island's best beaches are at **Calhau**, a weekend getaway 18km southeast of Mindelo. It's all but deserted during the week but comes alive on weekends, when locals storm the restaurant for lunchtime meals and beach time. Try the buffet with live music run by Chez Loutcha (p114) at its beachfront resto (CVE1600 with transfer) or the less touristy **Hamburg** (2329309; mains CVE800; ⊘ 9am-9pm), with a colourful patio set behind the beach.

Calhau is also the best gateway for boat trips to the uninhabited island of **Santa Luzia** across the way, with its blissfully empty beaches. A **boat trip** with one of the local fishermen, which takes about 1½ hours each way, typically costs CVE15,000 round-trip (for up to four people). The man to look for among the fishermen is Alcides, who speaks a little English and can make arrangements. It's also possible to camp overnight, arranging for pick-up for the next day, although this costs more. Note that any boat trip needs to be arranged at least a day ahead and departure depends on the weather; if the ocean is too rough, no boat will want to take you over.

The fishing village of **Salamansa** has a nice brown-sand beach around a lovely bay. There's a beach shack run by **Kitesurf NOW** (☎ 9871954; www.kitesurfnow.eu; ⊘ 8am-6pm), which serves snacks and offers windsurfing and kitesurfing classes as well as equipment rental. They can also arrange day trips to Santa Luzia (book ahead).

Baía das Gatas is another popular weekend escape, 12km from Mindelo, for swimming in its natural pools and beachfront restaurants. Near the airport is the quaint fishing village of São Pedro, with a pretty beach and harbour.

SANTO ANTÃO

POP 43,915

For many people the main reason for visiting Cape Verde is for spectacular Santo Antão, and it really is a good reason. This dizzyingly vertical isle, ruptured with canyons, gorges and valleys, offers some of the most amazing hiking in West Africa. The second-largest island in the archipelago, it is the only one that puts the *verde* in Cape Verde. As you approach it from São Vicente by ferry, you wouldn't guess how green it is, as the south side looks quite barren and harsh. But the northeast of the island, which is the most populated corner and the most popular with hikers, receives enough regular moisture for forests of pine trees to dominate the hilltops and tropical plants to flourish in the steamy valleys.

To really get the most out of this island, set aside several days, prepare for some blisters and set out along the valleys and up the mountains on foot. See the northeast first but then get off the beaten trails and head to the untrammelled western reaches of Santo Antão, with its mighty mountains and tourism that's only nascent but worth supporting.

During the high season, from early November through February, it's wise to book accommodation ahead.

ⓘ Getting There & Away

Due to dangerous cross winds, no flights currently operate to Santo Antão and the airstrip at Ponta do Sol has been shut down for years.

There are daily ferries between Mindelo and Santo Antão. While subject to change, the comfortable *Mar d'Canal* leaves Mindelo at 8am, returning at 10am (except on Sunday, when there's only the afternoon departure). It leaves Mindelo again at 3pm (except Sunday), returning at 5pm. The trip costs CVE770 and lasts just under one hour. You must buy tickets 30 minutes before departure at the ferry-dock offices on both islands.

ⓘ Getting Around

If you want to see a lot of the island in a single day, your best bet is to hire your own *aluguer*, though expect to pay around CVE8000 for a full

CAPE VERDE SANTO ANTÃO

HIKING SANTO ANTÃO

Dramatic canyons, cloud-soaked peaks and vertigo-inspiring drops all help to make Santo Antão a hiker's paradise. Walks here cover all ranges of abilities, from gentle hour-long valley hikes to strenuous ascents only for the fittest. If you're intending to do some serious hiking get hold of the *Goldstadt Wanderkarte* hiking map. You may also consider hiring a local guide; price depends on the hike and whether the guide speaks English, but rates are about CVE4000. Many of the hikes begin or end on the transisland road. From here you can hitch a ride on a passing *aluguer*, or arrange for a taxi to wait for you ahead of time.

The classic hike is from the Cova crater (1170m), with its fascinating patchwork of farms, down to the stunning **Valé do Paúl**. The steep downhill route, which can get dangerously slippery, passes through lush mountainside, verdant stands of bananas and fields of sugar cane, all the way down to the string of villages that line the country road leading to the coastal town of Vila das Pombas.

An easier hike is along the coastal track from **Ponta do Sol** to **Fontainhas**. This hour-long walk takes you along a narrow path carved out of the cliff face that in places is really high and steep. At the end, the village of Fontainhas clings like a spider to a little ridge high above its fertile valley and a small, rocky cove.

These are just two popular hikes; there are numerous other possibilities. Many inn owners offer guide service and/or advice on nearby hikes; they are typically the best source of info for their particular area.

day around the east side of the island. You can usually arrange one when you arrive at Porto Novo. Alternatively, you can join locals on an *aluguer* headed towards Ribeira Grande and Ponta do Sol (CVE400, 45 minutes). Note that *alugueres* use the new, faster coastal road; if you want to travel along the scenic mountain road, be prepared to negotiate with the driver and dish out extra. It's typically pretty easy to find *alugueres* anywhere you are on the island, especially if you time your journey according to the ferry timetables. If you want to explore the west of the island, you may want to overnight in Porto Novo to get an early start.

Porto Novo

Arriving by ferry, the grubby port town of Porto Novo will be your first impression of Santo Antão. Don't worry; things rapidly improve! If you do get stuck in Porto Novo (although that's quite unlikely), you'll find a few places to stay, including the basic but decent **Residencial Antilhas** (☎ 2221193; residencialantilhas@hotmail.com; s & d without breakfast CVE2520), where you should request an upstairs room with a balcony offering views of the harbour. The upscale **Santantao Art Resort** (☎ 2222675; www.santantao-art-resort.com; s/d from CVE4500/6500; ✻@☎☏) to the south of town has balconied rooms, a range of facilities and a small tropical garden.

Ponta do Sol

Ponta do Sol feels like the end of the world, which in many ways it is: it sits where the road ends, literally. The sense of raw power here, with monstrous Atlantic waves and sheer cliffs reaching for the clouds leaves you feeling in awe of nature. For quite some time it was the only place in the area with decent tourist facilities, but that has changed in the last few years with the opening of a clutch of lovely inns in nearby Paúl. Although now overdeveloped, the town is still a good base for a night or two, with its pretty cobbled centre and a handful of decent hotels and restaurants.

🛏 Sleeping & Eating

Casa Tambla B&B   GUESTHOUSE **$**
(☎ 9825059;   kasatambla@gmail.com;   s/d CVE2100/3750) Rooms here feature a cosy and cheerful vibe. Some come with kitchenettes, others with terraces; most have private bathrooms. It's just up from the ocean,

fronted by a tropical patio. The French multilingual owner is a fount of info about the island and can set you up with guided kayaking trips, mountain-bike rentals, donkey tours and excursions to the uncharted western section.

Por de Sol Arte   GUESTHOUSE **$**
(☎ 2251121; porsolarte@yahoo.fr; s CVE2200-3100, d CVE3000-4300) On the waterfront, this playfully bright guesthouse has four spacious rooms, three with shared bathroom and two with balconies overlooking the ocean.

Hotel Blue Bell   HOTEL **$**
(☎ 2251215; bluebell@cvtelecom.cv; s/d CVE3200/4800; ✻) The closest the town has to a real hotel, the Blue Bell on the main square has adequate rooms and friendly service. A couple of smaller ground-floor rooms cost CVE2500 for a single, CVE3200 for a double. Some rooms have air-con; you can catch wi-fi from the square in the breakfast room. Note that it often hosts tour groups.

★Calheta por Sol   SEAFOOD **$$**
(mains CVE850; ⊙11.30am-2.30pm & 6-10.30pm) Bistrolike restaurant with sidewalk tables on the waterfront, where the French owner conjures up a mix of European and Capeverdian specialities using prime local products. Start with the goat cheese *beignets* (pastries) and move on to the seafood *feijoada*.

Cantinho do Gato Preto   INTERNATIONAL **$$**
(mains CVE800; ⊙11am-2pm & 6.30-10.30pm) Popular spot along the main road leading to the oceanfront from the square, with international classics and some local faves, as well as a small patio with live music on Sunday evening.

Ribeira Grande

The municipal region of Ribeira Grande occupies the island's northeastern section. Officially Ponta do Sol belongs to Ribeira Grande, although it's a world of its own. The region's urban centre is the unseemly town of Ribeira Grande, known by its old name of Povoação.

Beyond the town are gorgeous valleys and mountains, and a couple of adorable towns worth taking in. Those include **Chã da Igreja**, a sweet little place surrounded by mountains and sugar cane plantations, and

CAPE VERDE PORTO NOVO

centred on the main plaza with a church. A couple of locals rent out basic rooms, cook simple meals and offer *aluguer* service; look for rooms above Mercearia Mite or Mercado Baptista.

The quiet coastal village of Cruzinha is home to a *residencial*-restaurant, Sonafish (✆ 2261027; s/d incl breakfast & dinner CVE2500/5000), with rooms in a blue and white building on a rock right above the ocean. The more upscale Pedracin Village (✆ 2242020; s/d CVE3300/4950, plus IVA; P ❄ 🛜 🛏) sits above the hamlet of Boca de Coruja, 12km from Povoação. The series of stone cottages is set around a lush hillside garden connected by cobblestone paths. There's a swimming pool, a restaurant and free wi-fi in the public areas.

Povoação

Except for a tiny colonial heart, the town of Ribeira Grande, known to locals by its old name, Povoação, is not beautiful, though its position between steep cliffs and the roaring Atlantic is impressive. If you do get stuck here for the night, try the central Residencial Top d'Coroa (✆ 2212794; www.residencial-topcoroa.com; s/d CVE3000/4250; ❄), which has clean if chintzy rooms with private bathrooms, air-con and TV, or Residencial Tropical (✆ 2211129; rochatropical2011@hotmail.com; Rua d'Horta; s/d CVE2865/3925; ❄), hidden away in a yellow-grey building near the church, with nicely appointed spacious rooms (request one with a window) and friendly service. For food, try the downhome Cantinho de Amizade (mains CVE750; ⏲ 8am-4pm & 7-10.30pm), in a street just off the main plaza.

Paúl

Located southeast of Ribeira Grande is the municipality of Paúl, home to its pretty main town of Vila das Pombas and, stretching behind the coast, the dreamy valley that winds up into the heart of the island.

Thousands of people live in villages and hamlets that dot this idyllic valley, known for its lush and fertile land. Flowers and fruit trees are everywhere – from breadfruit to bananas and bougainvilleas – as are sugar cane fields; Paúl is famed for its potent *grogue*. A scenic country road leads from Vila das Pombas up the valley, passing the villages of Eito, Passagem, Lombinho, Chã João Vaz and Cabo de Ribeira, where the road ends. A steep cobblestone footpath leads from Cabo de Ribeira to Cova, an extinct volcanic crater whose floor is a patchwork of farms and lush greenery.

To immerse yourself in all this beauty, it's worth staying at one of the inns scattered around the valley. The owners at all of these can set you up with local guides and transfers. The first one up from Vila das Pombas is Wahnon Guesthouse (✆ 2231355; www.wahnonguesthouse.com; s CVE1500-2500, d CVE2000-5500, campsites/attic per person CVE500/850) in Eito. It's a family estate with rooms showcasing mahogany floors and antique handcrafted furniture and space for camping amid banana, sugar cane, avocado and mango trees.

Next up following the country road is Casa das Ilhas (✆ 2231832; www.casadasilhas.com; s/d incl breakfast & dinner CVE4500/5500), a pleasant set of houses on a hillside, reachable along a 15-minute uphill footpath (they'll carry your luggage). The well-equipped rooms range in comfort and size but all come with amazing valley views.

Further inland, on a hillside away from the main road, is the charming Aldeia Manga (✆ 2231880; www.aldeia-manga.com; Lombo Comprido; s/d bungalow CVE3850/4950, 2-person house CVE6600; 🛜 🛏), which has four two-person adobe bungalows (cold water only) and a big house for families with soft pine furnishings and solar-heated showers. There's a lush garden with hammocks and a small natural pool with valley views. Meals are available and there's free wi-fi in the public area.

Along the road in Chã João Vaz is O Curral (mains CVE250; ⏲ 10am-6pm Mon-Sat, 11am-5pm Sun), known to locals as Alfred's, a straw-roofed restaurant, farm shop and *grogue* distillery run by an Austrian who's been living in the valley for decades. The earthy dining room made of natural and recycled materials is a great spot to fill up on organic food and local coffee after the walk from Cova crater.

In the last roadside village is the adorable Spanish-run Casa Cavoquinho (✆ 2232065; www.cavoquinho.com; s/d CVE4400/4900; 🛜) housed in an orange building nestled on a hillside, with three recently spruced-up doubles with private bathrooms, pine floors, and hot water on demand. There's a terrace with dazzling valley views and a hammock, and wi-fi (for a fee).

The last lodging option in the valley is **Chez Sandro** (📞2231941; sandro_lacarenza@yahoo.fr; s/d CVE2500/3500; @), a hostel-like guesthouse run by a Frenchman and his Capeverdian wife. There's computer use (for a fee), hot water in the mornings and free laundry after three days. Downstairs is a cosy bar-restaurant with 25 different kinds of local liqueur, homemade ice cream and good food (mains CVE650). Look for the big red building that says 'Sandro'.

Vila das Pombas

The main centre of Paúl is this pretty strip of pastel houses along the ocean. There's nothing much to do here except wander, ponder the waves and visit the family-run distillery, **Trapiche Ildo Benrós** (admission CVE100; ☺6am-7pm), where *grogue* is made using the 400-year-old *trapiche* (machine for juicing sugar cane). Sample drinks such as passionfruit *caipirinha* under tall almond trees, as a veritable zoo of animals roams around. Look for a small green and white sign for Trapiche Ildo Benrós along the coastal road.

🛏 Sleeping & Eating

Residencial Mar e Sol　　　GUESTHOUSE $
(📞2231294; s CVE1500, d CVE2500-3000) Friendly *residencial* on the waterfront, in a blue building with clean rooms that feature chintzy decor and private bathrooms. Ask for one of the three rooms with ocean views.

Aldeia Jerome　　　GUESTHOUSE $
(📞2232173; www.aldeiajerome.it.gg;　s/d CVE3000/3500; 📶) Lovely garden hideaway tucked away from the coastal strip along a footpath through banana and mango trees, with rooms and suites in two buildings. All are clean, colourful and cosy, and equipped with fans and fridges. Ask for a room with a garden view. Breakfast is served on the top-floor terrace, plus there's wi-fi (for a fee) on the garden patio.

Hotel Paul Mar　　　HOTEL $$
(📞2232300; st.hotelpaulmar@gmail.com; Rua Agostinho Neto; s/d CVE4300/5400; ❄📶) This seafront hotel has contemporary spick-and-span rooms with all trimmings such as air-con, safes, wi-fi (for a fee) and verandahs. Sea-view rooms have balconies perched right over the ocean.

Pizzeria Ti Lello　　　PIZZERIA $
(pizzas CVE500; ☺noon-11pm) At the entrance to town if coming from Ribeira Grande along the old road, across from the beach, this Italian-run spot with a covered open-air patio churns out the island's best pizzas (evening only) as well as good spaghetti and burgers.

Atelier　　　CAFE $
(meals CVE700; ☺9am-late) This artsy hideaway behind Hotel Paul Mar is the local hipster hang-out. Run by a young musician and his wife, it serves yummy snacks, traditional dishes and herb teas in the small interior or on the large terrace outside. There's live music on weekends, often featuring up-and-coming musicians.

Tarrafal

Lost in the burning desert beige of the west coast, the sleepy little oasis of Tarrafal, set along a beach of inky black sand, is a delightful place to rest, unwind and do nothing more strenuous than flip the pages of a book. The high cliffs here shelter the beach from the worst of the winds. The **Pensão Mar Tranquilidade** (📞2276012; www.martranquilidade.com; s/d CVE2000/2800) offers lovely stone-and-thatch cottages as well as good meals and all kinds of activities.

The journey to Tarrafal is long and bumpy. *Alugueres* (CVE700) normally leave Porto Novo every morning (except Sunday) after the ferry disgorges its passengers. Taxis charge a hefty CVE10,000 one way; to find them, head to the bar of Residencial Antilhas.

FOGO

POP 37,051

Whether you're being tossed and turned in the heavy seas during the boat ride from Praia or thrown about by unpredictable winds and turbulence in the small prop plane, the drama of Fogo begins long before you even set foot on its volcanic soils. The island of Fire (Fogo translates as fire) consists of a single, giant black volcano (which last erupted in 1995) that dominates every view and every waking moment.

Life here isn't just about macho tectonic movements, though: São Filipe is easily one of the most attractive towns in the archipelago and can be used as a base for great

CLIMBING MOUNT FOGO

The conical 2829m-high Pico do Fogo volcano, shrouded in black cinder, rises dramatically out of the floor of an ancient crater known as Chã das Caldeiras ('Chã'). Bound by a half-circle of precipitous cliffs, Chã was born when, sometime in the last 100,000 years, some 300 cu km of the island collapsed and slid into the sea to the east. The main cone has been inactive for more than 200 years, though there have been regular eruptions in Chã. The latest, in 1995, threatened the twin villages of Portela and Bangaeira, whose residents manage to grow grapes, coffee, beans and apples in this forbidding landscape.

There's fantastic hiking along the crater floor, but most people come to climb the peak. The majority do it as a day trip from São Filipe, departing around 6am; book one through Qualitur (p120) or Zebra Travel (p120). Others overnight in Chã, which is a more leisurely option. Most people climb Pico Grande, which isn't technically difficult but requires good physical condition, a hearty pair of boots and a local guide. There are plenty in Portela, and the going rate is around CVE4000. The taxing ascent – a climb of 1000m up a 30- to 40-degree slope – takes three to four hours, with some challenging scrambles near the top, but the views are magnificent (especially in spring; otherwise you may be staring down into cloud cover). Afterwards, you can run down through volcanic ash in 45 minutes!

For more of an adventure, you can go up Pico Grande and come down via Pico Pequeno, which is the more difficult descent: you go down a steep slope of loose volcanic rocks for some 200m before reaching the 'runway' of volcanic ash and sand and then run down all the way to the multicoloured Pico Pequeno crater.

Fatal accidents have happened on these routes, so don't take the hike lightly. Always go with a guide and start climbing early to avoid the noon heat. Leave São Filipe by 5am by taxi (CVE6000 return with waiting time, 90 minutes). The driver should be able to locate a guide. If you come by *aluguer* (CVE500; depart São Filipe around 11am), you will need to spend two nights in Chã. Spend the afternoon after you arrive exploring the crater, and then make the ascent the next morning. Recover in the afternoon and then head back to São Filipe the next morning by *aluguer*, which leaves around 6am.

Other options from Chã include visiting caves wedged between the walls of lava (you can even camp in some), walking along the *bordeira* (crater edge), rock climbing and undertaking the steep and slippery five-hour descent from the volcano to the town of Mosteiros.

In Portela you can stay at Pedra Brabo (☑2821521; pedrabrabo@cvtelecom.cv; s/d CVE2500/3600), with basic rooms around an arcaded courtyard filled with lava stone sculptures. Only two rooms have private bathroom, and all showers are cold water. There's a restaurant (mains CVE800) and guide services on offer. The same owners run Casa Mariza (☑2821662; s/d CVE2500/3600) in Bangaeira, where all the rooms have private bathrooms with hot water (the only one in Chã with this luxury).

About 11 households have built rooms (s CVE1200-2000, d CVE2000-2800) for tourists in their homes; none have hot water, some include breakfast. Enquire at the tourist info point (☑2821515; ☉9.30am-1.30pm & 3.30-6.30pm Mon-Fri & Sun) in a wooden roadside kiosk in Portela. The kiosk also has a small exhibit about the area, including some info about the famous François Louis Armand de Montrond, a French count who moved to Fogo in the late 19th century and apparently fathered 21 children with seven island wives. Two of the sons moved to the crater in the 1920s and founded Portela, so the legend goes; that explains why you still see many villagers with blue eyes and light hair, and why 80% of them carry the surname Montrond. The info point is being moved to the entrance of the village; it should be up and running by summer 2013.

Finally, after you've struggled up the peak, what better way to reward yourself than with a drop of locally produced wine? The vines are actually grown in the volcanic ash of the crater. For tastings and purchasing, visit Adega de Chã das Caldeiras, a small cooperative in Portela (hours are erratic). If you're staying overnight, don't miss the nightly performance (around 6pm) at Casa Ramiro, a grocery store where you can try local goat cheese and homemade *manecon* wine, and enjoy live music performed by Ramiro and his children.

hikes and pretty drives around the island's eastern side to the small town of Mosteiros, past terraced hillsides yielding mild Arabica coffee.

ⓘ Getting There & Away

TACV (🖉 281228; www.flytacv.com; ⊘ 8am-12.30pm & 3-5.30pm Mon-Fri) has one to two daily flights to/from Praia, which last 30 minutes. A taxi from the airport into São Filipe (2km) costs CVE300. Boats arrive at the port 3km from town (taxis charge CVE400), which looks like a giant construction site.

ⓘ Getting Around

Minibuses around the island are relatively scarce. Most are based around the timings of the central market in São Filipe. That means they head to São Filipe in the early morning, and then back home later in the day; plan accordingly. Fares depend on distance but shouldn't cost more than CVE500.

Qualitur (🖉 2811089; www.qualitur.cv; ⊘ 8am-6pm Mon-Fri, to noon Sat) and **Zebra Travel** (🖉 9914566; www.zebratravel.net; ⊘ 8am-5pm Mon-Fri, 9am-noon Sat) offer self-drive cars from CVE7000 to CVE7500 per day as well as island-wide tours. The going rate for hiring a taxi for the day is CVE6000; one of the best drivers on the island, who speaks English to boot, is **Albino** (🖉 9953231).

São Filipe

Set commandingly on the cliffs like the nest of a seabird, São Filipe is a town of grace, charm, immaculate Portuguese houses, and plazas full of flowers and sleepy benches. Below, at the base of the cliffs, lies a beach of jet-black sand and evil, dumping waves; beyond, tantalising on the horizon, squats the island of Brava. All this makes São Filipe one of the most compelling and charming towns in Cape Verde. Note that strong currents make the town beach unsafe for swimming, especially in winter.

⊙ Sights

Dja'r Fogo　　　　　　　　GALLERY
(🖉 9919713;　　djarfogo-agnelo@hotmail.com; ⊘ 9am-12.30pm & 3-6pm Mon-Fri, 9am-12.30pm Sat) A must-stop for visitors interested in history, culture and coffee. Run by a local artist who splits his time between Lisbon, Paris and Fogo, it serves as art gallery, cafe, information point and launch pad for informal trips around the island. It's also the best place to taste artisanal Fogo coffee; the

owner's family has had a coffee plantation since 1874 and, six generations later, he still roasts and packages it into neat little cotton bags.

If Agnelo, the owner, is on Fogo, he organises personalised island circuits as well as dinners at his 200-year-old family estate, **Quinta das Saudades**, in the village of Achada Lapa, 8km east from town in the mountains. This is a treat not to be missed (CVE1500 per person, with wine, plus CVE700 for transfer), featuring traditional corn-based dishes prepared by a woman who has been cooking for the family for 40 years. Email or call ahead of time to arrange the dinner.

If Agnelo is away, the gallery is still open; relax on the patio over a cup of coffee or check out the old photos, art and jewelry made of recycled materials and cards made with banana leaves and black sand.

Museu Municipal　　　　　　MUSEUM
(🖉 2812475; adult/student & child CVE100/free; ⊘ 10am-3pm Mon-Fri) Pop into this airy colonial mansion with two floors of exhibits, showcasing old photographs, traditional music instruments, sewing machines and sundry items. You can watch the 28-minute film about the 1995 volcano eruption (no subtitles), browse the souvenir shop and see the *funco,* a traditional circular abode made of volcanic rock, in the leafy courtyard.

Praia da Salina　　　　　　　BEACH
Join the locals at the lovely Praia da Salina. Protected by strange volcanic rock formations, the beach is 17km to the north of town on the route to Mosteiros.

★☆ Festivals & Events

On 1 May, the town celebrates **Nhô São Filipe**, its yearly citywide festival. Its **Mardi Gras** celebration is also raucous.

🛏 Sleeping

Pensão Las Vegas　　　　　PENSION **$**
(🖉 2812223; s/d CVE2000/3000) It might not be as glam as its namesake, but nevertheless this is a decent place to stay, and the cheapest digs in town. Half of the rooms have sea views, some come with terraces and all have hot-water showers in the private bathrooms.

Pousada Belavista　　　GUESTHOUSE **$**
(🖉 2811734;　　p_belavista@yahoo.com;　　s/d CVE2600/3600; ❋ 🛜) An understated, im-

peccably run hotel built around an old colonial home and a new adjacent building. Rooms are well furnished if a little stuffy, some have ocean views, and breakfasts are hearty. Rooms with air-con cost CVE200 extra.

Tortuga B&B GUESTHOUSE **$$**
(☏9941512; www.tortuga-fogo.eu; s/d CVE3520/4950; @) A heavenly little beach hideaway a 10-minute drive or a 30-minute walk along the beach from town. The live-in Italian owners take good care of their guests, who stay in four stylish rooms with an earthy look or the straw bungalow in the garden. Think hammocks between palm trees, the sound of crashing waves, a beach at your doorstep... Roberto cooks up amazing meals on request (CVE1600 for three courses), and a delicious breakfast of local products is included. It's also a good place to arrange a variety of island tours. Call ahead for a pick-up; taxis tend to overcharge for the rough road that comes down here.

Hotel Savana HOTEL **$$**
(☏2811490; www.hotelsavanafogo.com; s/d CV3900/4500; ❋▣) This startlingly yellow, renovated colonial building dressed up in showy pink bougainvillea is a comfortable base. The rooms are simple but have an old-fashioned elegance and the black volcanic rock decorations contrast nicely with the bright colours. The pricier suites come with sea vistas. There's a plunge pool in the inner courtyard.

Casa Beiramar GUESTHOUSE **$$**
(☏2813485; www.cabo-verde.ch; s CVE3000-4000, d CVE5500, apt CVE7500-8800) In a colonial building opposite the main church, this German-run house offers two spotless apartments with a pleasing stonewashed look. The double room upstairs is simple, with a lovely terrace showcasing an ocean view. There's also a basic single downstairs, without hot water. A good breakfast is served on the downstairs terrace. There's laundry service, dinners on request and info about island tours.

Colonial Guest House GUESTHOUSE **$$$**
(☏9914566; www.thecolonialguesthouse.com; s/d CVE6100/9100; ❋▣) This gorgeously renovated colonial mansion facing the ocean houses the town's nicest place to stay, run by a Danish-Capeverdian couple. Rooms come with antique furniture and wooden floors; some have terraces with ocean views. There's a terrace with a swimming pool, a

massage room and Jacuzzi in the basement and a pillow-strewn inner patio. Perks include free wi-fi and airport transfers. Zebra Travel (p122) is the place to book tours and make onward travel arrangements, while the adjacent Fogo Lounge (p123) serves as Fogo's travellers' hub.

🍴 Eating & Drinking

São Filipe is one of the best (and most reasonable) places in Cape Verde to try seafood.

For a special meal, make dinner reservations at Tortuga B&B (p123), where Italian owner Roberto cooks up innovative seafood dishes based on his father's old recipes, prepared using local ingredients and homemade products; wash it all down with the top-quality aged *grogue* from Brava.

Maria Augusta Bakery BAKERY **$**
(◷morning-evening Mon-Sat, to noon Sun) The friendly Maria Augusta churns out delicious bread and pastries from the giant wood-burning oven inside what looks like a garage. Look for an orange building on the edge of the sea near the church. Stock up on sweet goat-cheese tarts *(pudim de queijo)*, coconut biscuits and marmalade-filled doughnuts.

Cape Cod CAPEVERDIAN **$**
(mains CVE650; ◷7am-10pm Mon-Sat, 8am-8.30pm Sun) Popular lunchtime spot that locals storm for good and inexpensive daily specials. It's simple, downhome and friendly.

Fogo Lounge INTERNATIONAL **$$**
(mains CVE800; ◷7.30am-midnight) As the drinks flow, afternoons quickly slip through to evenings at this cosmopolitan outdoor restaurant–lounge bar. Meals rotate around sandwiches, pastas, burgers, pizzas and crepes, as well as more substantial mains. There are natural juices, a good choice of drinks, and occasional live music.

Tropical Club SEAFOOD **$$**
(mains CVE750; ◷8am-midnight) Just up from the main square, this cheerful restaurant with a palm-shaded terrace has an extensive menu of mainly seafood dishes; try the delicious Fogo-style tuna. On Friday night there's a *tocatina* (live traditional music performance).

Bidon CAPEVERDIAN **$$**
(mains CVE800; ◷7.30am-midnight Sun-Thu, to 2am Fri & Sat) A rambling music-themed spot

CAPE VERDE SÃO FILIPE

with straw-roof outdoor seating areas and lots of colourful artwork that pays homage to the US, where the owner lived for many years. It serves meals throughout the day and cheap lunch specials; live traditional music on Friday evening and DJs late night on Saturday. Snag the booth with a barrel offering an ocean view. It is on Rua Hospital, next door to BCA bank.

ℹ Information

For internet access there's **Stop Cafe** (⊙8am-1pm & 3-6pm Mon-Fri, 8am-noon Sat), slightly uphill from the centre; it charges CVE50 for 30 minutes and offers printing. The main plaza has free wi-fi, although with spotty signal. There are several banks with ATMs around the centre.

SAL

POP 25,765

Though flat, desolate and overdeveloped, Sal boasts more tourists than any other island. They fall into three categories: the package-holiday crowd, hardcore windsurfers and those in transit to more interesting islands. Our advice: Skip Sal if you can.

The largest town is Espargos, right next to the international airport, but most people stay near the fine beach in Santa Maria, 18km to the south.

ℹ Getting There & Away

AIR

The airport has left-luggage facilities (CVE220 per bag per 24 hours), an ATM, a bureau de change, free wi-fi and a tourist booth.

TACV (☑2411305) TACV has several flights daily to/from Praia and one daily to São Vicente, three weekly to Boa Vista and three a week to São Nicolau.

ℹ Getting Around

Minibuses ply the road between Santa Maria and Espargos (CVE100, 25 minutes); all stop on the main road just in front of the airport. Taxis from the airport to Santa Maria charge CVE1000 during the day, 30% more at night.

Santa Maria

The good news is the beach. A sublime strip of gentle sand and ever-so-blue waters with world-class windsurfing and lots of fun-in-the-sun activities. But avert your eyes from this view and you're in for a shock. Santa Maria, the king of Cape Verdean resorts, is a grim, wind-battered building site that in places resembles a war zone more than an international holiday resort.

There are several banks with ATMs (although they tend to run out of cash on weekends) and numerous internet cafes.

🏃 Activities

As far as activities go, you can't get bored on Sal. The accent is on water sports; there are a number of centres and schools, which cover anything from scuba diving, kitesurfing and snorkelling to windsurfing and sailing. Those include the **Orca Dive Club** (☑2421302; www.orca-diveclub-caboverde.com), **Surf Zone** (☑9978804; www.surfcaboverde.com) and **Manera Kite School** (☑9329894; www.manerakiteschool.com), among many others.

The hippest water-sports centre and beach hang-out is **Angulo Cabo Verde** (☑2421580; www.angulocaboverde.com), which is at Praia António de Sousa, 1km from the centre, east of the pier. It offers kitesurfing lessons, equipment rentals and food (mains CVE750) served on a wooden deck with parasols and loungers.

Other activities include shark-watching jaunts, **turtle-watching** (www.sostartarugas.org), horseback riding and island tours with a 4x4. A good one-stop shop for activities and excursions is the green and yellow **info kiosk** (☑9592030; ⊙9am-6pm) along the beach, near Hotel Morabeza. Or stop by **Barracuda Tours** (☑2422033; www.barracudatours.com) for various excursion options, including sailing trips.

🛏 Sleeping

Much of the accommodation in Santa Maria consists of large package-tour resorts that line the beachfront and privately rented apartments.

★ **Sakaroulé B&B** GUESTHOUSE $
(☑2421682; www.sakaroulecaboverde.com; s/d CVE2530/3300; @) In a very local neighbourhood 300m from the beach, Sal's loveliest B&B has stylish rooms that come in different sizes, pretty colours and with African decor touches. Owned by an Italian-French couple and run by a pair of live-in Croatians (a yoga teacher and a surfer) who can set up you up with tours and activities, Sakaroulé is a top choice away from the

tourist buzz, with a friendly, earthy and hip vibe.

Hotel Nhá Terra
HOTEL $

(☎2421109; nhaterra@hotmail.com; s/d from CVE4000/5000; ❋🏠❄) The hotel's a little dull but otherwise these spacious rooms are spick and span, with air-con and balconies (in some). There's also a small pool and a decent restaurant (closed Sunday). Sea-view rooms are pricier (by CVE300).

Pensão Les Alizés
PENSION $$

(☎2421446; www.pensao-les-alizes.com; s/d CVE4950/6600; @) The slightly old-fashioned rooms of the French-owned Les Alizés, right at the heart of town, are a little noisy but cosy, clean and equipped with verandahs. There's one pricier room (No 10) with an ocean-view terrace. Breakfast is served on the lovely 2nd-floor terrace.

Hotel Morabeza
HOTEL $$$

(☎2421020; www.hotelmorabeza.com; s/d from CVE14,445/22,055; ❋@🏠❄) Fronting a lively patch of beach, this grande dame of a beach hotel was the very first on the strip. Over 40 years later, it's still a great choice, with well-appointed rooms facing the beach or the gardens, several restaurants, two pools and lots of activities.

🍴 Eating & Drinking

★Cafe Criolo
CAPEVERDIAN $

(mains CVE600; ⊙7.30am-10pm Mon-Sat) The least touristy, most downhome place to eat in town, this low-key eatery with a streetside verandah serves delicious homemade food, like *cachupa* (beans and corn mixed with fish or meat; preorder it), fish stews and tuna steaks. The lunch specials are a steal.

D'Angela
SEAFOOD $$

(mains CVE750; ⊙8am-11pm) The oceanfront terrace is the highlight of this simple, always buzzing restaurant that dishes out reliably good seafood fare. Live music makes it even livelier on Fridays and Saturday evenings, and at lunchtime on Sundays.

Chez Pastis
ITALIAN $$$

(☎9843696; mains CVE1150; ✍) Reserve ahead at this tiny, narrow little restaurant, which serves top-quality (and priced accordingly) meat and seafood dishes with an Italian twist. Good vegetarian options, too.

Salbeach Club
BAR

(⊙8am-midnight) Hip beachfront spot with live music on weekends, good-value Sunday roast dinners, free wi-fi, a big TV screen and a small plunge pool.

Pub Calema
PUB

(⊙5pm-5am) Busy pub on the main strip, with sidewalk tables, nightly happy hour and DJ-spun tunes nightly from 11pm.

Tam Tam
PUB

(⊙9am-midnight, closed morning Sun & all day Thu) This Irish-owned pub-restaurant is a popular tourist drinking hole, with live music on Saturday night.

Espargos

Located near both the airport and the ferry dock, Espargos – the island's capital – is a small, dusty workaday town that feels more like the real Cape Verde than touristy Santa Maria. Both food and accommodation are cheaper here than in Santa Maria. If you want to use it as your base, try **Pensão Paz e Bem** (☎2411782; pensaopazbem@cvtelecom. cv; s/d CVE2120/3180), just to the south of the main square, with spacious and clean

---

OTHER ISLAND HIGHLIGHTS

A great attraction is the surreal, lunarlike **Pedra do Lume** (per person CVE550), the crater of an ancient volcano where seawater is transformed into shimmering salt beds. You can see the old salt-extraction machinery of the 1805 plant; float in the medicinal salt water; have a massage, salt scrub or mud treatment at the small Salinas Relax spa; and have a meal at the restaurant. Pedra do Lume is 6km southeast of Espargos; taxis from Santa Maria charge between CVE3500 and CVE4400, with a wait of two hours. It's often mobbed with tour groups.

Other points of interest include the fish market in **Palmeira**, the gorgeous **Igrejinha beach** at the far-eastern end of Santa Maria and the **Buracona** natural swimming pool (time your visit for noon to see the Blue Eye, a natural light effect in a small underground pool).

rooms. **Sivvy** (mains CVE500; ⊘10.30am-3pm & 7.30-10.30pm) on the square is a good old-fashioned cafe-bar that serves simple meals and drinks. Plenty of minibuses ply the road between Espargos and Santa Maria (CVE100).

BOA VISTA

POP 9162

With its feathery lines of peachy dunes, stark plains and scanty oases, Boa Vista looks as if a chunk of the Sahara somehow broke off the side of Africa and floated out to the middle of the Atlantic. Though the island offers some fantastic if wind-blown beaches, incredible windsurfing, the pretty little town of Sal Rei, and an ever-increasing number of resorts and hotels, it's this desert interior that is the real reason for venturing out here. Be ready for some rough off-roading, as most of Boa Vista's roads are treacherous.

◎ Sights

The long and beautiful **Praia da Santa Mónica** is on the island's southern coast, as well as the beaches of **Curralinho** and **Varandinha**. It's worth whizzing through the village of **Povoaçao Velha**, the **Viana Desert** (great to visit on a full-moon night; Migrante (p127) Guesthouse offers tours) and the oasis town of **Rabil**.

The **Morro Negro lighthouse** on a 150m-high cape is Cape Verde's most easterly point, with a great panorama. Another good destination is the spooky village of **Curral Velho**, abandoned due to near-endless drought and now the home of ghosts and the odd passing fisherman. Another, equally eerie sight is the wreck of the **Santa Maria**, a rusting hulk laid out on a stormy stretch of beach to the north of Sal Rei along Costa de Boa Esperança. While this makes a decent half-day walk, it's better not to attempt it as there have been muggings on this route; take a taxi or visit it as part of an island tour instead. There's also a string of pretty villages – **João Galego**, **Fundo das Figueiras** and **Cabeço das Tarafes** – in the island's interior.

While you can't take in all these sights in one day, two days is more than enough to see the entire island.

Activities

The attractive beach at Sal Rei is lined with beach clubs that offer water sports, food and occasional fun at night. Most are only open in wintertime, from November to April, which is the windy season.

Planet Allsports WATER SPORTS
(☑5963834; www.planetallsports.com) A great choice, with two centres near Sal Rei, one on Tortuga beach and another at Morabeza. They rent boards for around €65 per day and kites for €80 per day. Windsurfing courses start at around €65 for a two-hour taster; a two-hour kitesurf will set you back €75. Note that it costs less if you prebook. They also rent stand-up paddleboards and surfboards.

Submarine Dive Center DIVING
(☑9924865; atilros@gmail.com) Submarine Dive Center provides equipment, dives for experienced folk (€60 with equipment) and crash courses (€100) for novices. Kayaks are also available for rent (€50 for two hours).

Naturalia TURTLE-WATCHING
(☑2511558; www.naturaliaecotours.com) Turtles come to Boa Vista in massive numbers in order to lay eggs. Several agencies on the island offer turtle-watching tours in season (July to October), but Naturalia is the best and most environmentally sensitive; tours cost €50 per person and typically depart around 7.30pm, returning at midnight. Naturalia also offers **whale-watching excursions** (€65 per person per half-day) between February and May, when humpback whales travel the waters off Cape Verde; and **birdwatching** tours for €50 (there are 24 species on Boa Vista). It also arranges **snorkelling** trips to Baía das Gatas, where you swim among rich coral and nurse sharks.

Morena 4WD TOUR
(☑2511445; www.boavistamorena.com; ⊘9am-12.30pm & 4-7pm Mon-Fri, 9am-12.30pm Sat) If you're a landlubber, book a 4WD tour around the island with Morena; it has half-day trips for CVE4400 and full-day jaunts for CVE5500. Morena also offers horseback riding along the beach for CVE3300 per hour.

If you're feeling adventurous, you can hire a 4WD from CVE5500 to CVE7000 per day; look for La Perla and Olicar on the main square. Alternatively, hire a taxi with a driver (the going rate is between CVE6600 and CVE9900 per day, depending on where you want to go).

🛏 Sleeping

With an increasing number of tourists venturing to Boa Vista, accommodation can be tight. It's a good idea to book ahead.

Pensão Santa Isabel
PENSION $

(📞 2511252; s/d CVE2500/3000) This basic but friendly *pensão*, right on the main square, is the most decent budget pick in town, with a set of poky and dark rooms with private bathrooms.

Hotel Boa Vista
HOTEL $$

(📞 2511145; hotelboavista@cvtelecom.cv; s/d CVE5000/6500; ❋ 🛜) Functional hotel on the main road into town, with colourful and bright rooms that are generous with space and amenities; some have balconies. There's wi-fi, for a fee.

★ Migrante Guesthouse
GUESTHOUSE $$

(📞 2511143; www.migrante-guesthouse.com; s/d CVE6600/9900; @ 🛜) The gorgeous Migrante has four rooms set around a courtyard of mustard yellow and bougainvillea pink, with a giant palm tree. Each room has dark wood floors, big, soft beds and black-and-white portraits hanging on the icy white walls, which give it an arty feel. The downstairs cafe is lovely too. Rates include airport transfers.

★ Spinguera Eco Lodge
LODGE $$$

(📞 2511941; www.spinguera.com; s/d CVE18,000/24,000; 🅿 🛜) ✐ Boa Vista's most magical hideaway is an abandoned fishing village converted into a stunning eco-lodge by the Italian artist owner. Inside whitewashed cottages, stylish and minimalist rooms showcase reclaimed wood and clay floors and ocean views. The restaurant serves delectable food and there's a walkway down to your own little beach. A stay here is a splurge but a worthy one.

🍴 Eating & Drinking

For beachside meals during the day and night-time action (on weekends only), head to Estoril beach, which has several options. The best include Social Club Boa Vista, Tortuga and Morabeza; from Sal Rei, they appear in the order listed as you walk down.

Rosi's
SEAFOOD $

(mains CVE650; ⏱ 11am-3pm & 7.30-9.30pm Mon-Sat) Order ahead for a great-value feast of lobster (CVE2000) and octopus (CVE1000) at this old-fashioned eatery with wooden panelling, right across the road from Migrante.

Naida
CAPEVERDIAN $

(mains CVE750; ⏱ 1-2.30pm & 7-9pm) Grab a table in the back-room restaurant of this friendly traditional spot on the northeast side of the plaza for a simple and inexpensive meal of seafood or grilled meat.

Esplanada
CAFE $

(mains CVE750; ⏱ 7.30am-2am Mon-Sat) Good spot for a late lunch, when all restaurants are closed, right on the main plaza. Serves anything from pizzas and sandwiches to more substantial dishes.

Blue Marlin
SEAFOOD $$

(mains CVE850; ⏱ Mon-Sat) This tiny restaurant with graffiti-covered walls on the main square serves the island's best seafood and normally has an atmosphere to match. Book in advance.

Chandinho
ITALIAN $$$

(📞 9860718; mains CVE1100; ⏱ 7-11pm daily except Wed) Here you will find a bustling restaurant near the ocean, a five-minute walk from the plaza, with a colourful interior accented with tribal art. The menu features lots of pastas and seafood dishes with an Italian touch, plus there's a good wine list. Book ahead.

Wakan Bar
CAFE

(⏱ 9.30am-9pm Tue-Sat) Adorable little blue and white shack with a boat shape, right by the fishing boats on Praia de Diante. Expect no fewer than 46 cocktail varieties, nice snacks, good Italian coffee and a two-for-one happy hour.

Unico Amor
BAR

(⏱ 5.30pm-2am Tue-Sun) Loungy spot overlooking the port, behind the post office, it features DJ-spun tunes, live Cuban music and live drumming on the terrace and inner patio. Food is good, too (mains CVE900).

ℹ Information

There are several banks with ATM around the *praça*, which has free wi-fi.

ⓘ Getting There & Away

TACV (☑ 2511186) has three weekly flights to Praia (one hour) and three weekly to Sal (15 minutes). Irregular ferries sail to/from Boa Vista, Praia and Sal, but they are so sporadic you may lose many days waiting for one. *Aluguers* (from CVE200) ply the island's roads, but they're scarce. Taxis are readily available; the short hop from the airport to town costs CVE500.

OTHER ISLANDS

Brava

POP 5995

Except for the occasional car that braves the cobblestone, cross-island roads, Brava seems to reside firmly in the 19th century. Its terraced hillsides are farmed with the aid of mules and life moves at a pace that would make a sloth sleepy. Its mountainous interior is breathtaking and the coastline dramatic, though thanks to its distance from anywhere else and infrequent, erratic travel connections, the island receives little foreign tourism. You will see fancy mansions dotted around the island; these are built by US returnees – Brava's population has left in droves for US shores but some come back to build their lifelong dream.

Nova Sintra ('Vila'), the tiny capital, sits on a little plateau regularly engulfed by clouds. From Vila there are some short but lovely hikes: eastward down to the ghost village of Vinagre via Santa Barbara and westward to Cova Joana and then on to Nossa Senhora do Monte or Lima Doce, both nearby. Another highlight includes the 1½-hour walk to the mountainside hamlet of Baleia from the village of Mato Grande, 4km from Nova Sintra. The scenic village of Fajã d'Agua on the northwestern coast is set dramatically between a rocky cove and impressive cliffs. It's great to hike down to the village, along a sharp 7km descent with stunning views.

Aluguers ply the road between Nossa Senhora do Monte, Vila and the ferry port at Furna (CVE150 for each leg). You can find a car and driver for a full-day tour of the island for as little as CVE4000 – ask around among the *aluguer* drivers. To get to Fajã for a couple of hours, *aluguers* charge about

CVE2000. Plan ahead if you have a morning boat, as transport can be scarce.

🛏 Sleeping & Eating

Pensão Nova Sintra PENSION $
(☑ 2852037; pensao_novasintra@yahoo.com; s/d CVE2850/3850) On the main road into Vila, this newly built townhouse has clean, spacious rooms with private bathrooms and TVs. Solid choice in town.

Pensão Sol na Baia PENSION $$
(☑ 2852070; pensao_sol_na_baia@hotmail.com; s/d CVE4500/5500; @) The island's most attractive place to stay, oceanfront Sol na Baia offers a handful of tastefully appointed rooms (some with balconies), French-inspired meals and a delightful garden full of birds and bees.

O Poeta CAPEVERDIAN $
(mains CVE600; ⊘ 8am-midnight) On the main street leading up from the square, this restaurant with a terrace serves decent fish and meat dishes off a picture menu. There's live music on Saturday night, plus free wi-fi.

ⓘ Getting There & Away

There are no flights to Brava and until just a couple of years ago the only way to get there was with a tiny fishing trawler that crossed the treacherously rough channel between Fogo and Brava. That changed when **Cabo Verde Fast Ferry** (www.cvfastferry.com) came in, with its solid boat that runs between Praia, Fogo and Brava several times a week. Schedules change often, so it's best to consult the website for the latest. The journey from Fogo to Brava lasts 40 minutes and costs CVE1550; from Praia to Fogo it's 3½ hours and costs CVE3350 (if heading to Brava, a one way-ticket is CVE3750).

Note that the ferry from Fogo departs at night from the port outside São Filipe, which looks like a giant construction site. You may be confused when the taxi drops you off in a dark middle-of-nowhere surrounded by shipping containers – yes, surprisingly, you are in the right place and the boat will come.

Maio

POP 6952

Glittering like a white crystal in a sea of turquoise, Maio is a place of squeaky-clean beaches and days that drift slowly by in a haze of sunshine and long conversations. Aside from the pretty if slightly overdeveloped main town of **Vila do Maio** (also known as Porto Inglés), the sleepy fishing village of **Calheta** 11km to the north and the many **beaches**, the only other 'attraction' is the scrubby acacia-dotted interior with its string of 13 villages. But for the discerning traveller after something a little different, Maio is begging you to leave your footprints on its gorgeous beaches.

🛏 Sleeping

Residencial Bom Sossego   GUESTHOUSE **$**
(☎ 2551365; residencialbomsossego@hotmail.com; Vila do Maio; s/d from CVE2900/3550; ❄) On the main plaza, with basic rooms, some with fans and others with air-con, and a decent restaurant downstairs.

Torre Sabina   GUESTHOUSE **$$**
(☎ 2561299; www.inseltraum.biz; d CVE5500) One amazing double room with panoramic ocean vistas inside a funky tower right on Baixona beach in Calheta. Run by a German couple, it's surrounded by lovely gardens; there's a kayak you can use for free. Delicious breakfast is included and dinners are available on request.

🍴 Eating & Drinking

Kabana   SEAFOOD **$**
(mains CVE650; ❀ closed all day Tue & evening Sun) Wooden beach shack with a deck on the sand, with friendly service and simple fish and meat dishes.

Tropical   SEAFOOD **$**
(mains CVE600; ❀ Tue-Sun) Beachside spot with a travellers' vibe and a good range of food, such as spaghetti, pizzas, toasts and fish mains. There's a great sunset happy hour.

Wolf Djarmai   INTERNATIONAL **$**
(mains CVE700; ❀ 8am-11pm, closed Sat) Capeverdian and European food is dished out at this funky German-run spot inside a blue container fronted by a tree-shaded terrace, just up from the main square behind the church. The Friday night *tocatina* is the place to be.

Cala Grande Piano Bar   BAR
(☎ 2561140; ❀ 9am-11pm) Opened by well-known Capeverdian musician To Tavares, this small bar in Calheta serves as the island's unofficial cultural centre. There's a dance company and music school as well as traditional music concerts by a resident

band every Saturday. Food, prepared by village ladies, is available if you call a day ahead (CVE600 per dish), and there are a couple of basic rooms in the back (CVE3500).

ℹ Getting There & Around

TACV (☎ 2551916) has three flights weekly to/ from Praia (10 minutes). The transfer into town costs CVE250; look for Bemvindo, the island's most trustworthy driver. He charges CVE6000 for an island tour; you can find a cheaper pick-up for CVE4500.

São Nicolau
POP 12,817

São Nicolau hides its secrets well. First impressions are of a desolate and barren island, but hidden among those three ridges that dominate all views are lush and green valleys and soaring peaks that rise up to Mt Gordo – at 1312m the island's highest peak.

Near the mouth of the fertile Fajã Valley lies **Ribeira Brava**, the island's capital. Long Cape Verde's religious centre, it was built inland to protect its treasures from pirates. Its narrow, hillside streets and tiled roofs are still reminiscent of 17th-century Portugal. Ribeira Brava's **Carnival** celebration in February or March is second only to Mindelo's.

You can go to Ribeira Brava by minibus (CVE400) or taxi (around CVE3000) from the unbeautiful town of Tarrafal, the island's port. A great option is to get off halfway at Cachaço and hike down through the Fajã Valley to Ribeira Brava. The trail up to Mt Gordo also goes through Cachaço, passing through a protected pine forest before reaching the summit.

🛏 Sleeping & Eating

Pensão Jardim   PENSION **$**
(☎ 2351117; s/d CVE2600/3600) Located on a hill overlooking town and with breathtaking views in Ribeira Brava, this spotless *pensão* has quaint, comfortable rooms and a very good rooftop restaurant (mains CVE700; order ahead).

ℹ Getting There & Away

Ferries stop off at Tarrafal at least twice a week while travelling between Praia and São Vicente. TACV has three flights a week to Sal and one weekly to São Vicente. The airport is 5km southeast of Ribeira Brava (CVE500 by taxi).

UNDERSTAND CAPE VERDE

Cape Verde Today

In 2011, Cape Verde held both parliamentary and presidential elections. Three parties now hold seats in the National Assembly: PAICV, MPD and the Cape Verdean Independent and Democratic Union (UCID). The president is Jorge Carlos Fonseca of MPD. Cape Verde is presently the most prosperous West African nation, with the best-educated population. The country has Special Partnership status with the EU.

Tourism is the fastest-growing industry, which accounts for 29.8% of GDP (in 2011). Huge tourist-resort construction projects on Sal and Boa Vista have brought a steady stream of package tourists. However, the worldwide economic crisis and tourism downturn have halted mass development on other islands.

History

Slavery, Drought & Neglect

When Portuguese mariners discovered Cape Verde in 1456, the islands were uninhabited but fertile enough to attract the first group of settlers six years later. They founded Ribeira Grande (now Cidade Velha), the first European town in the tropics, on the island of Santiago. To work the land, settlers almost immediately began to import slaves from the West African coast. Plans by Genoese investors to create large sugar plantations never paid off, especially after the Caribbean proved productive. However, the islands' remote yet strategic position made them a perfect clearinghouse and victualling station for the transatlantic slave trade.

Cape Verde's first recorded drought occurred in 1747; from that date droughts became ever more common and, in the century from 1773, three droughts killed some 100,000 people. This cycle lasted well into the 20th century. At the same time, the island's economic clout fell as Britain, France and the Netherlands challenged Portugal's control over the slave trade. As a result, Lisbon invested little in Cape Verde. To escape hunger, many men left the islands, principally to work as hired hands on American whaling ships. Even today, Cape Verdean communities along the New England coast in the US rival the population of Cape Verde itself.

Cape Verde's fortunes revived with the advent of the ocean liner and the archipelago became an important stopover for coal, water and livestock. When the aeroplane replaced the ocean liner, Cape Verde opened an international airport on Sal in 1948 that was designed to service transatlantic flights.

Independence

Cape Verde's mostly mixed-race population tended to fare better than fellow Africans in other Portuguese colonies. Beginning in the mid-19th century, a privileged few received an education, many going on to help administer mainland colonies. By independence, 25% of the population could read (compared with 5% in Guinea-Bissau).

However, literate Cape Verdeans were gradually becoming aware of the nationalism simmering on the mainland. Soon, together with leaders of Guinea-Bissau, they had established a joint independence movement. In 1956 Cape Verdean intellectual Amilcar Cabral (born in Guinea-Bissau) founded the Marxist-inspired Partido Africano da Independência da Guinée Cabo Verde (PAIGC), later renamed the Partido Africano da Independência de Cabo Verde (PAICV).

As other European powers were relinquishing their colonies, Portugal's right-wing dictator António de Salazar propped up his regime with dreams of colonial greatness. From the early 1960s, one of Africa's longest wars of independence ensued. However, most of the fighting took place in Guinea-Bissau, and indeed many middle-class Cape Verdeans remained lukewarm about independence.

Eventually, Portugal's war became an international scandal and led to a nonviolent end to its dictatorship in 1974, with Cape Verde gaining full independence a year later. Cape Verde and Guinea-Bissau seriously considered uniting the two countries, but a 1980 coup in Guinea-Bissau ended talks.

Cape Verde Since Independence

On gaining power the PAICV created a one-party state but also instituted a remarkably successful health and education program.

But independence did not solve the problem of drought, and in 1985 disaster struck again. This time the USA and Portugal contributed 85% of the food deficit; their aid continues in a country that produces only about 20% of its food supply.

By the late 1980s there were increasing calls for a multiparty democracy, and in 1990 the PAICV acquiesced, allowing lawyer Carlos Veigo to found the Movimento para a Democracia (MPD). With a centre-right policy of political and economic liberalisation, the MPD swept to power in the 1991 elections. Privatisation and foreign investment – especially in tourism – brought only slow results, however, and in 2001 the PAICV reclaimed power and Pedro Pires became president.

Culture

If you arrive from mainland Africa, the lack of hustle among Cape Verdeans will likely come as a welcome relief. While they are gregarious, you may catch a whiff of a certain distance, even clannishness, due in part to the islands' isolation from the mainland and from each other. The European legacy is more marked here than in most parts of Portuguese-speaking Africa, yet Cape Verdeans will tell you their Crioulo culture is – at its core – African, citing especially their food and music. More recently, the huge expatriate community in the US has had an effect on attitudes, including a growing evangelical community and a general infatuation with the US.

Except for a small class of business owners and professionals who live like their Western counterparts, life in Cape Verde is not easy. Terraced farms require enormous effort and arid weather keeps yields small. While the infrastructure, from roads to water, is rapidly modernising, you will see women and children toting water from common wells. A high percentage of households consists of single mothers with children, a legacy of male-only emigration patterns that dates to the 18th century.

Cape Verde boasts by far the highest GDP per capita (US$3900) in West Africa. The country's literacy rate of 84% is also the highest in the region. Virtually all children of primary-school age attend school, though attendance at secondary schools is considerably lower.

People

Based on the UN's Africa Human Development Report 2012, Cape Verde comes out on top in West Africa. From 1975 to 2011, life expectancy leapt from 46 years to 74 years, far higher than the sub-Saharan African average. The country also has one of the lowest population-growth rates in the region. It's the only country in West Africa with a population of primarily mixed European and African descent. About 40% of the population lives on Santiago – mainly around the capital, Praia. The rest live largely in small towns clustered in the agriculturally productive valleys. As tourism grows, so do the once-tiny populations of arid Sal, Boa Vista and Maio, all of which have seen an influx of foreign residents.

Religion

The vast majority of Cape Verdeans are Roman Catholic. Evangelical Protestantism is making inroads. Traces of African animism remain in the beliefs of even devout Christians.

Arts & Crafts

Traditional crafts include weaving, ceramics, baskets, mat making and batik. Be aware that most craft shops sell objects from the African mainland rather than Cape Verde itself.

While Cape Verde has the smallest population of any country in West Africa, its literary tradition is one of the richest. However, little of that has been translated into anything but Portuguese. Prior to independence, a major theme in Cape Verdean writing was the longing for liberation. Poet, musician and national hero Eugénio Tavares (1867–1930) composed lyrical *mornas* in Crioulo rather than Portuguese. In 1936, a small clique of intellectuals founded a literary journal, *Claridade,* whose goal was to express a growing sense of Cape Verdean identity. Themes of contemporary literature, best expressed by poet Jorge Barbosa's *Arquipélago,* remain constant: *sodade* (longing and/or homesickness), mysteries of the sea and an attempt to come to terms with a history of oppression.

Much of Cape Verdean music evolved as a form of protest against slavery and other types of oppression. Today, two kinds of song dominate traditional Cape Verdean music:

CAPE VERDE CULTURE

mornas and *coladeiras,* both built on the sounds of stringed instruments like the fiddle and guitar. As the name suggests, *mornas* are mournful expressions of *sodade* – an unquenchable longing, often for home. With faster, more upbeat rhythms, *coladeiras,* in contrast, tend to be romantic love songs or else more active expressions of protest. Another popular style is *funaná,* built on fast-paced, Latin-influenced rhythms and underpinned by the accordion. The most African of music and dance styles is *batuko,* with lots of drumming and call-and-respond chanting.

Cesária Évora was hands-down the most famous practitioner of *morna* and *coladeiras.* Contemporary musicians to look for include the ensemble groups Simentera and Ferro Gaita, and singers Maria de Barros and Sara Tavares.

Environment

Cape Verde consists of 10 major islands (nine of them inhabited) and five islets, all of volcanic origin. Though none is more than about 50km from its closest neighbour, they represent a wide array of climates and landscapes. All are arid or semiarid, but the mountainous islands of Brava, Santiago, Fogo, Santo Antão and São Nicolau – all with peaks over 1000m – catch enough moisture to support grasslands as well as fairly intensive agriculture, particularly in windward-facing valleys. Still, only 20% of the land is arable. Maio, Boa Vista and Sal are flatter and almost entirely arid, with long, sandy beaches and desertlike interiors.

Cape Verde has less fauna than just about anywhere in Africa. Birdlife is a little richer (around 75 species), and includes a good number of endemics (38 species). The frigate bird and the extremely rare razo lark are much sought after by twitchers. The grey-headed kingfisher with its strident call is more common.

Divers can see a good range of fish, including tropical species such as parrotfish and angelfish, groupers, barracudas, moray eels and, with luck, manta rays, sharks (including the nurse, tiger and lemon) and marine turtles. Humpback whales breed in these waters; the peak is March and April. Five endangered species of turtle visit the islands on their way across the Atlantic. Cape Verde has the world's third-largest loggerhead turtle nesting population. Nesting takes place from June to October.

Environmental Issues

The greatest threats to the environment remain cyclical drought and soil erosion, exacerbated by deforestation and overgrazing – mostly by goats. To combat these problems, the country has constructed more than 15,000 contour ditches and 2500km of dams, and since the 1970s has been implementing a major reforestation program. On some islands, notably Santo Antão, Maio, Santiago and parts of Fogo, the tree cover has noticeably increased over the past couple of decades, but on islands like Sal a tree remains as rare as a rainy day. Overfishing is another issue to contend with.

Food & Drink

While Cape Verdean cuisine may include Portuguese niceties such as imported olives and Alentejo wines, it's built on a firm African base, with *milho* (corn) and *feijão* (beans) the ubiquitous staples. To these the

CESÁRIA ÉVORA

Undisputed queen of the *morna* and Cape Verde's most famous citizen, Cesária Évora wowed the world with a voice at once densely textured and disarmingly direct. She began to gain an international audience in the mid-1990s but vaulted to stardom in 1997 when, at the second annual all-African music awards, she ran away with three of the top gongs, including best female vocalist. Suddenly people around the world were swaying to the rhythms of Cape Verde's music, even if they couldn't point the country out on a map. Évora left her native Mindelo in favour of Paris, but the 'barefoot diva' never put on airs; she was known to appear onstage accompanied by a bottle of booze and a pack of ciggies. When she died at 70 in 2011, after a bout of illness, Cape Verde declared two days of national mourning and the Mindelo airport was renamed in her honour. Her music legacy very much lives on.

locals add *arroz* (rice), *batatas fritas* (fried potatoes) and *mandioca* (cassava). From the sea come excellent *atum* (tuna), *garoupa* (grouper), *serra* (sawfish) and *lagosta* (lobster). Other protein sources include *ovos* (eggs), *frango* (chicken) and, with increasing rarity, *cabrito* (goat), *porco* (grilled pork) and *carne de vaca* (beef). Vegetables – often *cenoura* (carrots), *couve* (kale) and *abóbora* (squash) – come in *caldeirada* (meat or fish stews), or simply steamed.

Meals tend to be very simple wherever you go: a piece of grilled or fried meat or fish, accompanied by rice or *xerém* (corn meal) and your choice of steamed vegetables or French fries. Practically nowhere will you pay less than CVE600, yet even the fanciest place will rarely charge more than CVE1100 (except for beef and shellfish, which cost significantly more). The classic dish is the ubiquitous *cachupa,* which consists of beans and corn mixed with whatever scraps of fish or meat that might be around. For those with a sweet tooth there are concoctions of *cóco* (coconut), *papaia* (papaya) and banana, as well as flanlike *pudim* of either *leite* (milk) or *queijo* (soft goat cheese).

Thanks to the large number of Italian tourists and expats, some reasonable pizza and pasta dishes are starting to appear on even the most out-of-the-way menus.

For drinks, there's *grogue,* the local sugar cane spirit; *ponch* (rum, lemonade and honey); some reasonable wines from Fogo (the white and rosé are the best); Strela, a decent bottled local beer; and, of course, Portuguese beers and wines. A decent caffeine fix is available everywhere (coffee even grows on the slopes of Mt Fogo and on Santo Antão), but tea is harder to find.

SURVIVAL GUIDE

❶ Directory A–Z

ACCOMMODATION

By West African standards, accommodation is expensive in Cape Verde, especially on Sal and Boa Vista and in Praia, where prices are some 30% more than in the rest of the country.

Most other places, you can expect to pay under CVE4000 for a basic but decent double with shared bathroom.For around CVE4000 to CVE9000, you can expect a comfortable mid-range double with hot water, TV and air-con.At

the top end, there are mostly resort hotels that cater to package tours, especially on Sal and Boa Vista.

There are no campsites, but camping on remote beaches, and on Santa Luzia, is possible and generally safe (except on Sal, Boa Vista and Santiago).

All rates listed include breakfast and VAT, unless otherwise stated.

ACTIVITIES

The main draws are windsurfing and kitesurfing, scuba diving and deep-sea fishing on Sal and Boa Vista.

There is trekking in the mountains of São Nicolau, Brava, Fogo and especially Santo Antão.

Surfing is growing in popularity on Sal and Santiago, though in both cases the waves are quite inconsistent.

Diving in Cape Verde is well known for the diversity of species that can be seen, plus a few wrecks; dolphins, whales, sharks and rays are all occasionally seen. Because of currents, not all sites are suitable for beginners or inexperienced divers. Note that there is currently no decompression chamber in Cape Verde. The best months are from March to November; Sal and Boa Vista are the best-organised places in which to dive.

Windsurfing and kiteboarding conditions are among the best in the world on Sal, Boa Vista and lesser-known Maio. Ponta Preta on Sal is a world-famous break. The best months are between mid-November and mid-May (particularly

January to March, when winds are strong and constant).

April to November (especially June to October) is good for fishing (rays, barracudas, marlins, wahoos and sharks).

Trekking and cycling are good year-round.

BOOKS

Publications in English about Cape Verde are scarce but include the *Historical Dictionary of the Republic of Cape Verde* by Richard Lobban, *Cape Verde: Politics, Economics and Society* by Colm Foy, *Antonio's Island: Cape Verde* by Marcelo Gomes Balla and *The Fortunate Isles* by Basil Davidson.

EMBASSIES & CONSULATES

French Embassy (☎ 2604511; Rua Manuel Duarte, Prainha) In Praia.

Portuguese Embassy (☎ 2626097; Avenida da OUA, Achada de Santo António) Also in Mindelo, São Vicente.

Senegalese Embassy (☎ 2615621; Rua Abilio Macedo) In Praia.

US Embassy (☎ 2608900; Rua Abilio Macedo 6) In Praia.

FESTIVALS & EVENTS

Cape Verde's main festivals include Mardi Gras (also known as Creole Carnival), which is held all over Cape Verde in February or March, the largest occurring in Mindelo (São Vicente); Nhô São Filipe (Fogo), held on 1 May; and the Festival de Música, held in Baía das Gatas (São Vicente) in August.

INTERNET ACCESS

The main towns of each island, and even other good-sized towns, have internet cafes with cheap and fast connections.

The main town squares on all major islands have free wi-fi.

Note that many hotels, even the upscale ones, charge for wi-fi.

INTERNET RESOURCES

Bela Vista (www.bela-vista.net) Travel and tourism-related info.

Cabo Verde (www.caboverde.com) Comprehensive tourism listings in English, Portuguese and Italian.

Cabo Verde 24 (www.caboverde24.com) General tourist information on the islands.

EMERGENCY

Fire (☎ 131)

Medical assistance (☎ 130)

Police (☎ 132)

MAPS

A good map of the islands is the German-produced AB Karten-Verlag *Cabo Verde* (1:200,000; 2001).

An excellent hiking map for Santo Antão is the (also German) *Goldstadt Wanderkarte* (1:50,000; 2001) with around 40 suggested walks. The same company also produces maps to several other islands.

MONEY

The unit of currency is the Cape Verde escudo (CVE), divided into 100 centavos. Though not a hard currency, it's stable; in January 2002 it was pegged to the euro. Most businesses also accept euros.

Banks are found in all the main towns and even some of the smaller ones; most have ATMs that accept bankcards and Visa (daily withdrawal limit is CVE20,000).

Many banks change travellers cheques and cash in all the main currencies (except the West African CFA franc).

Credit cards are not widely accepted; Visa is the most widespread. Even where accepted, there's typically a 3% to 5% commission for credit-card payments.

OPENING HOURS

Note that for posted hours days are often numbered according to the Portuguese system from 1º to 7º (1º is Sunday, 7º is Saturday).

Banks From 8am to 3pm Monday to Friday.

Businesses Generally 8am to noon and 3pm to 6pm Monday to Friday, and 8am to noon or 1pm Saturday.

Restaurants Mostly open from around noon to 3pm and 7pm to 10pm.

POST

The postal service is cheap, reliable and reasonably quick.

Correios (post offices) are generally open 8am to 3pm Monday to Friday and on Saturday mornings in Praia and Mindelo.

PUBLIC HOLIDAYS

New Year's Day 1 January
National Heroes' Day 20 January
Labour Day 1 May
Independence Day 5 July
Assumption Day 15 August
All Saints' Day 1 November
Immaculate Conception 8 December
Christmas Day 25 December

SAFE TRAVEL

Violent crime is on the rise in Praia, where it's highly advisable to take taxis at night, no matter where and how far you're going. Take cau-

PRACTICALITIES

➡ **Electricity** Voltage is 220V with European-style twin-pronged plugs.

➡ **Language** Portuguese is the official language. Most Cape Verdeans speak Crioulo, an African-inflected version of medieval Portuguese, as their first language. French is widely understood; English is not.

➡ **Newspapers** *A Semana*, *A Naçao* and *Expresso das Ilhas* are the weekly newspapers.

➡ **Radio & TV** Mostly limited to Portugal's, with Portuguese and Brazilian shows as well as Cape Verde news.

tion in Mindelo, too, where pickpocketing and muggings are not uncommon.

Some hiking trails have become sites of banditry in recent years, as on Boa Vista and around Tarrafal on Santiago; always ask locals before you set out.

The rest of the country is very safe, though petty crime like pickpocketing is always a possibility.

TELEPHONE

Every number for a fixed telephone line in Cape Verde has seven digits; all landlines start with '2'. No area code is necessary. The country code is ☎238.

Public telephone booths are fairly plentiful, but you'll need a phonecard (available in CVE50/150 denominations at any post office and many small shops).

Post offices often have call centres as well, which can be more convenient for expensive international calls, which start at around CVE200 per minute.

For better deals, keep an eye out for internet-based calling centres, which charge as little as CVE15 per minute to Europe.

Mobile phone reception is excellent. Mobile phone numbers are seven digits.

If bringing a phone from home with roaming facilities it will connect automatically; note that Cape Verde is not on the GPRS system, so internet phones will not work here.

Local SIM cards (from CVE50) are available at all mobile phone offices and will work with unlocked phones.

VISAS

All visitors (except holders of some African passports) require a visa.

Within West Africa, Dakar (Senegal) is one of the few places where you can get one.

A one-month tourist visa can be obtained without any problems on arrival at the airports and at the ports of Praia and Sal. It costs €25 (payable in euros only – don't expect change to be available).

Technically, there's a fine of CVE15,000 if you let your visa expire; in reality, if you're only a little over nobody is likely to care.

For an extension you need, in theory, to fill in a form, supply a photo and lodge the application at the **Direcção de Emigração e Fronteiras** (Rua Serpa Pinto, Praia); in reality, staff members here are likely to be highly confused if you turn up requesting an extension!

Visas for Senegal can be obtained at that country's embassy in Praia. They cost around CVE500 and take up to 48 hours to process.

WOMEN TRAVELLERS

Cape Verde is one of the safest countries in West Africa for solo women travellers – no special precautions are required.

🅸 Getting There & Away

ENTERING CAPE VERDE

Proof of yellow-fever vaccination is only required if you are coming from an infected area.

AIR

Most international flights land on Sal, though Praia and Boa Vista are seeing an increasing amount of international activity and São Vicente recently started receiving international flights.

TACV has five weekly flights to Lisbon from Praia and one weekly from Sal, São Vicente and Boa Vista. There are also weekly nonstop flights to Boston, Amsterdam, Fortaleza, Paris, Dakar and Bissau.

TAP has daily flights from Lisbon to Praia in peak season (five weekly otherwise), six weekly to Sal and two weekly to São Vicente.

Various charter flights fly to Sal and Boa Vista from the UK, Germany and Italy. These are generally the cheapest way of getting to the islands. See www.thomson.co.uk and www.tuifly.com for more.

From West Africa, TACV flies between Praia and Dakar (Senegal) three to four times weekly. Sénégal Airlines has four flights weekly to/from Dakar, with connections to most major West African cities.

Sénégal Airlines (☎2633249; www.senegal airlines.aero; Rua Serpa Pinto, Praia)

TACV (☎2608200; www.flytacv.com; Rua Serpa Pinto 5, Praia)

TAP (☎2615826; www.flytap.com; Praia International Airport)

ℹ Getting Around

AIR

TACV serves all the inhabited islands except Brava and Santo Antão.

Internal flights are slightly cheaper (note that we said cheaper, not cheap) if you buy tickets in Cape Verde.

If you're taking two or more internal flights, you may want to purchase TACV's Cabo Verde AirPass (available from travel agencies abroad but not in Cape Verde). You have to arrive by TACV to qualify.

Note that flights are regularly cancelled, often without passengers being advised. Always reconfirm your flight one day before.

If flights are full it's well worth flying standby as no-shows are common.

The cheapest TACV flights are at least CVE4500; the run between Praia and São Vicente, for example, is at least CVE7500.

BOAT

There are boat connections to all nine inhabited islands, although most on are cargo ships and not fit for passengers.

The only reliable scheduled services are between Praia, Brava and Fogo, and between Mindelo (São Vicente) and Santo Antão.

Seas can be rough and the crossings rocky, especially during winter months.

There are cafes on board the bigger boats, but it's always a good idea to bring a reserve of water and snacks.

CAR

You can rent cars on many islands, but the only three that make the expense worth it are Santiago, Boa Vista and possibly Fogo.

Consider a 4WD, especially on Boa Vista, as conditions are rough once you get off the few main roads.

Cars cost from CVE5500 per day, including tax and insurance. As tourism grows, international car-rental agencies are setting up shop. Check at airports upon arrival.

MINIBUS & TAXI

Ranging from comfortable vans to pick-up trucks with narrow wooden benches, *aluguers* provide connections between even relatively small towns on most islands. They pick up people at unmarked points around town, set off when they're more or less full, and drop passengers off anywhere on the way, on request.

Taxis are generally plentiful, with round-town fares rarely topping CVE500.

Airport runs and excursions are more costly.

Hitching is easy, though payment is sometimes expected. It's usually safe, but be aware of the possible risks.

Côte d'Ivoire

📞 225 / POP 21.9 MILLION

Best Places to Eat

➡ Aboussouan (p141)

➡ Mille Maquis (p139)

➡ Des Gateaux et Du Pain (p141)

Best Places to Stay

➡ La Licorne (p139)

➡ Beneath the forest canopy, Parc National de Taï (p147)

➡ Le Wafou (p139)

Why Go?

Blighted by recent conflict but bejewelled by beaches and rainforests, it would be a shame to sidestep Cote d'Ivoire because of its baggage.

Cote d'Ivoire is a stunner, shingled with starfish-studded sands, and forest roads so orange they resemble strips of bronzing powder.

In the south, the Parc National de Taï hides secrets, species and nut-cracking chimps under the boughs of its trees, while the peaks and valleys of Man offer a highland climate, fresh air and local art.

The beach resorts of low-key Assinie and arty Grand Bassam were made for weekend retreats from Abidjan, the capital in all but name, where lagoons wind their way between skyscrapers and cathedral spires pierce the blue heavens.

When to Go
Abidjan

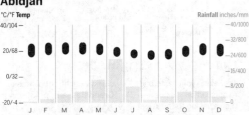

May–Jul Storms to rival those in Oct–Nov; be prepared for buckets of rain and lightning.

Jun–Oct Wet in the north but humid with bursts of rain in the south. Temperatures about 28°C.

Dec–Feb Prime beach season, with temperatures hitting 30°C and not a cloud in the sky.

ABIDJAN

POP 4.5 MILLION

Côte d'Ivoire's economic engine is strapped between lagoons and waterways, overlooking the crested waves of the Atlantic. At first glimpse, you wonder if these shiny scrapers can really be in West Africa.

Although Abidjan took a beating during the 2011 crisis, the engine rattled on, and new bars, bistros and hotels are opening regularly; this is, after all, one of Africa's sleekest party cities.

◉ Sights

Abidjan gets props for its breathtaking skyline. It all started with **La Pyramide** (Map p142; cnr Ave Franchet d'Esperey & Blvd Botreau-Roussel), by the Italian architect Olivieri.

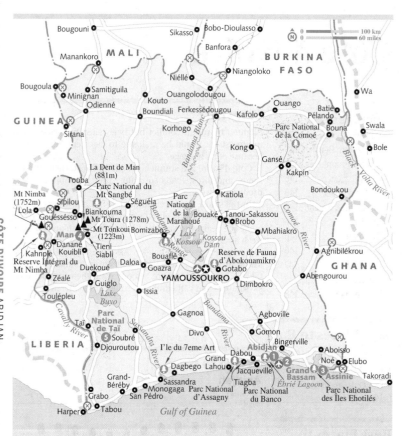

Côte d'Ivoire Highlights

① Taking your taste buds to *poisson braisé* heaven then swaying to the sweet sounds of *coupé-décalé* in the shadow of the stunning skyline in **Abidjan** (p138).

② Tapping into Côte d'Ivoire's artistic vibe, visiting galleries and the quirky beachfront bistros of **Grand Bassam** (p143).

③ Lazing in a *pirogue*, watching surfers slide to shore and tucking into fresh seafood under the stars of **Assinie** (p146).

④ Hiking to the point where three West African countries converge and feasting upon the green fields below, home to mask and jewellery makers, in **Man** (p147).

⑤ Exploring the dense **Parc National de Taï** (p147), home to a colony of nut-cracking chimps.

Cathedrale St Paul
CHURCH

(Map p140; Blvd Angoulvant, Le Plateau; ☺8am-7pm) FREE Designed by the Italian Aldo Spiritom, the Cathedrale St Paul is a bold and innovative modern cathedral. The stained glasswork is as warm and rich as that inside the Yamoussoukro basilica.

Musée National
MUSEUM

(Map p140; Blvd Nangul Abrogoua, Le Plateau; admission CFA2000; ☺9am-5pm Tue-Sat) This museum houses an interesting collection of traditional art and craftwork, including wooden statues and masks, pottery, ivory and bronze.

🛏 Sleeping

La Nouvelle Pergola
HOTEL $

(✐21-753501; Blvd de Marseille/Rue Pierre et Marie Curie; d CFA30,000; ✱🛜🏊) For reasonable rooms on a budget, La Nouvelle Pergola is an OK bet. There are over 130 rooms in this complex, which includes a pool and nightclub, and there's wi-fi and the usual creature comforts, although few of Côte d'Ivoire's charms.

Le Marly
BUNGALOW $$

(✐21-258552; Blvd de Marseille, Zone 4; s/d/ste CFA40,000/50,000/60,000; P✱🏊) Le Marly offers simple plantation-style huts in a pretty garden setting. At the end of a short track just off Blvd de Marseille.

Hotel Onomo
HOTEL $$

(✐08-939377; Blvd de l'Aéroport Félix Houphouet Boigny; d from CFA51,000) Within spitting distance of the airport, the Onomo – a chain hotel present in several African cities – is a reliable bet regardless of whether you have an early flight to catch. The rooms are sleek and comfortable, with a nod to local style, and there's fast wi-fi, a good restaurant and midrange hotel service.

⭐ La Licorne
BOUTIQUE HOTEL $$

(Map p140; ✐22-410730; www.licogriff.com; Rue des Jardins, Deux Plateaux Vallons; r CFA55,000-70,000; P✱@🛜🏊) La Licorne, like its sister hotel Le Griffon around the corner, is a pretty boutique hotel run by a friendly French family. Rooms are individually decorated, and there's wi-fi, a bar, a hot tub, book exchange and a decent restaurant.

⭐ Le Wafou
BOUTIQUE HOTEL $$$

(✐21-256201; Blvd de Marseille, Zone 4; standard r/ste CFA55,000/125,000; P✱🛜🏊) If the Flintstones won the lottery and moved to West Africa, they'd live somewhere like this. Set in large grounds, Le Wafou's gorgeous bungalows take cues from traditional Dogon villages in neighbouring Mali. At night you can enjoy great food and wine poolside. A hit with kids, too.

Novotel
HOTEL $$$

(✐20-318000; www.novotel.com; 10 Ave du Général de Gaulle; r from CFA70,000; P✱@🛜🏊) During the 2011 conflict, soldiers loyal to ex-leader Laurent Gbagbo stormed the Novotel, terrorising journalists sheltering inside. Don't let that dissuade you from staying here; there's a reason the Novotel was their place of choice, including smart rooms, four-star amenities and a large outdoor pool, all in the heart of Le Plateau. And great security.

Le Pullman
HOTEL $$$

(Map p142; ✐20-302020; www.sofitel.com; Rue Abdoulaye Fadiga, Le Plateau; r from CFA115,000; P✱@🛜🏊) This is the best of the upmarket chain hotels. Plush rooms equipped with wi-fi and everything you could possibly need.

🍴 Eating

Don't miss **Mille Maquis** (Map p140), an energy-infused local strip of *maquis* (rustic open-air restaurants) offering fresh Ivorian dishes served with a side of banter, at Place de la République and at Treicheville's Maquis Rue 19. There are two useful supermarkets: **Cash Center** (Map p142) and **Hypermarché Sococé** (Map p140; Blvd Latrille).

ⓘ SET YOUR BUDGET

Budget
➡ Basic hotel room CFA12,00
➡ Plate of *poisson braisé* CFA800
➡ Coffee from street vendor CFA200
➡ Shared taxi in Abidjan CFA300

Midrange
➡ Room with air-con CFA30,000
➡ Two-course meal CFA12,000
➡ Glass of wine CFA3000
➡ Private taxi hire, per hour CFA3500

Top End
➡ Hotel room with mod cons CFA60,000
➡ Meal for two with wine and dessert CFA50,000
➡ Cocktail in nightclub CFA5500
➡ 4x4 rental per day CFA65,000, plus petrol

CÔTE D'IVOIRE ABIDJAN

Abidjan

N
0 _____ 2 km
0 _____ 1 mile

CÔTE D'IVOIRE ABIDJAN

Blvd Latrille

Shared Taxis
for Adjamé
5

@
13

Rue de Williamsville

SGBCI Bank
& ATM
Rue J40

8
3

To Yopougon
(6.8km)

Train
Station

Shared Taxis for
Grand Bassam

11

To Bingerville
(16km)

LES DEUX
PLATEAUX

Blvd de Gaulle

Blvd Mitterrand

ADJAMÉ

Ave Mermoz

RIVIERA

Marché
d'Adjamé

7
12

Blvd de France
4

Marché de
Cocody

COCODY

2
1

Rue Washington

Ave Aka

10

Ébrié
Lagoon

See Le Plateau
Map (p142)

9

LE PLATEAU

Ébrié
Lagoon

Blvd Achalma
6

Train
Station

Gare de
Marcory
(Sotra)

Palais de
la Culture

MARCORY

Blvd du Cameroun

Marché de
Treichville

TREICHVILLE

Train
Station

14
Blvd Valéry Giscard d'Estaing

ZONE 4

Ave de la TSF

STC Bus Station
(Buses to Ghana)

To Félix Houphouët-
Boigny Airport (16km)

Blvd de Marseille

Agence Catran
(1.5km)

To American
Embassy (2km)

Rue des Jardins

Blvd Nangui Abrogoua

Abidjan

◉ Sights

◉ Sleeping

◉ Eating

◉ Entertainment

◉ Shopping

◉ Information

◉ Transport

Allocodrome AFRICAN $
(Map p140; Rue Washington, Cocody; mains around CFA2000; ☉dinner) *Brochettes* (kebabs), beer and beats: this fantastic outdoor spot, with dozens of vendors grilling meats, sizzles until late.

Urban Chic CAFE $
(Rue du Docteur Blanchard; mains from CFA4500; ❄🏵) Get past the sultry scarlet lounge seating and you'll find a great lunch and dinner menu, and an even better Saturday brunch one.

Le Nandjelet AFRICAN $
(opposite cemetery, Blockosso; mains from CFA2000; ☉dinner) Tucked away in Blockosso, this enchanting local spot offers good, basic fare. Make a beeline for one of the outdoor tables on the edge of the lagoon – they offer a breathtaking panorama of the Abidjan skyline.

★ Des Gateaux et Du Pain BAKERY $
(☎22-415538; Rue des Jardins, Deux Plateaux; ☉7am-8pm Mon-Sat; 🏵) Around the corner from La Licorne and Le Griffon hotels, this patisserie does exactly what it says: great freshly baked breads, chocolate puddings and divine fruit-topped cakes.

★ Aboussouan AFRICAN $$
(☎21-241309; Blvd Giscard-D'Estaing, Treichville; mains from CFA8000; ☉lunch & dinner Tue-Sat; 🏵) Take Côte d'Ivoire's best *maquis* dishes, ask top chefs to prepare them and add fine, innovative touches: that's Aboussouan. Foodie heaven, and there's an excellent wine list too.

Abidjan Cafe FRENCH $$
(Map p142; ☎20-224434; Rue Gourgas; mains from CFA7500; ☉lunch & dinner Tue-Sat; P🏵📶✎) This Plateau dining hall has a good French menu featuring everything from local grilled fish to *fois gras* and *créme brûlèe* infused with Nutella.

Hippopotamus FRENCH $$
(Map p142; Ave Chardy, Plateau; mains from CFA5000; ☉noon-11pm Mon-Sun; 🏵) French bistro chain Hippopotamus has swung its meaty hips onto the Abidjan restaurant scene: come for *steak frites*, cocktails and the best burgers in town.

🍷 Drinking & Nightlife

Parker Place BAR
(☎06-643381; Rue Paul Langevin, Zone 4; ☉evening Tue-Sun) Abidjan's most famous reggae bar, Alpha Blondy and Tikin Jah Fakoly played here before they were famous. The bar is still going strong and welcomes live acts most Thursday, Friday and Saturday nights (there's usually a cover charge).

Le Bidule BAR
(cnr Blvd du 7 Decembre & Rue Paul Langevin, Zone 4) Expats and travellers congregate here on weekends. It's a drinking lounge with walls the colour of Ivorian soil.

L'Acoustic LIVE MUSIC
(Rue des Jardins, Deux Plateaux) L'Acoustic's stage has held the feet of everyone from hip female vocalists to jazz and big-band ensembles. The place attracts an arty, music crowd. There's also a kitchen for late-night dinners.

La Mostra CLUB
(☎48-378709) Inside the Cafe de Rome complex (which also includes a hotel and a casino), La Mostra is a mainstay on the Abidjan clubbing scene, which otherwise changes regularly. Mingle with models and party people; a night here doesn't run cheap.

🛍 Shopping

Galerie d'Arts Pluriels ARTS & CRAFTS
(Map p140; ☎22-411506; Rue des Jardins, Deux Plateaux) This fantastic art gallery and shop is run by an Ivorian art historian. You can view

Le Plateau

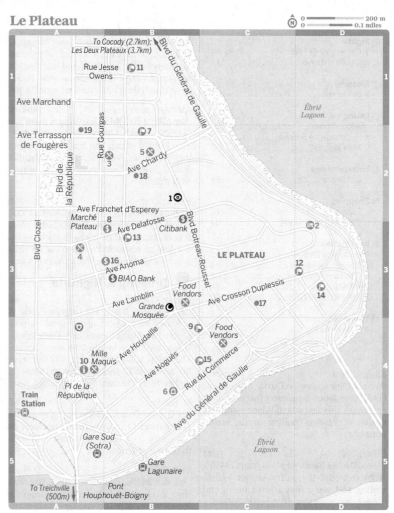

0 ———————— 200 m
0 ———————— 0.1 miles

To Cocody (2.7km);
Les Deux Plateaux (3.7km)

Blvd du Général de Gaulle

Rue Jesse Owens

Ave Marchand

Ave Terrasson de Fougères

Rue Gourgas

Ébrié Lagoon

Ave Chardy

Ave Franchet d'Esperey

Marché Plateau

Ave Delafosse

Citibank

Blvd de la République

Blvd Botreau-Roussel

Blvd Clozel

LE PLATEAU

Ave Anoma

BIAO Bank

Ave Lamblin

Food Vendors

Ave Crosson-Duplessis

Grande Mosquée

Ave Houdaille

Food Vendors

Ave Nogués

Mille Maquis

Rue du Commerce

Pl de la République

Train Station

Ave du Général de Gaulle

Gare Sud (Sotra)

Ébrié Lagoon

Gare Lagunaire

To Treichville (500m)

Pont Houphouët-Boigny

CÔTE D'IVOIRE ABIDJAN

and buy paintings, sculptures and jewellery from all over the continent.

Espace Latrille　　　DEPARTMENT STORE
(Map p140; Deux Plateaux) Contains a range of stores including the revered Hypermarché Sococé.

Woodin　　　CLOTHING
(Map p142; ☑ 20-310565; Rue du Commerce, Le Plateau) This is part of a highly regarded West African group that sells quality wax-clothing. Great for gifts.

ℹ Information

INTERNET ACCESS

Most hotels, and a growing number of restaurants and bars, offer wi-fi.

Inkoo (☑ 21-247065; Cap Sud Centre Commercial & Gallerie Sococé, Deux Plateaux; ☉ 9am-8pm) Speedy connections, a printing centre, phone booths, faxes and scanners.

MEDICAL SERVICES

The US embassy publishes a list of recommended practitioners on its website (http://abidjan.usembassy.gov).

Le Plateau

Polyclinique des Deux Plateaux (Map p140; ☑ 22-413320; Deux Plateaux)

PISAM (Polyclinique Internationale St Anne-Marie; ☑ 22-445132; off Blvd de la Corniche, Cocody) Recommended by UN staff. Has a 24-hour intensive-care unit.

MONEY

Euros and dollars can be changed at main branches of banks in Le Plateau. Most branches of SGBCI and Bicici have ATMs that accept Visa, MasterCard and Maestro.

Bicici Bank (Map p142; www.bibici.org; Ave Delafosse) Has an ATM.

SGBCI Bank (Map p142; www.sgbci.org; Ave Anoma) Good ATM option – accepts Visa, MasterCard and Maestro.

POST & TELEPHONE

For postal services, head to **La Poste** (Pl de la République; ⊙7.30am-noon & 2.30-4pm Mon-Fri), which also has a Western Union and poste restante. Mobile phone SIM cards are sold on the roadside all around town (from CFA2000). Inkoo has phone booths for local, national and international calls.

TOURIST INFORMATION

Côte d'Ivoire Tourisme (Map p142; ☑20-251610, 20-251600; Pl de la République, Le Plateau; ⊙7.30am-noon & 2.30-4pm Mon-Fri) There's a good map on the wall and the helpful staff will happily shower you with brochures.

TRAVEL AGENCIES

Agence Catran (☑21-759163; Blvd de Marseille, Zone 4)

Amak Agence (☑20-211755; www.amak-international.com; ground fl, Botreau Roussel Bldg, Le Plateau)

ℹ Getting There & Away

The shiny Félix Houphouët-Boigny International Airport takes all of the international air traffic. The main bus station is the chaotic Gare Routière d'Adjamé, some 4km north of Le Plateau. Most UTB and Sotra buses and bush taxis leave from here, and there's frequent transport to all major towns.

Bush taxis and minibuses for destinations east along the coast, such as Grand Bassam, Aboisso and Elubo at the Ghanaian border, leave primarily from the **Gare de Bassam** (Map p140; cnr Rue 38 & Blvd Valéry Giscard d'Estaing), south of Treichville.

ℹ Getting Around

Woro-woro (shared taxis) cost between CFA300 and CFA800, depending on the length of the journey. They vary in colour according to their allocated area. Those between Plateau, Adjamé, Marcory and Treichville, for example, are red, while those in Les Deux Plateaux and Cocody are yellow, and Yopougon's are blue.

A short hop in a cab from Le Plateau to Zone 4 costs around CFA2000. If you want to hire a taxi driver for a day, bank on anywhere between CFA15,000 and CFA30,000 depending on the strength of your negotiating skills (and the state of the economy).

THE EASTERN BEACHES

Grand Bassam

Arty and bathed in faded glory, beachside Bassam was Côte d'Ivoire's former French capital, until a yellow-fever epidemic broke out there, prompting the French to move their capital to Bingerville.

The city is laid out on a long spit of land with a quiet lagoon on one side and the turbulent Atlantic Ocean on the other. If you take a dip, watch the strong currents.

◉ Sights

A walk through town will take you past the colonial buildings the city is known for; some have been restored, while others are slowly falling apart. The Palais de Justice (Blvd Treich-Laplene) should be your first stop. Built in 1910, it was in this building that members of Côte d'Ivoire's PDCI-RDA political group – that of Houphouët-Boigny – were arrested by the French authorities in 1949, in the struggle that preceded independence. The Musée National du Costume (Blvd Treich-Laplene; admission by donation), in the former governor's palace, has a nice little exhibit showing housing styles of various ethnic groups.

If you're in the market for an Ivorian painting, head to Nick Amon's art gallery (Blvd Treich-Laplene). One of Côte d'Ivoire's most respected contemporary artists, he'll greet you with paint-splattered clothing and a warm smile. His canvases start at around CFA50,000; profits go to an organisation that gives street kids art classes.

Augustin Édou runs a horse-riding school (Blvd Treich-Laplene). You can arrange riding trips (one/two hours for CFA13,000/20,000) along the coast at sunrise. Dugout-canoe trips to see traditional crab fishers, mangroves and birdlife can be arranged with local boatmen.

🛏 Sleeping & Eating

There are guesthouses spread all along Blvd Treich-Laplene, Bassam's main road.

COUPÉ-DECALÉ: CUT & RUN

Picture the scene: it's 2002 and you're at the swish l'Atlantic nightclub in Paris. Around you, tight-shirted Ivorian guys are knocking back Champagne, throwing euros into the air and grinding their hips on the dance floor.

Coupé-decalé is one of the most important music movements to hit Côte d'Ivoire. From the French verb *couper*, meaning to cheat, and *decaler*, to run away, the term loosely translates as 'cut and run'. It evolved as a comment on the shrewd but stylish Ivorian and Burkinabé guys – modern-day Robin Hoods, if you like – who fled to France at the height of the conflict in 2002, where they garnered big bucks and sent money home to their families.

They splashed the rest of their cash on the Paris club scene. It wasn't unusual for them to shower audiences with crisp notes. The late Douk Saga, one of the founders of the movement, was famous for wearing two designer suits to his shows. Halfway through, he'd strip provocatively and throw one into the crowd.

Soon this music genre took off in Côte d'Ivoire, becoming increasingly popular as the conflict raged on. With curfews in place and late-night venues closed, Ivorians started going dancing in the mornings. The more that normal life was suppressed, the more they wanted to break free from the shackles of war. *Coupé-decalé*, the who-gives-a-damn dance, allowed them to do exactly that.

Early *coupé-decalé* was characterised by repetitive vocals set to fast, jerky beats. Lyrics were either superficial, facetious or flippant – 'we don't know where we're going, but we're going anyway', sang DJ Jacab. As the trend has matured, *coupé-decalé* lyrics have become smarter, more socially aware and dripping with double and triple entendres. The movement is now a national source of pride and, above all, a comment on Ivorian society; despite years of conflict, misery and fear, Ivorians have never stopped dancing.

Today's *coupé-decalé* is cheeky, crazy and upbeat, and to fully appreciate it you should get yourself to an Abidjan dance floor. Tracks to seek out include Bablée's 'Sous Les Cocotiers', Kaysha's 'Faut Couper Decaler', 'Magic Ambiance' by Magic System, DJ Jacab's 'On Sait Pas Ou On Va', 'Guantanamo' by DJ Zidane and Douk Saga's 'Sagacité'. The latter spawned the Drogbacité dance craze, inspired by the footballer Didier Drogba. In 2006 DJ Lewis' hugely popular 'Grippe Aviaire' did for bird flu what early *coupé-decalé* did for the conflict – it replaced fear with joy.

Grand Bassam

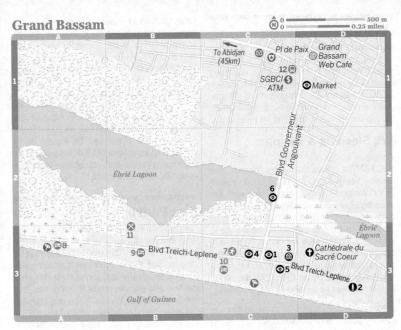

Grand Bassam

Hôtel Boblin la Mer   HOTEL $
(☑ 21-301418; Blvd Treich-Laplene; r with air-con CFA15,000-20,000; P ❄) Breezy and sunwashed, Boblin la Mer is easily the best value in Bassam. The rooms are decorated with masks and woodcarvings, and breakfast is served on the beach.

★**La Madrague**   HOTEL $$
(☑ 21-301564; Blvd Treich-Laplene; d CFA30,000) La Madrague taps into Grand Bassam's spirit, with its smart, lovingly decorated rooms. There's local art on the walls and Ivorian cloth swaddling the luxurious beds, and the humour of the owner is evident in the signs he hangs around the hotel.

Taverne la Bassamoise   BUNGALOW $$
(☑ 21-301062; Blvd Treich-Laplene; r/bungalows incl breakfast CFA29,000/35,000; P ❄ ≋) It's worth a visit just to check out the courtyard – wooden monkeys and parrots hang from every branch of a colossal tree. Bungalows (a little shabby) are hidden underneath a canopy of bougainvillea.

La Playa   AFRICAN $
(Blvd Treich-Laplene; dishes from CFA3000) A *maquis* that does a great line in upmarket versions of Senegalese and Ivorian dishes.

❶ Getting There & Away

Shared taxis (CFA700, 40 minutes) leave from Abidjan's Gare de Bassam. In Bassam, the *gare routière* (bus station) is beside the Pl de Paix roundabout, north of the lagoon.

Assinie

Quiet little Assinie tugs at the heartstrings of overlanders, washed-up surfers and rich weekenders from Abidjan who run their quad bikes up and down its peroxide-blonde beach. It's actually a triumvirate of villages: Assinie village, Assinie Mafia and Assouindé. Watch the rip tides; they can be powerful.

🛏 Sleeping & Eating

Coucoue Lodge   BUNGALOW $$
(☑ 07-077769; www.coucouelodge.blogspot.com; weekday/weekend d CFA65,000/85,000; P ❄ 🛜 ⚟) Colourful wooden bungalows spill out onto acres of white sand at Coucoue Lodge, a sweet getaway spot. If lounging on the beach or in the luxury rooms doesn't cut it, you can slice through the ocean on jet skis, rent inflatables or play a round of golf. The restaurant has a nice wine list, and there's a nightclub onsite (from the villas, the music is drowned out by the sound of the waves).

L'Eden   BUNGALOW $$
(☑ 05-780934; s/d CFA30,000/45,000; ❄ 🛜) Laid-back L'Eden is one of Assinie's sweetest spots, sandwiched between the beach and Assinie Mafia. A good bet for a relaxed weekend away with friends, there's nice Ivorian fare on offer and cool, calm, clean, comfortable rooms.

Akwa Beach   VILLA $$
(☑ 08 833 374; www.akwa-beach.com; d CFA45,000; P ❄ 🛜 ⚟) On the beach between Assinie and Assouindé, Akwa has sleek, comfortable rooms housed in modern whitewashed villas. There's a restaurant serving upscale French fare and a pool area with stylish beach furniture.

❶ Getting There & Around

Coming from Grand Bassam or Abidjan, take a shared taxi to Samo (CFA2000, 45 minutes). From here you can pick up another car to Assouindé, 15 minutes away. Once there, the rest of the area is accessible by *pirogue* (traditional canoe) or shared taxi.

THE WEST COAST

Sassandra & Around

Sassandra, a low-key beach resort in the far-western corner of Côte d'Ivoire, may be a little dog-eared these days, but there's some-

thing endearing – and enduring – here, for travellers keep going back. Perhaps it's the warm welcome at the gorgeous **Best of Africa** (☑ 34-720606; best@bestofafrica.org; bungalows CFA40,000-60,000; P ❄ @) resort, 35km east of Sassandra at Dagbego. The owners can help arrange trips in the area.

In Sassandra itself, **Hôtel le Pollet** (☑ 34-720578; lepollet@hotmail.fr; Rte du Palais de Justice; ☀ r/ste CFA17,000/38,000; ❄) overlooks the Sassandra River and **La Route de la Cuisine** (meals from CFA1000) throws the day's catch on the grill, sometimes including swordfish and barracuda.

San Pédro

Framed by a strip of soft, white sand on one side, and the distant shadows of the fertile Parc National de Taï (p147) on the other, a stop in San Pedro promises a sweet marriage of beach life and forest treks. It's also the best place to overnight if you're heading overland into Liberia via Tabou and Harper.

Located in the Balmer area of town, **Les Jardins d'Ivoire** (☑ 34-713186; Quartier Balmer; r CFA25,000; P ❄ ⚟) has a pretty garden, swimming pool and clean, smart rooms. **Le Cannelle** (☑ 34-710539; r CFA25,000) is a little more lively and has rooms in the same price range.

UTB buses link San Pédro with Abidjan once daily (CFA5000). Shared taxis go west to the balmy **beaches** of Grand-Béréby (CFA2500) and east to Sassandra (CFA3000). For Harper, just across the Liberian border, you can take a shared taxi to Tabou (about CFA4000), then continue on by a combination of road and boat; it's not worth attempting in the rainy season.

THE CENTRE

Yamoussoukro

Yamoussoukro (or Yamkro, as it's affectionately dubbed) isn't exactly its country's cultural epicentre, but it is worth a stop here, if only to marvel at the oddity of the capital that was built on the site of former President Félix Houphouët-Boigny's ancestral village.

◉ Sights

Yamoussoukro's spectacular **basilica** (Rte de Daloa; admission CFA2000; ☀ 8am-noon & 2-5.30pm Mon-Sat, 2-5pm Sun) will leave you

PARC NATIONAL DE TAÏ

There are many places in West Africa that could be dubbed one of the region's 'best-kept secrets', but perhaps none so as much as Taï (☎34-712353; www.parc-national-de-tai.org), a 5000-sq-km reserve of rainforest so dense that scientists are only just beginning to discover the wealth of flora and fauna that lies within.

Until about 2009, Taï was off limits due to the presence of militias, who set up camp beneath its birdsong-strung canopies. Now the only camp inside is an eco-camp, the year-round **Touraco Ecotel** (☎34-722299; www.parcnationaltai.com), which has a sprinkling of thatch-topped round huts and a restaurant on the edge of a forest clearing. It's early days; the camp was not yet complete at the time of research, but you can be among the first to discover Taï, taking forest hikes with local rangers, visiting the Hana River, Buya Lake and Mt Niénokoué, where you can stop at the primate research base famous for its nut-cracking chimps.

Taï is 213km from San Pédro; it's about a three-hour drive outside the rainy season. If you have your own vehicle, hit the road until you reach the village of Djouroutou, on the west side of the park. You can also reach Djouroutou via public transport, but it will take longer and you may have to change cars. In theory, there's a **shuttle** (☎34-722299) linking San Pedro to Tai, but you'll need to call ahead and make sure it's functioning before counting on it.

wide-eyed. It remains in tip-top shape, with English-speaking guides on duty. Don't forget to take your passport, which the guard holds until you leave. The **presidential palace**, where Houphouët-Boigny is now buried, can only be seen from afar. Sacred crocodiles live in the lake on its southern side and the keeper tosses them some meat around 5pm. In 2012, a veteran keeper was killed by one of the creatures during a photo op staged for UN peacekeepers.

The **tourist office** (☎30-640814; Ave Houphouët-Boigny; ☀8am-noon & 3-6pm Mon-Fri) arranges Baoulé dancing performances in nearby villages.

🛏 Sleeping & Eating

You'll find *maquis* all over town, concentrated at the *gare routière* and by the lake. The French-owned **Bouclier de Brennus** behind SIB bank serves upmarket Gallic fare with occasional helpings of televised rugby.

Residence Berah   HOTEL **$**
(☎30 64 17 80; r from CFA20,000; P❄🎖🏊) Over in *le quartier des millionaires* (yes, such a thing exists), Residence Berah isn't as swish as its address. But the rooms are clean and modern, with wi-fi and television, and there's a pool and restaurant.

Hôtel Président   HOTEL **$$$**
(☎30-641582; Rte d'Abidjan; s/d/ste US$65/ 80/150; ❄🏊) Yamoussoukro's signature hotel, imposing but faded. Rooms are old

but still swish, and there is an 18-hole golf course, as well as three restaurants (including a panoramic eatery on the 14th floor), four bars and a nightclub.

ⓘ Getting There & Away

MTT and UTB, whose bus stations are south of town, run buses frequently to Abidjan (CFA4500), with the latter also going frequently to Bouaké (CFA3800) and once daily to Man (CFA5000) and San Pédro (CFA6000).

THE NORTH

Man

When you've had your fill of the sun and sand in the south, or the hot winds and dust in the north, head to the green, green peaks and valleys of Man. Here the air is cooler, the food lighter and the landscapes muddier: perfect hiking territory.

For local art, check out the **Tankari Gallery** and **Jacky Gallery** in the centre of town.

Hôtel Amointrin (☎33-792670; Rte du Lycé e Professionel; r standard/superior CFA14,000/16,000; ❄) is probably Man's smartest hotel; the rooms come with hot water and pretty views out over the mountains. The centrally located **Hôtel Leveneur** (☎33-791776; Rue de l'Hôtel Leveneur; r CFA12,000; ❄) has the dishevelled backpacker thing down pat, though we suspect it's not deliberate. Less crumpled, clean and with all mod cons is Goulou Marie (☎ 33-784010; Rte du Lycee; r with air-con from CFA10,000; ❄).

Man has a host of decent maquis – Le Boss and Maquis Jardin Bis (Rte du Lycée Professionnel) both do great attiéké (grated cassava; a slightly bitter couscouslike dish) and brochettes. The Pâtisserie la Brioche (Rue du Commerce; croissants CFA240) is a fine place for breakfast or morning coffee.

You can reach Abidjan by shared taxi (CFA8000) or UTB bus (CFA7000). Taxis for N'zérékoré in Guinea run via Sipilou.

Around Man

If you're considering scaling Mt Tonkoui, give La Dent de Man (Man's Tooth) a shot first. Northeast of town, this steep, molar-shaped mountain hits a height of 881m. Allow at least four hours for the round trip and bring snacks. The hike starts in the village of Zobale, 4km from Man.

At 1223m, Mt Tonkoui is the second-highest peak in Côte d'Ivoire. The views from the summit are breathtaking and extend to Liberia and Guinea, even during the dusty harmattan winds. The route begins about 18km from Man.

The area around Man is also famous for La Cascade (admission CFA300), 5km from town, a crashing waterfall that hydrates a bamboo forest. You walk a pretty paved path to reach it.

One of Man's most celebrated neighbours is Silacoro, about 110km north, which is famous for its stilt dancing.

UNDERSTAND CÔTE D'IVOIRE

Côte d'Ivoire Today

In November 2011 former President Laurent Gbagbo was extradited to The Hague, and charged with war crimes committed during a 2010–11 post-election conflict, in which Gbagbo had contested election results and refused to cede power to current leader Alassane Ouattara. This sparked months of violence that, according to Human Rights Watch, left 3000 people dead and 500,000 homeless. Gbagbo's trial was scheduled to begin in late 2012. Human-rights groups have alleged that

atrocities, including the burning of inhabited homes and the hacking of limbs, were committed by both sides, and have called for allies of Ouattara to also be tried.

History

Côte d'Ivoire's troubles began in September 2002, when troops from the north gained control of much of the country. A truce was short-lived and fighting resumed, this time also over prime cocoa-growing areas. France sent in troops to maintain the ceasefire boundaries; meanwhile, Liberian tensions from that country's war began to spill over the border, which escalated the crisis in parts of western Côte d'Ivoire and foreshadowed future events.

In January 2003, Gbagbo and the leaders of the New Forces, a newly formed coalition of rebel groups, signed accords creating a 'government of national unity', with representatives of the rebels taking up places in a new cabinet. Curfews were lifted and French troops cleaned up the lawless western border, but the harmony was short-lived.

In March 2004 a peace deal was signed, and Guillaume Soro, formerly the secretary of the New Forces rebel coalition, was named prime minister. UN peacekeepers arrived, but on 4 November Gbagbo broke the ceasefire and bombed rebel strongholds, including Bouaké. Two days later, jets struck a French military base, killing nine French peacekeepers. In retaliation, the French destroyed much of the Ivorian air force's fleet. Government soldiers clashed with peacekeepers, while most French citizens fled, and dozens of Ivorians died.

Amid reports that Gbagbo was rebuilding his air force, a UN resolution backed his bid to stay in office until fair elections could be held. In April 2007 French peacekeepers began a staged pullback from the military buffer zone, to be replaced gradually by mixed brigades of government and rebel troops. Gbagbo declared the end of the war and the two sides moved to dismantle the military buffer zone.

In June that year a rocket attack on Prime Minister Soro's plane killed four of his aides, shaking the peace process further. Protests over rising food costs spread through the country in April 2008, causing Gbagbo to put the elections back to November. A month later, northern rebels began the long disarmament process. Just days before the planned elections, the government postponed them yet again, amid disorganised voter registration and uncertainty about the validity of identity cards.

Côte d'Ivoire began to embrace a wary peace and was looking to 2010 elections when tensions boiled over, sparking the conflict that has left the country in the state it is in today.

Culture

None of Côte d'Ivoire's conflicts have killed the population's *joie de vivre;* even in Abidjan, nightclubs remained open at the height of the fighting. Education and professional life are taken seriously in Abidjan and other large urban areas, and literature, art and creativity are valued; even in refugee camps on the Liberian border, you might come across book-club meetings and philosophical salons. In rural areas, family ties are deeply treasured and you'll meet many Ivorians who are supporting as many as 20 kin on their pay cheques.

Arts & Crafts

The definitive Ivorian craft is Korhogo cloth, a coarse cotton painted with geometrical designs and fantastical animals. Also prized are Dan masks from the Man region, and Senoufo wooden statues, masks and traditional musical instruments from the northeast.

Food & Drink

Côte d'Ivoire is blessed with a cuisine that's lighter and more flavoursome than that of its immediate coastal neighbours. There are three staples in Ivorian cooking: rice, *fufu* and *attiéké*. Fufu is a dough of boiled yam, cassava or plantain, pounded into a sticky paste. *Attiéké* is grated cassava and has a couscouslike texture. *Aloco,* a dish of ripe bananas fried with chilli in palm oil, is a popular street food. The most popular places to eat out are *maquis;* these are cheap, open-air restaurants, usually under thatch roofs, that grill meats each evening. *Poisson braisé,* a delicate dish of grilled fish with tomatoes and onions cooked in ginger, is a must to try.

The standard beer is Flag, but if you're after a premium lager, call for a locally brewed Tuborg or a Beaufort.

Environment

Côte d'Ivoire used to be covered in dense rainforest, but most of it was cleared during the agricultural boom, and what remains today is under attack from illegal logging. According to 2008 World Bank data, Côte d'Ivoire is still losing more than 3000 sq km of forested land per year.

Several peaks in the west rise more than 1000m, and a coastal lagoon with a unique ecosystem stretches 300km west from the Ghanaian border. The north is dry scrubland.

SURVIVAL GUIDE

ℹ️ Directory A–Z

ACCOMMODATION
Abidjan is expensive and not always good value for money. Elsewhere in the country, you'll find better deals, but standards of comfort are generally lower.

ACTIVITIES
Several spots on the coast, most notably Assinie and Dagbego, have decent surfing. Côte d'Ivoire also has a lot to offer birdwatchers, particularly during the (European) winter migration season from December to March. For hiking, head to Man or the beautiful Parc National de Taï.

BOOKS
There is a wealth of books in French about the country's trials and tribulations. Guillaume Soro's autobiography, *Pourquoi Je Suis Devenu Rebelle* (Why I Became a Rebel), is a page-turner. *Le Peuple n'Aime pas le Peuple* (The People Don't Like the People), by Kouakou-Gbahi Kouakou, describes the conflict well.

EMERGENCIES
Fire (☑ 180)
Medicins Urgence (Private Company) (☑ 07-082626)
SOS Medecins (Private Company) (☑ 185)

EMBASSIES & CONSULATES
The following embassies are in Abidjan.
Belgian Embassy (☑ 20-210088, 20-219434; Ave Terrasson des Fougères 01, 4th fl, Immeuble Alliance) Also assists Dutch nationals.
Burkinabé Embassy (☑ 20-211501; Ave Terrasson de Fougères) There's also a consulate in Bouaké.
Canadian Embassy (☑ 20-300700; www. dfait-maeci.gc.ca/abid jan; 23 Ave Noguès,

PRACTICALITIES

➡ **Electricity** Voltage is 220V/50Hz and plugs have two round pins.

➡ **Languages** The main languages are French, Mande, Malinke, Dan, Senoufo, Baoulé, Agni and Dioula.

➡ **Newspapers** Among the nearly 20 daily newspapers, all in French, *Soirinfo*, *24 Heures* and *L'Intelligent d'Abidjan* steer an independent course. *Gbich!* is a satirical paper.

➡ **Radio** Jam (99.3FM) and Radio Nostalgie (101.1FM) play hit music. The BBC World Service broadcasts some programs in English on 94.3FM.

Immeuble Trade Centre) Also assists Australian nationals.

French Embassy (☏20-200404; www.consul france-abidjan.org; 17 Rue Lecoeur)

German Embassy (☏22-442030; 39 Blvd Hassan II)

Ghanaian Embassy (☏22-410288; Rue des Jardins, Deux Plateaux)

Guinean Embassy (☏20-222520; Ave Crosson Duplessis, 3rd fl, Immeuble Crosson Duplessis)

Liberian Embassy (☏20-324636; Ave Delafosse, Immeuble Taleb)

Malian Embassy (☏20-311570; Rue du Commerce, Maison du Mali)

Senegalese Embassy (☏20-332876; Immeuble Nabil, off Rue du Commerce)

FESTIVALS & EVENTS

Fête du Dipri Held in Gomon, northwest of Abidjan, in March or April. An all-night and all-the-next-day religious ceremony where people go into trances.

Fête de l'Abissa Held in Grand Bassam in October or November. A week-long ceremony honouring the dead.

HEALTH

Whether you're travelling by air or by land, you'll need a yellow-fever certificate to enter Côte d'Ivoire. If you don't have one, you'll be ushered behind a curtain for an on-the-spot jab when you arrive.

MONEY

Visa ATMs are widespread in Abidjan, Grand Bassam, Yamoussoukro and major towns. Most SGBCI branches have ATMs that accept Visa, MasterCard and sometimes Maestro. There are no banks in Assinie, but there is a branch of SGBCI (with an ATM) in Grand Bassam.

OPENING HOURS

Banks From 8am to 11.30am and 2.30pm until 4.30pm Monday to Friday.

Government offices From 7.30am to 5.30pm Monday to Friday, with breaks for lunch.

Shops From 8am to 6pm.

PUBLIC HOLIDAYS

New Year's Day 1 January
Labour Day 1 May
Independence Day 7 August
Fête de la Paix 15 November
Christmas 25 December

SAFE TRAVEL

Abidjan and other parts of the south were safe at the time of research, although pockets of tension remained. If you're heading north or to the border with Liberia, check with locals first and follow news reports: tensions flare sporadically.

Take care when walking at night; it's unwise to walk alone outside of well-populated areas. Also beware of riding in cars without a seat belt. The Atlantic has fierce currents and a ripping undertow and people drown every year – often strong, overly confident swimmers.

TELEPHONE

If you have a GSM mobile (cell) phone, you can buy SIM cards from CFA2500. Street stalls also sell top-up vouchers from CFA550. Calls generally cost between CFA25 and CFA150 per minute. The Orange network is reliable and accessible in most parts of the country, even some rural areas, although it can be expensive. The country code is 225.

VISAS

Everyone except nationals of Economic Community of West African States (Ecowas) countries must arrange a visa in advance.

Visas can be extended at **La Sureté Nationale** (Blvd de la République, Police de l'Air et des Frontières, Immeuble Douane; ⊙8am-noon & 3-5pm Mon-Fri) in Le Plateau in Abidjan.

❶ Getting There & Away

AIR

Félix Houphouët-Boigny is Côte d'Ivoire's swish international airport, complete with wi-fi access.

Air France (AF; Map p142; ☏20-202424; www.airfrance.com; Rue Noguès, Immeuble Kharrat, Le Plateau)

Air Ivoire (VU; Map p142; ☏20-251561, 20-251400; www.airivoire.com; Pl de la République, Immeuble Le République)

Ethiopian Airlines (ET; Map p142; ☏20-215284; www.flyethiopian.com; Ave Chardy, Le Plateau)

Kenya Airways (KQ; Map p142; ☑ 20-320767; www.kenya-airways.com; Blvd de la République, Immeuble Jeceda, Le Plateau)

SN Brussels (SN; ☑ 27-232345; www.flysn.com) Off Blvd Valéry Giscard d'Estaing, Treichville.

South African Airways (SA; Map p142; ☑ 20-218280; www.flysaa.com; Blvd de la République, Immeuble Jeceda, Le Plateau)

LAND

Burkina Faso Passenger train services (36 hours, three times a week) run between Abidjan and Bobo-Dioulasso in Burkina Faso. Romantic in a gritty way, the Abidjan–Ouagadougou sleeper takes two days. Contact **Sitarail** (☑ 20-208000).

Ghana It will take you about three hours to reach the crossing at Noé from Abidjan. Note that the border shuts at 6pm promptly, accompanied by a fancy flag ceremony.

Guinea The most frequently travelled route to Guinea is between Man and N'zérékoré, either through Danané and Nzo or Biankouma and Sipilou. The Liberia–Guinea border closes at 6pm each day.

Liberia Minibuses and shared taxis make the quick hop from Danané to the border at Gbé-Nda. A bus takes this route from Abidjan to Monrovia (two days) several times a week. From Monrovia, plan on about three days to cross through Guinea and board a bus for Abidjan.

Mali Buses and shared taxis run from Abidjan, Yamoussoukro and Bouaké to Bamako, usually via Ferkessédougou, and Sikasso in Mali. The Mali–Côte d'Ivoire border closes at 6pm each day.

ⓘ Getting Around

AIR

When it's running, Air Ivoire offers internal flights throughout the country, but prices can be high.

BUS

The country's large, relatively modern buses are around the same price and are significantly more comfortable than bush taxis or minibuses.

BUSH TAXI & MINIBUS

Shared taxis (ageing Peugeots or covered pick-ups, known as *bâchés*) and minibuses cover major towns and outlying communities not served by the large buses. They leave at all hours of the day, but only when full, so long waits may be required.

TRAIN

The romantically named *Bélier* and *Gazelle* trains link Abidjan with Ferkessédougou (CFA12,000, daily).

The Gambia

POP 1.8 MILLION

Best Places to Stay

➡ Hibiscus House (p164)

➡ Ngala Lodge (p161)

➡ Mandina River Lodge (p164)

Best of Nature

➡ Abuko Nature Reserve (p164)

➡ Bijilo Forest Park (p157)

➡ Makasutu Culture Forest (p164)

Why Go?

The tiny sliver of Africa's smallest country is wedged into surrounding Senegal, and is seen as a splinter in its side, or the tongue that makes it speak, depending on who you talk to. For many, The Gambia is a country with beaches that invite visitors to laze and linger on package tours. But there's more than sun and surf.

Small fishing villages, nature reserves and historic slaving stations are all within easy reach of the clamorous Atlantic resorts. Star-studded ecolodges and small wildlife parks dot the inland like a green belt around the coast and The Gambia is a bird lovers' utopia: on a leisurely river cruise, you'll easily spot more than 100 species while your *pirogue* charts an unhurried course through mangrove-lined wetlands and lush gallery forests. You won't be able to resist wielding binoculars with the excellent network of guides.

When to Go
Banjul

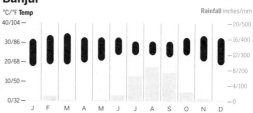

Nov–Feb The dry season and the best time to watch wildlife and birds.

Late Jun–Sep Rainy season. Many places close, but you'll avoid the crowds.

Oct & Mar–May Decent weather and ideal for bagging a shoulder-season discount.

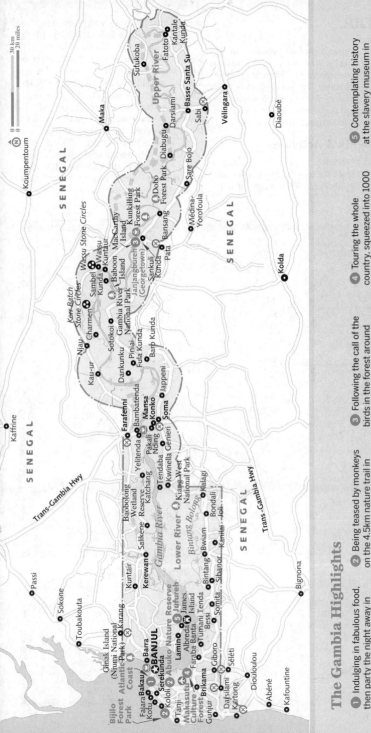

The Gambia Highlights

1 Indulging in fabulous food, then party the night away in the **Atlantic Coast resorts** (p156).

2 Being teased by monkeys on the 4.5km nature trail in **Bijilo Forest Park** (p157) and looking out for rare birds and giant crocodiles in tiny **Abuko Nature Reserve** (p164).

3 Following the call of the forest in the birds around **Janjangbureh (Georgetown)** (p166).

4 Touring the whole country, squeezed into 1000 hectares of abundant nature at **Makasutu Culture Forest** (p164).

5 Contemplating history at the slavery museum in the town to where Alex Haley traced his origins, **Jufureh** (p165).

BANJUL

POP 37,000

It's hard to imagine a more consistently ignored capital city. It sits on an island crossed by sand-blown streets and dotted with fading colonial structures. And yet, it tempts with a sense of history that the plush seaside resorts lack, and is home to a busy harbour and market that show urban Africa at its best.

⊙ Sights & Activities

★ **Albert Market**   MARKET

(Russell St) Since its creation in the mid-19th century the Albert Market, an area of fren-

zied buying, bartering and bargaining, has been Banjul's hub of activity. This cacophany of Banjul life is intoxicating, with its stalls stacked with shimmering fabrics, hair extensions, shoes, household and electrical wares and the myriad colours and flavours of the fruit and vegetable market.

Give yourself a good couple of hours to wander around – long enough to take in all the sights, smells and sounds – and get your haggling skills up to scratch. There are several drinks stalls and chop shops in the market to pacify shopped-out bellies. It's never calm here, but early in the morning or late in the afternoon is less crazed.

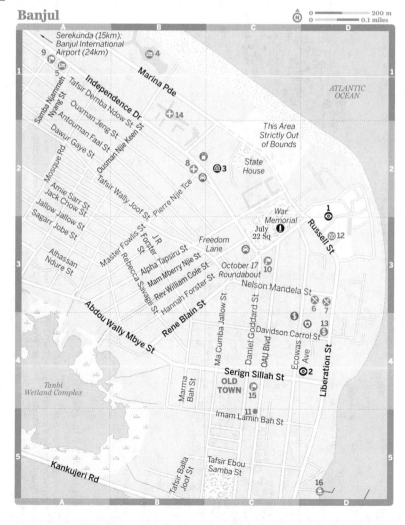

Banjul

★ **St Joseph's Adult Education & Skills Centre** SCHOOL
(☏ 4228836; stjskills@qanet.com; Ecowas Ave; ⊙ 10am-2pm Mon-Thu, to noon Fri) Tucked away inside an ancient Portuguese building, this centre has provided training to disadvantaged women for the last 20 years. Visitors can take a free tour of sewing, crafts and tie-dye classes, and purchase reasonably priced items such as patchwork products, embroidered purses and cute children's clothes at the on-site boutique.

Arch 22 MONUMENT
(Independence Dr; admission D100; ⊙ 9am-11pm) This massive, 36m-high gateway, built to celebrate the military coup of 22 July 1994, grants excellent views. There's also a cafe and a small **museum** (☏ 4226244) that enlightens visitors about the coup d'état and often houses good exhibitions.

National Museum MUSEUM
(☏ 4226244; www.ncac.gm; Independence Dr; admission D50; ⊙ 9am-6pm Mon-Thu, to 5pm Fri-Sun) Well-presented, if slightly dusty, displays of historical and cultural artefacts, including musical instruments, agricultural tools and ethnographic items. There's an interesting

---

Banjul

⊙ **Top Sights**
1 Albert Market D2
2 St Joseph's Adult Education &
     Skills Centre D4

⊙ **Sights**
3 National Museum C2

⊙ **Sleeping**
4 Laico Atlantic Hotel B1
5 Princess Diana Hotel A1

⊗ **Eating**
6 Ali Baba Snack Bar D3
7 King of Shawarma Café D3

ⓘ **Information**
8 Banjul Pharmacy B2
     Gamtel Internet Café .... (see 5)
9 German Embassy A1
10 Guinean Embassy C3
11 Immigration Office C5
12 Main Post Office D3
13 PHB Bank D4
14 Royal Victoria Teaching Hospital B1
15 Sierra Leonean Embassy C4

ⓘ **Transport**
16 Ferries D5

ⓘ **SET YOUR BUDGET**

Budget
➡ Hotel room D800
➡ Sandwich or *shwarma* (kebab) D150
➡ Soft drink D80
➡ Local bus ride D50

Midrange
➡ Hotel room D1500
➡ Two-course dinner D450
➡ Bottle of beer D90
➡ Short shared taxi ride D100

Top End
➡ Hotel room D3000
➡ Two-course dinner D700
➡ Glass of wine D100
➡ Private taxi ride D250

---

archaeological section reconstructing some of the earliest periods of human habitation of the region, and a history floor with photographs that lead right up to the present.

Old Town NEIGHBOURHOOD
West from the ferry terminal towards the wide Ma Cumba Jallow St (Dobson St) is a chaotic assembly of decrepit colonial buildings and Krio-style clapboard houses (steep-roofed structures with wrought-iron balconies and corrugated roofs). It's no coincidence they resemble the inner-city architecture of Freetown, Sierra Leone, as many of them still belong to families who came to Banjul from Freetown, some as early as the 1820s.

🛏 Sleeping

Not many tourists stay in Banjul, and the best hotels are along the coast.

Princess Diana Hotel HOTEL $
(☏ 4228715; 30 Independence Dr; r D900) This is slightly better than most Banjul dosshouses, simply because it has doors that lock plus occasional live music in the bar.

Denton Bridge Resort HOTEL $$
(☏ 7773777; s/d D1200/1500; 🛜 🏊) Near Oyster Creek, this is a breezy, decent hotel with large rooms. It also functions as a watersports centre, *pirogue* (traditional canoe) landing and excursion point.

Laico Atlantic Hotel   HOTEL **$$$**
(☑4228601; www.laicohotels.com; Marina Pde; s/d from D2500/3500; [P][✱][@][🛜][🏊]) This plush palace has all the makings of a classy hotel (good restaurants, massage centre, nightclub), modern swanky rooms, plus, it's within walking distance of the heart of Banjul.

✗ Eating

Banjul's restaurant scene is a culinary desert and many eateries roll down the blinds before the evening has even started. Around Albert Market you can find several cheap chop shops where plates of rice and sauce start at about D40. The Laico Atlantic Hotel restaurant offers international fare if you are looking for a more high-end experience.

★Nefertiti Bar & Restaurant   SEAFOOD **$**
(☑7776600; Marina Pde; meals D200-300; ⊙11am-11pm) Smack on the beach with a gorgeous view of the beach, this laid-back spot serves up local seafood and is a popular spot for drinks in the late afternoon and evening.

Ali Baba Snack Bar   MIDDLE EASTERN **$**
(☑4224055; Nelson Mandela St; dishes around D150-200; ⊙9am-5pm) Banjul's main snack bar has a deserved reputation for tasty *shwarmas* (sliced, grilled meat and salad in pita bread) and felafel sandwiches.

King of Shawarma Café   MIDDLE EASTERN **$**
(☑4229799; Nelson Mandela St; dishes D100-200; ⊙9am-5pm Mon-Sat) Friendly, fresh and happy to relax its opening hours, this place serves delicious meze and pressed fruit juice.

❶ Information

Banjul Pharmacy (☑4227470; ⊙10am-8.30pm) Across the road from the hospital.
Gamtel Internet Café (Independence Dr; per hr D40; ⊙9am-midnight) Internet access and phone service.
Main Post Office (Russell St; ⊙8am-4pm Mon-Sat) Has telephone facilities next door.
PHB Bank (☑4428144; 11 Liberation St; ⊙8am-4pm Mon-Thu, to 1.30pm Fri) Has an ATM and changes money.
Royal Victoria Teaching Hospital (☑4228223; Independence Dr) The Gambia's main hospital has an emergency department, but facilities aren't great.

SAFE TRAVEL
The Barra ferry is rife with pickpockets, and tourists are easy prey at the ferry terminals and at Albert Market.

❶ Getting There & Away

Banjul International Airport (BLJ; ☑4473117) is at Yundum, 24km from Banjul city centre and 16km from the Atlantic coast resorts. For more information about flights, see p169.

Ferries (☑4228205; Liberation St; passengers D15, cars D200-300) travel between Banjul and Barra, on the northern bank of the Gambia River. They are supposed to run every one to two hours from 7am to 9pm and take one hour, though delays and cancellations are frequent.

Gelli-gellis (minibuses) and shared taxis to Bakau (D12) and Serekunda (D15) leave from their respective taxi ranks near the National Museum. Note that you might have to pay a bit more for luggage. A private taxi to the coastal resorts will cost D200 to D400.

❶ Getting Around

TO/FROM THE AIRPORT
A tourist taxi from Banjul International Airport to Banjul costs around D300 to D400. There is no airport bus.

SHARED TAXI
A short ride across Banjul city centre (known as a 'town trip') in a private taxi costs about D30 to D60.

SEREKUNDA & THE ATLANTIC COAST

POP 326,000

Chaotic, splitting-at-the-seams Serekunda is the nation's largest urban centre, and appears to consist of one big, bustling market. The nearby Atlantic Coast resorts of Bakau, Fajara, Kotu Strand and Kololi are where the sun 'n' sea tourists flock. If you can manage to dodge the persistent ganja peddlers and bumsters (touts), this is a great place to spend long days on the beach and late nights on the dance floor.

◉ Sights & Activities

Botanic Gardens   GARDENS
(☑7774482; Bakau; adult/child D65/free; ⊙8am-4pm) Bakau's botanic gardens were established in 1924 and offer shade, peace and good bird-spotting chances.

★Kachikally Crocodile Pool   WILDLIFE RESERVE
(☑7782479; www.kachikally.com; off Salt Matty Rd, Bakau; admission D60; ⊙9am-dusk) One of Gambia's most popular tourist attractions is a sacred site for locals. As crocodiles represent the power of fertility in Gambia, women

who experience difficulties in conceiving often come here to pray and wash (any child called Kachikally tells of a successful prayer at the pool). The pool and its adjacent nature trail are home to 78 fully grown and several smaller Nile crocodiles that you can observe basking on the bank. If you dare, many are tame enough to be touched (your guide will point you in their direction). A small museum containing musical instruments and other cultural artefacts is also on the premises.

★ **Bijilo Forest Park**   WILDLIFE RESERVE
(☑9996343; Kololi; admission D30; ◷8am-6pm) This small reserve and community forest is a lovely escape. A 4.5km walk takes you along a well-maintained series of trails that pass through lush vegetation, gallery forest, low bush and grass, towards the dunes. You'll see green vervet, red colobus and patas monkeys, though feeding by visitors has turned them into cheeky little things that might come close and even steal items. Try not to feed them, as this only encourages them further. Monitor lizards will likely come and stare you down, too. Birds are best watched on the coastal side. The more than 100 species that have been counted here include several types of bee-eater, grey hornbill, osprey, Caspian tern, francolin and wood dove.

Sakura Arts Studio   ARTS CENTRE
(☑7017351; Latrikunda; ◷10am-5pm) Art lovers should visit Njogu Touray's Sakura Arts Studio for a private view of the acclaimed painter's colourful works.

★ **African Living Art Centre**   ARTS CENTRE
(☑4495131; Garba Jahumpa Rd, Fajara; ◷10am-7pm) A fairy-tale cross between an antique gallery, a cafe and an orchid garden, the African Living Art Centre is the hub of Gambia's arts scene. It hosts exhibitions, brings artists together, offers workshops and infuses Gambia's contemporary scene with life. You can arrange to meet artists here and talk to them about their work, and find out how to participate in creative exchanges. Or simply enjoy the shade of the garden setting and kick back with a cocktail at the loungy cafe.

Sportsfishing Centre   FISHING
(☑7765765; Denton Bridge) The Sportsfishing Centre is the best place in Serekunda to arrange fishing and *pirogue* excursions. Various companies are based there, including **African Angler** (☑7721228; www.african-angling.co.uk; Denton Bridge), which runs fishing excursions, and the **Watersports**

Centre (☑7773777; Denton Bridge), which can organise jet-skiing, parasailing, windsurfing or catamaran trips.

☞ Tours

Gambia Experience   GUIDED TOURS
(☑4461104; www.gambia.co.uk; Senegambia Beach Hotel, Kololi) Gambia's biggest tour operator. Does everything from charter flights and all-inclusive holidays to in-country tours.

Gambia River Excursions   GUIDED TOURS
(☑4494360; www.gambia-river.com; Fajara) Also has a base at Janjangbureh Camp in Janjangbureh. Renowned for its bird-and-breakfast excursions.

Gambia Tours   GUIDED TOURS
(☑4462602, 4462601; www.gambiatours.gm) Efficient, family-run enterprise.

★ **Hidden Gambia**   GUIDED TOURS
(☑Skype 0120-2884100; www.hiddengambia.com) Has a base at Bird Safari Camp in Janjangbureh and arranges trips from the coast. Great for tailor-made tours.

Tilly's Tours   GUIDED TOURS
(☑9800215; www.tillystours.com; Senegambia Strip, Kololi) Small company with responsible tourism products.

⌊ Sleeping

At the time of research, **Coconut Residence** (☑4463377; www.coconutresidence.com; Badala Park Way), one of the best top-end options, was closed for refurbishment but is due to reopen in late 2013. Check the website for details and updates.

★ **Fajara Guesthouse**   GUESTHOUSE $
(☑4496122; fax 4494365; Fajara; s/d D800/1100; ❄@) This cosy island cum resort exudes family vibes with its leafy courtyard and welcoming lounge. There's hot water and self-caterers can use the kitchen.

★ **Luigi's**   HOTEL $
(☑4460280; www.luigis.gm; Palma Rima Rd, Kololi; s/d incl breakfast D800/900, apt from D2200; ❄@ ⦿ ☲) This impressive complex has three restaurants and attractive lodgings set around the pool and Jacuzzi. Despite this tropical growth rate, the place manages to keep its family feel.

Bakau Lodge   LODGE $
(☑9901610; www.bakaulodge.com; Bakau market, Bakau; d from D700; ☲) This small place

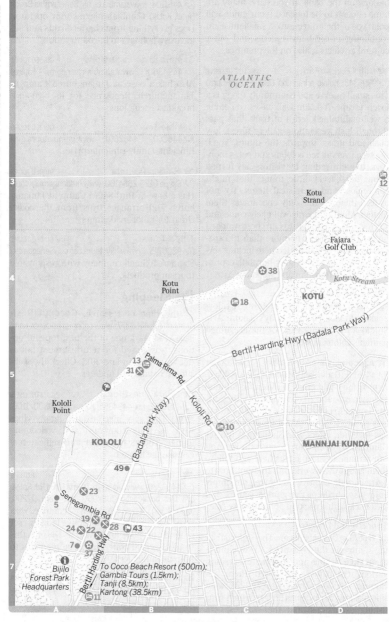

ATLANTIC OCEAN

Kotu Strand

Fajara Golf Club

Kotu Stream

KOTU

Kotu Point

Bertil Harding Hwy (Badala Park Way)

Palma Rima Rd

(Badala Park Way)

Kololi Rd

Kololi Point

KOLOLI

MANNJAI KUNDA

Senegambia Rd

Bertil Harding Hwy

Bijilo Forest Park Headquarters

To Coco Beach Resort (500m);
Gambia Tours (1.5km);
Tanji (8.5km);
Kartong (38.5km)

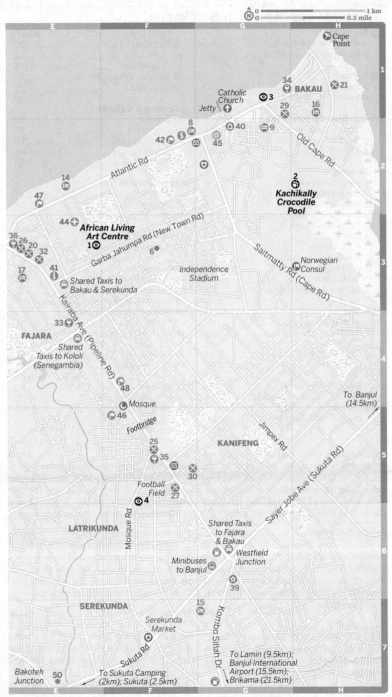

Cape Point

34 BAKAU 21

Catholic Church 3

Jetty

29

16

8 42 40 9

@ 45

Atlantic Rd

Old Cape Rd

14

47

2
Kachikally Crocodile Pool

44 African Living Art Centre
1

Garba Jahumpa Rd (New Town Rd)

6

36 26 20 32

17 41

Shared Taxis to Bakau & Serekunda

Independence Stadium

Saltmatty Rd (Cape Rd)

Norwegian Consul

Kairaba Ave (Pipeline Rd)

33

FAJARA

Shared Taxis to Kololi (Senegambia)

48

Mosque

46

Footbridge

To Banjul (14.5km)

KANIFENG

Jimpex Rd

25

35

30

Football Field

27

4

Mosque Rd

Sayer Jobe Ave (Sukuta Rd)

LATRIKUNDA

Shared Taxis to Fajara & Bakau

Westfield Junction

Minibuses to Banjul

39

SEREKUNDA

15

Serekunda Market

Kombo Sillah Dr

Sukuta Rd

To Lamin (9.5km); Banjul International Airport (15.5km); Brikama (21.5km)

Bakoteh Junction

50

To Sukuta Camping (2km); Sukuta (2.5km)

Atlantic Coast Resorts & Serekunda

surprises with large, two-room bungalows set around a swimming pool right in the heart of the Bakau neighbourhood. It's calm, considering the urban village setting, rooms come with tea-making facilities and the affable staff help in any way they can.

Sukuta Camping CAMPGROUND $
(☎ 9917786; www.campingsukuta.com; Sukuta; campsites per person D150, per car/van D22/30, s/d D280/480) This well-organised campground offers simple rooms for those who have tired of canvas. Facilities are great and there's an on-site mechanic.

Praia Hotel HOSTEL $
(☎ 4394887; Mame Jout St, Serekunda; r D550; ❀) This clean, spacious hostel with simple but clean rooms is bright, friendly and perfect for budget travellers.

Banana Ville HOTEL $
(☎ 9906054; njieadama@hotmail.com; off Kololi Rd, Kololi; d D800; ❀@) Very tiny and very simple, this is a great budget bet. The furniture looks a bit wonky, but beds are comfortable enough for a good night's sleep.

Seaview Gardens Hotel HOTEL $$
(☎ 4466660; www.seaviewgardens-hotel.co.uk; Bertil Harding Hwy, Kotu; s/d D1600/2200; ❀@🛜🛏) This tries hard to be a top-class place, and has quite a few attributes that point that way. It's pretty, tidy, friendly and bright.

African Village Hotel HOTEL $$
(☎ 4495384; Atlantic Rd, Bakau; s D750-1700, d D1400-2400; @🛏) Like a slightly scruffy, slightly bored little sister to the glitzy holiday clubs, this fills a gap somewhere between the bottom of the barrel and lofty palaces. The basic bungalows are a bit crammed

together, but the pool is great, the location practical and extra services like bicycle hire and exchange bureau welcome.

Safari Garden HOTEL $$
(4495887; www.safarigarden.com; Fajara; s/d D1300/1799; ❄@🛜🏊) The soul of this cute garden place with excellent food and service are managers Geri and Maurice, a couple so dedicated to the possibilities for ecotourism in Gambia that travellers tend to get drawn in. Rooms are bright with plenty of colourful bedspreads and an open, airy feel.

Roc Heights Lodge LODGE $$
(4495428; www.rocheightslodge.com; Samba Breku Rd, Bakau; s/d/apt D1800/2500/3500; ❄@🛜) This three-storey villa sits in a quiet garden that makes the bustle of Bakau suddenly seem very far away. Self-catering apartments, with an appealing decor of wood-and-tile simplicity, come with fully equipped kitchens, bathtub, hairdryer, TV, telephone and plenty of space (though 'penthouse' is a slightly ambitious label).

★ Coco Ocean Resort & Spa HOTEL $$$
(4466500; www.cocoocean.com; Bamboo Dr, Bijilo; d from D3500, ste from D4500; P❄@🛜🏊) With its full-service spa and endless chalk-white structures sprawling across vast tropical gardens, this is five-star pampering at its best. You won't get a feel for The Gambia hidden behind walls of bougainvillea, but for a dose of luxury you can't beat this place.

★ Ngala Lodge LODGE $$$
(4494045; www.ngalalodge.com; 64 Atlantic Rd, Fajara; ste per person from D2200; ❄@🏊) Now here's a hotel loved and fussed over by its owner. Even the simplest lodging in this red-brick

palace is a large suite with its own Jacuzzi and hand-picked paintings. Our favourite was the Rolling Stones room, kind of a stylish shrine to one of owner Peter's passions. It's not one for families but is perfect for couples, and the penthouse with sky-gazer dome and sea view is ideal for honeymoons. Perfect down to the frosted glasses and thoughtfully chosen book collection, the Ngala has also one of the top restaurants in Gambia.

🍴 Eating

Serekunda and Bakau are best for street food and cheap eateries. For supermarkets head to Kairaba Ave, where there's plenty of choice, including the large and well-stocked **Kairaba Supermarket** (Kairaba Ave, Serekunda).

Solomon's Beach Bar SEAFOOD $
(4460716; Palma Rima Rd, Kololi; meals D200-300) At the northern end of Kololi beach, this cute round house serves excellent grilled fish in a youthful atmosphere. As light and sunny as the reggae classics on loop.

Saffie J AFRICAN $
(9937645; Old Cape Rd; snacks D200) This is the low-key approach to restaurant management: purchase a few cheap seats, paint them with the Gambian flag, put them on the roadside and erect a semblance of a fence around it. Now you can serve simple snacks with street views.

La Paillotte FRENCH $
(4375418; Serekunda; dishes D70-200; ⊙noon-4pm) The restaurant of the Alliance Franco-Gambienne does cheap, tasty meals of the day.

Soul Food AFRICAN $
(4497858; Kairaba Ave, Fajara; meals from D150) This is a place for generous portions of solid

---

BEACHES

Most beaches in this area are relatively safe for swimming, but currents can sometimes get strong. Care should be taken along the beach in Fajara, where there's a strong undertow. Always check conditions before plunging in.

The erosion that used to eat its way right up to the hotels has largely been reversed, so that the beaches of Kotu, Kololi and Cape Point are once again wide, sandy and beautiful. **Kotu** is particularly attractive, with sand and palm trees, beach bars and juice sellers on one side, and an area of lagoons a bit further north, where Kotu Stream cuts into the land (that's where birdwatchers head to).

Cape Point, at the northern tip of Bakau, has the calmest beaches. As this is a more residential area, you get less hassle from touts.

If the Atlantic Ocean or fending off bumsters doesn't appeal, all the major hotels have swimming pools. Most places allow access to nonguests if you buy a meal or a drink, or pay a fee.

meals. Think platters of rice dishes, mashed potatoes and rich sauces.

Solar Project
AFRICAN **$**
(✆7053822; 18 Sainey Njie St, Faji Kunda; snacks D75-150; ☺7am-midnight Mon-Sat) All of the omelettes, meatballs, cakes and dried fruit served here are cooked on the parabolic solar cookers; you can watch them being made in the backyard.

Ali Baba's
MIDDLE EASTERN **$**
(✆9905978; Senegambia Strip, Kololi; meals around D200-300; ☺9.30am-2am) Everyone knows Ali Baba's, so it's as much a useful meeting point as a commendable restaurant. A fast-food joint during the day, it serves dinner with a show in its breezy garden. There are frequent live concerts (mainly reggae), and important football matches on a big screen.

★ Butcher's Shop
MOROCCAN **$$**
(✆4495069; www.thebutchersshop.gm; Kairaba Ave, Fajara; dishes D250-450; ☺8am-11pm) Driss, the Moroccan celebrity chef (and TV star), knows how to grill a pepper steak to perfection, subtly blend a sauce until the spices sing in harmony and present a freshly pressed juice cocktail like a precious gift. It does a mean Sunday brunch from 10am to 4pm, and even at this self-service occasion, Driss makes sure everything runs smoothly.

★ Gaya Art Café
INTERNATIONAL **$$**
(✆4464022; www.gaya-artcafe.com; Badala Park Way, Kololi; meals D400-600; ☺noon-midnight Mon-Sat; 🛜📶) Arty, veggie, healthy and organic, this is an unlikely addition to Senegambia's loud and boisterous food stations. The airy sculpture garden with its comfy armchairs is a great place to relax, the food absolutely fresh, the coffee made from freshly ground beans and the smoothies perfect for an energy boost after a walk around town.

Keur Bouba J & Cotton Club
INTERNATIONAL **$$**
(✆4498249; Kairaba Ave, Fajara; mains D300-400; ☺9am-6am) With two venues wrapped in one, this restaurant and music club only closes for three hours every night. That means morning coffee between its warm, red walls, a huge plate of rice for lunch, and à la carte dinners before enjoying live jazz or salsa.

Calypso
INTERNATIONAL **$$**
(✆4496292; Chez Anne & Fode, Bakau; dishes from D300; ☺9am-late) This cute, round beach bar serves delicious seafood, snacks and an Afri-can dish of the day between red-brick walls and attractive paintings, plus a full English breakfast.

Paradiso Pizza
PIZZA **$$**
(✆4462177; Senegambia Strip, Kololi; pizzas from D350) No one argues with Paradiso's claim of serving the best pizza in town. Amid the host of indistinguishable eateries that line the Senegambia Strip, this is a real find. Sticking with the Italian theme, the espresso here has flavour.

Luigi's Pizza & Pasta House
ITALIAN **$$**
(✆4460280; www.luigis.gm; Palma Rima Rd, Kololi; dishes from D350; ☺6pm-midnight; 🚗📶) A song of praise to Italy and its culinary achievements. The pasta is al dente, the pizzas are crisp and everything is cooked with the freshest ingredients.

Jojo's
INTERNATIONAL **$$**
(✆7295711; Senegambia; dishes D400-600; 🚗) Jojo's, with its earthy, minimalist ambience, sets out to rival established kitchens. The saltimbocca chicken is divine, and for vegetarians there's a great choice of salads.

Green Mamba
ASIAN **$$**
(✆6662622; www.greenmambagarden.com; Senegambia; woks D500-600; ☺7pm-midnight; 🚗) This inspired restaurant is built around the concept of an Asian grill, meaning you have the rare treat of choosing the raw ingredients for your personalised stir-fry and watching them being cooked – unless you wish to relax over an original local fruit cocktail while the attentive staff bring your plate over. Spread across a large garden, tables grant a couple-enticing amount of privacy.

★ Ngala Lodge
INTERNATIONAL **$$$**
(✆4494045; Atlantic Rd, Fajara; meals D700-1200) One of Gambia's most renowned restaurants, this has always been the top address for sumptuous and lovingly presented meals; service and sea-view setting are impeccable.

🍷 Drinking & Nightlife

Come Inn
PUB
(✆4391464; Serekunda; ☺10am-2am) For a good draught beer and a solid dose of local gossip, there's no better place than this German-style beer garden. It's popular with overlanders. Hearty international fare is useful to line the stomach with all that beer flowing freely.

Chapman's
PUB

(☑4495252; Atlantic Rd, Bakau; ⊙11am-10pm Thu-Tue) Very popular, this pub is usually packed with a mixed crowd. Good, varied meals are washed down with pints of draught beer and good conversation.

Sinatra's
BAR

(☑7781727; Atlantic Rd, Bakau) With a different program every day (movies on Monday, live music on Friday and Saturday, grill party on Sunday afternoon) and the fixed point of cheap draught beer to guide you through it all, this is a place you're unlikely to visit only once.

Blue Bar
BAR

(☑9991539; Kairaba Ave, Fajara; ⊙11am-3am) This cheerful, dimly lit bar has an excellent selection of drinks to be sipped in the relaxed vibe and good company on the outdoor terrace.

Weezo's
BAR

(☑4496918; Kairaba Ave, Fajara) Fajara's favourite Mexican diner undergoes a fascinating transformation around sunset, when the lights are dimmed, the tables readied for spontaneous dancing, and the sumptuous tortilla dishes replaced with one of the best cocktail menus on the coast.

Aquarius
CLUB

(☑4460247; Bijilo Forest Park Rd, Senegambia Strip; ⊙10am-3am) A smart cafe during the day, Aquarius turns into a glittering dance floor at night. The drinks are expensive and the atmosphere is strictly party-vibe.

Destiny's
CLUB

(Kotu Beach) This sparkling place is where parties go on until late, clothes are tight and tiny, and the beat is thumping. It's the nightlife version of a holiday beach club.

Jokor
CLUB

(☑4375690; 13 Kombo Sillah Dr, near Westfield Junction) This open-air club is a raucous local affair, and makes a convincing claim to be the most entertaining club of all. It's open, and packed, every night, and there's a live band, usually *mbalax* (percussion-driven, Senegalese dance music) or reggae, on Friday and Saturday.

 Shopping

A good place to pick up sculptures, batiks and souvenirs is **Bakau Market**.

FRESH FOOD ON THE FARM

Near Yundum, the **Gambia is Good Farm Yard** (☑9891560, 4494473; Alhagie Darboe; adult/child D30/20) is the public face of a socially engaged marketing company that has, since 2004, helped over 1000 poor (and mostly female) farmers sell the produce of their small agricultural farms. On a visit, you can learn about the farmers' horticultural techniques, attend cookery classes (minimum of four people, per person US$19) and taste an organic Gambian stew in the restaurant (US$9 including tour). Do phone before setting out so they can prepare for your visit. A return trip from the coastal resorts by taxi will cost around D80.

ℹ Information

INTERNET ACCESS
Wi-fi connections are becoming popular at restaurants and hotels, where they are typically free for guests. Connections are usually slow. Most internet cafes charge D30 per hour.

Net Bar (☑4498212; Atlantic Rd, Bakau; ⊙9am-midnight) Small snack bar outside.

MEDICAL SERVICES
Medical Research Council (MRC; ☑4495446; Fajara) If you find yourself with a potentially serious illness, head for this British-run clinic.

Stop Steps Pharmacy (☑4371344; Serekunda; ⊙9am-10pm Mon-Sat) Well stocked; has several branches.

SAFE TRAVEL
Crime rates in Serekunda are low. However, tourists (and especially women) will have to deal with the constant hustling by 'bumsters' or beach boys (see box, p169). Decline unwanted offers firmly – these guys are hard to shake off. Steer clear of the beaches after dark.

TOURIST INFORMATION
To find out about sustainable tourism options, drop into **Cultural Encounters** (☑4497675; www.asset-gambia.com; Fajara).

ℹ Getting There & Away

Bush taxis and *gelli-gellis* for most destinations in The Gambia leave from Westfield Junction and Tippa petrol station in Serekunda. Destinations include Brikama (D25, one hour), Soma (D100, five hours) and Gunjur (D30, 45 minutes). For journeys eastward, you're better off going to Barra and using the northbank road.

ℹ Getting Around

TO/FROM THE AIRPORT

A tourist taxi from Banjul International Airport to the coastal resorts costs around D12 to D15. Private taxis cost about D200 to D400.

TAXI

Shared taxis called *six-six* (a short hop costs D10) operate on several routes around the coastal resorts. They connect Bakau to Westfield Junction and Serekunda, passing through Sabina Junction near the Timbooktoo bookshop at Fajara. You can also get *six-six* from the traffic-lights junction in Fajara to Senegambia Strip in Kololi and from there to Bakau. Simply flag a taxi down, pay your fare and get off where you want.

You can also hire yellow or green taxis (they're more expensive) for trips around town. Rates are negotiable.

WESTERN GAMBIA

Abuko Nature Reserve

Abuko Nature Reserve (☑4375888; adult/child US$1.30/0.70; ⊙8am-6pm) is rare among African wildlife reserves: it's tiny, it's easy to reach, you don't need a car to go in, and it's well managed, with an amazing diversity of vegetation and animals. It is possibly the mightiest of Gambia's national parks.

More than 250 bird species have been recorded in Abuko's compact area, making it one of the region's best birdwatching haunts. Birds include sunbirds, green hylias, African goshawks, oriole warblers, yellowbills and leafloves. Abuko is also about the only place in Gambia where you can observe green and violet turacos, white-spotted flufftails, ahanta francolins and western bluebills. And among the 52 mammal species calling Abuko home are bushbucks, duikers, porcupines, bushbabies and ground squirrels, as well as three monkey types: the green or vervet, endangered western red colobus, and patas. The reserve is particularly famous for its Nile crocodiles and other slithering types such as pythons, puff adders, green mambas and forest cobras.

Be sure to pop into the reserve's Darwin Field Station and educational centre, packed with information on the animal species you'll encounter here. The animal orphanage here is a rehabilitation centre whose aim is to return injured or mistreated animals back to the wild. Many of the animals are baboons or monkeys that were previously kept as pets.

To get to Abuko, take a private taxi (D400 to D500) or a minibus headed for Brikama from Banjul or Serekunda (D15).

Makasutu Culture Forest & Ballabu Conservation Project

Like a snapshot of The Gambia, Makasutu Culture Forest bundles the country's array of landscapes into a dazzling 1000-hectare package. The setting is stunning, comprising palm groves, wetlands, mangroves and savannah plains, all inhabited by plenty of animals, including baboons, monitor lizards and hundreds of bird species.

A day in the forest includes a mangrove tour by *pirogue;* guided walks through a range of habitats, including a palm forest where you can watch palm sap being tapped; a visit to a crafts centre; and demonstrations of traditional dancing. The tours are well organised and run by excellent staff. This is a great day out, especially for families seeking a taste of nature away from the beaches and without the hassle of braving the roads upcountry.

If you feel like a treat, you can stay in the forest at the exclusive and very stunning eco-retreat Mandina River Lodge (☑9951547; www.mandinalodges.com; s/d withhalf board from D4000/7800; ✳✴), an elegant marriage of lavishness and respect for nature. It provides three types of lodge: in-the-jungle accommodation tucked away in the mangroves with roof terraces that beg you to perch for hours; solar-powered luxury lodges floating on the river; and stilt houses boasting open-air bathrooms and hammock- and day-bed filled terraces.

Phone or email beforehand to be picked up from Brikama in the morning and dropped off in the evening with the park's bus (D150 one way). A private taxi from Brikama costs around D200.

Tanji, Brufut & Around

Located just to the south of the Atlantic Coast resorts, Brufut has rapidly changed from a tranquil fishing village to a built-up tourist centre. Small and attractive Hibiscus

House (☎7982929; www.hibiscushousegambia.com; Brufut; s/d incl breakfast from D2800/3500; ✻ ✻) is tucked away at the end of a bougainvillea-lined road.

A short drive southward takes you to Tanji. Here, the charming Tanji Village Museum (☎9926618; tanje@dds.nl; adult/child D120/30; ☺9am-5pm) presents Gambian nature and life scenes by recreating a traditional Mandinka village, where you can peer into huts and learn about the country's history and artisan crafts. The Tanji River Bird Reserve (☎9919219; admission D40; ☺9am-6pm) is an area of dunes, lagoons and woodland, and contains Bijol Island, a protected breeding ground for the Caspian tern.

Tanji village, 3km south of the reserve office, has a couple of good lodgings. Nyanya's Beach Lodge (☎9808678; www.nyanyas-beach-lodge.com; s/d D500/600) has bright bungalows in a leafy garden on the bank of a Gambia River branch.

A little further south in Tujering, you can observe batik makers and weavers in the village. Put in a stop at the quirky and wonderful Tunbung Arts Village (☎9982102; www.tunbungartvillage.com; Tujering Village; admission free), a ragged assembly of skewed huts, wildly painted walls and random sculptures that peer out behind walls and from treetops. This is the creative universe of Etu Ndow, a renowned Gambian artist. It's fun to look at this piece of live art in progress, including the small museum displaying exhibits relating to local history. The arts centre also offers a few rooms (per person incl breakfast D350) in mud houses, decorated with bright colours and Ndow's whimsical style. Alternatively, Bendula Bed & Breakfast (☎7717481; www.bendula.com; s/d D570/850) offers a clutch of no-frills, colourful huts huddled on green terrain within walking distance of the beach.

The beautiful beaches of Sanyang, the next spot on the coast, are popular with tour groups from the Kombos. Rainbow Beach Bar (☎9726806; www.rainbow.gm; d from D500/700, mains from D200) has clean, thatched-roof bungalows, a generator and a chef who knows how to grill prawns properly, but it's best for relaxing with a beer with a view of the beach.

Gunjur

Ten kilometres south of Sanyang lies the tranquil fishing village of Gunjur, one of The Gambia's largest fishing centres. This place is all about fish, guts and nets, though the Gunjur Environmental Protection and Development Group (GEPADG; ☎8800986; gepadg.jilankanet.com) can introduce you to the ecological side of town, notably its community reserve and lagoon. Stay eco-friendly at the excellent Footsteps Eco Lodge (☎7411609; www.footstepsgambia.com; bungalows incl breakfast D2800; ✻ @ ✻) and indulge in the great food. Five kilometres further south, Balaba Nature Camp (☎9919012; www.balabacamp.co.uk; Medina Salaam; r with half board D850) is much more basic but also environmentally committed.

LOWER GAMBIA RIVER

Jufureh & James Island

When Alex Haley, the American author of *Roots*, traced his origins to Jufureh, the tiny village quickly turned into a favourite tourist destination. There's little to see, though the small slavery museum (☎7710276; www.ncac.gm/juffureh.html; Jufureh; admission D50; ☺10am-5pm Mon-Sat), which traces slavery in The Gambia and includes a replica slave ship, is worth a visit.

One of Gambia's most significant historical sights is James Island. It houses the remains of Fort James (1650s), an important British colonial trading post since 1661 and the departure point of vessels packed with ivory and gold as well as slave ships. Over subsequent decades, it was the site of numerous skirmishes. Variously held by British, French and Dutch traders, as well as a couple of privateers (pirates), it was completely destroyed at least three times before being finally abandoned in 1829.

The ruins of the fort are quite extensive, though badly neglected – the only intact room is a food store, which is often called the slave dungeon for dramatic effect. The biggest threat, though, is rapid coastal erosion, which literally pulls away the ground the ruins stand on.

The easiest way to visit Jufureh and James Island is with an organised tour. Otherwise, take the ferry to Barra and find a shared (D35) or hire taxi (return D400) or hop on a *pirogue* (from D600) from Albreda (the town next to Jufureh).

UPPER GAMBIA RIVER

Janjangbureh & Around

Janjangbureh (Georgetown) is a sleepy, former colonial administrative centre. It is situated on the northern edge of MacCarthy Island in the Gambia River, and is reached via ferry links from either bank. There is little in terms of infrastructure – no banks and no hospital. And persistent young kids in Janjangbureh haggle you more than the usual amount, so it's best to avoid loitering and head straight to a lodge or hut out of the town centre.

A walk around town does reveal a few historic buildings, including the old Commissioner's Quarter, a 200-year-old wooden house once inhabited by freed slaves, and the foundations of a colonial warehouse. The main reason to come here, however, is to stay in a local lodge and take advantage of the superb birdwatching opportunities. Some 2.5km west of Janjangbureh, near a patch of woodland, Bird Safari Camp (☑7336570, Skype 0120-2884100; www.bsc.gm; per person incl breakfast US$34; @☒) is the remotest of the accommodation available (not a problem if you come with a Hidden Gambia boat excursion), and fantastic if you're here for birdwatching. Janjangbureh Camp (☑9816944; www.gambia-river.com; per person D280) has quirky if dusty bungalows on a vast terrain between forest and water and is a good base for river trips.

Janjangbureh/MacCarthy Island can be reached by ferry (passenger/car D8/100) from either the southern or the northern bank of the river. Most bush taxis turn off the main road between Soma and Basse Santa Su to drop off passengers at the southern ferry ramp; request this when entering the taxi.

UNDERSTAND THE GAMBIA

The Gambia Today

After decades in power, Yahya Jammeh's leadership style has become increasingly authoritarian. Amnesty International, Reporters Without Borders and other human rights organisations have denounced what they say is a climate of fear felt by opposition voices and journalists. Jammeh also claims to have found cures for HIV/AIDS and asthma, which he administers in weekly TV shows. A 2009 televised declaration in which he threatened human rights activists with death heightened international concern.

In late 2011, The Gambia's presidential elections, in which Jammeh won another five-year term, were deemed corrupt by most of the international community and labelled 'not conducive for the conduct of free, fair and transparent polls' by the Economic Community of West African States (Ecowas).

In August 2012, Gambia again attracted international condemnation when Jammeh announced all death-row convicts would be executed – thought to be 40 or 45 people – by September 2012. After nine prisoners were killed by firing squad, Jammeh bowed to foreign pressure and halted the executions indefinitely.

History

Ancient stone circles and burial mounds indicate that this part of West Africa has been inhabited for at least 1500 years. The Empire of Ghana (5th to 11th centuries) extended its influence over the region, and by the 13th century the area had been absorbed into the Empire of Mali. By 1456 the first Portuguese navigators landed on James Island, turning it into a strategic trading point.

Built in 1651 by Baltic Germans, the James Island fort was claimed by the British in 1661 but changed hands several times. It was an important collection point for slaves until the abolition of slavery in 1807. New forts were built at Barra and Bathurst (now Banjul), to enforce compliance with the Abolition Act.

The British continued to extend their influence further upstream until the 1820s, when the territory was declared a British protectorate ruled from Sierra Leone. In 1886 Gambia became a Crown colony.

Gambia became self-governing in 1963, although it took two more years until real independence was achieved. Gambia became The Gambia, Bathurst became Banjul, and David Jawara, leader of the People's Progressive Party, became Prime Minister Dawda Jawara and converted to Islam, while the queen remained head of state.

High groundnut prices and the advent of package tourism led to something of a boom in the 1960s. Jawara consolidated his power, and became president when The Gambia became a fully fledged republic in 1970. The economic slump of the 1980s provoked social unrest. Two coups were hatched – but thwarted with Senegalese assistance. This cooperation led to the 1982 confederation of the two countries under the name of Senegambia, but the union had collapsed by 1989. Meanwhile, corruption increased, economic decline continued and popular discontent rose. In July 1994, Jawara was overthrown in a reportedly bloodless coup led by Lieutenant Yahya Jammeh. After a brief flirtation with military dictatorship, the 30-year-old Jammeh bowed to international pressure, inaugurated a second republic, turned civilian and won the 1996 election comfortably.

Culture

Holiday brochures like to describe Gambia as the 'Smiling Coast'. Hospitality certainly is part of Gambian culture, but it's more easily found upcountry, away from the large tourist centres.

Years of authoritarian rule have resulted in a climate of distrust. Conversations are often conducted with care, and few people will express their views on governmental politics openly – you never know who might be listening. Short-term travellers might not readily notice this. Yet being aware of the troubles the population faces will help you understand the country better and grant you an insight into the real Gambia that lies beyond the polished smiles and tourist hustling.

People

With around 115 people per square kilometre, The Gambia has one of the highest population densities in Africa. The strongest concentration of people is around the urbanised zones of the Atlantic Coast. Forty-five per cent of the population is under 14 years old.

The main ethnic groups are the Mandinka (comprising around 43%), the Wolof (about 15%) and the Fula (around 18%). Smaller groups include the Serer and Diola (also spelt Jola). About 90% of the population is Muslim. Christianity is most widespread among the Diola.

Arts & Crafts

The *kora*, Africa's most iconic instrument, was created in the region of Gambia and Guinea-Bissau after Malinké groups came here to settle from Mali. Famous *kora* players include Amadou Bansang Jobarteh, Jali Nyama Suso, Dembo Konte and Malamini Jobarteh.

In the 1960s, The Gambia was hugely influential in the development of modern West African music. Groups like the Afro-funky Super Eagles and singer Labah Sosse had a huge impact in The Gambia, Senegal and beyond. Today, it's locally brewed reggae and hip hop that get people moving. Even the president has been seen rubbing shoulders with the world's reggae greats, proud to hear his country nicknamed 'Little Jamaica'.

Banjul's national museum has a few good examples of traditional statues and carved masks on display. Leading contemporary artists Njogu Touray and Etu produce colourful works from mixed materials. Fabric printers such as Baboucar Fall and Toimbo Laurens push the art of batik in new creative directions.

Food & Drink

National dishes include *domodah* (rice with groundnut sauce) and *benachin* (rice cooked in tomato, fish and vegetable sauce). Vegetarians ought to try *niebbe*, spicy red beans that are served with bread on street corners.

The Gambia has great local juices, such as *bissap* (made from sorrel) and creamy *bouyi* (made from the fruits of the baobab tree). *Ataaya* (strong, syrupy green tea) is a great pick-me-up. For something more potent, try a cup of thick, yeasty palm wine or an ice-cold JulBrew beer.

Environment

At only 11,295 sq km, The Gambia is mainland Africa's smallest country. It's also the most absurdly shaped one. Its 300km-long territory is almost entirely surrounded by Senegal and dominated by the Gambia River that runs through it. The country is flat, and vegetation consists mainly of savannah woodlands, gallery forests and saline marshes. Six national parks and reserves protect 3.7% of the country's landmass. Some of the most interesting ones are Abuko, Kiang West and Gambia River. The Gambia boasts a few large mammals, such as hippos and reintroduced chimps, but most animal lovers are drawn to the hundreds of spectacular bird species that make The Gambia one of the best countries in West Africa for birdwatching. The main

PRACTICALITIES

➜ **Driving** Gambians drive on the right-hand side.

➜ **Electricity** 220V. Most plugs have three square pins (same as Britain); two round pins (same as continental Europe) are also in use.

➜ **Languages** English, Mandinka, Wolof, Pulaar (Fula).

➜ **Newspapers** *The Point* is a daily newspaper published in Bakau.

environmental issues are deforestation, over-fishing and coastal erosion.

SURVIVAL GUIDE

ℹ Directory A–Z

ACCOMMODATION

At the Atlantic Coast resorts of Bakau, Fajara, Kotu Strand and Kololi the choice of accommodation ranges from simple hostels to five-star hotels. Upcountry, your options are normally limited to basic guesthouses and hotels. All prices quoted are high-season rates (November to April). In low season, they may be 25% or even 50% lower.

ACTIVITIES

Beach-related activities such as swimming, water sports and fishing are popular around the coast. Upcountry, it's all about birdwatching tours around the national parks and *pirogue* excursions (see p157).

EMBASSIES & CONSULATES

German Embassy (☑4227783; 29 Independence Dr, Banjul; ⊙8am-1pm, closed Tue)

Guinean Embassy (☑909964, 4226862; 78A Daniel Goddard St, top fl, Banjul; ⊙9am-4pm Mon-Thu, 9am-1pm & 2.30-4pm Fri)

Guinea-Bissau Embassy (☑4226862; Atlantic Rd, Bakau; ⊙9am-2pm Mon-Fri, to 1pm Sat)

Malian Embassy (26 Cherno Adama Bah St, Banjul)

Mauritanian Embassy (☑4491153; Badala Park Way, Kololi; ⊙8am-4pm Mon-Fri)

Senegalese Embassy (☑4373752; off Kairaba Ave, Fajara; ⊙8am-2pm & 2.30-5pm Mon-Thu, to 4pm Fri)

Sierra Leonean Embassy (☑4228206; 67 Daniel Goddard St, Banjul; ⊙8.30am-4.30pm Mon-Thu, to 1.30pm Fri)

UK Embassy (☑4495134, 4495133; http://ukingambia.fco.gov.uk; 48 Atlantic Rd, Fajara; ⊙8am-1pm Mon-Thu, to 12.30pm Fri)

US Embassy (☑4392856; http://banjul.usembassy.gov; 92 Kairaba Ave, Fajara; ⊙8.30am-12.30pm)

Several European countries have honorary consuls, including Belgium (at the Kairaba Hotel, Kololi), Denmark, Sweden and Norway (Saitmatty Rd, Bakau).

EMERGENCIES

Ambulance (☑16)
Fire (☑18)
Police (☑17)

FESTIVALS & EVENTS

Held biannually, the one-week **Roots International Festival** (⊙ May-Jun) (formerly the Roots Homecoming Festival) features concerts by Gambian and diaspora artists, as well as seminars and lectures, held in various towns. The high point is the weekend in Jufureh, where local dance troupes and bands drown the village in music.

INTERNET ACCESS

It's easy to find a (sluggish) internet cafe along the coast. Upcountry, access is harder to find.

MONEY

The local currency, dalasi (D), fluctuates strongly. There aren't any official changing points at the border, just very persistent black-market changers. You'll be fine using CFA, though, until you get to the coast, where changing money is easier. Many hotels can recommend an informal changer, though the rates may be similar to those the banks propose. Many hotels will accept UK pounds sterling.

There are no ATMs upcountry, and you're best off changing all you need at the coast.

OPENING HOURS

Banks From 1pm to 4pm Monday to Thursday, with lunch break from 1pm to 2.30pm on Friday.

Government offices From 8am to 3pm or 4pm Monday to Thursday, 8am to 12.30pm on Friday.

Restaurants Lunch from 11am to 2.30pm, dinner from 6pm.

Shops and businesses From 8.30am to 1pm and 2.30pm to 5.30pm Monday to Thursday; from 8am until noon Friday and Saturday.

VACCINATION CERTIFICATES

A yellow-fever vaccination certificate is required of travellers coming from an infected area.

BEACH BOYS

A beach boy, also referred to as a *sai sai* or bumster, is a womaniser, a smooth operator, a charming hustler, a con man or a dodgy mixture of all of these. These guys are usually young, often good-looking men, who approach women (sometimes bluntly, sometimes with astonishing verbal skills) in towns, nightclubs, bars and particularly on beaches. While some of them are fairly harmless (just don't get your heart broken), others can pull some pretty sly jobs, involving sexual advances, tricking you out of money or downright stealing.

Use the same yardsticks you would at home before getting involved. It's best to ignore these guys completely. They might respond with verbal abuse, but it's all hot air.

PUBLIC HOLIDAYS

As well as religious holidays, there are a few public holidays observed in The Gambia:

1 January New Year's Day
18 February Independence Day
1 May Workers' Day
15 August Assumption

SAFE TRAVEL

Serious crime is fairly rare in The Gambia, though muggings and petty theft do occur, particularly around the tourist centres. Avoid walking around alone after dark. Kids will often hassle you for money or tours, but usually this is just a harmless annoyance. Beach boys are another matter.

TELEPHONE

The telephone country code is 220.

TOURIST INFORMATION

The **Gambia Tourism** (www.visitthegambia.gm) website has a wealth of information.

VISAS

Visas are not needed for nationals of the UK, Germany, Italy, Australia, Luxembourg, the Netherlands, and Scandinavian and Ecowas countries for stays of up to 90 days. For those needing one, visas are normally valid for one or three months and cost D1000 or 3000; you'll need to provide two photos. The **Immigration Office** (☎ 4228611; OAU Blvd, Banjul; ⊙ 8am-4pm) deals with visa extensions (D400). For onward travel, get your visa from the relevant embassy. Most embassies will deal with requests within 48 hours. You cannot buy visas on the borders with Senegal, but they will let you in to purchase one at the immigration office within 72 hours. If you are flying into the country, get your visa before you leave home.

ⓘ Getting There & Away

AIR

Brussels Airlines (☎ 4466880; www.brussels airlines.com; Badala Park Way, Kololi) is the only scheduled airline connecting Gambia and Europe. Most people arrive on charter flights with **Gambia Experience** (☎ in UK 0845 330 4567; www.gambia.co.uk). For inner-African flights, you'll usually have to go to Dakar first.

LAND

Minibuses and bush taxis run regularly between Barra and the border at Karang (D60), where Dakar-bound bush taxis and minibuses (D700, six hours) are normally waiting.

To get to southern Senegal (Casamance), minibuses and bush taxis leave from Serekunda petrol station (D200, five hours). Transport also goes from Brikama to Ziguinchor.

At the far-eastern tip of The Gambia, bush taxis run from Basse Santa Su to Vélingara (D70, 45 minutes; 27km), and from there bush taxis go to Tambacounda (D75, three hours).

ⓘ Getting Around

BOAT

There are no scheduled passenger boats, but several tour operators (p157) offer excursions, including tailor-made trips upriver.

CAR & MOTORCYCLE

Reliable car-hire companies include **Hertz** (☎ 4390041; Boketh Total petrol station).

LOCAL TRANSPORT

The southbank road from the coast eastward is in a perennial state of construction; the northbank road is a good alternative option for journeys upcountry. It's best to cross on the ferry from Banjul to Barra on foot and get a *sept-place* (shared seven-seater) taxi to Kerewan, from where you can change for transport heading further east. *Sept-place* taxis are by no means a comfy way of travelling; however, they are infinitely better than the battered *gelli-gelli* minibuses. A few green, government-owned 'express' buses also ply the major roads. You can get on at Tippa petrol station in Serekunda – prepare for a slow, bouncy ride.

Ghana

POP 25 MILLION

Includes ➡

Best Places to Eat

➡ Buka (p177)

➡ El Gaucho (p192)

➡ Khana Khazana (p177)

➡ Okorye Tree (p188)

➡ Nik's Pizza (p192)

Best Places to Stay

➡ Lake Point Guesthouse (p193)

➡ Green Turtle Lodge (p189)

➡ Four Villages Inn (p191)

➡ Mountain Paradise (p182)

➡ Aylos Bay (p181)

Why Go?

Hailed as West Africa's golden child, Ghana deserves its place in the sun. One of Africa's great success stories, the country is reaping the benefits of a stable democracy in the form of fast-paced development. And it shows: Ghana is suffused with the most incredible energy.

With its welcoming beaches, gorgeous hinterland, rich culture, vibrant cities, diverse wildlife, easy transport and affable inhabitants, it's no wonder Ghana is sometimes labelled 'Africa for beginners'.

It's easy to come here for a week or a month, but no trip can be complete without a visit to Ghana's coastal forts, poignant reminders of a page of history that defined our modern world.

Travel north and you'll feel like you've arrived in a different country, with a different religion, geography and cultural practices. The beauty is that this diversity exists so harmoniously, a joy to experience and a wonder to behold in uncertain times.

When to Go

Accra

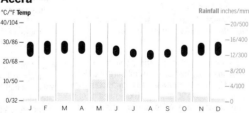

Apr–Jun The heaviest of the two rainy seasons (autumn can also be wet).

Nov–Mar The dry and easiest season to travel.

Dec–Apr Best for wildlife viewing, with good visibility and animals congregating at water holes.

ACCRA

POP 2.29 MILLION

Ghana's beating heart probably won't inspire love letters, but you might just grow to like it. The capital's hot, sticky streets are perfumed with sweat, fumes and yesterday's cooking oil. Like balloons waiting to be burst, clouds of dirty humidity linger above stalls selling mangoes, *banku* (fermented maize meal) and rice. The city's tendrils reach out towards the beach, the centre and the west, each one a different Ghanaian experience.

The city doesn't have any heavy-hitting sights like Cape Coast or Elmina, but it does have good shopping, excellent nightlife and definitely the best selection of eating options in Ghana.

⊙ Sights & Activities

Osu Castle (Map p174) is currently the seat of government and is off-limits to visitors, but at the time of research the government was scheduled to move to the brand-new **Flagstaff House** (Map p174) on Liberation Rd and for Osu Castle to open to the public.

Jamestown   NEIGHBOURHOOD
(Map p174) Jamestown originated as a community that emerged around the 17th century British James Fort, merging with Accra as the city grew. These days, Jamestown is one of the poorer neighbourhoods of Accra but it remains vibrant. For a great view of the city and the busy and colourful fishing harbour (haze and pollution permitting), climb to the top of the whitewashed **lighthouse** (admission C5).

There are several boxing gyms in Jamestown that have nurtured a long line of local kids into champions. You'll see plenty of posters around.

Kwame Nkrumah Park   MEMORIAL
(Map p178; High St; park & museum admission adult/child C6/1; ☉10am-5pm) It's all bronze statues and choreographed fountains at the Kwame Nkrumah park, dedicated in the early 1990s to Ghana's first president. The park **museum** houses a curious collection of Nkrumah's personal belongings, including his presidential desk, bookcase, jacket and student sofa, as well as numerous photos of him and various world leaders.

Independence Square   MONUMENT
(Map p174) Independence Sq is a vast, empty expanse of concrete overlooked by spectator stands of Stalinesque grace. The square is dominated by an enormous McDonald's-like

arch, beneath which the Eternal Flame of African Liberation, lit by Kwame Nkrumah, still flickers. It stands empty for most of the year, except for special commemorations. Super churches sometimes get the authorisation to preach here.

Across the street stands **Black Star Square** (Map p174), with an angular arch, crowned by a large black star, Ghana's national symbol. Note: taking photos is forbidden.

Makola Market   MARKET
(Map p178; ☉8am-6pm) There is no front door or welcoming sign to the Makola Market. Before you know it, you've been sucked by the human undertow from the usual pavements clogged with vendors hawking food, secondhand clothes and shoes to the market itself. For new arrivals to Africa, it can be an intense experience, but it's a fun – though perhaps a slightly masochistic – Ghanaian initiation rite.

Labadi Beach   BEACH
This is where Accra residents love to congregate and party at weekends. It does get extremely crowded, and the pumping music, food smells and heat can all become a bit too much, but there is no denying that this is typical Ghana-style partying. Labadi is about 8km east of Accra; to come here, take a *tro-tro* (minibus) at Nkrumah Circle in Central Accra or along the Ring Rd.

ℹ SET YOUR BUDGET

Budget
➡ Dorm bed C10
➡ Fried rice in chop bar C2
➡ Star beer C3
➡ Accra–Tamale by bus C40

Midrange
➡ Hotel room with bathroom & air-con C80
➡ Pizza C15
➡ Drink in a bar C6
➡ Flight Accra–Tamale C100

Top End
➡ Room in a lodge US$100
➡ Two-course meal C30
➡ Cocktail C10
➡ 4WD with driver, per day US$110

GHANA ACCRA

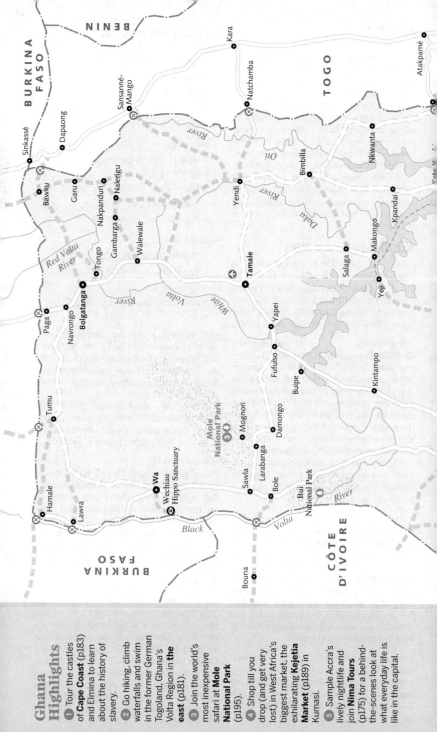

Ghana Highlights

1 Tour the castles of **Cape Coast** (p183) and Elmina to learn about the history of slavery.

2 Go hiking, climb waterfalls and swim in the former German Togoland, Ghana's Volta Region in **the east** (p181).

3 Join the world's most inexpensive safari at **Mole National Park** (p195).

4 Shop till you drop (and get very lost) in West Africa's biggest market, the exhilarating **Kejetia Market** (p189) in Kumasi.

5 Sample Accra's lively nightlife and join **Nima Tours** (p175) for a behind-the-scenes look at what everyday life is like in the capital.

6 Surf, chill and hike for a few days around **Busua** (p188).

LOMÉ

Aflao
Afloa

Denu
Akatsi
Keta
Anloga
Keta Lagoon
Dabala

Jasikan

Mt Afadjato (885m)
Wli
Klouto
Kpalimé

2 **Volta Region**

Hohoe
Liáti Wote
Kpandu
Tafi Atome
Tafi Abuipe
Mt Gemi

Kpetoe
Amedzofe
Ho
Mt Adaklu

Akatsi
Ada Kasseh
Ada

Sogakope

Ferry

Digya National Park
Kwadiokrom

Lake Volta

Akosombo
Atimpoku
Kpong

Volta River

Tema

Somanya
Aburi

ACCRA
Kokrobite

Nkawkaw

Koforidua

Winneba
Apam

Atebubu

Ejura

Boabeng-Fiema
Monkey Sanctuary
Nkoranza

Adanwomase
Mampong
Bonwire
Bobiri Forest Reserve
Konongo

Abono
Lake Bosumtwi
Ejisu
Kumasi **4**
Ntonso
Owabi Wildlife Sanctuary

Kade
Oda

Asamankese

Saltpond
Anomabu
Cape Coast
1 Kakum National Park

Wenchi
Techiman
Berekum
Sunyani

Bia River

Pra River

Obuasi
Dunkwa

Elmina
Shama
Takoradi
Sekondi

Bibiani

Tarkwa

Agona Junction
6 **Busua**
Dixcove
Akwidaa

Wiawso

Bia National Park

Ankobra
Axim
Cape Three Points

Ankasa Nature Reserve

Aboisso
Agniblékrou

Elubo
Half Assini
Beyin

ATLANTIC OCEAN
Gulf of Guinea

100 km
60 miles

0
0

N

Accra

Enlargement

OSU

Danquah Circle

Ring Rd East

11th La
10th La
9th La
8th La
First St
7th La
6th La
5th La
4th La
3rd La

14th La
15th La
16th La
17th La
18th La

6th St

Cantonments Rd

Mission St

To Nyaho Medical Centre (1.2km)

Borstal Rd
Lumumba Rd
Achimota Rd

17
12
10
22
16
13
33
11
18
7
31
23
15
19

0   400 m
0   0.2 miles

Kanda High Rd

2
28
27
20
30
26

Liberation Rd

To Crystal (9km)

8
9
Ring Rd Central

NORTH RIDGE

Sankara Interchange

35
37

Ring Rd West

36

Lampfey Circle

To Kaneshie Motor Park (450m)

Graphic Rd

Abasi Okai Rd

Farrar Ave

Kojo Thompson Rd

See Central Accra Map (p178)

Mango Tree Ave
Ridge Rd

29

25

Independence Ave
Osu St
Narser Ave
Angola St

Cathedral Square

Castle Rd

WEST RIDGE

Liberia Road Nth

Efua Sutherland Children's Park

Liberia Rd

Train Station

Kinbu Gardens
Kinbu Rd

Makola Market

VICTORIABORG

Commercial St
Selwyn Market St

USSHER TOWN

Nettey Rd
Lutterodt Intersection

Ring Rd West

Slater Ave

Guggisberg Ave

Stadium

Oval Rd

1
3
6

High St

Fishing Harbour

4

Ring Rd West

To Accra Mall (1.3km);
Lister Hospital (6km)

Amilcar Cabral Rd

Agostino Neto Rd

Kotoka International Airport

Liberation Rd

37 Circle

Giffard Rd

37 Military Hospital

Burma Camp Rd

Jawaharlal Nehru Rd

CANTONMENTS

Josef Broz Tito Ave

Cantonments Circle

Cantonments Rd

Ring Rd East

LABONE

Sithole Rd

See Enlargement

Ring Rd East

OSU

To Labadi Beach (3km);
Tema (28.5km)

Cantonments Rd

Labadi Rd

Accra

⊙ Sights
1	Black Star Square	D6
2	Flagstaff House	D3
3	Independence Square	D6
4	Jamestown	B7
5	Osu Castle	E6

⊟ Sleeping
6	Afia Beach Hotel	D6
7	Frankie's	B2
8	New Haven	C4
9	Paloma	C4

⊗ Eating
10	Buka	B1
11	Dynasty	B2
	Frankie's	(see 7)
12	Koala Supermarket	B1
13	Mamma Mia's	B2
14	Monsoon	B2
15	Nourish Lab Smoothy's	B3
	Paloma Restaurant	(see 9)

⊖ Drinking & Nightlife
16	Epo's Spot	A2
17	Firefly	B1
18	Republic Bar & Grill	B2
19	Ryan's Irish Pub	B3
	The Lexington	(see 9)

✪ Entertainment
20	+233	D4
21	Alliance Française	E2

⌂ Shopping
22	Global Mamas	B1
23	Vidya Books	C2

ⓘ Information
24	Australian High Commission	E4
25	British High Commission	D5
26	Canadian High Commission	D4
27	Dutch Embassy	D4
28	French Embassy	D3
29	German Embassy	C4
30	Immigration Office	D4
31	Ivorian Embassy	B2
32	Togolese Embassy	E4
33	Trust Hospital	B2
34	US Embassy	F3

ⓘ Transport
35	Neoplan Motor Park	B4
36	STC Ring Road	A5
37	VIP	A4

GHANA ACCRA

National Museum MUSEUM
(Map p178; Barnes Rd; admission C7; ⏲9am-4.30pm Mon-Sun) Set in pleasant grounds, the national museum features excellent displays on various aspects of Ghanaian culture and history. The displays on local crafts, ceremonial objects and the slave trade are particularly noteworthy.

★**Nima Tours** WALKING TOUR
(☎024-6270095; http://ghana-nima-tours.yolasite.com; Nima; per hr C5) Charles Sablah loves his neighbourhood. He also loves meeting new people, so he started welcoming couch-surfers in his home a few years ago. He showed them around Nima and what started as a standard friendly welcome has become a regular tour. Charles has done a lot of research to learn the history of the area and his enthusiasm and smile are infectious. He'll take you around the market, a primary school, local houses (all friends), bars and more. It's all tailored according to how long you have and what you'd like to do. A highly authentic and heartily recommended experience.

Sleeping

Accra has a good range of places to sleep, though prices are generally high.

New Haven HOTEL $
(Map p174; ☎030-2222053; newhavenhotel@yahoo.com; off Ring Rd Central, Asylum Down; s/d/tw C29/50/68) As far as budget places go in Accra, the New Haven is one of the best. Rooms are spacious and spotless, there is a pleasant courtyard and the location is excellent. The one problem is the extremely noisy generator used during power cuts (unfortunately still quite frequent).

Crystal GUESTHOUSE $
(☎030-2304634; www.crystalhostel.com; 27 Akorlu Cl, Darkuman; dm/s/d US$10/18.50/37; 📶) The hosts go out of their way to make travellers welcome at this lovely budget set-up in the quiet suburb of Darkuman. Rooms have TV and fridge. There's a leafy communal lawn area and a rooftop terrace.

Rising Phoenix Magic Beach Resort BACKPACKERS $
(Map p178; ☎024-4315416; www.magicbeachresort.com; off High St; r with/without bathroom C57/29) In theory, Rising Phoenix ought to rock with its central location and laid-back rasta vibes. In practice, cleanliness is borderline and the noise from the ocean and the beach bars can be defeaning. But as one of Accra's few real budget options, it remains popular.

Pink Hostel HOSTEL $$
(Map p178; ☎030-2256710; www.pinkhostel.com.gh; Asylum Down; dm US$20, s/d US$40/50; ❄@📶) This newish hostel ticks all the boxes: clean rooms, good facilities (terrace, hanging-out space, restaurant, internet), friendly staff and a good location. It's not exactly budget, though – the dorms (with four to eight beds per room) in particular are overpriced. Breakfast is included.

Afia Beach Hotel LODGE $$
(Map p174; ☎030-2681460; www.afiavillage.com; 2 Liberia Rd, Osu; s/d/f from US$85/100/200; ❄📶) The Afia Beach is all about location: beachfront and central. The rooms and bungalows are simple but pleasant. Service is a little blasé, a shame considering there are so few hotels in this price range. Prices include breakfast.

Paloma HOTEL $$
(Map p174; ☎030-2231815; www.palomahotel.com; Ring Rd Central; s/d US$110/130, bungalows US$150; ❄@📶) Cool rooms and bungalows with every comfort. The complex includes an excellent restaurant, a sports bar, a garden area and a cocktail bar. The hotel also has a free airport-shuttle service.

Frankie's HOTEL $$
(Map p174; ☎030-2773567; Cantonments Rd, Osu; ❄@📶) This well-known hotel-cum-diner was undergoing much-needed and extensive renovations at the time of our visit.

Villa Monticello BOUTIQUE HOTEL $$$
(☎030-2773477; www.villamonticello.com; No 1A Mantaka Ave Link, Airport Residential; s/d from $295/345; ❄@📶≋) Behind the austere khaki concrete facade hides a sleek boutique hotel. The opulent rooms were designed according to themes – Soho, Coco Chanel, Last Emperor, Out of Africa – and are furnished with exquisite taste.

Esther's Hotel BOUTIQUE HOTEL $$$
(☎030-2765751; www.esthers-hotel.com; No 4 Volta St, Airport Residential; s/d from $150/180; ❄📶) Long one of Accra's fancier addresses, Esther's now looks a little frumpy in the face of Accra's swanky new establishments. It's

still a lovely address, though, friendly and cosy. Prices include breakfast.

 Eating

Accra has the best choice of restaurants in the country, and the food will seem like haute cuisine if you're returning to the city after time spent elsewhere in Ghana. Osu has the widest choice of restaurants (many cluster along the main street, Cantonments Rd, which is universally referred to as Oxford St), but if you're not fussy you'll find the ubiquitous chop bars everywhere around town.

You'll also find supermarkets, cafes and fast-food outlets at the Accra Mall (p179).

★ **Khana Khazana** INDIAN **$**
(Map p178; www.khanakhazanaghana.getafrica online.com; Kojo Thompson Rd, Adabraka; mains around C10; ⏱9am-10pm) Tucked behind a petrol station (Engen), this outdoor Indian restaurant is a gem – cheap, delicious and with long opening hours. One of the house specialities are the *dosas* (savory parcels made of rice flour normally eaten for breakfast). Sunday is *thali* (set meals) day.

Cuppa Cappuccino CAFE **$**
(off Volta St, Airport Residential; sandwiches C7-15; ⏱8am-8pm Mon-Sat) This little cafe in the leafy Airport Residential Area is the king of sandwiches and juices. With its alfresco sitting area and fresh products, it's a top lunch choice.

Nourish Lab Smoothy's CAFE **$**
(Map p174; Cantonments Rd, Osu; smoothies C5, snacks from C4; ⏱8am-11pm Mon-Sat, from 9am Sun; ❊⏾) Escape the heat at this air-conditioned smoothie bar. The staff will whip up anything you fancy while you sit back on the sofas, use the free wi-fi or watch MTV. Tasty pies, sandwiches and cakes too.

Koala Supermarket SUPERMARKET **$**
(Map p174; Cantonments Rd, Osu; ⏱8.30am-9pm Mon-Sat, 11am-8pm Sun) An excellent, but expensive, range of products.

★ **Buka** AFRICAN **$$**
(Map p174; 10th Lane, Osu; mains from C15-20; ⏱noon-9pm) Dig into mouth-watering Ghanaian, Nigerian, Togolese and Senegalese specials at hip Buka. The stylish 2nd-floor open-air dining room seals the deal. Come early for *fufu* (cooked and mashed cassava, plantain or yam).

Mamma Mia's PIZZERIA **$$**
(Map p174; ☑024-4264151; 7th Lane, Osu; mains C21-32; ⏱6-10.30pm Tue-Fri, noon-10.30pm Sat & Sun) Expats swear by the pizza here and the pretty outdoor garden dining area makes everything taste better. Spaghetti and kid-friendly chicken fingers are also served.

Frankie's FAST FOOD **$$**
(Map p174; Cantonments Rd, Osu; mains C20-40; ⏱24hr; ❊) Stainless-steel tables, big-screen sports and a vast menu covering everything from hot dogs to meze. Though it feels a bit like the kind of diner you might find at a bowling alley, Frankie's is a crowd-pleaser.

Dynasty CHINESE **$$**
(Map p174; Cantonments Rd, Osu; mains C30-45; ⏱noon-3pm & 6-11pm Mon-Sat, noon-6pm Sun; ❊) Accra's most central Chinese restaurant is also its plushest, with white tablecloths and easy-listening music; Sunday is dim sum day.

Paloma Restaurant AFRICAN **$$**
(Map p174; Ring Rd Central; mains C12-20; ⏱6.30am-11pm; ❊) With its string of outdoor terraces, charming staff and great African cuisine, this is a nice place to stop for lunch. In the evenings, the restaurant shows English Premier League football games.

Monsoon JAPANESE **$$$**
(Map p174; Cantonments Rd, Osu; mains C20-50; ⏱6.30-11pm Mon-Sat; ❊) Sushi, sashimi, teppanyaki – the food at this swanky Japanese establishment is delicious. The roof terrace is popular with expats for post-work drinks.

La Chaumière FRENCH **$$$**
(☑030-2772408; Liberation Rd; mains C35-50; ⏱12.30-2.30pm & 6.30-10pm Mon-Fri, 6.30-10pm Sat; ❊) Accra's swishest dining establishment with soft lighting, polished wooden floors, classical music and delicious French fusion gastronomy. La Chaumière is renowned for its steaks, but there is plenty of seafood on the menu too. Bookings essential.

▼ Drinking & Entertainment

Accra's drinking scene is a moving target: new bars open every couple of months and the trend at the time of writing was for super-sleek cocktail bars, not unlike those of Soho or Manhattan.

Epo's Spot BAR
(Map p174; off 7th Lane, Osu; ⏱11am-late) Climb to the rooftop terrace of this low-slung building for cold drinks and good conversation. Epo's Spot is popular with Ghanaian

GHANA ACCRA

Central Accra

N
0 ————— 400 m
0 ————— 0.2 miles

Nkrumah
13 🏠 Circle

Ring Road

Paradise St

**ASYLUM
DOWN**

5

11

2nd Mango
Tree Ave

Akasanoma Rd

9 💲

Odanta St

Eseefo Rd

Samora Machel Rd

Afram St

Mango Tree Ave

Kanda High Rd

Ridge Rd

Kente St

Farrar Ave

Farrar Ave

Farrar Ave

Manyo Plange St

**ASYLUM
DOWN**

Castle Rd

Tackie Tawiah Ave

7 ⊗

Watson Ave Loop

Cathedral
Square

Castle Rd

ADABRAKA

Kojo Thompson Rd

Castle Rd

4 🏛

Eighth Ave

Kwame Nkrumah Ave

Education
Cl

**WEST
RIDGE**

Seventh Ave

Morocco Rd

6th Ave

Liberia Road Nth

Liberia Road Sth

Independence Ave

Liberia Rd

Graphic Rd

Adjaben Rd

Barnes Rd

🚉 Train
Station

Agbogbloshi Rd

Tudu Rd

Tudu Crescent Rd

**NORTH
ACCRA**

Barnes Rd

Kinbu
Gardens

Kinbu Rd

Kinbu Rd

Kinbu Rd

14

16

3 ⊙
Makola
Market

15

Okai-Kinbu Rd

Station Rd

Mamleshie Rd

Kimberly Ave

VICTORIABORG

28th February Rd

8

Commercial St

Derby Ave

**CITY
CENTRE**

Makola
Circle

Rawlings Park

2 ⊙

Selwyn Market St

Zongo La

Thorpe Rd

Hansen Rd

**USSHER
TOWN**

Lutterodt
Intersection

Pagan Rd

High St

Asafoatse Nettey Rd

Lutterodt St

12 ✉

10 💲

1 ⊕

6

Atlantic Ocean
(Gulf of Guinea)

Central Accra

couples who order simple dishes from the chop bar next door.

Republic Bar & Grill   BAR
(Map p174; 3rd Lane, Osu; ⊙noon-midnight; 🛜) With its bright red walls, b&w photos, vintage postcards and outdoor wooden deck, this fab new bar wouldn't look out of place in Brooklyn. Here, it delights happening young Ghanaians and expats in equal measure.

The Lexington   COCKTAIL BAR
(Map p174; www.thelexingtonaccra.com; Ring Rd Central, Paloma Hotel complex; ⊙5pm-late Mon-Fri, 9am-late Sat & Sun) Entirely renovated and given a sleek new lounge-bar look, the Lexington is one of Accra's most happening spots, with karaoke, live music, sports nights, pub quiz and more. It also has an extensive menu, with tapas, bar snacks and mains, so you can make a night of it.

Ryan's Irish Pub   PUB
(Map p174; behind Cantonments Rd, Osu; ⊙11am-late) This Osu gastro pub is homely and welcoming. Ever true to its roots, there's beer on tap, footy on TV and a stash of board games.

Firefly   LOUNGE BAR
(Map p174; ✆030-2777818; 11th Lane, Osu; ⊙4pm-late) Accra's sleekest cocktail bar, where the capital's beautiful people come to see and be seen; dancing generally starts around 10pm on Friday and Saturday nights.

★+233   LIVE MUSIC
(Map p174; Ring Rd East, Ridge; ⊙4.30pm-midnight) This 'Jazz Bar & Grill', as the strapline goes, is one of the best live music venues in Accra. Bands come from all over the continent and there is a great atmosphere.

Alliance Française   LIVE MUSIC
(Map p174; www.afaccra.com; Liberation Link, Airport Residential Area) With several concerts a week (rock, jazz, reggae, hip-hop), exhibitions, and various cultural events, the cultural arm of the French embassy is a good bet whenever you're in town. Concerts generally cost C10 to C20.

🛍 Shopping

The **Accra Mall** (www.accramall.com; near Tetteh Quarshie Interchange; ⊙10am-9pm Mon-Sat, noon-6pm Sun) has chain stores as well as supermarkets.

★Global Mamas   FASHION
(Map p174; www.globalmamas.org; 14th Lane, Osu; ⊙9am-8pm Mon-Sat, from 1pm Sun) This shop, which stocks pretty dresses, hats, tops, accessories (including lush scented shea butter), and kids clothes in colourful fabrics, is part of a bigger Fair Trade enterprise that is promoting sustainable income-generating activities for women.

Centre for National Culture   MARKET
(Arts Centre; Map p178; 28th February Rd; ⊙8am-6pm) A warren of stalls selling arts and crafts, known simply as the Arts Centre, this is the place to shop in Accra. The level of aggressive hassling may make you want to keep your cedis in your pocket, but if you have the patience and wherewithal, you can come away with good-quality handicrafts from all over Ghana.

Vidya Books   BOOKS
(Map p174; 18th Lane, Osu; ⊙9.30am-6pm Mon-Fri, to 5.30pm Sat) Accra's most popular stop for new fiction and magazines.

ℹ Information

In addition to the following you can ask your embassy for a list of recommended doctors and specialists. Pharmacies are everywhere. You'll find dozens of banks and ATMs all over town.

Abacar Tours (☏024-9574691; 39 Bobo St, Tesano) Reputable operator run by a Franco-Ghanaian team, with plenty of options in Ghana and the possibility to extend into neighbouring Togo, Benin and Burkina Faso.

Barclays Bank Headquarters (Map p178; High St; ⊙8.30am-4.30pm Mon-Fri) Changes cash and travellers cheques (max US$250); ATM.

Busy Internet (Ring Rd Central; per hr C2.50; ⊙6am-11pm; ☎) Fast browsing, printing services and a laptop lounge.

Easy Track Ghana (☏027-665 7036; www.easytrackghana.com) Set up by two friends, an American and a Ghanaian, Easy Track has a strong focus on sustainable tourism and runs tours all over the country as well as in the rest of West Africa.

Immigration Office (Map p174; ☏021-2021667; off Independence Ave, North Ridge; ⊙8.30am-2pm Mon-Fri) Three-month visa extensions cost C40 and take two weeks to process. You will need a photo and a letter of application explaining the reasons for your extension request.

Lister Hospital (☏030-3409030; www.listerhospital.com.gh; Airport Hills, Cantonments) Ultra-modern 25-bed hospital. Has lab, pharmacy and emergency services.

SharpNet (Ring Rd East; per hr C2; ⊙24hr; ☎)

Time Out Accra (www.timeoutaccra.com; C15) A fantastic, glossy annual magazine with the low-down on what's hot and what's not in Accra. Great features on Ghana's cultural scene plus a section on day trips. Available in the capital's bookshops and large hotels.

Trust Hospital (Map p174; ☏030-2761974; www.thetrusthospital.com; Cantonments Rd, Osu) A private, slightly shabby-looking hospital that nevertheless has decent general practitioner and lab services.

ℹ Getting There & Away

AIR

Kotoka International Airport (www.ghanairports.com.gh), just 5km north of the ring road, is the main international gateway to the country. There are also domestic flights to Kumasi, Takoradi and Tamale.

BUS

The main **STC** (Map p174; ☏030-2252849; www.stcghana.com.gh; Ring Rd West) bus station and the **VIP** (Map p174; ☏020-8402080; Ring Rd West) bus station are on Ring Rd West.

STC (Map p178) also has another depot in Tudu. For international services, see p202.

Services from Accra include:

➡ Kumasi (C18, 4½ hours, half-hourly, VIP station)

➡ Cape Coast (C9, two hours, three daily, STC Ring Rd station)

➡ Takoradi (C14, three hours, three daily, STC Ring Rd station)

➡ Tamale (C40, 11 hours, three daily, STC Ring Rd station

➡ Bolgatanga (C44, 18 hours, three weekly, STC Ring Rd station)

➡ Paga (C46, 20 hours, three weekly, STC Ring Rd station)

➡ Wa (C42, 13 hours, two weekly, STC Ring Rd station)

➡ Aflao (C12, three hours, one daily, STC Tudu station)

➡ Ho (C6, three hours, one daily, STC Tudu station)

➡ Hohoe (C9, four hours, one daily, STC Tudu station)

TRO-TRO

Tro-tros (minibuses or pick-ups) leave from four main motor parks. Every taxi knows exactly which services leave from where.

Kaneshie Motor Park (Kaneshie): Cape Coast (C10, 2½ hours), Takoradi (C11, three hours) and other destinations to the west.

Neoplan Motor Park (Map p174; Ring Rd West): Kumasi (C12, four hours), Tamale and northern destinations.

Tema station (Map p178): Tema (C4, one hour), Ho (C8, three hours), Hohoe (C10, four hours).

Tudu station (Map p178): Aflao (C10, three hours), Akosombo (C4, 1¼ hours), Ho (C8, three hours), Hohoe (C9, four hours).

ℹ Getting Around

TO/FROM THE AIRPORT

It is essential that you allow plenty of time to get to the airport: even though it is relatively close to the city centre, it can only be accessed through one of Accra's most congested roads. A one-hour journey is common, two or three hours not unheard of.

A taxi from the airport to the centre should cost around C10.

TRO-TROS & TAXIS

Shared taxis and *tro-tros* travel on fixed runs from major landmarks or between major circles, such as Danquah Circle, 37 Circle and **Nkrumah Circle** (Map p178) (usually just called 'Circle'), the centre of Accra's public-transport universe. It can be quite daunting for newcomers, but

Ghanaians are experts at navigating the system and will readily direct you or take you under their wing if they're travelling in the same direction.

➡ Major routes include Circle to Osu via Ring Rd; Circle to the main post office via Kwame Nkrumah Ave; Tudu station to Kokomlemle; 37 Circle to Osu; Makola Market to Osu; and Circle to the airport.

➡ Fares are usually very cheap, C0.2 to C0.40.

➡ *Tro-tros* run virtually 24 hours a day, with reduced frequency between midnight and 4am.

➡ Private taxis within the Ring Rd shouldn't cost more than C5.

THE EAST

The Volta region has to be Ghana's most underrated gem. The area is covered in lush, fertile farmland flanked by rocks, and mountains offering beautiful vistas. It is prime hiking territory and has great eco-tourism ventures.

Having your own car to explore the area really pays off here as the main points of interest are relatively scattered; *tro-tros* and charter taxis will get you everywhere – just not as quickly. Ho and Hohoe are the two main cities and transport hubs in the region, with regular buses and *tro-tros* to and from Accra (from Tudu station); allow three hours from Ho, four hours from Hohoe.

Akosombo

Built in the early 1960s to house construction workers involved in the completion of the hydroelectric dam of the same name, Akosombo is the site of the world's second-largest artificial lake (it was the largest until the Three Gorges Dam was completed in China).

Amazingly, you can visit the dam: the **Volta River Authority** (☎034-30220658) organises daily **tours** (per person C5; ⊗ on the hour, 10am-3pm), which explain its history and the essential role Akosombo plays in Ghana's economy. The agency also organises tours of the hydroelectric plant, although these must be booked in advance.

🛏 Sleeping & Eating

⭐ **Aylos Bay**   LODGE $$
(☎024-3374443, 034-3020093; aylosbay@yahoo. com; Atimpoku; campsites C15, bungalows with fan/air-con C70/80; ❋) Set in lush green grounds right on the Volta River, Aylos Bay has lovely bungalows. The air-con waterside bungalows are well worth the extra C10. There's a garden bar-restaurant and a beach, and you can rent canoes (C10). It's located just 500m from the Adomi Bridge on the Akosombo Rd.

Volta Hotel   HOTEL $$$
(☎034-3020731; www.voltahotel; Akosombo; s/d/ste US$150/180/250; ❋@🛜🏊) Built on a hill

---

GHANA READS

Ghana is one of the most interesting places to be in Africa right now, and there are tremendous books exploring the country's history.

➡ Ekow Eshun's *Black Gold of the Sun: Searching for Home in England and Africa* is an excellent account of the author's journey to reconcile his Ghanaian and British roots.

➡ *In My Father's Land*, by Star Nyanbiba Hammond, is part autobiography, part novel, inspired by the author's move from England to Ghana at the age of eight.

➡ Maya Angelou's *All God's Children Need Travelling Shoes* beautifully documents the author's emigration to Ghana.

➡ Albert van Dantzig's *Forts and Castles of Ghana* remains the definitive work on the early European coastal presence.

➡ *Kwame Nkrumah, The Father of African Nationalism* by David Birmingham is a comprehensive biography of the first African statesman; Nkrumah's own works give you an insight into the man and his beliefs.

➡ Paul Nugent's *Big Men, Small Boys and Politics in Ghana* is a good account of the Rawlings era.

➡ *My First Coup d'Etat: Memories from the Lost Decade of Africa* by the current president, John Dramani Mahama, chronicles his coming of age during the post-independence years.

overlooking the dam and the lake, it offers the most breathtaking panoramas. The interior looks a tad passé but the staff's professionalism and the spectacular setting are second to none. Rates include breakfast.

ℹ Getting There & Away

Akosombo is located about 7km north of the Accra–Ho road; the turn-off is at Atimpoku, just before the beautiful Adomi Bridge on the Volta River.

There are daily *tro-tros* from Accra to Akosombo (C4, 1½ hours). More likely, you'll have to change at Kpong (C4, one hour), a major transport hub on the Accra–Ho road, for onward travel to Atimpoku and Akosombo (C1, 30 minutes).

Amedzofe

Amedzofe's claim to fame is that, at 750m altitude, it is Ghana's highest settlement. The drive to the village, through the stunning Avatime Hills, is scenic and tortuous; it almost comes as a surprise when Amedzofe suddenly appears around a bend.

The village offers breathtaking vistas, a waterfall, forests, a cool climate and plenty of hiking opportunities. There's a fantastic community-run visitor centre (☏054-7297493; ⊗8am-6pm) where you can arrange hikes. Popular choices include a 45-minute walk to Amedzofe Falls (admission C5) – the last section is treacherous – and a 30-minute walk to the summit of Mt Gemi (611m; admission C5), one of the highest mountains in the area, where there is a 3.5m iron cross and stunning views.

You can stay at the Abraerica (☏054-7752361; www.abraericahospitalities.com; Amedzofe; s/d with fan C40/50, d/tw with air-con C65/75), a newly built hotel with squeaky-clean, slightly impersonal rooms but fabulous views. The nicest place to stay in the area, however, is Biakpa Mountain Paradise (☏024-4166226; www.mountainparadisebiakpa.com; Biakpa; campsites C9, s/d/f C25/40/50), a former government rest home converted into a lovely mountain hideaway near the village of Vane. It's a peaceful place, with a good restaurant, and staff can arrange hikes along the Kulugu River (C5) and bike rental (per hour C3).

For better or for worse, the (unsealed) road on which the guesthouse is located is about to become the main (sealed) Ho–Hohoe road. The traffic will definitely affect the site's tranquility but will also make it more accessible. At the moment, you can get as far as Vane by *tro-tro* but you then have to charter a taxi from Vane (C20).

There are *tro-tros* between Ho, Vane and Amedzofe (C3, one hour) except on Sunday. A private taxi between Ho and Amedzofe will cost C40.

Tafi Atome & Tafi Abuipe

These two small villages are worthy eco-tourism destinations in the region. Tafi Atome (admission C8) has long been known for its Monkey Sanctuary: the mona monkeys, revered by the villagers, are habituated and readily come to feed off the hand of visitors. Early in the morning and late in the afternoon, they can be seen roaming the village.

In Tafi Abuipe (admission C10), it is the village's kente weaving tradition that takes pride of place. You can visit the weaving room, tour the village and organise homestays (C7 per person per night). The kente in this part of Ghana is good value and with a bit of notice, villagers will produce any textile to any measurement and deliver it to where you're staying.

Tafi Atome and Tafi Abuipe lie a couple of kilometres west off the Ho-Hohoe road, not far off the village of Fume. If you don't have your own transport, you can charter a taxi from there for about C20.

Wli Falls

Ghana's tallest waterfalls, the Wli (pronounced 'vlee') falls stand amid an exquisite landscape of rolling hills, forests and bubbling streams.

It takes about 40 minutes to walk from the welcome centre to the lower waterfalls (C10) along an easy path. Much more challenging is the hike to the upper falls (C13), which takes about two hours and requires clambering in places. The falls are most impressive during the rainy season, when you can hear – and feel – the flow of water thundering down.

The excellent Wli Water Heights Hotel (☏020-9119152; wliheights@yahoo.com; r without/with bathroom C40/55, d with air-con C80) is a beautiful spot just 500m from the falls. The garden is the perfect place to wind down after a day of trekking.

Wli is right on the border with Togo. Regular *tro-tros* and shared taxis make the scenic run between Wli and Hohoe (C2, 40 minutes). If you're heading for Togo, the Ghanaian border post is on the eastern side of Wli (turn left at the junction as you enter the village).

THE COAST

Kokrobite

It seems that Kokrobite has become victim of its own success. Endowed with a long stretch of white sand just 45 minutes from Accra, it is a favourite of backpackers, volunteers and Accra weekenders. But a number of travellers have complained about the pollution on the beach (used as the local toilet), robberies and the poor service at Kokrobite's main hotel, Big Milly's Backyard (☏0249 999330; www.bigmilly.com; camping C8, dm C12, d without bathroom & with fan C35, d/tr with bathroom & air-con C59/79; ✳ @). Still, it remains a good party spot (particularly on Friday and Saturday nights, with live music and barbecue) and a pleasant place to relax with a beer and the sound of the ocean for a couple of days.

Tro-tros (C1.25, 45 minutes) to Kokrobite go from the western end of Kaneshie motor park in Accra. A taxi from Accra will cost around C40.

Anomabu

Many travellers rate Anomabu's stunning beaches as second only to those further west, like Busua and Akwidaa. The sands and ribbons of low-key surf are certainly a big draw, but the village has its charms too. Former slave fort Fort William is now open to the public. It is in a bad state of repair, having served as a prison from 1962 to 2000, but fortkeeper Philip's tours (per person C5) are lively and fascinating.

The town also has a number of *posubans* (the shrines of the city's Asafo companies, ancient fraternities meant to defend the city); Posuban No 6, in the shape of a ship, is one of the largest. To find it, walk west from Fort William for about 50m towards the yellow house. When you see Posuban No 7 on your right, turn left down some steps, where you'll find Posuban No 6. Company No 3's *posuban*, which features a whale between

two lions, is about 50m from the main road, opposite the Ebeneezer Hotel.

Anomabu Beach Resort (☏033-21291562; www.anomabo.com; campsites $15, huts with/without air-con US$45/75; ✳) is without a doubt the best place to stay here, and has attractive bungalows set within a sandy and shady grove of coconut palms. It tends to be very quiet during the week, and very busy at weekends and holidays when the restaurant puts on large barbecues. Wi-fi was in the works at the time of our visit.

You'll have no problem finding a *tro-tro* (C0.50, 15 minutes) to Cape Coast along the main road.

Cape Coast

POP 217,000

Forever haunted by the ghosts of the past, Cape Coast is one of the most culturally significant spots in Africa. This former European colonial capital, originally named Cabo Corso by the Portuguese, was once the largest slave-trading centre in West Africa. At the height of the slave trade it received a workforce from locations as far away as Niger and Burkina Faso, and slaves were kept locked up in the bowels of Cape Coast's imposing castle. From the shores of this seaside town, slaves were herded onto vessels like cattle, irrevocably altering the lives of generations to come.

Today, Cape Coast is an easygoing fishing town with an arty vibe, fanned by salty sea breezes and kissed by peeling waves. Crumbling colonial buildings still line the streets, while seabirds prowl the beaches and fishermen cast nets where slave ships once sailed. Many travellers use Cape Coast as a base to explore Kakum National Park, Anomabu and even Elmina.

◉ Sights & Activities

You'll notice the ruins of Fort William, which dates from 1820 and now functions as a lighthouse, and Fort Victoria, originally built in 1702, on the town's hills, but you are advised not to venture to either because of muggings.

★Cape Coast Castle   CASTLE
(Victoria Rd; adult/student/child C11/7/2, camera fee C20; ⊙9am-5pm) Cape Coast's imposing, whitewashed castle commands the heart of town, overlooking the sea. First converted into a castle by the Dutch in 1637 and

Cape Coast

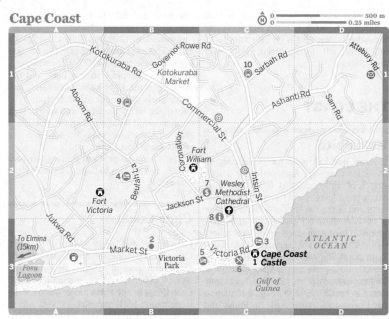

Cape Coast

expanded by the Swedes in 1652, the castle changed hands five times over the 13 tumultuous years that followed until, in 1664, it was captured by the British. During the two centuries of British occupation, it was the headquarters for the colonial adminis-

tration until Accra was declared the new capital in 1877.

Now extensively restored, Cape Coast Castle deserves as much time as you can give it. Mountains of rusty cannonballs line the route walked by slaves, and castle staff conduct excellent tours of the grounds every hour or so (less frequently on Sunday). You'll be shown into the dark, damp dungeons, where slaves sat waiting for two to 12 weeks, all the while contemplating rumours that only hinted at their fate.

A visit to the condemned-slave cell (not for the claustrophobic) contrasts sharply with the incredible governor's bedroom, blessed with floor-to-ceiling windows and panoramic views of the ocean. There's also an excellent **museum** on the 1st floor, detailing the history of Ghana, the slave trade and Akan culture.

The castle buildings, constructed around a trapezoidal courtyard facing the sea, and the dungeons below, provide a horrifying insight into the workings of the slave trade. Tours, which last about an hour, end with a passage through the Door of No Return.

★**Global Mamas**　　　　　COURSE
(📞 024-4973353; www.globalmamas.org; Market St) This fantastic outfit organises cook-

ing courses (C34), batik courses (C48) and drumming and dancing courses (C22, minimum two people). All courses last three hours and can be organised at short notice (the day before); drumming courses cannot be held on Wednesday for taboo reasons.

🛏 Sleeping

Baobab
GUESTHOUSE $
(📞 054-0436130; www.baobab-children-foundation.de; Commercial St; s/d/tr/q without bathroom C18/25/35/40; 📶) A lovely guesthouse with simple but well-kept rooms a stone's throw from Cape Coast Castle. All profits from the guesthouse go to the Baobab Children Foundation, which runs a school for disadvantaged children.

Oasis Guest House
HOSTEL $
(📞 024-3022594, 024-4089535; www.oasisbeach.net; seafront, Victoria Park; hut without/with bathroom C40/60, dm C12) Like a hip party spot, a night at Oasis is loud, hot and sweaty. Backpackers, volunteers and Cape Coast's beautiful people gravitate towards the beachfront bar, which does a good line in sandwiches, salads and cocktails. Staff are very friendly.

Sasakawa Guesthouse
GUESTHOUSE $
(📞 033-2136871; sasakawa@yahoo.com; University of Cape Coast, Newsite; s/d C50/60; 💠📶) Originally built to accommodate Cape Coast University's visiting lecturers, this modern facility on the university's beautiful campus is now open to all. It is an absolute bargain, with wi-fi, satellite TV, air-con and breakfast all included in the price, and it's a great place to meet young Ghanaians. The campus is about 5km out of town, served by a constant stream of taxis.

Mighty Victory Hotel
HOTEL $$
(📞 033-2130135; http://mightyvictoryhotel.com; Aboom Cl; r with fan/air-con C40/75; 💠📶) One of the best options in town: rooms are modern and cool, with crisp white sheets and hot running water. There's a good on-site restaurant, fast wi-fi in the reception area (per day C5) and helpful staff.

Kokodo Guesthouse
GUESTHOUSE $$
(📞 024-4673486; jcasmah@yahoo.co.uk; Residency Rd; r US$50-60; 💠📶) This gorgeous, modern villa – formerly the house of Barclays Bank's manager – sits atop a bluff in a pretty garden. Rooms are spacious and airy, with gigantic beds. There is a wonderful restaurant lounge (mains C15). The only drawback is the location, on the outskirts of town.

🍴 Eating

As well as the options listed here, Oasis Guest House and the Kokodo Guesthouse restaurant are open to nonguests, and are definitely recommended.

Baobab
VEGETARIAN $
(www.baobab-children-foundation.de; Commercial St; sandwiches C4.50, mains C6-7; ⊙7am-8pm; 📶📃) A tiny organic food bar with a wholesome touch, Baobab serves up great aubergine sarnies, soy lattes and refreshing pineapple or *bissap* juice (made from hibiscus and ginger).

The Castle
AFRICAN $
(Victoria Rd; mains C6-15; ⊙7am-11pm) Though not as impressive in size as its next-door neighbour (Cape Coast Castle), this wooden bar-restaurant is a charmer. The fare (a mix of Ghanaian and international dishes) is good, though not sensational.

ℹ Information

Barclays Bank (Commercial St; ⊙8am-5pm Mon-Fri) Can change travellers cheques and cash; has an ATM.

Coastal Foreign Exchange (Jackson St; ⊙8am-4.30pm Mon-Fri, 9am-1pm Sat) A good alternative to the perennially full Barclays for changing cash.

Cornell Internet (Commercial St; per hr C1; ⊙7am-7pm)

Ocean View Internet (Commercial St; per hr C1; ⊙7.30am-11pm) Printing, scanning, CD burning.

Tourist Office (King St; ⊙8.30am-5pm Mon-Fri) On the 1st floor of Heritage House, a gorgeous colonial building; staff can help with practical information such as transport and directions but little else.

ℹ Getting There & Away

BUS
The STC bus station is near the Pedu junction, about 5km northwest of the town centre. Destinations include Accra (C5, three hours, twice daily), Takoradi (C4, one hour, twice daily) and Kumasi (C9, five hours, twice daily).

TRO-TROS
Shared taxis and *tro-tros* to local destinations such as Anomabu (C0.50, 15 minutes) and Elmina (C1.10, 15 minutes) leave from **Kotokuraba station** (Johnston Rd).

For *tro-tros* to Accra (C10, 2½ hours) and Kumasi (C12, four hours) head to **Tantri station** (cnr Sarbah & Residential Rds).

GHANA CAPE COAST

GHANA'S COASTAL FORTS

The chain of forts and castles (the terms are used interchangeably) along Ghana's coast is an extraordinary historical monument, unique in West Africa. Most of the forts were built during the 17th century by various European powers, including the British, Danes, Dutch, French, Germans, Portuguese and Swedes, who were vying for commercial dominance of the Gold Coast and the Gulf of Guinea. Competition was fierce and the forts changed hands like a game of musical chairs. By the end of the 18th century, there were 37 along the coastline.

The forts were concentrated along this reasonably short (around 500km) stretch of coast because access to the interior was relatively easy compared with the more swampy coastlines elsewhere along the West African coast, and because the rocky shore provided building materials. They were fortified not against the locals, with whom they traded equitably, but against attack from other European traders.

The forts were originally established as trading posts to store goods brought to the coast, such as gold, ivory and spices. Later, as the slave trade took over, they were expanded into prisons for storing slaves ready for shipping. Slaves were packed into dark, overcrowded and unsanitary dungeons for weeks or months at a time. Thousands died during their sequestration. If you tour any of the forts, you'll leave with a deep impression of just how brutally the captives were treated. When a ship arrived, they were shackled and led out of the forts to waiting boats through the Door of No Return.

Cape Coast Castle and St George's Castle at Elmina are both Unesco World Heritage Sites and must-sees. There are many smaller forts along the coast too, some of them not as well preserved, others not open to the public, but they all tell the same poignant story.

Ciodu Station (Jukwa Rd) serves destinations west of Cape Coast, such as Kakum National Park (C3.50, 30 minutes) and Takoradi (C3.50, one hour).

Kakum National Park

An easy day trip from Cape Coast, **Kakum National Park** (☎ 020-0420831, 033-2196146; admission C1; ⊙ 8.30am-3.30pm) is home to over 300 species of bird, 600 species of butterfly and 40 mammal species – on paper, that is. In practice, you'll be lucky if you see a monkey.

The park is famous for its **canopy walk** (adult/student C30/15), a series of viewing platforms linked by a string of bouncy suspension bridges 30m above the ground. The trouble is that it is being sold as an attraction rather than a national park, with steep admission fees, raucous noise on visits (which are always done in large groups, with no insistence from rangers to keep quiet) and, consequently, very little wildlife. The short **nature walks** (adult/student C15/7) offered from the visitor centre are hardly more authentic.

If you would like to see wildlife, you will need to venture further into the park and make special arrangements with a guide the day before.

The cafe at the visitor centre serves basic food, snacks and homemade ginger juice.

Kakum is easily accessible by public transport. From Cape Coast, take a *tro-tro* from Ciodu Station (C3.50, 30 minutes).

Elmina

POP 32,800

The enchanting town of Elmina lies on a narrow finger of land between the Atlantic Ocean and Benya Lagoon. Here, the air is salty and the architecture is a charming mix of colonial remnants, elderly *posubans*, and an imposing historical legacy in the shape of St George's Castle.

◉ Sights & Activities

St George's Castle CASTLE
(Elmina Castle; adult/student/child C11/7/2, camera fee C20; ⊙ 9am-5pm) St George's Castle, a Unesco heritage site, was built by the Portuguese in 1482, and captured by the Dutch in 1637. From then until they ceded it to the British in 1872, it served as the African headquarters of the Dutch West India Company.

It was expanded when slaves replaced gold as the major object of commerce, and the storerooms were converted into dungeons. The informative tour (included in the entry fee) takes you to the grim dungeons, punishment cells, Door of No Return and the turret room where the British imprisoned the Ashanti king, Prempeh I, for four years. Later, soldiers of the Royal West African Frontier Force trained at the castle.

These days there are palm trees growing in the (dry) moat. The Portuguese church, converted into slave-auctioning rooms by the Protestant Dutch, houses a museum with simple but super-informative displays on the history and culture of Elmina.

Lagoon   NEIGHBOURHOOD
The traditional name of Elmina is Anomansa, meaning inexhaustible supply of water. Watching the colourful *pirogues* pull in and out of the lagoon, breathing in the salty air and listening to the cacophony of shouts at the crowded Mpoben port is like having front-row theatre seats. The vast fish market is also fascinating to wander around, particularly when the day's fishing catch is being unloaded in the afternoon.

★**Ghana Ecotours**   WALKING TOUR
(☑024-2176357; www.ghanaecotours.com; 1st fl, St George's Castle; 1-5 people C15) Run by the ebullient Felix, this sensational outfit offers highly informative walking tours (one hour) that retrace the city's history. Tours take in the local fish market, the town's *posuban*, colonial buildings, small alleyways and great panoramas.

🛏 Sleeping & Eating

★**Stumble Inn**   LODGE $
(☑054-1462733; www.stumbleinnghana.com; dm C10, d C50) This little slice of heaven gets rave reviews from travellers, and rightly so: the spotless huts and dorm are homely (and eco-friendly, with solar panels and dry-composting toilets), the location right on the beach with gorgeous grounds is dreamy, the food is delicious and the staff are exquisite. It's located about 4km west of town, just before the Elmina Bay Resort.

Almond Tree Guesthouse   B&B $$
(☑024-4281098; www.almond3.com; r C63-135; ❊☎) It is Byron, Sonia and Michelle's warm welcome that makes this guesthouse so special. Originally from Jamaica, the family settled in Britain and then here. The rooms are impeccable and homely; some have shared facilities while others enjoy their own little balcony. Prices include breakfast.

Coconut Grove Beach Resort   RESORT $$$
(☑033-2191213; www.coconutgrovehotelsghana.com; village d C100, resort d C260; ❊@☎❊) This beach resort offers a variety of upmarket rooms as well as a pool, ball court and nine-hole golf course. Rooms in the resort's extension – called 'the village' – are good value. The resort is 3km west of Elmina.

Bridge House   AFRICAN $
(mains C15; ☺11.30am-8pm; ❊) With a terrace overlooking the fort and the lagoon, Bridge House is the nicest place to eat in town. The Black Star special is recommended. Portions are huge.

ℹ Getting There & Away

From the main taxi and *tro-tro* station (outside the Wesley Methodist Cathedral) you can get *tro-tros* to Takoradi (C3, one hour) or passenger taxis to Cape Coast (C1.10, 15 minutes).

Takoradi
POP 445,000
Takoradi was just a fishing village until it was chosen as Ghana's first deep-water seaport; since then it has prospered. Now feeding on Ghana's oil boom, Takoradi (or Taadi, as it's known) is growing larger by the day.

There isn't much for visitors here, but the town is an important transport hub so you're bound to go through it at some stage.

🛏 Sleeping & Eating

Amenla Hotel   HOTEL $
(☑031-2022543; New John Sarbah Rd; d C35-40) A block from the STC station, a decent budget option, with plain rooms set around a pleasant courtyard.

Planter's Lodge   LUXURY HOTEL $$$
(☑031-2199271; www.planterslodge.com; d from US$200; ❊@☎❊) Originally built to accommodate British Royal Air Force flying officers, this exquisite compound is now a stylish hideaway popular with oil magnates and the Takoradi jet set.

Bocadillos   CAFE $
(☺6am-7pm Mon-Sat) Perfect for pastries and sandwiches.

North Sea   AFRICAN $$
(Axim Rd; meals from C15-30; ☺7am-9pm) A kitsch restaurant serving the usual Ghanaian staples.

❶ Getting There & Away

BUS

From the STC bus station, you'll find services to the following destinations:

➡ Accra (C11, four hours, three daily)

➡ Kumasi (C17, six hours, two daily)

➡ Tema (C12, five hours, two daily)

➡ Tamale (C33, 13 hours, one daily)

➡ Bolgatanga (C36, 16 hours, one daily)

TRO-TROS

Tro-tro stops are scattered around the main market roundabout. Everyone should be able to direct you. Destinations include Accra (C11, three hours), Kumasi (C13, five hours) and Agona Junction (C2, 40 minutes).

Busua

Some 30km west of Takoradi, the small village of Busua is a magnet for volunteers and backpackers, who love coming here to chill on the beach for a few days.

The surf here is some of the best in Ghana and there are some lovely excursions to do from the village. Make sure you contact local guide **Ebenezer** (☑027-5283759, 029-3522188; per hr C5) if you want to explore the surroundings: not only does he know the area inside out, he's great company and always partial to a laugh.

◉ Sights & Activities

★ Butre   VILLAGE

The stunning village of Butre is well worth the 3km walk from Busua. In fact, the walk itself is half the attraction: head east along the beach from Busua for about 2km then veer left along a path to go up a hill. The views of Butre when you reach the summit are a sight to behold, with the ruined Fort Batenstein nestled in palm trees on a bluff, Butre sandwiched between the ocean and the lagoon, and the ocean lapping a long, curvy beach beyond the lagoon.

Dixcove   VILLAGE

Dixcove (or Dick's Cove, as it was once known) is a large, bustling fishing village, with a very different feel from Busua. Its natural harbour is deep enough for small ships to enter – one of the reasons the British chose to settle here, building **Fort Metal Cross** in 1696.

Dixcove is just 20 minutes' walk over the headland to the west of Busua. Locals warn against walking the track alone, however, so heed their advice and take a local guide with you.

Black Star Surf Shop   SURFING

(☑026-1951360;   www.blackstarsurfshop.com) This stalwart surfing establishment rents longboards, shortboards (per hour C15) and bodyboards (C6). They also run regular surfing lessons (C40, two hours).

🛏 Sleeping

Alaska Beach Club   BACKPACKERS $

(☑020-7397311; huts with/without bathroom C50/25) Owned by an Alaskan with an eccentric sense of humour, the lovely Alaska offers an assortment of bungalows right on the beach. There is a large bar and restaurant too, complete with loud music and hammocks. All told, it offers the best value in town.

Busua Inn   GUESTHOUSE $$

(☑020-7373579; www.busuainn.com; r with fan & cold water C55, r with air-con & hot water C110; ❄️🛜) Busua's most charming midrange option. Owners Danielle and Olivier offer four clean, spacious and breezy rooms with sea views. There's a leafy terrace restaurant that backs onto the beach, serving good but overpriced French and West African dishes (mains C20 to C30) against a good wine list.

Busua Beach Resort   RESORT $$$

(☑031-2093307; www.busuabeach.com; s/d/ste US$132/162/187; ❄️@🛜🏊) This plush resort has a slight corporate feel with its manicured lawns and impersonal bungalows. That said, you can't fault the service and facilities, so if you're after a little pampering you can be sure that the Busua Beach Resort will see you right. Rates include buffet breakfast.

🍴 Eating

The hotels listed here all serve food too. Being so close to the coast, the seafood is usually excellent and cheap, including lobster.

★ Okorye Tree   CAFE $

(mains C7-15; ⏰7am-9pm) Attached to the Black Star Surf Shop, the Okorye Tree does a roaring trade in pancakes and big burritos. Grab a table on the wooden deck, order a frozen margarita and watch the waves break.

Julian's   AFRICAN $

(mains C4-8; ⏰8am-9pm) A cheerful and excellent local eatery that serves the usual fried rice and starch'n'sauce as well as very good thin-crust pizzas.

ⓘ Information

There are no banking facilities in Busua (the nearest are in Agona or Takoradi. Internet (per hour C6) is available at the Busua Inn Resort.

ⓘ Getting There & Away

Busua is about 12km from the main coastal road between Takoradi and Axim. To get there, get a *tro-tro* from Takoradi to Agona (C2, 40 minutes) and then a shared taxi to Busua (C1, 15 minutes).

To get to Akwidaa, you'll need to go back to Agona; from Akwidaa to Busua, however, you could stop at Dixcove and then walk from there.

Akwidaa & Cape Three Points

Akwidaa's unique selling point is its long, pristine white sandy beach, by far one of the best in Ghana. The village itself isn't as interesting as other settlements on the coast, but you can explore cocoa plantations and forests, organise canoe trips or visit the windswept Cape Three Points, Ghana's most southern point. The walk to the cape follows the local track for a while, which is monotonous landscape-wise but fascinating for local encounters (charcoal makers, *akpeteshie* – palm wine – distilleries etc).

By far and away the best place to stay in the area is Green Turtle Lodge (☑ sms only after 5pm 026 4893566; www.greenturtlelodge. com; Akwidaa Beach; dm C12, d without/with bathroom C30/60). Built entirely from locally sourced, natural materials, the lodge has cute bungalows dotted all over a private stretch of beach. The bar plays laid-back tunes, the restaurant churns out chocolate-covered bananas and there's a stack of board games. The beach is a turtle nesting site and the staff organise nightly tours, as well as guided tours to all local attractions (C8 to C15). Magical.

Akwidaa is about 16km south of the Takoradi–Axim road. Take a *tro-tro* from Takoradi to Agona (C2, 40 minutes) and then a *tro-tro* from Agona to Akwidaa (C2, one hour). The driver can drop you off at the Green Turtle Lodge. *Tro-tros* stop in Dixcove on the way, handy if you want to get to Busua.

THE CENTRE

Kumasi

POP 1.98 MILLION

Once the capital of the rich and powerful Ashanti kingdom, Ghana's second city is still dripping with Ashanti traditions. Its heart, the huge Kejetia market, throbs like a traditional talking drum and its wares spill into the city so that no matter where you are in Kumasi, it sometimes feels like one enormous marketplace.

Kumasi has some interesting sights but the city's constant traffic congestion can be oppressive. Consider staying at Lake Bosumtwe, a gorgeous spot just one hour from Kumasi, and visiting Kumasi as a day trip.

If you're coming from Accra or Tamale, you might feel a pleasant drop in temperature.

◎ Sights & Activities

★ Kejetia Market   MARKET

From afar, the Kejetia Market looks like an alien mothership landed in the centre of Kumasi. Closer up, the rusting tin roofs of this huge market (often cited as the largest in West Africa; there are 11,000 stalls and at least four times as many people working there) look like a circular shantytown. Inside, the throbbing Kejetia is quite disorienting but utterly captivating.

There are foodstuffs, secondhand shoes, clothes, plastic knick-knacks, glass beads, kente strips, Ashanti sandals, batik, bracelets and more.

Wandering around the market by yourself is absolutely fine: few tourists come here and shopkeepers will be pleasantly surprised to see you. Alternatively, go with a guide, who not only knows his or her way around but can also explain the more obscure trades and goods, and help you bargain and meet stallholders. Allow about C10 for a two-hour tour; contact the Ghana Tourist Authority or your hotel for recommendations.

Prempeh II Jubilee Museum   MUSEUM

(National Cultural Centre; adult/student/child C5/4/1; ⊙ 8am-5pm Mon-Fri, 10am-4pm Sat & Sun) This museum may be small, but the personalised tour included with admission is a fascinating introduction to Ashanti culture and history. Among the displays are artefacts relating to the Ashanti king Prempeh II, including the king's war attire, ceremonial clothing, jewellery, protective amulets,

Kumasi

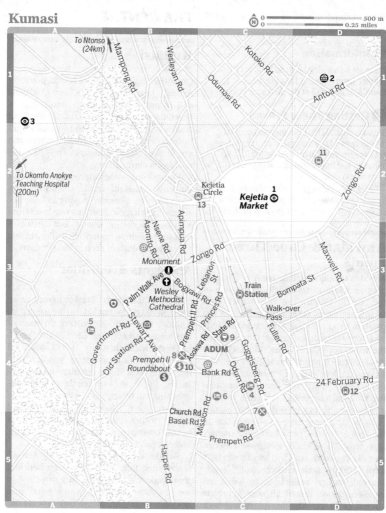

To Ntonso
(24km)

To Okomfo Anokye
Teaching Hospital
(200m)

Kejetia
Circle

Kejetia
Market

Monument

Wesley
Methodist
Cathedral

Train
Station

Walk-over
Pass

ADUM

Prempeh II
Roundabout

Bank Rd

Church Rd

Basel Rd

24 February Rd

GHANA KUMASI

personal equipment for bathing and dining, furniture, royal insignia and some fine brass weights for weighing gold.

Constructed to resemble an Ashanti chief's house, it has a courtyard in front and walls adorned with traditional carved symbols. Among the museum's intriguing photos is a rare one of the famous Golden Stool. The museum also contains the fake golden stool handed over to the British in 1900.

National Cultural Centre ARTS CENTRE
(☺8.30am-5pm) The National Cultural Centre is set within peaceful, shaded grounds

and includes craft workshops, where you can see brassworking, woodcarving, pottery making, batik cloth dyeing and kente cloth weaving, as well as a gallery and crafts shop.

Manhyia Palace Museum MUSEUM
(off Antoa Rd; adult/student C10/8; ☺9am-5pm)
Manhyia Palace was built by the British in 1925 to receive Prempeh I when he returned from a quarter of a century of exile in the Seychelles to resume residence in Kumasi. It was used by the Ashanti kings until 1974; the current Asantehene now lives in a modern compound behind the museum.

Kumasi

On display is the original furniture and assorted royal memorabilia. During the festivities of Adae, which take place every 42 days, the Asantehene receives visitors; it's a fairly formal occasion but travellers are welcome.

✦ Festivals & Events

The Ashanti calendar is divided into nine cycles of 42 days called Adae, which means 'resting place'. Within each Adae, there are two special days of worship, when a celebration is held and no work is done. The most important annual festival is the **Odwira festival**, which marks the last or ninth Adae. The festival features lots of drumming, horn blowing, food offerings and parades of elegantly dressed chiefs. Contact the tourist office for exact dates.

🛏 Sleeping

Accommodation in the budget and lower midrange categories is positively lacklustre in Kumasi.

Presbyterian Guesthouse GUESTHOUSE $
(☎ 032-2026966; Mission Rd; tw without bathroom C30, d with bathroom C50; P) Set in attractive green grounds, this two-storey guesthouse is the cheapest budget option in central Kumasi. The building and staff are rather austere and the bathrooms are only just clean. There's an on-site cafe, with meals from C2.50.

Ashanti Gold HOTEL $$
(☎ 032-2025875; www.ashantigoldhotel.com; s/d C40/65; ❄) This lemon-meringue building tucked behind the National Cultural Centre is a great midrange option, with friendly welcome, super-clean rooms and a certain charm with its ornamental fountain and kitsch furniture.

Fosua Hotel HOTEL $$
(☎ 032-2037382; Aseda House; s/d C50/60; ❄) Occupying the top floor of the Aseda Complex a block from the STC station, the rooms here are clean and comfortable. The place doesn't have much soul, but for the price and location it's as good as it gets in Kumasi.

Kumasi Catering Rest House GUESTHOUSE $$
(☎ 032-2026506; kcrhouse@yahoo.com; Government Rd; s/d/ste C65/80/125; ❄@🖧) This charming guesthouse set within shady grounds a short walk from the centre gets top marks for its friendly service, huge and impeccable rooms and excellent on-site bar and restaurant (mains C10 toC15).

★ Four Villages Inn GUESTHOUSE $$
(☎ 032-2022682; www.fourvillages.com; Old Bekwai Rd; s/d US$80/90; ❄@🖧) The Ghanaian-Canadian owners have pulled out all the stops at this impressive guesthouse. Each of the four enormous air-conditioned rooms is decorated in a different style and there's a TV lounge and a tropical garden.

Chris and Charity are wonderful, knowledgeable hosts and can help you organise all manner of tours, including tip-top market tours with their local guide and excursions around Kumasi (C60 per person per day plus fuel). Prices include breakfast but exclude the 15% VAT.

Sir Max Hotel HOTEL $$
(☎ 032-2025222; sirmaxhotel@live.com; Ahodwo; d/tr US$80/100; ❄🖧🏊) The rooms at Lebanese-run Sir Max are rather ordinary,

but it's the facilities that really make the place: lovely pool, excellent travel agency, fab restaurant. Sir Max, it seems, does have it all.

Eating

Good Ghanaian chop houses (basic local-style restaurants) are dotted all over Kumasi.

Vic Baboo's INTERNATIONAL $
(Prempeh II Rd; mains C7-20; ⊙11am-9.30pm; ※) Vic Baboo's is an institution among travellers and expats. With the biggest menu in town, this place is whatever you want it to be – Indian takeaway, decent burger joint, Lebanese deli or cocktail bar. It also has ice cream, cashew nuts and popcorn. Last orders are around 9pm.

A-Life Supermarket SUPERMARKET $
(Asafo Interchange; ⊙8am-5pm Mon-Sat) A good range of snacks, ideal ahead of long bus journeys.

★**Nik's Pizza** PIZZERIA $$
(off Old Bekwai Rd; pizza from C17; ⊙2-9pm) New Image Kitchen, or Nik's as it's known, is a Kumasi gem. Friendly waiters serve excellent pizza (and only pizza) in a quiet, leafy garden setting. You're advised against walking here after dark because of the lack of street lighting. Go there with a taxi and keep his phone number to call him once you're finished. To find it: from Apino Plaza on the Old Bekwai Rd, turn left, and Nik's is signposted from there.

Chopsticks Restaurant CHINESE $$
(Old Bekwai Rd; mains C15-20; ⊙11am-2.30pm & 6-10pm) Looking like the remains of a restaurant, Chopsticks is only a few outdoor tables with plastic chairs serving standard Chinese dishes and delicious large pizzas.

Moti Mahal Restaurant INDIAN $$$
(www.motimahalgh.com; Southern Bypass Rd; mains C17-30; ⊙noon-3pm & 7-11pm; ※) One of the most expensive restaurants in Kumasi, Moti Mahal is a formal place serving a large and excellent selection of Indian cuisine; because everything is a la carte (bread and rice must be ordered separately) the bill quickly adds up. Note too that prices do not include the 15% VAT, which can leave a sour note at the end of your meal...

★**El Gaucho Restaurant** GRILL $$$
(Ahodwo; mains C17-40; ⊙11am-10pm; ☎) As the name suggests, Sir Max's restaurant prides itself in its grill: every kind of meat is thrown on the huge barbecue, including suc-culent (and pricey) T-bone steaks. El Gaucho also does an excellent line in Lebanese food (the owners are from Lebanon) and some fine pizzas.

Drinking & Nightlife

El Gaucho Restaurant and Nik's Pizza are some of the nicest bars in town (it's 'buy one drink and get one free' at El Gaucho on Tuesday).

Eclipse BAR
(Adum Rd; ⊙11am-11pm) A friendly beer joint with an outdoor patio on the street; inside it's all diamond-shaped mirrors and big-screen sports.

Funkies BAR
(⊙11am-11pm) Big outdoor space, English premiership football and blaring music are the staples at this low-key bar.

ℹ Information

There are half a dozen banks in the centre, all with ATMs and foreign exchange facilities. Pharmacies are dotted all over town.

Barclays Bank (Prempeh II Roundabout; ⊙8.30am-4.30pm Mon-Fri) Changes travellers cheques; ATM.

Ghana Tourist Authority (National Cultural Centre; ⊙7am-5pm Mon-Fri) In the National Cultural Centre complex. Staff can help arrange guided tours of the city and surrounding villages: their prices at the time of our visit were outrageous, though (about six times the going rate), so just get the information you need and arrange a guide through your hotel instead.

Okomfo Anokye Teaching Hospital (☎032-2022301; www.kathhsp.org; Bantama Rd) Kumasi's main public hospital with 700-plus beds.

State Internet Café (Asomfo Rd; per hr C1; ⊙7.30am-8pm)

Unic Internet (Bank Rd; per hr C1; ⊙8am-7pm)

ℹ Getting There & Away

AIR

Kumasi airport is on the northeastern outskirts of town, about 2km from the centre. **Fly 540 Africa** (www.fly540africa.com) and **Antrak Air** (www.antrakair.com) both offer regular flights to Accra (one way starts around US$25). A taxi from the centre to the airport costs about C10. Allow plenty of time because of the traffic.

BUS

You will find the following bus services:
➡ Accra (C17, four hours, half-hourly; operated by VIP)

→ Cape Coast (C9, five hours, twice daily; operated by STC)

→ Takoradi (C17, six hours, twice daily; operated by STC)

→ Tamale (C25, eight hours, once daily; operated by STC)

→ Ouagadougou (Burkina Faso; C36, 15 hours, three weekly; operated by STC)

TRO-TRO

There are three main motor parks in Kumasi, each with its allocated destinations:

Asafo station (Asafo): Cape Coast (C10, four hours), Accra (C10, four hours), Kunatase (C2, 45 minutes)

Alaba station (Alaba): Wa (C20, six hours), Tamale (C15, five hours)

Kejetia station (Kejetia Circle): for local tro-tros around Kumasi

Around Kumasi

The area around Kumasi is famed for its craft villages. Some have become quite touristy, but a couple of community-run initiatives are well worth a day trip.

The easiest way to visit these scattered villages is to hire a private taxi (about C70 for a full day).

Ntonso

Ntonso, 15km north of Kumasi, is the centre of adinkra cloth printing. Adinkra symbols represent concepts and aphorisms; they are traditionally printed on cotton fabric by using a natural brown dye and stamps carved out of calabash. You can see the whole process explained at **Ntonso's Craft Centre** (admission C3) and even create your own works; strips of fabric are sold for C10 and make a lovely keepsake.

Tro-tros travelling north from Kejetia station stop at Ntonso (C1).

Adanwomase

This kente-weaving and cocoa-growing village wins the Palme d'Or of eco-tourism in Ghana. Villagers here have put a huge amount of effort into developing fun, informative tours.

There are two visits on offer: a kente tour and a village tour (C5 each, or C7 combined). The kente tour takes you through the kente production process, from thread to finished product, and lets you try your hand at spinning and weaving. The village tour for its part takes you through the cocoa plantations, to local shrines and the local palace.

There are direct *tro-tros* (C1.10) from Kejetia station in Kumasi.

Lake Bosumtwe

With a depth of 86m, Lake Bosumtwe (also spelled Bosumtwi) is a crater lake that was formed from the impact of a huge meteorite. The lake is hugged by lush green hills in which you can hike, cycle and ride horses. Local hotels are your best bet to organise excursions. **The Green Ranch** (☑ 020 2917058; Lake Bosumtwe) offers horse-riding (per hour C30).

Located 38km southeast of Kumasi, the village of **Abono** is the gateway to Lake Bosumtwe; it is a popular weekend holiday spot for Kumasi residents, who come here to relax and swim (the water is bilharzia free). It's also a sacred site. The Ashanti people believe that their souls come here after death to bid farewell to the god Twi. Historically, dugout canoes and boats were forbidden on the lake, but the tide has turned and Bosumtwe becomes a haven for water-sport enthusiasts on the weekends.

Foreign visitors will be charged C2 upon arriving in Abono.

🛏 Sleeping & Eating

Lake Bosumtwe makes a great alternative to Kumasi for exploring Ashanti country: the accommodation is better value and the setting is, well, unrivalled. The downside is that there is less choice.

⭐ **Lake Point Guesthouse** LODGE $
(☑ 024-3452922; Lake Bosumtwe; dm/d/tr C10/38/46) This little piece of heaven sits right on the shore of Lake Bosumtwe, in a secluded spot about 2km east of Abono. The bungalows, bright and charming, are scattered on the slopes of a beautiful garden. Stephen, the Ghanaian owner, is a delightful host and can help you organise excursions around the lake and Ashanti country. His restaurant is the best in the area, with a daily changing menu (mains C12 to C25) and, a rare thing in Ghana, desserts.

Rainbow Garden Village LODGE $$
(☑ 024-3230288; Lake Bosumtwe; dm/d/bungalows C15/50/65) The Rainbow used to be the place to stay in Bosumtwe, but the hotel is looking a little tired these days. The location, right on the lakeside, is as enchanting as

ever, but the service and rooms need a new lease of life. It's located 4km west of Abono.

❶ Getting There & Away

You can sometimes find tro-tros travelling directly between Kumasi and Abono, but it's more likely you'll need to go to Kunatase first (C2, 45 minutes) and then catch a shared taxi from there (C1, 15 minutes).

THE NORTH

Tamale

POP 538,000

If the northern region is Ghana's breadbasket, Tamale is its kitchen. If you can take the heat, you'll discover a town with some good food, charm and a whole lot of soul. (If you can't, don't panic: Mole National Park is generally cooler.)

Tamale's population is largely Muslim and there are several interesting mosques around town, notably on Bolgatanga Rd. The National Culture Centre (off Salaga Rd) is a lively place, with craft shops and regular dance and music performances.

🛏 Sleeping

TICCS Guesthouse
GUESTHOUSE $

(☑ 037-2022914; www.ticcs.org/residence; s/d with fan C20/23, with air-con C27/30) Set in lovely grounds, this Christian guesthouse offers clean, simple rooms, serene surroundings and the great roof-terrace Jungle Bar. The full breakfast (fruit, porridge, bread, omelette, hot drink) is well worth the C8.

Catholic Guesthouse
GUESTHOUSE $

(☑ 037-2022265; Gumbihini Rd; s/d with fan C21/36, with air-con C25/48; P ❄) Simple, air-conditioned rooms wrapped around a pretty courtyard.

African Dream Hotel
GUESTHOUSE $$

(☑ 037-2091127; www.africandreamhotel.com; Bolgatanga Rd; r US$75-80; ❄ 🖥) A dream indeed to find this boutique guesthouse 10km north of Tamale. The work of a Franco-Ghanaian-Swiss couple, African Dream offers gorgeous rooms in pretty landscaped grounds. Because the guesthouse is outside of town, Abu Prince offers pick-ups and drops from town and the airport. He can also arrange tours to Mole National Park and northern Ghana.

✕ Eating & Drinking

Swad Fast Food
INDIAN $

(Gumbihini Rd; mains C7-13; ⊙ 9am-10pm) The name might not be a winner, but this is one of the best places to grab a bite in Tamale. The speciality is Indian, but there are also such delights as French onion soup, red red (a Ghanaian dish with beans) and fish-finger sandwiches.

Sparkles
CAFE $

(Culture Centre; mains C6-10; ⊙ 8am-8pm) A simple cafe serving good Ghanaian food alongside Western staples such as sandwiches. It's popular with local volunteers.

Jungle Bar
BAR

(TICCS Guesthouse, Gumbihini Link Rd; ⊙ 4-9pm) The Jungle Bar, on the grounds of the TICCS Guesthouse, is on a leafy balcony with an all-wood bar, cable TV and comfy benches and is probably the nicest spot for a drink in Tamale. Also serves food.

Giddipass
BAR

(Crest Restaurant, Salaga Rd; ⊙ 10am-10pm) Sit on the rooftop terrace and let an ice-cold beer and the sweet sounds of northern hiplife into your world at this decent drinking spot.

❶ Information

Barclays (Salaga Rd; ⊙ 8.30am-5pm Mon-Fri) Changes cash and travellers cheques; ATM.

Stanbic (Salaga Rd; ⊙ 8.30am-4.30pm Mon-Fri) Changes cash; ATM.

Tamale Teaching Hospital (☑ 037-2022454; Salaga Rd) The main hospital in Northern Ghana, 2km southeast of town.

Vodafone (internet per hr C1.40; ⊙ 9am-10pm; 🖥) The fastest connection in town (still pretty slow at busy times); it's right next to the towering radio mast near the STC bus station.

❶ Getting There & Away

Buses and tro-tros congregate around the Total petrol station and the radio mast in the centre of town. There are regular tro-tros to Bolgatanga (C6, three hours) and Wa (C15, six hours).

Air The airport is about 20km north of town; a private taxi there costs around C20. Antrak Air and Fly 540 Africa fly between Tamale and Accra from US$50 one way.

Bus STC buses go to Accra (C40, 12 hours, daily), Kumasi (C25, six hours, daily), Cape Coast and Takoradi (C33 to C35, 13 hours, twice a week). The daily Metro Mass bus to Mole National Park (C5, four to six hours) leaves in theory at 2.30pm (but in practice much later) from the bus station behind the

Total petrol station. Buy a ticket in advance or arrive at the bus station well before the scheduled departure time to be sure of a seat.

Mole National Park

With its swaths of saffron-coloured savannah, Mole National Park (☎027-7564444, 024-4316777; www.molemotelgh.com; adult/student C10/5, car C4, driver C5) offers what must surely be the cheapest safaris in Africa. There are at least 300 species of bird and 94 species of mammal, including African elephants, kob antelopes, buffalos, baboons and warthogs.

The park organises walking and driving safaris (2hr safari per person C6; ☺7.30am & 3.30pm). If you do not have your own vehicle, you can rent the park's for C100 for the two-hour safari; park rangers are happy to let you pool with other travellers.

The safaris are excellent and sightings of elephants are common from December to April. You're guaranteed to see other mammals year-round, however. Sturdy, covered footwear is a must; if you come without, the rangers will insist on lending you a pair of Wellington boots for a fee of C2.

🛏 Sleeping & Eating

Mole Motel   HOTEL **$$**
(☎024-4316777, 027-7564444; www.molemotelgh.com; Mole National Park; dm C24, r without/with aircon C70/90, bungalows C105; ❋❋) The park's only accommodation, Mole Motel is overpriced, with tired rooms and blasé service, but the location is stupendous (and the pool a godsend): at the top of an escarpment, with a viewing platform overlooking plains

teeming with wildlife. There's also a reasonable restaurant, serving a mix of Ghanaian and international fare (mains from C12 to C18). The hotel gets very busy, so make sure you book well in advance.

❶ Getting There & Away

A daily Metro Mass bus from Tamale (C5) arrives at the park motel around 7pm, if all goes well. The same bus overnights at the park, returning to Tamale the next day, leaving the park at around 4am.

A daily Metro Mass bus from Tamale to Wa (C8) passes through Larabanga around 9am or 10am; Mole Motel can arrange transport to Larabanga (C5).

Bolgatanga

POP 66,685

Bolgatanga – usually shortened to Bolga – was once the southernmost point of the ancient trans-Saharan trading route, running through Burkina Faso to Mali.

Bolga doesn't have much in the way of sights, but the city is laid-back and a fine base to explore the surrounding area – and it's the last stop on the road to Burkina.

Tanga Tours (☎024-9874044; tangatoursgh@gmail.com; Black Star Hotel, Bazaar Rd) offers guided scooter/bike excursions in the region. The renowned crafts market, where you'll find some of the best selections of textiles, leatherwork, baskets and the famous Bolga straw hats, takes place every three days.

For internet, head to Sirius Click Internet Café (Black Star Hotel, Bazaar Rd; per hr C1; ☺7.30am-9pm). Banks congregate around the main *tro-tro* station off Zuarungu Rd.

CULTURE AT MOLE

As well as the fantastic wildlife, Mole has some cultural gems to offer. Larabanga, the nearest village to the national park on the Tamale–Wa road, is famous for its mud-and-stick mosque, reputedly the oldest of its kind in Ghana.

Travellers have reported a fair bit of hassle at Larabanga in the past. To avoid complications, make sure you go with a local guide (C5), which you can easily arrange at the park's visitor centre.

About 10km east of the visitor centre, the village of Mognori (canoe trip 1-5 people C25, village tour per person C8, cultural performance 1-4 people C30) has become a flourishing ecotourism venture. The village sits right on the edge of the national park and villagers offer canoe safaris on the river (there are monkeys, birds and crocodiles), village tours (where you can learn about shea-butter production and traditional medicine), and drumming and dancing performances. Homestays can also be arranged (C10 per person per night, C10 for breakfast and dinner).

Tours are informative and the village very pretty and it makes a nice change from the Mole Motel if you're there for a few days.

🛏 Sleeping & Eating

Nsamini Guesthouse GUESTHOUSE $
(☎027-7316606, 038-2023403; off Navrongo Rd; r without/with bathroom C16/20) A popular choice, this cute courtyard set-up is one of Bolga's best budget buys. Rooms are clean and Koffi, the affable owner, will make you feel at home. It's up a lane leading off the Navrongo Rd.

Sands Garden Hotel HOTEL $
(☎038-2023464; sandgardenshotel@yahoo.com; off Zuarungu Rd, behind Metro Mass station; r with fan/air-con C30/50) A very pleasant establishment, with simple but impeccable rooms and very friendly management. The courtyard restaurant (mains C7 to C15) is one of the more popular in town. Rates include breakfast.

Black Star Hotel HOTEL $
(☎038-2022346; Bazaar Rd; s/d without bathroom C28/36, with bathroom C40/48; ❄ @) The prices say budget, but the hotel definitely feels mid-range, with air-con throughout and good facilities including a bar and an internet cafe. Some of the ground-floor rooms feel a little claustrophobic; ask to see a couple before you choose.

Swad Fast Food INTERNATIONAL $
(off Navrongo Rd; mains C10; ⊙11am-9pm) The outdoor terrace is lovely, but if the heat is too much, you can always retreat to the air-con dining room. The menu is eclectic – Indian, Chinese, Ghanaian – but excellent overall.

ℹ Getting There & Away

Tro-tros to Tamale (C6, three hours) and Paga (C4, 40 minutes) leave from the motor park off Zuarungu Rd, past the police station.

The STC bus station is 500m south of the centre, on the road to Tamale. There are daily services to Kumasi (C30, eight hours) and Accra (C44, 12 hours).

THE NORTHWEST

This remote corner of Ghana is hard to reach and seldom visited for that reason.

Wa

The capital of the Upper Northwest region is basically an overgrown village. If you happen to overnight here (to visit Wechiau or break the journey between Bobo-Dioulasso

---

PAGA'S CROCODILE PONDS

If you've ever dreamt of a *Crocodile Dundee* photo opportunity, make a beeline for **Paga's Crocodile Ponds** (adult/student C7/6, chicken to feed the croc C5). The ponds' reptiles, which are held sacred by the locals, are reputed to be the friendliest in Africa and, while we're not totally convinced, plenty of visitors do indeed safely pose with the crocs. Local women even do their laundry in the pond while kids frolic in the water. It is frankly disarming when you know how dangerous crocodiles can be.

Legend has it that this state of blissful cohabitation goes back to a pact the town's founders made with local crocodiles not to hurt each other.

There are two ponds to visit: Chief's Pond on the main road and Zenga Pond, about 500m east off the main road. Both are signposted.

---

and Kumasi), check out the town's mud-and-stick mosque.

The **Tegbeer Catholic Guesthouse** (☎039-2022375; r with shared bathroom & fan C30, s/d with bathroom & air-con C28/45; ❄), about 3km north of town, is an excellent option with clean, good rooms and a nice on-site bar-restaurant (mains C7). More upmarket is **Upland Hotel** (☎039-2022180; s/d C60/80), west of the town centre, which is popular with the town's businesspeople and has air-con and DSTV in the rooms. The restaurant serves international cuisine (mains C10).

There are regular *tro-tros* and buses to Wechiau (C2, one hour), Tamale (C15, six hours), Hamale (C6, three hours) and Kumasi (C20, six hours).

Wechiau Hippo Sanctuary

This much-hyped **hippo sanctuary** (www.ghanahippos.com; adult/student C7/5) on the Black Volta River was initiated by local village chiefs in 1999. Hippos can usually be seen from December to August; once the rainy season is under way, however, hippos disappear and the site becomes very hard to reach – probably not worth the considerable effort it takes to get to this remote corner of Ghana.

When you arrive, report at the community centre in Wechiau village, where you'll pay your fees and organise activities.

Options include river safaris, birdwatching, village tours and nature walks. All activities cost C6 per person per hour.

Accessing Wechiau is no small feat, even if you have your own vehicle. The village is located about 50km southwest of Wa, about an hour's drive; the sanctuary is then a further 20km (of bad tracks) from Wechiau. *Tro-tros* run between Wa and Wechiau (C2, one hour); the community centre can then help you hire a bicycle/motorbike/*tro-tro* for C5/10/20 to cover the last leg of the journey.

Unless you have your own vehicle, you'll have to overnight at the sanctuary. There is a very basic guesthouse (rooms C10); meals are not available, so you'll need to bring all your food.

UNDERSTAND GHANA

Ghana Today

Ghana is regarded by international analysts as West Africa's golden child: one of the continent's most stable democracies and fastest-growing economies.

Since the country discovered oil off the coast in 2007, the economy has gone into overdrive. Signs of this newfound prosperity abound, especially around Takoradi, the epicentre of the oil industry, and Accra: cranes work around the clock on new real estate developments, traffic congestion is horrendous, smart phones are everywhere – it definitely feels more like South Africa than Guinea or the DRC.

This is way too simplistic a portrait of Ghana, however. If you're a middle-class young professional living in the leafy 'burbs of Accra, life is good. Chances are you have running water, power, street lights and a fair wage.

But in Accra's poorest suburbs or the rural parts of northern Ghana, development is a work in progress. People defecate in the open for lack of sanitation; school-aged children sell water sachets in the street and women still spend many hours fetching water at the village pump.

The 2012 presidential elections made much of the debate on universal education and sharing the profits of wealth. John Dramani Mahama (who succeeded John Atta Mills as leader of the NDC after he died in July 2012) won, although his victory was being challenged at the time of writing by opposition candidate Nana Akufo-Addo on the grounds of alleged rigging.

History

Present-day Ghana has been inhabited since 4000 BC, filled by successive waves of migrants from the north and east. By the 13th century several kingdoms had developed, growing rich from the country's massive gold deposits and gradually expanding south along the Volta River to the coast.

Power & Conflict

By the 16th century one of the kingdoms, the Ashanti, emerged as the dominant power, conquering tribes left, right and centre and taking control of trade routes to the coast. Its capital, Kumasi, became a sophisticated urban centre, with facilities and services equal to those in Europe at the time. And it wasn't long until the Europeans discovered this African kingdom. First the Portuguese came prospecting around the coast; the British, French, Dutch, Swedish and Danish soon followed. They all built forts by the sea and traded slaves, gold and other goods with the Ashanti.

But the slave trade was abolished in the 19th century, and with it went the Ashanti domination. By that time the British had taken over the Gold Coast, as the area had come to be known, and began muscling in on Ashanti turf. This sparked several wars between the two powers, culminating in the British ransacking of Kumasi in 1874. The British then established a protectorate over Ashanti territory, which they expanded in 1901 to include areas to the north. The Gold Coast was now a British colony.

The Road to Independence

By the late 1920s the locals were itching for independence, and they set up political parties dedicated to this aim. However, parties like the United Gold Coast Convention (UGCC), formed in 1947, were too elitist and detached from those they were meant to represent – the ordinary workers. So the UGCC's secretary-general, Kwame Nkrumah, broke away in 1948 and formed the Conventional People's Party (CPP), which became an overnight success. Nkrumah was impatient for change and called for a national strike in 1949. The British, anxious about his popularity, jailed him. Despite this, the

CPP won the elections of 1951. Nkrumah was released and he became prime minister.

Independence & the Nkrumah Years

When Ghana finally won its independence in March 1957, Nkrumah became the first president of an independent African nation. His speeches, which denounced imperialism and talked about a free, united Africa, made him the darling of the pan-African movement.

But back home Nkrumah was not popular among traditional chiefs and farmers, who were unimpressed with the idea of unity under his rule. Factionalism and regional interests created an opposition that Nkrumah tried to contain through repressive laws, and by turning Ghana into a one-party state.

Nkrumah, however, skilfully kept himself out of the fray and concentrated on building prestige projects, such as the Akosombo Dam and several universities and hospitals.

But things were starting to unravel. Nkrumah expanded his personal bodyguard into an entire regiment, while corruption and reckless spending drove the country into serious debt. Nkrumah, seemingly oblivious to his growing unpopularity, made the fatal mistake of going on a state visit to China in 1966. While he was away his regime was toppled in an army coup. Nkrumah died six years later in exile in Guinea.

Dr Kofi Busia headed a civilian government in 1969 but could do nothing to overcome corruption and debt problems. Colonel Acheampong replaced him in a 1972 coup, but few things changed under his tenure.

The Rawlings Years

By 1979 Ghana was suffering food shortages and people were out on the streets demonstrating against the army fat cats. Enter Jerry Rawlings, a good-looking, charismatic, half-Scottish air-force pilot, who kept cigarettes behind his ear and spoke the language of the people. Nicknamed 'Junior Jesus', Rawlings captured the public's imagination with his calls for corrupt military rulers to be confronted and held accountable for Ghana's problems. The military jailed him for his insubordination, but his fellow junior officers freed him after they staged an uprising. Rawlings' Armed Forces Revolutionary Council (AFRC) then handed over power to a civilian government (after a general election) and started a major 'house cleaning'

operation – that is, executing and jailing senior officers.

The new president, Hilla Limann, was uneasy with Rawlings' huge popularity, and later accused him of trying to subvert constitutional rule. The AFRC toppled him in a coup in 1981, and this time Rawlings stayed in power for the next 15 years.

Although Rawlings never delivered his promised left-wing revolution, he improved the ailing economy after following the orders of the International Monetary Fund (IMF). During part of the 1980s, Ghana enjoyed Africa's highest economic growth rates.

The Democratic Era

By 1992 Rawlings was under worldwide pressure to introduce democracy, so he lifted the 10-year ban on political parties and called a general election. However, the hopelessly divided opposition couldn't get their act together, and Rawlings won the 1992 elections freely and fairly, with 60% of the vote. Still licking their wounds, the opposition withdrew from the following month's parliamentary elections, giving Rawlings' newly formed National Democratic Congress (NDC) an easy victory. In 1996 he repeated this triumph in elections that were again considered free and fair. At much the same time, the appointment of Ghanaian Kofi Annan as UN secretary-general boosted national morale.

After eight years of Rawlings and the NDC (the constitution barred Rawlings from standing for a third term in the 2000 presidential elections), his nominated successor and former vice-president, Professor John Atta Mills, lost to Dr John Kufuor, leader of the well-established New Patriotic Party (NPP). Some fun-loving members of Accra's growing middle class say his biggest legacy is the creation of the Accra Mall, a shiny shopping mall on the outskirts of town, complete with the country's first multiscreen cinema. Under the Kufuor administration, primary-school enrolment increased by 25% and many of Ghana's poor were granted access to free health care.

The 2008 election was widely regarded as a test of Ghana's ability to become a modern democracy. Atta Mills won by a slim margin and, despite the tensions with NPP competitor Nana Akufo-Addo, the election passed without serious violence.

People of Ghana

Ghana's population of 25 million makes it one of the most densely populated countries in West Africa. Of this, 44% are Akan, a grouping that includes the Ashanti (also called Asante), whose heartland is around Kumasi, and the Fanti, who fish the central coast and farm its hinterland. The Nzema, linguistically close to the Akan, fish and farm in the southwest. Distant migrants from present-day Nigeria, the Ga are the indigenous people of Accra and Tema. The southern Volta region is home to the Ewe.

In the north, the Dagomba heartland is around Tamale and Yendi. Prominent neighbours are the Gonja in the centre, Konkomba and Mamprusi in the far northeast, and, around Navrongo, the Kasena. The Sisala and Lobi inhabit the far northwest.

Religion

Ghana is a deeply religious country and respect for religion permeates pretty much every aspect of life, from hilarious sideboards ('Jesus Loves Fashion', 'If God Says Yes Snack Bar') to preachers on public transport and street corners, ubiquitous religious celebrations such as funerals, and the wholesale takeover of Ghana's airwaves by God (and his workers) on Sunday.

You'll come across churches of every imaginable Christian denomination; even the smallest village can have two or three different churches. About 70% of Ghanaians are Christian. Pentecostal and Charismatic denominations are particularly active, as are the mainline Protestant and Catholic churches. If you can bear the length (three to four hours), attending a service is an enlightening experience, whatever your creed.

Christianity was introduced by European missionaries, who were also the first educators, and the link between religion and education persists.

About 15% of the population is Muslim; the majority are in the north, though there are also substantial Muslim minorities in southern cities such as Accra and Kumasi.

Many Ghanaians also have traditional beliefs, notably in spirits and forms of gods who inhabit the natural world. Ancestor veneration is an important part of this tradition. Many people retain traditional beliefs alongside Christian or Muslim beliefs.

The Arts

Music

There's no doubt about it: Ghana's got rhythm. Whichever part of the country you visit, Ghana's soundtrack will be a constant travel companion. From the age of three or four children are taught to dance: it's not unusual to see little kids copying the hip-grinding and ass-shaking that characterises the average Ghanaian party.

Traditional music doesn't have the popular following that it has in countries such as Burkina. It tends to be reserved for special occasions and associated with royalty.

Contemporary music, on the other hand, is thriving. Highlife, a mellow mix of big-band jazz, Christian hymns, brass band and sailor sonnets, hit Ghana in the 1920s, and popular recordings include those by ET Mensah, Nana Ampadu and the Sweet Talks. Accra trumpeter ET Mensah formed his first band in the 1930s and went on to be crowned the King of Highlife, later performing with Louis Armstrong in Ghana.

WWII brought American swing to Ghana's shores, prompting the first complex fusion of Western and African music. Hiplife, a hybrid of rhythmic African lyrics poured over imported American hip-hop beats, has now been ruling Ghana since the early 1990s.

Imported American hip-hop and Nigerian music closely compete for the number two spot after highlife. Gospel music is also big, as is reggae.

Arts & Crafts

Ghana has a rich artistic heritage. Objects are created not only for their aesthetic value but as symbols of ethnic identity or to commemorate historical or legendary events, to convey cultural values or to signify membership of a group.

The Akan people of the southern and central regions are famous for their cloth, goldwork, woodcarving, chiefs' insignia (such as swords, umbrella tops and linguist staffs), pottery and bead-making.

Around Bolgatanga in the north, fine basket weaving and leatherwork are traditional crafts. Drums and carved *oware* boards – the game of *oware* has various names throughout West Africa – are also specialities.

TEXTILES

Kente cloth, with its distinctive basketwork pattern in garish colours, is Ghana's signature cloth. Originally worn only by Ashanti royalty, it is still some of the most expensive material in Africa. The cloth can be single-, double- or triple-weaved and the colour and design of the cloth worn are still important indicators of status and clan allegiance.

Kente is woven on treadle looms, by men only, in long thin strips that are sewn together. Its intricate geometric patterns are full of symbolic meaning, while its orange-yellow hues indicate wealth.

Food & Drink

Fiery sauces and oily soups are the mainstay of Ghanaian cuisine and are usually served with a starchy staple like rice, *fufu* (cooked and mashed cassava, plantain or yam) or *banku* (fermented maize meal).

About the most common dish you'll find is groundnut stew, a warming, spicy dish cooked with liquefied groundnut paste, ginger and either fish or meat. Palm-nut soup (fashioned from tomatoes, ginger, garlic and chilli pepper, as well as palm nut) takes its bright red colour from palm oil. Red-red is a delicous bean stew normally served with fried plantain.

Cold water is sold everywhere in plastic sachets (called 'pure water') for about C0.10. Fresh fruit juices are, oddly, rather hard to find. Beer, on the other hand, isn't: popular brands include Star, Club, Gulder and Guinness. For something stronger, look no further than *akpeteshie* (palm wine), the fiery local spirit made from palm wine.

SURVIVAL GUIDE

ℹ Directory A–Z

ACCOMMODATION

➡ If you're looking for a bargain, Ghana probably isn't it.

➡ Budget hotels don't often provide a top sheet, so pack a sleeping liner.

➡ Despite the high prevalence of malaria in Ghana, remarkably few hotels have mosquito nets; wear repellent and cull before you go to sleep.

➡ Rooms with bathrooms are generally called 'self-contained'.

EMBASSIES & CONSULATES
The following are all in Accra.

Australian High Commission (Map p174; ☑ 030-2216400; www.ghana.embassy.gov.au; 2 Second Rangoon Cl, Cantonments)

British High Commission (Map p174; ☑ 30-2213250; http://ukinghana.fco.gov.uk; 1 Osu Link)

Burkinabe Embassy (Map p178; ☑ 030-2221988; 2nd Mango Tree Ave, Asylum Down)

Canadian High Commission (Map p174; ☑ 030-2211521; www.canadainternational. gc.ca/ghana; 46 Independence Ave, Sankara Interchange)

Dutch Embassy (Map p174; ☑ 030-214350; www.ambaccra.nl; 89 Liberation Rd, Ako Adjei Interchange)

French Embassy (Map p174; ☑ 030-2214550; www.ambafrance-gh.org; 12th Lane, off Liberation Rd)

German Embassy (Map p174; ☑ 030-2211000; www.accra.diplo.de; 6 Ridge Rd, North Ridge)

Ivorian Embassy (Map p174; ☑ 030-774611; 18th Lane, Osu)

Togolese Embassy (Map p174; ☑ 030-777950; 4th Circular Rd)

US Embassy (Map p174; ☑ 030-2741000; http://ghana.usembassy.gov; 4th Circular Rd)

EMERGENCY
Call ☑ 193 for ambulance, ☑ 192 for fire and ☑ 191 for police.

ETIQUETTE

➡ Ghanaians are an affable lot and greetings are of paramount importance. You will always be welcomed, greeted and asked how you are and it is expected you do the same in return.

➡ Humour is entrenched in Ghanaian culture and always the best way to deal with tricky situations; for instance, when calls of 'Obroni' (meaning white person) become too much, it's fine to call back 'Bebeni' (meaning black person).

➡ In Muslim areas, remember not to pass food or shake hands with your left hand.

➡ The only way to call somebody or get their attention is by hissing or making a 'tsssss' sound; this is also how people will try to get your attention.

FESTIVALS & EVENTS

Ghana has many festivals and events, including the Fetu Afahye Festival (first Saturday of September) in Cape Coast, the Bakatue Festival (first Tuesday in July) in Elmina, the Fire Festival (dates vary according to the Muslim calendar) of the Dagomba people in Tamale and various year-round Akan celebrations in Kumasi. Pana-fest, an arts festival, is celebrated biennially in Cape Coast.

INTERNET ACCESS
You can get online pretty much anywhere in Ghana these days. Many hotels offer wi-fi, all mobile-phone networks have 3G and there are internet cafes in every town and city (connection costs C1 to C2.50 per hour).

MONEY
In 2007 four zeros were lopped off the value of the old Ghana cedi (divided into 100 pesewas), making it the highest-value currency in West Africa. For the most part, Ghanaians have adjusted, but you'll still hear people asking for C10,000 when they really want C1.

➤ The best currencies to bring are US dollars, UK pounds and euros, in that order.

➤ Barclays is the only bank to exchange travellers cheques; there is a maximum of US$250 per transaction.

➤ Foreign-exchange bureaus are dotted around most major towns: note that they give lower exchange rates for small USD denominations, so pack your $50 and $100 notes.

➤ There are ATMs virtually everywhere; almost every bank accepts Visa. Stanbic accepts Mastercard and Maestro.

➤ Midrange and top-end hotels tend to accept credit cards, but at a surcharge.

OPENING HOURS
Administrative buildings From 8am until 2pm or so. Embassies tend to keep similar hours.
Banks 8am-5pm Monday to Friday; some additionally run until noon on Saturday.
Markets 7am-5pm; in predominately Muslim areas, Friday is quieter; in Christian areas, it's Sunday.
Shops 9am-5pm or 6pm every day except Sunday, when only large stores open.

PUBLIC HOLIDAYS
New Year's Day 1 January
Independence Day 6 March
Good Friday March/April
Easter Monday March/April
Labour Day 1 May
May Bank Holiday 1st Monday in May
Africa Unity Day 25 May
Republic Day 1 July
Founders Day 21 September
Christmas Day 25 December
Boxing Day 26 December

Ghana also celebrates Muslim holidays, which change dates every year.

SAFE TRAVEL
Ghana has proved to be a stable and generally peaceful country. Take care of your valuables on beaches and avoid walking alone at night. If swimming, beware strong currents; ask locals before diving in.

TELEPHONE
➤ Ghana's country code is +233.

➤ Mobile (cell) phones are ubiquitous in Ghana and the network coverage is virtually universal and excellent value.

➤ If you have an unlocked phone, SIM cards (C5) can be picked up in shopping centres and communication centres.

➤ MTN, Vodafone, Tigo and Airtel are the main networks; all have 3G.

➤ International SMS costs about C0.1, international calls from C0.13 per minute.

TOURIST INFORMATION
As a rule, tourist information is pretty useless in Ghana, and staff working in tourist offices have little understanding of what travellers need.

NCRC (www.ncrc-ghana.org) The driving force behind Ghana's most successful community-tourism ventures and a good source of information on the topic.

No Worries Ghana (www.noworriesghana.com) Published by the North American Women's Association, this guide (both paper and electronic) is more targeted at people moving to rather

PRACTICALITIES

➤ **Newspapers** Accra's best dailies are *Daily Graphic* (www.graphic.com.gh) and *Ghanaian Chronicle* (www.ghanaian-chronicle.com).

➤ **BBC World Service** Listened to widely; in Accra it's 101.3FM.

➤ **Radio** Local Ghanaian stations include the excellent Joy FM (news and music; 99.7FM), Choice FM (102.3) and Gold FM (90.5).

➤ **TV** Ghana's biggest TV stations are GTV, Metro TV and TV3. Satellite TV is increasingly available in midrange and upmarket hotels.

➤ **Electricity** 230V and three-pin British-style plugs are used. Power cuts remain frequent.

➤ **Languages** English, plus nine local languages.

than travelling to Ghana; nonetheless, the dozens of eating, drinking and entertainment listings as well as the information on shipping, transport and so on is very useful.

Touring Ghana (www.touringghana.com) Ghana's official tourism portal; worth a look for inspiration and general information.

VISAS

Visas are required by everyone except Economic Community of West African States (Ecowas) nationals. Though it's technically possible to pick up a visa upon arrival, they only get granted in rare cases, so it is highly advisable you get one ahead of travelling.

➡ Single-entry three-month visas (US$60/£50) and multiple-entry six-month visas (US$100/£70) are standard.

➡ You can get a visa extension at the immigration office (p180) in Accra near the Sankara Interchange.

Visas for Onward Travel

Most nationalities need a visa for onward travel throughout West Africa.

Burkina Faso The embassy issues visas for three months (C73), usually in 24 hours. You need three photos.

Côte d'Ivoire A three-month visa costs CFA65,000 and requires a hotel confirmation. See full list of requirements at www.snedai. com. The Visa de l'Entente, available in Burkina Faso, is a much more expedient and cheaper process.

Togo The embassy issues visas for one month on the same day. Alternatively, you can get a visa at the border at Aflao, but it's only valid for seven days and you'll need to extend it in Lomé.

VOLUNTEERING

Ghana is one of Africa's top volunteering spots, and you'll find literally hundreds of organisations that arrange short-term and long-term placements.

Many guesthouses listed in this book can help arrange short-term placements within their communities or local schools. The government-sponsored US Peace Corps and UK Voluntary Service Overseas are both active in Ghana.

❶ Getting There & Away

You need a yellow-fever vaccination certificate to enter Ghana.

AIR

Kotoka International Airport in Accra is Ghana's international gateway and an increasingly important hub for regional African air travel.

➡ Every major European airline flies to Accra; Emirates now also flies daily to Dubai, open-

ing a host of easy connections to Asia-Pacific. There are direct flights to the US east coast.

➡ You'll find plenty of direct flights to other parts of Africa, including South Africa, Kenya, Ethiopia, Egypt, Morocco and most neighbouring West African countries.

LAND

Ghana has land borders with Côte d'Ivoire to the west, Burkina Faso to the north and west, and Togo to the east. Crossing is generally straightforward. The main border crossings:

➡ With Côte d'Ivoire: Elubo, Sunyani-Agnibilékrou and Bole-Ferkessédougou

➡ With Burkina Faso: Paga and Hamale

➡ With Togo: Aflao and Wli

Border crossings are normally open 6am to 6pm, except Afloa, which shuts at 10pm.

Burkina Faso

➡ Direct STC buses run to Ouagadougou from Accra (C48 + CFA1000, 24 hours) and Kumasi three times a week.

➡ From Paga, there are frequent *tro-tros* to Bolgatanga (C4, 40 minutes); on the Burkina side, you'll find plenty of onward transport to Pô and Ouagadougou.

➡ There were rumours that a direct bus service between Kumasi and Bobo-Dioulasso via Wa would start running in 2013. Until then, you'll need to get a *tro-tro* from Wa to Hamale. On the Burkina side, you'll find transport to Diebougou and then Bobo-Dioulasso.

Côte d'Ivoire

➡ STC buses run daily between Accra and Abidjan (C39 + CFA1000, 12 hours).

➡ Otherwise you'll find *tro-tros* running between Takoradi and Elubo (three hours), from where you can cross into Côte d'Ivoire and find onward transport to Abidjan.

Togo

➡ The easiest way to cross into Togo is to catch a bus or a *tro-tro* to Aflao, pass the border on foot and catch a taxi on the other side to central Lomé.

➡ Overlanders may prefer to cross at the less hectic Wli border post near Hohoe.

❶ Getting Around

AIR

➡ Antrak Air (p192) and Fly 540 Africa (p192) operate domestic flights in Ghana.

➡ There are several daily flights from Accra to Kumasi (45 minutes), Takoradi (35 minutes) and Tamale (1¼ hours). They tend to be relatively cheap and a huge time saver when travelling north.

BUS

➤ Buses are preferable to *tro-tros* for long journeys as they tend to be more comfortable and reliable.

➤ **STC** (http://beta.stcghana.com.gh) is Ghana's main long-haul bus company; its route network is extensive, it is fairly reliable and despite the sometimes unbearably loud music/film/radio, it's relatively comfortable (air-con).

➤ Other relevant bus companies for travellers include **VIP**, which runs half-hourly buses between Accra and Kumasi, and **Metro Mass** (www.metromass.com), which runs local services in various parts of the country.

➤ It's wise to book in advance as tickets get snapped up fast on the more popular routes.

➤ Services are usually less frequent on Sunday.

➤ There is always a charge for luggage. Theoretically, it should be per kilogram, but in practice, large rucksacks or suitcases just tend to be charged a flat C1.

CAR & MOTORCYCLE

➤ Driving is on the right in Ghana.

➤ Most main roads are in pretty good condition, though almost all secondary roads are unsealed.

➤ You will need an international driver's license.

➤ Hiring a car with a driver is a good option if you're short on time; travel agencies can usually arrange this. Depending on the distance,

car and driver experience, factor in anything from US$70 to US$120 per day, plus fuel.

TAXIS

➤ Within towns and on some shorter routes between towns, shared taxis are the usual form of transport. They run on fixed routes, along which they stop to pick up and drop off passengers. Fares are generally very cheap (C0.30 to C0.50).

➤ Private taxis don't have meters and rates are negotiable. It's best to ask a local in advance for the average cost between two points.

➤ Taxis can be chartered for an agreed period of time, anything from one hour to a day, for a negotiable fee.

TRO-TRO

Tro-tro is a catch-all category that embraces any form of public transport that's not a bus or taxi. Generally they're minibuses.

➤ *Tro-tros* cover all major and many minor routes.

➤ They don't work to a set timetable but leave when full.

➤ Fares are set but may vary on the same route depending on the size and comfort (air-con) of the vehicle.

➤ There is generally an additional luggage fee.

➤ The area where *tro-tros* and buses congregate is called, interchangeably, lorry park, motor park or station.

Guinea

Fast Facts

➡ **Capital** Conakry

➡ **Population** 10.8 million

➡ **Languages** French, Malinke, Pulaar (Fula) and Susu

➡ **Area** 245,857 sq km

➡ **Currency** Guinean franc (GFr)

➡ **Visa requirements** 90-day visa and yellow-fever certificate required

➡ **Tourist information** www.ontguinee.org

Rugged Landscapes & Vibrant Beats

Imagine you're travelling on smooth highway, and then get tempted by a tiny, dusty turn-off into rugged terrain, where surprising beauty and treacherous vistas define the route. Guinea is that turn-off. This is a country blessed with amazing landscapes; from the mountain plateau Fouta Djalon to wide Sahelian lands and thick forests.

Overland drivers are drawn here by rugged tracks, and the challenge of steering their vehicles over rocks and washed-out paths. Nature lovers can lose themselves on long hikes past plunging waterfalls, proud hills and tiny villages, or track elephants through virgin rainforest. While Guinea is not famed for its beaches, those it does have are stunning, and often deserted.

Guinea Top Sights

➡ **Îles de Los** Stretch out on palm-fringed strands, sipping fresh coconut juice

➡ **Fouta Djalon** Ramble through the mountains and swim in the waterfalls of this majestic mountain plateau

➡ **Bossou** Come face to face with chattering chimps

➡ **Conakry** Hop through the capital's dubious dives, getting drunk on some of West Africa's best live music

➡ **Forêt Classée de Ziama** Track elephants in the virgin rainforest

➡ **Parc National du Haut Niger** Look for chimps and buffaloes in one of West Africa's last tropical dry-forest ecosystems

➡ **Kankan** Squeeze through narrow market streets and visit the beautiful Grand Mosquée in this lively university town

UNDERSTAND GUINEA

Guinea Today

Following the death in 2008 of president Lansana Conté, an army contingent under Captain Moussa Dadis Camara took power in a coup d'état. 'Dadis' promised that he'd quickly clean up the Guinean house, organise elections and return to the army barracks. His initial measures, such as cracking down on Guinean drug rings (Guinea is one of West Africa's hubs of the cocaine trade), and announcing anti-corruption measures and new mining deals (Guinea is hugely rich in natural resources, owning 30% of the world's bauxite resources), gained him many followers.

However, his announcement in 2009 that he would consider standing in the upcoming elections, and increasing violence committed by members of the army, provoked furious reactions. On 28 September 2009, army elements quashed a large demonstration with extreme violence. A UN commission denounced the events as a crime against humanity, and it is thought that over 150 people were killed. Two months later, 'Dadis' was shot (but not killed) following a dispute with his aide-de-camp Toumba Diakite.

After meeting in Ouagadougou in January 2010, 'Dadis', his vice-president Sekouba Konaté and Blaise Compaoré, president of Burkina Faso, produced a formal statement of 12 principles promising a return of Guinea to civilian rule within six months. A provisional government supervised the transition to civilian rule at the end of 2010.

After half a century in opposition, Alpha Conde, from the Malinke ethnic group, was declared winner in Guinea's first democratic election since independence from France in 1958. However, the vote kindled ethnic tensions. Conde's defeated rival, Cellou Dalein Diallo, is a member of the Fula ethnic group,

ℹ️ COUNTRY COVERAGE

At the time of research very few travellers were heading to Guinea, so we're providing historical and cultural information rather than reviews and listings. A good source of information for on-the-ground travel in Guinea is Lonely Planet's Thorn Tree on-line travel forum www.lonelyplanet.com/thorntree. Another source of good internet-based information is www.ontguinee.org.

to which 40% of Guineans belong. Diallo has consistently accused the president of marginalising his constituents, including many Fula.

Conde's Conakry residence suffered an armed attack in July 2011. The building was partially destroyed, but Conde was unharmed.

Travel here can be difficult. Guinea is not as set up for tourism as some other countries in the region, and beyond the capital creature comforts are scarce. Taxis and buses are poorly maintained and unreliable, and for overlanders, rugged tracks, steep laterite and washed-out paths can be a challenge.

There were serious riots and violent demonstrations in Conakry in late 2012 and early 2013. Muggings at gunpoint are increasingly common across the country.

History

Guinea was part of the Empire of Mali, which covered a large part of western Africa between the 13th and 15th centuries; the empire's capital, Niani, is in eastern Guinea. From the mid-1400s Portuguese and other European traders settled Guinea's coastal region, and the country eventually became a French colony in 1891.

The end of French West Africa began with Guinea. In 1958, Sekou Touré was the only West African leader to reject a French offer of membership in a commonwealth, and instead demanded total independence. French reaction was swift: financial and technical aid was cut off, and there was a massive flight of capital.

Sekou Touré called his new form of state a 'communocracy', a blend of Africanist and communist models. It didn't work; the economy went into a downward spiral, and his growing paranoia triggered a reign of terror.

'Conspiracies' were being sensed everywhere; thousands of supposed dissidents were imprisoned and executed. By the end of the 1960s over 250,000 Guineans lived in exile.

Towards the end of his presidency Touré changed many of his policies and tried to liberalise the economy. He died in March 1984.

Days after Touré's death, a military coup was staged by a group of colonels, including the barely known, barely educated Lansana Conté, who became president. He introduced austerity measures, and in 1991 bowed to pressure to introduce a multiparty political system. Initial hopes for a new era of freedom and prosperity were quickly dashed. Conté claimed victory in three highly disputed elections, and there were incidents of obstruction and imprisonment of opposition leaders. In 2007 demonstrations were violently quashed, though a few concessions (such as the nomination of a prime minister) were made. Severely ill and barely able to govern, Conté stayed in power until his death in December 2008.

Music & Culture

Overshadowed on the international stage by neighbouring Mali and Senegal, Guinea still packs a punch when it comes to musical tradition.

Sekou Touré's form of communism may have been an economic disaster, but the government's emphasis on nationalist *authenticité* in the arts, and state patronage of artistic institutions, was a bonus. Musicians were funded and allowed time to perfect their art, paving the way for the sound most commonly associated with Guinean music – that of the great dance orchestras of the 1960s and '70s. They, in turn, were strongly influenced by the traditions of the Mande *griots* (West Africa's hereditary praise singers).

The first orchestra to leap to fame was the Syli National Orchestra, whose guitarist, 'Grand' Papa Diabaté, became one of the greatest stars of Guinea's music scene. They perfected the Guinean rumba, a fusion of traditional songs and Latin music. Bembeya Jazz would achieve even greater recognition, thanks, in part, to their guitarist, Sékou 'Diamond Fingers' Diabaté, one of the most talented musicians of his generation.

Legendary South African singer and activist Miriam Makeba lived in exile in Guinea from the late 1960s until the early 1980s, recording with and performing alongside some of the top local musicians.

In the early 1980s, Guinea's dire economic situation had worsened and large orchestras became difficult to fund, forcing many artists to Abidjan, where 90% of all Guinean releases were recorded. The centre of the pop world soon shifted to Paris, where acclaimed Guinean vocalist and kora player Mory Kanté was based.

Alongside Kanté and Sekouba Diabaté, who joined Bembeya Jazz at the age of 19 before going solo in the 1990s, popular musicians today include Ba Cissoko (a band whose sound has been described as 'West Africa meets Jimi Hendrix'), and *kora* player and vocalist Djeli Moussa Diawara. Guinea also has a vibrant hip-hop scene, with many young artists using their music to lash out at Guinea's poor living conditions and political corruption. The best-known name in Guinean hip-hop is Bill de Sam.

Dance is also popular in Guinea. The dance group Les Ballets Africains today remains the 'prototype' of West African ballet troupes, while Circus Baobab mixes trapeze shows and acrobatics with their dance shows.

Camara Laye, author of *L'Enfant Noir*, is the country's best-known writer.

To pick up some typical arts and crafts, try the indigo and mud-cloth cooperatives in many towns.

When it comes to eating out, proper restaurants are rare outside Conakry, though most towns have a couple of basic eating houses serving *riz gras* (rice fried in oil and tomato paste and served with fried fish, meat or vegetables) or simple chicken and chips. In Fouta Djalon, creamy sauces made from meat and potato leaves (*haako putte*) or manioc leaves (*haako bantara*) are common.

Guinea's main ethnic groups are the Fula (about 40% of the population), Malinke (about 30%) and Susu (about 20%). Fifteen other groups, living mostly in the forest region, constitute the rest of the population. Susu predominantly inhabit the coastal region; Fula, the Fouta Djalon; and Malinke, the north and centre. The total population is about 9.8 million. About 85% of the population is Muslim (the Fouta Djalon being a centre of Islam), 8% are Christian and the remainder follow traditional animist religions (especially in the forest region and the Basse Côte).

GUINEA MUSIC & CULTURE

Guinea-Bissau

♪ 245 / POP 1.5 MILLION

Why Go?

For a country that consistently elicits frowns from heads of state and news reporters, Guinea-Bissau will pull a smile from even the most world-weary traveller. The jokes here, like the music, are loud but tender. The bowls of grilled oysters are served with a lime sauce spicy enough to give a kick, but not so strong as to mask the bitterness. The buildings are battered and the faded colonial houses bowed by sagging balconies, but you'll see beauty alongside the decay.

Here, bare silver trees spring up like antler horns between swathes of elephant grass, and cashew sellers tease each other with an unmistakably Latin spirit. Board a boat for the Bijagós, where you can watch hippos lumber through lagoons full of fish and spot turtles nesting.

Despite painful wars, coups and cocaine hauls, Guinea-Bissau buzzes with joy, even when daily life is tough and the future bleak. There must be magic in that cashew juice.

Best Places to Eat

➡ Oysters on Quinhámel beach (p215)

➡ Dom Bifana (p212)

➡ Adega do Loureiro (p211)

➡ Berca do Rio (p215)

Best Places to Stay

➡ Ponta Anchaca (p214)

➡ Kasa Afrikana (p214)

➡ Pensão Creola (p209)

When to Go
Bissau

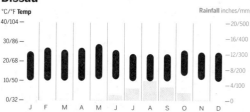

Dec–Feb The year's coolest months, when sea turtles emerge from their nests.

Mar–Jul Hot, humid and sweaty; travel with plenty of water and sunscreen.

Aug–Oct Batten down the hatches or dance in the rain; the rainwater will just keep fallin'.

BISSAU

POP 450,000

In the early evening, the fading sunlight lends the crumbling colonial facades of Bissau Velho (Old Bissau) a touch of old-age glamour. Dozens of generators set the town trembling, and ignite the lights of stylish bars and restaurants that form something of a modern, indoor city in startling contrast with the worn exterior.

Sights

Bissau Velho (Old Bissau), a stretch of narrow alleyways and derelict buildings, is 'guarded' by the **Fortaleza d'Amura** (off the southern end of Av Amílcar Cabral), an imposing fort that is not accessible to visitors. With its bombed-out roof and shrapnel-riddled neoclassical facade, the **former presidential palace** (Praça dos Heróis Nacionais) sends a powerful message about Guinea-Bissau's simmering conflicts. The rebuilt and brushed-up **Assembleia Ministério da Justiça**, by contrast, is an architectural expression of democratic hopes.

Festivals & Events

Carnaval   CARNIVAL
Bissau and Bubaque's Carnaval is the country's biggest party. It takes place every year in February or early March during the week leading up to Ash Wednesday and the beginning of Lent. Music, masks, drinking and dancing are the order of the day.

Sleeping

Bissau has a mix of accommodation for most budgets.

Pensão Creola   PENSION $
(☑ 6633031; www.pensaobissau.com; Ave Domingos Ramos; s/d from CFA15,000/18,000) Run by a knowledgeable Swiss-Guinean couple, this is Bissau's best budget stop. Rooms in the pretty colonial-style villa are ideal for groups, with two or three single beds and a shared bathroom. At the back of the house, single rooms with fans, showers and desks are housed in a wooden extension that backs onto the garden. There's 24-hour power, but, at the time of research, no wi-fi or air-con.

GUINEA-BISSAU BISSAU

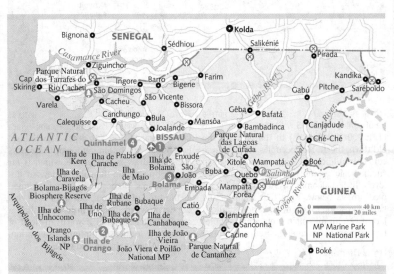

Guinea-Bissau Highlights

❶ Dancing tango in cobbled streets by candlelight, after a dinner of *bacalau* (salted flakes of cod) and red wine at **Bissau Velho** (p209)

❷ Locking eyes with hippos as they emerge from the warm saltwater lagoons of **Ilha de Orango** (p214)

❸ Sitting on the steps of the abandoned town hall, with its crumbling Greek-style pillars, on the island of **Bolama** (p214)

❹ Dipping oysters in hot lime sauce after a day in the water at **Quinhámel** (p215)

Bissau

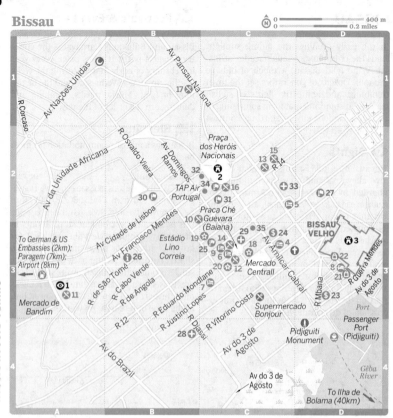

Hotel Ta Mar   HOTEL **$**

(☎6606744; Rua 3, Bissao Velho; s/d CFA15,000/25,000; ❄🛜) In the heart of the old town, the Ta Mar occupies a Portuguese colonial building. Gloomy corridors lead to small, basic rooms that are redeemed by lovely little balconies overlooking the cobbled streets below. Note that some of the bathrooms don't have doors. There's an adjacent restaurant/coffee shop, and the hotel has 24-hour power and, theoretically, wi-fi.

Hotel Diarama   HOTEL **$$**

(☎6716000, 5651255; http://bissau-hoteldiarama. com; Ave Pansau Na Isna ; s/d CFA40,000/50,000; ❄🛜) Popular with visiting NGO workers, the Diarama has modern, bright, clean rooms with 24-hour power, air-con, wi-fi and decent bathrooms. From here it's a five-minute walk to the old town, and you can hail a taxi outside the front door.

Hotel Kalliste   HOTEL **$$**

(☎6765662; kallistebissau@hotmail.com; Praça Ché Guevara; d CFA35,000; ❄🛜) The Kalliste is a Bissau institution, although these days the main draw is the terrace, which is far more atmospheric than the somewhat unloved rooms. Renovations were planned at the time of research, but until then this Corsican-owned hotel is little more than a scruffy fallback option if you're in need of a centrally located last-minute reservation. There's security, air-con and wi-fi.

★Coimbra Hotel   BOUTIQUE HOTEL **$$$**

(☎3201490, 3213467; www.hotelcoimbra.net; Ave Amílcar Cabral; r from CFA76,000; ❄@🛜) The Coimbra has smart, modern rooms decked out with African art and speakers. Climb the steps to the bougainvillea-fringed terrace or head downstairs into the main building, which houses a bar, piano room, chess tables and a spa. The restaurant does an excel-

Bissau

lent lunch and dinner buffet with a choice of wines, and the breakfast bar is easily the best in town. Call ahead for airport pick-up.

Hotel Malaika HOTEL **$$$**
(☎6710010, 3207474; http://hotelinbissau.blogspot. de; Ave Osvaldo Vieira; s/d from CFA80,000/100,000; ❄☏) Despite its African name, you could be anywhere in the world when you step into the chain hotel–like lobby of the Malaika. The rooms are smart, stylish and comfortable, with the usual creature comforts, and there's a bar and ATM downstairs.

✖ Eating

Spicy local dishes, waters brimming with fresh fish and Portuguese culinary influences make Bissau a foodie's paradise.

Restaurant Samaritana AFRICAN **$**
(☎6131392; off Ave Pansau Na Isna; mains CFA2500) It's made from a cut-out container and buzzes with Guineans of all ranks and incomes eager to sample the reliably delicious meals.

Adega do Loureiro PORTUGUESE **$**
(Rua 5 de Julho; mains from CFA4000; ❄☏) There are wooden chairs, patterned tablecloths, terracotta ceiling tiles and carafes of red wine at this old-style Portuguese restaurant. The *bacalau* (salted flakes of cod) is salty

and succulent, the pork chops are flavorsome and the little red pots of beans and rice are the perfect comfort food.

Morabeza INTERNATIONAL **$**
(Praça Ché Guevara; meals from CFA2000) Order fast food at the counter downstairs or climb the rickety stairs to the terrace, where you can eat *brochettes* (kebabs), pizza, steak and salads under a sky full of stars.

O Bistro FRENCH **$**
(☎3206000; Rua Eduardo Mondlane; mains CFA4000; ⊙noon-3pm & 7pm-late; ❄⊿) This Belgian-owned spot has all the right ingredients: excellent, reasonably priced mains including fresh catches, sautéed vegetables and *crepes au chocolat,* friendly service, a well-stocked bar and a warm ambience that transcends the air-con. Bring mosquito spray if you want the big table on the verandah.

Mamaputcha CAFE **$**
(Rua Eduardo Mondlane; meals from CFA2000) Scratched tables spill out onto the pavement outside Mamaputcha, owned by the sister of Super Mama Djombo bandleader Atchuchi. If you're after glamour, you won't find it here. But you will find warm bowls of fries begging to be dipped in mayonnaise and plates of *brochettes* marinated to perfection.

Kalliste Restaurant
FRENCH **$$**

(☑6765662; Praça Ché Guevara; meals from CFA4000) If the potted plants lining Hotel Kalliste's terrace had ears, what stories they would tell...this central bar/restaurant buzzes at night, attracting everyone from tired UN lawyers to politicians, activists, conservation volunteers and mosquitoes. There's live music most evenings and the pizzas are pretty good.

Pastelaria Imperia
BAKERY **$$**

(pastries from CFA500) Across the roundabout from the presidential palace, the *pastelaria* (cake shop) has the largest selection of cakes, pastries and ice cream in Bissau. Swing by here to pick up breakfast fodder, or head to the big covered terrace for mid-afternoon coffee and cake.

Dom Bifana
EUROPEAN **$$**

(✱) Adjacent to Bissau's parliament building, this classy restaurant serves up more than just *bifanas* (Portuguese sandwiches). Expats and parliamentarians come for steak, finely grilled shrimp and divine desserts. There's a decent wine list and a tranquil atmosphere in the semialfresco dining room.

ⓘ SET YOUR BUDGET

Budget

➜ Hotel room CFA15,000

➜ Rice, fish and spicy okra sauce CFA2000

➜ Imported Cristal beer CFA600

➜ Shared taxi ride in Bissau CFA350

Midrange

➜ Hotel room CFA35,000

➜ Bowl of grilled oysters for two CFA7000

➜ Gin and tonic in a bar CFA2500

➜ Private taxi ride in Bissau CFA1000

Top End

➜ Hotel room CFA76,000

➜ Steak in upmarket restaurant CFA7000

➜ Glass of wine CFA3000

➜ 4x4 with driver, per day outside Bissau CFA70,000

🍷 Drinking & Nightlife

X Club
CLUB

(☑3213467; Rua Osualdo Vieira) At X (pronounced 'sheesh') Club, join the odd assembly of hard-working UN staff, shady businessmen and sparkling party folk on their glitzy trip through the night.

Insonias
CLUB

Get lost among the plastic palm trees and plastic people at Insonias, a bizarrely decorated club popular with the NGO and UN crowd at weekends. Open until dawn.

Saboura
CLUB

Guineans and expats head to Saboura (in Pilom) to dance until the sun comes up. The place is usually teeming on Thursday nights.

Centre Culturel Franco-Bissao-Guinéen
PERFORMING ARTS

(☑3206816; Praça Ché Guevara; ⊙9am-10pm Mon-Fri; 🛜) This bright, modern centre houses a library/workspace, an art gallery, a performance space and a small cafe. There are regular performances by dance and theatre groups and the centre hosts film screenings. The cafe does coffees, breakfast sandwiches and great-value mains for lunch. Specials include lasagne, baked fish and salads and prices start at around CFA2000. Wi-fi access is available for CFA2000 per day.

🛍 Shopping

Diagonally across from Ta Mar Restaurant is **Cabaz di Terra** (Ave Pansau Na Isna), which stocks gorgeous, fairly produced Guinean throws, handbags and jewellery. Part of the store is devoted to condiments such as honey, cashew juice and *fleur du sel*. At nearby **Bibas** (Ave Pansau Na Isna) you can flip through the racks of vintage and recycled dresses.

Bissau's main market is at **Bandim**, a five-minute cab ride in the direction of the airport. Here you can pick up everything from fresh cherry tomatoes to oysters to black-and-white cloth embroidered with the image of Amílcar Cabral.

ⓘ Orientation

Bissau's main drag is the wide Ave Amílcar Cabral, running between the port and Praça dos Heróis Nacionais. On the northwestern edge of the centre is the Mercado de Bandim. From here, Ave de 14 Novembro leads northwest to the main *paragem* (bus and taxi park), the airport and all inland destinations.

WARNING

Although beautiful, Guinea-Bissau is unstable, and even periods of calm can be followed by violent flare-ups. Although attacks and coup attempts rarely wound civilians or visitors, human rights abuses have been documented. If the current situation looks calm, however, don't let the chronic instability dissuade you from visiting – people here will be thrilled to welcome you, and tourism could help get Guinea-Bissau on its feet again. Do note that shops, banks, businesses and, more rarely, borders may close during tense periods.

ℹ Information

INTERNET ACCESS

For wi-fi access, head to the terrace of the Hotel Kalliste (CFA2000 per day) or the Centre Culturel Franco-Bissao-Guinéen (p212; CFA2000 per day). Both places have accessible power sockets and will allow you to linger. Where the road to the airport meets Bairro Ajudda is **Lenox**, a sports cafe/performance space that has a small cybercafe inside.

MEDICAL SERVICES

Pharmacia Nur Din (Rua Vitorino Costa) A reasonably well-stocked pharmacy.

Policlinica (☑ 3207581; info@policlinica. bissau.com; Praça Ché Guevera) A better option for illnesses than a trip to the hospital.

Simão Mendes (☑ 3212861; Ave Pansau Na Isna) Bissau's main hospital; in a poor state.

MONEY

It's wise to travel with a supply of cash. At the time of research, there were only two ATMs in the country that accepted international Visa cards (MasterCard was not compatible); one is inside Hotel Malaika, the other across the road from Hotel Kalliste. Hotels do not take payment by credit or debit cards, although some, such as the Coimbra Hotel, accept wire transfers. To change money, either ask your hotel for an informal moneychanger or try Ecobank or Banco da Africa.

BAO (Banco da Africa Occidental; ☑ 3202418; Rua Gerra Mendes)

Ecobank (☑ 7253194; Ave Amílcar Cabral) Changes dollars and euros.

ℹ Getting There & Away

There are daily flights to Bissau with TACV Cabo Verde Airlines, TAP Air Portugal, Senegal Airlines and Royal Air Maroc.

Once in Bissau, you can get *sept-place* taxis (Peugeot 504s with 'seven seats') and *transporte misto* (literally 'mixed transport') buses to just about anywhere in the country at the *paragem* (bus park), about 4km (CFA1000 by taxi) west outside town.

ℹ Getting Around

The airport is 9km west of the town centre. A taxi to town should be around CFA3000.

Shared taxis – generally blue, well-worn Mercedes – are plentiful and ply all the main routes. Trips cost CFA350. Rates for longer routes vary and have to be negotiated.

Blue-yellow *toca-tocas* serve main city routes (for CFA100), including Ave de 14 Novembro towards the *paragem* and airport.

ARQUIPÉLAGO DOS BIJAGÓS

The Bijagós islands look like the perfect postcard from paradise. Protected by swift tides, treacherous sandbanks and the Unesco heritage fund, the Bijagós, a matriarchal people, eluded Portuguese control until the 1930s.

You need to bring either time or money, as transport to and between the islands is either difficult or pricey. Life swings to the rhythm of the tide – and mind the stingrays lurking in the waters.

ℹ Getting There & Away

Ilha de Bubaque is the gateway to the rest of the Bijagós, with the exception of Ilha de Bolama and the private resort islands. The former Greek island ferry **Expresso dos Bijagós** (☑ 6538739; Bissau Velho; tickets CFA3500-12,500) normally leaves Bissau port for Bubaque every Friday, returning from Bubaque on Sunday. Exact departure times depend on the tide but are between 9am and 3pm; posters advertise the exact time the evening before. On other days, your choice is between rough and risky *canoas* (motor canoe; per person CFA2500, six hours), private plane (from CFA250,000 per person) or speedboat (per four-seater boat CFA200,000 to CFA300,000, two hours).

The Expresso dos Bijagós also ferries passengers between Bissau and Bolama once a week but timings vary; ask around at the port for the latest departure times. If you miss the ferry, *canoas* operate three times per week, but be warned: one sank on this route in 2012, killing many of those on board. You can also reach Bolama by taking a *sept-place* to Buba (three hours), where you can overnight before hiring motorbikes for the journey (three hours, CFA15,000) along rough forest roads to the *pirogue* hopper at São João.

The 1950s cruise ship **Africa Queen** can take you island hopping for a week (from CFA700,000); ask at the port or your hotel for information. It's wise to exercise caution when contemplating taking any kind of boat from Bissau during heavy rains.

Ilha de Bolama

Geographically closer to Bissau than any other island in the Bijagós, eerily beautiful Bolama feels worlds away, both aesthetically and socially. The Portuguese capital of Guinea-Bissau until 1943, Bolama's shores are awash with crumbling relics that were abandoned after independence. Tree-lined boulevards are mapped out by lamp posts that no longer shine, and the colonial barracks have been recast as a hospital, now – like much of the island – in a dark and desolate state.

The former **town hall**, flanked by Greek-style pillars, was built in 1870; these days huge splinters hang like stalactites from its ceilings. The turrets of the once grandiose **Hotel Turismo** sit in an overgrown nest of lianas, 3m-tall weeds and snakes. It's worth walking out to Ofires Beach, an hour's stroll from the town, to see the spooky sweeping **staircase** of a beach hotel that no longer exists.

You can rent a breezy room at the **fishing training centre** (☑ call Ivan Gomes for reservations 5286345; r incl breakfast CFA12,500) close to the port. There is electricity at the centre, but the rooms do not have fans. Alternatively, ask for directions to the smarter **Hotel Ga Djau** (r CFA13,000), a 15-minute walk from the market. The rooms do have fans, but the generator shuts off late at night.

Feisty **Lionessa** (meals CFA1000) serves up fresh fish and potatoes most evenings if you order in advance. Find her cafe about halfway up the main road, on the right-hand side if you're walking from the port.

Ilha de Bubaque

At the centre of the Bijagós, Bubaque is home to the archipelago's largest town, which serves as its major transport hub. If you can't make it to more remote islands, Bubaque makes a comfortable place to unwind and a good weekend getaway from Bissau. Its best beach is **Praia Bruce** on the southern tip.

There's an internet cafe, the research and information centre **Casa do Ambiente** (☑ 3207106) and a small **museum** (☑ 6115107; admission CFA1000; ◷ 10am-1pm & 4-7pm).

You can lay your head at pretty **Casa Dora** (☑ 6928836, 5967714, 6925836; susybubaque@gmail.com; s/d CFA10,000/15,000), housed in a colourful garden, or from November to May at **Le Calypso** (☑ 5949207, 6106436; calypso@gtelecom.gw; s/d CFA20,000/22,000; ✸), which has a pool and bar. At the top of Bubaque's game is **Kasa Afrikana** (☑ 5949213, 7243305; www.kasa-afrikana.com; per person from CFA40,000; ✸ 🤖 ✸), a fishing lodge that hits the right ratio of charm to luxury, with comfortable rooms, a pool and on-site chef.

Orango Islands National Park

Ilha de Orango (Bijagós Archipelago; boat to Eticoga village from Bubaque) is the heart of Orango Islands National Park. The island is home to rare saltwater hippos, and is also the burial site of the Bijagós kings and queens. Pretty **Orango Parque Hotel** (☑ 6615127; laurent.durris@cbd-habitat.com; r incl full board CFA30,000) is run in association with the local community, and guides can take you **hippo spotting** (around CFA150,000). You can reach Orango by speedboat transfer from Ilha de Kere or by scheduled *pirogue* from Bubaque. For the latter, you'll need to have time and tides on your side.

Other Islands

The islands of Kere and Rubane are home to luxury fishing lodges. The latter's **Ponta Anchaca** (☑ 6056032, 6394352; www.pontaanchaca.com; r per day with half board from €100) is divine, with a pool, spa, masseuse and gorgeous wooden huts bedecked with four-poster beds and Jacuzzis under the stars. You can travel by speedboat from Bissau (€460 per boatload) or board a private plane from Senegal's Cap Skirring for €530. On **Kere** (http://bijagos-kere.fr) prices are slightly cheaper for a similar experience. Contact Manuel (☑ 5909531), the booking agent in Bissau, for more information. Trips can be arranged from there to Biombo and other islands.

On the idyllic island of João Vieira lies **João Viera e Poilão National Marine Park**, a nesting area for endangered sea turtles. The owner of the guesthouse Chez Claude can arrange speedboat pick-up from Bubaque (CFA200,000 per boatload). Close to Bubaque, the large island **Canhabaque** (one hour by *pirogue*) is a good place to experience village life in the Bijagós.

THE NORTHWEST

Quinhámel

Quinhámel, 35km west of Bissau, makes an interesting day or weekend trip. You can overnight at Mar Azul (☏ 6760990, 6656086; r incl lunch CFA40,000), where rooms overlook the pool, gardens and ocean. The restaurant serves grilled oysters served with a hot citrus sauce. About 2km away, nestled between the mangroves, is a local beach popular with families and young people at the weekends. The inspiring community project Artissal (☏ 6604078; artissal@gmail.com; ☉ 9am-5pm) introduces visitors to the region's unique weaving traditions.

Transporte misto from Bissau costs CFA500; a private taxi is around CFA15,000 return.

Varela

The 45km road from São Domingos is rough, even in a good 4WD – and that's why the white-sand, windswept beaches of Varela remain deserted. There are plans to tarmac the road, but until that happens, Varela's charm lies in its remoteness.

Transporte misto leaves every afternoon from São Domingos (CFA3000) taking around four hours and returning the following morning. If you're driving by 4WD, plan on at least two hours. You can also come in from Senegal, via Kabrousse, but this route involves several hours' walk and arranging a *pirogue* with local fishermen in advance.

To reach the main beach from Fatima's place, turn right out of the gate and drive until you reach the end of the main road. Turn right again, and follow the long track for about five minutes until you hear the sound of the waves.

Chez Fatima   GUESTHOUSE $
(Aparthotel Chez Helena; ☏ 5120036, 6640180; d/ste CFA15,000/20,000; ℗) Friendly owners Fatima and Franco offer nine brightly coloured huts in a pretty garden setting. The huts are lovingly decorated, with fans, mosquito nets and bathrooms. There's Italian food and fresh juices (they grow their own tomatoes and passion fruits) on hand in the restaurant. Call ahead for information on road conditions. The generator kicks in after dark.

THE NORTHEAST

Bafatá & Gabú

Bafatá ('the place where the rivers meet' in the Mandinga language), feels surprisingly hot and dry. Independence hero Amílcar Cabral was born here in 1924 and Unesco has transformed his childhood home into a museum that's open daily (ask for the '*casa rosa Amílcar Cabral*').

You can sleep at the basic but clean Hotel Maimuna Capé (☏ 6648383; s/d CFA10,000/15,000; ❀) or try the yellow Apartamento Imel (r CFA5000) in the centre of town. Ponto de Encontro (☏ 6921690; Chez Celia; dishes around CFA3500), at the end of the main street, is run by a charming older Portuguese couple. Head there for hearty fare and a glimpse into Bafatá's past.

Transporte misto to Bissau (CFA1750, two hours) and Gabú (CFA800) departs from the petrol station area.

Gabú, once the capital of the eponymous 19th-century kingdom is mainly a stopover on the way to Guinea, or a base for excursions to the rocky lands of Boé (40km from Gabú). The best hotel in town is the Boca-Branco (☏ 7229065, 6744403; r from CFA24,000). There's also the central Residencial Djaraama (☏ 6938442; r/d without bathroom CFA15,000/20,000), or the simple Hotel Baga Baga ('Termite Mound' in Crioulo; s CFA15,000), near the entrance to town.

THE SOUTH

Buba

With its calm streets and pretty, tranquil lakes and lagoons, Buba comes as a surprise. You can bed down at the pleasant Berca do Rio (☏ 5208020, 6619700; r CFA12,000), a short walk from the lake, where Slow Food chef Abdon, who trained in Cotonou, serves up wonderful three-course meals with wine using innovative, local ingredients. He can also arrange picnics and *pirogue* trips through the mangroves.

Transporte misto run regularly along the asphalt road from Bissau to Buba (CFA3000, three hours).

Jemberem & Parque Natural de Cantanhez

The hardest-to-reach places are often the most beautiful, and so it goes with Jemberem. You'll need a 4WD, time and patience to get here, but if you do, you can stay at the clean and simple **U'Anan Camp** (☑ 6637263, 6060019; d/q CFA15,000/25,000) on the edge of **Parque Natural de Cantanhez**, which supports a fully fledged ecotourism project. The camp can arrange forest treks into the chimp- and elephant-inhabited park.

UNDERSTAND GUINEA-BISSAU

Guinea-Bissau Today

In 2012, President Malam Bacai Sanha died from illness, plunging the country into another bout of instability and adding another name to the long list of presidents who have failed to complete a full term in power. A coup d'etat ousted the prime minister and election frontrunner three months later and a transitional government was installed, headed by Manuel Serifo Nhamadjo, who was chosen by West African bloc Ecowas. Nhamadjo's time in power was shaken by coup attempts and attacks, and fresh elections were tentatively planned for 2013. At the time of research tensions were rising between the Balanta and other ethnic groups.

History

In around 1200, when a group of Malinké was led to present-day Guinea-Bissau by a general of Sunjata Keita, the region became an outpost of the Empire of Mali. In 1537, it became a state in its own right – the Kaabu Empire. Gabù became the capital of this small kingdom.

European Arrival & Colonisation

Portuguese navigators first reached the area around 1450, and established lucrative routes for trading slaves and goods. With the abolition of the slave trade in the 19th century, the Portuguese extended their influence beyond the coast towards the interior in order to continue extracting wealth.

Portuguese Guinea descended into one of the most repressive and exploitative colonial regimes in Africa, particularly accentuated when right-wing dictator António Salazar came to power in Portugal in 1926.

War of Liberation

By the early 1960s African colonies were rapidly winning independence, but Salazar refused to relinquish control. The result was a long and bloody war of liberation for Guinea-Bissau and Cape Verde, fought on Guinean soil. Many Guineans were recruited to fight for the Portuguese, essentially pitting brothers against brothers and neighbours against neighbours.

The father of independence was Amílcar Cabral, who in 1956 helped found the Partido Africano da Independência da Guiné e Cabo Verde (PAIGC). In 1961 the PAIGC started arming and mobilising peasants, and within five years controlled half of the country. Cabral was assassinated in Conakry in 1973, but independence had become inevitable. When Salazar's regime fell in 1974, the new Portuguese government recognised the fledgling nation.

Independence

Once in power, the PAIGC government faced staggering problems of poverty, lack of education and economic decline. In 1986 a coup attempt forced President João Vieira to privatise state enterprises.

Intractable poverty and growing corruption under Vieira culminated in national strikes in 1997, which spiralled into civil war. Vieira was killed in a 2009 coup and instability has been endemic ever since, fuelled by deep tensions between the government and the military, which includes ageing officers who fought in the war of independence. The squabble for profits from Bissau's main cash cow – not the humble cashew, but cocaine – is a symptom of these tensions.

Culture

Despite grinding poverty, a severely damaged infrastructure and wide religious and ethnic differences, Bissau-Guineans are generally united in their approach to the troubles in their country – although tensions have

SUPER MAMA DJOMBO

In the tiny, nigh-on-impossible to access village of Cobiana, a spirit rose to prominence during the independence era of the late 1960s and early 1970s. Her name was Mama Djombo, and she was said to protect the independence fighters as they waged a bloody battle against Portugal. A few years earlier, musician Ze Manel (then seven years old) and his compatriots created a band at their summer scout camp in Bissau. They named it Super Mama Djombo, after the forest spirit, and later shot to fame, accompanying independence figures to neighbouring countries, to Cuba and to Europe.

Today, the re-formed Super Mama Djombo is Bissau's most famous band, performing their woozy independence era harmonies throughout the region and as far afield as Iceland and Hong Kong. With tracks like 'Djan Djan', about the ship on which bandleader Atchutchi sailed to Senegal during the civil war, and 'Guine Cabral', their music contains the sad notes and the euphoria of the independence era – and then some. 'The people of Guinea-Bissau are like termite mounds,' Ze Manel told us, referring to the track 'Baga Baga'. 'Knock us down and we get right back up.'

brewed in recent years between the Balanta ethnic group and rivals. While many feel detached from the military-government chaos, its impact is felt on a daily basis, in everything from making banking transactions to the challenges of the decrepit healthcare system.

Politeness and sincerity are deeply respected in Guinea-Bissau. Among the citizens of neighbouring countries, Guineans are known as relentless partygoers, but people in Guinea-Bissau will tell you they just know how to let their hair down properly. There's a spirit of liberty, joy and acceptance in many situations.

People

Guinea-Bissau's 1.5 million inhabitants are divided among some 23 ethnic groups. The two largest are the Balanta (30%) in the coastal and central regions and the Fula (20%) in the east and south. Other groups include the Manjak, Papel, Fulup and the Mandinka. The offshore islands are mostly inhabited by the Bijagós people. In the last few years, tensions have been growing between the Balanta and other ethnic groups.

About 45% of the people are Muslims and 10% Christians. Animist beliefs remain strong along the coast and in the south.

Arts & Crafts

The Bijagós people are famous for their traditions of mask making and sculpture – you will see these come out in carnival season.

The traditional Guinean beat is *gumbé*, though contemporary music is mainly influenced by zouk from Cape Verde. Guinea-Bissau's classic band is Super Mama Djombo; Manecas Costa and Justino Delgado are two contemporary stars.

Food & Drink

Seafood is the highlight of Guinean cuisine, including shrimp, oysters and meaty *bica* (sea bream), best served sautéed with onion and lime. A national favourite is *chabeu*: deep-fried fish served in a thick palm-oil sauce with rice.

Local brews include palm wine and the very potent liquors *caña* (rum) and *cajeu* (cashew liquor). The best beers are the imported Portuguese brands.

Environment

Tiny Guinea-Bissau has an area of just over 36,000 sq km. The natural savannah woodlands have largely been replaced by cashew plantations.

In the Bijagós archipelago you find rare saltwater hippos, aquatic turtles, dolphins, manatees and sharks. The rainforests of the southeast are the most westerly home of Africa's chimpanzee population.

Among the main environmental issues are mangrove destruction, deforestation, soil erosion and overfishing. A number of areas are protected, including the Bolama-Bijagós Biosphere Reserve. For more information, contact IBAP (☑ 3207106; Rua São Tomé), the institute that oversees all the parks from Bissau.

GUINEA-BISSAU PEOPLE

SURVIVAL GUIDE

 Directory A–Z

ACCOMMODATION

While Bissau has a range of accommodation to suit most budgets, conditions are generally more basic elsewhere in the country (the luxury fishing lodges of the Bijagós are an exception). National electricity is severely limited, forcing hoteliers to rely on expensive generator power.

ACTIVITIES

The waters around the Bijagós are renowned for their deep-sea fishing spots. Snorkelling is also possible, as is forest trekking.The national parks are fabulous for birdwatchers.

BUSINESS HOURS

Banks and government offices Usually 8am to noon and 2pm to 5pm Monday to Friday, although hours vary.

Shops From 8am or 9am until 6pm Monday to Saturday. Some close for lunch.

EMBASSIES & CONSULATES

All embassies and consulates are in Bissau. The consul for the UK and the Netherlands is **Jan van Maanen** (☑ 6622772; Rua Eduardo Mondlane, Supermercardo Mavegro, Bissau).

French Embassy (☑ 3201312; cnr Ave de 14 Novembro & Ave do Brazil)

German Embassy (☑ 3255020; escritorio-bissau@web.de; SITEC Bldg; ☺ 9-11am Mon-Fri)

Guinean Embassy (☑ 3201231; Rua 12; ☺ 8.30am-3pm Sat-Thu, to 1pm Fri) East of the central stadium.

Portuguese Embassy (☑ 3203379; Ave Cidade de Lisboa; ☺ 8am-noon)

Senegalese Embassy (☑ 3212944; off Praça dos Heróis Nacionais; ☺ 8am-noon)

Spanish Embassy (Praça dos Heróis Nacionais; ☺ 8am-noon)

FESTIVALS & EVENTS

Guinea-Bissau's main event is Carnaval (p209). The biggest party happens in Bissau, but Bubaque has the more interesting masks and costumes.

HEALTH

A certificate with proof of yellow-fever vaccination is required for all travellers.

INTERNET ACCESS

Wi-fi is increasingly common in hotels and restaurants in Bissau. Roaming is possible on phones and iPads, but connections are generally slow. Don't count on internet access outside the capital.

MONEY

Some ATMs in the capital accept international visa cards. Try the Malaika Hotel or the ATM opposite the Kalliste Hotel.

The unit of currency is the West African CFA franc.

POST

The postal service is slow. You're better off posting mail home from Senegal or The Gambia.

PUBLIC HOLIDAYS

Islamic feasts, such as Eid al-Fitr (at the end of Ramadan) and Tabaski, are celebrated. Guinea-Bissau also celebrates a number of public holidays.

New Year's Day 1 January

Anniversary of the Death of Amílcar Cabral 20 January

Women's Day 8 March

Easter March/April

Labour Day 1 May

Pidjiguiti Day 3 August

Independence Day 24 September

Christmas Day 25 December

TELEPHONE

You can pick up an Orange or MTN SIM card for an unlocked phone, and buy top-up credit on the street. Service can be unreliable in remote areas, including the Arquipélago dos Bijagós.

VISAS

All visitors, except nationals of Ecowas countries (who must pay CFA1000 on entry), need visas before arrival. Visas can be valid for single or multiple entries and the price varies depending on the point of issue.

Visa Extensions

Extensions are easy to obtain at **Serviço de Estrangeiros** (Praça dos Heróis Nacionais, Bissau). For virtually all nationalities, 45-day visa extensions cost around CFA4000 and are ready the same day if you apply early.

☺ Getting There & Away

AIR

Guinea-Bissau's international airport is on the outskirts of Bissau. The main airlines flying to Guinea-Bissau are TAP Air Portugal, Royal Air Maroc, Senegal Airlines and TACV Cabo Verde Airlines. Private planes can also be arranged.

TACV Cabo Verde Airlines (VR; ☑ 3206087; www.tacv.com; Ave Amílcar Cabral)

TAP Air Portugal (TP; ☑ 3201359; www.flytap.com; Praça dos Heróis Nacionais)

PRACTICALITIES

⇒ **Radio** National radio and TV stations broadcast in Portuguese. Most interesting for travellers is Radio Mavegro FM (100.0MHz), which combines music with hourly news bulletins in English from the BBC.

⇒ **Newspapers** Newspapers come and go quickly in Bissau. If you sit at one of the city's cafes or restaurants, a vendor will quickly offer you the latest options. If you can read Portuguese or Crioulo, it's worth checking out the Friday editions for the serialised fiction.

⇒ **Electricity** Supply is 220V and plugs are of the European two-round-pin variety.

⇒ **Language** Portuguese is the official language, though the tongue that unites Bissau-Guineans of diverse ethnic groups is the soft and rhythmic Crioulo. French is also fairly widely spoken.

LAND
Guinea

Transport for Guinea (plan on 24 to 48 hours to reach Conakry, depending on road/taxi conditions) leaves from Gabu and traverses a rough pass through the beautiful Fouta Djalon mountains via Labe. There is an alternative, tougher route via Quebo and Pitche.

Senegal

From Dakar, the cheapest, and most scenic, way to reach Bissau is by taking the biweekly overnight ferry to Ziguinchor (cabin beds from CFA18,000), collecting a visa from the consulate in Ziguinchor (issued on the spot; single entry CFA10,000) and travelling onwards by *sept place* (CFA3500 plus small luggage fee, four hours). There are also regular flights on Senegal Airlines.

ⓘ Getting Around

BOAT

The main boat connection is the Expresso dos Bijagós (p213) that links Bissau to Ilha de Bubaque. *Canoas* (motor canoes) also go between individual islands.

SEPT PLACE & TRANSPORTE MISTO

Sept places are Peugeot 504 seven-seaters that link the main towns. More common and far less comfortable are large minibuses called *transporte misto* (literally 'mixed transport'). Mornings (before 8am) are the best time to get transport.

The main roads between Bissau and Bafatá, Gabú, São Domingos and Buba are all tar and generally in a good state. Stretches between Buba and Jemberem and São Domingos and Varela are unpaved and in bad condition.

Liberia

📞 231 / POP 4.1 MILLION

Best Places to Eat

➡ Fresh seafood on Buchanan beach (p227)

➡ Ministry of Fruit (p223)

➡ Sharing a bowl of palm butter upcountry

Best Places to Stay

➡ Camping beneath Robertsport's cotton tree (p227)

➡ Mamba Point Hotel (p227)

➡ Libassa Eco-Lodge (p227)

Why Go?

It wasn't long ago that Liberians talked with obvious nostalgia of 'normal days'. Now, over a decade after the war has ended, 'normal days' are back in this gorgeous green land.

They can be seen in the Liberian designer who's launched a fashion store in Monrovia; the former refugee who runs a motorbike-taxi business; the Liberian surfer who's touring West Africa and the salesman investing in ecotourism.

You might be among his customers, leaning back in a string hammock on the edge of a forest singing with tropical birds. Or you might visit Monrovia, exploring the relics of Liberia's rich history and the American influence that still shapes it. Sapo National Park is one of the most stunning patches of rainforest left in West Africa, while the sands of pretty Robertsport are shingled with fishing canoes and huge granite gems.

Today's 'normal days' are the spark that will light your travels in Liberia.

When to Go
Monrovia

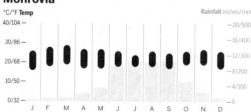

Jan–May This is the hot, dry season, so head to the beaches. The mercury can easily top 32°C.

Jun–Oct Spectacular storms and impressive surf, but country roads are impassable.

Oct–Dec A touch of harmattan breeze from the Sahel occasionally cools the air.

MONROVIA

POP 1.8 MILLION

Monrovia has been everything over the decades – a splendid African capital brimming with elegant stores and faces, a party city monitored by sheriffs wearing secondhand US police uniforms, a war zone marred by bullet holes and a broken-hearted city struggling to climb to its feet. Now aid workers are packing their bags, Liberians are returning from the US and Europe and the city is forging a fresh identity.

Walk along Broad St, Monrovia's main boulevard, and you'll hear the original beat of locally brewed hip-co and the gentle rhythm of Liberian English. You'll see the architectural ghosts of Monrovia's past and the uniformed schoolchildren of its future. You'll watch entrepreneurs climb into sleek, low-slung cars, market men sell coconuts from rusty wheelbarrows and models sashay

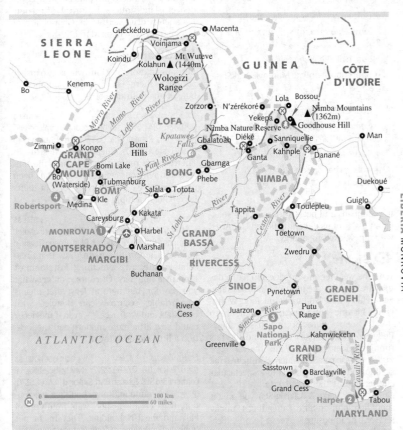

Liberia Highlights

① Gaining a history lesson walking around the Liberian capital **Monrovia** (p221).

② Hitting the long, bumpy road to **Harper** (p228), a town blessed with southern American architecture and an end-of-the-line feel.

③ Exploring the habitat of the endangered pygmy hippo, camping beneath the forest canopy and listening to the sounds of the rainforest at **Sapo National Park** (p228).

④ Riding the waves with Liberian surfers, running your hands through the phosphorescent swell and eating fresh lobster in the shade of the cotton tree in **Robertsport** (p227).

ⓘ SET YOUR BUDGET

Budget

➡ Sachet of drinking water $0.10

➡ Bed in convent guesthouse $20

➡ Bowl of palm butter and rice $2

➡ Monrovia–Robertsport by bush taxi $3.50

Midrange

➡ Bottled cola in air-conditioned bar $2

➡ Simple hotel room with fan and wi-fi $65

➡ Lunch at Lebanese cafe $6

➡ Short hop in private Monrovia taxi $5

Top End

➡ Cocktail in upmarket hotel bar $6

➡ Centrally-located hotel room with air con and wi-fi $200

➡ Sushi dinner for two with wine $70

➡ 4x4 hire per day upcountry $120, plus petrol

in tight jeans and heels. Monrovia has shaken off many of its old epithets and is infused with a new, exciting energy.

◉ Sights

With the weather on your side and half a day to spare, you can see most of Monrovia's major architectural landmarks on foot. Worthwhile historic buildings include the retro **Rivoli Cinema** (Broad St), which still shows Bollywood movies (just don't mind the rats running under your feet) and the **EJ Roye building** (Ashmun St), which dominates the skyline and was once home to a spectacular auditorium. At the **First United Methodist Church** (cnr Gurley & Ashmun Sts) you might spot Ellen Johnson-Sirleaf attending a Sunday service. The imposing **Masonic Temple** (Benson St) overlooks the city at the western end of Broad St, in the shadow of the abandoned **Hotel Ducor**; this was West Africa's finest hotel in the 1970s, where Idi Amin swam in the pool and Miriam Makeba sang in the bar.

Liberia National Museum   MUSEUM
(☑077-232 682; Broad St; admission US$5; ⊙9am-4pm Mon-Sat, 2-4pm Sun) The museum's collection was depleted during the war years, but renovations have created

space for photo and art exhibitions as well as the ethnic and historical exhibits. Wander through the light-filled 2nd and 3rd floors, where you can see founding father Joseph Jenkins Roberts' dining table – a gift from England's Queen Victoria. The building was the former legislature.

Providence Island   ISLAND
There isn't much to mark the spot where freed American slaves first disembarked, but the government has plans to turn Providence Island into a historical attraction. It's a short drive across the Gabriel Tucker bridge from Waterside Market.

🛏 Sleeping

Accommodation in Monrovia is expensive, although there is a growing number of budget and midrange beds.

St Theresa's Convent   HOSTEL $
(☑0886-784 276; archdiocesanpastoralcenter@yahoo.com; Randall St; r US$30, without bathroom US$20, ste US$50) Cheap and cheerful St Theresa's has rooms that back onto the convent and religious centre. Security has been upped since we last heard reports of thefts here. There's a 10pm curfew.

Corina Hotel   HOTEL $$
(☑077-514 708, 0886-514 708; www.corinahotel.com; cnr 26th St & Tubman Blvd, Congo Town; d US$65) The Corina's main draw is its reasonable ratecard, something lost to most Monrovia hoteliers. Of course you get what you pay for, but here at least that means comfortable, secure, clean doubles with breakfast and wi-fi access – even if the decor could be a little more modern and the location a little closer to town.

Bella Casa   BOUTIQUE HOTEL $$
(☑077-444 110, 077-692 272; www.bellacasaliberia.com; cnr 3rd St & Tubman Blvd, Sinkor; d from US$120; P❄🖳) A sound midrange boutique-style option, Bella Casa is a short walk from Capitol Hill and the UN building. They might not quite evoke dreams of Italy, but the rooms are comfortable and clean and come with air-con, desk and free wi-fi. The suites are large, with stylish bed linen and a more luxurious touch.

Cape Hotel   HOTEL $$
(☑077-006 633; http://thecapehotelliberia.com; UN Dr, Mamba Point; d US$160; P❄🖳🖳) The Mamba Point Hotel's next-door neighbour may forever be in its shadow, but it is a more reasonably priced option and there's

an on-site terrace restaurant, friendly staff, parking and a pool. Ask for one of the renovated rooms, which are sleeker and more stylish than the rest.

★ Mamba Point Hotel   LUXURY HOTEL $$$

(☑ 06-544 544, 06-440 000; mambapointhotel@ yahoo.com; r/ste US$200/350; P ✳ 🛜 ⊠) Monrovia's finest hotel is an institution. It has 60-plus beautiful rooms, decked out with stylish furnishings and luxurious bathrooms (the suites are divine, with stunning sea views). There's an excellent terrace restaurant, adjacent sushi bar, casino and pool, and there are plans to add a spa, gym and cocktail bar.

Royal Hotel   LUXURY HOTEL $$$

(☑ 077-777 788; royalhotelliberia@yahoo.com; cnr 15th St & Tubman Blvd; r/presidential ste US$200/800; P ✳ 🛜) Recent renovations have turned the Royal into the most talked about hotel in town. The new complex holds 58 plush rooms (including two presidential suites), coffee shop, hair salon, art gallery, Asian fusion restaurant and rooftop cocktail bar.

✖ Eating

Sweet Lips   LIBERIAN $

(Newport St; meals US$1.50-2.50; ⊙ 11am-9pm Mon-Sat) This firm favourite is said to serve up the very best Liberian food in town – try the excellent *fufu* (puréed, fermented cassava) and palm butter.

Shark's Ice Cream   ICE CREAM $

(Airfield, Sinkor; P ✳ 🍴) Head here for American-dreamt, Liberia-made ice cream. There are usually a handful of flavours on offer, such as chocolate and passion fruit, although many regulars swear by the creamy vanilla. There's also a sandwich and burger menu, a popcorn machine, rides for toddlers and, upstairs, sports on the big screen.

Sajj House   LEBANESE $$

(☑ 06-830 888; cnr Tubman Blvd & 18th St, Sinkor; mains US$5-10; ⊙ 9am-10pm; P 🛜 🍴) Lebanese meze, cheese-and-spinach pies, sandwiches and pizzas are served beneath the awnings of a large, traditional Liberian garden hut. Popular with salsa-dancing expats on Friday nights, Sajj has a fully stocked bar, blender (try the frozen strawberry juice) and dessert menu, featuring chocolate crepes. The volume dial turns with the clock.

Evelyn's   INTERNATIONAL $$

(☑ 0777-001 155, 0886-710 104; 80 Broad St; mains US$8-20; ⊙ 11am-8pm Mon-Sat; ✳ 🛜) One of Monrovia's best lunch spots, Evelyn's offers up-market Liberian dishes (such as palm butter and rice; from US$8), American mains including sandwiches, and an all-you-can-eat lunch buffet on Wednesday. You can order sides of cassava fries, stuffed plantain and fried chicken, while for dessert there's papaya pie and cornbread muffins.

Bishoftu   ETHIOPIAN $$

(☑ 0886-639 120; cnr 11th St & Payne Ave) For a change from Monrovia's plethora of American, Lebanese – and of course Liberian – restaurants, there's Ethiopian restaurant Bishoftu in Sinkor, which has an outdoor courtyard. The *injera* (flatbread) gets mixed reviews.

Embassy Suites   LEBANESE, AMERICAN $$

(☑ 0886-985 985; www.embassysuiteslib.com; near US Embassy, Mamba Point) The friendly staff at Embassy Suites (also a good hotel) will bring over bowls of popcorn before you start your meal. On the menu is a mix of Lebanese and American dishes, including fresh salads, steaks and pizzas. There's live music most Saturdays.

Golden Beach   INTERNATIONAL $$

(5th St, Sinkor; meals US$5-12; ⊙ noon-late Mon-Sun; P 🍴) Life in Liberia doesn't get better than this. Exhale, kick off your shoes and start your evening here, where tables sink into the sand and sunsets dip behind gin 'n' tonics. Nobody's in a hurry here, including the chefs, who prepare Liberian, European and Thai food.

★ Ministry of Fruit   CAFE $$

(Cheeseman Ave & 17th St, Sinkor; meals from US$5; ⊙ 8am-9pm Mon-Fri, 10am-9pm Sat, 10am-2pm Sun; 🛜 ✍) 🍴 Climb the red spiral staircase for Chris' freshly squeezed juices, coffee, sweet smoothies, great sandwiches and homemade banana bread. You can even sip on a root-beer float while you flick through the bookshelves or access the wi-fi. The Sunday brunch (US$5 to US$10) crowd is a mix of locals and expats – something that's reflected in the ethos, warm welcome and decor.

Blue House   LIBERIAN $$$

(☑ 0880-888 884; Oldest Congo Town) A smart restaurant serving creative dishes made from local ingredients, a glam cocktail bar, and the occasional live jazz act, Blue House

Monrovia

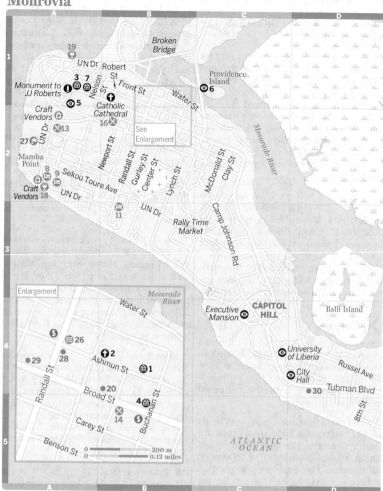

fits the bill for a date or special evening. In the furthest part of Congo Town, it's about a 20- to 30-minute drive from the city centre.

🍷 Drinking & Nightlife

Lila Brown's
BAR

(UN Dr; ☺ 5pm-late Mon-Sun) Lila B's is a duplex bar nestled between the Mamba Point Hotel and the Atlantic. Downstairs, there's a food menu and a party vibe on weekend nights. Climb the wooden staircase for sea views, waiter service and relaxed tables shielded

from rainy-season downpours by stylish shower curtains.

Tides
BAR

(✆ 0777-666 444; UN Dr, near Swedish Embassy; ☺ 4pm-late Tue-Sun) Wicker armchairs and loveseats line the wide verandah at Tides, which looks out over the ocean. Inside, find the cocktail list scribbled on a blackboard (try the bissap margarita), a pool table and a long bar beneath a safari-lodge ceiling. The kitchen – which serves sandwiches, cassava fries and crispy fried plantain, known

Monrovia

⊙ Sights

1	EJ Roye building	B4
2	First United Methodist Church	B4
3	Hotel Ducor	A1
4	Liberia National Museum	B5
5	Masonic Temple	A1
6	Providence Island	C1
7	Rivoli Cinema	A1

⊜ Sleeping

8	Cape Hotel	A2
9	Mamba Point Hotel	A2
10	Royal Hotel	E5
11	St Theresa's Convent	B3

⊗ Eating

12	Bishoftu	E5
13	Embassy Suites	A2
14	Evelyn's	B5
15	Sajj House	F5
16	Sweet Lips	B2

⊖ Drinking & Nightlife

17	Jamal's Boulevard Cafe	E5
18	Lila Brown's	A2
19	Tides	A1

⊕ Information

20	Bureau of Immigration	B4
21	Côte d'Ivoire Consulate	E5
22	Ghanian Embassy	E4
23	Guinean Embassy	F5
24	JFK Hospital	F5
	Karou Voyages	(see 9)
25	Lucky Pharmacy	F5
26	Main Post Office	A4
27	US Embassy	A2

⊕ Transport

	British Airways	(see 17)
28	Brussels Airlines	A4
29	Kenya Airways	A4
30	Royal Air Maroc	D4

as *kelewele* – opens after 4.30pm. There are movie nights and special events.

JR's Beach Bar　BAR

(Mamba Point beach; ☉ afternoons & evenings) Take any one of the beach tracks from Mamba Point Rd and you'll stumble upon JR's Beach Bar, Rasta Bar, Miami Beach or any of the other beach bars that are popping up here. Rasta Bar has a pool table.

Jamal's Boulevard Cafe　BAR

(cnr 14th St & Tubman Blvd, Sinkor; ☉ 5pm-late Mon-Fri, 10am-late Sat & Sun; 🛜) This Sinkor institution comes alive on weekend nights,

and has drinks specials, karaoke, quiz nights and special events. There's also food, including good pizza (call ahead for delivery), and wi-fi. Sunday brunch includes the likes of mimosas and bloody Marys.

Deja Vu　CLUB

(📱 05-555 000; Airfield Short Cut, Sinkor; ☉ 10pm-4am Tue-Sat) Join the shimmering, moneyed party people at Liberia's sleekest club, which hosts DJs and regular special nights. No shorts or sandals for men.

Palm Spring Resort　CASINO

(📱 0880-606 060; www.liberiapalmspring.com; Tubman Blvd, Congo Town; 🛜) Friday nights at the Palm Spring Resort in Congo Town herald live music in the bar, before the mass exodus into the casino, where the younger generations of Liberia's political elite mingle with Russian croupiers, curious expats and elegant ladies of the night.

🛍 Shopping

For souvenirs, visit the Guinean craft vendors opposite Mamba Point Hotel or on the hilltop above the US Embassy, where you can strike a good bargain.

Kasawa (📞0886-698 005; www.kasawa.org; 1st St, Sinkor) is a fair-trade initiative that brings together clothing designers and producers from Robertsport, while Jola House (📞0880-652 933; Duport Rd, Paynesville) stocks fairly produced bags, place mats and cushions. Afropolitan (📞0880-514 514; cnr Benson & Newport Sts) has a colourful range of clothing, laptop bags, purses, souvenirs and jewellery.

German entrepreneur Manfred (📞0886-963 969) creates bottle openers and candlesticks from old war weapons and Benjamin Somon (📞077-027 751) makes chess sets from discarded AK-47 bullets. Leslie Lumeh (📞0886-430 483) sells his watercolour and acrylic paintings.

ℹ Orientation

The heart of town is around Benson and Randall Sts, and along Broad St, where you'll find most shops and businesses. Southwest of here at Mamba Point are hotels, restaurants and NGO offices. To the southeast is Sinkor, with more hotels, eateries and businesses. It leads into Congo Town, Elwa junction and Red Light Motor Park.

ℹ Information

Lucky Pharmacy (Tubman Blvd; ⊘8.30am-late Mon-Sun) Right opposite JFK Hospital, this pharmacy is trusted by international organisations and has knowledgeable staff.

SOS Clinic (📞0886-841 673; Tubman Blvd, Congo Town) Head here in the first instance if you fall sick; this clinic is the best equipped in the country, trusted by expats. It's between the YWCA and Total Garage.

JFK Hospital (Tubman Blvd, Sinkor) Monrovia's main hospital is fine for basic needs (they can do malaria tests) but should be avoided for more serious matters, unless the hospital's annual flying surgeons are in town.

Karou Voyages (📞0886-517 454; Mamba Point Hotel, UN Dr) Good for continent-wide flight bookings. It's run from an office inside the Mamba Point Hotel complex.

Main Post Office (cnr Randall & Ashmun Sts; ⊘8am-4pm Mon-Fri, to noon Sat)

Barefoot Safari (The Sole Explorers of Liberia; 📞06-841 582) Run with enthusiasm and expertise, Barefoot offers trips into Sapo National Park, Monrovia city tours, canoe excursions and tailor-made itineraries. Highly recommended.

SAFE TRAVEL

Be careful around Waterside and avoid West Point and most of the beaches in town, for both security and health reasons. Watch your back (and head) if you choose to zip around on the back of a *pen-pen* (motorbike taxi) – medical care is limited in Liberia.

ℹ Getting There & Around

Flights arrive at **Roberts International Airport** (ROB; Robertsfield), 60km southeast of Monrovia, from where a taxi into the city costs around US$70. There is also the smaller Spriggs Payne Airport (MLW) in Sinkor.

Bush taxis for Robertsport and the Sierra Leone border leave from Duala Motor Park, 9km northeast of the town centre. Transport for most other domestic destinations leaves from the Red Light Motor Park, Monrovia's main motor park, 15km northeast of the centre. Nearby Guinea Motor Park has buses heading to Guinea and Côte d'Ivoire.

THE COAST

Around Monrovia

About 15km southeast of town is the pretty Silver Beach (📞0886-522225), where Layal serves up platters of grilled grouper, shrimp and lobster against a Sunday backdrop of salsa dancing (US$10 by charter taxi). Another 2km further south is Thinker's Beach, popular with a party crowd on weekends. In the shadow of the now-skeletal Hotel Africa is CeeCee Beach, 40 minutes west of Monrovia. Soil erosion is claiming the restaurant, but you can still swim in a lagoon sheltered by rocks.

Just beyond Careysburg is the quirky Wulki Farms (📞0886-327 637), owned by a former minister in Charles Taylor's cabinet, where you can ride horses (US$10), visit the zoo and order steak in the restaurant.

Marshall

A short drive from Robertsfield International Airport and 45 minutes or so from Monrovia is the rural area surrounding Marshall, which makes for an easy weekend escape from the city. You can camp on the quiet beaches here (speak to the locals to find a good spot, and be mindful of security) or see Monkey Island, a small archipelago that's home to chimpanzees evacuated from a hepatitis research lab during the war. Call the animals' feeder Joseph (☑0886-537 942) for information on joining a food run. Just don't get too close; these chimps know how to throw mangoes.

Nearby is Wolokor Cultural Village, where you can watch performances from a talented cultural troupe. If you're passing Harbel, it's worth taking a detour into Firestone Rubber Plantation, the world's largest rubber plantation, which is leased from the government on a controversial 99-year plan. You can play a round at the 18-hole golf course.

★ **Libassa Eco-Lodge** LODGE $$
(☑05-940 930, 0888-555 563; www.libassa.com; day entry fee US$10, huts US$125, honeymoon ste US$250; P🐾) 🐾 With pretty, solar-powered huts (named after endangered Liberian species) on the edge of the forest, Libassa makes for a gorgeous weekend retreat near Marshall. Pack your swimsuit; there's a pool, a lagoon and a beach as well as a lunch buffet run by helpful staff. The 2km stretch of road beyond Kpan Town is rough and only accessible by 4WD (45 minutes from Monrovia).

RLJ Kendeja RESORT $$$
(☑from the US 240-744 7850, 0886-219 939; www. rljkendejaresort.com; r from US$205; P❄🐾📶) This sleek, dreamy resort is spread across a beach in the environs of the airport. Interlinked walkways take you to the pool, the plush bar and restaurant, and the spa. Sunday brunch is a hit with expat NGO workers and there are romantic getaway deals.

Robertsport

Framed by gold-spun beaches, phosphorescent waves and a thick mane of forest, pretty Robertsport was just a fishing village a few years ago. Now, as you emerge from the rust-red roads and wind your way through the old town with its architecture in various states of undress (look out for the stunning scarlet ruins of the defunct Tubman Center of African Culture), you're greeted by surf lodges and body-boarding tourists.

Thankfully, the capital of Grand Cape Mount has largely retained its simple, paradise-found feel and you can still pitch your tent beneath the fabled cotton tree (☑Prince at Robertsport Community Works 0886-546 214; per person US$5). The lodges offer breakfast, lunch and dinner, or you can drive into the lively Grassfields part of town for Liberian food.

For the best surf breaks, wait for the rainy season and head to Fisherman's Point (good for beginners), Cotton Trees (along a shallow sand bar) or the more ambitious Cassava Point, which heaves towards the shiny granite rocks.

★ **Kwepunha Villas** GUESTHOUSE $
(☑0888-132 870; www.kwepunha.com; Fisherman's Beach, Robertsport; s/d US$25/35; P) 🐾 Run by Californian surfers in conjunction with community initiatives, this blue-and-yellow beach house offers pleasant, breezy rooms with wooden four-poster beds. You can join grassroots-style surf retreats here, or book the rooms independently. The house is situated on Fisherman's Beach (a 15-minute walk from Nana's along the sand), where you can tuck into fish tacos and margaritas.

Nana's Lodge LODGE $$
(☑086-668 332; Cassava Beach; canvas/wooden bungalows for 2 from US$60/110; P) 🐾 Robertsport's original ecolodge, Nana's has 11 bungalows overlooking the beach. The wooden huts are pricier than the canvas ones, but both styles of accommodation come with two comfortable double beds, fans and balconies. The sandy cantina down on the beach is a top sunset spot.

Buchanan

Liberia's second port hosts wild, beautiful beaches that are perfect for camping, plus an annual dumboy festival in January: two good reasons to make it here. You can sleep at the clean, reasonably comfortable Teepro Lodge (☑0880-961 568; Roberts St; r with net & fan US$25), next to the Buchanan Renewables site. The owners can advise on beach camping – it's advisable to hire an overnight security guard and watch the strong currents if you swim. In town, Black and White is a nightclub that also serves food, and there are beach bars along the coastal strip.

Bush taxis ply the route from Monrovia (L$350, three hours) or you can charter a car (US$100 one way) or a 4WD (US$150 plus petrol per day) for the 125km to Buchanan, which is mostly paved.

NORTH OF MONROVIA

Gbarnga

Liberia's most prestigious seat of learning, the country's second city and capital of the county of Bong is home to Cuttington University, on the site of the old Africana Museum, which once had a 3000-piece collection. Gbarnga's historical significance runs deeper than that; it is the site of Charles Taylor's farm (on the outskirts of town), from where he masterminded rebel operations in Sierra Leone and Liberia. An hour outside of Gbarnga is Kpatawee waterfall, a pretty picnic and swimming spot.

You can sleep at the Hill Top Hotel (☑0886-423 702; r US$50), 5km from town on the Ganta Hwy, or Paulma's Guesthouse (☑0886-771 297; r US$25) nearby. By bush taxi, Gbarnga can be reached in about five hours from Monrovia (L$400).

Mount Nimba

When the heat gets too much in Monrovia, there's only one thing for it – head for higher climes. Beautiful Mt Nimba is Liberia's tallest peak, 1362m above sea level, and you can feasibly climb it if you have a few days on your hands.

The jumping-off point is the curious town of Yekepa, a 10-hour drive from Monrovia and a *Truman Show*–esque mining town owned by Arcelor Mittal. The road to Mt Nimba is paved for almost three-quarters of the way to the top; you can drive to the peak using a 4WD, and camp along the way if you have your own equipment, hiking along the peaks. Bring GPS and warm clothing as it can get misty and very cool at night. Accommodation in Yekepa is available at the Noble House Motel (☑077-285 158; r from US$12).

THE SOUTHEAST

Zwedru

Flanked by thick, lush rainforest that runs along the Côte d'Ivoire border, Zwedru is the capital of Grand Gedeh, one of Liberia's greenest counties. It's only 200km from Monrovia, but you'll need to allow at least 10 hours to get there by road, for the route is long, rough and bumpy. This is the hometown of Samuel Doe, who stole power in a bloody coup in 1980. His mark is still evident in Zwedru, where he installed pavements and was in the process of constructing a house on the edge of town when he was murdered. Many people in Grand Gedeh, particularly those who feel forgotten by the Monrovia administration, remain vocal supporters of Doe.

The best place to stay is the Munnah Guesthouse (☑0886-485 288; r from US$30), also used by NGOs working in the area's Ivorian refugee camps. The modern, airy rooms have fans. The other option is the more basic Monjue Hotel (☑0880-748 658), which can be noisy at weekends. Florida restaurant, on the main road that runs through town, is a popular meeting spot that serves cheap Liberian dishes and European mains.

Sapo National Park   PARK
(scnlib2001@yahoo.com) FREE Sapo, Liberia's only national park, is a lush 1808-sq-km tract of rainforest containing some of West Africa's last remaining primary rainforest, as well as forest elephants, pygmy hippos, chimpanzees, antelopes and other wildlife, although these populations suffered greatly during the war. If you'd like to visit, your best bet is to go with a tour organised by the likes of Barefoot Safari (p226), as the park is not set up for independent travel. The park is in Sinoe Province. You'll need to allow at least a full day's travel to reach Sapo from Monrovia. Take a 4WD from Monrovia to Greenville, then head north to Juarzon and then southeast to Jalay's Town.

Harper

Reachable after two days on some of Liberia's worst roads, deliquescent, small-town Harper feels like the prize at the end of a long treasure hunt. The capital of the once-autonomous Maryland state, this gem is shingled with decaying ruins that hint at its former grandeur.

The drive from Monrovia to Harper can be broken up in Zwedru (10 hours), from where it's around five hours further south. It's inadvisable to attempt this route during the rainy season, even if you're travelling by 4WD.

◎ Sights

In the early evenings, the soft light gives an eldritch feel to the shell of the presidential mansion of former president William Tubman, who was born in Harper, and the remnants of the Morning Star Masonic Lodge, built by Tubman, himself a Grand Master Freemason.

Cape Palmas Lighthouse is no longer functional but can be climbed for an outstanding panoramic view of the cape. It's on a UN base, so get permission first, and don't attempt to scale the small, slippery steps during the rainy season. Don't miss the stunning, palm-lined beach at nearby Fish Town (not to be confused with the larger town of the same name), but take care with the currents if you swim.

⌂ Sleeping

The town's best-established hotel is Adina's Guest House (☑0886-620 005; r US$25), which has several basic rooms with fans. If it's fully booked, as is often the case, you can try your luck at Tubman University campus 6.5km north of town or the Pastoral Centre of the Catholic archdiocese.

✕ Eating & Drinking

Jade's   LIBERIAN $
(cnr Water & Rushman Sts) Jade's (or Sweet Baby, as some locals lovingly call it) serves fish, chicken and rice for US$5 per helping, as well as sandwiches and pizzas if the delivery truck has brought supplies.

Sophie's   LIBERIAN $
(Mechlin St) Sophie's offers good potato greens and cassava-leaf stew.

Bobby's   CAFE $
(Maryland Ave) Bobby's tea shop does the best breakfasts in town: think beans, spaghetti, instant coffee and greasy egg baps.

Pak Bat   ASIAN $
There's great south Asian food to be had at Pak Bat, the Pakistani UN peacekeepers' battalion, so long as you're prepared to pay US$3 and can pull off an NGO worker vibe.

Oceanview   BAR
(Printey St) For beachside drinks, Oceanview can't be beaten.

UNDERSTAND LIBERIA

Liberia Today

Liberia's Nobel Peace Prize–winning president, Ellen Johnson-Sirleaf, won a second term in power in 2011, after rival party Congress for Democratic Change (CDC) – led by Winston Tubman and former AC Milan footballer George Weah – boycotted the second round of the violence-ridden vote, complaining of fraud. 'Ellen', as she is widely known, enjoys support from a loyal band of Liberians. Others criticise her for being a part of the old set of politicians and accuse her of failing to understand their woes.

Ellen also failed in 2010 to implement the findings of Liberia's Truth and Reconciliation Commission, a post-conflict justice organ that was modelled on South Africa's. The body's final report recommended that the president herself be barred from holding public office for 50 years, after she admitted partially bankrolling former leader Charles Taylor's rebellion that sparked the civil war.

Taylor was sentenced to 50 years behind bars by a UN-backed war-crimes tribunal in The Hague in 2011. Many Liberians expressed frustration that Taylor was tried not for his role in the painful Liberian conflict but for masterminding rebel operations during Sierra Leone's war.

Many middle-class Liberians are excited about the country's new dawn, but for others – particularly those outside Monrovia – the fresh coats of paint and eager investors in the capital do little to heal old wounds. Justice, they say, is still a way away.

History

The Love of Liberty

Liberia was ruled along ethnic lines until American abolitionists looking for a place to resettle freed slaves stepped off the boat at Monrovia's Providence Island in 1822. They saw themselves as part of a mission to bring civilisation and Christianity to Africa, but their numbers were soon depleted by tropical diseases and hostile indigenous residents.

The surviving settlers, known as Americo-Liberians, declared an independent republic in 1847, under the mantra 'The Love of Liberty Brought Us Here'. However, citizenship excluded indigenous peoples, and every president until 1980 was of American freed-slave ancestry. For nearly a century, Liberia foundered economically and politically while the indigenous population suffered under forced labour. They were not afforded the right to vote until 1963.

During William Tubman's presidency (1944–71) the tide began to turn. Foreign investment flowed into the country, and for several decades Liberia sustained sub-Saharan Africa's highest growth rate. Firestone and other American companies made major investments, and Tubman earned praise as the 'maker of modern Liberia'.

Yet the influx of new money exacerbated existing social inequalities, and hostilities between Americo-Liberians and the indigenous population worsened during the era of Tolbert, who succeeded Tubman. While the elite continued to live the high life, resentment among other Liberians quietly simmered.

Death in Pyjamas

Master-sergeant Samuel Doe crept into the presidential palace one night in 1980 and killed Tolbert, who was ready for bed in his pyjamas. For the first time, Liberia had a ruler who was not an Americo-Liberian, giving the indigenous population a taste of political power and an opportunity for vengeance. One of Doe's first moves was to order the execution of 13 of Tolbert's ministers on a beach in Monrovia. Ellen Johnson-Sirleaf, a member of Tolbert's cabinet, narrowly escaped.

The coup was widely condemned both regionally and internationally. While relations with neighbouring African states soon thawed, the post-coup flight of capital from the country, coupled with ongoing corruption, caused Liberia's economy to plummet.

Doe struggled to maintain power, but opposition forces began to gain strength and inter-tribal fighting broke out. On Christmas Eve 1989, Charles Taylor launched an invasion from Côte d'Ivoire. By mid-1990, Taylor's forces controlled most of the countryside. Doe was murdered in 1991, his death captured on a video tape that shows Prince Johnson – who came third in the 2012 presidential race – sipping a beer while shouting instructions to the killers.

Following a series of failed peace accords interspersed with factional fighting, the 1996 elections brought Charles Taylor to the presidency with a big majority. His election slogan was: 'He killed my ma, he killed my pa, I'll vote for him'.

In August 2003, with rebel groups controlling most of the country, and under heavy pressure from the international community (and from Johnson-Sirleaf), Charles Taylor went into exile in Nigeria. A transitional government was established, leading to elections in late 2005. Johnson-Sirleaf's winning candidature made her the first elected female president in Africa.

Culture

Liberia remains a country of exceptions. The old inequality hang-ups haven't gone away; you'll notice that Americo-Liberians and returning, educated Liberians often enjoy better treatment than those with indigenous roots. Various initiatives are under way to even things out, but the road to cultural equality is likely to be long.

Regardless of their roots, one thing all Liberians have in common is their devotion to family. Many people you meet will be supporting a dozen others. Religion is also important, with Christian families regularly attending revivals at churches.

The Liberian handshake (practised mostly by men) has Masonic origins and involves a snappy pull-back of the third finger, often accompanied by a wide grin.

People

The vast majority of Liberians are of indigenous origin, belonging to more than a dozen major tribal groups, including the Kpelle in the centre, the Bassa around Buchanan and the Mandingo (Mandinka) in the north. Americo-Liberians account for barely 5% of the total. There's also an economically powerful Lebanese community in Monrovia.

Close to half of the population are Christians and about 20% are Muslim, with the remainder following traditional religions.

Arts & Crafts

Liberia has long been famed for its masks, especially those of the Gio in the northeast, including the *gunyege* mask (which shelters a power-giving spirit), and the chimpanzee-like *kagle* mask. The Bassa around Buchanan are renowned for their *gela* masks, which often have elaborately carved coiffures, always with an odd number of plaits.

Food & Drink

Rice and spicy meat sauces or fish stews are popular Liberian dishes. Palm butter with fish and potato greens are two favourites. Other popular dishes include palava sauce (made with plato leaf, dried fish or meat and palm oil) and *jollof rice* (rice and vegetables with meat or fish). American food is popular in Monrovia. Club beer is the local brew.

Environment

Illegal logging both during and after the conflict has threatened a number of species in Liberia, including the forest elephant, hawk, pygmy hippo (nigh-on impossible to see), manatee and chimpanzee. Liberia's rainforests, which now cover about 40% of the country, comprise a critical part of the Guinean Forests of West Africa Hotspot, an exceptionally biodiverse area stretching across 11 countries in the region.

Liberia's low-lying coastal plain is intersected by marshes, creeks and tidal lagoons, and bisected by at least nine major rivers. Inland is a densely forested plateau rising to low mountains in the northeast. The highest point is Mt Nimba (1362m).

SURVIVAL GUIDE

ⓘ Directory A–Z

ACCOMMODATION

Accommodation prices in Monrovia have been driven up by the presence of private companies and NGOs. You can expect to pay top dollar in the capital, with a few exceptions. Upcountry, both prices and standards are lower.

BOOKS

Journey Without Maps, Graham Greene's tale of adventuring across Liberia in the 1930s, is the Liberia classic. Less well-known but equally recommended is *Too Late to Turn Back*, written by Greene's cousin and travelling companion Barbara.

President Ellen Johnson-Sirleaf's autobiography, *This Child Will be Great*, explores pre- and postwar Liberia, including Johnson-Sirleaf's backing of Taylor's rebellion.

MOVIES

Pray the Devil Back to Hell is a 2008 documentary that focuses on Nobel Prize–winner Leymah Gbowee's efforts to bring the war to an end. *An Uncivil War* includes disturbing images of the conflict and America's alleged failure to help.

Shot in the years following the war, *Sliding Liberia* is a short surf documentary that beautifully captures post-conflict Liberia and a local surfer's effort to catch the waves, rather than go under.

EMBASSIES & CONSULATES

Canadians and Australians should contact their high commissions in Abidjan (Côte d'Ivoire) and Accra (Ghana), respectively.

Côte d'Ivoire Consulate (☑0886-519 138; Warner Ave btwn 17th & 18th Sts, Sinkor)

French Embassy (☑031-235 576; German Compound, Congo Town)

German Embassy (☑0886-438 365; Tubman Blvd, UNMIL Bldg, Congo Town)

Ghanian Embassy (☑077-016 920; cnr 15th St & Cheesman Ave, Sinkor)

Guinean Embassy (☑0886-573 049; Tubman Blvd btwn 23rd & 24th Sts, Sinkor)

Nigerian Embassy (☑0886-261 148; Tubman Blvd, Nigeria House, Congo Town)

Sierra Leonean Embassy (☑0886-427 404; Tubman Blvd, Congo Town)

UK Embassy (☑06-516 973; chalkleyroy@ aol.com; UN Dr, Clara Town, Bushrod Island) Honorary consul, emergency assistance only; otherwise contact the British High Commission in Freetown, Sierra Leone.

US Embassy (☑077-054 826; http://monro via.usembassy.gov/; UN Dr, Mamba Point)

HEALTH

You will need a valid yellow-fever vaccination certificate in order to enter Liberia. Malaria is endemic and prophylaxis is recommended. Typhoid is also relatively common, so take care to wash your hands before eating.

MONEY

Liberia has two units of currency; the Liberty dollar (L$, or LD) and the US dollar, which is accepted in most places. There are between 60 and 73 Liberty dollars to one US dollar. For small purchases such as newspapers, shared taxi rides and cheap meals, Liberians use Liberty dollars. For anything else, it's US dollars.

PRACTICALITIES

→ **Electricity** Voltage is 110V. Plugs are a mixture of US-style (two flat pins) and European style. Grid power is gradually improving in Monrovia, although most hotels and apartment blocks still rely on fuel-heavy generators. Outside of the capital, it's generators all the way.

→ **Language** Liberian English – which to the untrained ear sounds something like Caribbean-lilted English, with southern American undertones and missing consonents – is the main language. Upcountry, as many as 25 languages are spoken, including Bassa, Mende, Vai and Kpelle.

→ **Newspapers** There are dozens of national newspapers; among the best-regarded are the *New Dawn*, the *Observer* and *Front Page Africa*.

If you have a Visa (not MasterCard) card, Ecobank's ATMs are reasonably reliable in Monrovia. Elsewhere, carry cash. Western Union and Moneygram operate in most towns.

OPENING HOURS

Banks Generally open 9am to 4pm Monday to Friday and 9am to noon on Saturday.

PUBLIC HOLIDAYS

New Year's Day 1 January
Armed Forces Day 11 February
Decoration Day Second Wednesday in March
JJ Roberts' Birthday 15 March
Fast & Prayer Day 11 April
National Unification Day 14 May
Independence Day 26 July
Flag Day 24 August
Liberian Thanksgiving Day First Thursday in November
Tubman Day 29 November
Christmas Day 25 December

SAFE TRAVEL

Liberia – notably the beaches in and around Monrovia – has some of the strongest rip currents in the world, and expat drownings transcend tropical diseases as one of the most common causes of death. Check with locals before you swim, never swim alone and learn how to negotiate rip tides before you dip your toes into the ocean. Poor sanitation facilities in many waterside communities mean that central Monrovia's beaches aren't the healthiest places to sunbathe or swim, but clean white sands await on the outskirts of town.

Otherwise, the biggest dangers are the roads. The security situation is stable, although it's wise not to walk in Monrovia after dark. Exercise caution if using motorbike taxis – medical care is limited – and don't be afraid to ask the driver to go slow. Electric shocks are common in badly wired buildings; wear shoes before plugging in appliances if you're worried.

TELEPHONE

The country code is 231.There are no area codes or landlines. You can call the US (but not Europe) cheaply from most mobile networks. You can pick up a Cellcom, Comium or Lonestar SIM card from booths on the street for US$5.

VISAS

Visas are required by all (except nationals of Ecowas countries), with costs varying depending on where they are procured. In the US a three-month single-entry visa for US citizens costs US$140. In a pinch, airport visas can be secured, but you must have a company apply to immigration ahead of time and someone must bring the visa to meet your plane at the airport.

Visa Extensions

Visas can be extended at the **Bureau of Immigration** (Broad St; ☉ 9am-5pm Mon-Fri, to 3pm Sat) in Monrovia.

Visas for Onward Travel

Côte d'Ivoire Bring one passport photo and leave your passport between 9am and 1pm or 2pm and 3pm Monday to Friday. A one-month single-entry visa costs US$75 for all nationals. Processing usually takes five working days but can be done faster at no extra cost if you're in a hurry.

Guinea Bring two passport photos and leave your passport between 9.30am and 4pm Monday to Friday. One-month single-entry visas cost US$65 for citizens of the EU, Australia and New Zealand, or US$100 for US and Canadian nationals. Processing takes 24 hours.

Sierra Leone You'll need two passport photos and a photocopy of your passport to get a visa. Applications are accepted only between 10am and 2pm on Monday, Wednesday and Friday, and single-entry visas valid for up to three months cost US$100 for citizens of the EU, Canada, Australia and New Zealand. US citizens are charged US$131.

ⓘ Getting There & Away

AIR

A number of airlines serve Monrovia.

Air France (www.airfrance.com; Broad St)
British Airways (www.ba.com; Royal Hotel, Tubman Blvd, Sinkor)

Brussels Airlines (www.brusselsairlines.com; Randall St)

Delta Air Lines (DL; www.delta.com)

Kenya Airways (KQ; ☎ 06-511 522, 06-556 693; www.kenya-airways.com; Broad St, KLM Bldg)

Royal Air Maroc (AT; ☎ 06-956 956, 06-951 951; www.royalairmaroc.com; Tubman Blvd)

LAND

Côte d'Ivoire

Border crossings with Côte d'Ivoire are just beyond Sanniquellie towards Danané, and east of Harper, towards Tabou.

From Harper, you must cross the Cavally River by ferry or canoe to reach the Ivorian border. Plan on two days if you want to reach Abidjan via San Pedro using public transport along this route.

Alternatively, daily bush taxis go from Monrovia to Ganta and Sanniquellie, from where you can continue in stages to Danané and Man (12 to 15 hours).

Guinea

For Guinea, the main crossing is just north of Ganta. From just north of Ganta's Public Market you can take a *moto-taxi* the 2km to the border and walk across. Once in Guinea, there are frequent taxis to N'zérékoré. From Sanniquellie's bush-taxi rank, known as the 'meat packing', there are irregular bush taxis via Yekepa to the Guinean town of Lola (US$6.50). A place in a shared taxi is the same price. A *moto-taxi* (if you can find one!) from Yekepa to the border should cost only US$0.50, after which there are Guinean vehicles to Lola. There is also a border crossing at Voinjama to Macenta via a bad road from Gbarnga (often impassable in the wet season).

Sierra Leone

Using a 4WD, you can reach Freetown in about 12 hours. The main Sierra Leone crossing is at Bo (Waterside). There are frequent daily bush taxis between Monrovia and the Bo (Waterside) border (three hours), from where it's easy to find onward transport to Kenema (about eight very rough hours further), and then on to Freetown.

Getting Around

BUSH TAXI & BUS

Bush taxis go daily from Monrovia to most destinations, including Buchanan, Gbarnga, Ganta, Sanniquellie and the Sierra Leone border, although distant routes are severely restricted during the rainy season. Minivans (called 'buses') also ply most major routes, although they're more crowded and dangerous than bush taxis.

CAR & MOTORCYCLE

Vehicle rental can be arranged through better hotels from about US$150 per day plus petrol for a 4WD. You can travel by private taxi in Monrovia for US$5 per short hop; contact the well-run and trusted network of Guinean taxi drivers, **Alpha** (☎ 0886-600 022), for more information, including on airport pick-ups. Motorbike taxis known as *pen-pens* ply the streets of Monrovia and other cities. In the capital they have a 10pm curfew for a reason; ride with caution.

Mali

♪ 223 / POP 14.5 MILLION

Fast Facts

➡ **Capital** Bamako

➡ **Population** 15 million

➡ **Area** 1,240,140 sq km

➡ **Languages** French, Bambara, Fulfulde, Tamashek, Dogon and Songhai

➡ **Money** West African CFA franc; US$1 = CFA504.29, €1 = CFA656

➡ **Seasons** Hot (October to February), very hot (April to June), wet (July to August)

➡ **Tourist Information** www.le-mali.com/omatho/index.htm

➡ **Visa** One- to three-month visas available at Mali embassies; short-stay and transit visas may be issued at borders depending on security situation.

Rugged Land of Sahelian Sands & Lush Forests

Like an exquisite sandcastle formed in a harsh desert landscape, Mali is blessed by an extraordinary amount of beauty, wonders, talents and knowledge.

Yet for now, it's landscapes, monuments, mosques and music bars are off-limits, sealed from tourists by a conflict that is threatening the culture of this remarkable country.

The beating heart of Mali is Bamako, where Ngoni and Kora musicians play to crowds of dancing Malians from all ethnicities, while in the Dogon country, villages still cling to the cliffs as they did in ancient times.

Further west, Fula women strap silver jewellery to their ears and their belongings to donkeys, forming caravans worthy of beauty pageants as they make their way across the *hamada* (dry, dusty scrubland).

And in the northeast, the writings of ancient African civilizations remain locked in the beautiful libraries of Timbuktu.

Mali Top Sights

➡ **Dogon Country** Rose-coloured villages, big blue skies, sacred crocodiles and sandstone cliffs

➡ **Djenné** Stunning mud-brick town with a fairy-tale mosque overlooking a clamorous Monday market

➡ **Bamako** Spicy grilled fish, live music, sprawling markets and motorbikes purring along the banks of the Niger river

➡ **Timbuktu** Few places in the world hold a pursuit of knowledge so dear, with its ancient libraries, monuments and never-digitized texts on philosophy and astronomy

➡ **Segou** Acacia trees, shea butter, pottery and waterside griots

➡ **Niger River** Africa's third-longest river, bending and twisting on its way to the ancient Sahelian trading kingdoms

UNDERSTAND MALI

Mali Today

Mali's fall from grace in 2012 came as a surprise to many, although not to close watchers of former President Amadou Toumani Toure (commonly referred to as ATT) who was ousted in a coup in April 2012. A band of mutinous soldiers ousted the president and his cabinet in the run-up to elections in which ATT was not planning to stand, claiming the leader was not adequately supporting the under-equipped Malian army against an Tuareg rebellion in the northeast of the country.

Somewhat ironically, the coup only worsened the situation in the northeast, allowing Islamist groups to gain hold of the region. They in turn pushed out the Tuareg groups and went on to install sharia law in the ancient towns of Gao and Timbuktu, destroying ancient monuments, tombs and remnants of history. 700,000 civilians were forced to flee in 2012 and early 2013, winding up in refugee camps in neighbouring countries as French forces and Regional West African Ecowas (Economic Community of West African States) troops launched air raids and ground attacks, successfully pushing back the Islamists from many of their strongholds. French forces began to draw down in April 2013, but the majority of the displaced had not returned home at the time of research, and Jihadi attacks continued.

Visiting Mali was dangerous and strongly unrecommended at the time of research. Although there is some semblance of normality in the capital, Bamako, the risk of kidnapping and violence remains. Venturing further north or east than Mopti and Sevare should be done with extreme caution.

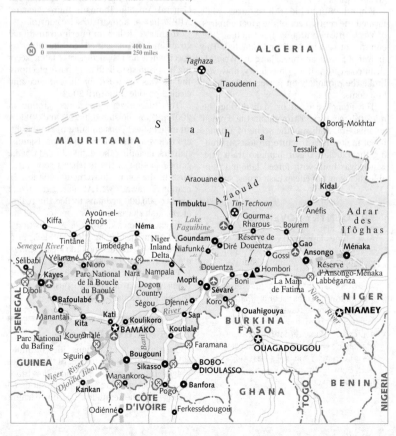

The instability is deeply felt by most Malians; many businesses have closed, tourism revenue has dropped dramatically; with the destruction of important sites in Gao and Timbuktu, many sadly feel that it is not only Mali's future that is under threat but its long-celebrated culture and history.

History

Early Empires

Rock art in the Sahara suggests that northern Mali has been inhabited since 10,000 BC, when the Sahara was fertile and rich in wildlife. By 300 BC, large organised settlements had developed, most notably near Djenné, one of West Africa's oldest cities. By the 6th century AD, the lucrative trans-Saharan trade in gold, salt and slaves had begun, facilitating the rise of West Africa's great empires.

From the 8th to the 16th centuries, Mali formed the centrepiece of the great empires of West African antiquity, most notably the empires of Ghana, Mali and Songhaï. The arrival of European ships along the West African coast from the 15th century, however, broke the monopoly on power of the Sahel kingdoms.

The French arrived in Mali during the mid-19th century. Throughout the French colonial era, Mali was the scene of a handful of major infrastructure projects, including the 1200km Dakar–Bamako train line, which was built with forced labour to enable the export of cheap cash crops, such as

---

ⓘ COUNTRY COVERAGE

At the time of research very few travellers were heading to Mali so we're providing historical and cultural information rather than reviews and listings. A good source of information for on-the-ground travel in Mali is Lonely Planet's Thorn Tree online travel forum www.lonelyplanet.com/thorntree. Other sources of good internet-based information are www.maliactu.net (local news in French) and blogs like Bridges from Bamako (http://bridges frombamako.com).

---

rice and cotton. But Mali remained the poor neighbour of Senegal and Côte d'Ivoire.

Independence

Mali became independent in 1960 (for a few months it was federated with Senegal), under the one-party rule of Mali's first president, Modibo Keïta. In 1968, Keïta was overthrown by army officers led by Moussa Traoré.

During the Cold War, Mali was firmly in the Soviet camp; food shortages were constant, especially during the devastating droughts of 1968-74 and 1980-85. One bright spot came in 1987 when Mali produced its first grain surplus.

The Tuareg rebellion began in 1990, and the following year a peaceful prodemocracy demonstration drew machine-gun fire from security forces. Three days of rioting followed, during which 150 people were killed. The unrest finally provoked the army, led by General Amadou Toumani Touré (General ATT as he was known), to seize control.

Touré established an interim transitional government and gained considerable respect when he resigned a year later, keeping his promise to hold multiparty elections. But he was rewarded for his patience and elected president in April 2002.

The Tuareg rebellion gained ground in 2007 and was bolstered in 2011 and 2012 by an influx of weapons and unemployed fighters following the Libyan civil war. Islamist fighters, including those linked to Al Qaeda, gained footing in the northeast soon after, ousting the main Mouvement pour le Liberation d'Azawad (MNLA) Tuareg group and forcing 400,000 civilians to flee the region after harsh sharia law was imposed and ancient monuments destroyed. A transitional government, headed by Dioncounda Traore, was installed, but deemed too weak to handle the crisis alone. French forces and later ECOWAS troops launched air and ground offensives in an attempt to push back the Islamists in January 2013.

Arts & Culture

For the majority of Malians, life continues as usual, although the impact of the conflict weighs heavily on their minds. For those who eke out a living working in shops or businesses, the emphasis is on earning

AND THE BANDS PLAYED ON

The backdrop of the events of 2012 shook artists and musicians as well as politicians, interrupting album recordings and forcing Tuareg musicians to leave the country. The famous *ngoni* player Bassekou Kouyate, who also served as a griot to ousted President ATT was in the middle of recording an album when the coup hit. He finished the record, but the mark of the coup on it – and perhaps his future sales – is indelible.

Tinariwen, an intoxicating Tuareg group of former rebels from Kidal, were caught up in the crisis multiple times in 2012, with some of their members going missing and turning up in refugee camps in neighboring countries. Sadly the Festival in the Desert, usually held in January and organized by Tuareg musicians, has become another victim of the crisis. Amano Ag Issa, who recently toured the world with his Tuareg group Tartit, fled the country in the wake of the 2012 Tuareg rebellion. 'I was living quietly in my country, until the day that shook all our lives. Everything changed!' he told us. 'My Tuareg people were attacked and killed for no reason. That's what made me leave Mali. I had to go, we really didn't have much choice but to leave our homeland,' he said.

Fortunately, music is harder to destroy than the threatened ancient monuments and libraries of Timbuktu but the crisis has certainly silenced some musicians, restricting access to funding, electricity and inspiration. In the northeast, sharia law has meant that live bands and dancing venues have been silenced.

Outside of Mali, the music plays on, including bluesy stuff such as that from the late Ali Farka Touré. Other much-loved blues performers include many from Ali Farka's stable, among them Afel Bocoum, Ali Farka's son Vieux Farka Touré, Baba Salah and Lobi Traoré. Some scholars believe that the roots of American blues lie with the Malian slaves who worked on US plantations.

The breadth and depth of Mali's musical soundtrack is attributable not just to centuries of tradition but also to the policies of Mali's postindependence government. As elsewhere in West Africa, Mali's musicians were promoted as the cultural standard-bearers of the newly independent country and numerous state-sponsored 'orchestras' were founded. The legendary Rail Band de Bamako (actual employees of the Mali Railway Corporation) was one of the greatest, and one of its ex-members, the charismatic Salif Keita, has become a superstar in his own right. We have yet to see what kind of sounds the next, tense chapter in Mali's history will produce.

enough to take care of their (large) families on a day-to-day basis. But many have placed long-term plans on hold, as they simply can't predict what the future will bring.

In the northeast of the country, life has changed drastically. The imposition of sharia law has meant that many bars and restaurants have been closed. The majority of Malians are Muslim, but the strain of Islam that is followed is moderate and liberal – many enjoy dancing, drinking and being social butterflies. Now women must cover their heads, couples are stoned to death for having sex outside of marriage and live music is banned. For those who have not fled from the towns of Kidal, Gao and Timbuktu, life has become fairly miserable. For those in refugee camps in neighbouring countries, it's worse still.

Malians hold fast to tradition and politeness is respected. Malians find it rude to ask questions or stop someone in the street without first asking after their health and their families.

People

Mali's population is growing by almost 3% per year, which means that the number of Malians doubles every 20 years; 48% of Malians are under 15 years of age.

Concentrated in the centre and south of the country, the Bambara are Mali's largest ethnic group (33% of the population). Fulani (17%) pastoralists are found wherever there is grazing land for their livestock, particularly in the Niger inland delta. The lighter-skinned Tuareg (6%), traditionally nomadic pastoralists and traders, inhabit the fringes of the Sahara.

Between 80% and 90% of Malians are Muslim, and 2% are Christian. Animist beliefs often overlap with Islamic and Christian practices, especially in rural areas.

Mauritania

📞 222 / POP 3.36 MILLION

Why Go?

If West Africa is a playground for overlanders, then Mauritania often seems to be little more than a transit between the better-known attractions of Marrakesh, Dakar or Bamako. That's a shame because Mauritania has some tremendous secrets to reveal.

Just as impressive as the cultural diversity is some of the continent's grandest scenery. The Adrar region offers epic sand dunes, eye-popping plateaus and Africa's biggest monolith. The Tagânt has similar charms, and both hide ancient (and World Heritage–listed) caravan towns – Chinguetti, Ouadâne and Oualâta. The World Heritage feast continues along the coast at Parc National du Banc d'Arguin, which attracts millions of migratory birds and is a renowned bird-watching site.

If you just breeze through, you'll miss out on a truly incredible country. No one in Mauritania is in a rush, and you shouldn't be either.

Best Places to Eat

➡ Restorante Galloufa (p245)

➡ Le Méditerranée (p242)

➡ Bla Bla Thé (p242)

Best Places to Stay

➡ Auberge Bab Sahara (p245)

➡ Auberge La Gueïla (p247)

➡ Maison d'Hôtes Jeloua (p241)

➡ Eco-lodge du Maure Bleu (p249)

When to Go
Nouakchott

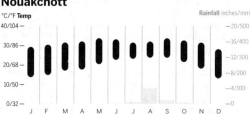

Nov–Mar The most pleasant months to visit the desert, although nights can be cold.

Jun-Aug The *rifi* (hot winds) send temperatures soaring to 45°C and above.

Jul–Sep The short rainy season in Nouakchott can be prone to flooding after downpour.

NOUAKCHOTT

POP 1 MILLION

Barely 50 years old, Nouakchott has to be simultaneously one of Africa's strangest and most unassuming capital cities. This is urban planning nomad style: a city simply plonked down 5km from the coast as if on an overnight caravan stop and left to grow by accident. Most travellers use it as a staging post before the Adrar, Parc National Banc d'Arguin or the next international border.

Although it's not a highlight of the country, Nouakchott is sleepily idiosyncratic and you could do worse than spend an afternoon at the gloriously frantic fish market (one of the busiest in West Africa), treat yourself to a comfy guesthouse or feast in a good restaurant. It's also laidback and amazingly safe – bliss after the rigours of the desert.

◉ Sights & Activities

Major landmarks in the centre include the **Grande Mosquée** (Rue Mamadou Konaté), also

Mauritania Highlights

❶ Wake up at the crack of dawn in order to catch a glorious sunrise from the labyrinthine lanes of the old city in **Chinguetti** (p247).

❷ Experience the magic of the Sahara and sleep beneath the star-studded skies at the saffron dunes in the **Adrar** (p245).

❸ Pack your binoculars and observe vast flocks of birds from a traditional *pirogue*

in **Parc National du Banc d'Arguin** (p245).

❹ Hop on the **iron-ore train** (p244) – one of the world's longest trains – and be ready for the most epic journey of your life!

Nouakchott

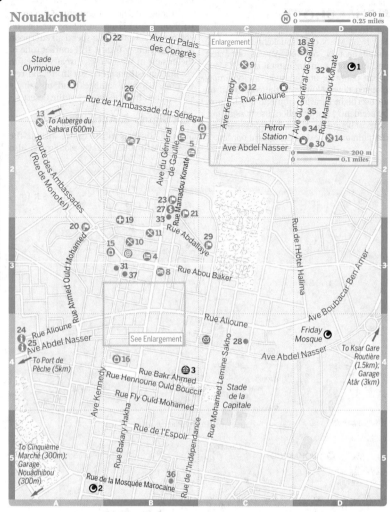

called the Mosquée Saoudienne, with its slender minarets, and the large **Mosquée Marocaine** (Rue de la Mosquée Marocaine), which towers over a bustling market area.

Port de Pêche
MARKET

(Fish Market) The Port de Pêche is Nouakchott's star attraction. Both lively and colourful, you'll see hundreds of teams of mostly Wolof and Fula men dragging in heavy fishing nets. Small boys hurry back and forth with trays of fish, which they sort, gut, fillet and lay out on large trestles to dry.

The best time is in the late afternoon, when the fishing boats return.

It's pretty safe as long as you're vigilant and sensible with your possessions, although people can be sensitive about photography. Take a taxi to get there from the centre.

Musée National
MUSEUM

(Rue Mohamed el Habib; admission UM300; ☉8am-3.30pm Mon-Fri) Moderately worthwhile for anyone with an interest in Moorish culture. On the 1st level is a prehistoric gallery with archaeological exhibits while

Nouakchott

the 2nd level is taken up with more recent ethnographic displays from Moorish society. The building is labelled as the Ministry of Culture.

Nouakchott beach SWIMMING

There are two decent beaches around 5km north of the centre, **Plage Pichot** and **Plage Sultan**. Both have small restaurants and shade, and are popular with the small expat community on weekends. Beware of undertows.

🛏 Sleeping

Nouakcott has a reasonable selection of accommodation. The big news is the construction of a five-star Rotana Hotel in the Ribat Al Bahar district, to open in late 2014.

Auberge du Sahara GUESTHOUSE $

(🖉 4764 1038; www.auberge-sahara.fr/; tent per person UM2000, dm UM2500, r UM6000-8000, parking UM1500; 🅿 ❄ 🛜) Well-signed on the road to Nouâdhibou. Dorms and rooms are plain, but functional, and shared bathrooms are kept in good nick. Other pluses are the outdoor areas, a kitchen for guests' use and a rooftop terrace.

Auberge Menata GUESTHOUSE $

(🖉 4643 2730; auberge.menata@voila.fr; off Ave du Général de Gaulle; tent per person UM2000, dm UM3000, s/d with air-con UM5000/10,000, parking UM2000; 🅿 ❄ 🛜) A centrally located and perennially popular haunt for backpackers and overlanders, the laidback Menata is a decent option. Good meals are available upon request or you can use the kitchen.

★ Maison d'hôtes Jeloua GUESTHOUSE $$

(🖉 3636 9450, 525 0914, 643 2730; maison.jel oua@voila.fr; r UM10,000-12,000, r without bathroom UM5000; 🅿 ❄ @🛜) Run by the same people as the Auberge Menata, this is a lovely *maison d'hôtes* (B&B). It's charmingly decorated and the garden has its own restaurant. Deservedly popular.

Maison d'hôtes la Bienvenue GUESTHOUSE $$

(🖉 4525 1421; dominiqueidris@hotmail.com; Ave du Général de Gaulle; s/d UM12,000/14,000; ❄🛜) Although it's on the main drag, this *auberge* (small hotel) is surprisingly peaceful and there's a pleasant leafy garden at the front, ideal for breakfast – the front of the hotel has been converted into the great (and fuschia-pink) Bla Bla Thé cafe. Rooms (all with bathrooms) are good value for the price tag.

ⓘ SET YOUR BUDGET

Budget

➡ Hotel room UM2000

➡ Street food UM500

➡ Tea in nomad's tent Free

➡ Nouakchott taxi ride UM200

Midrange

➡ Hotel room UM14,000

➡ Pizza UM1500

➡ Coffee UM800

Top End

➡ Hotel room UM35,000

➡ Two-course meal UM3000

➡ Can of beer UM1200 (if available)

➡ 4WD with driver, per day UM30,000

Hôtel Halima   HOTEL $$$

(☎4525 7921; www.hotel-halima.com; Rue de l'Hôtel Halima; s/d UM30,700/34,400; ❄) Sure, the well-run Halima doesn't claim the glitz of its top-end competitors but for the price it's a good bet in this bracket, with well-organised rooms, good facilities and a tough-to-beat location. Accepts credit cards.

Hôtel Tfeila   HOTEL $$$

(☎4525 7400; www.hoteltfeila.com; Ave du Général de Gaulle; s from UM45,200, d from UM47,200; P❄🛜🏊) Forget the blinding orange and yellow facade of this former Novotel; the interior shows money and a classy eye bonded with impeccable service. From swish rooms to free wi-fi, a good restaurant and a pool, this is by some degree Mauritania's best hotel.

✖ Eating & Drinking

Unless otherwise stated, all restaurants are open for lunch and dinner every day. In principle, alcohol is available at higher-end places.

Rue Alioune between Ave Kennedy and Ave du Général de Gaulle is good for fast food, with most places open until 11pm or later – most have a Lebanese bent.

Le Prince   FAST FOOD $

(Rue Alioune; mains UM500-1300) A bit grander than most fast-food joints, Le Prince claims to be Nouakchott's oldest restaurant. Plonk yourself on a wobbly chair in the room at the back and tuck into a plate of well-prepared

shwarma (a kebab-like dish), sandwiches, salads and ice cream – all great value.

Café Tunisie   CAFE $

(Ave Kennedy; set breakfast UM1000) Next to Tunis Air, this cafe is fine for coffee and smoking a water pipe, but comes into its own with fantastic breakfasts – freshly squeezed orange juice, bread, jam, pastries, yoghurt, coffee and a bottle of mineral water. A fine way to start the day.

Rimal   INTERNATIONAL $

(☎4525 4832; Ave Abdel Nasser; mains about UM1000; ⊘closed lunch Sun) This place thoroughly lacks any pretensions but is all the better for it. The surroundings might have seen better days, but the service is fast and the food piping hot. There are good salads, chicken dishes and a variety of tasty fish straight from the Port de Pêche.

★ Bla Bla Thé   CAFE $$

(☎tel, info 3669 1073; www.facebook.com/blablathe; Ave du Général de Gaulle; mains from UM1400, juices UM800) A fresh and funky cafe inside Maison d'hôtes la Bienvenue.

Pizza Lina   PIZZERIA $$

(☎4525 8662; Rte des Ambassades; mains UM1500-3500) A long-established player on the Nouakchott dining scene, Pizza Lina now faces stiff competition from the many similar places along this stretch of Rte des Ambassades. All the same, you'll find decent crispy pizzas and a selection of pasta and meat dishes.

★ Le Méditerranée   FRENCH $$

(☎3318 1240; off Ave du Général de Gaulle; mains from UM2000; ⊘closed Fri & lunch Sat) Good French and continental dishes, served up in a pleasant garden. Excellent service with a hint of sophistication rare in Nouakchott.

La Salamandre   FRENCH $$$

(☎4524 2680; off Rte des Ambassades; mains UM2000-4000; ⊘Mon-Sat) La Salamandre enjoys a decent reputation for lip-smacking French cooking, but throws in a little Mexican and even Japanese for variety. The sleek setting, with lashings of bright colours splashed all over the walls, is another draw.

☆ Entertainment

Pick up a copy of the excellent (French-language) monthly magazine *City Mag* (distributed free at many hotels) for listings of events, exhibitions and concerts.

Institut Français Mauritanie PERFORMING ARTS
(4529 9631; www.institutfrancais-mauritanie.com; next to French Embassy) Pick up a program for the Institut from many hotels; it's an excellent place for concerts by local musicians, films, talks, art exhibitions and dance lessons.

CIMAN LIVE MUSIC
(2500 1288; ciman.nkc@gmail.com) Conservatoire International de Musique et des Arts de Nouakchott (CIMAN) has regular classical and traditional music concerts.

Shopping

You'll find a bit of everything at **Marché Capitale** (Grand Marché; Ave Kennedy), including brass teapots, silver jewellery, traditional wooden boxes and colourful fabrics.

Zein Art ARTS & CRAFTS
(4651 7465; www.zeinart.com; ⊙3.30-7.30pm Mon-Wed, 10am-7.30pm Thu & Sat, closed Fri & Sun) A new gallery, curating the very best work from Mauritanian artists and craftsmen. Full of beautiful things to buy.

Artisans Shops JEWELLERY
(cnr Ave Kennedy & Rte des Ambassades) Check these places out for wooden boxes with silver inlay, daggers and jewellery.

ℹ️ Information

Bureaus de Change There are bureaus de change on Ave du Général de Gaulle and on Ave du Gamal Nasser, as well as in the Marché Capitale. CFA and Moroccan dirhams can be changed.

Cabinet Médical Fabienne Sharif (4525 1571) English-speaking doctor, recommended by expats.

Cyber Neja (off Ave Kennedy; per hr UM200; ⊙8am-midnight)

Main Post Office (Ave Abdel Nasser; ⊙8am-3pm Mon-Thu, to noon Fri) Postal services.

Societe Generale (Ave du Général de Gaulle) Two branches 100m apart; both have ATMs.

TOUR AGENCIES

Le Phare du Désert (4644 2421; www.desertmauritanie.com; info@desertmauritanie.com) Reliable tour operator around Mauritania by 4WD and camel, including the Adrar and Banc d'Arguin.

ℹ️ Getting There & Away

AIR

The major airlines have offices in Nouakchott.

Regional Air – Rega Tours (632 8735, 524 0422; Ave du Général de Gaulle; ⊙8am-5pm Mon-Thu, 8am-noon Fri) For purchasing domestic or international air tickets.

Air Algérie (4525 2059; www.airalgerie.dz; cnr Ave du Général de Gaulle & Ave Abdel Nasser)

Air France (4525 1808, 525 1802; www.airfrance.com; Ave Kennedy)

Mauritania Airlines (4524 4767; www.mai.mr; Rue Mamadou Konaté)

Royal Air Maroc (4525 3564; www.royalairmaroc.com; Ave du Général de Gaulle)

Sénégal Airlines (4525 6363; www.senegalairlines.aero; Ave du Général de Gaulle)

Tunis Air (4525 8762; www.tunisair.com.tr; Ave Kennedy)

BUSH TAXI

There are specific garages for Mauritania's different regions.

For Nouâdhibou (about UM5000, six hours), Garage Nouâdhibou is close to Cinquième Marché; for Rosso (about UM2000, 3½ hours), Garage Rosso is just over 5km south of the centre. For Atâr (UM4500, six hours), Garage Atâr is on the road to Atâr, about 3km north of the airport. Ksar Gare Routière (bus station; near the airport) serves destinations to the southeast including Kiffa, Ayoûn el-Atroûs and Néma. You should also be able to find bush taxis to Tidjikja from here.

ℹ️ Getting Around

A taxi ride within the centre costs around UM200. From the airport, the standard taxi fare to the centre is about UM1000, but it's cheaper to hail a taxi from the highway nearby (UM300).

THE ATLANTIC COAST

No tacky resorts. No pollution. This coastline is a rapturous place for tranquillity seekers and nature lovers. It's mostly occupied by the Parc National du Banc d'Arguin, something of a pilgrimage site for birdwatchers.

Nouâdhibou

POP 80,000

With the new tar road connecting the Moroccan border to Nouakchott, the fishing port of Nouâdhibou has lost much of its *raison d'être* for travellers, who prefer to dash to the capital or to the Adrar region. It's a good base, though, if you plan to visit Banc d'Arguin. The setting is also appealing: Nouâdhibou is on the Baie du Lévrier,

AN EPIC JOURNEY ON THE IRON-ORE TRAIN

Africa offers some pretty wild train trips, but the train ferrying iron ore from the mines at Zouérat to Nouâdhibou might just be the wildest. One of the longest trains in the world (typically a staggering 2.3km long), when it arrives at the 'station' in Nouâdhibou, a decrepit building in the open desert, a seemingly endless number of ore wagons pass before the passenger carriage at the rear finally appears. The lucky ones find a place on one of the two long benches (UM2500); the rest stand or sit on the floor. There are also a dozen 'berths' (UM3000) that are so worn out you can see the springs. It's brutally basic. It's also possible to clamber into the ore cars and travel for free. Impossibly dusty, it's only for the hardcore. Plastic sheets are essential to wrap your bags (and person), plus plenty of warm clothes, as the desert can get fearsomely cold at night, as well as food and drink.

The train leaves Nouâdhibou at around 2pm to 3pm daily. Most travellers get off at Choûm, 12 hours later, where bush taxis wait to take passengers to Atâr, three hours away. In the other direction, the train leaves Zouérat around midday and passes through Atâr at about 5.30pm.

in the middle of a narrow 35km-long peninsula.

◉ Sights & Activities

Réserve Satellite du Cap Blanc   WILDLIFE RESERVE

(admission UM2000; ◎10am-5pm Tue-Sat) A small nature reserve with an excellent information centre, dedicated to the colony of endangered Mediterranean monk seals (*phoque moin*) that live here. Resembling elephant seals, these grey-skinned animals were hunted since the 15th century for their valuable skins and oil. The protected colony here of roughly 150 seals is one of the last on earth. The colony is at the foot of the cliffs; you have a reasonable chance of seeing them swimming offshore.

The reserve is near the lighthouse at the southern tip of Cap Blanc. To get there, cross the railtracks near the SNIM refinery on the edge of Nouâdhibou; the *piste* (track) is rough. Also near the lighthouse is the spectacular wreck of the *United Metlika*, a cargo ship beached on a wide sandy beach and looking all the world like the set of a Hollywood movie.

🛏 Sleeping

In the centre, you'll find a slew of cheap restaurants along Rue de la Galérie Mahfoud. They're nothing fancy, serving fish and *mafé* (groundnut-based stew) for around UM300 a plate.

Camping Chez Abba   CAMPGROUND $

(☑4574 9896; fax 574 9887; Blvd Médian; tent per person UM1500, s/d UM2000/4000; ℗) A good

overlanders' haunt, with plenty of space to park and pitch a tent, and a few decent rooms with their own bathrooms and hot water. Recommended.

Camping Baie du Lévrier   HOSTEL $

(☑4574 6536, mobile 650 4356; Blvd Médian; s/d UM3000/5000; ℗) Also known as Chez Ali, this *auberge*-style place has a good location. Rooms are a bit cell-like, and bathroom facilities are shared, but there is a tent to relax in and cooking facilities.

Hôtel Al Jezira   HOTEL $$

(☑4574 5317; Blvd Maritime; s/d incl breakfast UM13,000/15,000; ℗❄) Nouâdhibou isn't overrun with top-class accommodation, but this midrange hotel slightly north of the centre just about works out. Rates are slightly high for what's on offer, but the rooms are fair, and occasionally border on the comfy.

Hotel Sahel   HOTEL $$$

(☑4574 3857; info@hotel-sahel.com; Rte de l'Aeroport; s/d from UM24,000/28,000; 🛰) Top of the hotel spectrum as far as Nouâdhibou goes, the Sahel is a solidly comfortable business-class option.

🍴 Eating

Restaurant-Pâtisserie Pleine Lune   CAFE $

(☑574 9860; off Blvd Médian; mains UM1000-1500) We like this place for its breakfasts – decent coffee and a good selection of pastries, but it's good at any time of day, with pizzas and sandwiches as quick fillers, or grilled fish and *brochettes* (kebabs) for something more substantial.

⭐ **Restorante Galloufa** SPANISH $$
(☑2216 8770; Rte de l'Aeroport; mains from UM1500; ☎) Excellent laid-back Spanish restaurant, with a heavy emphasis on seafood.

ℹ Information

There are several bureaus de change along the city's main drag, Blvd Médian, as well as two ATMs; most of the internet outlets along here also double as telephone offices.

ℹ Getting There & Away

Mauritania Airlines (☑4574 4291; Blvd Médian) flies four times a week to Nouakchott (UM20,000, one hour), and three times a week to Casablanca in Morocco.

There are plenty of minibuses and bush taxis from the *gare routière* to Nouakchott (UM5000, six hours). You can also get transport from here to Morocco (Western Sahara). Taxis go most days to Dakhla (UM11,500, eight hours). Arrive early – any later than 8am and you'll be facing a long wait for the vehicles to fill and go.

There is also a train that runs from Nouâdhibou to Choûm and Zouérat. The train 'station' is about 5km south of town.

Parc National du Banc d'Arguin

This World Heritage–listed **park** (www.mauritania.mr/pnba; per person per day UM1200) is an important stopover and breeding ground for multitudes of birds migrating between Europe and southern Africa, and as a result is one of the best birdwatching sites on the entire continent. It extends 200km north from Cape Timiris (155km north of Nouakchott) and 235km south of Nouâdhibou. The ideal way to approach the birds is by traditional fishing boat (UM15,000, plus UM3000 for the guide), best organised from the fishing village of **Iwik**.

Inside the park there are official **camp-sites** (per tent UM3000-6000) that are equipped with traditional tents. Meals can also be ordered. There's no public transport, so you'll need to hire a 4WD with a knowledgeable driver, either in Nouakchott or in Nouâdhibou, allowing a couple of days for the trip. Permits are issued either at the entrance gates or in Nouâdhibou at the **park office** (☑574 6744; Blvd Médian; ⊘8am-4pm Mon-Thu, to noon Fri). Both this office and the Nouakchott **Parc National du Banc D'Arguin headquarters** (Map p240; ☑525 8514; Ave Abdel Nasser) sell a map and guide to the park, including GPS waypoints.

THE ADRAR

The Adrar is the undoubted jewel in Mauritania's crown. It's epic Saharan country, and shows the great desert in all its variety: the ancient Saharan towns of Chinguetti and Ouadâne, mighty sand dunes that look sculpted by an artist, vast rocky plateaus and mellow oases fringed with date palms. For desert lovers, the Adrar is a must.

Atâr

POP 25,000

With the grandiose Adrar on its doorstep, this secluded town in the middle of the desert is an excellent place in which to organise camel or 4WD forays into the dunefields.

A large *rond-point* (roundabout) marks the centre of Atâr and the market is just north of it. You'll find several bureaus de change, telephone offices and internet cafes on or around the main drag.

🏃 Activities

There are over a dozen agencies in Atâr that can arrange **camel rides** or **4WD tours**, so shop around. The main costs are the vehicle and driver, so trips are a lot cheaper if you're in a group. Count on paying up to UM21,000 per day for a Toyota Hilux plus petrol. Add about UM2000 per day per person for food. Camel trips start at UM12,000 per day with food and lodging.

🛏 Sleeping & Eating

⭐ **Auberge Bab Sahara** GUESTHOUSE $
(☑4647 3966; www.bab-sahara.com; tent per person UM2000, caravan/stone hut UM5000/8000; ℙ❄) Off Rte de Azougui, Bab Sahara has been a little slice of overlanders' heaven for over 15 years. There's a selection of *tikits* (stone huts; with air-con), caravans and tents, plus a campsite in another compound and a mechanic's workshop. Meals are available on request. The Dutch-German couple who run it are great sources of local information and travel advice.

Auberge du Bonheur GUESTHOUSE $
(☑546 4537; fax 546 4347; tent/hut per person UM1500, r UM4000; ❄@) Those wanting a

BEN AMIRA

Big rocks don't come much more awesome than Ben Amira. Rising 633m out of the desert, it's Africa's biggest monolith, and in size is second only to Australia's Uluru (Ayers Rock). It's clearly visible from the train between Nouâdhibou and Zouérat, but if you have a 4WD it makes a brilliant one-night camping trip from Atâr.

There are actually two granite monoliths. Ben Amira is the largest, with slightly smaller Aïsha to the west. While Ben Amira is more massively spectacular, Aïsha holds a delightful surprise of her own. In December 1999, a symposium of 16 international sculptors was held here to celebrate the millennium, turning many of the boulders at the base of Aïsha into art. The natural shapes of the rocks were reinterpreted as animals, birds, faces and abstract creations. It's a wonderful spot, all the more so for being completely unheralded by its surroundings.

The monoliths are 4km north of the train track between Nouâdhibhou and Choûm, at Km 395 (Ben Amira village sits next to the tracks here). The route is sand rather than gravel *piste*. Aïsha is 5km west of Ben Amira. To find the sculptures, head for the eastern side of Aïsha, where it appears to join a lower mound made of giant 'melted' rocks: the sculptures are here.

reliable base could do worse than this welcoming outfit, a five-minute stroll from the centre. It's nicely turned out, with simple but decent rooms, a large tent in the courtyard and everything kept scrubbed pretty clean.

Camping Inimi CAMPGROUND $
(☑ 2229 4127; camping.inimi@yahoo.fr; Rte de Nouakchott) Cheap but welcoming overlanders' option on the main road south from Atâr.

Auberge Andaloss GUESTHOUSE $
(☑ 2229 3592; aubtwe@gmail.com; r UM6000-7000) Simple, bright green guesthouse with lots of rooms and plenty of lounging space (the more expensive have air-con). Meals on request, and are even prepared for free if you buy your own ingredients.

Hotel Waha HOTEL $$
(☑ 4421 1692; hotelwaha@gmail.com; s/d UM12,000/15,000, dinner UM4000; ☎) Atâr's fanciest option, with two-dozen *tikit*-style rooms, all with air-con and fridge. Good facilities mainly aimed at tour groups.

Restaurant du Coin AFRICAN $
(market, off Rte de Chinguetti; meals UM300) From the *rond-point* head down the Chinguetti road for a block, then turn left. This place is on the right-hand corner, marked by a tiny sign. It's as down-at-heel as you can get, serving up great quantities of rice, fish and Senegalese *mafé*. It's always busy, and the food piping hot and delicious.

Restaurant Agadir AFRICAN $
(Rte de Chinguetti; mains UM500-700) Near the *rond-point*, this cheap and cheerful eatery

rustles up some good couscous and tajines as well as sandwiches and lighter bites.

❶ Getting There & Away

The main *gare routière*, in the heart of town, is where you can get vehicles for Nouakchott (UM3500, six hours) and Choûm (UM1500, three hours). Choûm transport is timed to meet the train heading to/from Nouâdhibou (see p244).

Vehicles for Chinguetti (car/4WD UM1500/2500, about two hours) leave once a day from near a shop a block north of Hotel Monod. Most days there is also transport to Ouadâne (bush taxi/4WD UM3000/4000, about four hours), leaving from a street north of the *rond-point* (ask for '*gare de Ouadâne*'). For Azougui (UM500, 20 minutes) and Terjît (UM1000, one hour), infrequent 4WDs leave from near the *rond-point*.

Terjît

We've never visited an oasis quite like Terjît. About 40km south of Atâr, a streak of palm groves is hemmed in by great red cliffs. At its head, two springs tumble out of the rocks. One is hot, the other cold, and they mix to form a natural swimming pool the perfect temperature for a dip. It's simply bliss. You pay UM1000 to enter the site.

The main spring has been taken over by **Auberge Oasis de Terjît** (☑ 644 8967, in Atâr 546 5020; tent/hut per person UM1500), where a mattress in a tent by the trickling stream is on offer. A meal costs about UM1500. The only other place to stay is the **Auberge des Caravanes** (☑ 4593 1381; r/tikit per person

UM1500, dinner UM1500, breakfast UM1000; P),
a traveller-friendly place at the entrance of
the village.

To get here by private car, drive 40km
south of Atâr on the road to Nouakchott,
then turn left at the checkpoint and follow
a sandy track for 11km. By public transport,
take anything headed towards Nouakchott
and hitch a ride from the checkpoint.

Chinguetti

POP 4000

One of the more attractive of the ancient
caravan towns in the Sahara, Chinguetti is
shrouded with a palpable historic aura. It
was once famous for its Islamic scholars, and
was the ancient capital of the Moors; some
of the buildings date from the 13th century.
Chinguetti butts up against Erg Warane,
Mauritania's biggest stretch of dunes, and
is more than enough to meet traveller's ex-
pectations of the great Saharan sand ocean.

The highlight of any visit is a wander
through the labyrinthine lanes of Le Ksar
(Old Town). The principal attraction is the
16th-century stone mosque (no entry to
non-Muslims). Also of great interest are the
five old libraries, which house the fragile-
as-dust ancient Islamic manuscripts of
Chinguetti.

The best way to see the fascinating dunes
around Chinguetti is by camel. Numerous
méharées (camel trips) are available. Standard costs start from UM8000 per person per
day for the camel, food and guide. Any reputable travel agency in Atâr or *auberge* owner
can arrange camel rides. If you don't want
to sweat it out, you can hire a 4WD and driver. They cost from UM17,000 per day, petrol
not included.

🛏 Sleeping & Eating

Most places have shared bathroom unless
otherwise stated. Breakfast and meals are
available on request (about UM2000 per
meal). The tourist industry has collapsed in
recent years in Chinguetti, so many guesthouses are closed – all those listed are currently open for business.

Auberge des Caravanes   GUESTHOUSE $
(☑ 540 0022; fax 546 4272; r per person UM2000)
With its eye-catching, traditional architecture, it's hard to miss this place right in the
centre of town. Rooms are pretty simple,
and it can feel a bit impersonal, but it's adequate for the price.

★ **Auberge La Gueïla**   GUESTHOUSE $$
(☑ 2205 5056; www.lagueila.com; s/d UM8000/
12,800, dinner UM2800; 🖥) A fabulous, newly
built, French-run place, with six charming
rooms, excellent food (to be taken in the
courtyard garden), a library and even a mas-
sage room for real unwinding.

L'Eden de Chinguetti   GUESTHOUSE $$
(☑ 2220 38844; mahmoudeden@yahoo.fr; r
UM8000) This impressive *auberge* is a great
place to stay. It's neat, well tended and embellished with well-chosen knick-knacks
and a nice garden. The English-speaking
owner is a mine of information. It's on the
road to Atâr, not far from Auberge La Rose
des Sables.

ℹ Getting There & Away

There is at least one vehicle a day to/from Atâr
(car/4WD from UM1500/2500, two hours) They leave
from just behind the market. There are no bush
taxis between Chinguetti and Ouadâne; you'll
have to go back to Atâr.

Ouadâne

Sitting on the edge of the Adrar plateau,
120km northeast of Chinguetti, Ouadâne is
one of the more enchanting semighost towns
of the Sahara. As you arrive across the sands
or plateau from Atâr or Chinguetti, the
stone houses of Le Ksar al Kiali (Old Quarter;
admission UM1000) seem to tumble down the
cliff. The top of the hill is dominated by the
minaret of the new mosque, which is a mere
200 years old, while at the western end, at
the base of the town, is the 14th-century old
mosque. In between, the crumbling structures seem to have been piled up higgledy-
piggledy by some giant child playing with
building blocks. Like Chinguetti, Ouadâne
was a place of scholarship and is home to
over 3000 manuscripts held in private libraries. Only 20 to 30 families still live in
the old town.

🛏 Sleeping & Eating

All places to stay can prepare meals for their
guests (about UM2000 for lunch or dinner) – try the *ksour*, a local thick pancake
made of wheat. Most places are down on the
plateau. Mellow Auberge Vasque – Chez
Zaid (☑ 681 7669; tikit per person UM2000, r with
bathroom & air-con UM10,000) is run by Zaida, a
congenial lady who goes out of her way to
make your stay a happy one. There are five

tikits and a couple of nomads' tents. Rooms at Auberge Warane (☑ 4687 3508; r/tent per person UM1500) are a bit bunkerlike but the place is friendly enough. Auberge Agouei-dir – Chez Isselmou (☑ 4525 0791; agoueidir@ yahoo.fr; tikit/tent per person UM1200/2500, s/d UM5000/7000) is the grandest outfit, but was block-booked by oil workers when we visited.

❶ Getting There & Away

Without your own vehicle, getting to Ouadâne isn't always straightforward. Atâr is the place to look for transport, and vehicles run between the two most days, usually in the morning (bush taxi/4WD UM3000/4000, about four hours). Direct transport between Ouadâne and Chinguetti runs next to never.

If driving you have two alternatives: the southerly Piste du Batha, which passes through sand dunes and requires a 4WD and guide, and the northerly Piste du Dhar Chinguetti along the plateau, which is in very good condition. The latter departs the Atâr–Chinguetti road 18km before Chinguetti.

Tanouchert

This charming oasis, approximately halfway between Chinguetti and Ouadâne, is a popular stop for 4WD trips and camel treks. Nestled around a freshwater source, it's complete with palm trees and surrounded by superb date fields, miles from anywhere.

You'll need to hire a 4WD with driver to get to Tanouchert. Otherwise, if you do a camel trek from Chinguetti to Ouadâne, you'll probably spend a night here.

🛏 Sleeping & Eating

Oasis Tanouchert   CAMPGROUND $
(Chez Chighaly; ☑ 4654 1885; Azougi; bed UM1500, breakfast/dinner UM800/1500) Unsophisticated (mattresses under palm-frond shelters) but welcoming. If there's a group, the host can organise a *méchoui* (nomads') feast.

THE ROAD TO MALI

The Rte de l'Espoir (Road to Hope) from Nouakchott to Néma (around 1100km) is now entirely tarred, giving a smooth (if still very long) trip to the border. Check trusted security sources before travelling towards the border.

The first major town on the road to the Malian border is Kiffa (population 30,000), an important regional trading centre and crossroads, where you can bunk down at Auberge Le Phare du Désert (☑ 644 2421; pharerim@yahoo.fr; tikit UM10,000; ❀) on the outskirts.

You could also break up your journey at lively Ayoûn el-Atroûs, which is a good place to spend your last ouguiyas before crossing into Mali. For accommodation, try the unpretentious Hôtel Ayoûn (☑ 515 1462; s/d UM5000/8000; ❀), which is in the centre, or Auberge Saada Tenzah (☑ 641 1052, 515 1337; r UM2500-6000), about 3km east of the centre on the road to Néma.

The tarred road ends at the town of Néma, the jumping-off point for Oualâta. You'll find several petrol pumps here, a couple of modest stores and a police station at which you can get your passport stamped. You can base yourself at Compiexe Touristique N'Gady (☑ 513 0900; bungalow s/d UM7000/9000; r 12,000-15,000; ⓟ❀), a few kilometres west of the centre.

Oualâta

Possibly one of Mauritania's best-kept secrets, Oualâta is another ancient Saharan town high on atmosphere and personality. Dating from 1224, it used to be the last resting point for caravans heading for Timbuktu. It's about 100km north of Néma but is definitely worth the gruelling ride to get here.

Entering the town you'll be struck by the red mudbrick houses adorned with decorative paintings on the exterior and interior. There's a small museum and a library, which houses ancient Islamic manuscripts. There are also several rock paintings and archaeological sites in the vicinity. Various camel trips can be organised (ask your hosts).

Although you're miles from anywhere, you'll find about six guesthouses to rest your weary limbs, including Auberge Tayib/ Gamni – Auberge de l'Hotel de Ville (r per person UM3000) and Auberge Ksar Walata (r per person UM5000), which features a lovely patio and attractive rooms. They all serve meals.

There are two dirt tracks between Néma and Oualâta (approximately 110km). Land Rovers ply the route between the two towns

(UM2000, 2½ hours) on an infrequent basis. Ask around in Néma market.

THE ROAD TO SENEGAL

Parc National Diawling

This little known national park is a sister to the Djoudj National Bird Sanctuary in Senegal on the opposite side of the border. It has important mangroves and an acacia forest, as well as large coastal dunes. Incredibly rich in birdlife, it's well-worth a detour if you have a 4WD. Facilities are almost completely undeveloped; the Eco-Lodge du Maure Bleu offers the best access as well as being involved with local communities to receive visitors.

🛏 Sleeping & Eating

★ Eco-Lodge du Maure Bleu   LODGE $$
(☑ 4412 0379; www.ecolodgemaurebleu.net; 2-bed tent UM12,500, meals UM1000-3500) A gorgeous off-grid tent-camp offering a surprising degree of comfort and home-cooked food, as well as arranging walking and *pirogue* (traditional canoe) tours in the national park.

UNDERSTAND MAURITANIA

Mauritania Today

The rule since 2008 of General Mohamed Ould Abdel Aziz has seen mixed fortunes for Mauritania. The economy has grown, in part due to mineral extraction, gas exploration and new factory fishing licences given to EU and Chinese fleets, but a prolonged drought in 2011 led to rocketing food prices and an increase in aid dependency for swathes of the population.

Mauritania's long border with Mali has also seen it receive large numbers of refugees, and the government has had to tread carefully to avoid being dragged into the Malian conflict. In October 2012, Aziz survived an 'accidental' shooting by one of his soldiers, the exact circumstances of which still remain unclear.

History

From the 3rd century AD, the Berbers established trading routes all over the Western Sahara, including Mauritania. In the 11th century, the Marrakesh-based Islamic Almoravids pushed south and, with the assistance of Mauritanian Berber leaders, destroyed the Empire of Ghana, which covered much of present-day Mauritania. That victory led to the spread of Islam throughout Mauritania and the Western Sahara. The descendants of the Almoravids were finally subjugated by Arabs in 1674.

As colonialism spread throughout Africa in the 19th century, France stationed troops in Mauritania, but it was not until 1904 that, having played one Moorish faction off against another, the French finally managed to make Mauritania a colonial territory. Independence was fairly easily achieved in 1960 because the French wanted to prevent the country from being absorbed by newly independent Morocco. Mokhtar Ould Daddah became Mauritania's first president.

Ould Daddah took a hard line, especially against the (mainly black African) southerners, who were treated like second-class citizens and compelled to fit the Moors' mould. Any opposition was brutally suppressed.

The issue of Western Sahara (Spanish Sahara) finally toppled the government. In 1975 the very sandy Spanish Sahara (a Spanish colony) was divided between Morocco and Mauritania. But the Polisario Front launched a guerrilla war to oust both beneficiaries from the area. Mauritania was incapable, militarily and economically, of fighting such a war. A bloodless coup took place in Mauritania in 1978, bringing in a new military government that renounced all territorial claims to the Western Sahara.

A series of coups ensued. Finally, Colonel Maaouya Sid' Ahmed Ould Taya came to power in 1984. For black Africans, this was even worse than being under Ould Daddah. Ethnic tensions culminated in bloody riots between the Moors and black Africans in 1989. More than 70,000 black Africans were expelled to Senegal, a country most had never known.

In 1991 Mauritania supported Iraq during the Gulf War, and aid dried up. To counter criticism, Taya introduced multiparty elections in 1992, which were boycotted by the opposition. Riots over the price of bread in 1995 worsened the political situation. Cosmetic elections were held in 2001, with Taya still holding the whip hand.

The 2000s have been marked by coups. In June 2005, Taya was toppled in a bloodless coup led by Colonel Ely Ould Mohamed Vall. Vall was largely popular and formulated a new constitution and voluntarily gave up power by holding elections in March 2007. Sidi Ould Cheikh Abdallahi was returned as Mauritania's first democratically elected president. He openly condemned the 'dark years' of the late 1980s, and sought rapprochement with the expelled black Moors – a move that angered the traditional elites and which led, in part, to his overthrow by General Mohamed Ould Abdel Aziz in a coup in August 2008. Despite international condemnation, his position was consolidated the following year in elections that saw Azis narrowly returned as president.

Culture

Mauritanian society is changing fast. Tourism development in the heart of the desert, the internet and mobile phones have played a crucial role in the last decade. But despite the profound social changes, the extended family, clan or tribe remains the cornerstone of society, especially with the Moors.

As in many Muslim countries, religion continues to mark the important events of life. Although slavery was declared illegal in 1980, it is still widespread and the caste system permeates society's mentality.

The iconic image of nomadic Moors sipping a cup of tea under a tent in the desert belongs to the past. Over the past three decades, drought has resulted in a mass exodus of traditionally nomadic Moors from the desert to Nouakchott.

Women are in a fairly disadvantaged position. Only a third as many women as men are literate and few are involved in commercial activities. Female genital mutilation and forced feeding of young brides are still practised in rural communities. However, Mauritanian women do have the right to divorce and exert it routinely.

People

Of Mauritania's estimated three million inhabitants, about 60% are Moors of Arab and Berber descent. The Moors of purely Arab descent, called 'Bidan', account for 40% of the population, and hold the levers of political power. The other major group is black Africans, ethnically split into two groups. The Haratin (black Moors), the descendants of people enslaved by the Moors, have assimilated the Moorish culture and speak Hassaniyya, an Arabic dialect. Black Mauritanians living in the south along the Senegal River constitute 40% of the total population and are mostly Fulani or the closely related Tukulor. These groups speak Pulaar (Fula). There are also Soninke and Wolof minorities.

More than 99% of the population are Sunni Muslims.

Arts & Crafts

Mauritania has a strong tradition of arts and craftwork, especially silverwork. Most prized are wooden chests with silver inlays, but there are also silver daggers, silver and amber jewellery, earthtone rugs of camel hair, and hand-dyed leatherwork, including colourful leather cushions and leather pipe pouches, camel saddles and sandals.

The traditional music of Mauritania is mostly Arabic in origin, although along its southern border there are influences from the Wolof, Tukulor and Bambara. One of the most popular Mauritanian musicians is Malouma. She has created what is called the 'Saharan blues' and is to Mauritania what Cesária Évora, is to Cape Verde.

There's some superb traditional architecture in the ancient Saharan towns in the Adrar as well as in Oualâta.

Food & Drink

The desert cuisine of the Moors is rather unmemorable and lacks variety. Dishes are generally bland and limited to rice, mutton, goat, camel or dried fish. With negligible agriculture, fruit and vegetables are imported, and hard to find outside Nouakchott. Mauritanian couscous, similar to the Moroccan variety, is delicious. A real treat is to attend a *méchoui* (traditional nomads' feast), where an entire lamb is roasted over a fire and stuffed with cooked rice.

The cuisine of southern Mauritania, essentially Senegalese, has more variety, spices and even a few vegetables. Look for rice with fish and *mafé* (a groundnut-based stew).

SLAVERY IN MAURITANIA

Mauritania has one of the most stratified caste systems in Africa. The system is based on lineage, occupation and access to power, but colour has become a major determinant of status, splitting the population into Bidan and Haratin – White and Black Moors. At the bottom of the social pile are slaves and ex-slaves.

Chattel slavery has long been apart of Mauritanian culture, with the owning of slaves a sign of social status. Incredibly, it was only in 1980 that the government finally declared slavery illegal. Despite this, the head of Mauritania's Human Rights Commission has said that antislavery laws are rarely enforced, despite tougher punishments legislated for in 2007. Estimates vary, but a 2010 UN special report on slavery suggests that upwards of 340,000 Mauritanians may still be enslaved. The Mauritanian antislavery organisation SOS-Esclaves ('SOS-Slaves'; www.sosesclaves.org) works with runaway slaves.

Mauritanian tea is also ubiquitous, invariably strong, sweet and endlessly decanted between tiny glasses to produce a frothy head. It's polite to accept the first three glasses offered. *Zrig* (unsweetened curdled goat or camel milk) often accompanies meals served in private homes. Alcohol is technically forbidden but is sometimes openly (and expensively) available in Nouakchott restaurants.

Environment

Mauritania is about twice the size of France. About 75%, including Nouakchott, is desert, with huge expanses of flat plains broken by occasional ridges, sand dunes and rocky plateaus, including the Adrar (about 500m high).

The highest peak is Kediet Ijill (915m) near Zouérat. Mauritania has some 700km of shoreline, including the Parc National du Banc d'Arguin, one of the world's major bird-breeding grounds and a Unesco World Heritage site. The south is mostly flat scrubland.

Major environmental issues are the usual suspects of desertification, overgrazing and pollution. Overfishing is another concern, with hundreds of tonnes of fish caught every day off the Mauritanian coastline.

SURVIVAL GUIDE

❶ Directory A–Z

ACCOMMODATION

In general, you can expect to spend less than US$15 per person in budget places and up to US$50 for midrange. There's also a sprinkle of air-conditioned hotels meeting international standards in Nouakchott and, to a lesser extent, Nouâdhibou and Atâr. In the desert, you'll find numerous basic *auberges* or *campements*. They consist of a series of *tikits* (stone huts) or *khaimas* (tents) that come equipped with mattresses on the floor.

ACTIVITIES

Camel rides and 4WD expeditions in the desert are the most popular activities. For birdwatching, nothing can beat the Parc National du Banc d'Arguin, one of the world's greatest birdlife-viewing venues.

BUSINESS HOURS

Mauritania is a Muslim country, and for business purposes Mauritania adheres to the Monday to Friday working week. Friday is the main prayer day, so many businesses have an extended lunch break on Friday afternoon. Many shops are open every day.

Government offices, post offices & banks Usually open 8am to 4pm Monday to Thursday and 8am to 1pm on Friday.

CUSTOMS REGULATIONS

It is illegal to bring alcohol into the country.

EMBASSIES & CONSULATES

The majority of embassies and consulates have locations in Nouakchott.

French Embassy (☑ 4525 2337; Rue Ahmed Ould Mohamed)

German Embassy (☑ 4525 1729; Rue Abdallaye)

Malian Embassy (☑ 4525 4081, 525 4078)

Moroccan Embassy (☑ 4525 1411; Ave du Général de Gaulle)

Senegalese Embassy (☑ 4525 7290; Rue de l'Ambassade du Sénégal)

US Embassy (☑ 4525 2660; fax 525 1592; Rue Abdallaye)

INTERNET ACCESS

You can get online in any reasonably sized town, although outside Nouakchott connection speeds can often be wanting. Expect to pay around UM200 an hour.

MONEY

The unit of currency is the ouguiya (UM). There are a handful of ATMs in Nouakchott and Nouâdhibou accepting international bank cards, but take euros or US dollars as back-up. Credit cards are accepted only at top-end hotels and larger businesses.

PUBLIC HOLIDAYS

New Year's Day 1 January
National Reunification Day 26 February
Workers' Day 1 May
African Liberation Day 25 May
Army Day 10 July
Independence Day 28 November
Anniversary of the 1984 Coup 12 December
Mauritania also celebrates the usual Islamic holidays.

SAFE TRAVEL

Mauritania is generally one of the safest countries in Africa, particularly the capital and the main tourist region of the Adrar.

In 2008, the Paris–Dakar Rally was cancelled due to threats against the Mauritanian leg by Islamist groups. Although there have subsequently been a small number of incidents, these have been restricted to remote areas unvisited by foreigners. On the main roads, regular police checkpoints take note of all foreigners passing through for security. In the southeast, however, security problems in Mali have threatened to spill across the border. Coupled with periodic reports of banditry on the roads, travellers should take trusted advice before planning to travel in this region.

TELEPHONE

You can make international calls and send faxes at post offices. The innumerable privately run phone shops in the major cities and towns cost about the same and are open late. A GSM SIM card for the Mauritel, Chinguitell or Mattel networks costs around UM2000.

There are no telephone area codes.

VISAS

Visas are required for all except nationals of Arab League countries and some African countries. In countries where Mauritania has no diplomatic representation, including Australia, French embassies often issue visas. For overlanders heading south, Rabat (Morocco) is a good place for visas (US$45). Visas are no longer issued at the Morocco–Mauritania border.

One-month visa extensions can be obtained for UM5000 at the **Sûreté** (off Ave Abdel Nasser; ◷ 8am-3pm Mon-Thu) in Nouakchott.

Visas for Onward Travel

In Nouakchott you can get visas for most neighbouring countries.

Mali

One-month visas are issued the same day (UM6500). You need two photos and a passport photocopy.

Morocco

Most nationalities do not require visas, and simply get an entry stamp valid for 90 days on arrival. Nationalities that do (mostly Africans, including Mauritanians) must pay UM8700 and provide two photos and passport photocopies and (according to whim) an air ticket.

Senegal

One-month visas (UM1500) are issued in 24 hours. You need to supply four photos plus passport photocopies.

WOMEN TRAVELLERS

Mauritania is a conservative Muslim country, but it is by no means the most extreme in this regard. Women might receive the odd bit of sexual harassment, but it's nothing in comparison with some North African countries. It's wise to dress modestly, covering the upper legs and arms and avoiding shorts or skimpy T-shirts.

ⓘ Getting There & Away

AIR

Nouakchott, Nouâdhibou and Atâr have international airports. Nouakchott's airport handles most traffic.

The only direct flights from Europe are through Paris, with Air France.

Mauritania Airlines flies twice a week between Nouakchott and Dakar, six times to Bamako (three of which continue to Abidjan, Cotonou and Brazzaville). Senegal Airlines flies five times a week to Dakar. For other Saharan or

---

PRACTICALITIES

→ **Electricity** Current is 220V AC, 50Hz and most electrical plugs are of the European two-pin type.

→ **Languages** Hassaniya (Arabic), French, Fula, Soninké and Wolof.

→ **TV** Mauritania's only TV station is TVM, with programs in Hassaniyya and French, but top-end hotels have satellite TV.

→ **Newspapers** For the news (in French), pick up Le Calame or Horizons.

sub-Saharan countries, you'll have to change in Dakar or Abidjan.

Mauritania is well connected to North Africa. Royal Air Maroc operates between Casablanca and Nouakchott five times a week, while Tunis Air connects Tunis with Nouakchott (three times a week). Air Algérie flies to Algiers twice a week. Mauritania Airlines has four flights a week to Casablanca from Nouakchott, and twice weekly from Nouâdhibou.

LAND
Mali

All border information is subject to security advice as to the situation in Mali.

At the time of research, the most straightforward route to Mali was from Ayoûn el-Atroûs to Nioro. You can also cross at Néma, Timbedgha (both connecting with Nara in Mali) and Kiffa (connecting with Nioro in Mali).

From Nouakchott, you can catch bush taxis to Néma and Ayoûn el-Atroûs. From these places you can catch a bush taxi to Nara or Nioro. It's also possible to travel from Sélibaby to Kayes.

If crossing into Mali, have your passport stamped by police at the first town you reach after crossing the border. You must also clear customs, which is done in Néma or Ayoûn el-Atroûs.

Morocco

The trans-Sahara route via Mauritania is a very popular route from North Africa into sub-Saharan Africa. This crosses the internationally disputed territory of Western Sahara, although the border itself is administered by Morocco.

The only border crossing between Morocco/Western Sahara and Mauritania is north of Nouâdhibou. Crossing this border is straightforward and the road is entirely tarred to Nouakchott, except for the 3km no-man's land that separates the two border posts.

There are direct bush taxis heading north from Nouâdhibou to Dakhla (Western Sahara), but travelling in the opposite direction you'll need to change vehicles at the border. The 425km trip can easily be accomplished in a long day.

Senegal

The main border crossing for Senegal is at Rosso (by ferry), but it's also possible to cross by bridge at Diamma (Keur Masséne), west of Rosso. The latter is a much calmer experience (officials at Rosso often give travellers hassle) although road conditions make Diamma largely a dry-season option.

From Dakar to Nouakchott by public transport usually takes from 11 to 13 hours depending on the wait at the border. At Rosso, most travellers without vehicles cross by *pirogue* (UM200/CFA500, five minutes) as the ferry crosses only

PAPERS PLEASE

Mauritania is a country in love with police roadblocks, and you'll frequently be asked to produce ID, especially when entering or leaving a town. This is usually a straightforward procedure and police are generally polite. Your details are registered, so to speed things up make your own form (*fiche* or *ordre de mission*) to hand over. List all the personal details from your passport (including visa number), occupation and destination. If you're driving, include your vehicle's make, colour and registration number. Make plenty of photocopies.

four times daily. The border is open 8.30am to noon and 3pm to 6pm.

Vehicles cost CFA5000 (foot passengers free). Customs fees are around UM1500 if you're entering Mauritania, CFA2000 for Senegal, but officials here are reported to be notoriously greedy, so keep your paperwork (and vehicle) in good order.

❶ Getting Around

AIR

Mauritania Airlines flies daily from Nouakchott to Nouâdhibou (UM20,000, one hour), three times a week via Zouérat (UM39,000, three hours).

CAR & MOTORCYCLE

Mauritania's road network is mostly good, with tarred roads leading from the border with Western Sahara to Nouakchott, and on to the Senegalese and Malian borders at Rosso and Nioro respectively. The roads from the capital to Atâr and Tidjikja are also tarred. Elsewhere, *piste* is the order of the day, although great swathes of the country are little more than sandy tracks (at best). Police checkpoints abound; make your own form *(fiche)* to hand over. List all the personal details from your passport (including visa number), home address, occupation and parents' names, plus your vehicle's make, colour and registration number. Make plenty of photocopies.

Consider renting a 4WD and driver if you want to reach more remote parts of the country. The standard Toyota Hilux usually costs around UM21,000 per day for the vehicle, plus petrol.

MINIBUS & BUSH TAXI

Minibus routes stitch together the main towns and cities linked by tarmac roads. Where tarmac is replaced by *piste,* the bush taxi *(taxi brousse)* – often Mercedes 190s and Peugeot 504s – take over, along with pick-up trucks for the rougher routes.

TOURS

There are numerous travel agencies in Nouakchott that offer tours around the country, but it's not a bad idea to arrange a tour with a more regional-focused company – eg in Atâr for the Adrar or the Tagânt. If there are at least four travellers, prices should average around UM20,000 per person per day.

TRAIN

The Nouâdhibou–Zouérat train is certainly an epic adventure (see boxed text, p244). It's an iron-ore train with no passenger terminals, but it's become a passenger train for lack of better alternatives. The trip takes 16 to 18 hours, but most travellers get off at Choûm (close to Atâr), 12 hours from Nouâdhibou.

Morocco

♪ 212 / POP 33.3 MILLION

Best Places to Eat

➡ Le Salama (p281)

➡ Outdoor Fish Grill Stands (p269)

➡ Ty Potes (p263)

➡ Café Clock (p275)

➡ Rick's Café (p267)

Best Places to Stay

➡ Dar Finn (p273)

➡ Le Pietri Urban Hotel (p263)

➡ Dar el Janoub (p287)

➡ Dar Baraka (p261)

➡ La Tangerina (p259)

Why Go?

For many travellers Morocco might be just a short hop by budget airline, or by ferry from Spain, but culturally it's a much further distance to travel. On arrival, the regular certainties of Europe are swept away by the full technicolour arrival of Africa and Islam. It's a complete sensory overload.

Tangier – that faded libertine on the coast – has traditionally been a first port of call, but the winds quickly blow you along the coast to cosmopolitan, movie-star-famous Casablanca and the whitewashed fishing-port gem Essaouira. Inland the great imperial cities of Marrakesh and Fez attract visitors in droves; the winding streets of their ancient medinas hold enough surprises to fill a dozen repeat trips.

If you really want to escape from everything, Morocco still has a couple of trump cards. The High Atlas Mountains seem custom-made for hiking, with endless trails between Berber villages, and North Africa's highest peak to conquer.

Morocco can feel like another world, but you don't need a magic carpet to get there.

When to Go
Marrakesh

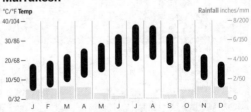

| Mid-Mar–May Morocco is at its best in spring, when the country is lush and green. | Sep–Nov Autumn is also good, when the heat of summer has eased. | Nov–Jul In winter, head for the south – but be prepared for bitterly cold nights. |

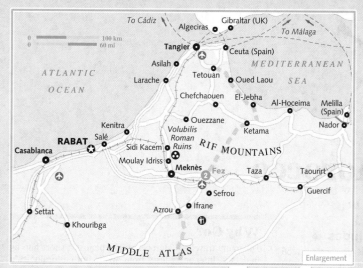

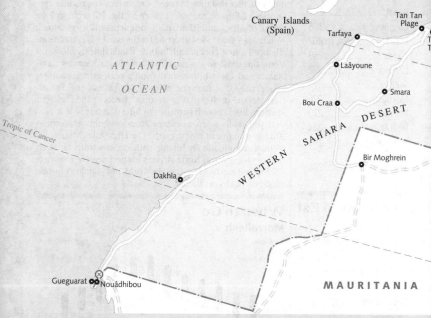

Morocco Highlights

1 Dive into the clamour and endless spectacle of Morocco's most dynamic city, **Marrakesh** (p279).

2 Lose yourself in the exotic charms of a medieval city replete with sights, sounds and smells in **Fez** (p273).

3 Laze by the sea in Morocco's coolest and most evocative resort at **Essaouira** (p267).

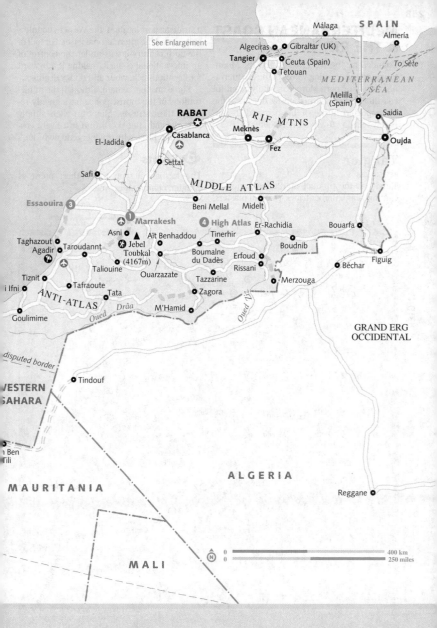

SPAIN

Málaga
Almería

See Enlargement

Algeciras ○ Gibraltar (UK)
Tangier ○ Ceuta (Spain)
Tetouan

MEDITERRANEAN
SEA

To Sète

Melilla
(Spain)
Saidia

RIF MTNS

RABAT ☆
Meknès
Oujda

Casablanca

El-Jadida ○
Fez

Settat

Safi ○

Essaouira ❸
MIDDLE ATLAS

Beni Mellal
Midelt

Marrakesh ❶
❹ High Atlas
Er-Rachidia
Bouarfa

Asni ○
Aït Benhaddou
Tinerhir

Taghazout ○ Taroudannt
Jebel
Toubkal
(4167m)
Boumalne
du Dadès
Erfoud
Boudnib

Agadir ○
Boumalne
du Dadès
Figuig

Taliouine
Rissani
Béchar

Tiznit ○
Ouarzazate
Tazzarine

i Ifni ○ Tafraoute
ANTI-ATLAS
Tata
Zagora
Merzouga

Goulimime
Oued   Drâa
M'Hamid

Oued Ziz

GRAND ERG
OCCIDENTAL

disputed border

WESTERN
SAHARA
○ Tindouf

ALGERIA

n Ben
Tili

MAURITANIA

Reggane ○

MALI

Ⓝ 0 ———————— 400 km
   0 ———————— 250 miles

❹ Trek deep into a world of
stunning scenery and isolated
Berber villages in the **High
Atlas** (p284).

MEDITERRANEAN COAST & THE RIF

Bounded by the red crags of the Rif Mountains and the crashing waves of the Mediterranean Sea, northern Morocco's wildly beautiful coastline conceals attractions as diverse as the cosmopolitan hustle of Tangier, and the superbly relaxing town of Chefchaouen.

Tangier

POP 688,000

Tangier is the product of 1001 currents, including Islam, Berber tribes, colonial masters,

a strategic port location, the Western counter-culture and the international jetset. For half of the 20th century it was under the control of an international council, making it a byword for licentious behaviour and dodgy dealings.

Some hustlers remain, although the ministrations of the tourist police have greatly reduced these stresses. Many travellers simply pass through, but you'll find it a lively, cosmopolitan place with an energetic nightlife.

◉ Sights

The Kasbah sits on the highest point of Tangier, behind stout walls.

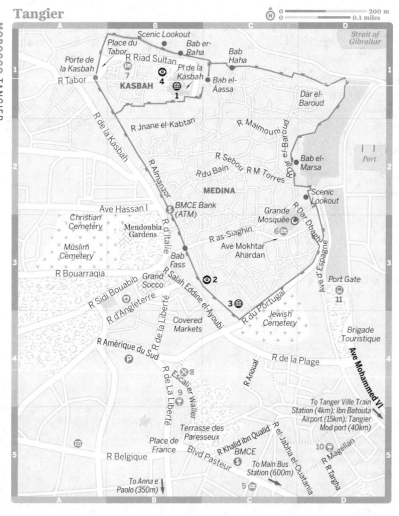

Tangier

Kasbah Museum · MUSEUM
(☑ 0539 932097; admission Dh10; ☺ 9am-12.30pm & 3-5.30pm Wed, Thu & Sat-Mon, 9am-12.30pm Fri) Enter the medina through Bab el-Aassa, the southeastern gate, to find the Kasbah Museum. Housed in the 17th-century palace of Dar el-Makhzen, this is a worthwhile museum devoted to Moroccan arts. Before leaving, take a stroll around the Andalucían-style **Sultan's Gardens**.

Old American Legation Museum · MUSEUM
(☑ 0539 935317; www.legation.org; 8 Rue d'Amerique; donations appreciated; ☺ 10am-1pm & 3-5pm Mon-Fri) The Old American Legation Museum is an intriguing relic of the international zone, with a fascinating collection of memorabilia from the international writers and artists who passed through Tangier.

★ Festivals & Events

Le Festival International de Théâtre Amateur · THEATRE
(☑ 039 930306; fondationlorin@gmail.com; 44 Rue Touahine, Fondation Lorin; ☺ 11am-1pm & 3.30-7.30pm Sun-Fri) A week of Arabic- and French-speaking theatre, traditionally held every May, run by Fondation Lorin.

⊨ Sleeping

Hôtel Mamora · HOTEL $
(☑ 0539 934105; www.hotelmamora.site.voila.fr; 19 Rue des Postes; low season s/d with toilet

ⓘ WHEN TO VISIT
The timing of Ramadan (the traditional Muslim month of fasting and purification, which is likely to occur during June or July when you are reading this) is an important consideration when planning your trip to Morocco, as many restaurants and cafes close during the day and general business hours are reduced.

Dh100/150, with shower Dh200/230) With a variety of rooms at different rates, this is a good bet. It's a bit institutional, but clean, well run and strong value for money. The rooms overlooking the green-tiled roof of the Grande Mosquée are the most picturesque, if you don't mind the muezzin's call.

Hotel de Paris · HOTEL $
(☑ 0539 9931877; 42 Blvd Pasteur; s/d with bathroom & breakfast Dh350/450) This reliable choice in the heart of the Ville Nouvelle has a variety of room types and prices depending on bathroom arrangements and balconies. All are clean and modern, but those overlooking Blvd Pasteur can get noisy. The helpful front desk makes for a pleasant stay.

La Tangerina · HOTEL $$
(☑ 0539 947733; www.latangerina.com; Rue Riad Sultan, Kasbah; d incl breakfast Dh 600-1620) A perfectly renovated riad (traditional courtyard house) at the very top of the Kasbah, La Tangerina has 10 rooms of different personality. Bathed in light and lined with rope banisters, it feels like an elegant, Berber-carpeted steamship cresting the medina, with the roof terrace overlooking the ancient crenellated walls of the Kasbah. Dinner is available on request.

✗ Eating

In the medina there's a host of cheap eating possibilities around the Petit Socco and the adjacent Ave Mokhtar Ahardan, with rotisserie chicken, sandwiches and *brochettes* (kebabs) on offer. In the Ville Nouvelle, try the streets immediately south of Place de France, which are flush with fast-food outlets and sandwich bars.

Anna e Paolo · ITALIAN $
(☑ 0539 944617; 77 Ave Prince Heretier; mains from Dh60) This is the top Italian bistro in the city: a family-run restaurant with Venetian owners who make you feel like you've been invited for Sunday dinner. Expect a highly

MOROCCO TANGIER

SET YOUR BUDGET

Budget

➡ Hotel room Dh130
➡ Street food Dh30
➡ Glass of mint tea Dh10
➡ Petit taxi ride Dh9

Midrange

➡ Hotel room Dh350
➡ Tajine Dh70
➡ Drink in a bar Dh50
➡ Intercity train ticket (2nd class, four hours) Dh80

Top End

➡ Hotel room Dh1500
➡ Two-course meal Dh200

international crowd, lots of cross-table conversations about the events of the day, wholesome food and a shot of grappa on your way out the door.

Populaire Saveur de Poisson   SEAFOOD $$$
0539 336326; 2 Escalier Waller; set menu Dh150; ⊘12.30-4pm & 7-10pm Sat-Thu) This charming little seafood restaurant offers excellent, filling set menus in rustic surroundings. The owner serves inventive plates of fresh catch, with sticky *seffa* (sweet couscous) for dessert, all of it washed down with a homemade 15-fruit juice cocktail. Not just a meal, but a whole experience.

🍷 Drinking & Entertainment

Tangier's nightlife picks up in the summer, and nightclubs cluster near Place de France and line the beach. Tangier's gay scene has long since departed for Marrakesh, but the **Tanger Inn** (1 Rue Magellan, Hotel el-Muniria; beer Dh10; ⊘10.30pm-1am, to 3am Fri & Sat) and some of the bars along the beach attract gay clientele, particularly late on weekends.

Caid's Bar   BAR
(El-Minzah; 85 Rue de la Liberté; wine from Dh20; ⊘10am-midnight) Long the establishment's drinking hole of choice, this el-Minzah landmark is a relic of the grand days of international Tangier, and photos of the famous and infamous adorn the walls.

❶ Information

Blvd Pasteur and Ave Mohammed V are lined with numerous banks with ATMs and bureau-de-change counters. Blvd Pasteur also has plenty of internet places.

BMCE (Banque Marocaine du Commerce Extérieur; Blvd Pasteur; ⊘9am-1pm & 3-7pm Mon-Fri, 10am-1pm & 4-7pm Sat & Sun) One of several in this area.
Clinique du Croissant Rouge (Red Cross Clinic; ✆0539 946976; 6 Rue al-Mansour Dahabi) Medical service.
Main Post Office (Blvd Mohammed V)

❶ Getting There & Away

FERRY

Ferries go to and from Tarifa (Spain) from Tanger Port, in the city; all other destinations (including Algeciras) sail from Tanger Med. There's a free shuttle bus to Tanger Med from the CTM bus station. For more information, see p292.

BUS

The **CTM bus station** (✆0539 931172) is beside the port gate. Destinations include Casablanca (Dh130, six hours), Rabat (Dh100, 4½ hours), Fez (Dh110, six hours), Meknès (Dh90, five hours) and Chefchaouen (Dh40, three hours). Cheaper bus companies operate from the **main bus station** (gare routière; ✆0539 946928; Place Jamia el-Arabia), 2km south of the city centre.

TAXI

Grands taxis (shared taxis) leave from a lot next to the main bus station. Destinations include Tetouan (Dh25, one hour; change for Chefchaouen) and, for Ceuta, Fnideq (Dh40, one hour).

TRAIN

Five trains depart daily from Tanger Ville, 3km southeast of the city centre, to Casablanca (Dh125, five hours), Rabat (Dh95, 3½ hours), Fez (Dh80, 4½ hours) and Marrakesh. Some services involve changing at Sidi Kacem. A night service goes all the way to Marrakesh (seat/couchette Dh205/350, 12 hours).

❶ Getting Around

Petits taxis (blue with yellow stripes) journey around town for Dh7 to Dh10. From **Ibn Batouta airport** (✆0539 393720), 15km southeast of the city, take a cream-coloured *grand taxi* (Dh150).

Chefchaouen

POP 50,000

Set beneath the striking peaks of the Rif Mountains, Chefchaouen has long been charming travellers. One of the prettiest towns in Morocco, its old medina is a delight of Moroccan and Andalucían influences, with red-tiled roofs, bright-blue buildings and narrow lanes converging on a delightful square.

◎ Sights

Chefchaouen's medina is one of the loveliest in the country, with blinding blue-white hues and a strong Andalucían flavour. At its heart is the cobbled Plaza Uta el-Hammam, which is dominated by the red-hued walls of the kasbah (✆039 986343; admission incl museum & gallery Dh10; ☉9am-1pm & 3-6.30pm Wed-Mon, 9-11.30am & 3-4.30pm Fri) and the Grande Mosquée (Plaza Uta el-Hammam), noteworthy for its octagonal minaret. Inside the kasbah's gardens is a modest ethnographic museum, where the photos of old Chefchaouen are the highlights.

🛏 Sleeping

Hostal Guernika   GUESTHOUSE $
(✆0539 987434; hostalguernika@hotmail.com; 49 Onssar; d/tr Dh200/300) This is a warm and charming place, not too far from Plaza Uta el-Hammam. There are several great, streetside rooms – large and bright, facing the mountains – but others are dark. All have showers.

Dar Baraka   GUESTHOUSE $
(✆0614 682480; www.riad-baraka.com; Derb Ben Yacoub; d Dh240-280, q per person Dh120; 🛜) Friendly and bright guesthouse, with comfortable, spotless facilities. The terrace is great, with a chill-out room with DVDs. A few rooms share bathrooms.

Casa Hassan   HOTEL $$
(✆0539 986153; www.casahassan.com; 22 Rue Targui; s/d/tr incl half board from Dh500/650/800; ❄) Large hotel with a boutique feel, this long-established choice has sizeable rooms with creative layouts, plus in-house *hammam* (traditional bathhouse). The terrace provides an elegant lounge, and the cosy Restaurant Tissemlal a warm hearth.

✗ Eating

A popular eating option is to choose one of about a dozen plaza cafe-restaurants (Plaza Uta el-Hammam; breakfast from Dh15, mains from Dh25; ☉8am-11pm) on the main square. Menus are virtually identical – Continental breakfasts, soups and salads, tajines and seafood – but the food is generally decent and the ambience lively.

Assaada   MOROCCAN $
(✆0666 317316; Bab el-Ain; set menu Dh40) Located on both sides of the alley just prior to Bab el-Ain, it offers the usual *menu complet,* but also great fruit shakes and a funky graffiti rooftop terrace that exudes an urban charm. The staircase is not for the fainthearted.

Restaurant Les Raisins   MOROCCAN $$
(✆0667 982878; 7 Rue Sidi Sifri; tajines Dh20, set menu from Dh40; ☉7am-9pm) A bit out of the way, this family-run place is a perennial favourite with locals and tourists alike, and known for its couscous royal. Late,

MOROCCO CHEFCHAOUEN

CEUTA

Jutting out east into the Mediterranean, this 20-sq-km peninsula has been a Spanish enclave since 1640. Its relaxed, well-kept city centre, with bars, cafes and Andalucían atmosphere, provides a sharp contrast to the other side of the border. Nonetheless, Ceuta is still recognisably African. Between a quarter and a third of the population are of Rif Berber origin, giving the enclave a fascinating Iberian-African mix.

Ceuta makes a good alternative entry point by ferry from Spain to Morocco. Its ferry port *(estación marítima)* is west of the town centre, and has several daily high-speed ferries to Algeciras (around €28, 35 minutes). Bus 7 runs up to the Moroccan border *(frontera)* every 10 minutes from Plaza de la Constitución (€0.60). For Tangier, take a *grand taxi* to Fnideq (Dh5, 10 minutes), just south of the border, and change there.

Ceuta's main attraction is its Royal City Walls (✆956 511770; Ave González Tabla; ☉10am-2pm & 5-8pm) FREE, and there's a helpful tourist office (✆956 200560; Baluarte de los Mallorquines; ☉8.30am-8.30pm Mon-Fri, 9am-8pm Sat & Sun). If you get stuck for the night, try the Pensión La Bohemia (✆956 510615; 16 Paseo de Revellín; s/d €25/35); you'll find good restaurants around the harbour. Remember that Ceuta is on Spanish time and uses the euro.

Chefchaouen

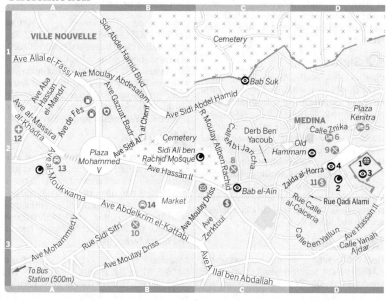

lazy lunches are best, with the front terrace catching the afternoon sun.

ℹ️ Information

Banque Populaire (Plaza Uta el-Hammam; ⏰9.30am-1pm & 3.30-9pm Mon-Fri) Has an ATM.

Hospital Mohammed V (☎0539 986228; Ave al-Massira al-Khadra) Medical service.

Post Office (Ave Hassan II; ⏰8am-4.30pm Mon-Fri, to noon Sat & Sun)

ℹ️ Getting There & Away

Many bus services from Chefchaouen originate elsewhere, so book in advance if possible. **CTM** (☎039 987669) services include Casablanca (Dh115, eight hours), Rabat (Dh85, six hours), Fez (Dh70, four hours) and Tangier (Dh40, three hours).

Grands taxis heading to Tetouan (Dh30, one hour) leave from just below Plaza Mohammed V – change for Tangier or Ceuta.

THE ATLANTIC COAST

Morocco's Atlantic shoreline is surprisingly varied, with sweeping beaches and lagoons, the economic motor of the urban sprawl around the political and economic capitals

of Rabat and Casablanca, respectively, and the pretty fishing ports/tourist drawcards of Essaouira and Asilah.

Rabat

POP 1.7 MILLION

Relaxed, well kept and very European, flag-waving capital Rabat is just as cosmopolitan as Casablanca down the coast but lacks the frantic pace and grimy feel of its economic big brother. Its elegant, tree-lined boulevards and imposing administrative buildings exude an unhurried, diplomatic and hassle-free charm that many travellers grow to like.

👁️ Sights

Barely 400 years old, Rabat's medina is tiny compared to that of Fez or Marrakesh, although it still piques the senses with its rich mixture of spices, carpets, crafts, cheap shoes and bootlegged DVDs.

The Kasbah des Oudaias sits high up on the bluff overlooking the Oued Bou Regreg and contains within its walls a 12th-century mosque. The southern corner of the kasbah is home to the Andalucían Gardens (⏰sunrise-sunset), laid out by the French during the colonial period. The centrepiece

MOROCCO RABAT

is the grand 17th-century palace containing the **Musée des Oudaia** (☏ 0537 731537; admission Dh10; ⊙ 9am-noon & 3-5pm Oct-Apr, to 6pm May-Sep).

Le Tour Hassan TOWER
(Hassan Tower; off Blvd Abi Radraq) Towering above the Oued Bou Regreg is Rabat's most famous landmark. This 44m unfinished minaret was begun in 1195; the beautifully designed and intricately carved tower still lords over the remains of the adjacent mosque.

Mausoleum of Mohammed V MAUSOLEUM
(⊙ sunrise-sunset) **FREE** The cool, marble Mausoleum of Mohammed V (and since 1999 Hassan II), built in traditional Moroccan style with intense *zellij* (mosaic tiles), lies opposite the tower.

🛏 Sleeping

Hôtel Splendid HOTEL $
(☏ 0537 723283; 8 Rue Ghazza; s/d Dh128/187, without bathroom Dh104/159) In the heart of town, this hotel has spacious, bright rooms with high ceilings, big windows, cheerful colours and simple wooden furniture. Bathrooms are new, and even rooms without bathrooms have a hot-water washbasin. The hotel is set around a pleasant courtyard.

Hôtel Balima HOTEL $$
(☏ 0537 707755; www.hotel-balima.com; Ave Mohammed V; s/d Dh453/716; ✻) The grand dame of Rabat hotels isn't as grand as she used to be but still offers comfortable rooms with views over the city. The hotel has a glorious shady terrace facing Ave Mohammed V, a great place for lazy coffees.

Le Pietri Urban Hotel HOTEL $$
(☏ 0537 707820; www.lepietri.com; 4 Rue Tobrouk; s/d Dh720/790; ✻ @) This is a good-value boutique hotel in a quiet side street. The spacious, bright rooms, with wooden floors, are well equipped and decorated in warm colours and a contemporary style. The hotel has an excellent, trendy restaurant with a small garden for elegant alfresco dining.

🍴 Eating

For quick eating, go to Ave Mohammed V just inside the medina gate, where you'll find a slew of hole-in-the-wall joints dishing out tajines, *brochettes*, salads and chips.

Ty Potes CAFE $
(☏ 0537 07965; 11 Rue Ghafsa; set menu Dh70-105; ⊙ closed Mon & dinner Tue/Wed) A pleasant and welcoming lunch spot, serving sweet and savoury crepes and salads. It's popular with well-heeled locals. The atmosphere is more

Central Rabat

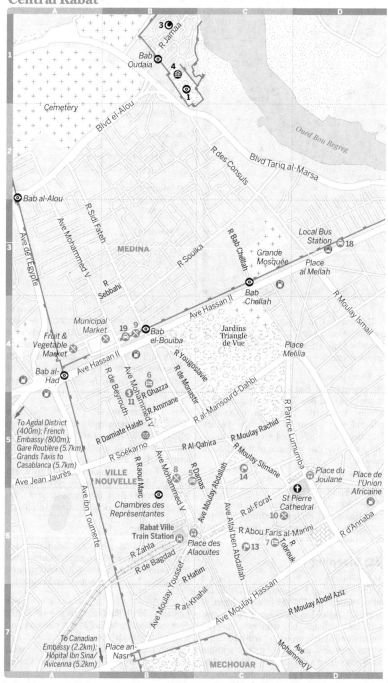

Cemetery

Bab Oudaia

R Jamaa

3

Bab Oudaia

4

1

Blvd el-Alou

Oued Bou Regreg

Blvd Tariq al-Marsa

R des Consuls

Bab al-Alou

Ave de l'Egypte

Ave Mohammed V

R Sidi Fateh

MEDINA

R Souika

R Sebbahi

R Bab Chellah

Grande Mosquée

Local Bus Station 18

Place al Mellah

Ave Hassan II

Bab Chellah

R Moulay Ismail

Municipal Market

19 9

Bab el-Bouiba

Fruit & Vegetable Market

Bab al-Had

Ave Hassan II

R de Beyrouth

Ave Mohammed V

6

R Ghazza

11

R Ammane

R Yougosiavie

R de Monastir

R al-Mansourd-Dahbi

Jardins Triangle de Vue

Place Melilia

R Patrice Lumumba

To Agdal District (400m); French Embassy (800m); Gare Routière (5.7km); Grands Taxis to Casablanca (5.7km)

R Damiate Halab

R Soékarno

R Al-Qahira

R Moulay Rachid

R Moulay Slimane

Ave Jean Jaurès

VILLE NOUVELLE

Ave Raoul Marc

Ave Mohammed V

8

5 R Damas

R Moulay Abdallah

14

Place du Joulane

Place de l'Union Africaine

Ave Ibn Toumerte

Chambres des Représentants

Ave Mohammed V

St Pierre Cathedral

10

R al-Forat

R d'Annaba

Rabat Ville Train Station

Place des Alaouites

R Zahla

R de Bagdad

R Abou Faris al-Marini

13

7 R Tobrouk

Ave Moulay Youssef

R Hatim

R al-Khahil

Ave Allal ben Abdallah

Ave Moulay Hassan

R Moulay Abdel Aziz

To Canadian Embassy (2.2km); Hôpital Ibn Sina/ Avicenna (5.2km)

Place an-Nasr

MECHOUAR

Ave Mohammed V

MOROCCO RABAT

European, with a little garden at the back, and alcohol is served.

Restaurant el-Bahia MOROCCAN **$**
(☑ 0537 734504; Ave Hassan II; mains Dh50; ⊙ 6am-midnight, closes 10.30pm winter) Built into the outside of the medina walls, and a good spot for people-watching, this laid-back restaurant has the locals lapping up hearty Moroccan fare. Choose to sit on the pavement terrace, in the shaded courtyard or upstairs in the traditional salon.

Le Grand Comptoir FRENCH **$$**
(☑ 0537 201514; www.legrandcomptoir.ma; 279 Ave Mohammed V; mains Dh95-175) Oozing the charms of an old-world Parisienne *brasserie*, this suave restaurant and lounge bar woos customers with its chic surroundings and classic French menu. Go for the succulent steaks or be brave and try the *andouillette* (tripe sausage) or veal kidneys.

ℹ Information

Numerous banks (with ATMs) are concentrated along Ave Mohammed V.

BMCE (Ave Mohammed V; ⊙ 8am-8pm Mon-Fri) Bank with ATM.

Hopital Ibn Sina/Avicenna (☑ 0537 674450, for emergencies 0537 672871; Place Ibn Sina, Agdal) Medical service.

Main Post Office (cnr Rue Soékarno & Ave Mohammed V)

ⓘ Getting There & Away

Rabat Ville train station (☑ 0537 736060) is in the centre of the city. Trains run twice hourly to either Casa-Port or Casa Voyageurs in Casablanca (Dh35, one hour), with services to Fez (Dh80, 3½ hours, eight daily) via Meknès (Dh65, 2½ hours), Tangier (Dh95, 4½ hours, seven daily) and Marrakesh (Dh120, 4½ hours, eight daily).

Rabat has two bus stations: the main **gare routière** (☑ 0537 795816) and the less-chaotic **CTM station** (☑ 0537 281488), both on the outskirts of the city. CTM has daily services to Casablanca (Dh35, 1½ hours), as well as Essaouira (Dh120, three hours), Fez (Dh70, 3½ hours), Marrakesh (Dh130, five hours) and Tangier (Dh100, 4½ hours).

Grands taxis leave for Casablanca (Dh35) from just outside the intercity bus station. Other *grands taxis* leave for Fez (Dh65), Meknès (Dh50) and Salé (Dh4) from a lot off Ave Hassan II behind the Hôtel Bouregreg.

ⓘ Getting Around

Rabat's blue *petits taxis* are plentiful, cheap and quick. Short rides will cost about Dh10. Trams run by Rabat's **Tramway** (www.tram-way.ma) link the city to Salé. Tickets cost Dh6 and are sold at kiosks.

Casablanca

POP 4 MILLION

Many travellers stay in 'Casa' just long enough to change planes or catch a train, but Morocco's economic heart offers a unique insight into the country. This sprawling, European-style city is home to racing traffic, simmering social problems, wide boulevards and parks. The facades of imposing Hispano-Moorish and art deco buildings stand in sharp contrast to Casablanca's modernist landmark: the enormous, incredibly ornate Hassan II mosque.

⊙ Sights

Central Casablanca is full of great art deco and Hispano-Moorish buildings. Get the best taste by strolling the area around the Marché Central and Place Mohammed V. This grand square includes the law courts, the splendid Wilaya, the Bank al-Maghrib and the main post office. After that, explore the slightly dilapidated 19th-century medina near the port.

Hassan II Mosque   MOSQUE

The Hassan II Mosque is the world's third-largest mosque, built to commemorate the former king's 60th birthday. The mosque (and its 210m minaret) rises above the ocean on an outcrop northwest of the medina, a vast building that holds 25,000 worshippers and a further 80,000 in the squares around it. To see the interior you must take a **guided tour** (☑ 0522 482886; adult/child/student Dh120/30/60; ⊙ 9am, 10am, 11am & 2pm Sat-Thu).

⏢ Sleeping

Hôtel Astrid   HOTEL $

(☑ 0522 277803; hotelastrid@hotmail.com; 12 Rue 6 Novembre; s/d Dh315/368; ☎) Tucked away on a quiet street south of the city centre, the Astrid offers the most elusive element of Casa's budget hotels: a good night's sleep. There's little traffic noise here and the spacious, well-kept rooms with frilly decor all have bathrooms.

Hôtel Guynemer   HOTEL $

(☑ 0522 275764; www.guynemerhotel.net; 2 Rue Mohammed Belloul; s/d/tr incl breakfast Dh398/538/676; ✸@☎) The 29 well-appointed and regularly updated rooms here are tastefully decked out in cheerful colours. Fresh flowers, plasma TVs, wi-fi access, new bathroom fittings and firm, comfortable beds make rooms a steal at these rates, and the service is way above average.

Hôtel Transatlantique   HOTEL $$

(☑ 0522 294551; www.transatcasa.com; 79 Rue Chaouia; s/d/tr Dh600/750/950; ✸☎) Set in one of Casa's art deco gems, this 1922 hotel – shaped like a boat – has buckets of neo-Moorish character. The grand scale, decorative plaster, spidery wrought iron and eclectic mix of knick-knacks, pictures and lamps at the front of the house give the Transatlantique a whiff of colonial-era decadence crossed with '70s retro. It has a lovely outdoor seating area, but the rooms themselves are a little plain, though comfortable.

✗ Eating

Rue Chaouia, opposite the central market, is the best place for a quick bite, with a line of rotisseries, stalls and restaurants serving roast chicken, *brochettes* and sandwiches

Taverne du Dauphin
FRENCH $

(☑0522 221200; 115 Blvd Houphouët Boigny; mains Dh70-90, set menu Dh110; ☺Mon-Sat) A Casablanca institution, this traditional Provençal restaurant and bar has been serving up *fruits de mer* (seafood) since it opened in 1958. A humble, family-run place with food that leaves you smitten.

Sqala Café Maure
& Restaurant
MOROCCAN $$

(☑0522 260960; Blvd des Almohades; mains Dh70-160; ☺8am-10.30pm Tue-Sun, daily in summer) Nestled in the walls of the *sqala* (an 18th-century fortified bastion), this lovely restaurant has a rustic interior and a delightful garden surrounded by flower-draped trellises – a lovely spot for a Moroccan breakfast or a selection of salads for lunch. Tajines are a speciality.

Rick's Café
INTERNATIONAL $$

(☑0522 274207; 248 Blvd Sour Jdid; mains Dh130-160; ☺noon-3.30pm & 6pm-midnight) This bar, lounge and restaurant has furniture, fittings and nostalgia inspired by the film *Casablanca*. Lamb chops, chilli, hamburgers and American breakfasts – as well as a few French and Moroccan specialities – are all on the menu. It also boasts an in-house pianist and Sunday jazz session.

🍷 Drinking & Entertainment

The beachfront suburb of Aïn Diab is the place for late-night drinking and dancing in Casa. Expect to pay at least Dh100 to get into a club and as much again for drinks.

Café Alba
CAFE

(☑0522 227154; 59-61 Rue Indriss Lahrizi; ☺8am-1am) High ceilings, swish, modern furniture, subtle lighting and a hint of elegant colonial times mark this cafe out from the more traditional smoky joints around town. It's hassle-free downtime for women and a great place for watching Casa's up-and-coming.

La Bodéga
BAR

(☑0522 541842; 129 Rue Allah ben Abdellah; ☺12.30-3pm & 7pm-midnight) Hip, happening and loved by a mixed-ages group of Casablanca's finest, La Bodega is essentially a tapas bar where the music (everything from salsa to Arabic pop) is loud and the Rioja flows freely. It's a fun place with a lively atmosphere and a packed dance floor after 10pm.

ℹ Information

There are banks – most with ATMS and bureaus de change – on almost every street corner in the centre of Casablanca.

Crédit du Maroc (☑0522 477255; 48 Blvd Mohammed V) Central bureau de change.

Gig@net (☑0522 484810; 140 Blvd Mohammed Zerktouni; per hr Dh10; ☺24hr) Internet.

Main Post Office (cnr Blvd de Paris & Ave Hassan II)

ℹ Getting There & Away

All long-distance trains depart from **Casa-Voyageurs train station** (☑0522 243818). Destinations include Marrakesh (Dh90, three hours), Fez (Dh110, 4½ hours) via Meknès (Dh90, 3½ hours), and Tangier (Dh125, 5¾ hours). **Casa Port station** (☑0522 223011) commuter services to Rabat (Dh35, one hour).

There are two bus stations – the **CTM bus station** (☑0522 541010; 23 Rue Léon L'Africain) and the **Gare Routière Ouled Ziane** (☑0522 444470), 4km southeast of the centre.

CTM services from Casablanca include:
➡ Essaouira (Dh145, seven hours, two daily)
➡ Fez (Dh100, five hours, 10 daily)
➡ Marrakesh (Dh90, four hours, nine daily)
➡ Meknès (Dh90, four hours, 11 daily)
➡ Rabat (Dh35, one hour, hourly)
➡ Tangier (Dh145, six hours, six daily)

ℹ Getting Around

Trains run hourly from 6am to midnight from Casa Voyageurs to Blvd Mohammed V international airport (Dh35, 35 minutes); a *grand taxi* between the airport and the city centre will cost you Dh250.

Casablanca's red *petits taxis* are notorious for arguing about using their meters. Trams run by the city's new **Tramway** (www.casatramway.ma) network were due to start in 2013; stops will include Casa Voyageurs, along Blvd Mohammed V and out towards Aïn Diab.

Essaouira

POP 70,000

The port town of Essaouira has long been a favourite of the travellers trail: laid-back and artsy, with sea breezes and picture-postcard ramparts. Although it can appear swamped with visitors in summer, once the day-trippers get back on the buses there's more than enough space to sigh deeply and just soak up the atmosphere.

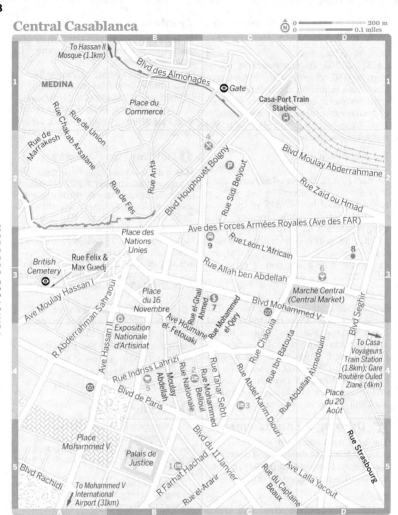

Central Casablanca

MOROCCO ESSAOUIRA

◉ Sights & Activities

The narrow winding streets of Essaouira's walled medina are a great place to stroll. Its late-18th-century fortified layout is a prime example of European military architecture in North Africa. The easiest place from which visitors can access the ramparts is the impressive sea bastion Skala de la Ville. By the harbour, the Skala du Port (adult/child Dh10/3; ⊘8.30am-noon & 2.30-6pm) offers picturesque views over both the fishing port and the Île de Mogador (boats from Port du Peche).

It's possible to rent water-sports equipment to Essaouira's wide sandy beach.

Océan Vagabond (☑0524 783934; www.oceanvagabond.com; ⊘9am-6pm daily) has surfboards (Dh750 for three days' rental) plus lessons in surfing (two hours, Dh440), kitesurfing (six hours, D2310) and windsurfing (two/six hours Dh825/1750). Beware the strong Atlantic currents.

🎉 Festivals & Events

Gnaoua & World Music Festival MUSIC
The Gnaoua & World Music Festival (the third weekend of June) is a four-day extravaganza with concerts on Place Moulay Hassan.

Central Casablanca

🛏 Sleeping

Hotel Beau Rivage HOTEL $
(☑ 0524 475925; beaurivage@menara.ma; 14 Place Moulay Hassan; s/d/tr Dh250/350/450, d without bathroom Dh200, breakfast Dh20) A longtime backpackers' favourite, this cheery hotel on the central square could hardly be better located. Rooms are clean, comfortable and airy.

Riad Nakhla HOTEL $
(☑ tel/fax 0524 474940; www.essaouiranet.com/riad-nakhla; 2 Rue d'Agadir; s/d Dh225/325, ste Dh400-500) Riad Nakhla greets weary travellers with a friendly reception in a beautiful courtyard with elegant stone columns and a trickling fountain. The well-appointed bedrooms are simple but comfortable. Breakfast on the roof terrace with views over the ocean and town is another treat.

Lalla Mira HOTEL $$
(☑ 0524 475046; www.lallamira.net; 14 Rue d'Algerie; s/d/ste Dh436/692/920; @) This gorgeous little place has simple rooms with wrought-iron furniture, natural fabrics and solar-powered underfloor heating. The hotel also has a *hammam* and a restaurant serving a decent selection of vegetarian food.

🍴 Eating & Drinking

Outdoor Fish Grill Stands SEAFOOD $
(port end of Place Moulay Hassan; around Dh40) These unpretentious stands offer a definitive Essaouira experience. Just choose what you want to eat from the colourful displays of freshly caught fish and shellfish at each grill, cooked on the spot and served with a pile of bread and salad.

Restaurant Ferdaous MOROCCAN $$
(☑ 0524 473655; 27 Rue Abdesslam Lebadi; mains Dh60-80, set menu Dh105; ⊘closed Mon) Delightful Moroccan restaurant, and one of the few places in town that serves real (as in home-cooked) traditional Moroccan food. The seasonal menu offers an innovative take on traditional recipes, the service is good, and the low tables and padded seating make it feel like the real McCoy.

Taros Café MEDITERRANEAN $$
(☑ 5247 476407; 2 Rue du Skala; mains Dh70-120; ⊘8am-11pm Mon-Sat) At this rooftop restaurant and bar, you can sip your drink under giant lamps and huddle round your table to fend off the wind whipping up from the sea. The restaurant is heavy on fish.

ℹ Information

There are several banks with ATMs around Place Moulay Hassan. There are also plentiful internet cafes, most opening from 9am to 11pm and charging Dh8 to Dh10 per hour.
Délégation du Tourisme (☑ 0524 783532; www.essaouira.com; 10 Rue du Caire; ⊘9am-noon & 3-6.30pm Mon-Fri) Very helpful staff.
Hôpital Sidi Mohammed ben Abdallah (☑ 0524 475716; Blvd de l'Hôpital) For emergencies.
Main Post Office (Ave el-Mouqawama)

ℹ Getting There & Away

CTM (☑ 0524 784764) has buses daily to Casablanca (Dh135, six hours), Marrakesh (Dh75, 2½ hours) and Agadir (Dh60, three hours). Other companies run cheaper and more frequent buses to the same destinations, as well as to Taroudannt (Dh70, six hours).

Supratours (☑ 0524 475317) runs buses to Marrakesh train station (Dh70, 2½ hours), connecting with trains to Casablanca. Book in advance.

Agadir

POP 680,000

Levelled by an earthquake in 1960, Agadir rose from its ruins to become Morocco's main beach resort, with a glitzy marina. Rebuilt into a neat grid of residential suburbs and wide boulevards, the town feels strangely bereft of the sort of bustling life often associated with Moroccan cities. Its lure, however, lies in its huge sandy bay, which is more sheltered than many other Atlantic beaches.

Essaouira

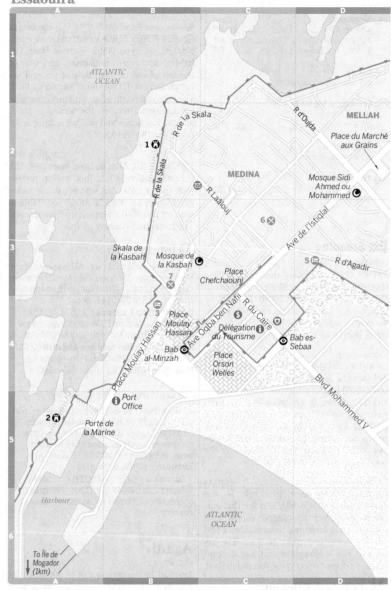

MOROCCO AGADIR

🛏 Sleeping

Hôtel Tiznine HOTEL **$**
(📞 0528 843925; 3 Rue Drarga; s/d Dh100/150,
with shower Dh120/150) One of Agadir's best
budget places, with a dozen good-sized rooms
around a green-and-white tiled flowering

courtyard. Some rooms have bathrooms, but
even the communal facilities are spotless.

Hôtel Kamal HOTEL **$$**
(📞 0528 842817; www.hotel-kamal.com; Ave Has-
san II; s/d Dh405/462) A popular and well-run

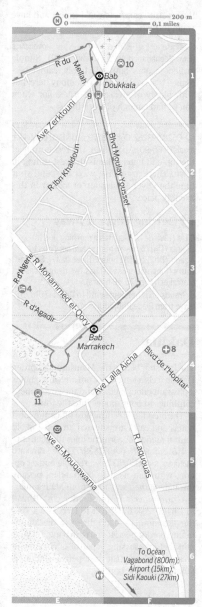

🍴 Eating

The cheap snack bars in Nouveau Talborjt and around the bus stations are open after hours. The **fish stalls** (meals around Dh50) at the entrance to the commercial port are excellent. There are plenty of places along the beach to chill at midday or toast the sunset. Some places along Palm Beach stay open till 1am in summer.

Bab Marrakesh MOROCCAN $
(📞0528 826144; Rue de Massa; sandwiches Dh25-35, couscous Dh70, tajine for 2 Dh100) Near Souq al-Had, this is the real thing – far removed from the tourist traps near the beach. Highly regarded by locals, it serves authentic Moroccan food at authentic prices.

La Scala MOROCCAN $$$
(📞0528 846773; Rue du Oued Souss; meal incl wine Dh350) An excellent Moroccan restaurant, La Scala has a pleasantly cosmopolitan atmosphere. The food is elegant and fresh, and beautifully presented.

ℹ Information

Banks with ATMs and internet places proliferate along Blvd Hassan II.

ℹ Getting There & Away

Although a good number of buses serve Agadir, it is quite possible you'll end up in the regional transport hub of Inezgane, 13km south – check before you buy your ticket. Plenty of *grands taxis*

hotel in a modernist white block near the town hall, the Kamal manages to appeal to a wide range of clients, including package-tour groups and travelling Moroccans. Rooms are bright and clean, and there's a pool large enough to swim laps in.

(Dh8) and local buses shuttle between there and Agadir.

CTM has buses to Casablanca (Dh180, eight hours, six daily), Marrakesh (Dh80, four hours, seven daily) and Essaouira (Dh60, two hours, one daily). There are more bus options at the regional transport hub of Inezgane, 13km to the south.

The main *grand taxi* rank is at the south end of Rue de Fès. Destinations include Inezgane (Dh8), Taroudannt (Dh35) and Essaouira (Dh70).

WESTERN SAHARA

Ask any Moroccan about the status of the Western Sahara and they'll insist it's sovereign soil, yet international law is clear that this is still under dispute. For travellers, it's mainly an empty windswept stretch of country for transiting to or from Mauritania.

There's no officially designated border between Morocco and the Western Sahara. Although the region is peaceful you'll be more aware of military and police checkpoints.

Laâyoune

POP 200,000

The former Spanish phosphate-mining outpost of Laâyoune has been turned into the principal city of the Western Sahara. Now neither Sahrawi nor Spanish, its population is mostly Moroccan, lured from the north by the promise of healthy wages and tax-free goods.

The town's showpiece is the vast Place du Méchouar, but there's no obvious centre. The post office, banks and most hotels are along either Blvd Hassan II or Blvd de Mekka.

🛏 Sleeping & Eating

There are many cafes and simple restaurants around Place Dchira. Lively food stalls can be found at the Souq Djemal.

Hôtel Jodesa   HOTEL $
(🖉 0528 992064; 223 Blvd de Mekka; s/d Dh100/144, with shower Dh144/155) North of Place Dchira, this modern hotel is a good budget option. Rooms are basic but reasonably spacious.

Hôtel Parador   HOTEL $$$
(🖉 0528 892814; Ave de l'Islam; s/d Dh1100/1400; ❄ 🏊) Built in Spanish hacienda style around gardens, the Parador has a faintly colonial bar and a good, if expensive, restaurant (set menu Dh200). Rooms are equipped with all

the creature comforts you'd expect and have small terraces.

Restaurant el-Bahja   MOROCCAN $
(Blvd Mohammed V; set menu Dh20) Simple grilled meat – lamb, certainly, camel perhaps – is served without ceremony here, but with plenty of grease and frites. For when you've had enough of fresh fish.

Le Poissonier   SEAFOOD $$
(🖉 0528 993262, 0661 235795; 183 Blvd de Mekka; meals Dh60-90) Apart from the restaurants at the top-end hotels, this is the best dining in town. There are worse ways to spend your time than over a fish soup or lobster in this friendly place.

❶ Getting There & Away

CTM (Blvd de Mekka) has a morning bus to Dakhla (Dh175, seven hours) and services to Agadir (Dh220, 10½ hours, three daily). **Supratours** (Place Oum Essad) has two daily buses to Marrakesh (Dh270, 16 hours).

Grands taxis heading south to Dakhla (Dh175) leave from Place Boujdour.

Dakhla

POP 40,000

The last stop before the Mauritanian border, Dakhla feels a long way from anywhere but is a pleasant enough place and the government continues to pour money into the town.

The bus offices, central post office and most hotels and cafes are situated around the old central market. A corniche lines the seafront.

Hôtel Sahara (🖉 0528 897773; Ave Sidi Ahmed Laaroussi; s/d Dh80/100) is a reliable budget option, with staff used to overlanders passing through on their way to or from Mauritania.

Grands taxis to the border cost Dh250 to Dh400. Ask the driver to ferry you across the 3km no-man's-land direct to the Mauritanian border post. If you're driving, fill your tank before crossing – petrol is cheaper in Western Sahara (the last petrol station is 80km before the border).

IMPERIAL CITIES & THE MIDDLE ATLAS

The rolling plains that sweep along the base of the Middle Atlas are Morocco's breadbasket, dotted with olive groves and wheat fields. Several important cities have also taken root here, including ancient Fez, Meknès and the Roman city of Volubilis – Morocco's most interesting archaeological site.

Fez

POP 1 MILLION

At 1200 years old Fez is Morocco's spiritual heart. Its medina (Fez el-Bali) is the largest living medieval Islamic city in the world. A first visit can be overwhelming: an assault on the senses through bazaars, winding alleys, mosques, workshops, people and pack animals that seem to take you out of the 21st century and back to imagined *Arabian Nights*.

◉ Sights

The Medina (Fez el-Bali)

Within the old walls of Fez el-Bali lies an incredible maze of twisting alleys, blind turns and hidden souqs. Navigation can be confusing and getting lost is a certainty, but this is part of the medina's charm: you never quite know what discovery lies around the next corner.

Kairaouine Mosque MOSQUE

(Map p276) The Kairaouine Mosque is Fez's true heart. Built in 859 by refugees from Tunisia, and rebuilt in the 12th century, it can accommodate up to 20,000 people at prayer. Non-Muslims have to be content with glimpses of its seemingly endless columns from the gates on Talaa Kebira and Place as-Seffarine.

Medersa Bou Inania NOTABLE BUILDING

(Map p276; admission Dh10; ☺9am-6pm, closed during prayers) Located 150m east of Bab Bou Jeloud, the 14th-century Medersa Bou Inania is the finest of Fez's theological colleges. The *zellij, muqarna* (plasterwork) and woodcarving are amazingly elaborate.

Nejjarine Museum of Wooden Arts & Crafts MUSEUM

(Map p276; ☎0535 740580; Place an-Nejjarin; admission Dh20; ☺10am-7pm) Located in a wonderfully restored *funduq* (caravanserai for travelling merchants), with a host of fascinating exhibits. Photography is forbidden. The rooftop cafe has great views over the medina.

Tanneries NEIGHBOURHOOD

(Map p276) The tanneries are one of the city's most iconic sights (and smells). Head northeast of Place as-Seffarine and take the left fork after about 50m; you'll soon pick up the unmistakeable waft of skin and dye that will guide you into the heart of the leather district.

Fez el-Jdid (New Fez)

Only in a city as old as Fez could you find a district dubbed 'new' because it's only 700 years old. It's home to the Royal Palace, whose entrance at **Dar el-Makhzen** (Royal Palace; Map p274; Place des Alaouites) is a stunning example of modern restoration; palace grounds are closed to the public.

In the 14th century, Fez el-Jdid became a refuge for Jews, thus creating a *mellah* (Jewish quarter). The *mellah's* southwest corner is home to the fascinating **Jewish Cemetery & Habarim Synagogue** (Map p274; donations appreciated; ☺7am-7pm).

★ Festivals & Events

Fez Festival of World Sacred Music MUSIC

(☎0535 740691; www.fesfestival.com) Every June the Fez Festival of World Sacred Music brings together musicians from all corners of the globe. It's an established favourite on the 'world music' festival circuit.

🛏 Sleeping

Medina

Hôtel Cascade HOTEL $

(Map p276; ☎0535 638442; 26 Rue Serrajine, Bab Bou Jeloud; dm/r Dh80/160, breakfast Dh20) One of the grandaddies of the Morocco budget-hotel scene. You shouldn't expect much for the price, but if you're up for meeting plenty of like-minded travellers, then this might be the place for you.

Funky Fes HOSTEL $

(Map p276; ☎0535 633196; www.funkyfes.com; Arset Lamdisi, Bab Jdid; dm Dh130-170) Fez's first proper hostel, offering up good, cheap backpacker accommodation, with activities, tours, cooking and more.

Dar Finn GUESTHOUSE $$

(Map p276; ☎0535 740004; www.darfinn.com; r Dh850-1200; ▣ ☎) A lovingly restored guesthouse, with high-Fassi style in the front and a sunny back courtyard with plunge pool. Very welcoming, with delicious breakfasts.

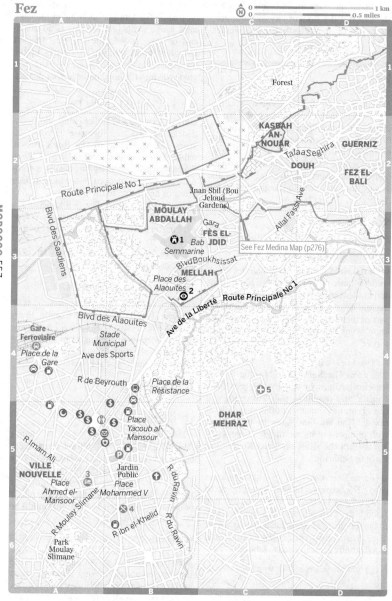

Ville Nouvelle

Hôtel Splendid   HOTEL **$**
(Map p274; ☎ 0535 622148; splendid@iam.net.
ma; 9 Rue Abdelkarim el-Khattabi; s/d Dh318/412;

❄ ☒) This hotel makes a good claim for
three stars. It's all modern and tidy, plus
there's a pool for the heat and a bar for the
evenings.

Fez

Sights

1 Dar el-Makhzen....................................B3
2 Jewish Cemetery & Habarim
   Synagogue B3

Sleeping

3 Hôtel Splendid A5

Eating

4 Restaurant Marrakech.....................B6

Information

5 Hôpital Ghassani C4

✖ Eating & Drinking

✖ Medina

In the medina, you won't have to walk far to find someone selling food – tiny cell-like places grilling *brochettes,* cooking up cauldrons of soup or just a guy with a pushcart selling peanut cookies. Bab Bou Jeloud has quite a cluster of options, with streetside tables for people-watching.

Café Clock   CAFE **$$**

(Map p276; ☑ 0535 637855; www.cafeclock.com; 7 Derb el-Mergana, Talaa Kebira; mains Dh55-80; ⊙9am-10pm; 🛜) In a restored townhouse, this funky place has a refreshing menu with offerings such as falafel, some interesting vegetarian options and a monstrously large camel burger. Its 'Clock Culture' program includes sunset concerts every Sunday (cover charge around Dh20), attracting a good mix of locals, expats and curious tourists.

Médina Café   MOROCCAN **$$**

(☑ 0535 633430; 6 Derb Mernissi, Bab Bou Jeloud; mains Dh70-100; ⊙8am-10pm) Just outside Bab Bou Jeloud, this small restaurant is good for a quick bite or a fruit juice; in the evening better Moroccan fare is on offer.

Mezzanine   CAFE

(Map p276; ☑ 5356 633430; 17 Kasbah Chams; tapas selection from Dh100 or per dish around Dh30; ⊙noon-1am) Scoring highly on the fashion meter, this new bar is the hippest thing in the medina – more Ibiza than Moulay Idriss. The terrace overlooking Jnan Sbil gardens is a good place to chill with a beer or cocktail, and there's tapas too if you want some finger food.

✖ Ville Nouvelle

Restaurant Marrakech   MOROCCAN **$$**

(Map p274; ☑ 0535 930876; 11 Rue Omar el-Mokhtar; mains from Dh55; ✳) A charming restaurant with red walls and dark furniture, plus a cushion-strewn salon at the back. The menu's variety refreshes the palate, with dishes like chicken tajine with apple and olive, or lamb with aubergine and peppers (there's also a set three-course menu).

ⓘ Information

There are plenty of banks (with ATMs) in the Ville Nouvelle along Blvd Mohammed V.

Cyber Batha (Derb Douh; per hr Dh10; ⊙9am-10pm) Internet; has English as well as French keyboards.

Hôpital Ghassani (Map p274; ☑ 0535 622777) One of the city's biggest hospitals; located east of the Ville Nouvelle in the Dhar Mehraz district.

Main Post Office (cnr Ave Hassan II & Blvd Mohammed V) Poste restante is at the far left; the parcels office is through a separate door.

Post Office (Place Batha) In the medina.

ⓘ Getting There & Away

BUS

The main station for **CTM buses** (☑ 0535 732992) is near Place Atlas in the southern Ville Nouvelle.

Non-CTM buses depart from the **main bus station** (Map p276; ☑ 0535 636032) outside Bab el-Mahrouk.

CTM services from Fez include:

➡ Casablanca (Dh105, five hours, seven daily)
➡ Chefchaouen (Dh45, four hours, three daily)
➡ Marrakesh (Dh150, nine hours, two daily)
➡ Meknès (Dh25, 1½ hours, six daily)
➡ Rabat (Dh70, 3½ hours, seven daily)
➡ Tangier (Dh115, six hours, three daily)
➡ Tetouan (Dh100, five hours, two daily)

TAXI

There are several *grand taxi* ranks dotted around town. Taxis for Meknès (Dh20) and Rabat (Dh60) leave from in front of the main bus station (outside Bab el-Mahrouk) and from near the train station.

TRAIN

The **train station** (☑ 0535 930333) is in the Ville Nouvelle. Trains depart every two hours to Casablanca (Dh110, 4½ hours), via Rabat (Dh80, 3½ hours) and Meknès (Dh20, one hour); there are also services to Marrakesh (Dh195, eight hours) and Tangier (Dh105, five hours).

❶ Getting Around

Drivers of the red *petits taxis* generally use their meters without any fuss. Expect to pay about Dh9 from the train or CTM stations to Bab Bou Jeloud.

Meknès

POP 690,000

Morocco's third imperial city is often overlooked by tourists, but Meknès (Map p280) is worth getting to know. Quieter and smaller than nearby Fez, it's more laid-back and

Fez Medina

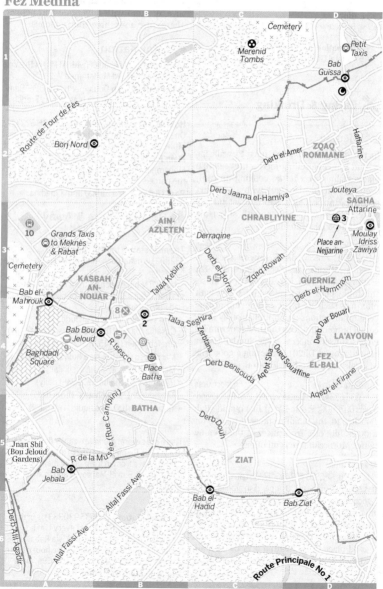

less hassle, but still awash with the winding, narrow medina streets and grand buildings befitting a one-time capital of the sultanate.

Meknès is also the ideal base from which to explore the Roman ruins at Volubilis and the hilltop holy town of Moulay Idriss, two of the country's most significant historical sites.

Sights

The heart of Meknès' medina lies to the north of the main square, Place el-Hedim, with the *mellah* to the west. To the south, Moulay Ismail's imperial city opens up through one of the most impressive monumental gateways

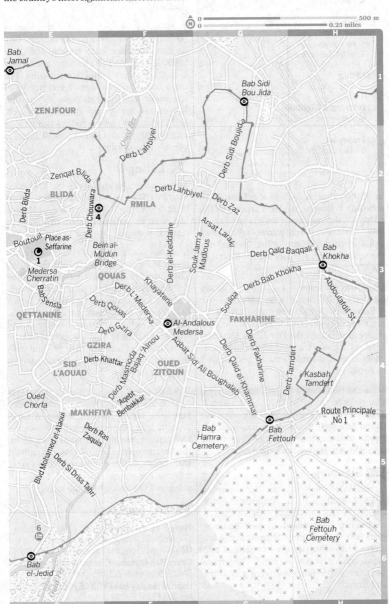

Fez Medina

⊙ Sights
1 Kairaouine Mosque E3
2 Medersa Bou Inania........................... B4
3 Nejjarine Museum of
    Wooden Arts & Crafts D3
4 Tanneries E2

⊜ Sleeping
5 Dar Finn C3
6 Funky Fes E6
7 Hôtel Cascade................................... B4

⊗ Eating
8 Café Clock B4

⊙ Drinking & Nightlife
9 Mezzanine A4

⊙ Transport
10 Main Bus Station A3

in all of Morocco, **Bab el-Mansour** (Place el-Hedim). Following the road around to the right, you'll come across the grand **Mausoleum of Moulay Ismail** (donations appreciated; ⊙8.30am-noon & 2-6pm Sat-Thu), named for the sultan who made Meknès his capital in the 17th century.

Dar Jamaï Museum   MUSEUM
(☑0535 530863; Place el-Hedim; admission Dh20; ⊙9am-noon & 3-6.30pm Wed-Mon) Overlooking Place el-Hedim on the north is the 1882 palace that houses the Dar Jamaï Museum. Exhibits include traditional ceramics, jewellery, rugs and some fantastic textiles and embroidery.

Medersa Bou Inania   NOTABLE BUILDING
(Rue Najjarine; admission Dh20; ⊙9am-noon & 3-6pm) Deep in the medina, opposite the Grand Mosquée, the Medersa Bou Inania is typical of the exquisite interior design that distinguishes Merenid monuments.

🛏 Sleeping

Maroc Hôtel   HOTEL $
(☑0535 530075; 7 Rue Rouamzine; s/d/tr Dh100/200/270) Perennially popular, the Maroc has kept its standards up over the many years we've been visiting. Friendly and quiet, rooms (with sinks) are freshly painted and the shared bathrooms are clean. The terrace and orange tree–filled courtyard add to the ambience.

Hôtel Majestic   HOTEL $
(☑0535 522035; 19 Ave Mohammed V; s/d Dh159/210, with shower Dh231/322) Built in the 1930s, this grand old lady carries her age well. There's a good mix of rooms (all have sinks) and there's plenty of character to go around, plus a peaceful patio and panoramic roof terrace.

Ryad Bahia   GUESTHOUSE $$
(☑0535 554541; www.ryad-bahia.com; Derb Sekkaya, Tiberbarine; r incl breakfast Dh670, ste Dh950-1200; ❄ 🔊) This charming guesthouse is a stone's throw from Place el-Hedim. The main entrance opens onto a courtyard and the whole place has an open, airy layout. Rooms are pretty and carefully restored, and the owners (keen travellers themselves) eager to swap travel stories as well as guide guests in the medina.

🍴 Eating

Take your pick of any one of the ~~sandwich~~ stands (Place el-Hedim; sandwiches around Dh30; ⊙7am-10pm) lining Place el-Hedim, and sit at the canopied tables to watch the scene as you eat.

Marhaba Restaurant   MOROCCAN $
(23 Ave Mohammed V; tajines Dh25; ⊙noon-10pm) The essence of cheap and cheerful; we adore this basic, canteen-style place. Do as everyone else does and fill up on a bowl of *harira* (a thick soup made from lamb stock, lentils, chickpeas, onions, tomatoes, fresh herbs and spices) or a plate of *makoda* (potato fritters) with bread and hard-boiled eggs – and walk out with change from Dh15. We defy you to eat better for less.

Dar Sultana   MOROCCAN $$
(☑0535 535720; Derb Sekkaya, Tiberbarine; mains from Dh70, 3-course set menu Dh150) A small restaurant in a converted medina house, the tent canopy over the courtyard gives an intimate atmosphere, set off by walls painted with henna designs and hung with bright fabrics. The spread of cooked Moroccan salads is a big highlight of the menu.

⊙ Information

There are plenty of banks with ATMs in both the Ville Nouvelle (mainly on Ave Hassan II and Ave Mohammed V) and the medina (Rue Sekkakine).
Cyber Bab Mansour (Zankat Accra; per hr Dh6; ⊙9am-midnight) Internet.
Hôpital Moulay Ismail (☑0535 522805) Off Ave des FAR.

Main Post Office (Place de l'Istiqlal) The parcel office is in the same building, around the corner on Rue Tetouan.

🛈 Getting There & Away

Meknès has two train stations; use the more central **El-Amir Abdelkader** (☎ 0535 522763). There are plentiful trains to Fez (Dh20, one hour), and Casablanca (Dh90, 3½ hours) via Rabat (Dh65, 2¼ hours), five for Marrakesh (Dh174, seven hours) and one for Tangier (Dh85, four hours) – or take a westbound train and change at Sidi Kacem.

CTM bus departures include Casablanca (Dh90, four hours, six daily) via Rabat (Dh55, 2½ hours), Marrakesh (Dh160, eight hours, daily) and Tangier (Dh100, five hours, three daily). The main bus station lies just outside Bab el-Khemis, west of the medina.

The principal *grand taxi* rank is at Bab el-Khemis. There are regular departures to Fez (Dh16, one hour) and Rabat (Dh44, 90 minutes). *Grands taxis* for Moulay Idriss (Dh12, 20 minutes) leave from opposite the Institut Français.

CENTRAL MOROCCO & THE HIGH ATLAS

Marrakesh is the queen bee of Moroccan tourism, but look beyond it and you'll find great trekking in the dramatic High Atlas, and spectacular valleys and gorges that lead to the vast and empty sands of the Saharan dunes.

Marrakesh

POP 2 MILLION

Marrakesh grew rich on the camel caravans threading their way across the desert, although these days it's cheap flights from Europe bringing tourists to spend their money in the souqs that fatten the city's coffers. But Marrakesh's old heart still beats strongly enough, from the time-worn ramparts that ring the city to the nightly spectacle of the Djemaa el-Fna that leaps from the pages of the *1001 Nights* on the edge of the labyrinthine medina.

◎ Sights

The focal point of Marrakesh is **Djemaa el-Fna** (⊙ approx 9am-1pm, later during Ramadan), a huge square in the medina and the backdrop for one of the world's greatest spectacles. Djemaa el-Fna comes into its own at dusk, when the curtain goes up on rows of open-air food stalls smoking the immediate area with mouth-watering aromas. Jugglers, storytellers, snake charmers, musicians, acrobats and spectators fill the remaining space.

Southwest of Djemaa el-Fna is the 70m-tall minaret of Marrakesh's most famous monument, the **Koutoubia Mosque** (cnr Rue el-Koutoubia & Ave Mohammed V; ⊙ mosque & minaret closed to non-Muslims, gardens open 8am-8pm). Visible for miles in all directions, it's a classic example of Moroccan-Andalucían architecture.

The largest and oldest-surviving of the mosques is the 12th-century **Ali ben Youssef Mosque** (⊙ closed to non-Muslims), which marks the intellectual and religious heart of the medina. Next to the mosque is the 14th-century **Ali ben Youssef Medersa** (☎ 0524 441893; Place ben Youssef; admission Dh40; ⊙ 9am-6pm winter, to 7pm summer), a peaceful and meditative place with some stunning examples of stucco decoration.

Marrakesh has more gardens than any other Moroccan city, offering the perfect escape from the hubbub of the souqs and the traffic. The rose gardens of Koutoubia Mosque, in particular, offer cool respite near Djemaa el-Fna.

Palais de la Bahia　　　　PALACE
(☎ 0524 389564; Rue Riad Zitoun el-Jedid; admission Dh10; ⊙ 8.30-11.45am & 2.30-5.45pm Sat-Thu, 8.30-11.30am & 3-5.45pm Fri) Located near Place des Ferblantiers, La Bahia (The Beautiful) boasts floor-to-ceiling decoration begun by Grand Vizier Si Moussa in the 1860s and further embellished in 1894–1900 by slave-turned-vizier Abu 'Bou' Ahmed. The painted, gilded, inlaid woodwork ceilings still have the intended effect of subduing

---

WORTH A TRIP

VOLUBILIS & MOULAY IDRISS

In the midst of a fertile plain about 33km north of Meknès, **Volubilis** (Ouailili; admission Dh20, parking Dh5, guide Dh140; ⊙ 8am-sunset) are the largest and best-preserved Roman ruins in Morocco. One of the country's most important pilgrimage sites, the lovely whitewashed hill town **Moulay Idriss**, is only about 4.5km from Volubilis.

A half-day outing by *grand taxi* from Meknès will cost around Dh350, including a stop at Moulay Idriss.

Meknès

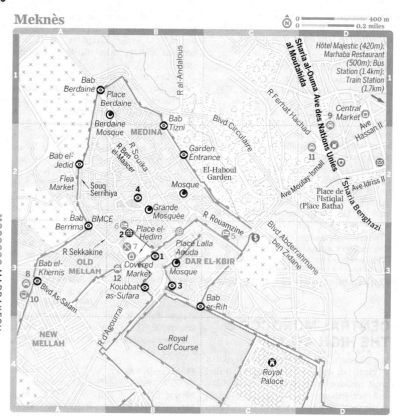

Meknès

crowds, while the carved stucco is cleverly slanted downward to meet the gaze.

Saadian Tombs TOMBS
(Rue de la Kasbah; admission Dh10; ⊙8.30-11.45am & 2.30-5.45pm) Long hidden from intrusive eyes, the area of the Saadian Tombs, alongside the Kasbah Mosque, is home to ornate tombs that are the resting places of Saadian princes.

Jardin Majorelle GARDENS
(☏0524 301852; www.jardinmajorelle.com; cnr Ave Yacoub el-Mansour & Ave Moulay Abdullah; garden Dh30, museum Dh15; ⊙8am-6pm summer, to 5pm winter) In the Ville Nouvelle, the Jardin Majorelle is a sublime mix of art deco buildings and psychedelic desert mirage.

🛏 Sleeping

Hôtel Central Palace HOTEL $
(☏0524 440235; hotelcentralpalace@hotmail.com; 59 Derb Sidi Bouloukat; d Dh305, with shower

Dh205, without bathroom Dh155) Sure it's central, but palatial? Actually, yes! With 40 clean rooms on four floors arranged around a burbling courtyard fountain, and a roof terrace lording it over the Djemaa el-Fna, this is a rare example of a stately budget hotel.

Jnane Mogador
GUESTHOUSE $

(☎0524 426323; www.jnanemogador.com; 116 Riad Zitoun el-Kedim, Derb Sidi Bouloukat; s/d/tr/q Dh360/480/580/660; @) An authentic 19th-century riad with all the 21st-century-guesthouse fixings: prime location, in-house *hammam,* double-decker roof terraces and owner Mohammed's laid-back hospitality. Perennially popular; book in advance.

Riad Nejma Lounge
GUESTHOUSE $$

(☎0524 382341; www.riad-nejmalounge.com; 45 Derb Sidi M'Hamed el-Haj, Bab Doukkala; d incl breakfast Dh495-795; ❋@❄) Lounge lizards chill on hot-pink cushions in the whitewashed courtyard, and graphic splashes of colour make wood-beamed guest rooms totally mod, though the rustic showers can be temperamental. Handy for Ville Nouvelle restaurants and shops.

Dar Soukaina
GUESTHOUSE $$$

(☎0661 245238; www.darsoukaina.com; 19 Derb el-Ferrane, Riad Laârouss; s/tr incl breakfast Dh790/1150, d incl breakfast Dh970-1400; ❋❄) Sister riads: the original is all soaring ceilings, cosy nooks and graceful archways, while the newer extension across the street is about sprawling beds, the grand patio and handsome woodwork. A 20-minute walk from the Djemaa, but worth the discovery.

Eating

The cheapest and most exotic place in town to eat remains the **food stalls** (☉sunset-1am) on Djemaa el-Fna, piled high with fresh meats and salads, goats' heads and steaming snails.

Just before noon, the vendors at a row of stalls in **Mechoui Alley** (250g lamb with bread Dh30-50; ☉11am-2pm), on the east side of Souq Ablueh (Olive Souq), start carving up steaming sides of *mechoui* (slow-roasted lamb), with bread and spices.

Earth Café
VEGETARIAN $$

(2 Derb Zouak, Riad Zitoun el-Kedim; mains around Dh60; ☉9am-11pm; ✍) Run by an enthusiastic Moroccan-Australian, Earth Café claims to be Morocco's first vegetarian/vegan restaurant. The atmosphere is laid-back hippy-

chic, and the food fresh and fabulous (we fell in love with the ricotta-and-squash *bastilla,* a multilayer pastry). Produce comes from the owner's nearby farm, to which visits can be arranged.

Le Salama
MOROCCAN $$

(☎0524 391300; www.lesalama.com; 40 Rue des Banques) Low lighting and dark Moroccan decor lend atmosphere to this upscale dining experience – more than just traditional tajines, and with a rooftop bar that's the closest place to Djemma el-Fna where you can get a drink.

Terrasse des Épices
MOROCCAN $$

(☎0524 375904; 15 Souq Cherifia; set meals Dh100-150) Head to the roof for lunch on top of the world in a mudbrick *bhou* (booth). Check the chalkboard for the Dh100 fixed-price special: Moroccan salads followed by chicken-leg tajine with fries, then strawberries and mint. Reservations handy in the high season.

🍷 Drinking

Dar Cherifa
CAFE

(☎0524 426463; 8 Derb Cherifa Lakbir; tea/coffee Dh15-25; ☉noon-7pm) Revive souq-sore eyes at this serene late-15th-century Saadian riad, near Rue Mouassine, where tea and saffron coffee is served with contemporary art and literature downstairs or terrace views upstairs.

Café Arabe
BAR

(☎0524 429728; www.cafearabe.com; 184 Rue el-Mouassine, Medina; ☉10am-midnight) Gloat over souq purchases with cocktails on the roof at sunset or a glass of wine next to the Zen-*zellij* courtyard fountain. The food is mixed.

🛍 Shopping

Marrakesh is a shopper's paradise: its souqs are full of skilled artisans producing quality products in wood, leather, wool, metal, bone, brass and silver. The trick is to dive into the souqs and treat shopping as a game.

Ensemble Artisanal
ARTS & CRAFTS

(Ave Mohammed V; ☉8.30am-7.30pm) To get a feel for the quality of merchandise it is always good to start at this government-run spot in the Ville Nouvelle.

Cooperative Artisanale Femmes de Marrakesh
ARTS & CRAFTS

(☎0524 378308; 67 Souq Kchachbia; ☉9.30am-12.30pm & 2.30-6.30pm) A hidden treasure worth seeking in the souqs, with breezy

Marrakesh

MOROCCO| MARRAKESH

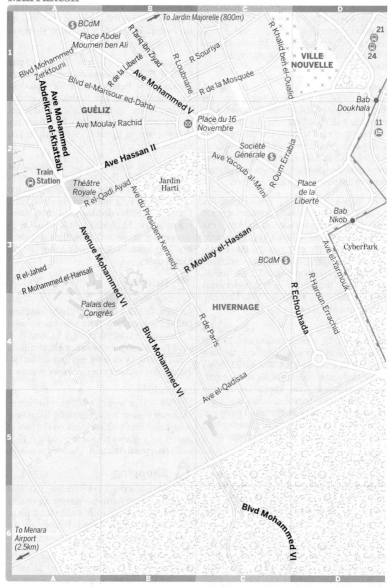

cotton clothing and household linens made by a Marrakesh women's cooperative, and a small annexe packed with varied items from nonprofits and women's cooperatives from across Morocco.

ℹ Information

Cybercafes ringing the Djemaa el-Fna charge Dh8 to Dh12 per hour; just follow signs reading 'c@fe'. There are plenty of ATMs along Rue de Bab Agnaou off the Djemaa el-Fna.

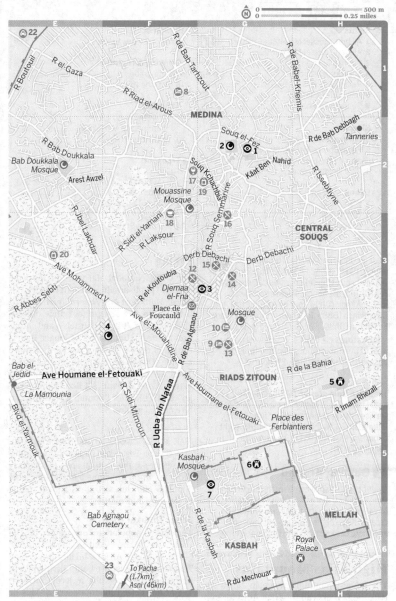

Main Post Office (☎0524 431963; Place du 16 Novembre; ⏰8.30am-2pm Mon-Sat)

Polyclinique du Sud (☎0524 447999; cnr Rue de Yougoslavie & Rue Ibn Aicha, Guéliz; ⏰24hr) Private hospital for serious cases and emergency dental care.

🛈 Getting There & Away

BUS

Most buses arrive and depart from the **main bus station** (☎0524 433933; Bab Doukkala), just outside the city walls. A number of companies run buses to Fez (from Dh130, 8½ hours, at

Marrakesh

least six daily) and Meknès (from Dh120, six hours). **CTM** (☑ 0524 434402; Window 10, Bab Doukkala bus station) operates daily buses to Fez (Dh160, 8½ hours). There are also services to Agadir (Dh90, four hours, nine daily), Casablanca (Dh85, four hours, three daily) and Essaouira (Dh80, 2½ hours, three daily).

Supratours (☑ 0524 435525; Ave Hassan II), west of the train station, operates three daily buses to Essaouira (Dh65, 2½ hours).

TRAIN

The swish **train station** (☑ 0524 447768; cnr Ave Hassan II & Blvd Mohammed VI, Guéliz) has services to Casablanca (Dh90, three hours), Rabat (Dh120, four hours), Fez (Dh185, eight hours) via Meknès (Dh174, seven hours) and Tangier (Dh205).

ⓘ Getting Around

A *petit taxi* to Marrakesh from the airport (6km) should cost no more than Dh60. Alternatively, bus 11 runs irregularly to Djemaa el-Fna. The creamy-beige *petits taxis* around town cost anywhere between Dh5 and Dh15 per journey.

High Atlas Mountains

The highest mountain range in North Africa, the Berbers call the High Atlas Idraren Draren (Mountain of Mountains) and it's easy to see why. Flat-roofed, earthen Berber villages cling tenaciously to the valley sides, while irrigated terraced gardens and walnut groves flourish below.

Hiking

The Office National Marocain du Tourisme (ONMT) publishes the excellent booklet *Morocco: Mountain and Desert Tourism*, with lists of *bureaux des guides* (guide offices), *gîtes d'étape* (hikers' hostels) and other useful information. Hikes of longer than a couple of days will almost certainly require a guide (Dh300 per day) and mule (Dh100). There are *bureaux des guides* in Imlil, Setti Fatma, Azilal, Tabant (Aït Bou Goumez Valley) and El-Kelaâ M'Gouna, where you can hire official guides.

Club Alpin Français   HIKING
(CAF; ☑ 0522 270090; 50 Blvd Moulay Abderrahman, Quartier Beauséjour, Casablanca) Operates key refuges in the Toubkal area, particularly those in Imlil, Oukaïmeden and on Jebel Toubkal. The club website is a good source of trekking information.

Jebel Toubkal Hike

The most popular hiking route in the High Atlas is the ascent of Jebel Toubkal (4167m), North Africa's highest peak. The Toubkal area is just two hours' drive south of Marrakesh and accessible by local transport.

You don't need mountaineering skills or a guide to reach the summit, provided you follow the standard two-day route and don't do it in winter. You will, however, need good boots, warm clothing, a sleeping bag, food and water, and should be in good physical condition before you set out. It's not particularly steep, but it's a remorseless uphill trek all the way.

The starting point is the village of Imlil, where you can stock up on supplies. There's plenty of accommodation here – try Café-Hotel Soleil (☎ tel/fax 0524 485622; d incl breakfast Dh220, without bathroom Dh170, per person without/with bathroom & half board Dh170/220) or Dar Zaratoustra (☎ 0524 485601; http://toubkal-maroc.voila.net/; d with half board Dh350-500; ☺ Mar-Oct).

The first day's walk (10km; about five hours) winds steeply through the villages of Aroumd and Sidi Chamharouch to the large Toubkal Refuge (☎ 0664 071838; dm CAF member/HI nonmember Dh46/69/92), at 2307m.

The ascent to the summit on the second day should take about four hours and the descent about two. It can be bitterly cold at the summit, even in summer.

Frequent local buses (Dh15, 1½ hours) and *grands taxis* (Dh30, one hour) leave south of Bab er-Rob in Marrakesh to Asni, where you change for the final 17km to Imlil (Dh15 to Dh20, one hour).

Other Hikes

In summer, it's quite possible to do an easy one- or two-day trek from the ski resort of Oukaïmeden, which also has a CAF refuge, southwest to Imlil or vice versa. You can get here by *grand taxi* from Marrakesh.

From Tacheddirt there are numerous hiking options. One is a pleasant two-day walk northeast to the village of Setti Fatma (also accessible from Marrakesh) via the village of Timichi, where there is a welcoming *gîte*. A longer circuit could take you south to Amsouzerte and back towards Imlil via Lac d'Ifni, Toubkal, Tazaghart (also with a refuge and rock climbing) and Tizi Oussem.

Aït Benhaddou

Aït Benhaddou, 32km from Ouarzazate, is one of the most exotic and best-preserved kasbahs in Morocco. It's regularly used as a film set, starring in everything from *Lawrence of Arabia* and *Gladiator* to *Game of Thrones*.

From Ouarzazate, take the main road towards Marrakesh as far as the signposted turn-off (22km); Aït Benhaddou is another 9km. *Grands taxis* run from outside Ouarzazate bus station when full (Dh20 per person).

Drâa Valley

A ribbon of Technicolor palmeraies (palm groves), earth-red kasbahs and Berber villages, the Drâa Valley is a special place. Eventually seeping out into the sands of the desert, it helped control the ancient trans-Saharan trade routes that built Marrakesh's wealth.

Zagora

The iconic 'Tombouktou, 52 jours' ('Timbuktu, 52 days') signpost was recently taken down in an inexplicable government beautification scheme, but Zagora's fame as a desert outpost is indelible. It feels very much like a border town, fighting back the encroaching desert with its lush palmeraie. Though modern and largely unappealing, the spectacular Jebel Zagora, rising up across the other side of the river Drâa, is worth climbing for the views.

🏃 Activities

Camel rides are practically obligatory in Zagora. Count on around Dh300 per day if you're camping; ask about water, bedding, toilets and how many other people will be sharing your campsite.

Caravane Dèsert et Montagne   DESERT EXCURSIONS
(☎ 0524 846898; www.caravanedesertetmontagne. com; 112 Blvd Mohammed V)

Caravane Hamada Drâa   DESERT EXCURSIONS
(☎ 0524 846930; www.hamadadraa.com)

🛏 Sleeping & Eating

Most hotels have their own restaurants. Moroccan fare with less flair can be had at cheap restaurants along Blvd Mohammed V.

Hôtel la Rose des Sables   HOTEL $
(☎ 0524 847274; Ave Allal Ben Abdallah; s/d Dh80/150, without bathroom Dh60/90) Off-duty desert guides unwind in these basic, tidy rooms right off the main drag. You might be able to coax out stories of travellers over tasty tajine meals at the outdoor cafe (set menu Dh40 to Dh50).

Dar Raha   GUESTHOUSE $
(☎ 0524 846993; www.darraha.com; Amezrou; s/d with half board Dh235/310) 'How thoughtful!' is the operative phrase here, with oasis-appropriate details such as local palm

mats, recycled wire lamps and thick straw *pisé* (earthen) walls eliminating the need for a pool or air-con. Enjoy home-cooked meals and check out the exhibition of local paintings and crafts.

ℹ Information

Banks with ATMs and normal banking hours are on Blvd Mohammed V, along with internet cafes.

ℹ Getting There & Away

The **CTM bus station** (☎ 0524 847327) is at the southwestern end of Blvd Mohammed V, and the main bus and *grand taxi* lot is at the northern end. CTM has a daily service to Marrakesh (Dh100) and Casablanca (Dh175) via Ouarzazate. Other companies also operate buses to Boumalne du Dadès (Dh75) and Erfoud (Dh85).

M'hamid

M'hamid's star attraction is Erg Chigaga, a mind-boggling 40km stretch of golden Saharan dunes. It's 56km away – a couple of hours by 4WD or several days by camel. A closer alternative is Erg Lehoudi (in bad need of rubbish collection). Sahara Services (☎ 0661 776766; www.saharaservices.info) and Zbar Travel (☎ 0668 517280; www.zbar-travel.com) offer tours – an overnight camel trek should start at about Dh400. M'Hamid Bali, the old town, is 3km away across the Oued Drâa, with a well-preserved kasbah.

If you're not sleeping with your camel in the dunes, Dar Sidi Bounou (☎ 0524 846330; www.darsidibounou.com; s/d with full board in tent/hut/r Dh330/420/540) is a desert dream. Camping Hammada du Drâa (☎ 0524 848080; campsites/Berber tents per person Dh15/50, per car Dh20) offers simpler fare.

There's a daily CTM bus to Zagora (Dh25, two hours), Ouarzazate (Dh70, seven hours) and Marrakesh (Dh120, 11 to 13 hours), plus an assortment of private buses, minibuses and *grands taxis*.

Merzouga & the Dunes

Morocco's greatest Saharan *erg* (sand sea) is Erg Chebbi. It's an impressive, drifting chain of sand dunes that deserves much more than the sunrise or sunset glimpse many visitors give it. The largest dunes are near the villages of Merzouga and Hassi Labied. At night, you only have to walk a little way into the sand, away from the light, to appreciate the immense clarity of the desert sky and the brilliance of its stars.

Some 50km south of Erfoud is Merzouga, a tiny village with Téléboutiques, general stores, a mechanic and, of course, a couple of carpet shops. It also has a reputation for some of the pushiest touts in Morocco.

Most hotels offer excursions into the dunes, which can range from Dh80 to Dh200 for a couple of hours' sunrise or sunset camel trek. Overnight trips usually include a bed in a Berber tent, dinner and breakfast, and range from Dh300 to Dh650 per person. Outings in a 4WD are more expensive – up to Dh1200 per day for a car taking up to five passengers.

🛏 Sleeping & Eating

Chez Julia   GUESTHOUSE $
(☎ 0535 573182; s/d/tr/q Dh200/400/600/800) Pure charm in the heart of Merzouga, Chez Julia offers nine simply furnished rooms in soft, sun-washed colours, with immaculate white-tiled shared bathrooms. The

---

WORTH A TRIP

TODRA GORGE

The spectacular canyons of Todra Gorge, at the end of a lush valley thick with palmeraies and Berber villages, are one of the highlights of the south. A massive fault in the plateau dividing the High Atlas from Jebel Sarhro, with a crystal-clear river emerging from it, the gorge rises to 300m at its narrowest point. It's best in the morning, when the sun penetrates to the bottom of the gorge, turning the rock from rose pink to a deep ochre.

About a 30-minute walk beyond the main gorge is the Petite Gorge. This is the starting point of many pleasant day hikes, including one starting by the Auberge-Camping Le Festival, 2km after the Petite Gorge. A good accommodation option is Dar Ayour (☎ 0524 895271; www.darayour.com; Km 13, Gorges du Todra, Tinghir; r without/ with bathroom Dh100/150, r incl breakfast/half board Dh200/350).

Todra Gorge is near Tinerihr, accessible by bus from Marrakesh (Dh105, five daily) via Ouazazarte. *Grands taxis* run throughout the day to Todra Gorge (Dh8).

Moroccan ladies who run the place can cook up a storm of delicious meals.

Dar el Janoub GUESTHOUSE **$$**
(☑ tel/fax 0535 577852; www.dareljanoub.com; d standard/large/ste per person Dh580/725/800; ❋ ❋) In Hassi Labied, 5km north of Merzouga, the architect here stuck to elemental building shapes, because when you're facing the dunes, why compete? For the price, you get great rooms with a million-dirham view, half board, a pool and pure poetry.

❶ Getting There & Away

Most hotels are located at least 1km off the road at the base of the dunes, but all are accessible by car. Supratours has a daily service to Marrakesh (Dh185) and there are plentiful *grands taxis* to Rissani (and further transport).

UNDERSTAND MOROCCO

Morocco Today

Mohammed VI has ruled since 1999 and overseen small but reformist steps, including elections, and the Mudawanna, a legal code protecting women's rights to divorce and custody. The king has also forged closer ties with Europe and overseen a tourism boom, aided in great part by the arrival of European budget airlines. Morocco's human-rights record is one of the cleaner in North Africa and the Middle East, though repressive measures were revived after September 11 and the 2003 Casablanca bombings.

Clever politicking by Mohammed VI saw the sting drawn from the Arab Spring when revolutionary events overtook Tunisia and Egypt. The nascent 20 February protest movement was overtaken by the announcement of a new constitution in 2011, drafted without consultation but approved in a national referendum. Amazigh, the main Berber language, was granted official language status, although political power continues to be concentrated in the palace rather than in a move to a more constitutional monarchy.

History

Berbers & Romans

Morocco's first-known inhabitants were Near Eastern nomads who may have been distant cousins of the ancient Egyptians. Phoenicians appear to have arrived around 800 BC. When the Romans arrived in the 4th century BC, they called the expanse of Morocco and western Algeria 'Mauretania' and the indigenous people 'Berbers', meaning 'barbarians'.

In the 1st century AD, the Romans built up Volubilis into a city of 20,000 (mostly Berber) people, but emperor Caligula declared the end of Berber autonomy in North Africa in AD 40. However, Berber rebellions in the Rif and the Atlas ultimately succeeded through a campaign of near-constant harassment.

As Rome slipped into decline, the Berbers harried and hassled any army that dared to invade, to the point where the Berbers were free to do as they pleased.

Islamic Dynasties

In the second half of the 7th century, the soldiers of the Prophet Mohammed set forth from the Arabian Peninsula. Within a century, nearly all the Berber tribes of North Africa had embraced Islam, although local tribes developed their own brand of Islamic Shi'ism, which sparked rebellion against the eastern Arabs.

By 829, local elites had established an Idrissid state, with its capital at Fez, dominating Morocco. Thus commenced a cycle of rising and falling Islamic dynasties, which included the Almoravids (1062–1147), who built their capital at Marrakesh; the Almohads (1147–1269), famous for building the Koutoubia Mosque; the Merenids (1269–1465), known for their exquisite mosques and *madrassas* (Quranic schools), especially in Fez; the Saadians (1524–1659), responsible for the Palais el-Badi in Marrakesh; and the Alawites (1659–present), who left their greatest monuments in Meknès.

France took control in 1912, making its capital at Rabat and handing Spain a token zone in the north. Opposition from Berber mountain tribes continued to simmer away and moved into political channels with the development of the Istiqlal (independence) party. Sultan Mohammed V proved vocally supportive of movements opposing colonial rule and was exiled for his pains.

Morocco Since Independence

France allowed Mohammed V to return from exile in 1955, and Morocco successfully negotiated its independence from France and Spain in 1956.

When Mohammed V died in 1961, King Hassan II became the leader of the new nation. Hassan II consolidated power by cracking down on dissent and suspending parliament for a decade. With heavy borrowing and an ever-expanding bureaucracy, Morocco was deeply in debt by the 1970s.

In 1973 the phosphate industry in the Spanish Sahara started to boom. Morocco staked its claim to the area with the 350,000-strong Green March into Western Sahara in 1975. It settled the area with Moroccans while greatly unsettling indigenous Sahrawi people agitating for self-determination. The UN brokered a cease-fire in 1991, but the promised referendum, in which the Sahrawis could choose between independence and integration with Morocco, has yet to materialise, and Western Sahara's status remains undecided in international law.

However, the growing gap between the rich and the poor ensured that dissent against the regime was widespread. Protests against price rises in 1981 prompted a government crackdown, but sustained pressure from human-rights activists achieved unprecedented results in 1991, when Hassan II founded the Truth and Reconciliation Commission to investigate human-rights abuses that occurred during his own reign – a first for a king.

Culture

Culturally, Moroccans cast their eyes in many directions – to Europe, the economically dominant neighbour; to the east and the lands of Islam; and to their traditional Berber heartland. The result is an intoxicating blend of the modern and the traditional, the liberal and the conservative, hospitality and the need to make a dirham. Away from the tourist scrum, a Moroccan proverb tells the story – 'A guest is a gift from Allah'. The public domain may belong to men, but they're just as likely to invite you home to meet the family. If this happens, consider yourself truly privileged, but remember to keep your left hand firmly out of the communal dish.

In present-day Morocco, *jellabas* (flowing cloaks) cover Western suits, turbans jostle with baseball caps, European dance music competes with sinuous Algerian rai and mobile phones ring in the midst of perhaps the greatest of all Moroccan pastimes – the serious and exuberant art of conversation. An inherently social people, Moroccans have a heightened sense of mischief, love a good laugh and will take your decision to visit their country as an invitation to talk...and drink tea and perhaps buy a carpet, a very beautiful carpet, just for the pleasure of your eyes...

People

Morocco's population is of mixed Arab-Berber descent. The population is young, growing and increasingly urbanised. Nearly 60% of Moroccans live in cities and the median age is just 25 years and decreasing – two trends that present the country with clear social and economic challenges. Fundamentalism is discouraged but remains a presence – especially among the urban poor, who have enjoyed none of the benefits of economic growth. That said, the majority of Muslims do not favour such developments and the popularity of fundamentalism is not as great as Westerners imagine.

Emigration to France, Israel and the US has reduced Morocco's once-robust Jewish community to approximately 7000 from a high of around 300,000 in 1948. The Jewish communities that once inhabited the historic *mellahs* (Jewish quarters) of Fez, Marrakesh, Essaouira and Meknès have largely relocated to Casablanca.

Arts & Crafts

Architecture

Moroccan religious buildings are adorned with hand-carved detailing, gilded accents, chiselled mosaics and an array of other decorative flourishes. A mosque consists of a courtyard, an arcaded portico and a main prayer hall facing Mecca. Great examples include the 9th-century Kairaouine Mosque in Fez and the colossal Hassan II Mosque in Casablanca. While all but the latter are closed to non-Muslims, the *madrassas* that bejewel major Moroccan cities are open for visits.

Although religious architecture dominates, Casablanca in particular boasts local architectural features grafted onto whitewashed European edifices in a distinctive crossroads style that might be described as Islamic geometry meets art deco.

The street facades of the Moroccan riads (traditional courtyard houses; also called *dars*) usually conceal an inner courtyard that allows light to penetrate during the day and cool air to settle at night. Many classy guesthouses occupy beautifully renovated traditional riads.

Music

The most renowned Berber folk group is the Master Musicians of Jajouka, who famously inspired the Rolling Stones and collaborated with them on some truly experimental fusion. Joyously bluesy with a rhythm you can't refuse, Gnaoua music, which began among freed slaves in Marrakesh and Essaouira, may send you into a trance – and that's just what it's meant to do. To sample the best Gnaoua, head to Essaouira on the third weekend in June for the Gnaoua & World Music Festival.

Rai, originally from Algeria, is one of the strongest influences on Moroccan contemporary music, incorporating elements of jazz, hip-hop and rap. A popular artist is Cheb Mami, famous for vocals on Sting's 'Desert Rose'.

Food & Drink

Influenced by Berber, Arabic and Mediterranean traditions, Moroccan cuisine features a sublime use of spices and fresh produce.

It would be a culinary crime to skip breakfast in Morocco. Sidewalk cafes and kiosks put a local twist on a Continental breakfast, with Moroccan pancakes and doughnuts, French pastries, coffee and mint tea. Follow your nose into the souqs, where you'll find tangy olives and local *jiben* (fresh goat's or cow's milk cheeses) to be devoured with fresh *khoobz* (Moroccan-style pita bread baked in a wood-fired oven).

Lunch is traditionally the biggest meal of the day in Morocco. The most typical Moroccan dish is tajine, a meat-and-vegetable stew cooked slowly in an earthenware dish. Couscous, fluffy steamed semolina served with tender meat and vegetables, is another staple. Fish dishes also make an excellent choice in coastal areas, while *harira* is a thick soup made from lamb stock, lentils, chickpeas, onions, tomatoes, fresh herbs and spices. *Bastilla,* a speciality of Fez, includes poultry (chicken or pigeon), almonds, cinnamon, saffron and sugar, encased in layer upon layer of very fine pastry.

Vegetarians shouldn't have any problems – fresh fruit and vegetables are widely available, as are lentils and chickpeas. Salads are ubiquitous, particularly *salade marocaine* made from diced green peppers, tomatoes and onion. Ask for your couscous or tajine *sans viande* (without meat), or go for beans *(loubiya)* or pea-and-garlic soup *(bsara)*.

For dessert, Moroccan patisseries concoct excellent French and Moroccan sweets. Local sweets include flaky pastries rich with nuts and aromatic traces of orange-flower water. Another variation is a *bastilla,* with toasted almonds, cinnamon and cream.

Cafe culture is alive and well in Morocco, and mint tea – the legendary 'Moroccan whisky' – is made with Chinese gunpowder tea, fresh mint and copious amounts of sugar. Fruit juices, especially freshly squeezed orange juice, are the country's greatest bargain. It's not advisable to drink tap water in Morocco. Beer is easy to find in the Villes Nouvelles – local brands include Casablanca and Flag. Morocco also produces some surprisingly good wines from the Meknès area: try President Cabernet and Medallion Cabernet for reds, or the whites Coquillages and Sémillant Blanc.

Environment

Morocco's three ecological zones – coast, mountain and desert – host more than 40 different ecosystems and provide habitat for many endemic species, including the iconic and sociable Barbary macaque (also known as the Barbary ape). The pressure upon these ecosystems from ever-more-sprawling urban areas and the encroachment of industrialisation in Morocco's wilderness has ensured that 18 mammal and 11 bird species are considered endangered.

Pollution, desertification, overgrazing and deforestation are the major environmental issues facing Morocco. Despite plantation programs and the development of new national parks, less than 0.05% of Moroccan territory is protected, one-third of Morocco's ecosystems are disappearing, 10% of vertebrates are endangered and 25,000 hectares of forest are lost every year.

SURVIVAL GUIDE

ℹ️ Directory A–Z

ACCOMMODATION

Hotels vary dramatically, ranging from dingy dives to fancy five-star options (the latter mostly in larger cities). Cities that see many tourists also offer gorgeous guesthouses in the style of a riad (traditional courtyard house).

Expect to pay up to Dh400 for budget-style accommodation, Dh400 to Dh800 for midrange and over Dh800 for top end. Exceptions to this are Casablanca, Essaouira, Fez, Rabat and Tangier, where budget accommodation may cost up to Dh600, midrange Dh600 to Dh1200 and top end more than Dh1200. Places include a private bathroom unless otherwise stated. Prices given are for high season and include tax; always check the price you are quoted is TTC (all taxes included).

Advance reservations are highly recommended for most places, especially in summer.

ACTIVITIES

Camel Treks & Desert Safaris

Exploring the Moroccan Sahara by camel is one of the country's signature activities and one of the most rewarding wilderness experiences, whether done on an overnight excursion or a two-week trek. The most evocative stretches of Saharan sand are Erg Chigaga (the Drâa Valley) and Erg Chebbi (Merzouga).

Autumn (September to October) and winter (November to early March) are the only seasons worth considering. Prices hover around Dh350 to Dh450 per person per day but vary depending on the number of people involved and the length of the trek.

Hammams

Visiting a *hammam* (traditional bathhouse) is a ritual at the centre of Moroccan society. Every town has at least one public *hammam*, and the big cities have fancy spas – both are deep-cleaning and relaxing. A visit to a standard *hammam* usually costs Dh10, with a massage costing an extra Dh15 or so.

Hiking

Morocco is a superb destination for mountain lovers, offering a variety of year-round hiking possibilities. It's relatively straightforward to arrange guides, porters and mules for a more independent adventure. Jebel Toubkal (4167m), the highest peak in the High Atlas, attracts the lion's share of visitors, but great possibilities exist throughout the country, including in the Rif Mountains around Chefchaouen. The Dadès and Todra Gorges also offer good hiking opportunities. Spring and autumn are the best seasons for trekking.

EMBASSIES & CONSULATES

For details of all Moroccan embassies abroad and foreign embassies in Morocco, go to www.maec.gov.ma.

Many countries have representation in Rabat. Ireland has no embassy, but some consular services are provided by the Canadian embassy.

Belgian Embassy (☑0537 268060; info@ambabel-rabat.org.ma; 6 Ave de Marrakesh)

Canadian Embassy (☑0537 687400; fax 0537 687430; 13 Rue Jaafar as-Sadiq, Agdal)

French Embassy (☑0537 689700; www.ambafrance-ma.org; 3 Rue Sahnoun, Agdal) There is also a French Consulate-general (☑037 268181; Rue Alla Ben Abdallah, Rabat; ⊙visa applications 8.30-11.30am Mon-Fri, visa pick-up 1.30-3pm Mon-Fri). Consulates-General are also in Agadir, Casablanca, Tangier, Marrakesh and Fez.

German Embassy (☑0537 709662; www.amballemagne-rabat.ma; 7 Rue Madnine)

Italian Embassy (☑0537 706598; ambaciata@iambitalia.ma; 2 Rue Idriss el-Azhar)

Japanese Embassy (☑0537 631782; fax 0537 750078; 39 Ave Ahmed Balafrej, Souissi)

Mauritanian Embassy (☑0537 656678; ambassadeur@mauritanie.org.ma; 7 Rue Thami Lamdaouar, Soussi)

Dutch Embassy (☑0537 219600; nlgovrab@mtds.com; 40 Rue de Tunis)

Spanish Embassy (☑0537 633900; emb.rabat@mae.es; Rue Ain Khalouiya, Km 5.300, Rte des Zaers, Souissi) Consulates are also located in Agadir, Casablanca, Nador, Rabat, Tangier and Tetouan.

UK Embassy (☑0537 238600; www.britain.org.ma; 17 Blvd de la Tour Hassan)

US Embassy (☑0537 762265; www.usembassy.ma; 2 Ave de Marrakesh)

EMERGENCIES

Ambulance (☑15)
Fire (☑16)
Police (☑19)

FESTIVALS & EVENTS

Religious festivals are significant for Moroccans. Local *moussems* (saints days) are held all over the country throughout the year and some draw big crowds. The Fez Festival of World Sacred Music (p273) is always a favourite.

Gnaoua & World Music Festival (www.festival-gnaoua.co.ma; Essaouira) Held in June.

Moussem of Moulay Idriss II (Fez) September/October.

GAY & LESBIAN TRAVELLERS

Homosexual acts are officially illegal in Morocco. Discretion is the key and public displays of affection should be avoided (aggression towards gay travellers is not unheard of). This advice applies equally to heterosexual couples.

Marrakesh and Tangier are more gay-friendly, with 'gay' bars found here and there. Lesbians shouldn't encounter any problems.

It is also worth bearing in mind that the pressures of poverty mean some young men will consider having sex for money or gifts; and exploitative relationships can be an unpleasant dimension of the Moroccan gay scene.

INTERNET ACCESS

Internet access is widely available, efficient and cheap (Dh5 to Dh10 per hour) in internet cafes. One irritant for travellers is the widespread use of French or Arabic (non-qwerty) keyboards.

Most top-end and many midrange hotels offer wi-fi, and it's more or less standard in most riads and maisons d'hôtes.

MONEY

The Moroccan currency is the dirham (Dh), which is divided into 100 centimes. It's forbidden to take dirhams out of the country. The Spanish enclaves of Ceuta and Melilla use the euro.

ATMs (guichets automatiques) are widespread and generally take international bank cards. Major credit cards are widely accepted in the main tourist centres. Australian, Canadian and New Zealand dollars are not quoted in banks and are not usually accepted.

Tipping

Tipping and bargaining are integral parts of Moroccan life. Practically any service can warrant a tip, and a few dirham for a service willingly rendered can make your life a lot easier. Tipping between 5% and 10% of a restaurant bill is appropriate.

OPENING HOURS

Cafes 7am to 11pm.

Restaurants Noon to 3pm and 7pm to 11pm.

Shops 9am to 12.30pm and 2.30pm to 8pm Monday to Saturday (often closed longer from noon on Friday).

Tourist offices 8.30am to 12.30pm and 2.30pm to 6.30pm Monday to Thursday.

POST

Post offices are distinguished by the 'PTT' sign or the 'La Poste' logo. You can sometimes buy stamps at tabacs, the small tobacco and newspaper kiosks you see scattered about the main city centres.

The postal system is fairly reliable but not terribly fast. The parcel office, indicated by the sign 'colis postaux', is generally in a separate part of the post-office building. Take your parcel unwrapped for customs inspection. Some parcel offices sell boxes.

PUBLIC HOLIDAYS

All banks, post offices and most shops are shut on the main public holidays.

PRACTICALITIES

➡ **Newspapers** For a full list of Moroccan newspapers online, go to **onlinenewspapers.com.** (www.onlinenewspapers.com/morocco.htm)

➡ **Radio** Moroccan radio encompasses a handful of local AM and FM stations, the bulk of which broadcast in either Arabic or French. Midi 1 at 97.5 FM covers northern Morocco, Algeria and Tunisia, and plays reasonable contemporary music.

➡ **TV** Satellite dishes are everywhere in Morocco and pick up dozens of foreign stations. There are two government-owned stations, TVM and 2M, which broadcast in Arabic and French.

➡ **Electricity** Electric current is 220V/50Hz but older buildings may still use 110V. Moroccan sockets accept the European round two-pin plugs.

➡ **Languages** Moroccan Arabic (Darija), French and Berber.

New Year's Day 1 January

Independence Manifesto 11 January

Labour Day 1 May

Feast of the Throne 30 July

Allegiance of Oued-Eddahab 14 August

Anniversary of the King's and People's Revolution 20 August

Young People's Day 21 August

Anniversary of the Green March 6 November

Independence Day 18 November

In addition to secular holidays there are many national and local Islamic holidays and festivals, all tied to the lunar calendar.

Eïd al-Adha Marks the end of the Islamic year. Most things shut down for four or five days.

Eïd al-Fitr Held at the end of the month-long Ramadan fast, which is observed by most Muslims. The festivities last four or five days, during which Morocco grinds to a halt. Ramadan will most likely fall in summer when you read this.

Mawlid an-Nabi (Mouloud) Celebrates the birthday of the Prophet Mohammed.

SAFE TRAVEL

Plenty of kif (marijuana) is grown in the Rif Mountains, but possession is illegal and drug busts are common.

A few years ago the brigade touristique (tourist police) was set up in the principal tourist centres to clamp down on Morocco's notorious faux guides and hustlers. Anyone convicted of operating as an unofficial guide faces jail time and/or a huge fine. This has reduced but not eliminated the problem of faux guides. You'll still find plenty of these touts hanging around the entrances to medinas and train stations (and even on trains approaching Fez and Marrakesh), and at Tangier port. Remember that their main interest is the commission gained from certain hotels or on articles sold to you in the souqs.

If possible, avoid walking alone at night in the medinas of the big cities; knife-point muggings aren't unknown.

TELEPHONE

Privately run Téléboutiques can be found in every town and village on almost every corner. Public payphones are card operated, with télécartes (phonecards) sold in general stores and news kiosks.

All domestic phone calls in Morocco require a 10-digit number, which includes the four-digit area code. The country code is ☑ 212.

Morocco has three GSM mobile phone networks, Méditel, Maroc Telecom and Inwi, which cover 90% of the population. A local SIM card costs around Dh20; top-up scratch cards are sold everywhere.

TOURIST INFORMATION

The national tourism body, **Office National Marocain du Tourisme** (ONMT; www.visit-morocco.com), has offices in the main cities, with the head office in Rabat. These offices are often called Délégation Régionale du Tourisme. Regional offices, called Syndicat d'Initiative, are to be found in smaller towns. Most tourist offices inside Morocco offer little more than standard brochures and helpless smiles.

VISAS

Most visitors to Morocco do not require visas and are allowed to remain in the country for 90 days on entry. Exceptions to this include nationals of Israel, and most sub-Saharan African countries (including South Africa). Moroccan embassies have been known to insist that you get a visa from your country of origin. Should the standard 90-day stay be insufficient, it is possible (but difficult) to apply at the nearest police headquarters (Préfecture de Police) for an extension – it's simpler to leave (eg travel to the Spanish enclaves of Ceuta and Melilla) and come back a few days later. Your chances improve if you re-enter by a different route. The Spanish enclaves have the same visa requirements as mainland Spain.

Visas for Onward Travel

Algeria Although Algeria has now emerged from over a decade of civil war, the border with Morocco remains closed and visas are not being issued.

Mauritania Everyone, except nationals of Arab League countries and some African countries, needs a visa, which is valid for a one-month stay. These are issued in 24 hours at the Mauritanian embassy in Rabat (apply before noon). Visas cost Dh340, with two photos and a passport photocopy. An onward air ticket to Nouakchott is not required. Get to the embassy well before the 9am opening time, and be prepared to fight for your place in the queue.

WOMEN TRAVELLERS

Women can expect a certain level of sexual harassment when travelling in Morocco. It comes in the form of nonstop greetings, leering and other unwanted attention but is rarely dangerous. If possible, it's best to try and ignore this attention. Women can save themselves a great deal of grief by avoiding eye contact, dressing to cover their knees and shoulders, and refraining from walking around alone at night.

ℹ Getting There & Away

AIR

Morocco's two main international entry points are **Mohammed V international airport** (☑ 022 539040; www.onda.ma), 30km southeast of Casablanca, and Marrakesh's **Ménara Airport** (☑ 0524 447865). Other international airports are in Fez, Tangier and Agadir.

International Airlines in Morocco

Air Algérie (AH; ☑ 0522 314181; www.air algerie.dz)

Air France (www.airfrance.com)

Alitalia (AZ; ☑ 0522 314181; www.alitalia.it)

British Airways (BA; ☑ 0522 229464; www.ba.com)

EasyJet (EZY; www.easyjet.com)

Iberia (IB; ☑ 0522 279600; www.iberia.com)

KLM-Royal Dutch Airlines (KL; ☑ 0522 203222; www.klm.com)

Lufthansa Airlines (LH; ☑ 0522 312371; www.lufthansa.com)

Royal Air Maroc (RAM; ☑ 0522 311122; www.royalairmaroc.com)

Ryanair (www.ryanair.com)

Tunis Air (TU; ☑ 0522 293452; www.tunisair.com.tn)

LAND

The Moroccan bus company **CTM** (☑ in Casablanca 0522 458080; www.CTM.co.ma) operates buses from Casablanca and most other main cities to France, Belgium, Spain, Germany and Italy. It's part of the **Eurolines** (www.euro lines.com) consortium.

Algeria

The border with Algeria has been closed since 1994 and is not expected to open any time soon.

Mauritania

The trans-Saharan route via Mauritania is now the most popular route from North Africa into sub-Saharan Africa. This crosses the internationally disputed territory of Western Sahara, although the border itself is administered by Morocco.

The only border crossing between Morocco/Western Sahara and Mauritania is at Guegarat, north of Nouâdhibou. Crossing this border is straightforward and the road is entirely tarred to Nouakchott, except for the 3km no-man's-land that separates the two border posts. For more detailed information see p253.

SEA

Regular ferries run to Europe from several ports along Morocco's Mediterranean coast. The most trafficked is Tangier, from where there are boats to Algeciras (60 to 70 minutes) and Tarifa (35 minutes, five daily) in Spain, and Gibraltar. Ferries also run from Ceuta to Algeciras. Typical fares are around €35. Bringing a bicycle costs €8 to €15 extra, while a car adds €60 to €80. Children are half price.

ⓘ Getting Around

AIR

Royal Air Maroc (RAM; 0890 000800; www.royalairmaroc.com) dominates the Moroccan airline industry, with Casablanca as its hub. For most routes, flying is an expensive and inconvenient option compared to road or rail.

BUS

A dense network of buses operates throughout Morocco, with many private companies competing for business alongside the comfortable and modern buses of the main national carrier, CTM (p292).

The ONCF (p293) train company runs buses through Supratours to widen its train network; for example, running connections from Marrekesh to Essaouira. Morocco's other bus companies are all privately owned and only operate regionally. It's best to book ahead for CTM and Supratours buses, which are slightly more expensive than those of other companies.

CAR & MOTORCYCLE

Taking your own vehicle to Morocco is straightforward. In addition to a vehicle registration document and an International Driving Permit (many foreign licences, including US and EU ones, are acceptable), a Green Card is required from the car's insurer. Not all insurers cover Morocco.

Renting a car in Morocco isn't cheap, with prices starting at Dh3500 per week or Dh500 per day for a basic car with unlimited mileage. International rental companies are well represented; booking in advance online secures the best deals.

In Morocco drive on the right-hand side. On a roundabout, give way to traffic entering from the right.

LOCAL TRANSPORT

Cities and bigger towns have local *petits taxis*. They are not permitted to go beyond the city limits, are licensed to carry up to three passengers and are usually metered. Fares increase by 50% after 8pm.

The old Mercedes vehicles belting along roads and gathered in great flocks near bus stations are *grands taxis* (shared taxis), linking towns to their nearest neighbours. *Grands taxis* take six cramped passengers and leave when full.

TRAIN

Morocco's train network is run by **ONCF** (www.oncf.org.ma). There are two lines that carry passengers: from Tangier in the north down to Marrakesh; and from Oujda in the northeast, also to Marrakesh, joining with the Tangier line at Sidi Kacem.

Trains are comfortable, fast and generally preferable to buses. There are different 1st- and 2nd-class fares, but 2nd class is usually more than adequate on any journey. Couchettes are available on the overnight trains between Marrakesh and Tangier. Children aged under four travel free. Those aged between four and 12 years get a reduction of 10% to 50%, depending on the service.

Niger

Fast Facts

➡ **Capital** Niamey

➡ **Population** 16.3 million

➡ **Languages** French, Hausa, Djerma, Fulfulde, Tamashek

➡ **Area** 1,267,000 sq km

➡ **Currency** CFA franc

➡ **Visa requirements** A tourist visa is required, valid for three months

➡ **Tourist information** www.friendsofniger.org

Haunting Desertscapes & Ancient Cities

Niger only seems to make the news for negative reasons: its recent coup, the Tuareg Rebellion, a devastating famine. But visit this desert republic and you'll find a warm and generous Muslim population and superb tout-free travel through ancient caravan cities at the edge of the Sahara.

To the north, the stark splendour of the Aïr Mountains hides Neolithic rock art and stunning oasis towns. Within the expansive dunes of the Ténéré Desert you'll find dinosaur graveyards and deserted medieval settlements. Head south and the ancient trans-Saharan trade-route town of Agadez and the sultanate of Zinder are home to magnificent mazes of mudbrick architecture. For nature lovers, there's the fantastically diverse Parc Regional du W and herds of wild giraffes at Kouré.

The security situation meant that much of Niger was off limits to travellers at the time of writing. Attacks against foreigners have occurred across the Sahel, and the threat of kidnapping remains high.

Niger Top Sights

➡ **Agadez** Spiral up to the spiky summit of a majestic mud mosque for incredible views over the Sahara and beyond

➡ **Kouré** Wander in wonder with West Africa's last wild herd of giraffes

➡ **Zinder** Explore the Birni Quartier and soak up the brutal history at the sultan's palace in this fascinating Hausa city

➡ **Parc Regional du W** Come face to face with lions, crocodiles, monkeys and elephants in this incredibly diverse national park

➡ **Ténéré Desert** Dive into the deep end with an expedition to this sublime section of the Sahara

➡ **Aïr Mountains** Make tracks with camels through red sands and blue rocks in these mystical mountains

UNDERSTAND NIGER

Niger Today

A series of unpleasant events have defined Niger to the outside world in recent years. In 2007 the Tuareg in the north of the country began a rebellion against Niger's government, whom it accused of hoarding proceeds from the region's enormous mineral wealth and failing to meet conditions of previous ceasefires, in a conflict that has reignited at regular intervals since the early 20th century.

A year later Niger again made headlines around the world for less-than-positive reasons when in a landmark case an Economic Community of West African States (Ecowas) court found Niger guilty of failing to protect a young woman from the continued practice of slavery in the country. According to anti-slavery organisations, thousands of people still live in subjugation (see p389).

There have been several high-profile kidnappings of tourists and foreign workers over the past few years by gunmen linked to al-Qaeda factions operating in the Sahel and Sahara zone – in April and September 2010 near Arlit, and in January 2011 near Niamey. The Islamist takeover of northern Mali in 2012 created a security vacuum and opened up a safe haven for extremists and organised-crime groups in the Sahara desert. Tens of thousands of refugees flooded into the country.

The country's main export, uranium, is prone to price fluctuations and the industry has been hurt by the threat of terrorism and kidnapping. Niger began producing and refining oil in 2011 following a US$5 billion joint-venture deal with China.

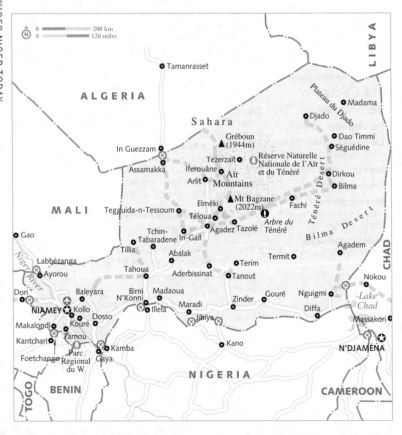

History

Before the Sahara started swallowing Niger around 2500 BC, it supported verdant grasslands, abundant wildlife and populations thriving on hunting and herding. Long after the desert pushed those populations southward, Niger became a fixture on the trans-Saharan trade route. Between the 10th and 18th centuries, West African empires, such as the Kanem-Borno, Mali and Songhaï, flourished in Niger, trafficking gold, salt and slaves.

The French strolled in late in the 1800s, meeting stronger-than-expected resistance. Decidedly unamused, they dispatched the punitive Voulet-Chanoîne expedition, destroying much of southern Niger in 1898–99. Although Tuareg revolts continued, culminating in Agadez's siege in 1916–17, the French had control.

French rule wasn't kind. They cultivated the power of traditional chiefs, whose abuses were encouraged as a means of control, and the enforced shift from subsistence farming to high-density cash crops compounded the Sahara's ongoing migration.

In 1958 France offered its West African colonies self-government in a French union or immediate independence. Countless votes disappeared, enabling France to claim that Niger wished to remain within its sphere of influence.

Maintaining close French ties, Niger's first president, Hamani Diori, ran a repressive one-party state. After surviving several coups, he was overthrown by Lieutenant Colonel Seyni Kountché after food stocks were discovered in ministerial homes during the Sahel drought of 1968–74. Kountché established a military ruling council.

Kountché hit the jackpot in 1968 when uranium was discovered near the town of Arlit. Mining incomes soon ballooned, leading to ambitious projects, including the 'uranium highway' between Agadez and Arlit. Yet not everyone was smiling: inflation skyrocketed and the poorest suffered more than ever.

The 1980s were unkind to all: uranium prices collapsed, the great 1983 drought killed thousands, and one-party politics hindered democracy. By the 1990s, Nigeriens were aware of political changes sweeping West Africa and mass demonstrations erupted, eventually forcing the government into multiparty elections in 1993. However, a military junta overthrew the elected president, Mahamane Ousmane, in 1996.

ℹ COUNTRY COVERAGE

At the time of research very few travellers were heading to Niger so we're providing historical and cultural information rather than reviews and listings. A good source of information for on-the-ground travel in Niger is Lonely Planet's Thorn Tree on-line travel forum www.lonelyplanet.com/thorntree. Other sources of good internet-based information are www.friendsofniger.org and http://voyageforum.com/forum/niger/.

In 1999, during widespread strikes and economic stagnation, president Mainassara (a 1996 coup leader) was assassinated and democracy re-established. Peaceful elections in 1999 and 2004 witnessed victory for Mamadou Tandja.

In 2009 Mamadou Tandja won a referendum allowing him to change the constitution to allow him to run for a third term. In the presidential elections that year Tandja won by a large margin, though Ecowas did not accept the result and suspended Niger's membership. The tables were turned on Tandja in February 2010 when a military coup in Niamey led to his arrest. A year-long military junta ended when veteran opposition leader Mahamadou Issoufou was declared winner of a presidential poll in March 2011.

Culture

Niger boasts the highest birth rate in the world: women have a staggering average of eight children each. The population is predicted to reach 21.4 million by 2025.

More than 90% of Nigeriens live in the south, which is dominated by Hausa and Songhaï-Djerma, making up 56% and 23% of Niger's populace respectively. The next largest groups are nomadic Fulani (8.5%) and Tuareg (8%), both in Niger's north, and Kanuri (4.3%), located between Zinder and Chad.

Nigeriens are predominantly Muslim (over 90%), with small percentages of Christian urban dwellers. Several rural populations still practise traditional animist religions. Due to the strong influence of Nigeria's Islamic community, some Muslims around the border town of Maradi call for sharia law.

Despite most Nigeriens being devoutly Muslim, the government is steadfastly secular and Islam adopts a more relaxed aura than in nations with similar demographics. Women don't cover their faces, alcohol is quietly consumed and some Tuareg, recognising the harshness of desert life, ignore Ramadan's fast.

While Islam plays the greatest role in daily life, shaping beliefs and thoughts, little is visible to visitors. The biggest exceptions are *salat* (prayer), when Niger grinds to a halt – buses even break journeys to partake.

Religion aside, survival occupies most people's days. Around 90% make their tenuous living from agriculture and livestock, many surviving on US$1 or less per day. Producing numerous children to help with burdening workloads is a necessity for many, a fact contributing to population growth. The fact of children being obliged to work has led to staggering adult illiteracy rates.

Niger's best-known artisans are Tuareg silversmiths, who produce necklaces, striking amulets, ornamental silver daggers and stylised silver crosses, each with intricate filigree designs representing areas boasting Tuareg populations. The most famous cross is the *croix d'Agadez*. To Tuareg, crosses are powerful talismans protecting against ill fortune.

Leatherwork by *artisans du cuir* is well regarded, particularly in Zinder, where traditional items – such as saddlebags, cushions and tasselled pouches – rank alongside attractive modernities like sandals and briefcases.

Beautifully unique to Niger are vibrant *kountas* (Djerma blankets), produced from bright cotton strips.

Food & Drink

Dates, yoghurt, rice and mutton are standard Tuareg fare, while *riz sauce* (rice with sauce) is omnipresent in Niger's south. Standard restaurant dishes include grilled fish (particularly capitaine, or Nile perch), chicken, and beef *brochettes* (kebabs). Couscous and ragout are also popular. Outside Niamey vegetarian options diminish.

Sitting for a cup of Tuareg tea is rewarding and thirst-quenching. For a wobble in your step, try Bière Niger. For a serious stagger, down some palm wine.

Environment

Three-quarters of Niger is desert, with the Sahara advancing 10km a year. The remaining quarter is Sahel, the semidesert zone south of the Sahara. Notable features include the Niger River (Africa's third-longest), which flows 300km through Niger's southwest; the Aïr Mountains, the dark volcanic formations of which rise over 2000m; and the Ténéré Desert's spectacularly sweeping sand dunes.

Desertification, Niger's greatest environmental problem, is primarily caused by overgrazing and deforestation. Quartz-rich soil also prevents topsoil from anchoring, causing erosion.

The southwest's dry savannah woodland hosts one of West Africa's better wildlife parks, Parc Regional du W.

Nigeria

📞 234 / POP 162 MILLION

Best Places to Shake Your 'Yansh'

➡ New Afrika Shrine (p304)

➡ Elegushi Beach (p305)

➡ Likwid (p305)

Best Places to Worship Orishas

➡ Osun Sacred Grove (p310)

➡ Oòni's Palace (p310)

➡ Olumo Rock (p308)

Why Go?

Nigeria is a pulsating powerhouse: as the most populous nation on the continent it dominates the region economically and culturally, spreading the fruits of its rapid development throughout Africa with fury. Lagos, Nigeria's main city, is bursting at the seams: with burgeoning technology and telecommunications industries, posh restaurants and clubs, and an absolutely exploding music and arts scene, this megacity is the face of modern Africa.

In villages and towns outside Gidi (as Lagosians call their city), you may often feel as if you're a lone explorer getting a glimpse of the raw edges of the world. Immersing yourself in the deep and layered cultures, histories, and surroundings – from the ancient Muslim cities of the north to the river deltas, from Yoruba kingdoms and spiritual shrines to the legacy of tribal conflict and the slave ports, and among simply stunning natural environments – provides a worthy antidote to a sometimes exhausting journey.

When to Go
Lagos

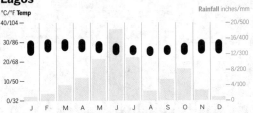

Oct–Jan Your best bet for dry weather.

Dec–Jan Lots of events and festivals; also the busiest (and most expensive) time of year.

Jun–Aug Nigeria's rainy season and usually quite wet, but not necessary to avoid.

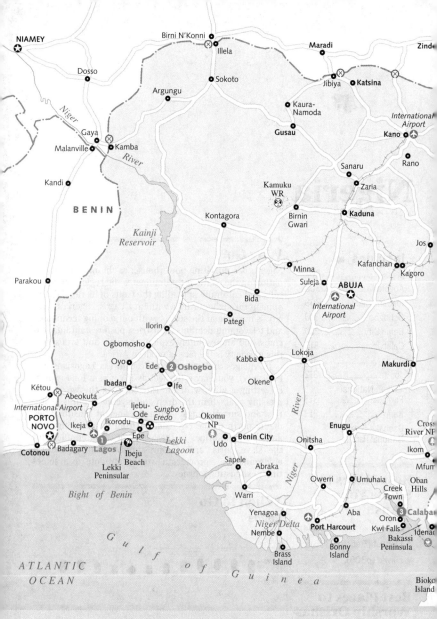

Nigeria Highlights

1 Joining the gold rush of **Lagos** (p302), the newly moneyed, fastest growing, and largest African city on the continent.

2 Learning about the traditional arts and ancient spiritual shrines in **Oshogbo** (p310), the centre of Yoruba culture.

3 Taking in colonial history and cutting-edge conservation in the easygoing old river port, **Calabar** (p310).

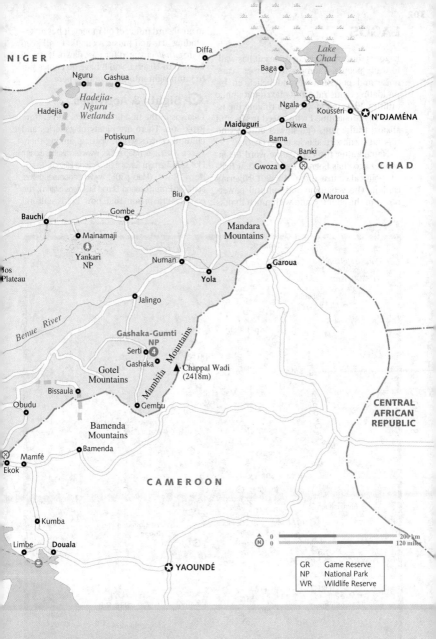

NIGER

Diffa

Lake
Chad

Baga

Nguru Gashua

Hadejia

*Hadejia-
Nguru
Wetlands*

Ngala Kousséri ☆ N'DJAMÉNA

Maiduguri Dikwa

Potiskum Bama

Banki

CHAD

Gwoza

Biu Maroua

Bauchi Gombe Mandara
Mountains

Mainamaji

Yankari
NP

Numan Garoua

Jos
Plateau Yola

Jalingo

Benue River

Gashaka-Gumti
NP

Serti ●❹

Gashaka Chappal Wadi
(2418m)

Gotel
Mountains

Mambila Mountains

CENTRAL
AFRICAN
REPUBLIC

Bissaula

Obudu Gembu

Bamenda
Mountains

Mamfé Bamenda

Ekok

CAMEROON

Kumba

Limbe Douala

☆ YAOUNDÉ

Ⓝ 0   200 km
    0   120 miles

GR	Game Reserve
NP	National Park
WR	Wildlife Reserve

❹ Heading into the real wilds
to explore, **Gashaka-Gumti
National Park** (p314), a newly
reorganised mountain-meets-
savannah national park.

LAGOS

⌐ 01 / POP 25 MILLION

Lagos is the largest city in Africa; it has wall-to-wall people, bumper-to-bumper cars, noise and pollution beyond belief, an intimidating crime rate, and maxed-out public utilities. Elevated motorways ringing the island city are jammed with speed freaks and absurd traffic jams ('go-slows') on top, and tin-and-cardboard shacks underneath.

Named after the Portuguese word for lagoon, Lagos has been a Yoruba port, a British political centre and, until 1991, Nigeria's capital. The economic and cultural powerhouse of the country, and with much thanks to an absurd influx of oil money, it has an exploding arts and music scene that will keep your *yansh* engaged far past dawn. If you're headed to Nigeria, you'll have no choice but to jump right into the madness here.

⊙ Sights & Activities

Lagos is in the middle of an arts and culture explosion. There are plenty of galleries and cultural centres worth visiting, among them **Terra Kulture** (Map p308; www.terrakulture.com; Plot 1376 Tiamiyu Savage St, Victoria Island), **Freedom Park** (Map p306; www.freedomparklagos.com; Old Prison Ground, Broad St, Lagos Island), the colonial-era prison that now holds cultural

Lagos

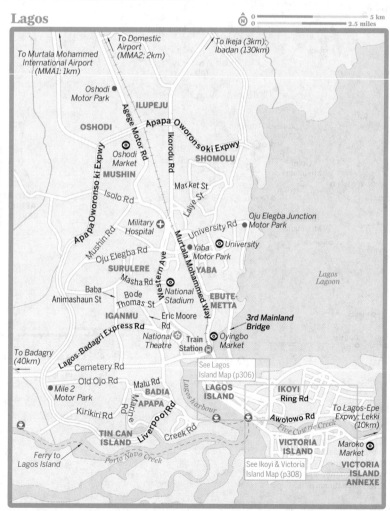

events, the **African Artists' Foundation** (Map p308; www.africanartists.org/; 54 Raymond Njoku St, Ikoyi), a contemporary arts gallery, and **Quintessence** (Map p308; ✆0803 3275401; Falomo Shopping Centre, Awolowo Rd, Ikoyi).

For markets try **Jankara Market** (Map p306; off Adeyinka Oyekan Ave), full of fabric, *juju* ingredients, and crafts. **Balogun Market** (Map p306; off Breadfruit St) sells fabric from across West Africa. **Lekki Market** (Elegushi Market; off Epe Expressway, Lekki) has the best selection of crafts from around Nigeria and West Africa.

On Lagos Island look out for examples of old Brazilian architecture in the distinctive houses built by former slaves and their descendants who returned from Brazil.

Also head to Lagos institution **Jazz Hole** (Map p308; Awolowo Rd), a bookshop, a record store and a lovely cafe.

⭐ **Kalakuta Republic Museum**   MUSEUM
(Gbemisola St, Ikeja) Legendary musician Fela Kuti's former house and revolutionary headquarters is now a fascinating museum, with everything intact from Fela's bedroom to his underwear. Breathe deep and you may even catch a high.

⭐ **Nike Art Gallery**   GALLERY
(✆0803 4096 656; www.nikeart.com; 2nd Roundabout, Epe Expressway, Lekki) **FREE** One of Nigeria's most important artists, Nike Davies-Okundaye, runs this enormous gallery full of contemporary and traditional Nigerian arts. Nike herself is practically an incarnation of love and beauty, which is reflected in this astonishing four-storey space. If you're lucky she'll be there and may grace you with a new Yoruba name. Cultural tours to other Yoruba towns can be arranged through the gallery.

🛏 Sleeping

It's hard to find a cheap place to rest your head in this surprisingly expensive city. While there are plenty of small midrange guesthouses with basic rooms, there is an absolute boom in high-end hotels.

Peerage Retreat   HOTEL **$$**
(Map p308; ✆01 271 9650; peerageretreat@yahoo.com; 1 Olabode George St, Victoria Island; r N10,000; ❄) The best option for the money on the island, this family-run hotel is clean, friendly and well run. Given the deal, it fills up fast.

Hotel Victoria Palace   HOTEL **$$**
(Map p308; ✆01 262 5901; victoriapalace@gmail.com; 1623 Sake Jojo St; s/d N12,500-14,000; P ❄)

Basic rooms and a friendly staff, a good budget-ish choice on Victoria Island. The **Bombay Palace** (Map p308; Awolowo Rd; mains from N1200; ⏱ noon-3pm & 6-10pm) on the top floor serves good Indian food.

Bogobiri House   BOUTIQUE HOTEL **$$$**
(Map p308; ✆01 270 7436; www.bogobirilagos.com; 9 Maitama Sule St, Ikoyi; r incl breakfast from N30,000; ❄@🔊) This charming boutique hotel, beautifully decorated with paintings and sculptures by local artists, serves as the hub of the vibrant art and cultural scene. Its side-street location provides a calm escape from the Lagos buzz. The restaurant has some of the best Nigerian favourites in the city, and there is often excellent live music.

The Wheatbaker   BOUTIQUE HOTEL **$$$**
(✆01 277 3560; www.legacyhotels.com; 4 Onitolo Rd, Ikoyi; r from N88,000; P❄@🔊☒) A luxury boutique hotel, The Wheatbaker ranks at the absolute top. Experience the secluded grounds and gorgeous pool at Sunday brunch to get a taste of the elite Lagos lifestyle.

🍴 Eating

Broad St and Campbell St in Lagos Island are good for chophouses and *suya* (Nigerian kebab); the better restaurants are in Ikoyi and Victoria Island. Some of the best places to eat are attached to hotels and cultural centres, such as Bogobiri, Terra Kulture and **Purple at The Blowfish** (✆014631298;

NIGERIA LAGOS

WARNING: BOKO HARAM

Since 2009, Boko Haram, a jihadist organisation based in the northeast of Nigeria, has waged a low-level war against Christian communities and the central government, killing thousands. Known for bombing churches and markets, assassinating police, and motorcycle drive-bys, the group, whose name means 'Western education is sinful' in Hausa, has made travel to northern Nigeria a dicey proposition.

Attacks are sporadic and have taken place in Adawama, Gombe, Yobe, Jigawa and Plateau States, occasionally in an outskirt of Abuja or Jos, with many incidents centred on Maiduguri, the capital of Borno State.

Boko Haram's goal is ostensibly to impose sharia law. But Nigerians in the south have other suspicions about their motivations. The 2010 death of northern-born President Yar'Adua ushered in the current president Goodluck Jonathan – a southern native – losing the north the seat of governmental power. Boko Haram's continued terrorism may be seen as angling for more resources and control.

While Lagosians will tell you flat out not to go north, the astounding sites there make it alluring to explore. Travellers should proceed with extreme caution: check the news reports and ask locals with specific knowledge before attempting to go.

www.theblowfishhotel.com; 17 Oju Olobun, Victoria Island).

Ikoyi Hotel Suya AFRICAN $
(Map p308; Kingsway Rd, Ikoyi Hotel, Ikoyi; suya from N100; ⏰10am-10pm) Lagosians claim the best *suya* in town can be found at the stall outside the Ikoyi Hotel. Not just beef and goat, but chicken, liver and kidney, plus some great fiery *pepe* (pepper) to spice it all up.

Pizze-Riah PIZZA $$
(Map p308; 13 Musa Yardua St, Victoria Island) Brick-oven pizza in a lovely outdoor setting.

Bangkok Restaurant THAI $$
(Map p308; Muri Okunola St; ⏰11am-11pm) With the best Thai food in Lagos, the Bangkok is a treat. The cooks and waitresses are all Thai, and offer you a broad menu of fragrantly spiced dishes. Portions are very generous, and if you can't finish your meal, they're used to sending people home with a doggie bag.

Cactus BAKERY $$
(Map p308; Maroko Rd; mains from N1200; ⏰8am-10pm) This place labels itself primarily as a patisserie, but it also serves up proper meals throughout the day. Breakfasts of pancakes or bacon are good, as are the pizzas, and the club sandwiches with salad and chips are simply huge – excellent value at N1800.

Yellow Chilli AFRICAN $$
(Map p308; 27 Ojo Olubun Cl, Victoria Island; mains N1500-2500; ⏰11am-10pm; 🖊) Well-presented Nigerian dishes in swish surroundings. It's carried off well, with tasty dishes in reasonable portions and good service – a great way to eat your way around the country without leaving your table.

 Drinking & Nightlife

As they say in Lagos, what happens in Gidi stays in Gidi. In other words, Lagos' nightlife is legendary. Be prepared to stay up past dawn and arrive home sore. Note that what's hot is constantly changing. Ask around for the best nights out. Drink spots are best up until midnight when dance spots then heat up.

New Afrika Shrine LIVE MUSIC
(Adeleye St, Ikeja (mainland); cover charge N500; ⏰Thu-Sun 6pm-1am) Just by showing up you'll get a political education, a scandalising lesson in shakin' it, and a contact high. Though Fela Kuti's original Shrine was burnt down, this replacement run by his children is possibly the best show in town. Femi Kuti plays free on Thursday night and does a paid show on Sunday. Fela's most approximate reincarnation, the younger Seun Kuti, plays the last Saturday of the month. Snacks, ice cream, palm wine, and more are on offer. Smoking encouraged.

Bogobiri II/Nimbus BAR
(Map p308; Maitama Sule St, Ikoyi; ⏰8am-11pm) Part of Bogobiri House (p303), this is a lovely place for a drink (and eat) – mellow in the day and happening at night. There's an attached art gallery with works from local artists, and at weekends there's usually live music.

Motherlan'   LIVE MUSIC
(Opebi Rd, Ikeja; cover charge N1000; ⊙ Thu-Sun)
Owned by renowned musician Lagbaja, this
is a big outdoor venue with lots of live music
and a robust local following.

Likwid Lounge   BAR
(Map p308; Samuel Manuwa St, Victoria Island)
Starts late, gets good even later. Nigeria's
elites, socialites and pop stars come here
for the post-party partying. If you get the
munchies, head across the street, outside the
gate of 1004 Housing Estates, to Chopbox;
it's always open.

Sip Lounge   BAR
(Map p308; Akin Adesola St, Victoria Island) Another swank late-night drinking hole for the
fancy-inclined.

Elegushi Beach   BAR
Dancing bumper-to-bumper, bottles of the
hard stuff, lots of ladies – the party does not
get better than Elegushi Beach on a Sunday
night. Go with a local; there have been robberies. Not for the faint of heart. During the
day, pay a fee (N1000) to enjoy the semi-
private beach.

ℹ Orientation

For the traveller, there are three main areas
dividing Lagos: the mainland, a massive area of
upper, middle, and working-class neighbourhoods along with innumerable business centres
and some universities; Lagos Island, the heart
of the city, including Ikoyi, an elite suburb, some
embassies and top-end hotels; and Victoria
Island (VI), an even smarter suburb facing the
Atlantic Ocean with the bulk of the embassies
and a number of top-end hotels. Beyond VI is the

Lekki Penninsula. The islands are connected by
elevated expressways and bridges constantly
clogged with traffic.

ℹ Information

INTERNET ACCESS
Internet cafes are everywhere and cost upwards
N200 per hour. Many upscale restaurants and
cafes also have wi-fi. Have lunch at Bogobiri
House (p303) for a fast connection. Satisfy your
sweet tooth and wireless needs at the bakery-
restaurant **Cafe Royale** (Map p308; No 267A,
Etim Inyang Cres, Victoria Island; ⊙7am-10pm;
✽ ⊚).

MEDICAL SERVICES
Healthplus Integrative Pharmacy (Map p308;
☑0802 802 5810; Unit 54, The Palms Shopping Centre, Lekki; ⊙8am-7pm Mon-Sat) With
branches in Ikeja, Yabo and the airport.
St Nicholas Hospital (Map p306; ☑0802 290
8484; http://saintnicholashospital.com; 57
Campbell St) Has a 24-hour emergency clinic.

MONEY
ATMs are ubiquitous. GTB bank is the most
reliable for foreign cards.

At money changers, high-denomination bills
trade at a much better rate. Find them at Alade
Market on the mainland, or outside Federal Palace and Eko Meridien hotels on Victoria Island.

SAFE TRAVEL
Contrary to popular perception, violent crime
has decreased in recent years. Most crime
against foreigners targets expats in expensive
cars, and travellers are unlikely to encounter any
serious problems. Still, never carry more money
than is necessary and avoid flaunting valuables
and walking outside at night – particularly

NIGERIA LAGOS

FELA KUTI: MUSIC IS THE WEAPON

The impact of Fela Anikulapo Kuti's music in Nigeria, and worldwide, cannot be over-
stated. Fela Kuti (1938–97) is Africa's musical genius, the creator of Afrobeat – a
genre combining traditional African highlife, jazz, James Brown funk grooves and Latin
rhythms into a unique mix that is wholly his own – and a revolutionary. Fela's politically
inflammatory songs laid bare the corruption, violence and greed of the ruling regimes in
his country and beyond. He was arrested over a hundred times by the Nigerian government, and ultimately 1000 soldiers invaded and destroyed the Kalakuta Republic – Fela's living and performing compound that he shared with his 27 wives – sending nearly
all of the inhabitants to the hospital, or worse. Despite the death of his own mother due
to the siege, Fela never stopped fighting the powers of imperialism, colonialism and
racism with – as the legend himself put it – music as his weapon. Due to the recent
re-release of his music worldwide and, interestingly, a Broadway musical based on his
life, Fela's legacy is now enjoying renewed attention and a reinvigorated profile in Nigeria. The Lagos government even donated money to launch the new Kalakuta Museum
(p303), and Felabration is celebrated each year around his birthday on 15 October.

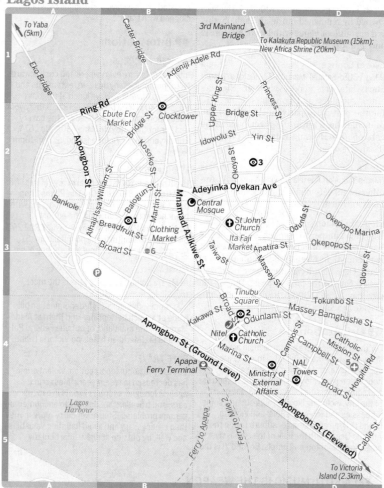

around hotels and restaurants frequented by foreigners.

ⓘ Getting There & Away

Murtala Mohammed International Airport (MMA1) is the main gateway to Nigeria and is roughly 10km north of Lagos Island. The domestic terminal (MMA2) is 4km away; tickets can be bought on departure or from an agent. Though there are airline offices at the airport and in Lagos, it's best to use a travel agency that can sort your flights all-in-one.

Ojota Motor Park (with Ojota New Motor Park next door), 13km north of Lagos, is the city's main transport hub. Minibuses and bush taxis leaving to all destinations depart from here. Sample fares are Benin City (N3000, four hours), Ibadan (N1000, two hours), Oshogbo (N2500, three hours) and Abuja (N5000, 10 hours).

Mile-2 Motor Park serves destinations east of Lagos, including the Benin border at Seme (N800, 90 minutes). You'll also find a few minibuses going as far north as Ibadan from here.

ABC Transport (Map p308; ☎ 01 740 1010; www.abctransport.com) is a good intercity 'luxury' bus company, serving many major cities, as well as destinations in Benin, Ghana and Togo. The depot is at Jibowu Motor Park, but there's a useful **booking office** (☎ 01 740 1010; Awolowo

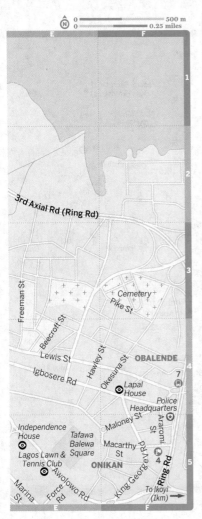

Ghana International Airlines (Map p308; ☑01 266 1808; www.fly-ghana.com; 130 Awolowo Rd, Ikoyi)

Kenya Airways (Map p308; ☑01 271 9433; www.kenya-airways.com; Badaru Abina St, Churchgate Tower)

KLM (Map p308; ☑0703 415 3801; www.klm. com; 1 Adeola Odeku St, Sapetro, Victoria Island)

Lufthansa (Map p306; ☑01 461 2222; www. lufthansa.com; Churchgate Tower, Victoria Island)

South African Airlines (Map p308; ☑01 270 0712; www.flysaa.com; 28c Adetukonbo Ademola St, Victoria Island)

ⓘ Getting Around

Traffic in Lagos is legendary – and it's not getting any better – especially with occasional governmental edicts outlawing *okada*, small (and sometimes unsafe) motorcycles that are your best best for skirting the 'go-slow'.

A taxi costs from N4000 to reach Lagos Island. Always allow way more time than you think to get to the airport when catching a flight. There are no airport buses.

Arriving in Lagos can be complicated and you may be dropped at one of several motor parks – Oshodi, Yaba and Oju Elegba Junction are the likeliest candidates. Minibuses run from these to more central points, such as Obalende Motor Park on Lagos Island.

Yellow minibuses (*danfos;* fares N70 to N250 according to distance) serve points all over Lagos – prices increase when you cross a bridge from one part of Lagos to another. Yellow private taxis start at N500.

Keke Napep (motorised tricycles that can carry three passengers) are useful for short-distance travel and have replaced the services previously provided by *okada*.

A decent, cheap option to avoid traffic, the official city Bus Rapid Transit (BRT) buses have

Rd, Block D, Falomo Shopping Centre) inside a shoe shop at Falomo Shopping Centre.

Aero Contractors (☑01 628 4140; www.acn. aero; airport desk)

Air France (Map p308; ☑01 461 0777; www. airfrance.com; Idejo Danmole St)

Arik Air (☑01 279 9999; www.arikair.com; Lagos Murtala Muhammed International Airport)

Cameroon Airlines (Map p308; ☑01 261 6270; Oko Awo Cl)

Ethiopian Airlines (Map p308; ☑01 774 4711; www.flyethiopian.com; 3 Idowu Tayor St, Victoria Island)

NIGERIA LAGOS

Ikoyi & Victoria Island

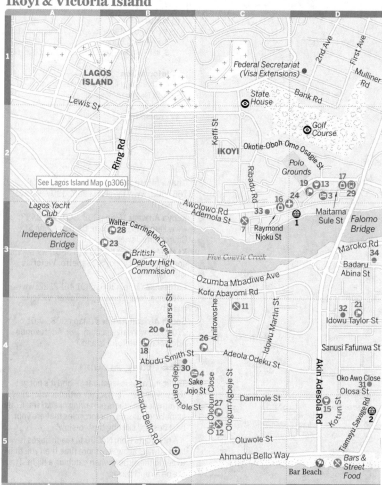

See Lagos Island Map (p306)

routes that stretch from Lagos Island to the mainland. Buy tickets (N70 to N150) at terminals scattered around Lagos. Boarding may require waiting on long queues.

SOUTHERN NIGERIA

Abeokuta

About 100km north of Lagos, Abeokuta is well known as the birthplace of many famous Nigerians, notably former president Obasanjo and Fela Kuti.

The founding site of Abeokuta, the famed **Olumo Rock** (admission N200) has a rich history and great spiritual significance. Hire a guide (dash around N500) and climb the rock. You'll see shrines, sacred trees, the elderly women of the god of thunder, tribal war-time hideouts, and ultimately, at the top, an astonishing view of the city.

To make the two-hour trip from Lagos take a bush taxi (N300) from Ojota Motor Park. You'll arrive at Kuto Motor Park, where you can hop on an *okada* (N100) or taxi.

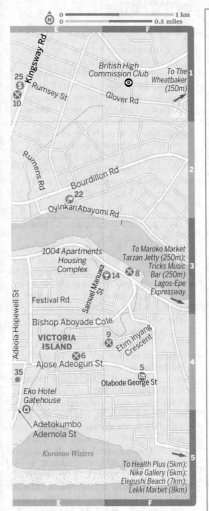

Ibadan

🖉 02 / POP 2.7 MILLION

The word sprawling could have been invented to describe Ibadan. You're likely to pass through this major transport junction, but there's little to keep you here.

Hotels are generally shoddy and expensive. The best bet on the higher end is **Kakanfo Inn** (www.kakanfoinn.com; 1 Nihinlola St, Ring Rd, Ibadan; P🚿@🛜🚗), which has a decent Indian restaurant. A cheaper option is the **University of Ibadan Guest House** (🖉 012 273 9865; University of Ibadan Campus; P🚿@). If you want something other than local chophouses, go to **Pancho Vino** (off Town Planning, Oluyole; pizzas around N1400; ⊙ noon-3pm & 6-11pm) for pizzas and Lebanese food in clean, modern surroundings.

The Gbagi market has an enormous selection of fabric.

Iwo Rd is Ibadan's major motor park; minibuses run to all points from here, including Lagos (N500, 90 minutes), Abuja (N2000, eight hours) and points north. For Oshogbo (N300, 90 minutes), go to Gate Motor Park in the east of the city.

Oshogbo

This quiet city has been a traditional centre for Yoruba spirituality and, since the 1950s, the birthplace for much contemporary Nigerian art.

The best sight is the Osun Sacred Grove believed to be the dwelling of Osun, the Yoruba fertility goddess. In the late 1950s, Austrian-born artist Susanne Wenger, later accepted as a high Yoruba priestess, revived the neglected grove, filling it with her own and her many pupils' sculptures and shrines revering traditional deities.

For an extra fee, tour the groves with one of Susanne's adopted children (and traditional priests) Sangodare (☑ 0803 226 2188) or Doyin Faniyi (☑ 0803 226 2188). Also visit Susanne's remarkable house and the cooperative shop run by the artists of the New Sacred Movement (41A Ibokun Rd).

There's no reason to stay anywhere else but the divine Nike Ambassador Guest House (r N5000-7000) with lovely gardens (including giant tortoises and peacocks) and an incredibly friendly staff. They can take you to Nike's traditional Yoruba craft workshops for Nigerian youth as well as the village where local women make traditional black soap.

There are several contemporary art galleries where you can buy fantastic crafts including the Nike Centre for Arts & Culture (Old Ede Rd) and Jimoh Buraimoh's African Heritage Gallery (1 Buraimoh St).

Also wander through the Oja Oba Market across from the Oba's Palace – it's packed with stalls selling *juju* material.

Okefia Rd is the main motor park. Minibuses leave regularly for Ibadan (N500, 90 minutes) and Lagos (N700, three hours).

Benin City

☑ 052

Benin City, which served as the capital of the Benin Kingdom, starting in the 15th century, gave rise to one of the first African art forms to be accepted internationally – the Benin brasses. Today the city is the centre

WORTH A TRIP

ILE-IFE

Ile-Ife is considered the traditional birthplace of Yoruba civilisation, and holds some of the most revered spiritual sites where people still worship traditional deities. Head to Oòni's Palace, where one of the king's servants will, for a small fee, show you the shrine within the palace walls, take you to see Oduduwa's staff, and teach you fantastic Yoruba creation stories including the tales of Moremi the warrior-princess, Obatala and Obameri. To get to Ile-Ife, take a bush taxi (N400, 45 minutes) from Oshogbo.

of Nigeria's rubber trade, and a sprawling metropolis.

The National Museum (King's Sq; admission N100; ☺ 9am-6pm) has displays of beautiful brasses. On nearby Brass Casters St sculptors reviving the 'lost-wax' sculpture technique can show you their works in progress, and sell you one of your own.

The totally bizarre Revelation Tourist Palazzo on Victor Awaido Ave has simulations of slave markets, ritual practices, ancestral shrines, and odd punitive practices.

For budget sleeping, try Edo Motel Plaza. The Lixborr Hotel (☑ 05 225 6699; Sakowpba Rd; s N3000, d N3250-5000; ✸) is a popular, well-run place with comfortable rooms. Opposite Brass Casters St, look for the giant statue of the Benin woman.

Arik Air (p307) and Aero Contractors (☑ 764 7571; www.acn.aero) have daily flights from Lagos (N45,000, 40 minutes). Iyaro Motor Park is the main place for minibuses to Lagos (N1600, six hours), and to Calabar (N1900, eight hours). Also try the depot next to the Edo-Delta Hotel on Akpakpava Rd which serves most destinations.

Calabar

☑ 087 / POP 500,000

Tucked into Nigeria's southeastern corner, the capital of Cross River State has a rich history and is well worth a trip. Originally a cluster of Efik settlements, Calabar was once one of Nigeria's biggest slave ports, and later a major exporter of palm oil. A popular stopover for travellers heading to Cameroon, this tourist-friendly city has an amazing museum and two excellent primate-conservation centres.

⊙ Sights

Calabar Museum
MUSEUM
(Court Rd; admission N100; ⊙ 9am-6pm) Housed in the beautiful old British governor's building overlooking the river, the museum has a fascinating collection covering Calabar's days as the Efik kingdom, the slave and palm-oil trade, and the colonial period.

Drill Ranch
WILDLIFE SANCTUARY
(✆0803 5921262; www.pandrillus.org; Nsefik Eyo Layout, off Atekong Rd; donations appreciated; ⊙9am-5pm) Home to a colony of rescued drill monkeys and chimpanzees, the Drill Ranch is home to Pandrillus, one of Africa's most progressive primate-conservation bodies, which places emphasis on local education to combat poaching and the bushmeat trade. Spending time with Liza, Peter and Tunje at the Calabar headquarters is fascinating. The organisation can arrange trips to its excellent **Afi Mountain Drill Ranch** (community charge N250, guides N1000, per car/motorbike N500/250, campsites N2000, huts N6000) near Cross River National Park. This is one of Nigeria's highlights, with a rainforest-canopy walk and close primate encounters.

Cercopan
WILDLIFE SANCTUARY
(www.cercopan.org; Mary Slessor Ave; donations appreciated; ⊙9am-5pm) On the other side of town from the Drill Ranch, Cercopan in the Botanic Gardens works with smaller monkeys such as guenons and mangabeys. The gardens (www.irokofoundation.org) are worth visiting to learn about the amazing biodiversity of the area.

🛏 Sleeping & Eating

For traditional dishes (N500) and palm wine with the locals, head to Atimbo, on the way to Akpabuyo town. The swish hotel Le Chateau has fine upscale local meals (N3000).

Nsikak Sea Side Hotel
HOTEL $
(45 Eden St; r N1000) At 59 years old, this hotel, smack in the middle of colonial Old Calabar, is a throwback to a different era. It's incredibly dilapidated, and the staff will be pleased to host foreigners (their clientele is nearly all Nigerian). There's no air-con, and the electricity only works when there's national power, but get the top room with a balcony overlooking the sea and you'll find yourself transported. A very local experience.

Nelbee Executive Guesthouse
GUESTHOUSE $
(✆08 723 2684; Dan Achibong St; r from N3500; P ✳) Close to Watt Market is this handy budget option. Rooms are comfortable, the management is friendly, and there's a terrifically formal dining room.

Jacaranda Suites
HOTEL $$
(✆08 723 9666; off Atimbo Rd; r from N12,000; P ✳ ⊠) Lovely suites, a lively outdoor thatch-roof bar with secluded cabanas, and a restaurant serving Cross River specialities and grilled fish, Jacaranda is an easy choice for high-end sleeping and eating.

Marian Hotel
HOTEL $$
(✆08 722 0233; Old Ikong Rd; r N7000-8000; P ✳) Well located, the Marian has had a lick of paint and a tidy-up since our last visit, and is all the better for it. Rooms are spacious, tidy and comfortable.

K's Court
AFRICAN $
(74 Ndidan Usang Iso Rd; dishes from N300; ⊙11am-late) An open-air chophouse and bar, this place gets going later in the day. It serves up fiery bowls of cow-leg soup with plantain, and once that's gone, pushes back the tables and cranks up the music to dance the weekend nights away.

🛈 Getting There & Away

Aero Contractors (www.acn.aero) and Arik Air (p307) fly daily to Lagos and Abuja (for around N55,000).

Fakoships (✆0806 9230753) sails every Wednesday and Friday around 7am to Limbe in Cameroon (N6000, seven hours).

The main motor park is tucked between Mary Slessor Ave and Goldie St. Sample minibus fares

NIGERIA CALABAR

WORTH A TRIP

CREEK TOWN

For a worthwhile day trip from Calabar, head to Creek Town by boat (N400) from the wharf on Marina Rd, leaving around 7am and noon, coming back at 4pm.

Once there, get in touch with **Itaeyo** (✆0803 741 2894), who will show you the prefab colonial buildings and artifacts, traditional architecture and the king's palace (bring booze as a gift for the king). Also learn about the legacy of missionary Mary Slessor, who ended the traditional practice of killing twins.

include Lagos (N3200, 10 hours) and Ikom (for Afi Mountain Drill Ranch; N700, three hours).

NORTHERN NIGERIA

Abuja

POP 2.5 MILLION

Nigeria's made-to-measure capital, Abuja was founded during the boom years of the 1970s. After the divisive Biafran war, the decision was made to move the capital from Lagos to the ethnically neutral centre of the country. Clean, quiet and with a good electricity supply, sometimes Abuja hardly feels like Nigeria at all. There's not much to do, but it's a good place to catch your breath and do some visa shopping.

Abuja tends to empty at weekends, with people leaving for more exciting destinations, so many hotels offer discounts for Friday and Saturday nights.

Good budget options include **African Safari Hotel** (📞09 234 1881; Plot 11, Benue Cres; r from N3000-7000; ❄ @), which has Area 1 Shopping Centre nearby (good for street food), **Browelf Hotel** on Lagos Cres, and **Dannic Hotel** (which has a great restaurant).

For something more upscale, **The Nordic Villa** (📞0703 682 9922; http://thenordicvilla.com/; No 52, Mike Akhigbe Way; r from N19000) is a modern Scandinavian-style guesthouse with helpful staff, a calm atmosphere and good internet access.

The main draw at **Smi Msira Restaurant** (Moshood Abiola Way; dishes from N700) is being able to sit out in the pleasant leafy surroundings – something of a genuine beer garden.

For a splurge, hit the many restaurants at the Hilton and Sheraton hotels.

The airport is 40km west of Abuja (N3500 by taxi). Flights depart hourly for Lagos with several airlines (N54,000, one hour). There are also daily flights to Kano and Port Harcourt, as well as flights several times a week to Ibadan, Calabar and Maiduguri.

Jabi Motor Park (also called Utoka) is the main terminus for Abuja. Transport goes to all points from here; sample minibus fares include Kano (N1000, four hours), Jos (N800, three hours), Ibadan (N1500, eight hours) and Lagos (N2600, 10 hours).

Okadas have been banned in Abuja. Instead, there are plentiful green taxis (around N200 a drop).

TRAVELLING IN THE NORTH

Due to the activities of Boko Haram and the subsequent unstable security situation, we were unable to travel independently in Kano, Jos, Yankari, and Gashaki-Gumpti National Park to update this chapter. Research for this part of the country was done using local contacts, the internet and other sources.

Jos

📷073

The temperate climes of the Jos plateau are perhaps the oldest inhabited parts of Nigeria. The earliest known Nigerians, the Nok people, originated in the area, witnessed by the famed Nok terracottas. At 1200m above sea level, it's noticeably cooler than most other parts of the country – in colonial times it was a recommended holiday destination for British officers. A former tin-mining centre, Jos now sits astride one of Nigeria's major Christian–Muslim fault lines. With communal violence not unknown, it's essential to keep your ear to the ground before planning a visit.

The **Jos National Museum** (admission N50; ◷8.30am-5.30pm) has a superb collection of pottery, including several Nok terracotta sculptures – at over 2500 years old, they're Africa's oldest figurative sculptures. On the same site, the **Museum of Traditional Nigerian Architecture** (◷8.30am-5.30pm) **FREE** has full-scale reproductions of buildings from each of Nigeria's major regions.

Good meals can be found at **Old Airport Junction** (old airport junction near Nasco; meals from N500) – pull up a table and munch on grilled fish, Suya or masa (meals from N500). **Decency Restaurant** (Beach Rd; meals from N300) provides traditional Nigerian cuisine. Afrione/Net Café is a great meeting place and serves western and Mexican dishes, baked goods and ice creams.

The areas around Jos hold some spectacular landscapes. To the east, Shere Hills offer a prime view of the city below, good hiking and rock climbing.

Kurra Falls is a great place for camping, boating, hiking and rock climbing. The area includes several lakes, a cascading waterfall and many hills and rock formations. Having a local guide is useful for finding the way and security measures.

There is a daily flight between Jos and Lagos with Arik Air (p307). You can book in the mornings at Hill Station Hotel. The airport is 30km south of Jos (N1800 by taxi).

Head for Plateau Riders Motor Park at Tafawa Balewa St near Terminus to go anywhere in the country. Cars and buses run to Bauchi (N800, two hours), Kano (N1500, five hours) and Abuja (N1500, four hours)

The motor park opposite NTA also offers taxis to cities close to Jos.

Cocin Guesthouse GUESTHOUSE **$**
(☑ 07 345 2286; 6 Noad A St; dm N600, r N1400) One of two church missions on this street. Accommodation is clean, yet spartan, and bathroom facilities are shared, but it's hard to beat the price. Next door, **Tekan Guesthouse** (☑ 07 345 3036; 5 Noad St; dm N350, r N1000) has more of the same.

Les Rosiers B&B **$$**
(☑ 0803 357 5233; https://sites.google.com/site/lesrosiersjos/; 1 Rest House Rd; r from N9000; P ☢ ✴) This bungalow B&B is a delightfully unexpected find with a couple of chalets amid pleasant gardens. The French-Nigerian hosts are a good source of information and can help organise hiking trips and further travel. Entrance is opposite the Plateau Hotel.

Yankari National Park

Yankari, 225km east of Jos, is Nigeria's best-known **national park** (admission N300, car N500, photo permit N1250) for observing wildlife. The park still holds reasonable numbers of buffaloes, waterbucks, bushbucks, hippos and plenty of baboons. The biggest draw is the 300-strong population of elephants – a few lions also survive there. The birdwatching is excellent.

The best time to see wildlife is from late December to late April, before the rains, when the thirsty animals congregate at the Gaji River. You're permitted to drive your own vehicle if you take a guide; otherwise, the park has a safari truck that takes two-hour tours (N300) at 7.30am and 3.30pm daily.

Yankari's other attraction is the **Wikki Warm Spring** (admission N200), near the park campground. The crystal-clear water is a constant 31°C, forming a lake 200m long and 10m wide. Bring your swimming gear – the spring is a real highlight and shouldn't be missed.

Set high above the spring, the **Wikki Camp** (campsites per person N600, bungalows from N9000; ✴) has chalets for rent (from N9000) and a serene view over the lush area. There's a decent restaurant and bar.

You can get to the park gate at Mainamaji by minibus from Bauchi (N600, five hours). After paying the entrance fee (N300), you'll need to arrange transport to the camp – around N3000 in a taxi or N1000 by *okada*.

Kano

☑ 064 / POP 10 MILLION
Founded around 1400 years ago, Kano is the oldest city in West Africa and Nigeria's second largest. It was a major crossroads in the trans-Saharan trade routes and, from the Middle Ages, an important centre for Islamic scholarship.

But Kano is now at the forefront of the imposition of sharia law, with issues such as gender segregation of public transport cutting across community fault lines. Boko Haram have been active in the area. Kano has some fascinating sights, but proceed only with extreme caution.

◉ Sights

With thousands of stalls in a 16-hectare area, **Kurmi Market** is one of the largest markets in Africa and is the city's main attraction. It's a centre for African crafts, including gold, bronze and silver work, and all types of fabric. Away from the throng are the **Kofar Dye Pits** (Kofar Mata Gate; ◷ 7am-7pm), where indigo cloth has been dyed for hundreds of years. Finished cloth is for sale, starting from around N1500 according to the design.

The **Gidan Makama Museum** (Emirs Palace Rd; admission N200; ◷ 8am-6pm) stands on the site of the original emir's palace (the modern one sits opposite) and is a wonderful example of traditional Hausa architecture. The museum has a fascinating photographic history of Kano, and displays on Nigerian Islam and traditional culture. The **Gidan Dan Hausa** (Dan Hausa Rd; admission N100; ◷ 8am-4pm Mon-Thu, to 1pm Fri) is another museum in a beautifully restored traditional house showcasing regional crafts and ceremonial costumes.

✭ Festivals & Events

Held annually just after the end of Ramadan (exact dates vary), is the Kano Durbar – the biggest and best festival of its kind in Nigeria. It includes an exquisite cavalry procession featuring ornately dressed men and colourfully bedecked horses flanked by musicians. Finishing outside the emir's palace, there is drumming, singing and massed cavalry charges.

Sleeping

Ecwa Guesthouse   GUESTHOUSE $
(06463 1410; 1 Mission Rd; r N1500-3500;) This Christian mission guesthouse is a great budget option. The cheapest rooms are in the old block, are fan only, and some have shared facilities; the more expensive rooms in the new block have bathroom, TV and aircon. Alcohol is forbidden on site.

Prince Hotel   HOTEL $$$
(06 498 4251; Tamandu Rd; r N16,200-21,000;) Professionally understated with a posh restaurant and bar, 24-hour power, wi-fi and a swimming pool, the Prince is a classy operation in a quiet part of town. Rooms are modern and exceedingly comfortable. The Calypso Restaurant is a popular meeting place for expats and journalists.

Eating & Drinking

Kano is the home of *suya*, so if you're looking for a quick 'meat-on-a-stick' eat, you'll be in heaven here.

The best 'food-is-ready' fare is found in Sabon Gari. Enugu Rd has plenty of **chophouses** (dishes from N250; 8am-late), most doubling as bars.

Al-Amir   AFRICAN $
(12B Club Rd; dishes N250-400; 11am-10pm) If you want to eat like a local, head here. The 'special plate' has a bit of everything in a serving, but also try northern specialities like *miyan taushe* (pumpkin-seed soup) and *tuwo shunkafa* (pounded rice), washed down with a glass of *zobo* (hibiscus tea).

Fasania   CHINESE $$
(Ahmadu Bello Way; mains N680-1100; noon-11pm) This Chinese restaurant has a better-than-average selection of dishes, all cooked and served efficiently. Alcohol is served.

Spice Food   INDIAN $$
(Magasin Rumfa Rd; dishes from N550; noon-3.30pm & 6-11pm) If you've been craving some vegetarian food, this fantastic Indian restaurant will answer your prayers (meat dishes are also served) and the owner loves talking to backpackers.

Information

When in doubt, head to the Sabon Gari, a kind of foreigners area of the city.

Try the money changers at the craft stalls outside the Central Hotel; they'll also exchange West African CFA francs. The tourist office has a bureau de change.

Friends Internet (Murtala Mohammed Way; per hr N200) Also serves coffee, cakes and sandwiches.

Kano State Tourist Board (06 464 6309; Bompai Rd, Tourist Camp) A rarity in Nigeria – a working tourist office. Has pamphlets and can arrange guides to the Old City (N1500 per hour).

See & Sweet Bakery Cybercafé (Bompai Rd; per hr N250) Also a good place for a quick bite.

Getting There & Away

The airport is 8km northwest of Sabon Gari – N150 by *okada*, three times that in a taxi.

There are daily flights to Lagos (N20,000, 90 minutes) and Abuja (N15,000, one hour).

Overnight luxury buses to Lagos are found at the Sabon Gari and cost around N4000.

Kuka Motor Park is the motor park for the north and the Niger–Nigerian border. Naiwaba Motor Park serves points south and west. Sample fares are: Zaria (N500, 90 minutes), Kaduna (N700, three hours), Maiduguri (N2000, six hours), Sokoto (N900, six hours) and Jos (N700, four hours).

Gashaka-Gumti National Park

Nigeria's largest national park, Gashaka-Gumti (admission N1000, vehicles N500) is also the remotest and least-explored part of the country. Its 6700-sq-km area contains rolling hills, savannah, montane forest – as wild and spectacular a corner of Africa as you could wish for. It also holds incredible diversity and is one of West Africa's most important primate habitats, as well as supporting lions, elephants, hippos and buffaloes.

The park is open year-round, although access is easiest during the dry season (December to March). The best way to visit is through the Gashaka Primate Project (www.ucl.ac.uk/gashaka), a UK-based conservation group that works with the park to protect the watershed and wildlife within. They have rooms for around N1500 a night, but you must bring your own food. It's important to get in touch with them first because you need to be prepared. There are also volunteer opportunities.

The park entrance is at Serti, 10 hours from Jos; from there head to the riverside park headquarters at Gashaka (campsites N200, chalets N300), or take an *okada* to Kwano (a further 12km), where the primate researchers are mainly based. Exploring with a guide, you can go chimp-tracking by foot (there are plentiful other monkeys to see too), or do a great two- or three-day hike to the mountains, via several Fulani villages. It's a truly magical place.

UNDERSTAND NIGERIA

Nigeria Today

After years of coups and military rule, Nigeria now has an elected leadership – international bodies declared President Goodluck Jonathan's 2011 victory as relatively free of violence and voter fraud. And Nigeria's explosive economic growth – due almost entirely to the influx of oil money – has ushered in a time of leaps in modernisation and development. But these advances haven't addressed entrenched government mismanagement, inaction and corruption. Images of barefoot children hawking fruit alongside slick SUVs are a reminder that new wealth doesn't often trickle down. While Lagos is awash in glitz, once outside major cities people often live as they did a hundred years ago.

In addition, President Goodluck Jonathan's government faces the challenge of stemming the jihadist-fueled violence of northern separatist group Boko Haram, who seek to overthrow the government and establish an Islamic state. The conflict has taken the lives of thousands in attacks that break along ethnic and religious fault lines.

History

Early Nigeria

Northern and southern Nigeria are essentially two different countries, and their histories reflect this disparity. The first recorded empire to flourish in this part of West Africa was Kanem-Borno around Lake Chad, which grew rich from the trans-Saharan trade routes. Islamic states based in the Hausa cities of Kano, Zaria and Nupe also flourished at this time.

Meanwhile, the southwest developed into a patchwork of small states, often dominated by the Yoruba. The Ijebu kingdom rose in the 10th century and constructed the mysterious earthworks at Sungbo's Eredo. Most famously the Benin kingdom became an important centre of trade and produced some of the finest metal artwork in Africa. In the southeast, the Igbo and other agrarian peoples never developed any centralised empires, instead forming loose confederations.

Colonial Era

The first contact between the Yoruba empires and the Europeans was made in the 15th century, when the Portuguese began trading in pepper and, later, slaves. In contrast, the northern Islamic states remained untouched by European influence until well into the 19th century.

In the early 19th century, the British took a lead in suppressing slavery along the Niger delta, leading to the annexation of Lagos port – a first colonial toehold. This led to further annexation to thwart the French, who were advancing their territory along the Niger River. By the beginning of the 20th century, British soldiers had advanced as far north as the cities of Kano and Sokoto, where Islamic revivalism had created a rapidly expanding caliphate.

Nigeria was divided in two – the southern, mainly Christian, colony and the northern Islamic protectorate. The British chose to rule indirectly through local kings and chiefs, exacerbating ethnic divisions for political expediency.

Military Misrule

These divisions came back to haunt Nigeria when independence came in October 1960. Politics split along ethnic lines, and in 1966 a group of Igbo army officers staged a coup. General Johnson Ironsi took over as head of state. Another coup quickly followed on its heels, along with massacres of Igbos, which in 1967 provoked civil war by secessionist Igbos.

The war dragged on for three years. Biafra was blockaded, and by the time its forces capitulated in 1970, up to a million Igbos had died, mainly from starvation.

An oil boom smoothed Nigeria's path to national reconciliation, but as the army jockeyed for political control, the next two decades were marked by a series of military coups, with only a brief democratic interlude in the early 1980s. When General Ibrahim Babangida offered elections in 1993, he annulled them when the result appeared to go against him, only to be toppled in a coup soon after by General Sani Abacha.

Abacha was ruthless, purging the army and locking up intellectuals, unionists and pro-democracy activists. His rule reached a nadir in 1995 with the judicial murder of the Ogoni activist Ken Saro-Wiwa, an act that led to Nigeria's expulsion from the Commonwealth.

Salvation finally came in June 1998, in what Nigerians called the 'coup from heaven'. Aged 54, and worth somewhere between US$2 billion and US$5 billion in stolen government money, Abacha died of a heart attack while in the company of two prostitutes. His successor immediately announced elections and, in February 1999, Olusegun Obasanjo, a former military leader, was returned as president.

Culture

With nearly 165 million people, Nigeria has a huge and expanding population. The main ethnic groups are the Yoruba (in the southwest), Hausa (north) and Igbo (southeast), each making up around a fifth of the population, followed by the northern Fulani (around 10%). It's thought that up to 250 languages are spoken in Nigeria.

Ordinary Nigerians struggle against systematic corruption through the natural entrepreneurship of one of Africa's better-educated populations.

American-style evangelical mega-churches have sprouted up everywhere, though in villages many traditional belief systems remain intact. The north is predominantly Muslim.

Chinua Achebe *(Things Fall Apart)* was probably Nigeria's most famous author; he died in March 2013. Equally acclaimed writers from Nigeria include the Nobel Laureate Wole Soyinka, Booker Prize–winner Ben Okri *(The Famished Road)* and Chimamanda Ngozi Adichie *(Half a Yellow Sun)*.

Some of Africa's best-known musicians have been Nigerian. Two styles have traditionally been dominant, Afrobeat and *juju*, with their respective masters being the late Fela Kuti and King Sunny Ade.

Food & Drink

Nigerians like their food ('chop') hot and starchy. The classic dish is a fiery pepper stew ('soup') with a little meat or fish and accompanied by starch – usually pounded yam or cassava *(garri, eba,* or the slightly sour *fufu).* Another popular dish is *jollof* – peppery rice cooked with palm oil and tomato. Cutlery isn't generally used – the yam or cassava is used to soak up the juices of the stew. As in most of Africa, you only eat with your right hand.

Environment

The north touches on the Sahel and is mostly savannah with low hills. Mountains are found only along the Cameroon border in the east, although there is a 1500m-high plateau around Jos in the centre of the country. The coast is an almost unbroken line of sandy beaches and lagoons running back to creeks and mangrove swamps and is very humid most of the year.

An underfunded national parks service does exist, but in practice very little land in Nigeria is effectively protected. The expanding population has contributed to widespread deforestation – 95% of the original forests have been logged. However, the oil industry has caused the greatest number of environmental problems: oil spills and gas flaring have damaged the fishing industry, with little of the industry's wealth trickling down to the local level.

SURVIVAL GUIDE

ⓘ Directory A–Z

ACCOMMODATION

Hotels are of a fair standard throughout Nigeria, but they're expensive.

Lagos is particularly expensive; rooms are either very cheap and shoddy or very expensive – there's not much middle ground.

Watch and listen for the ubiquitous power cuts and the sound of generators striking up.

EMBASSIES & CONSULATES

Some embassies have yet to relocate from Lagos to Abuja.

Australian Embassy (✆ 09 461 2780; www.nigeria.embassy.gov.au; 48 Aguyi Ironsi St, 5th fl, Oakland Centre, Maitama, Abuja)

Beninese Embassy Abuja (✆ 09 413 8424; Yedseram St; ⊙ 9am-4.30pm Mon-Fri); Lagos (Map p308; ✆ 01 261 4411; 4 Abudu Smith St, VI; ⊙ 9am-11am Mon-Fri).

Burkinabé Embassy (Map p308; ✆ 01 268 1001; 15 Norman Williams St, Ikoyi, Lagos)

Cameroonian Embassy (✆ 01 261 2226; 5 Elsie Femi Pearse St, VI) Calabar (✆ 087-222782; 21 Ndidan Usang Iso Rd; ⊙ 9am-3.30pm Mon-Fri);

Lagos (Map p308; 📞 261 2226; 5 Femi Pearse St, VI; ⏰ 8am-11am Mon-Fri).

Canadian Embassy Abuja (📞 09 413 9910; 15 Bobo St, Maitama); Lagos (Map p308; 📞 01 262 2616; 4 Anifowoshe St, VI).

Dutch Embassy (📞 01 261 3005; 24 Ozumba Mbadiwe Ave, VI, Lagos)

French Embassy (Map p308; 📞 01 269 3430; 1 Oyinkan Abayomi Rd, Ikoyi, Lagos)

German Embassy (Map p308; 📞 01 261 1011; 15 Walter Carrington Cres, VI, Lagos)

Ghanaian Embassy (📞 01 263 0015; 23 King George V Rd, Lagos Island, Lagos)

Irish Embassy (📞 09 413 1751; Plot 415 Negro Cres, off Aminu Kano, Maitama, Abuja)

Ivorian Embassy (📞 01-261 0963; 5 Abudu Smith St, VI, Lagos)

Nigerien Embassy Abuja (📞 01 413 6206; Pope John Paul II St; ⏰ 9am-3pm Mon-Fri); Kano (📞 0806 548 1152; Airport Roundabout; ⏰ 9am-3pm Mon-Fri); Lagos (Map p308; 📞 01 261 2300; 15 Adeola Odeku St, VI; ⏰ 9am-2.30pm Mon-Fri).

Spanish Embassy (📞 01 261 5215; 21c Kofo Abayomi St, VI, Lagos)

Togolese Embassy (Map p308; 📞 01 261 7449; Plot 976, Oju Olobun Cl, VI, Lagos)

UK Embassy Abuja (📞 09 413 4559; www.ukinnigeria.fco.gov.uk; Aguyi Ironsi St, Dangote House, Maitama); Lagos (📞 01 261 9531; 11 Walter Carrington Cres, VI).

US Embassy Abuja (📞 09 461 4000; http://nigeria.usembassy.gov; Plot 1075, Diplomatic Dr, Central Business District); Lagos (Map p308; 📞 01 261 0150; 2 Walter Carrington Cres, VI).

FESTIVALS & EVENTS

Thousands descend on Oshogbo in late August for the Osun Festival held in honour of the river goddess. Music, dancing and sacrifices form one of the centrepieces of the Yoruba cultural and spiritual year.

Calabar hosts a festival throughout December with concerts from national and international stars scheduled closer to Christmas. The highlight of the festival is the cultural masquerade carnival, when tens of thousand of costumed revellers descend on the city.

The Eyo Festival in Lagos is a large Yoruba masquerade organised to commemorate the life of a recently passed spiritual leader.

Around mid-February, the spectacular three-day Argungu Fishing and Cultural Festival in Argungu is held. Possibly the most interesting in the country, the festival has sadly been cancelled for the past few years due to politics.

Some of the most elaborate festivals are the celebrations in northern Nigeria (particularly in Kano, Zaria and Katsina) for two important

DASH

Used freely as both a noun and a verb, dash is a word you'll hear a lot in Nigeria. It can mean either a bribe or a tip. The most frequent form of dash you're likely to encounter is at police roadblocks. In large-scale corruption, money is referred to as 'chopped' (literally 'eaten'). Although you're actually unlikely to be asked for dash as a bribe, dashing someone who performs a service for you, such as a guide, is often appropriate.

Islamic holidays: the end of Ramadan, and Tabaski, 69 days later, which feature colourful processions of cavalry. Ramadan can be a tiring time to travel in the north – head for the Sabon Gari (foreigners' quarter) in each town, where food is served throughout the day.

The Igue (Ewere) Festival, held in Benin City, usually in the first half of December, has traditional dances, a mock battle and a procession to the palace to reaffirm loyalty to the oba. It marks the harvest of the first new yams of the season.

INTERNET ACCESS

Decent connections are widespread in major towns, for around N200 per hour. Never use internet banking in a Nigerian cybercafe.

MONEY

The unit of currency is the naira (N). Bring higher-denomination dollars or pounds for the best exchange rate. ATMs are increasingly widespread and many are connected to international systems like Mastercard or Visa. GTB is the most reliable. Credit cards are accepted only a few places, and use them with caution. Notify your bank before you use your cards in Nigeria as fraud scams have made it a red-flag country for transactions.

There are money changers in each town and they are almost always Hausa.

Western Union branches are useless unless you have a Nigerian bank account.

OPENING HOURS

General business hours are from 8.30am to 5pm Monday to Friday. Sanitation days are held on the last Saturday of the month – traffic isn't allowed before 10am for street cleaning.

Banks 8am to 4pm weekdays, closed Saturday and Sunday.

Government offices 7.30am to 3.30pm Monday to Friday.

POST

Mail sent to or from Nigeria is notoriously slow. Worldwide postcards cost about N80. For parcels, use an international courier like DHL or FedEx, which have offices in most towns.

PUBLIC HOLIDAYS

New Year's Day 1 January
Easter March or April
May Day 1 May
National Day 1 October
Christmas 25 December
Boxing Day 26 December

Islamic holidays are observed in northern Nigeria.

SAFE TRAVEL

Lagos has a reputation for petty and violent crime, not always undeserved, although it's been on the decline in the past few years. As a traveller you're unlikely to have trouble with large-scale corruption and bribery. Police roadblocks are common, but fines and bribes are paid by the driver. Some caution should be exercised on the major highways into Lagos, where armed robbery is a problem at night.

Currently the most dangerous region is northern Nigeria, where Boko Haram, a militant jihadist organisation, wages a low-grade war against the federal government. Most Nigerians will tell you to avoid northern Nigeria altogether.

A previously troubled region of the country is the Niger delta. Recent amnesty agreements have quelled long-running grievances between the local population and the big oil companies.

Enugu has a reputation for kidnapping schemes, but they're more likely after wealthy oil execs rather than scruffy backpackers.

TELEPHONE

Nigeria is in love with the mobile phone, and cellular networks are more reliable than landlines. Having a local SIM card to use in a smart phone is extremely useful. The best service is Etisalat (SIMs cost N300), though MTN has the widest coverage. Street vendors everywhere sell top-up scratch cards.

Calls at roadside phone stands are quick and easy to make, costing around N20 per minute inside Nigeria, and around N60 for an international call. Most mobile numbers start with ☑ 080. The country code is ☑ 234.

VISAS

Everyone needs a visa to visit Nigeria, and applications can be quite a process. Many Nigerian embassies issue visas only to residents and nationals of the country in which the embassy is located, so it's essential to put things in mo-

NIGERIA DIRECTORY A–Z

PRACTICALITIES

Newspapers Privately owned English-language daily newspapers include the *Guardian, This Day, Punch* and *Vanguard*.

TV There are more than 30 national and state TV stations, broadcasting in English and all major local languages. South African satellite DSTV is hugely popular.

Electricity Supply is 220V. Plugs are square British three pin, but most hotels have European two-pin adaptors.

Languages English, Pidgin, Hausa, Yoruba, Igbo, Edo, Efik.

tion well before your trip. Exact requirements vary, but as a rule of thumb, forms are required in triplicate, along with proof of funds to cover your stay, a round-trip air ticket, and possibly confirmed hotel reservations. You also need a letter of invitation from a resident of Nigeria or a business in the country. The cost of a 30-day visa is from US$70 to US$190, according to nationality.

If you're travelling overland to Nigeria, the embassy in Accra (Ghana) is consistently rated as the best place in West Africa to apply for a visa, as no letter of introduction is required. The embassy in Niamey (Niger) also claims to issue visas the same way.

Visa Extensions

Visas can reportedly be extended at the **Federal Secretariat** (Alagbon Cl, Ikoyi) in Lagos, but it's a byzantine process of endless forms, frustration and dash, with no clear sense of success.

Visas for Onward Travel

Benin One-month visas cost CFA15,000 (CFA, not naira), with two photos, and take 24 hours to issue. The embassy in Lagos carries an uninviting reputation, and unexpected extra fees are not unknown.

Cameroon A one-month single-entry visa costs CFA50,000 (CFA, not naira), with two photos, and is issued in a day. As well as Lagos and Abuja, there's a useful consulate in Calabar.

Chad Two photos and N5500 will get you a one-month single-entry visa, which you can pick up the next day.

Niger Best obtained in Abuja, a one-month single-entry visa costs N5300 with two photos, and is issued in 48 hours. The consulate in Kano (where the fee can also be paid in CFA) is also an excellent and speedy place to apply – take three photos.

🛈 Getting There & Away

AIR

The vast majority of flights to Nigeria arrive in Lagos, although there are also international airports in Abuja, Port Harcourt and Kano. Airports are well organised and have official porters, but plenty of touts outside.

LAND
Benin

The main border crossing is on the Lagos to Cotonou (Benin) highway. Expect requests for bribes. There's a good direct Cotonou–Lagos bus service run by Nigerian bus company **ABC Transport** (⌨ 01 326 1919, 01 879 3070; www. abctransport.com). An alternative border crossing is further north at Kétou on the Benin side.

Cameroon

There are two main border crossings. The northern border post is at Bama, 2½ hours from Maiduguri, across to Banki in Cameroon. A remote alternative crossing is at Ngala (Nigeria), which is used mainly for transiting to Chad.

The southern border crossing is at Mfum (Nigeria), near Ikom. The road infrastructure collapses pretty much as soon as you cross to Ekok (Cameroon), making this border problematic during the rainy season, so consider taking the Calabar–Limbe ferry instead during the wettest months.

Chad

Although there are no official border crossings between the two countries, it's possible to make a quick transit across Cameroon. In Nigeria, the border crossing into Cameroon is at Ngala. On the Cameroon side ask for a laissez-passer to allow you to make the two-hour traverse to the Chad border point at Kousséri.

Niger

There are four main entry points into Niger. The busiest is the Sokoto route, which crosses at Ilela (Nigeria). Minibuses and bush taxis run daily to the border, just past Ilela. Crossing to Birni N'Konni, you can get on a bus straight for Niamey. Travelling between Kano (Nigeria) and Zinder (Niger) is equally straightforward. The final option is between Katsina and Maradi.

From Niger, it's easiest to cross at Gaya. You'll probably have to hire a bush taxi to take you from the Nigerian side at Kamba on to Sokoto. Beware the potholes.

Note that there is heavy presence of security and more scrutiny because of Boko Haram, as it is believed that they have operations in Niger.

SEA

A ferry sails from Calabar to Limbe every Tuesday and Friday evening (N6000, five hours), returning on Monday and Thursday. It's an overnight trip in each direction. Your passport is collected on boarding and returned at immigration. Try to keep hold of your luggage – if it gets stowed in the hold, you'll be waiting hours to get it back.

🛈 Getting Around

AIR

Internal flights are a quick way of getting around Nigeria. Flights start at around N20,000. Most cities are linked by air to Lagos.

The most reliable domestic airlines with the best connections are Arik Air (p307) and Aero Contractors (p310).

CAR & MOTORCYCLE

Nigeria's road system is good. But the smooth, sealed roads allow Nigerians to exercise their latent talents as rally drivers and accident rates are high. The only real road rule is survival of the fittest.

Foreigners driving in Nigeria shouldn't get too much hassle at roadblocks, particularly if your vehicle has foreign plates. If you get asked for dash, a smile and some patience will often defuse the request. It's a legal requirement to wear a seatbelt; not doing so leaves you open to both official and 'unofficial' fines. Petrol stations are everywhere, but fuel shortages are common, causing huge queues and worsening the already terrible traffic. Diesel can sometimes be hard to come by, so keep your tank topped up.

LOCAL TRANSPORT

Each town has at least one motor park serving as the main transport depot full of minibuses and bush taxis.

Vehicles have signs on their roofs showing their destination, while touts shout out destinations. Minibuses don't run on any schedule but depart when full.

Bush taxis cost about 25% more, though true pricing is nearly impossible to ascertain.

MOTORCYCLE-TAXI

The quickest way to get around town is on the back of a motorcycle-taxi called an okada (achaba in the north). Because of their general lawlessness, the government has banned okada in a few of the major cities, badly affecting traffic and driving up the prices with drivers who are willing to flout the law.

TRAIN

There are still old rail lines in Nigeria, but no services are currently available. A project to relaunch the national railway service, starting in 2009, has stalled.

Senegal

POP 13.8 MILLION

Includes ➡

Best Places to Eat

➡ Chez Agnes (p339)
➡ Le Patio du Mar y Sol (p335)
➡ Cabane des Pêcheurs (p329)

Best Places to Stay

➡ Chez Valerie (p333)
➡ Lodge des Collines de Niassam (p335)
➡ La Maison Rose (p337)

Why Go?

One of West Africa's most stable countries is definitely not dull: the capital, Dakar, is a dizzying, street-hustler-rich introduction to the country. Perched on the tip of a peninsula, elegance meets chaos, noise, vibrant markets and glittering nightlife while nearby Île de Gorée and the beaches of Yoff and N'Gor tap to slow, lazy beats. In northern Senegal, the enigmatic capital of Saint-Louis, a Unesco World Heritage Site, tempts with colonial architecture and proximity to lucious national parks. Along the Petite Côte and Cap Skiring, wide strips of beaches beckon and the broad deltas of the Casamance River reveal hundreds of bird species, from the gleaming wings of tiny kingfishers to the proud poise of pink flamingos. Whether you want to mingle with the trendsetters of urban Africa or be alone with your thoughts and the sounds of nature, you'll find your place in Senegal.

When to Go
Dakar

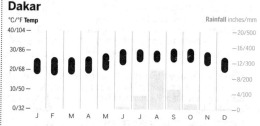

Nov–Feb Senegal's main tourist season is dry and cool.

Dec & Mar–Jun When most music festivals are on, including the Saint-Louis Jazz Festival (p339).

Jul–late Sep Rainy, humid season, but hotels reduce prices by up to 40%.

DAKAR

POP 2.9 MILLION

Once a tiny settlement in the south of the Cap Vert peninsula, Dakar now spreads almost across its entire triangle, and keeps growing. This is a city of contrasts, where horse-cart drivers chug over swish highways and gleaming SUVs squeeze through tiny sand roads, where elegant ladies dig skinny heels into dusty walkways and suit-clad businessmen kneel down for prayer in the middle of the street. A fascinating place – once you've learned how to beat its scamsters, hustlers and traders at their own game.

◉ Sights

Place de l'Indépendance   SQUARE
(Map p326) Dakar's central Place de l'Indépendance is the beating heart of the city. Symmetrically laid out and home to countless cars, crooks and 1960s concrete blocks, the square also contains majestic colonial buildings, including the Gouvernance (governor's office) and the Chambre de commerce (chamber of commerce).

Palais Présidentiel   HISTORIC BUILDING
(Map p326; Ave Léopold Senghor) Surrounded by sumptuous gardens and guards in colonial-style uniforms, the presidential palace was originally built for the governors but now serves as the residence of the current sitting president. You can't go inside, but it's a popular spot to take photos of the stately 1907 structure and its regal guards.

Musée Théodore Monod   MUSEUM
(Musée IFAN; Map p326; ☑ 33 823 9268; Pl de Soweto; adult/child CFA2300/200; ⊙ 9am-6pm Tue-Sun) The Musée Théodore Monod is one of the best museums in West Africa. The museum is a testament to African art and culture with over 9000 objects on display. Lively exhibits show masks and traditional dress across the region (including Mali, Guinea-Bissau, Benin and Nigeria) and provide an excellent overview of styles, without bombarding you with more than you can take in.

You can also see beautiful fabrics and carvings, drums, musical instruments and agricultural tools. A gallery behind the main building often houses excellent exhibitions of contemporary art.

Medina   NEIGHBOURHOOD
A bustling popular quartier with tiny tailor's shops, a busy Marché Tilène and streets brimming with life, the Medina was built as a

SENEGAL DAKAR

township for the local populace by the French during colonial days and is the birthplace of Senegalese superstar and current minister of culture Youssou N'Dour. Besides being a very real neighbourhood, where creative ideas and new trends grow between crammed, make-shift homes, it's also home to Dakar's 1664 **Grande Mosquée** (Map p324), impressive for its sheer size and landmark minaret.

★ Village des Arts   ARTS CENTRE
(Map p330; ☑ 33 835 7160; www.levillagedesarts.com; Rte de Yoff) An arts tour around Dakar is simply not complete with a visit to this famous art complex, where some of Senegal's most promising and established photographers, painters and sculptors create, shape and display their works in a large garden space. The on-site gallery shows a selection of their work and it's easy to grab a drink and chat to the friendly artists at the nearby restaurants.

Layen Mausoleum   MONUMENT
(Map p330; Mbenguene & the beach; ⊙ 10am-6pm Sun-Thu) In Yoff village, take a look at the Layen Mausoleum, a shrine to the founder of the Layen Muslim brotherhood. Residents of Yoff are noted for their strong Islamic culture: smoking and drinking are not allowed and visitors should be appropriately dressed (meaning long skirts or trousers). It's right on the beach and its floors are made of sand.

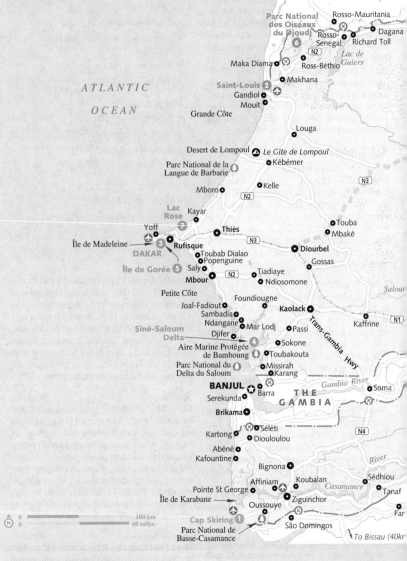

Senegal Highlights

① Weaving your way via tiny villages to Senegal's best beaches on **Cap Skiring** (p343) and kicking back for a day of doing absolutely nothing.

② Wandering in the footsteps of history in West Africa's first French settlement and Unesco World Heritage Site **Saint-Louis** (p337).

③ Spending sleepless nights touring the vibrant nightclubs, bars and concerts of **Dakar** (p329).

④ Winding through the mangroves of the **Siné-Saloum**

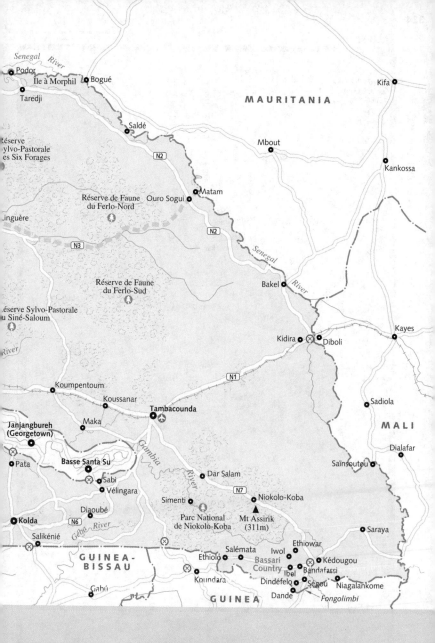

Delta (p334) in a *pirogue* (traditional canoe).

⑤ Contemplating history at **Maison des Esclaves** (p333) and breathing in the atmosphere of ancient peaceful **Île de Gorée** (p333).

⑥ Enjoying peaceful birdwatching at **Parc National des Oiseuax du Djoudj** (p340).

⑦ Floating on the salt-heavy **Lac Rose** (p334) and snap the otherworldly pics of the pink water contrasted with the bright blue sky.

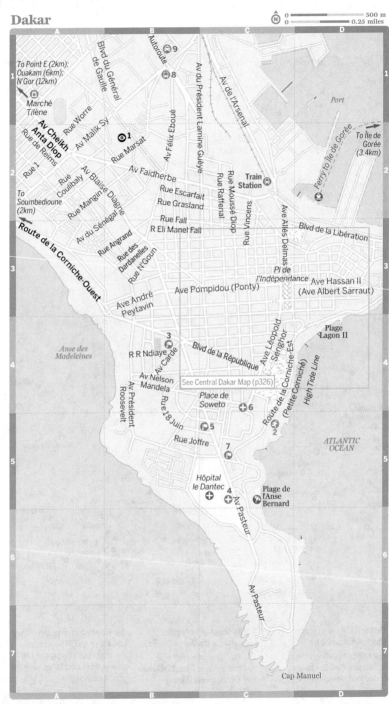

Dakar

0 — 500 m
0 — 0.25 miles

To Point E (2km);
Ouakam (6km);
N'Gor (12km)

Marché
Tilène

**Av Cheikh
Anta Diop**

Blvd du Général de Gaulle

Rue Worre

Rue de Reims

Rue 1

Rue Coulibaly

Av Blaise Diagne

Rue Mangin

Av du Sénégal

Rue Angrand

Rue des Dardanelles

Rue N'Goun

Av Malik Sy

Av Félix Eboué

Rue Marsat

Av Faidherbe

Rue Escarfait

Rue Grasland

Rue Fall

R Eli Manel Fall

Autoroute

Av du Président Lamine Guèye

Av de l'Arsenal

Rue Mousse Diop

Rue Raffenai

Rue Vincens

Av Allés Delmas

Train
Station

Port

Ferry to Île de Gorée

To Île de
Gorée
(3.4km)

Blvd de la Libération

Pl de
l'Indépendance

Ave Pompidou (Ponty)

Av Hassan II
(Ave Albert Sarraut)

Route de la Corniche-Ouest

To
Soumbedioune
(2km)

Ave André
Peytavin

Anse des
Madeleines

R R Ndiaye

Av Carde

Blvd de la République

Av Nelson
Mandela

Rue 18 Juin

Place de
Soweto

Av Léopold Senghor

Plage
Lagon II

See Central Dakar Map (p326)

Route de la Corniche-Est
(Petite Corniche)

High Tide Line

ATLANTIC
OCEAN

Rue Joffre

Hôpital
le Dantec

Av Président
Roosevelt

Plage de
l'Anse
Bernard

Av Pasteur

Av Pasteur

Cap Manuel

Dakar

◎ Sights
1 Grande Mosquée B2

⊕ Activities, Courses & Tours
2 Océanium C5

⊕ Information
3 Canadian Embassy.............................B4
4 Clinique de Cap..................................C5
5 German Embassy C5
6 Hôpital Principal C4
7 UK Embassy.......................................C5

⊕ Transport
8 Car Mouride Bus Stop........................B1
9 Gare Routière Pompiers B1

🏃 Activities

Dakar's best beaches are found in the north of the peninsula. **Plage de N'Gor** (Map p330; admission CFA500) is often crowded; if so, you're better off catching the frequent *pirogues* (roughly CFA500 to CFA700 one way) to Île de N'Gor, which has two small beaches. In Yoff, **Plage de Virage** (Map p330) is good; **Plage de Yoff** (Map p330) is rubbish strewn in parts, but waves are strong enough for surfing. Dakar has decent waves and a growing surf scene. **Tribal Surf Shop** (Map p330; ☑33 820 5400; www.tribalsurfshop.net; Yoff Virage; ⊙10am-7pm) and **Pantcho Surf Trip** (Map p330; ☑77 534 6232; www.senegalsurf.com/pantchosurftrip; Plage de N'Gor) can point out additional surf spots, run courses and hire out boards.

Piscine Olympique   SWIMMING
(Map p330; ☑33 869 0606; Tour de l'Œuf, Point E) The 50m pool of the Piscine Olympique is for serious swimmers.

Océanium   WATERSPORTS
(Map p324; ☑33 822 2441; www.oceaniumdakar. org; Rte de la Corniche-Est; ⊙Mon-Sat) The environmental agency Océanium runs recommended kayak, diving and snorkeling excursions.

🛏 Sleeping

Dakar has a range of accommodation, from filthy doss houses to palatial hotels – although everything is expensive and the steadily increasing prices are only justified in a few places.

SenegalStyle Bed & Breakfast GUESTHOUSE **$**
(Map p330; ☑77 791 5469; SenegalStyle@gmail. com; Ouest Foire, Cite Africa; per person CFA32,000; 🖥) Affable American-Senegalese owners who make you feel at home and happily arrange tours, ferry tickets, excursions, drumming lessons and more paired with snug, Africa-themed rooms a short walk from the beach make this of the best-value sleeps in town.

Keur Diame   HOTEL, HOSTEL **$**
(Map p330; ☑33 855 8908; www.keurdiame-senegal.com; Parcelles Assainies; s/d incl breakfast CFA15,000/23,000; @🖥) In a busy, local neighbourhood and close to Plage de Yoff, this friendly Swiss-owned hotel-hostel offers spotless rooms with mosquito nets and fans, plus a roof terrace.

Chez Nizar   HOSTEL **$**
(Map p326; ☑77 319 1224; 25 Ave Pompidou; r CFA16,000) Nizar's basic rooms boast the charm of social housing, *but* this is essentially Dakar's backpacker hub and the cheapest digs in the city centre.

LES MAMELLES – DAKAR'S BREASTS

Mamelles means 'breasts', and you don't need a great amount of imagination to guess why the pair of sloping mounds that form Dakar's only two hills have been given that name. The pretty white 1864 **Mamelles lighthouse** (Map p330) graces the top of the first hill – a leisurely 25-minute walk up is rewarded with a sweeping view across the town and water.

The second hill is topped by the massive, North Korean–built **African Renaissance** (Map p330; admission CFA6500; ⊙10am-6pm) monument. Allegedly Africa's highest statue, at 49m high it's taller than New York City's Statue of Liberty and Rio de Janeiro's Christ the Redeemer and was unveiled in 2010 to commemorate Senegal's 50 years of independence from France. The Soviet-style bronze of a man, woman and child looking out to sea has been heavily criticised for its cost (over US$30 million), the un-African shapes of its figures and the scantily dressed female, which offers a partial view of her breast and thighs. You can walk around the base for free; the entry fee is for the interior of the monument. A small display explains its construction and an elevator whisks you up to the head of the male figure, boasting expansive views of Dakar.

Central Dakar

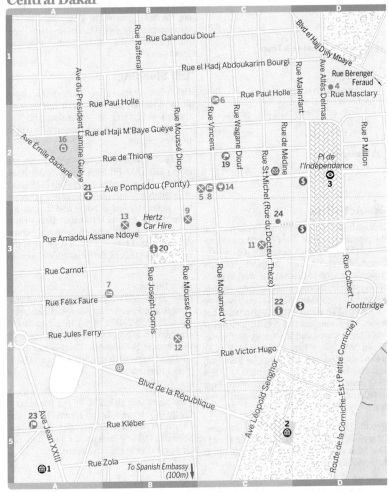

Hôtel du Phare HOTEL **$**

(Map p330; ☎ 33 860 3000; www.lesmamelles. com; Les Mamelles; s with/without bathroom CFA25,000/18,000, d CFA31,000/23,000; ✳ @ 🛜) This family-friendly, patio-adorned guesthouse has a handful of rooms with simple charm and a homely ambience.

★**La Demeure** GUESTHOUSE **$$**

(Map p330; ☎ 33 820 7679; www.lademeure-guest house.com; Rte de Ngor; d CFA59,000-79,000; ✳ 🛜 ⊠) Oozing laid-back elegance, this little guesthouse offers pleasant rooms (all with balconies) in a rambling, well-maintained house filled with a clutch of tasteful art collected by its engaging owner. It boasts a fantastic terrace and kitchen access in the afternoons and evenings.

La Brazzérade HOTEL **$**

(Map p330; ☎ 33 820 0683; www.labrazzerade.com; Plage de N'Gor; d/ste CFA30,000/50,000; ✳ @ 🛜) Known for its fabulous grill, this place has a hotel floor perched above the restaurant like a half-forgotten afterthought (or your little hideaway). The more expensive rooms have a small balcony and views over Île de N'Gor – an investment you should make.

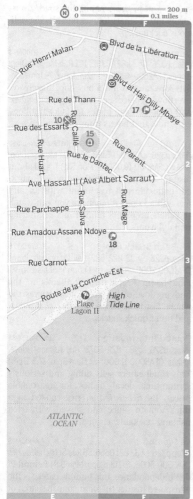

Central Dakar

◎ Sights
1	Musée Théodore Monod	A5
2	Palais Présidentiel	C5
3	Place de l'Indépendance	D2

⊕ Activities, Courses & Tours
4	Sahel Découverte Bassari	D1

⊜ Sleeping
5	Chez Nizar	C2
6	Hôtel Farid	C1
7	Hôtel Saint-Louis Sun	B3

⊗ Eating
8	Ali Baba Snack Bar	C2
9	Chez Loutcha	B3
10	Le Cozy	E2
11	Le Djembé	C3
12	Le Toukouleur	B4
13	Point d'Interrogation	B3
	Restaurant Farid	(see 6)

⊜ Drinking & Nightlife
14	Le Viking	C2

⊜ Shopping
15	Marché Kermel	E2
16	Marché Sandaga	A2

⊕ Information
17	Cape Verdean Embassy	F1
18	French Embassy	F3
19	Gambian Embassy	C2
20	Institut Français Léopold Sédar Senghor	B3
21	Pharmacie Guigon	A2
22	Senegal Tours	C4
23	US Embassy	A5

⊕ Transport
24	Senegal Airlines Agency	C3

Hôtel Saint-Louis Sun
HOTEL **$**

(Map p326; ☏ 33 822 2570; htlstlouisun@orange. sn; Rue Félix Faure; s/d CFA25,000/33,000; ❉ @) Rooms are pretty basic, but the central courtyard with huge palm trees turns the space into a calm oasis in the heart of Dakar.

Maison Abaka
HOTEL **$**

(Map p330; ☏ 33 820 6486; www.maison-abaka. com; Plage de N'Gor; r from CFA38,000; ❉ @ ☎ ≋) This surfers' favourite has airy and lovingly decorated rooms located right behind the beach.

Hôtel Farid
HOTEL **$$**

(Map p326; ☏ 33 821 6127; www.hotelfarid.com; 51 Rue Vincens; s/d from CFA41,000/45,000; ❉ @ ☎) This small place with a fabulous Lebanese restaurant is by no means luxurious but is a safe and comfortable option in the city centre.

Ambre
GUESTHOUSE **$$**

(Map p330; ☏ 33 820 6338; www.ambre.sn; Rte des Almadies; r from CFA52,000; ❉ @ ☎ ≋) Green, art adorned and beautifully designed, this small guesthouse is as friendly as a smile. A unique gem close to the city's best hotels and bars.

GETTING UNDER DAKAR'S SKIN

A brilliant way of getting to know Dakar and the rest of the country, its changeable moods and early-morning faces is by staying with a local family, sharing their lives for a few days and finding out what their world is really like. **Senegal Chez l'Habitant** (☑ 77 517 2666; www. senegalchezlhabitant.com) maintains a regularly updated register of families across Senegal who would like to open their houses to foreigners and puts you in touch with recommended families. The organisation checks the places it recommends and takes time to connect you with a home that fits your profile, from the most basic to the more luxurious stay.

Le Djoloff
HOTEL $$

(Map p330; ☑ 33 889 3630; www.hotel djoloff.com; 7 Rue Nani, Fann Hock; s/d/ste CFA55,000/70,000/130,000; ❄ @ ☎) Designed to make you feel like Malian royalty, this place comes with a wide, wonderful roof terrace and a solid restaurant.

Radisson Blu
HOTEL $$$

(Map p330; ☑ 33 869 3333; www.radissonblu. com; Rte de la Corniche-Ouest; d from CFA150,000; P ❄ @ ☎ ⊠) As one of Dakar's most luxurious hotel, with a contemporary, business feel, this plush spot is a decadent place to enjoy all the standard upmarket trimmings.

✖ Eating

Dakar's restaurant scene unites the scents and flavours of the world, though you need a healthy budget to eat out. If you're getting by on a few crumpled CFA notes a day, stop at the ubiquitous street stalls selling rice and sauce or one of the many *shwarma* places. The best-stocked supermarket is **Casino** (Map p330; ☑ 33 820 3361; Rte de N'Gor, in the Dakar City shopping complex; ◷ 8am-8pm).

★ Le Cozy
INTERNATIONAL $$$

(Map p326; ☑ 33 823 0606; www.lecozy.com; Rue des Essarts; dishes CFA8000-14,000; ◷ noon-3pm & 7pm-midnight) Waltz through Le Cozy's heavy wooden doors and you're instantly swept off the market streets into a temple of refined cuisine. Presentation and service are as perfect as the swanky restaurant and bar

spaces and in the evening, the space transforms into a smart lounge bar, serving delicious cocktails.

Chez Loutcha
AFRICAN $

(Map p326; ☑ 33 821 0302; 101 Rue Moussé Diop; dishes CFA2500-4000; ◷ noon-3pm & 7-11pm Mon-Sat) A restaurant like a bus stop, this always overflowing place serves up huge Senegalese and Cape Verdean plates to its loyal followers – note that it gets rammed at lunch.

Le Toukouleur
AFRICAN, INTERNATIONAL $$$

(Map p326; ☑ 33 821 5193; 122 Rue Moussé Diop; mains CFA6000-10,000; ◷ Mon-Sat) It's all about tasteful African chic in this mud-red painted, patio-adorned restaurant with an airy feel and an open kitchen, so you can watch the chefs prepare a refined mix of international flavours.

Ali Baba Snack Bar
FAST FOOD $

(Map p326; ☑ 33 822 5297; Av Pompidou; items CFA1000-2000; ◷ 8-2am) Dakar's classic fast-food haunt keeps turning thanks to the undying love of the Senegalese. Serves the whole fast-food range: kebabs, *shwarmas* and other quick snacks.

Point d'Interrogation
SENEGALESE $$

(Map p326; ☑ 33 822 5072; Rue Assane Ndoye; dishes CFA5000-11,000; ◷ 11am-3pm & 5-11pm) This small eatery sells filling and seriously scrumptious local dishes for reasonable prices. Its *tiéboutienne* (rice cooked in a thick tomato sauce and served with fried fish and vegetables) is divine.

Le Djembé
AFRICAN $

(Map p326; ☑ 33 821 0666; 56 Rue St Michel; dishes CFA3500-5000; ◷ 11am-5pm Mon-Sat) Behind Pl de l'Indépendance, this humble eatery is the whispered insider tip for anyone in search of a filling platter of *tiéboudienne*.

Restaurant Farid
LEBANESE $$

(Map p326; ☑ 33 823 6123; 51 Rue Vincens; dishes CFA5800-14,000; ◷ noon-11pm; ☑) Squeezed between grey inner-city walls, this little oasis serves the best Lebanese meze in town, plus quality grilled meat and fish.

Le Ngor
SEAFOOD $$

(Map p330; ☑ 77 504 3006; Corniche des Almadies; dishes CFA5000-7500; ◷ 11am-11pm Tue-Sat) At this quirky, seashell-adorned place, waves lap at your feet while you enjoy a perfectly grilled fish.

Le Récif des Almadies   SEAFOOD $$

(Map p330; ☑ 33 820 1160; Pointe des Almadies; mains CFA5500-7800; ☺ noon-midnight Thu-Tue) Occupying a prime location right on the Pointe des Almadies with views across the Atlantic; the menu here is as big as a book and packed with seasonal dishes.

Sao Brasil   ITALIAN $$

(Map p330; ☑ 33 820 0941; Rte de N'Gor, Station Shell; pizzas CFA6000; ☺ noon-4pm & 6.30pm-midnight; 🐾) Very confusingly named, this is one of Dakar's favourite restaurants (especially among the local expat community). Pizzas come with a huge diameter, a thin base and a large range of toppings.

★ Cabane des Pêcheurs   SEAFOOD $$

(Map p330; ☑ 33 820 7675; Plage de N'Gor; dishes CFA6000-10,000; ☺ 11am-3pm & 7-11pm) Dakar's best fish restaurant serves you absolutely fresh treats, such as amberjack and dolphin-fish, that you'll find hardly anywhere else in the city.

🍷 Drinking & Nightlife

There are bars to suit every taste in Dakar, but glam venues are mainly in the Les Almadies area. Live-music venues with dance floors are extremely popular, but nights on the dance floor start late – most places don't start to boogie before 1am. And always, always overdress. Bars are usually free, but cover charges at clubs and live-music venues are roughly CFA4000 to CFA12,000.

Le Viking   PUB

(Map p326; ☑ 77 244 8056; 21 Ave Pompidou) At this old-style, beer-scented pub, the pints spill over and the guests are red-faced. Women will feel safer if they've come with a few friends.

INSTITUT FRANÇAIS LÉOPOLD SÉDAR SENGHOR

Dakar's **Institut Français Léopold Sédar Senghor** (Map p326; ☑ 33 823 0320; www.ifdakar.org; 89 Rue Joseph Gomis), a spacious arts centre occupying a whole city block, is one of the main hubs of cultural activity in Dakar. It features an open-air stage (a fantastic place to catch a live-music gig), a good cafe, and exhibition and cinema rooms, and also houses a couple of artists' workshops and shops in its vast garden.

DAKAR MARKETS

You need plenty of energy and a safe place to hide your purse for a Dakar market tour. **Marché Sandaga** (Map p326; cnr Ave Pompidou & Ave du Président Lamine Guèye) in the centre is the largest market, with rickety stalls that claim most of the area around Ave Pompidou. **Marché des HLM** (Map p330; Av CA Bamba) is stacked with dazzling African fabrics. **Marché Tilène** is chock-full of fruits, vegetables and tiny tailor shops. The **Village Artisanal Soumbédioune** (Map p330) is the most popular place for buying souvenirs such as wood carvings, metal work and batiks. Also in the town centre, the historical, covered **Marché Kermel** (Map p326) includes both souvenir and food stalls.

Le Patio   BAR

(Map p330; ☑ 33 820 5823; Rte de N'Gor) Past the broad-shouldered bouncers and across the red carpet, this large outdoor place serves excellent cocktails within stumbling distance of the nightclubs.

New Africa   BAR

(Map p330; ☑ 33 827 5371; 9794 Sacré Cœur III) This may be the only bar where there's no pressure to dress up and sparkle. The Friday salsa nights are fantastic.

Just 4 U   LIVE MUSIC

(Map p330; ☑ 33 824 3250; www.just4udakar.com; Ave Cheikh Anta Diop; ☺ 11am-3am) If you only have time for one live music venue, don't miss Just 4 U. The small stage of this outdoor restaurant has been graced by the greatest Senegalese and international stars, from jazz to rap to folk and reggae. There's a concert on every day, and you often get to catch the big names.

Pen'Art   BLUES, JAZZ

(Map p330; ☑ 33 864 5131; Blvd du Sud) This cosy jazz club always impresses with good bands in a relaxed atmosphere.

Thiossane   CLUB

(Map p330; Rue 10) Owned by Youssou N'Dour, one of Africa's most notable musicians and Senegal's tourism and culture minister, this legendary club is always packed and jamming to anything from *mbalax* to international beats.

Greater Dakar

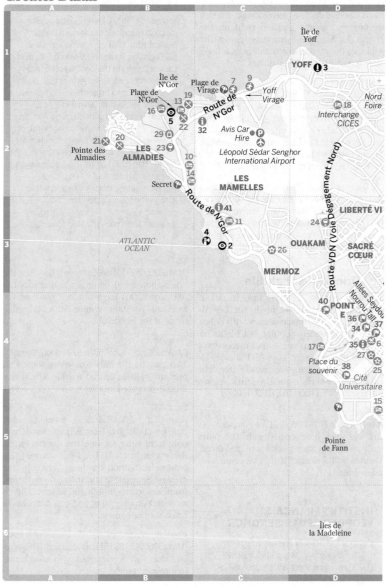

Le Balajo   LIVE MUSIC

(Map p330; ☎ 33 864 51 00; Ave Cheikh Anta Diop; ☉ Thu-Sun) Excellent bar and venue for live music with mainly African bands.

 Orientation

The expansive Pl de l'Indépendance is the city's heart. From here, major streets lead in all directions, including Ave Léopold Senghor and Ave Pompidou, which leads west to Marché Sandaga.

centre, and north of there are Les Almadies, Yoff and N'Gor, with Dakar's best beaches.

ℹ Information

CULTURAL CENTRES

British Council (Map p330; ☎ 33 869 2700; Rue AAB-68, Amitié Zone A&B) Has English magazines and occasional events.

Goethe Institut (Map p330; ☎ 33 869 8880; www.goethe.de/ins/sn/dak; cnr Rue de Diourbel & Piscine Olympique) The German cultural centre frequently hosts exhibitions and shows films.

INTERNET ACCESS

There are a few internet cafes, and wi-fi is spreading fast; it's offered free for customers in dozens of hotels and restaurants.

Espacetel Plus (☎ 33 822 9062; Blvd de la République; per hr CFA400; ⏰ 8am-midnight)

MEDIA

The exhaustive website www.au-senegal.com gives you an answer to almost any question about Senegal. Most parts of this French site are available in software-translated English.

The 221 section (CFA100) contains a cultural calendar, as well as interesting write-ups on music, arts and sports around the country.

MEDICAL SERVICES

Hospitals are understaffed and underequipped; for faster service try a private clinic. Pharmacies are plentiful in Dakar; most are open 8am to 8pm Monday to Saturday but rotate with 24-hour shifts.

Clinique de Cap (Map p324; ☎ 33 821 6146; www.cliniqueducap.com; Ave Pasteur) One of the biggest private medical clinics in Dakar.

Hôpital Principal (Map p324; ☎ 33 839 5050; www.hopitalprincipal.sn; 1 Ave Nelson Mandéla) Main hospital and emergency department.

Pharmacie Guigon (Map p326; ☎ 33 823 0333; 1 Ave du Président Lamine Guèye; ⏰ 8am-11pm Mon-Sat) One of the best-stocked options.

MONEY

ATM-equipped banks are never too far away in Dakar. Main branches are at Place de l'Indépendance.

POST & TELEPHONE

There are many small *télécentres* (call centres); post offices also have telephone facilities.

SAFE TRAVEL

Dakar's notorious street hustlers and hard-to-shake-off traders do a pretty good job at turning any walk around town into mild punishment, particularly for women. Stride purposefully on, and throw in a brief *bakhna* ('it's OK') and they'll

From here, Ave du Président Lamine Guèye goes north to Gare Routière Pompiers. The quickest route out of the centre is the coastal Rte de la Corniche-Ouest. To the north of the city centre lie the suburbs Point E, Fann, Mermoz and Ouakam, all of which have good bars and restaurants. The airport is 19km north of the town

Greater Dakar

eventually leave you alone. Many of them also double as pickpockets – be particularly vigilant at markets and in town.

Muggings – often at knifepoint or from passing scooters – are not uncommon. Avoid walking around after dark. Trouble spots include the Petite Corniche (behind the presidential palace), the Rte de la Corniche-Ouest and the beaches.

TRAVEL AGENCIES

ATG (Map p330; ☑ 33 869 7900; www.africa-travel-group.com; Rte de N'Gor; ⊙10am-6pm Mon-Fri, to 1pm Sat) Great for tours.

Nouvelles Frontières (Map p330; ☑ 33 859 4447; www.nfsenegal.com; Rte des Almadies, Lot 1 Mamelles Aviation; ⊙ 8.30am-6pm Mon-Fri, 9am-12.30pm Sat)

Senegal Tours (Map p326; ☑ 33 839 9900; www.senegal-tours.sn; 5 Pl de l'Indépendance; ⊙9am-6pm Mon-Fri, to noon Sat) Large tour operator that does ticketing and tours.

ⓘ Getting There & Away

AIR

Léopold Sédar Senghor International Airport (p347) is in Yoff. Senegal Airlines (p348) flies to and from 15 destinations across Central and West Africa (including Cap Skiring and Ziguinchor in Senegal and Banjul in the Gambia), at the time of research, with plans to expand the network. It also operates a **ticket office downtown** (Map p326; ☑ 33 839 77 77; Rue Amadou Assane Ndoye/Rotunda Building; ⊙ 9am-6pm Mon-Fri, to noon Sat).

BOAT

Aline Sitoé Diatta Ferry Dakar-Ziguinchor Ticket Office (☑33 849 4893; 1 Blvd de la Libération; one way CFA16,000-31,000) The Aline Sitoé Diatta ferry travels between Dakar and Ziguinchor twice weekly in each direction, leaving Dakar every Tuesday and Friday at 8pm, arriving in Ziguinchor the next day at 10am. Note that you *cannot* buy tickets over the phone.

BUSH TAXI

Road transport for long-distance destinations leaves from Gare Routière Pompiers, off Ave Malik Sy (a taxi from Place de l'Indépendance should cost around CFA2000). Rates are fixed but change frequently with fluctuations in the cost of petrol. Main destinations include Mbour (CFA3000), Saint-Louis (CFA4900), Karang at the Gambian border (CFA5800), Tambacounda (CFA9800) and Ziguinchor (CFA12,000).

TRAIN

Dakar's train station is 500m north of Place de l'Indépendance. In the past there has been an unreliable line between Dakar and Bamako (Mali), but at the time of research it was not running.

❶ Getting Around

Most car-hire agencies in Dakar (see map p330) are at the airport or in the city centre.

BUS

Dakar Dem Dikk (DDD; www.demdikk.com) buses are a pretty good way of travelling cheaply. There are several connections to the town centre. Fares cost beween CFA150 and CFA275. They're quite reliable and only crammed full during rush hour. Check the website for a detailed list of DDD routes.

More frequent but less user-friendly are the white Ndiaga Ndiaye minivans and the blue-yellow *cars rapides,* Dakar's battered, crammed and dangerously driven symbols of identity. Unless you know your way around, it's hard to find out where they are going. They stop randomly and suddenly – tap a coin on the roof to signal that you're getting off.

TAXI

Taxis are the easiest way of getting around town. Rates are entirely negotiable. A short hop costs from CFA600 upwards. Dakar centre to Point E is around CFA1700; it's up to CFA2700 from the centre to N'Gor and Yoff.

The official taxi rates for trips from Léopold Sédar Senghor International Airport are put up outside the airport. Don't pay more.

AROUND DAKAR

Île de Gorée

Ruled in succession by the Portuguese, Dutch, English and French, the historical, Unesco-designated Île de Gorée is enveloped by an almost eerie calm. There are no sealed roads and no cars on this island, just narrow alleyways with trailing bougainvilleas and colonial brick buildings with wrought-iron balconies – it's a living, visual masterpiece. But Gorée's calm is not so much romantic as meditative, as the ancient, elegant buildings bear witness to the island's role in the Atlantic slave trade.

You pay a tourist tax of CFA600 at the booth to the left of the ferry landing. If you need a guide, you can arrange it there, but the island is easily explored independently.

◎ Sights & Activities

Gorée is an internationally famous symbol of the tragedy of the Atlantic slave trade. Though relatively few slaves were actually shipped from here, the island was a place where much of the trade was orchestrated. Many artists also live here and their work is displayed at various small art galleries around town.

★**Maison des Esclaves**　　　MUSEUM
(Slave House; admission CFA600; ◎10am-noon & 2.30-6.30pm Tue-Sun) Set in a former grand home, allegedly used as a departure point for slaves (see boxed text p334), this is one of the most important monuments to the slave trade and features the famous 'doorway to nowhere' opening directly to the sea.

IFAN Historical Museum　　　MUSEUM
(☑33 822 2003; admission CFA600; ◎10am-noon & 2.30-6pm Tue-Sat) Contains ancient island maps, photos and artefacts under low, white arcs. Note: when you walk upstairs you're greated by fabulous views of Dakar.

Castel　　　HILL
Climb to the top of the Castel, the southern tip of the island, for great views, and seek out the cluster of tiny arts workshops filled with pieces by local artists.

🛏 Sleeping & Eating

Many Gorée residents keep a spare room for unexpected (and paying) visitors – just ask around and someone will show someone. Prices per person start at around CFA9000 per night.

For cheaper food options than the Hostellerie, check out any of the many eateries opposite the jetty.

★**Chez Valerie**　　　GUESTHOUSE $
(☑33 821 8195; csaodakar@orange.sn; 7 Rue St Joseph; r CFA15,000-20,000; 🛜) One of the prettiest and friendliest private options is Chez Valerie, an old Goréen house.

Hostellerie du Chevalier de Boufflers　　　FRENCH $$
(☑33 822 5364; r from CFA18,000-23,000; 🛜) Set in one of Gorée's classic elegant old homes, this place is mainly famous for its garden restaurant serving seafood-focused fare (meals CFA5000-7000) but also offers five tasteful rooms.

THE SLAVE HOUSE

Île de Gorée was an important trading station during the 18th and 19th centuries, and many merchants built houses in which they would live or work in the upper storey and store their human cargo on the lower floor.

La Maison des Esclaves (The Slave House; p333) is one of the last remaining 18th-century buildings of this type on Gorée. It was built in 1786 and renovated in 1990 with French assistance. With its famous 'doorway to nowhere' opening directly from the storeroom onto the sea, this building has enormous spiritual significance for some visitors, particularly African Americans whose ancestors were brought from Africa as slaves.

Walking around the dimly lit dungeons, you can begin to imagine the suffering of the people held here. It is this emotive illustration that really describes La Maison des Esclaves as a whole – its historical significance in the slave trade may not have been huge, but the island's symbolic role is immense.

The island's precise status as a slave-trading station is hotly debated. Of the 20 million slaves that were taken from Africa, the general belief is that only around 300 per year may have gone through Gorée (historians and academics dispute the exact number and some argue that no slaves passed through this specific house) and, even then, the famous doorway would not have been used – ships could not get near the dangerous rocks and the town had a jetty a short distance away.

But the number of slaves transported from here isn't what matters in the debate around Gorée. The island and museum stands as a melancholy reminder of the suffering the Atlantic slave trade inflicted on African people.

ⓘ Getting There & Away

A **ferry** (☑ 33 849 7961, 24hr info line 77 628 1111) runs regularly from the wharf in Dakar to Gorée (CFA6000 return for nonresidents, 20 minutes).

Lac Rose

Also known as Lac Retba, this shallow lagoon surrounded by dunes is a popular day-trip destination for *dakarois* and tourists alike, all coming to enjoy the calm and catch the lake's magic trick – the subtle pink shimmer that sometimes colours its waves. The spectacle is caused by the water's high salt content, which is 10 times that of your regular ocean. It's a beautiful sight but can only be enjoyed when the light is right. Your best chance is in dry season, when the sun is high. But even if nature refuses to put on her show, a day out here is still enjoyable. You can swim in the lake, buoyed by the salt, or check out the small-scale salt-collecting industry on its shores. And up until the demise of the Dakar rally, Lac Rose is where the Sahara drivers would arrive and celebrate their victories or drown their woes.

Most hotels here are clustered near the Village Artisanal, a spot that's plagued by touts and hustlers. One of the cheapest is Chez Salim (☑ 33 836 2466; www.chez-salim.com; d CFA20,000; ☜), with well-maintained bungalows set in a garden, but the best place is Chevaux du Lac (☑ 77 630 0241; www.chevaux dulac.com; half board CFA22,000; horseback tours 1½/3hr CFA12,000/20,000; ❋☜) on the other end of the lake. It's friendly and welcoming and offers tours around the lake on horseback.

Trying to get here by public transport involves a journey by minibus, *car rapide* (CFA600) or DDD bus 11 to Keur Massar; from there it's a 5km walk to the lake. It's much easier to hire a private taxi (round trip with some waiting time costs around CFA18,000).

PETITE CÔTE & SINÉ-SALOUM DELTA

The 150km Petite Côte stretches south from Dakar and is one of Senegal's best beach areas. Where the Siné and Saloum Rivers meet the tidal waters of the Atlantic Ocean, the coast is broken into a stunning area of mangrove swamps, lagoons, forests and sand islands. It forms part of the magnificent 180-sq-km Siné-Saloum Delta.

Mbour & Saly

Eighty kilometres south of Dakar, Mbour is the main town on the Petite Côte and the region's most vibrant and important fishing centre. Nearby Saly, with its strip of big ocean-front hotels, is the heavier weight when it comes to tourism.

Mbour's busy, slightly nauseating fish market on the beach, where the catch is immediately gutted and dispatched, is a sight to behold. **Chez Martine La Suissesse** (33 957 3109; Mbour; d incl breakfast CFA12,000-18,000) is a mere 100m from the beach and offers simple, clean rooms. **Tama Lodge** (33 957 0040; www.tamalodge.com; Mbour; s/d from CFA35,000/48,000;) has exquisitely designed bungalows, an eclectic art collection scattered around the property and a great restaurant, while the simple **New Blue Africa** (33 957 0993; Rte de Niakhniakhal, Mbour; s/d CFA35,000/42,000) sits on Mbour's finest dune. Perennially popular **Chez Paolo** (33 957 1310; Mbour; mains CFA3000-4500) is the local favourite and serves up super Senegalese dishes in modest digs.

If it's a beach holiday you're after, then Saly is the perfect corner for soaking up the sun and sipping cocktails. **Ferme de Saly & Les Amazones** (77 638 4790; www.farmsaly.com; Saly; d CFA20,000-36,000, apt CFA40,000-50,000) is a classic with overlanders, a place of sound sleep, good food and the generous company of host Jean-Paul. Nearer Saly village, **La Medina** (33 957 4993; Terrain de Football, Saly village; s/d CFA17,000/22,000;) has good, clean rooms surrounding a leafy patio. For a splurge try the bright and classy bungalows with private, sunny terraces at **Espadon** (33 939 7099; www.espadon-hotel.com; Saly; s/d incl breakfast CFA72,000/120,000;) – the hotel restaurant (international fare) is stellar and there's a great wellness centre for relaxation. For a daytime dose of fresh seafood with a view of the beach hit **Les Tables du Marlin** (33 957 2477; Saly; mains CFA3000-8000, 10am-7pm), but the best food is dished up at **Le Patio du Mar y Sol** (33 957 0777; Saly; mains CFA5000-9000), where you can dine on luscious French fare, poolside with a chilled beverage.

Joal-Fadiout

The twin villages of Joal and Fadiout are located south of Mbour at the end of the tar road. Joal sits on the mainland, while Fadiout is on a small island made of clam and oyster shells (even the houses, streets and cemeteries!), reached by an impressive wooden bridge. It's dreamy to wander around the island's narrow alleys, admire the shell-world and pop into artisan workshops dotted around. Your best bets for lodging are on Joal, but it's an easy hop to the island. Culturally, the local citizens are proud of their tolerance – this is a place where Christians and Muslims live in harmony.

The tiny auberge **Le Thiouraye** (77 515 6064; Joal; s/d incl breakfast CFA12,000/14,000;) has basic riverside rooms and a menu composed by one of Senegal's top chefs. **Keur Seynabou** (33 957 6744; www.keurseynabou.com; Joal; r CFA35,000-40,000;) sparkles with magazine-perfect lodgings overlooking a pool.

Minibuses go to/from Mbour (CFA800) and Palmarin (CFA1400). A *sept-place* taxi goes directly to Dakar most mornings (without changing at Mbour) for CFA3000.

Palmarin

Palmarin, with its soft lagoons, tall palm groves and labyrinthine creeks, is one of Senegal's most beautiful, and secret, spots.

There's a seductive choice of *campements* (guesthouses). The straw huts of **Yokam** (77 567 0113; Palmarin Facao; per person incl breakfast CFA9000) are cheap and lightweight, but the company is good. The red-mud structure of **Lodge de Diakhamor** (33 957 1256; Palmarin; s/d with half board CFA26,000/46,000;) is a stylish redbrick place where *pirogue* excursions, horse riding, and bicycle and fishing trips are all included in the price. **Lodge des Collines de Niassam** (77 639 0639; www.niassam.com; Palmarin; per person with half board CFA59,000;) is one of Senegal's most original *campements*. You can sleep in classy tree houses that cling to the mighty branches of baobabs, or sit on stilts in the river.

Palmarin is most easily reached by minibus from Mbour, via Joal-Fadiout and Sambadia (where you may have to change). The fare from Joal to Sambadia is CFA600 in a Ndiaga Ndiaye, and from Sambadia to Palmarin it's CFA450.

Ndangane & Mar Lodj

Siné-Saloum Delta's Ndangane is a thriving traveller centre along the coast from where you can take a *pirogue* to almost any point in the delta. Ndangane's cheapie is the lively

BIRDWATCHING & MORE IN PARC NATIONAL DU DELTA DU SALOUM

Covering over 76,000 hectares of mangrove-lined creeks, sandy islands, large sea areas and woodland, the **Parc National du Delta du Saloum** (admission CFA2000) is Senegal's second-largest national park. Beyond the mangrove swamps and a large marine section its main attraction is the fantastically varied landscape and the hundreds of bird species it attracts in the south. In the gallery forest and savannah woodlands of the Forêt de Fathala you might also spot wild boars and patas monkeys. You need a bit of luck to view the park's common duikers, bushbucks and red colobus monkeys – they're becoming very rare as human settlements, deforestation and hunting impact on the park, despite its protected status.

But if birds are your focus, Toubakouta offers enough bird life to have keen spotters stay here for days. It's mostly an area for sea birds and waders, though the nearby forest areas house some other species, including hornbills and sunbirds.

A good place to start a birdwatching tour is Diorom Boumag, an ancient seashell mound where giant baobabs have taken root, a 20-minute *pirogue* ride from Toubakouta. In their branches nestle numerous Senegalese parrots and rose-ringed parakeets. It's best to visit this place by *pirogue* in the late afternoon and move further along the river to arrive around dusk at the Reposoir des Oiseaux, where you can watch swarms of pelicans, cormorants, egrets and plenty of other species prepare noisily for the night.

The northern creeks and wetlands of the park can be explored on *pirogue* tours from Palmarin, Dionewar or Djifer. The Forêt de Fathala and the southern islands are best reached from Missirah.

Le Barracuda (Chez Mbacke; ☎ 33 949 9815; Ndangane; r per person CFA7000), with great views from the restaurant terrace. Brightly coloured **Auberge Bouffe** (☎ 33 949 9313; www.aubergebouffe.com; Ndangane; d CFA22,000; @ 🛜 🛏) has well-maintained rooms and plenty of character. Opposite, **Les Cordons Bleus** (☎ 33 949 9312; www.lescordonsbleus.com; Ndangane; s/d/tr CFA34,000/46,000/58,000; P 🚻 @ 🛜 🛏) has the best rooms in town.

Mar Lodj island is a much calmer choice, especially if you bunk at **Le Bazouk** (☎ 77 633 4894; www.bazoukdusaloum.com; Mar Lodj; per person with half board CFA18,000), with its spacious bungalows scattered over a vast, sand-covered garden in which bougainvilleas lend shade and palm trees carry hammocks. **Essamaye** (☎ 77 555 3667; www.senegalia.com; Marfafako; per person with full board CFA22,000) on the other side of the island is a place like a hug from a loved one – highly recommended for family vibes and its impressive Casamance-style *case à l'impluvium* (large, round traditional house).

Take any bus between Kaolack and Mbour, and get off at Ndiosomone, from where bush taxis shuttle back and forth to Ndangane. For Mar Lodj, contact your *campement* for *pirogue* pick-up, or hire a boat at the **GIE des Piroguiers** (☎ 77 226 6168, 77 213 7497), the boat owners association at the jetty in Ndangane.

Toubakouta & Missirah

Toubakouta is a fantastically calm and pretty spot in the south of the Siné-Saloum Delta, and is one of the country's best places for birdwatching. In town, **Keur Youssou** (☎ 33 948 7728; www.keuryoussou.com; Toubakouta; s/d CFA7700/13,000; 🚻) has beautifully furnished rooms and a relaxed ambience. **Keur Thierry** (☎ 77 439 8605; Toubakouta; d incl breakfast CFA14,000; 🚻) has equally lovely rooms but the better kitchen and colder beers. **Hôtel Keur Saloum** (☎ 33 948 7715; www.keursaloum.com; Toubakouta; s/d incl breakfast CFA38,000/58,000; P 🚻 @ 🛜 🛏) is the classiest place in town. A *pirogue* and donkey-cart ride away, **Keur Bamboung** (☎ 77 510 8013; www.oceanium.org; bungalows with half/full board CFA17,000/22,000) is the hub of the Marine Protected Area surrounding it. Things are simple and green, and the location is stunning. Phone to arrange pick-up from Toubakouta.

South of Toubakouta, Missirah is the point of entry to the Parc National du Delta du Saloum. The peaceful **Gîte de Bandiala** (☎ 33 948 7735; www.gite-bandiala.com; Missirah; per person with half/full board CFA16,900/23,200) sits right on its edge, has a water hole on site and organises tours through the Forêt de Fathala.

A private taxi from Toubakouta to Missirah costs around CFA6200.

NORTHERN SENEGAL

Saint-Louis

POP 172,000

With its crumbling colonial architecture, horse-drawn carts and peaceful ambience, West Africa's first French settlement has a unique historical charm – so much so it's been a Unesco World Heritage Site since 2000. The old town centre sits on an island in the Senegal River, but the city sprawls into Sor on the mainland, and onto the Langue de Barbarie, where you'll find the lively fishing community of Guet N'Dar.

The island is reached via the 500m-long Pont Faidherbe, a feat of 19th-century engineering.

◉ Sights & Activities

Place Faidherbe   SQUARE

With its statue of the French governor who led the colonial expansion eastwards and initiated many ambitious infrastructural projects, this square sits adjacent to several intact 19th-century houses, including the Governor's Palace and the 1837 Rognât Casernes on its north and south. Next to the governor's palace, you'll find a lovely 1828 cathedral (Rue de l'Eglise) with a neoclassical facade worth admiring. This central space is where Saint-Louis splits into its southern part (Sindoné) and northern part (Lodo); the former the old Christian town, the latter the original home to the Muslim population.

★ Pont Faidherbe   BRIDGE

(Senegal River) Transferred to Saint-Louis in 1897, the metal arches of this bridge designed by Gustav Eiffel and originally built to cross the Danube, the Pont Faidherbe is the city's most significant landmark. You'll cross its steel planks when driving into town; it links the mainland and island. The bridge is a grand piece of 19th-century engineering – 507m long with a noteworthy middle swing span that rotates to allow ships to steam up the Senegal River. The entire bridge was rehabilitated in stages between 2008 and 2012, with sections of the original bridge's crumbling metal spans replaced piece by piece with steel replicas of the original design.

IFAN Museum   MUSEUM

(☑ 33 961 1050; Quai Henri Jay; adult/child CFA600/350; ⊙ 9am-noon & 3-6pm) This heritage, art and culture museum contains photos of famous Saint-Louis personalities, an informative history section (in French) and exhibits on local culture and topography including antique dolls and exhibits on local flora and fauna.

Grand Mosque   RELIGIOUS, SPIRITUAL

(Ave Jean Mermoz) The Maghreb-style building of the Grand Mosque in the north was constructed in 1847 on order of the colonial administration to appease the growing Muslim population. The oddity of an attached clock tower betrays the designers' religious affiliation.

Les Ateliers Tèsss   ARTS CENTRE

(☑ 33 961 6860; www.tesss.net; Rue Khalifa Ababacar Sy; ⊙ 9am-1.30pm, 3-8pm Mon-Sat) Les Ateliers Tèsss displays beautiful woven products (you can see the artisans at work).

Guet N'Dar   VILLAGE

On the Langue de Barbarie, Guet N'Dar is a fantastically busy fishing town worth checking out to observe local culture. Come here to watch dozens of *pirogues* being launched in the morning, and fish being brought in, gutted and smoked on the shore in the afternoon.

✷ Festivals & Events

Saint-Louis Jazz Festival   FESTIVAL

(http://saintlouisjazz.net) The most internationally renowned festival in West Africa is held annually in early May and attracts jazz greats from around the world. The main event usually happens at the Quai des Arts or on an open-air stage in Place Faidherbe, and there are fringe events all over town.

Les Fanals   FESTIVAL

Celebrated the last week of December around Christmas, this historic lantern procession has its roots in the *signares'* (p339) lantern-lit marches to midnight Mass. Today it evokes Saint-Louisian history and reaffirms the town's unique identity.

🛏 Sleeping

Hotel Dior & Camping Océan   HOTEL $

(☑ 33 961 3118; www.hotel-dior-senegal.com; Hydrobase; campsites CFA6,000, s CFA25,000-33,000, d CFA32,000-37,000; @ 🛜) With Mauritanian tents tucked away behind sand dunes, this overlander favourite feels like a desert

home. For more comfort, rent a bungalow with hot water and minibar.

Auberge de la Vallée　　　　　　HOTEL $
(🕿 33 961 4722; Ave Blaise Diagne; d/tr from CFA16,000/18,000; ❈@🛜) A basic but friendly choice in the heart of the city, with bright, simple rooms and friendly staff.

★ **Hôtel Mermoz**　　　　　BOUTIQUE HOTEL $$
(🕿 33 961 3668; www.hotelmermoz.com; Rte de l'Hydrobase; d CFA25,000-40,000, with sea view CFA40,000-55,000; 🅿❈🛜🏊) With huts and bungalows spaced out in a large, sandy garden, and all buildings connected by meandering paths, this place oozes character. It has free bikes for guests to use, and offers a range of seaside excursions and sports.

La Résidence　　　　　　　　HOTEL $$
(🕿 33 961 1260; www.hoteldelaresidence.com; Ave Blaise Diagne; s/d/ste from CFA35,000/ 42,000/50,000; ❈@🛜) The Bancals, the old Saint-Louisian family that owns this classic place, have done a great job of evoking history. Each item and picture in the guest rooms has a meaningful link to Saint-Louis' colourful past.

Jamm
GUESTHOUSE **$$**

(Chez Yves Lamour; ☑77 443 4765; www.jamm-saintlouis.com; Rue Paul Holle; s/d incl breakfast CFA55,000/62,000; ❋@🛜) One of Saint-Louis' most beautifully restored houses offers four tiled and brick-walled rooms with ceilings high enough to impress even regular churchgoers. Every tiny decorative detail has been restored with care.

★ La Maison Rose
HOTEL **$$$**

(☑33 938 2222; www.lamaisonrose.net; Rue Blaise Diagne; d CFA67,000-85,000, ste CFA94,000-140,000; P❋; taxi) Old-time elegance meets contemporary luxuries in one of Saint-Louis' most famous old buildings: every room and suite here is unique, though they all exude a spirit of old-time comfort. The classic furniture and wonderful art works on display are all part of the extensive collections of the daughter of Senegal's former president, who owns the place. It's romantic, classy and oozes luxury.

 Eating

★ Chez Agnes
AFRICAN **$**

(Complexe Aldiana; ☑33 961 4044; Rue Duret; mains CFA2500-4000) In this pretty, tree-lined patio-restaurant, lovely Agnes serves portions of Senegalese rice and sauce that are so generous the word generosity itself ought to be redefined.

Pointe Nord
AFRICAN, SEAFOOD **$$**

(☑33 961 8716; Ave Jean Mermoz; mains CFA3500-5500; ⊙11am-4pm & 7pm-midnight Mon-Sat) This laughter-filled greasy spoon is Saint-Louis' best place for grilled fish served Côte D'Ivoire-style, with *athieke* (cassava couscous) and *aloko* (fried plantains).

Layalina
MIDDLE EASTERN **$$**

(☑33 961 8102; Rue Blaise Diagne; mains CFA5000-9,000) In the morning, hot croissants, cakes and pastries entice you to a lush breakfast in this Moroccan-style restaurant; later in the day, you can stop here for rich kebabs and other fast food, before relaxing into the cushions of the dimly lit teahouse for an elegant dinner.

🍷 Drinking & Nightlife

Flamingo
BAR

(☑33 961 1118; Quai Bacre Waly Guèye; ⊙11am-2am) Any night out here starts at the pool-adorned riverside bar Flamingo. Always packed, it's Saint-Louis' best place for live music.

Le Papayer
CLUB

(☑77 566 8382; Carrefour de l'Hydrobase; ⊙10am-5am) On Hydrobase, Le Papayer is the party place of choice.

Quai des Arts
ARTS CENTRE

(☑33 961 5656; Ave Jean Mermoz) The biggest concerts in town (including the main acts of the jazz festival) happen at the vast Quai des Arts.

❶ Orientation

The city of Saint-Louis straddles part of the Langue de Barbarie Peninsula, Île de N'Dar and the mainland. From the mainland you reach the island via the 500m-long Pont Faidherbe; Pont Mustapha Malick Gaye links the island to the peninsula, where the thriving fishing community of Guet N'Dar inhabits the areas of the old African quarter.

❶ Information

Internet Cafe (Ave de Gaulle; per hr CFA500; ⊙8am-11pm) Decent terminals and several phone booths.

Sahel Découverte (☑33 961 4263; www.saheldecouverte.com; Rue Blaise Diagne) Quite simply the best address for exploring the northern region.

Syndicat d'Initiative (☑33 961 2455; www.saintlouisdusenegal-tourisme.com; Gouvernance; ⊙9am-noon & 2.30-5pm) A haven of regional information with excellent tours.

❶ Getting There & Away

There are frequent *sept-place* taxis between Dakar and Saint-Louis (CFA4900, five hours,

---

SIGNARES

Founded in 1659, Saint-Louis was the first French settlement in Africa. A busy centre for the trade of goods and slaves, it had developed into a large and wealthy town by the 1790s, marked by the cosmopolitan culture of a large *métis* (mixed race) community, which defines Saint-Louis' cultural make-up to this day. The *signares* (women of mixed race who married wealthy European merchants temporarily based in the city) are the most famous example of this. They were essentially bourgeois female entrepreneurs and formed a key part of the economic, social, cultural and political make up of Saint-Louis, controlled most of the river trade and supported local Catholic institutions.

264km). You'll be dropped off at the *gare routière* (bus station), 3.5km south of Saint-Louis. A taxi to the island costs CFA600.

Parc National des Oiseaux du Djoudj

With almost 300 species of bird, this 16,000-hectare park (☑ 33 968 8708; admission CFA2400, pirogue CFA3800, car CFA5200; ☺ 7am-dusk Nov-Apr) is one of the most important bird sanctuaries in the world. Flamingos, pelicans and waders are most plentiful, and large numbers of migrating birds travel here in November. The park is best explored by *pirogue*. Boat trips can be arranged at the park entrance or at the hotels.

The main hotel is the large **Hôtel du Djoudj** (☑ 33 963 8702; www.hotel-djoudj.com; r CFA29,000, pirogue & bike hire half/full day CFA3000/6000; ☺ Nov-May; ❊ ☎ ☒) near the park headquarters. It arranges *pirogue* rides around the park, and rents bikes.

The park is 25km off the main road, and there's no public transport. You can either negotiate a private taxi from Saint-Louis (around CFA28,000) or join an organised tour.

CENTRAL SENEGAL

Tambacounda

The junction town Tambacounda is all about dust, sizzling temperatures and lines of traffic heading in all directions. It's a jumping-off point for Mali, Guinea and Gambia and is a fine place to base yourself to visit the Parc National de Niokolo-Koba.

Bloc Gadec (☑ 77 531 8931; dm/r CFA3000/8000) is a friendly hostel in the centre of town with clean rooms and shared toilets. **Hôtel Niji** (☑ 33 981 1250; www.hotel-niji.com; s/d CFA18,500/22,000; ℗ ❊ @ ☒) has everything from simple bungalows to lush (but soulless) quarters. Try **Oasis Oriental Club** (☑ 33 981 1824; www.oasisoriental.com; Rte de Kaolack; s/d incl breakfast CFA27,500/34,500; ℗ ❊ @ ☒) for some comfort and service.

Relais du Rais (☑ 77 552 7096; dishes from CFA2500; ☺ noon-2.30pm & 6-11pm) serves filling plates of rice and sauce, and **Saveur Orientale** (☑ 77 322 5619; Garage Kothiary; pizzas CFA2500; ☺ 11am-1am) is a step above the grubby usual in these parts and does good pizzas and snacks. **Chez Nanette** (sand-wiches CFA1800-2200; ☺ 8am-midnight), right outside Bloc Gadec, is a busy, rootsy drinking hole that offers snacks and sandwiches.

If you're travelling on to Mali, you get your *sept-place* taxi to Kidira (CFA6000, three hours) at Garage Kothiary on the eastern side of town. Vehicles to other destinations go from the larger *gare routière* near the market.

Parc National de Niokolo-Koba

Niokolo-Koba, at 900 sq km, is Senegal's largest national park. It's listed as a World Heritage Site in danger, as park resources barely suffice to adequately protect the remaining animals (including elephants, lions, warthogs, and various monkey and antelope species).

You can explore the park by 4WD, though sightings of the rare mammals are far from guaranteed. The best option is a river tour (CFA6500), where you'll most certainly spot hippos and crocodiles, combined with an exploration of Simenti, the centre of the park. The water hole nearby is a good viewing spot.

The park is officially open from 15 December to 30 April, as most areas are inaccessible during the wet months. The entrance fee (adult/child under 10 years CFA2000/free, vehicles CFA5000) gives you access for 24 hours. You get your obligatory guide (CFA8000) at the entrance gate.

To spend a night in the park, your best bets are to pitch a tent or stay in the rustic but tidy thatched huts of **Camp du Lion** (☑ Park headquarters 33 981 2454; campsites CFA5000, s/d CFA9000/12,500).

You will need a vehicle to enter the park. It's best to hire a 4WD (CFA90,000 to CFA130,000) in Tambacounda. Enquire at the *gare routière*, at the hotels or at the **National Park Office** (☑ 33 981 2454; Tambacounda; ☺ 8am-5pm). You won't save any money using public transport, as pick-up and drop-off from the park entrance and the tours will also add up to around CFA90,000.

CASAMANCE

With its lush tropical landscapes, watered by the graceful, winding Casamance River, and the unique culture of the Diola, this area seems far from Dakar and its surroundings, in every sense. That's what many locals feel as well, so strongly that separatist rebellions have troubled the region for years. Things have largely calmed down, but they've left a destabilising legacy of banditry that flares up regularly – check recent travel advisories and news before you go.

If the area is safe enough for visits, you'll discover a fascinating place. Between the sleepy capital, Ziguinchor, and the wide, sandy beaches of Cap Skiring, the banks of the Casamance River are dotted with tiny community *campements* that nestle between mangroves and lagoons.

Ziguinchor

POP 157,000

Ziguinchor is the largest town in southern Senegal, and the main access point for travel in the Casamance region. With its old houses, tree-lined streets and busy markets, this former colonial centre exudes real atmosphere. The city has no major sights per se but does boast some colourful historical buildings, including colonial beauty and central post office (Rue du Général de Gaulle) and the old Conseil Régional (regional council). The huge *case à impluvium* (large, round traditional house) of the Alliance Franco-Sénégalaise (☎33 991 2823; ☺9.15am-noon & 3-7.15pm Mon-Sat), with its stunning South African–Casamançais decor, is a beauty worth admiring. At Africa Batik (☎77 653 4936), you can try your hand at making batiks.

For *pirogue* excursions, ask at your hotel or speak to the boat owners at the *pirogue* jetty near Le Perroquet (☎33 991 2329; perroquet@orange.sn; Rue du Commerce; s/d CFA12,000/14,000), Zig's favourite budget place where dozens of yellow-billed storks attract you with their noisy chatter as you enter the place. Invest in a 1st-floor room for the river views. Alteratively, the three log cabins on the croc farm Ferme de Djibelor (☎33 991 1701; s/d CFA17,000/23,000) are cosy and strangely reminiscent of ski chalets, until the lush gardens remind you where you are.

Humble outdoor eatery Le Erobon (☎991 2788; Rue du Commerce; mains CFA 3500-5500; ☺10am-1am) boasts carefully spiced grilled fish served with a sea view. The ambience is wonderfully relaxed and often includes live music like a sole guitar player or a small local band. Le Kassa (☎33 991 1311; Rond-Point Jean-Paul II; mains CFA2800-4400; ☺8am-2am), a patio-pretty place on the roundabout, offers an African-food-focused kitchen that stays open late, and there's live music on weekends. L'Abondance (Rue du Général de Gaulle;

☺5pm-2am) is a small bar-cum-*dibiterie* (grilled-meat place) where you can round off a night out on the town with pork skewers, grilled lamb and cold beers. Lastly, Le Bombolong (☎33 938 8001; Rue du Commerce; cover CFA1800-3500) has the most raucous party for clubbers. There's also a small Superette (Rue Lemoine; ☺9am-10pm), as well as a good pâtisserie (Rue Javelier; cakes CFA300-500) in the centre of town. Diambone Voyages (☎77 641 5132; www.diambonevoyages.com; Rue de France) offers flight bookings, tours, car hire and more. The Aline Sitoé Diatta ferry travels between Dakar and Ziguinchor twice weekly in each direction, leaving Dakar every Thursday and Sunday at 3pm, arriving in Dakar the next day at 6pm. Buy your ticket (CFA16,000 to CFA31,000 one way) in advance and in person at the port.

The *gare routière* is to the east of the city centre. There are frequent *sept-place* taxis to Dakar (CFA12,000, nine hours, 454km) and Cap Skiring (CFA1600). To get anywhere around town by private taxi costs CFA600.

Oussouye

Roughly halfway between Ziguinchor and Cap Skiring, relaxed Oussouye is the main town in the Basse Casamance. For the local Diola population, this town is of significance because it's home to an animist king who is often sought for advice.

Bikes can be hired and tours booked at Casamance VTT (Chez Benjamin; ☎33 993

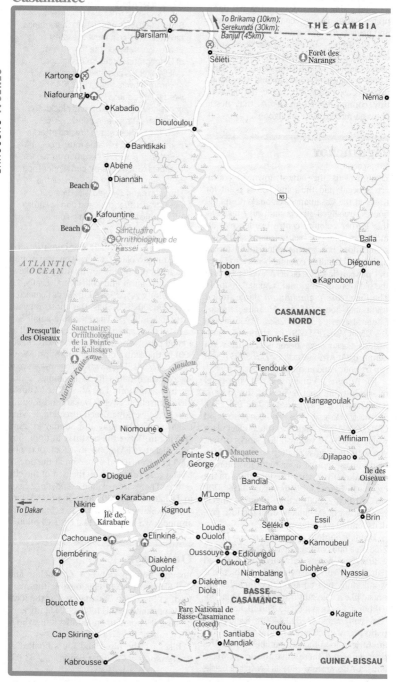

To Brikama (10km);
Serekunda (30km);
Banjul (45km)

THE GAMBIA

Darsilami

Séléti

Forêt des
Narangs

Kartong

Niafourang

Kabadio

Néma

Diouloulou

Bandikaki

Abéné

Diannah

Beach

Kafountine

Beach

Sanctuaire
Ornithologique de
Kassel

Baïla

ATLANTIC
OCEAN

Tiobon

Diégoune

Kagnobon

CASAMANCE
NORD

Presqu'île
des Oiseaux

Sanctuaire
Ornithologique
de la Pointe
de Kalissaye

Tionk-Essil

Tendouk

Marigot de Diouloulou

Mangagoulak

Niomoune

Affiniam

Casamance River

Pointe St
George

Manatee
Sanctuary

Djilapao

Île des
Oiseaux

Dioqué

Bandial

To Dakar

Nikine

Karabane

M'Lomp

Kagnout

Etama

Essil

Brin

Île de
Karabane

Séléki

Cachouane

Elinkine

Loudia
Ouolof

Enampor

Kamoubeul

Diembéring

Diakène
Ouolof

Oussouye

Edioungou

Oukout

Diohère

Nyassia

Niambalang

Diakène
Diola

BASSE
CASAMANCE

Boucotte

Parc National de
Basse-Casamance
(closed)

Kaguite

Youtou

Cap Skiring

Santiaba
Mandjak

Kabrousse

GUINEA-BISSAU

1004; www.casamancevtt.com; half-/full-day bike or kayak hire CFA8000/15,500; ⊙10am-5pm).

Campement Villageois d'Oussouye (☑33 993 0015; http://campement.oussouye.org; s/d CFA5500/6500) and **Campement Emanaye** (☑77 573 6334; emanaye@yahoo.fr; s/d CFA4800/7300) are striking two-storey mud dwellings, an architectural style typical of the region. **Aljowe** (Chez François; ☑77 517 0267; s/ apt per person CFA6000/8000) has cute rooms and mini-apartments in a redbrick structure. **Le Kassa** (mains CFA3000) serves up tasty Senegalese dishes under the cool shade of a massive kapok tree.

All bush taxis between Ziguinchor and Cap Skiring pass through Oussouye (CFA1600).

Elinkine & Île de Karabane

Elinkine is a busy fishing village and jumping-off point for the peaceful Île de Karabane, a former French trading station (1836–1900). On the island, you can still see the Breton-style church, with dusty pews and crumbling statues and visit the dilapidated cemetery where settlers and sailors were laid to rest.

The simple but charming **Campement Villageois d'Elinkine** (☑77 376 9659; campe mentelinkine@free.fr; Elinkine; per person CFA9000) offers basic rooms and friendly service. **Campement Le Barracuda** (☑77 659 6001; Karabane; r with half/full board CFA7700/10,200) has a recommended fishing and excursions centre, and helpful management. **Hôtel Carabane** (☑77 569 0284; hotelcarabane@ya hoo.fr; r with half/full board CFA16,500/25,000), in the former Catholic mission, is the most upmarket option on the isle.

For drinks and Senegalese dishes try **Africando** (☑77 533 3842; Île De Karabane; mains CFA2000-4000), nestled among the giant roots of a kapok tree.

Elinkine can be reached by minibus from Ziguinchor (CFA2400, two hours) or Oussouye (CFA700, one hour). For Karabane, take the public *pirogue* from Elinkine (CFA1550, five minutes, twice daily). Hiring a private *pirogue* costs around CFA17,000 one way.

Cap Skiring

The beaches at Cap Skiring are some of the finest in West Africa and, better still, they are usually empty. Most *campements* and hotels are on the beach, 1km from the village, at the end of a dirt track off the Ziguinchor road.

Ziguinchor

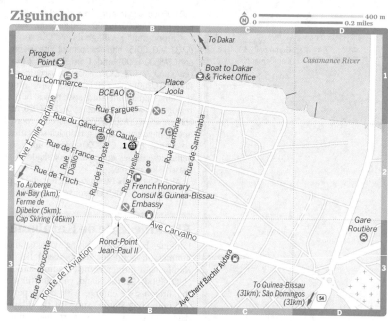

N 0 — 400 m
0 — 0.2 miles

To Dakar

Casamance River

Pirogue Point
Rue du Commerce
Boat to Dakar & Ticket Office
BCEAO
Place Joola
Rue Fargues
Ave Émile Badiane
Rue du Général de Gaulle
Rue Lemoine
Rue de Santhiaba
Rue de France
Rue de la Poste
Rue Diallo
Rue de Truch
Rue Javeller
To Auberge Aw-Bay (1km); Ferme de Djibelor (5km); Cap Skiring (46km)
French Honorary Consul & Guinea-Bissau Embassy
Ave Carvalho
Gare Routière
Rue de Boucotte
Route de l'Aviation
Rond-Point Jean-Paul II
Ave Cherif Bachir Aïdara
To Guinea-Bissau (31km); São Domingos (31km)

Ziguinchor

Most hotels offer a mix of activities like kayaking, quad hire and fishing trips.

Le Paradise (📞 33 993 5303; r CFA15,000; ❄) is the best of a row of cheap *campements*. In Cap Skiring village, the small **Auberge Le Palmier** (📞 33 993 5109; d from CFA12,000; ❄) is a decent budget bet, while the riverside **Kaloa**

les Palétuviers (📞 33 993 5210; www.hotel-kaloa. com; s/d incl breakfast CFA15,000/26,000; ❄ ⊠) is more upmarket and sits among lovely mangroves. **La Maison Bleu** (📞 33 993 5161; www. lamaisonbleue.org; r per person from CFA45,000; ❄) is an airy place that oozes sophistication, rooms with individual colour schemes and weekend trips to Guinea-Bissau's archipelago, the Bissagos Islands. Other excellent options on the beach include **Villa des Pêcheurs** (📞 33 993 5253; www.villadespecheurs. com; s/d incl breakfast CFA25,000/29,000; ❄), which also has a brilliant restaurant and offers the best fishing expeditions in town, and tiny **Mansa Lodge** (📞 33 993 5147; www.capsafari.com; s/d CFA35,000/48,000; ❄ ⊠), where family vibes reign.

Cap Skiring has a lively and delicious restaurant scene. Try **Chez Les Copains** (📞 77 548 1593; Allée du Palétuvier; mains CFA3000) for Senegalese food, **Bar de la Mer** (📞 33 993 5280; Kabrousse; mains CFA3000-5000) for seafood on the beach. **Casa Bambou** (mains CFA2500-5500) offers tasty French cuisine and live music (often jazz) but morphs to more of a club towards midnight. **Bakine** (📞 33 641 5124; Croisement du Cap; ◷ 10pm-3am) hosts rootsy drumming jam sessions.

Cap Skiring's airport (📞 33 993 5194) is served by Senegal Airlines (p348) with flights to and from Dakar. Otherwise it's a *sept-place* taxi (CFA1600) from Ziguinchor.

UNDERSTAND SENEGAL

Senegal Today

Senegal's February 2012 presidential elections were controversial: the Senegalese constitution prohibited a president from serving more than two terms, but then-sitting President Wade amended the constitution in 2011 to enable him to run for a third term. Several youth opposition movements contested the amendment. However, former prime minister Micky Sall won, and Wade conceded the election to Sall. The smooth democratic transition was heralded by many foreign observers as a sign of peace and stability.

History

Senegal was part of several West African empires, including the Empire of Ghana (8th century), and the Djolof kingdom, in the area between the Senegal River and Dakar (13th and 14th centuries). In the early 16th century, Portuguese traders made contact with coastal kingdoms and became the first in a long line of 'interested' foreigners: soon the British, French and Dutch jostled for control of strategic points for the trade in slaves and goods. In 1659, the French built a trading station at Saint-Louis; the town later became the capital of French West Africa.

Dakar, home to tiny fishing villages, was chosen as capital of the Senegalese territory, and as early as 1848 Senegal had a deputy in the French parliament.

Independence

In the run-up to independence in 1960, Senegal joined French Sudan (present-day Mali) to form the Mali Federation. It lasted all of two months, and in August 1960, Senegal became a republic. Its first president, Léopold Sédar Senghor, a socialist and poet of international stature, commanded respect in Senegal and abroad. His economic management, however, didn't match his way with words. At the end of 1980, he voluntarily stepped down and was replaced by Abdou Diouf, who soon faced a string of mounting crises.

The early 1980s saw the start of an ongoing separatist rebellion in the southern region of Casamance. Seven years later a minor incident on the Mauritanian border led to riots and deportations in both countries, as well as a three-year suspension of diplomatic relations and hundreds of casualties. Tensions mounted in other parts of the country as a result of austerity measures.

The arrest of opposition leader Abdoulaye Wade in February 1994 only increased his huge popularity. In March 2000, Wade won in a free and fair presidential election, thanks to his hope-giving *sopi* (change) campaign. Diouf peacefully relinquished power. The following year, a new constitution was approved, allowing the formation of opposition parties and consolidating the prime minister's role.

In 2002 the country was shaken by a huge tragedy when the MS *Joola,* the ferry connecting Dakar and the Casamance capital, Ziguinchor, capsized due to dangerous overloading, leaving almost 2000 people dead.

In 2009 Wade declared in a very early announcement that he intended to stand as candidate at the 2012 elections. There wasn't much cheering; after promising initial measures, Wade's government has not been able to lead the country out of crisis. The steadily rising cost of living, increasing power cuts and widening gap between rich and poor provoke anger and despair among the population. The images of young Senegalese emigrants crossing to the Canary Islands in tiny boats have been beamed around the world. In 2009, 2011 and 2012, conflicts flared up again in Casamance, which had been calm since the peace deal in 2004.

Culture

'A man with a mouth is never lost' goes a popular Wolof saying, and indeed, conversation is the key to local culture, and the key to conversation is a great sense of humour. The Senegalese love talking and teasing, and the better you slide into the conversational game, the easier you'll get around.

Personal life stories in Senegal tend to be brewed from a mix of traditional values, global influences, Muslim faith and family integration. More than 90% of the population is Muslim, and many of them belong to one of the Sufi brotherhoods that dominate religious life in Senegal. The most important brotherhood is that of the Mourides, founded by Cheikh Amadou Bamba. The *marabouts* who lead these brotherhoods play a central role in social life and wield enormous political and economic power (possibly the power to make or break the country's leaders).

The dominant ethnic group is the Wolof (44% of the population), whose language is the country's lingua franca. Smaller groups include the Fula (around 23%); the Tukulor, a sub-branch of the Fula (10%); the Serer (14%); and the Diola (4%). Senegal's population is young: around 40% are under 14 years old. The greatest population density is found in the urban areas of Dakar.

Senegal has a vast music scene; names such as Youssou N'Dour and Baaba Maal are famous worldwide. The beat that moves the nation is *mbalax*. Created from a mixture of Cuban music (hugely popular in Senegal in the 1960s) and traditional, fiery *sabar* drumming, *mbalax* was made famous by Youssou N'Dour in the 1980s.

Hip-hop is also an exciting scene in Senegal, with leading names including Didier Awadi and Daara J. 'Urban folk', led by Carlou D, is on the rise.

Visual arts are also huge (and celebrated every two years during the Dak'Art Biennale). Leading artists include Soly Cissé, Souleymane Keita and Ndaary Lô. Moussa Sakho, Babacar Lô and Gora Mbengue are famous artists practising *sous-verre* (reverse-glass painting).

The doyen of Senegalese cinema is the late Ousmane Sembène, and there's a new generation producing exciting work.

Food & Drink

Senegal's national dish is *tiéboudienne* (rice cooked in a thick tomato sauce and served with fried fish and vegetables). Also typical are *yassa poulet* or *poisson yassa* (marinated and grilled chicken or fish) and *mafé* (peanut-based stew).

Local drinks include *bissap,* made from sorrel flowers, and *bouyi,* made from the fruits of the baobab. The best local beer is Flag.

Environment

Senegal consists mainly of flat plains, cut by three major rivers: the Senegal River in the north, which forms the border with Mauritania; the Gambia River; and the Casamance River in the south, watering the lush green lands of Casamance.

The national parks of the coastal regions, including the Siné-Saloum Delta, the Parc National de la Langue de Barbarie and the Parc National des Oiseaux du Djoudj, are noted for their spectacular birdlife. Parc National de Niokolo-Koba has some large mammals, though they're hard to spot.

Overfishing, deforestation, desertification, and coastal erosion, largely caused by uncontrolled illegal sand mining, are the main environmental issues the country faces. The dwindling of fish stocks also threatens the economy.

SURVIVAL GUIDE

❶ Directory A–Z

ACCOMMODATION

Senegal has a very wide range of places to stay, from top-class hotels to dirty dosshouses. Dakar has the biggest choice, though you're hard-pushed to find a budget place there. Many rural areas, particularly the Casamance, have pleasant *campements*.

EMBASSIES & CONSULATES

If you need to find an embassy that is not listed here, check www.ausenegal.com/practique_en/ambassad.htm. Most embassies close late morning or early afternoon Monday to Friday, so set off early.

Canadian Embassy (Map p324; ☑ 33 889 4700; 45-47 Blvd de la République, Immeuble Sorano, 3rd fl, Plateau)

Cape Verdean Embassy (Map p326; ☑ 33 821 3936; 3 Blvd el Haji Djily Mbaye, Plateau)

Ivorian Embassy (Map p330; ☑ 33 869 0270; www.ambaci-dakar.org; Allées Seydou Nourou Tall, Point E)

French Embassy (Map p326; ☑ 33 839 5100; www.ambafrance-sn.org; 1 Rue Amadou Assane Ndoye, Dakar)

Gambian Embassy (Map p326; ☑ 33 821 7230; 11 Rue de Thiong)

German Embassy (Map p324; ☑ 33 889 4884; www.dakar.diplo.de; 20 Ave Pasteur)

Ghanaian Embassy (Map p330; ☑ 33 869 4053; Rue 6, Point E)

Guinea-Bissau Embassy Dakar (Map p330; ☑ 33 824 5922; Rue 6, Point E; ☺ 8am-12.30pm Mon-Fri); Ziguinchor (☑ 33 991 1046; ☺ 8am-2pm Mon-Fri)

Guinean Embassy (Map p330; ☑ 33 824 8606; Rue 7, Point E)

Malian Embassy (Map p330; ☑ 33 824 6252; 23 Rte de la Corniche-Ouest; ☺ 9am-1pm Mon-Fri)

Mauritanian Embassy (Map p330; ☑ 33 823 5344; Fann Mermoz; ☺ 8am-2pm Mon-Fri)

Moroccan Embassy (Map p330; ☑ 33 824 3836; Ave Cheikh Anta Diop, Mermoz)

Spanish Embassy (☑ 33 821 3081; 18-20 Ave Nelson Mandela)

UK Embassy (Map p324; ☑ 33 823 7392; 20 Rue du Dr Guillet) One block north of Hôpital le Dantec.

US Embassy (Map p326; ☑ 33 823 4296; Ave Jean XXIII)

EMERGENCIES

Fire (☑ 18)
Police (☑ 17)
SOS Medecin (☑ 33 889 1515)
SUMA Urgences (☑ 33 824 2418)

FESTIVALS & EVENTS

December, May and June are the best times for music and arts festivals, including the Saint-Louis Jazz Festival (p337), the **Dak'Art Biennale** (☑ 33 823 0918; www.dakart.org) and **Kaay Fecc** (☑ 33 824 5154; www.kaayfecc.com).

INTERNET ACCESS

Internet cafes are plentiful, and the number of wi-fi spaces is increasing almost daily (particularly in Dakar). Surfing costs from CFA400 to CFA500 per hour; wi-fi in hotel lobbies and bars is usually free with a purchase.

MONEY

The unit of currency is the West African CFA franc. Banks with ATMs are found in all larger towns across the country. Banks and exchange bureaux tend to offer similar rates; the currencies most easily changed are the euro and US dollars.

OPENING HOURS

Banks Usually close around 4pm; only a few open Saturday morning.

Business and government offices Open 8.30am to 1pm and 2.30pm to 5pm Monday to Friday.

Restaurants Offer lunch from noon to 2.30pm and dinner from 7pm onwards; many are closed on Sunday.

POST

Senegal's postal service is inexpensive though not entirely reliable.

PUBLIC HOLIDAYS

As well as Islamic religious holidays, Senegal celebrates a few principal public holidays.

New Year's Day 1 January
Independence Day 4 April

PRACTICALITIES

➡ **Languages** French, Wolof, Malinke, Pulaar (Fulfulde), Diola.

➡ **Electricity** 220V. Plugs have two round pins (same as continental Europe).

➡ **Newspapers** *Le Soleil* (www.lesoleil. sn) is the main daily newspaper.

Workers Day 1 May
Assumption 15 August

SAFE TRAVEL

There are two main dangers you may encounter in Senegal: civil unrest in Casamance and street crime in Dakar.

TELEPHONE

Good mobile-phone coverage means that most of the public *télécentres* have now closed. You'll still find them, but it's much easier to buy a SIM card. Top-up credit is available absolutely anywhere. Network coverage (especially for Orange) is excellent across the country.

The country code is ☑ 221. For directory assistance dial ☑ 1212.

TIME

Senegal is at GMT/UTC. There is no daylight-saving time.

VISAS

At the time of writing, visa requirements were in flux and Senegal now requires that visitors from nations that require entry visas from Senegalese citizens are required to obtain a visa for travel to Senegal. This includes citizens of the EU, EEA, Switzerland, Canada, USA and Australia. Tourist visas for one to three months cost between US$30 to US$80.

Visa Extensions

If you don't need a visa, just hop across the Gambian border and earn another three months on re-entry to Senegal.

ⓘ Getting There & Away

AIR

Dakar's **Léopold Sédar Senghor International Airport** (DKR; ☑ 24hr info line 77 628 1010; www.aeroportdakar.com) is one of Africa's transport hubs, with links across Africa, Europe and America.

Major airlines servicing Senegal, many with offices in Dakar, are as follows:

Air France (AF; ☑ 33 839 7777; www.air france.fr)

Brussels Airlines (SN; ☒33 823 0460; www.brusselsairlines.com)

Ethiopian Airlines (ET; ☒33 823 5552; www.flyethiopian.com; 16 Ave Léopold Sédar Senghor)

Kenya Airways (www.kenya-airways.com)

Royal Air Maroc (AT; ☒33 849 4748; www.royalairmaroc.com)

Senegal Airlines (www.senegalairlines.aero) Senegal's national airline flies to Ziguinchor, Cap Skiring and various cities throughout West Africa and at the time of research it had just started nonstop flights to Paris via its partner airline Corsair. Check the website for details.

South African Airways (SA; ☒33 869 4000; www.flysaa.com)

TACV Cabo Verde Airlines (VR; ☒33 821 3968; www.flytacv.com)

TAP Portugal (TAP; www.flytap.com)

LAND

The Gambia

From Dakar there are *sept-place* taxis south to Karang (CFA6800, six hours) at the Gambian border, where you connect to Barra and then via ferry to Banjul.

From southern Senegal, *sept-place* taxis run regularly between Ziguinchor and Serekunda (CFA4900, five hours), and between Kafountine and Brikama (CFA3500, two hours).

In eastern Senegal, *sept-place* taxis go from Tambacounda to Vélingara (CFA1800, three hours), and from there to Basse Santa Su (CFA1400, 45 minutes, 27km).

Guinea

Most traffic is by *sept-place* from Diaoubé (Senegal), via Koundara (Guinea), where you may have to change; some go via Kédougou (Senegal). The very rough ride costs CFA22,000 and takes up to 48 hours.

Guinea-Bissau

Sept-place taxis leave every morning from Ziguinchor for Bissau (CFA6600, four hours, 147km), via the main border post at São Domingos, and Ingore. The road is sealed and in good condition.

Mali

Sept-place taxis leave regularly from Tambacounda to Kidira (CFA5500, three hours), where you cross the border to Diboli in Mali, from where long-distance buses run to Kayes and Bamako. If you're brave, you can do Dakar–Bamako by long-distance bus (CFA24,000); buses leave from Gare Routière Pompiers in Dakar.

The legendary Dakar–Bamako 'express' train was no longer running at the time of research.

Mauritania

Sept-place taxis run regularly from Dakar to the main border point at Rosso (CFA7000, six hours, 384km), a crowded, hasslesome place, where four daily ferries (CFA2500/3500 per passenger/car) cross to Rosso-Mauritania.

If you have your own wheels, you can cross at the Maka Diama dam, 97km southwest of Rosso and just north of Saint-Louis, where the border crossing is swift.

ⓘ Getting Around

AIR

Senegal Airlines flies between Dakar, Ziguinchor and Cap Skiring.

LOCAL TRANSPORT

The quickest (though still uncomfortable) way of getting around the country is by *sept-place* taxi – battered Peugeots that negotiate even the most ragged routes. Slightly cheaper but infinitely less reliable are the minibuses (Ndiaga Ndiaye or *grand car*), carrying around 40 people. Vehicles leave from the *gare routière* when they're full, and they fill up quickest in the morning, before 8am.

Taxi prices are theoretically fixed, though they're steadily increasing as petrol prices rise. There's an extra, negotiable charge for luggage (10% to 20% of the bill).

Cars mourides (large buses, financed by the Mouride brotherhood) connect major towns in Senegal. Book ahead of travel. In Dakar, go to **Gare Routière Pompiers** (Map p324; ☒33 821 8585; off Ave Malick Sy), where most *sept-places* also go from. Arriving in Dakar, *sept-places* stop at Gare Routière Colobane.

Sierra Leone

🎵 232 / POP 5.4 MILLION

Best Places to Eat

➡ Seafood at Franco's (p357)

➡ Oasis (p354)

➡ Picnic at Turtle Islands (p359)

Best Places to Stay

➡ Tokeh Sands (p357)

➡ Tiwai Island (p359)

➡ Tribe Wanted (p357)

Why Go?

West Africa's secret beach destination rises from the soft waters of the Atlantic, dressed in sun-stained hues, rainforest green and the red, red roads of the north. Sierra Leone: the land so-named because it's shaped like a mountain lion. Sweet Salone, the locals say.

In Freetown, colourful stilted houses remember the days when freed slaves from the Caribbean were resettled upon these shores. Some landed on the peninsula, blanketed with sands as white and soft as cotton wool.

In the north, the Loma Mountains form the highest point west of Cameroon. Further east, streams cut national parks and mangrove swamp water swathes rainforest that shelter endangered species like the shy, waddling pygmy hippo.

The curtains have been drawn on the painful past, and it's time for a new act in Sierra Leone. Join the island-hoppers and sun-seekers, swim in the clear blue waters, explore the archipelagos and crack open fresh lobster in the shade of skinny palms and rope-strung hammocks.

When to Go
Freetown

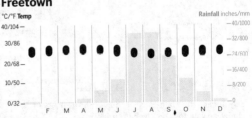

Nov–Jun The dry season is marked by mild, dusty harmattan winds from December until February.

April The average daytime temperature is 32°C.

Jun–Nov The rainy season sees spectacular storms and up to 3200mm of precipitation.

FREETOWN

022 / POP 1.1 MILLION

Strung between the mountains and the sea, Sierra Leone's capital is a cheeky, quicksilver capital bubbling with energy, colour and charm. One minute it's calm, offering up quiet beaches, friendly Krio chat and warm plates of soup and rice. The next it's frenzied and playing dirty, throwing you into the back of a shared taxi and hurtling you up and down its pretty little hills.

And it might just be the only capital in the world where when you emerge from the airport, blinking after an overnight flight, you find yourself standing on the wooden deck of a port flanked by a backdrop of mountains, beaches and palm trees so idyllic you wonder if it's real. Well it's all real, all of it – the chatter and the chaos and the colour and the dirt and the lush lobster dinners and the devastating war history – and those lovely white sands too.

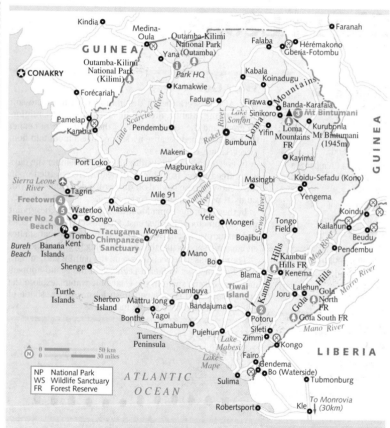

NP — National Park
WS — Wildlife Sanctuary
FR — Forest Reserve

Sierra Leone Highlights

① Feeling the white sand between your toes on **River No 2 Beach** (p356) and other Freetown beaches that line the stunning peninsula.

② Tracking colobus monkeys and joining the search for the elusive pygmy hippo on **Tiwai Island** (p359).

③ Pushing through the cool mist as you scale, **Mt Bintumani** (p358) West Africa's highest peak this side of Cameroon.

④ Soaking up the spirit of **Freetown** (p350), the colourful, cheeky capital.

⑤ Sleeping in tree houses in **Tacugama Chimpanzee Sanctuary** (p358) while rescued chimps chatter in the rainforest below.

◎ Sights & Activities

Cotton Tree
GARDENS

(Map p354) Freetown's most famous landmark is the fat Cotton Tree in the centre of the old part of town. Nobody's sure if it can be quite that old, but some say the city's poor black settlers rested in its shadows when they landed in Freetown in 1787. Either way, the tree has witnessed a lot, including the invasion of a huge colony of chirpy bats that were kicked out by authorities in 2010 – rumour has it that one day the bats will return.

Sierra Leone National Museum
MUSEUM

(Map p354; ☑ 223555; Siaka Stevens St; ⊙ 10.30am-4pm Mon-Fri) **FREE** The Sierra Leone National Museum has a small but fascinating collection of juju trinkets and historical artefacts, including Temne Guerrilla leader Bai Bureh's drum, clothes and sword.

State House
HISTORIC BUILDING

(Map p354; Independence Ave) The State House, up on Tower Hill and overlooking the Downtown area, is an example of the area's old Krio architecture, which features brightly washed buildings and higgledy-piggledy window frames. This building incorporates the bastions and lion gate from Fort Thornton (built at the turn of the 19th century).

St John's Maroon Church
CHURCH

(Map p354; Siaka Stevens St) Built around 1820, St John's Maroon Church is a squat white building with big windows. An example of the area's Krio architecture, it was built by returned slaves from Jamaica. It's located two blocks southwest of the Cotton Tree.

Old Boundary Cannons
HISTORIC SITE

(Map p352) Over at the junction of Kissy Road – known locally as Up Gun community – you can see one of the three old boundary cannons that were used to mark the mapped-out limes of Freetown. It is believed to date back to about 1805.

King's Yard Gate
HISTORIC SITE

(Map p354; Wallace Johnson St) The ancestors of nearly all present-day Krios passed through King's Yard Gate, atop Tower Hill in the strategic military Martello Tower, built in 1805. Here they awaited resettlement and medical care by the British. Now the site of Connaught Hospital, this is where the British brought rescued slaves to begin their new lives. Many of these new arrivals climbed the nearby Old Wharf Steps, sometimes erroneously called the Portuguese Steps.

National Railway Museum
MUSEUM

(Map p352; Cline St; ⊙ 9.30am-5pm Mon-Sat) **FREE** Visitors to the National Railway Museum are rare, but the short tour around these restored engines and cars is fairly interesting. You don't have to be a rail fan to enjoy this Clinetown museum, where there's a surprising collection of restored locomotives, including one commissioned for the Queen of England in 1961.

Lumley Beach
BEACH

With every patch of beachfront property purchased and many construction projects underway, it's not hard to imagine what Lumley Beach will look like in a few years, but for now development is pretty much limited to a few bamboo and thatch beershacks. Lifeguards and beach wardens are on duty and the public toilets and showers are kept clean, but the beach is not. Lumley Beach is the busiest beach on the peninsula, teeming with bars and lunch spots. If it's relaxation you're after, better to head out of town to River No 2 or one of the islands.

Bureh Beach Surf Club
SURFING

If you want to catch some waves, Bureh Beach Surf Club – initially set up before the war by a Peace Corps volunteer – is now in the hands of Irish surfer Shane, who works with local surf legends to boost tourism through surf trips, lessons and board rentals.

Greater Freetown

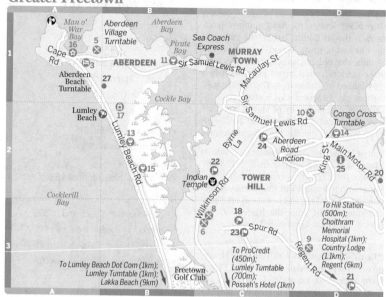

🛏 Sleeping

Freetown has a good mix of accommodation, with new options opening regularly.

Hotobah Lodge HOTEL $$
(Map p352; ☑076-241212; www.thehotobahlodge.com; 5 Boyle Lane, off Murray Town Rd; d/ste US$75/85; P❄🔊) A gem of a hotel that opened in 2013, Hotobah sits at Murray Town junction – on the main route into town from the west, dubbed 'Banana Wata' – and has smart, clean rooms with wi-fi and TVs (the generator is switched on in the evenings only). A friendly, great value place.

Family Kingdom HOTEL $$
(Map p352; ☑076-77794, 22236133; Lumley Beach Rd; P❄🔊) Don't mind the deer, they're tame, and part of the weird, wonderful family at this Lumley Beach hotel. The rooms here are upmarket and spacious, with 24-hour air-con and wi-fi, and you've good access to the eating and drinking spots that line the main beach drag.

Kona Lodge HOTEL $$
(Map p354; ☑076-611793; 32 King St; r from US$55; ❄🔊) Favoured by NGO workers, Kona Lodge is a sound option for a good night's work and sleep: there's 24-hour power, reliable wi-fi and the rooms are clean and modern.

The Place RESORT $$$
(Map p354; ☑079-685494; 42 Rawdon St; P❄🔊🏊) The Place has been transformed from a budget hotel to a luxury, boutique retreat. Renovations are expected to result in a sleek new pool and spa.

Country Lodge HOTEL $$$
(☑076-691000; www.countrylodgesl.com; Hill Station; r US$150-195, ste US$250-300; P❄🔊@🔊🏊) Country Lodge is Freetown's most upmarket address, popular with the odd combination of glittering celebrities and suited development consultants. There's a lap-length pool, a gym, a tennis court and free wi-fi. The only downside to the fabulous hilltop location is reaching it – you'll need your own car or a private taxi.

🍴 Eating

You can find local chop houses serving *plasas* (pounded potato or cassava leaves cooked with palm oil) all over town around lunchtime.

Dee's Bazaar RESTAURANT $
(Map p354; cnr Liverpool & Siaka Stevens Sts) Both the name and the food beat the decor at this local *plasas* spot. The menu changes daily, according to what's on-hand, but you can ex-

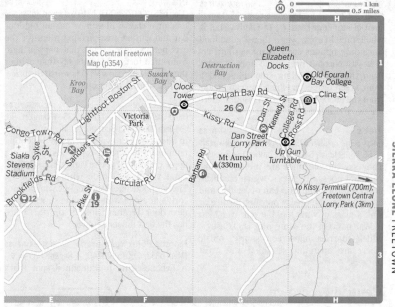

Greater Freetown

◎ Sights
1 National Railway Museum	H1
2 Old Boundary Cannons	G2

◉ Sleeping
3 Family Kingdom	A1
4 Hotobah Lodge	F2

✕ Eating
5 Alex's	A1
6 Bliss	C3
7 Caribbean Restaurant	E2
8 Crown Express	C3
9 Mamba Point Restaurant	D3
10 Oasis	D2

◉ Drinking & Nightlife
11 Atlantic	D1
12 China House	E2
13 O Bar	B2
14 Plum Store	D2
15 Roy's	B2

★ Entertainment
16 Ace's	A1

⬤ Shopping
17 Lumley Beach Arts & Crafts Market	B2

ⓘ Information
18 British High Commission	C3
19 Conservation Society of Sierra Leone	E2
20 DHL	D2
21 German Embassy	D3
22 Guinean Embassy	C2
23 Liberian Embassy	C3
24 Malian Consulate	C2
25 Visit Sierra Leone	D2

ⓘ Transport
Diamond Hovercraft	(see 16)
26 Poda-podas to Waterloo	G1
27 UTAir	B1

pect to fill up with cassava leaves or simple rice and fish for less than Le10,000.

Caribbean Restaurant CARIBBEAN $
(Map p352; ☎078-102813; Sanders St; ☞) Krio goes back to its roots at this old but colourful Caribbean joint. There are great freshly squeezed juices to be had, as well as an all-you-can-eat Wednesday lunch buffet brimming with banana balls, jerked chicken and fried plantains. For dinner, you must book in advance.

★ Oasis
RESTAURANT $$

(Map p352; www.freetownoasis.com; 33 Murray Town Rd, near Boyle Lane; 🖉) 🍃 Gladys' spot is wholesome in every way – there's good food (including options such as mango and vegies with coconut rice) made from produce from the garden, filling smoothies and a calm, green terrace in which you can escape from the chaos of Freetown. Upstairs, there are two rooms for rent.

Alex's
RESTAURANT $$

(Map p352; 🖉076-679272; off Cape Rd; meals US$6-28; ⏲lunch Sat & Sun, dinner Tue-Sun; ℗) They say the old ones are the good 'uns, and so it goes with Alex's, which has been around for a while. You can order fish and lobster from the breezy outdoor terrace or sink a glass of wine looking out over Man o' War bay. On the same plot is O'Casey's, which marries big-screen sports, music (there are open-mic sessions) and great burgers.

Bliss
RESTAURANT $$

(Map p352; 🖉078-609312; 110 Wilkinson Rd; ❄🗚) Freetown classic Bliss now has an outdoor bar and garden area, making room for the arts performance events that happen here from time to time. Expats say that neither the food nor the slow wi-fi is worth the price, yet this place is never empty.

Crown Express
RESTAURANT $$

(Map p352; 🖉077-447744; 125 Wilkinson Rd; ⏲10am-10pm Mon-Sun; ❄) A slice of London in Freetown, Crown Express is becoming famous for its hip, air-con-cooled decor and apple crumble. If you're eating, the staff will hand you a wi-fi code with your cutlery. There's no alcohol licence, but you can uncork a bottle of wine from the supermarket next door. Freetown insider tip: this place has the best toilets in town.

Mamba Point Restaurant
RESTAURANT $$$

(Map p352; 🖉076-618240; 4 Regent Rd; ❄🗚) A Lebanese-run, multimenued spot that's

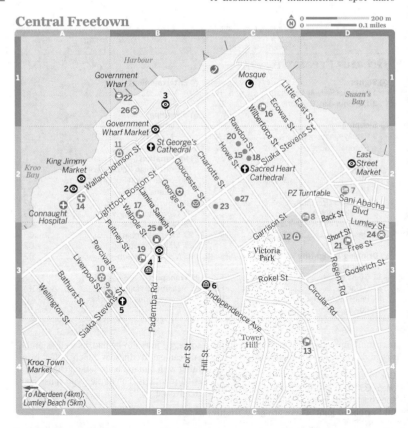

Central Freetown

the sister restaurant of Monrovia's famous Mamba Point. The bar area is styled like a typical English gastropub, but it's the (expensive) sushi bar that's the main draw here. It's also a decent hotel.

Drinking & Nightlife

O Bar BAR
(Map p352; Lumley Beach; ☉ 4pm-late Tue-Sun) You'll feel the strain on your wallet – and maybe your ears – at this swanky outdoor lounge that has banging music on the weekends. Popular with moneyed Sierra Leoneans and Lebanese, it also has an indoor club that's separated from the beach bar by the road.

Plum Store BAR
(Map p352) Cute Plum Store is shielded from the busy Congo Cross junction by greenery, making it an ideal spot for a quick drink on your way back from town.

Atlantic BAR
(Map p352; 63 Sir Samuel Lewis Rd) Toufic, the owner, will greet you with a weary grin at this old-time bar right on the water. Anything seems to go at the Atlantic – you can grind to Nigerian hip-hop, shoot some pool, catch a live band or chew on a sandwich.

Roy's BAR
(Map p352; ☎33405060) Watch the sun go down and the party people wake up on the deck at Roy's, a perfect sundowner's spot on Lumley Beach. It's hard to find a problem with this place – everyone from backpackers to ministerial employees seems to come here.

China House BAR
(Map p352; Youyi Building, cnr Main Motor & Brookfield Rds) Mingle with ministers at China House, strangely located in the compound of the ministerial building. There's live reggae music on Fridays, although you might want to watch who you elbow on your way to the bar.

Ace's CLUB
(Map p352; 74 Cape Rd; ☉ 7pm-late) It's all smoke and mirrors at Ace's, a club that doesn't really get going until the wee small hours. Cultural groups occasionally interrupt the DJ sets here, soaring above the party people on trapezes. Out the back, there's an outdoor area, ping-pong and pool tables.

Balanta Music Academy DANCE
(Map p354) On the last Friday of every month, Balanta Music Academy opens its doors to the public for a great evening of student performers, attracting an artsy crowd – there's everything from African dance to a capella and big-band joy.

Shopping

Victoria Park Market MARKET
(Map p354; Garrison St) This is the place to find colourful local wax cloths and *gara* (thin tie-died or batik printed sheet).

Big Market MARKET
(Basket Market; Map p354; Wallace Johnson St;
⊙7am-7pm Mon-Sat) The top floor of the Big
Market, also known as Basket Market, has
a larger selection than markets in Lumley.
What makes this the best place to shop for
souvenirs is the traditional household goods
on the ground floor.

ⓘ Orientation

Central Freetown is set out on a grid pattern
with Siaka Stevens St as the main thoroughfare.
Budget hotels are clustered near PZ Turntable,
which stays busy late into the night. Aberdeen
and Lumley lie 30 minutes to an hour west, depending on traffic.

ⓘ Information

CULTURAL CENTRES
British Council (Map p354; ☑224683; www.
britishcouncil.org; Tower Hill; ⊙8.30am-4.30pm
Mon-Thu, 8.30am-2pm Fri) Cultural Centre.

DANGERS & ANNOYANCES
Freetown has less crime than you'd imagine,
but it still makes sense to be cautious and avoid
walking alone late at night or leaving apartment
doors unlocked. Walking on the beach alone,
even during the day, is a bad idea.

By far the most dangerous creatures in
Freetown are not the mosquitoes but the (ad-
mittedly cheap) motorbike taxis, which buzz
far more loudly and swoop up and over the hills
like there's no tomorrow. There might not be
if you take one – do so at your peril and wear a
helmet.

EMERGENCY
The emergency services (☑999) are unreliable
in Sierra Leone.

INTERNET ACCESS
Most of the good hotels and some of the restaurants listed in the eating section offer access to
wi-fi. Most expats get by with USB pay-as-you-go
internet sticks. You can also pick up internet-
ready SIM cards for smartphones and iPads.

MEDICAL SERVICES
Central Pharmacy (Map p354; ☑076-615503;
30 Wallace Johnson St) Reasonably well-
stocked pharmacy.
Choitram Memorial Hospital (☑232598; Hill
Station) Freetown's best hospital.

MONEY
Forex bureaus are found throughout the city.
Rates at the airport's exchange bureau aren't
too bad, but you'll do better in town.

ProCredit Central (Map p354; 11 Rawdon St)
Lumley (157 Wilkinson Rd) Has Visa card-linked
ATMs, as do most major banks and some of the
hotels in the upper price-bracket.

POST
DHL Central (Map p354; ☑033-315299) Greater
(Map p352; ☑236156; 30 Main Motor Rd)
Post Office (27 Siaka Stevens St)

TOURIST INFORMATION
Conservation Society of Sierra Leone (Map
p352; ☑033-470043; cssl_03@yahoo.com; 2
Pike St; ⊙9am-5pm Mon-Fri) Very helpful for
travellers to Sierra Leone's natural reserves,
including the Turtle Islands.

TRAVEL AGENCIES
Visit Sierra Leone (Map p352; ☑076-877618;
www.visitsierraleone.org; 28 Main Motor Rd)
Brilliant one-stop shop for tours, information,
transport, guides and historical knowledge.

ⓘ Getting There & Away

From the main bus station, reasonably well-
maintained buses operate to cities such as
Bo, Kabala, Kenema, Koidu-Sefadu (Kono) and
Makeni and Conakry (Guinea). Shared bush taxis
head to the same destinations, stopping at villages and communities along the way. They leave
from **Freetown Central Lorry Park** (Bai Bureh
Rd), also known as Clay Factory, at Texaco Junction on the far east side of town. Taxis to Conakry
park along Free St near Victoria Park Market.

For airlines serving Sierra Leone and overland options to Liberia, see Getting There & Away (p233).

ⓘ Getting Around

Shared taxis and *poda-podas* (minibuses) cost
Le1000 per short hop and run on fixed routes
around town. You can also bargain for a charter
taxi, which feels like the lap of luxury after being
squashed into the back of a shared ride with four or
five others. The motorbike taxis, known as *okadas*,
as they are in Nigeria, can be downright reckless:
ride with caution, or even better, don't ride at all.

AROUND FREETOWN

Beaches

Freetown's tongue stretches out along the
coast, kissing beaches lined with tall, elegant
palms and iced with sand that's white as snow.

River No 2 shot to fame after the Bounty
chocolate bar ad was filmed here, and the
sugary white sands don't disappoint. The
eponymous River No 2 Guesthouse is a

TO & FROM THE AIRPORT

Sierra Leone has something rare: a journey to and from the airport that is arguably more spectacular than the views you'll see from the air. Lungi International Airport is located across the Sierra Leone River on an island, and you have five options to reach it: choppers (when they're running), a hovercraft, speedboat and water taxis.

Lungi International Airport is inconveniently located across the Sierra Leone River from Freetown. The fastest way to town is by **UTAir** (Map p352; ☏ 033-807420; one way US$80) helicopter, followed by **Diamond Hovercraft** (Map p352; ☏ 076-614888). Both drop and depart at Aberdeen, but they don't meet every flight. **Sea Coach Express** (☏ 033-111118; one way US$40) runs slower, smaller boats to Aberdeen Bridge for every flight. **Allied Marine** (Map p354; ☏ 033-664545; one way US$40) uses buses and ferries to take you to Government Wharf in the city centre. Other companies also plan to enter the airport transport game.

The helicopters are by far the most expensive (in more than one way) option, with prices starting at US$80 for the five-minute ride, and there have been several crashes throughout the years. Then there's the hovercraft, which can be booked at the Visit Sierra Leone office for US$40 one-way. Speedboats arranged through Pelican or Sea Coach Express cost US$40 and the boats are well maintained with life-jackets for all. They run in coordination with the airport's flight schedule. The two-to-three-hour ferry was not running at the time of research, and there were several other water taxi companies beginning operations.

You can find a taxi from any of the landing sites, although you might want to book ahead if you're arriving early or late.

community-run spot that has simple, clean rooms and red wooden tables sunk into the sand. The food – skewers of lime-soaked barracuda, or lobster and chips – is hearty and fresh. Boat trips can be arranged up the river to waterfalls, and down the peninsula to the Banana Islands.

Around the bend and cradled by the mountains behind is Tokeh Beach (you can walk here from River No 2, using a boat over the river at high tide), one of the most spectacular beaches on the peninsula, purportedly popular with European celebs before the war. Tokeh Sands (☏ 078-911111; r US$60-180), which has sleek, white rooms with 24-hour power and air-con, opened here in 2013. You can swim out to the old helipad nearby, or kick off your sandals and nap in one of the hammocks strung between the palms while you wait for the daily dinner menu – which features the likes of seared tiger prawns and homemade sorbet – to fall into your palms.

About 20km south of Freetown along the peninsula is John Obey Beach, home to the unusual ecotourism project Tribe Wanted. Guests stay in tents (US$50), hip beach bungalows (US$80) or smooth clay honeydomes (US$80) that look as if they were created in a pottery class. There are eco-toilets and showers open to the stars. Meals at the open beach 'chop house' are included, and you're expected to pitch in or get involved

with the community projects to make the most of the experience.

Half an hour from Freetown is the Sierra Leone foodie institution Franco's (☏ 078-366366), sprawled on Sussex Beach (beside the lagoon). Run by an Italian–Sierra Leonean couple, this is a favourite spot for a long, wine-fuelled Sunday lunch. It's worth ordering in advance as food can take a while to prepare at busy times of the year.

Ask someone in York, an interesting Krio village, to show you the caves on York Beach where slaves supposedly stayed before being loaded onto ships. From here you can look across Whale Bay to deserted and tough-to-reach Black Johnson Beach. It may be possible to walk here in the dry season; otherwise get a boat in York or follow the unmarked mile-long dirt road (veer right at the first junction) that begins after the Whale River Bridge.

At the tip of the peninsula is Kent, with its ruined fort and frequent transport to the Banana Islands.

Thanks to a freshly paved road, shared transport now runs down the coast all the way to Tokeh (US$2) and onto Kent.

Banana Islands

Dublin (*doo-blin*), Ricketts and Mes-Meheux are the three bananas in this pretty archipelago, hanging from the southern tip of the peninsula like a ripe bunch of fruit. The islands were first settled by the Portuguese in the 17th century and were later inhabited by freed slaves from the Caribbean – the descendents of those who live here now.

★**Banana Island Guest House** (☎076-989906; www.bananaislandguesthouse-biya.org; r US$65-115) has cute, solar-powered bamboo-style chalets on Dublin Island. The owners can organise sea transport from Kent. The 25-minute crossing costs Le150,000 per boatload. There's also **Dalton's Banana Guest House** (☎076-570208; per person Le30,000), which is a cheaper accommodation option.

Alternatively, you can make your own way to the islands by shared boat; a seat on a regular transport boat will cost you just under US$2.

Bunce Island

The former slave-trading post of Bunce Island lies some 30km up the Sierra Leone River from the ocean. Slave traders began operations here around 1670, and before the British outlawed the industry in 1807 some 30,000 men, women and children were shipped off into exile by four British slave-trading companies. Among those who have been traced back to here are the Gullah families of South Carolina.

You can visit the island and fort by boat from Freetown's Kissy Terminal, where you can charter a small boat for US$100, reaching Bunce in about two hours. A speedboat (about US$300 per boatload) can do it in under an hour from Man o' War Bay.

Tacugama Chimpanzee Sanctuary

Up and over Sugar Loaf Mountain, Sri Lankan founder Bala created **Tacugama Chimpanzee Sanctuary** (☎076-611211; www.tacugama.com; adult/child US$10/3.50; ☺tours by appointment 10.30am & 4pm), a leafy, waterfall-framed hideaway set up with the purpose of educating humans about one of our closest relatives. This excellent sanctuary remained operational throughout the war.

You can sleep here, bedding down in tree houses (from US$90) that overlook the sanctuary, or you can come for the day, watching rescued chimps lark around in enclosures or spotting those who have been released

to a larger area in the mountains beyond. Ninety-minute tours of the sanctuary run by appointment at 10.30am and 4pm each day and you can follow walking trails around the area.

A short drive from Freetown in the Peninsula Mountains, Tacugama is off the Regent/Bathurst road. The last stretch of the route follows a rough, unpaved path through the rainforest that can only be reached by 4WD or on foot (20 minutes).

THE NORTH

Makeni

POP 105,000

Makeni mixes politics with football as the birthplace of both Ernest Bai Koroma and the Wusum Stars, Sierra Leone's oldest football club. It's a good base for exploring the northern highlands. Any of the city's hotels will be able to advise you on getting out into the countryside, including rock climbing and hiking.

Straight-talking Irish Sister Mary will welcome you into the fold at **St Joseph's School for the Deaf**, where you can sleep in one of the lovely, fan-blown rooms with high-ceilings and bathrooms (from Le129,000). You can also tour the well-run school, eat meals here, book in for a massage and take a look at the arts and crafts on sale.

Or you can head to the fancier **Wusum Hotel** (☎076-341079; wusum.hotel@yahoo.co.uk; 65 Teko Rd; s/d US$88/110, chalets US$117; P ❄ @ ☎), which is more of a luxury resort (with a pool and conference facilities) than just a place to lay your head.

About 45 minutes from Makeni is **Rogbonko Village** (☎08-8631079), where you can go back to basics, overnighting in a thatched guest hut and sampling local country food.

Bush taxis and *poda-podas* run to many destinations including Freetown (two hours).

Mt Bintumani

Also known as Loma Mansa, the breathy King of the Mountains, 1945m-high Mt Bintumani is West Africa's highest peak – until you hit Cameroon. The mountain range is rich in highland birds and mammal species, including duikers, colobus monkeys, buffaloes, leopards and snakes. Any climbing attempt should be taken seriously – you might want to stay away during the slippery rainy season and come prepared with a GPS and hiking and camping equipment.

The main climbing route winds up from the village of Sokurala via Kurubonla, about 180km from Kabala. You can also stay overnight in Yifin, or if you're coming from Makeni in the east, follow the dirt road all the way to Sinekoro. Neither village had a guesthouse at the time of research, but you can take an offering to the local chief and ask if you might rent sleeping space from a local family. You can also hire local porters if you have camping gear you'd like to safely lug to the top. There are two campsites located just before the mountain becomes steep.

It's well worth the four-to-five day adventure; the spectacular summit looks out over most of West Africa, veiled by soft cool mist.

Outamba-Kilimi National Park

About 300km north of Freetown, Outamba-Kilimi seems like something out of East Africa rather than a treasure of the west, with its rolling savannah, elephant watering holes and hippo-trodden rivers. There are nine species of primates here, and there have been leopard and pygmy hippo sightings.

Sadly much of the park facilities were destroyed during the war, but efforts are underway to rebuild. Until then, you can stay in huts on the outskirts of the park for a small fee, and guides (US$5) can be arranged to accompany you on the trails. Fifteen kilometres to the south, Kamakwie is the nearest town. You can hire motorbikes (from US$12) or 4WDs (which cost much more) from here to reach the reserve.

THE SOUTH

Bo

POP 245,000

Sierra Leone's second-largest city, Bo escaped the scars of the war and is in better shape than many other urban centres. Still, there isn't much to do besides sleep, eat, chat and wander – just don't stray too far as this is somewhat sketchy diamond territory too.

For low budgets, there's **Madame Woki's** in the centre of town, while the **Sahara Hotel** ([☎]033908929; New Gerihun Rd; r Le50,000 incl breakfast) has comfortable rooms.

Bush taxis to Freetown (four hours) depart frequently each morning from Maxwell Khobe Park near the centre. Abess buses (US$6) leave from Tikonko Rd around midnight. The quickest way to Kenema is usually to go out to Shell-Mingo on the highway and jump in a taxi there.

Turtle Islands

This beautiful, remote eight-island archipelago in Sierra Leone's southwest peninsula is made from soft white sand, thick shavings of palm fronds and the purest turquoise water. Tethered to a traditional way of life, the islands swing to their own rhythms. You can explore most of them with the exception of Hoong, which is a male-only island reserved for rites of passage.

The Conservation Society of Sierra Leone (p356) can arrange boats (US$600 per boatload) from Freetown and accommodation at a basic lodge, or you can talk to Visit Sierra Leone (p356) to arrange to take a speedboat down (US$300 per person) and camp on the shores.

Tiwai Island

'Big Island' in the Mende language, 12-sq-km Tiwai Island ([☎]076-755146; www.tiwai island.org; day-trip/overnight US$10/20) certainly packs a punch when it comes to its primate population. Set on the Moa River, the entire island is run as a conservation research project. There are more than 700 different plant species, 11 species of primates – including Diana monkeys and chimpanzees – 135 bird species, plus otters, sea turtles and the endangered, elusive pygmy hippopotamus.

From Bo or Kenema, the departure point for Tiwai is Poturu; from Freetown, head to Kambama (eight hours). Speedboats (US$10 per person including island entrance fee) carry you the short distance to the island, where you can stay overnight on canopied platforms (US$20 per person) and drift off to sleep, listening to the midnight chatter of the rainforest.

Guided forest walks cost between US$4 and US$6 per person, depending on the size of the group. Canoe tours cost US$10 per person.

Gola Forest Reserve

Part of the same tract of rainforest as Tiwai Island, the Gola Forest Reserve (☏ 076-420218) is home to an abundance of creatures great and small, from rare, intricately patterned butterflies to lost, lumbering forest elephants having a hard time locating the rest of their species (as in most parts of West Africa, their numbers are critically low). The reserve, which has been declared a national park, runs from Tiwai Island in the south (a short boat ride away) up to the rocky Malema hills in the north (an hour's drive from Kenema).

There's a simple, reasonably priced guesthouse at the southern tip in the village of Belebu, or you can rent camping equipment (US$25) and rough it in the rainforest. The park entrance fee is US$10, and the forest guides charge US$10 per day (plus a tip).

Kenema

POP 160,000

Unless you're caught up in the murky world of diamonds there isn't much to bring you to the red roads of Kenema, although the surrounding countryside is pretty and a visit to the area will give you an idea of what life is like upcountry. It's also a good stopping point on the way to the Gola Forest Reserve or Tiwai Island.

Ericsons (☏ 076-410722) has clean, spacious doubles, while Capitol Hotel (☏ 033-161616; 51 Hangha Rd; s/d/ste US$52/85/138; P ❀ ⛵) has all the mod-cons and a central location.

Bush taxis to Bo (1½ hours), Potoru (three hours), Freetown (five hours) and the Liberian border depart from the bus station in the centre of town.

UNDERSTAND SIERRA LEONE

History

The North American slave trade was effectively launched from Freetown in 1560 and by the 18th century Portuguese and British trading settlements lined the coast. In the late 1700s, freed slaves from places such as Jamaica and Nova Scotia were brought to the new settlement of Freetown. Soon after, Britain abolished slavery and Sierra Leone became a British colony. Many subsequent settlers were liberated from slaving ships intercepted by the British navy and brought here. These people became known as Krios and assumed an English lifestyle together with an air of superiority.

But things didn't run smoothly in this brave new world. Black and white settlers dabbling in the slave trade, disease, rebellion and attacks by the French were all characteristics of 19th-century Sierra Leone. Most importantly, indigenous people were discriminated against by the British and Krios, and in 1898 a ferocious uprising by the Mende began, ostensibly in opposition to a hut tax.

Diamonds Are Forever

Independence came in 1961, but the 1960s and 1970s were characterised by coups (once there were three in one year, an all-African record), a shift of power to the indigenous Mende and Temne peoples, and the establishment of a one-party state (which lasted into the 1980s). By the early 1990s the country was saddled with a shambolic economy and rampant corruption. Then the civil war began.

It's entirely possible that buried in the depths of Foday Sankoh's Revolutionary United Front (RUF) was a desire to end the corruption and abuses of power committed by the ruling military-backed elites in Freetown, who had turned the country into a basket case. But any high ideals were quickly forgotten, replaced by a ferocious desire for Sierra Leone's diamond and goldfields, with looting, robbery, rape, mutilation and summary execution, all tools of the RUF's trade. While their troops plundered to make ends meet, Charles Taylor, the former president of Liberia, and the RUF's leaders enriched themselves from diamonds smuggled south.

The Sierra Leone government was pretty ineffective and tried using South African mercenaries against the RUF, who, bolstered by disaffected army elements and Liberian irregulars, were making gains across the country. In 1996 elections were held and Ahmad Tejan Kabbah was declared president, but a year later, after peace talks had brought some hope, the Armed Forces Revolutionary Council (AFRC) grabbed control of government and decided to share power with the RUF. By this time fractionalisation and desertion on both sides had led to an utter free-for-all, with the civilian population suffering atrocities at every turn.

Hopes & Fears

In March 1998 the Economic Community of West African States Monitoring Group (Ecomog), a Nigerian-led peacekeeping force, retook Freetown and reinstated Kabbah. Some sort of peace held until January 1999, when the RUF and AFRC launched 'Operation No Living Thing'. The ensuing carnage in and around Freetown killed 6000 people, mutilated many more (lopping a limb off was an RUF calling card) and prompted the government to sign the Lomé Peace Agreement. A massive UN peacekeeping mission (Unamsil) was deployed, but 10 months later it came under attack from the RUF. Three hundred UN troops were abducted, but as the RUF closed in on Freetown in mid-2000 the British government deployed 1000 paratroopers and an aircraft carrier to prevent a massacre and shift the balance of power back to Kabbah's government and UN forces. By February 2002 the RUF was disarmed and its leaders captured. Elections were held a few months later; Kabbah was re-elected and the RUF's political wing was soundly defeated.

Unamsil became the largest and most expensive peacekeeping mission in UN history up until that time, and also one of its most effective. The last of the 17,500 soldiers departed in 2005. Peace had won.

The road to justice, however, was just beginning. The Special Court for Sierra Leone, a UN-backed judicial body charged with investigating war crimes during the conflict, was set up in 2002 and headquartered in Freetown. It took 10 years for proceedings against more than 15 people to be completed; among them Issa Sesay, the RUF's senior military officer and commander, who received 52 years – the court's highest sentence – behind bars in Rwanda. The court's most famous convictee was Charles Taylor, the former president of next-door Liberia, who received a jail sentence of 50 years in 2012. His case was transferred to The Hague, amid fears it could spark a resurgence of unrest in Liberia and Sierra Leone. At the time of research Taylor was appealing his sentence.

Sierra Leone Today

Former insurance broker Ernest Bai Koroma won a second – and, according to the constitution, final – term in power in November 2012, with 59% of the votes cast. The poll, Sierra Leone's second since the post-conflict period began, passed largely without violence and was hailed as a marker of the peaceful postwar era. The country now has one of the fastest-growing economies in Africa, and the ongoing boost and interest in tourism is likely to continue to drive that.

Culture

The two largest of the 18 tribal groups, the Temnes of the north and Mendes of the south, each make up about one-third of the population. Krios, mostly living in Freetown, constitute about 1.5% of the population but a large percentage of the professional class.

About 75% of Sierra Leoneans are Muslim; most of the remaining are Christian, who live in the south. Sierra Leoneans are very tolerant and mixed marriages are common.

The Mendes and Temnes operate a system of secret societies responsible for maintaining culture and tradition. For example, if you see young girls with their faces painted white, you'll know that they're in the process of being initiated. They wear coloured beads when they have finished.

When Sierra Leoneans get together, talk always seems to turn to politics, development and corruption. The war did much to foster nationalism (everyone suffered together), but the elections showed that a significant north-south, Temne–Mende divide remains and it has become natural for the political parties to exploit it. Some people worry about how this will play out in coming years.

Handicrafts

Sierra Leone is known for its fabrics, especially country cloth, a coarse, naturally dyed cotton material, and *gara,* a thin tie-dyed or batik-printed sheet. Distinctive Temne basketry also makes a good souvenir.

Books

For a classic, there's Graham Greene's colonial-era *The Heart of the Matter,* set in Freetown. Aminatta Forna's *The Memory of Love* is a thrilling, poignant take on the effect of the conflict in Sierra Leone.

Food & Drink

Sierra Leone is known for its cuisine, and every town has at least one *cookery* (basic eating house) serving *chop* (meals). Rice is the staple and *plasas* (pounded potato or cassava leaves, cooked with palm oil and often fish or beef) is the most common sauce. Other typical dishes include okra sauce, groundnut stew and pepper soup. Street food, such as fried chicken, roasted corn, chicken kebabs and *fry fry* (simple sandwiches), is easy to find.

Star, the top-selling beer, is reasonable. *Poyo* (palm wine) is light and fruity, but getting used to the smell and the wildlife floating in your cup takes a while.

Environment

Sierra Leone's coast is lined with cracking beaches, mangrove swamps and many islands. The Freetown peninsula is one of the few places in West Africa where mountains rise near the sea. Inland are sweeping plains punctuated by random mountains, including Mt Bintumani (1945m), one of West Africa's highest peaks. About 30% of the country is forested and significant patches of primary rainforest remain in the south and east.

Outamba-Kilimi National Park (which still has elephants) in the north, and Tiwai Island (incredible for primates) in the south are worth a visit, but don't expect East African–style wildlife encounters.

SURVIVAL GUIDE

ⓘ Directory A–Z

ACCOMMODATION
Freetown has a growing number of accommodation choices, although you may have to pay through the roof for 24-hour power, water and internet. Elsewhere in the country, choices are more limited, but you can still find some gems.

BUSINESS HOURS
Banks Usually Monday to Friday 8.30am to 4pm, with a select few also open Saturday 9am to 1pm.

General shops and offices 9am to 5.30pm Monday to Saturday, though some places close at 1pm on Saturday.

EMBASSIES & CONSULATES
Most embassies are located in Freetown.

British High Commission (Map p352; ☑232961; http://ukinsierraleone.fco.gov.uk; 6 Spur Rd) Assists French nationals.

Gambian High Commission (Map p354; ☑225191; 6 Wilberforce St)

German Embassy (Map p352; ☑231350; 3 Middle Hill Station)

Ghanaian High Commission (Map p354; ☑223461; 13 Walpole St)

Guinean Embassy (Map p352; ☑232496; 6 Carlton Carew Rd)

Liberian Embassy (Map p352; ☑230991; 2 Spur Rd)

Malian Consulate (Map p352; ☑033-422994; 40 Wilkinson Rd)

Nigerian Embassy (Map p354; ☑224229; 37 Siaka Stevens St)

Senegalese Consulate (Map p354; ☑030-230666; 7 Short St, 2nd fl)

US Embassy (☑076-515000; http://freetown.usembassy.gov; Leicester Rd)

FESTIVALS & EVENTS
Freetown's recently revived **Lantern Parade** is a procession of illuminated floats on 26 April, the night before Independence Day.

INTERNET ACCESS
Most of the good hotels, and some of the restaurants listed in the Eating section, offer access to wi-fi. Most expats get by with USB pay-as-you-go internet sticks. You can also pick up internet-ready SIM cards for smartphones and iPads.

MONEY
The most easily exchangeable currencies in Sierra Leone are US dollars, UK pounds and euros, in that order. Large denominations get the best rates. Forex bureaus (and street traders, though avoid them unless somebody you trust makes the introduction) invariably offer better rates than banks.

PRACTICALITIES

➤ **Electricity** i230V/50Hz. Plugs have three large pins, like the UK.

➤ **Newspapers** *Awoko* and *Concord Times* are the most respected newspapers, though the satirical *Peep* is more popular.

➤ **Magazines** *Newsweek* and *BBC Focus On Africa* are sold at supermarkets.

➤ **TV** Sierra Leone's two TV stations are the government-owned SLBS and the private ABC, both of whose most popular programming is Nigerian soap operas.

➤ **Radio** The BBC World Service is heard on 94.3FM and Voice of America on 102.4FM. SKYY (106.6FM) plays the most local music.

➤ **Languages** Include English, Krio, Mende and Temne.

You can rarely pay with a credit card in Sierra Leone, but some Rokel Commercial Bank branches give cash advances (up to US$2000) on Visa cards and ProCredit Bank has ATMs in Freetown that spit out up to US$100 per day for those with Visa credit and debit cards. Don't rely on them too heavily, as they sometimes don't work.

POST & TELEPHONE
Cell phone service is good and so popular that landlines are disappearing. SIM cards cost US$5.

Sierra Leone's regular post is semi-reliable if you send something from Freetown.

PUBLIC HOLIDAYS
Besides the Islamic and Christian holidays, Sierra Leone celebrates New Year's Day (1 January) and Independence Day (27 April).

SAFE TRAVEL
Sierra Leone is generally safe, although the biggest dangers are the roads and the tides, both of which can claim travellers who aren't vigilant about safety. Read up on rip tides before you travel, and be sure to wear a seatbelt whenever possible: driving safety standards aren't always the highest. Avoid walking on Freetown's beaches alone – you should be fine on the peninsula – and it's best to walk in a group at night. Motorbike taxis are not the safest way to travel, especially in Freetown and other places with smooth roads.

TOURIST INFORMATION
The **National Tourist Board** (www.welcome-tosierraleone.org) might be helpful, but the best source of pre-departure information is Visit Sierra Leone (p356).

VISAS
Everyone from outside Ecowas (Economic Community of West African States) countries needs a visa. Prices and rules vary widely by nationality of applicant and embassy of issuance, but generally you need a plane ticket and a letter of invitation (a hotel reservation should suffice), and your passport needs one year of validity, rather than the typical six months. The regulations are generally more relaxed in embassies of neighbouring countries.

Some people manage to get visas on arrival for an extra fee, but this is unofficial and you risk being turned away.

Visa Extensions
Visas can be easily extended for 30 days at the **Immigration Department** (Map p354; ☎223220; Rawdon St; ⊙10am-3.30pm Mon-Fri) in Freetown.

ℹ Getting There & Away

AIR
British Airways (☎076-541230; www.flybmi.com; 14 Wilberforce St) flies to London for

around £700 return, while **Brussels Airlines** (☎076-333777; www.brusselsairlines.com; 30 Siaka Stevens St) serves its hub in Brussels.

Kenya Airways (☎076-536899; www.kenya-airways.com; 13 Lamina Sankoh St) flies from Nairobi for around US$1300 return and **Royal Air Maroc** (☎076-221015; www.royalairmaroc.com; 19 Charlotte St) flies from Casablanca for around £600.

For regional flights, Asky routes go via its hub in Lome and Arik Airlines flies to Dakar (and onwards to London).

LAND
Guinea
The main route to Guinea is via Pamelap. Bush taxis from Freetown to Conakry run regularly. The journey usually takes eight to 10 hours, depending on the season and the state of the roads.

From Kamakwie to Kindia (Guinea) there's little transport on the Sierra Leone side, where the road is quite bad. 4WDs usually leave Kamakwie every two or three days (US$10, eight to 10 hours). Alternatively, hire an *okada* to the border (they'll ask for US$20), where it's about a 1.5km walk to Medina-Oula in Guinea, which has plenty of transport.

The road from Kabala to Faranah (Guinea), is also in bad shape and only has 4WDs (US$13.50, four to eight hours, twice weekly). *Okada* drivers will take you to Faranah for US$50 in four hours or you could stop in Hérémakono to get a taxi.

Liberia
You can reach Liberia via the Mano River Bridge by Bo (Waterside), provided the raft ferry is running (otherwise you'll have to leave your car and take a pirogue, which is not recommended for safety reasons). Taxis (US$13.50) and sometimes *poda-podas* (US$12) depart from Bo and Kenema to the border post at Gendema (taking six to eight hours in the dry season and 10 to 12 hours in the wet), where you walk over to Liberia and continue in one of the frequent taxis to Monrovia. If you have your own 4WD, you can reach Monrovia in 10 to 12 hours from Freetown.

ℹ Getting Around

BOAT
Pam-pahs (large cargo and passenger boats) operate to several towns, most notably between Mattru Jong and Bonthe.

Speedboat hire costs from US$300 per day while slower *pam-pahs* (which hold up to 20 people) cost around US$165. In Freetown, inquire at Man o' War Bay, Government Wharf, Kissy Terminal and the Conservation Society of Sierra Leone.

CAR

Car hire is expensive (starting at around US$100 in Freetown, much more to head upcountry), but don't choose a company only on the price; ask about the terms too.

You could also just charter *(chatah)* a taxi. In Freetown you can usually negotiate an hourly rate of US$5 for one hour, and US$4 per hour for several hours.

LOCAL TRANSPORT

Bush taxis and *poda-podas* link most towns; except for departures to and from Freetown and between Bo and Kenema, you'll find that traffic is usually pretty sparse, especially on Sunday. Buses will usually cost a little less, but they are slower.

Togo

POP 6.9 MILLION

Best Places to Eat

➡ Côté Jardin (p370)

➡ La Belle Époque (p370)

➡ Le Fermier (p373)

➡ Centre Grill (p374)

Best Places to Stay

➡ Hôtel Napoléon Lagune (p367)

➡ Côté Sud (p367)

➡ Le Geyser (p372)

➡ Coco Beach (p371)

➡ La Douceur (p374)

Why Go?

For those fond of travelling off the beaten track, Togo will prove a rewarding destination. It offers a great diversity of landscapes, from the lakes and palm-fringed beaches along the Atlantic coastline to the rolling forested hills in the centre. As you head further north, the landscape leaves its mantle of lush forest green for the light green and yellowy tinges of savannah land. The cherry on top is Lomé, the low-key yet elegant capital, with its large avenues, tasty restaurants and throbbing nightlife – not to mention the splendid beaches on its doorstep. Togo is also an excellent playground for hikers – there's no better ecofriendly way to experience the country's savage beauty than on foot.

Another highlight is the culture. Togo is a melting pot. The fortified compounds of Koutammakou are a reminder that the country's ethnically diverse population didn't always get along. Nowadays, however, voodoo, Muslim, Christian and traditional festivals crowd the calendar and are often colourful celebrations for all.

When to Go
Lomé

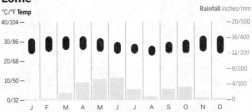

| **Nov–Feb** The best time to visit, with pleasant temperatures. Perfect for outdoor activities. | **Mid-Jul–mid-Sep** There's a dry spell in the south, which makes transport less challenging. | **Mar & Apr** The hottest period throughout the country is best avoided. |

Togo Highlights

1 Soaking up the the mellow vibes of **Lomé** (p367), the coastal capital.

2 Unwinding on blissful **Coco Beach** (p371).

3 Relaxing on the shores of **Lac Togo** (p371).

4 Hiking in lush forested hills and taking in the chilled vibe of **Kpalimé** (p372).

5 Tracking buffaloes and antelopes at **Parc Sarakawa** (p374), Togo's most underrated wildlife reserve.

6 Seeking out northern Togo's remote clay-and-straw fortresses, the *tata* compounds, around **Koutammakou** (p375).

BURKINA FASO

BENIN

GHANA

0   80 km
0   50 miles

Sinkasse

● Dapaong

Nano ●

Sansanné-Mango ●

Natitingou ●

Nadoba ● ● Boukoumbé
6
Koutammakou

Kandé ●

Parc Sarakawa **5** Pya ●   ● Djougou
Sarakawa ●   Kétao
                Kémérida
        Kabou
Yendi ●   ● Natchamba   **Kara**
                Bafilo ●
        Bassar   ● Aledjo Fault

Oti River

        Sokodé ●

Fazao ●

        Sotouboua ●

        Blitta ●

    ● Yégué
                Langabou ●

Lake Volta

                Anjé ●

    Badou ●

        Danyi Plateau
                Atakpamé ●

Mt Klouto (710m) ▲   ● Adéta   *Cascade de Womé*
Kpandu ●   ▲ Mt Agou   Tohoun ●
    Kpalimé **4**   (986m)   **Notsé** ●

        Ho ●

                    Tabligo ●

        Tsevié ●   **Vogan** ● Hilla-Condji
                Lac   **3** Aného
                Togo   Togoville
Aflao ● **1** **2**   Agbodrafo
        LOMÉ **Coco Beach**   *Gulf of Guinea*

Mono River

LOMÉ

POP 750,000

Togo's capital may be a shadow of its former self, when it was dubbed 'the pearl of West Africa', but it retains a charm and nonchalance that is unique among West African capitals. You'll probably appreciate its human scale and unexpected treats and gems: from tasty *maquis* (informal street-side eateries) to colourful markets and palm-fringed boulevards.

◎ Sights

Marché des Féticheurs   MARKET
(Fetish Market; ☑ 227 20 96; Quartier Akodessewa; admission & guide CFA3000, plus per camera/video CFA5000/10,000; ◎ 8.30am-6pm daily) The Marché des Féticheurs, 4km northeast of the centre, stocks all the ingredients for traditional fetishes, from porcupine skin to serpent head. It's all a bit grisly but it's important to remember that a vast majority of Togolese retain animist beliefs and fetishes are an integral part of local culture. To get there charter a taxi (CFA1000) or a *taxi-moto* (motorbike taxi; CFA500).

Grand Marché   MARKET
(Rue du Grand Marché; ◎ to 4pm Mon-Sat) The labyrinthine Grand Marché is Togo at its most colourful and entrepreneurial. You'll find anything at this market from Togolese football tops to cheap cosmetics.

⊨ Sleeping

Auberge Le Galion   HOTEL $
(☑ 22 22 00 30; www.hotel-galion.com; 12 Rue des Camomilles, Kodjoviakopé; r with fan CFA7000-10,000, with air-con CFA13,000-17,000; ✳ ☎) This Swiss-owned hotel is the stalwart of budget accommodation in Lomé. The 24 rooms are basic but clean and the restaurant (mains CFA1800 to CFA4900) and bar are very popular, particularly for the live-music session on Friday night. The more expensive rooms have hot water. It's in a quiet residential area.

My Diana Guesthouse   GUESTHOUSE $
(☑ 91 25 08 80; Rue des Jonquilles; r CFA6000-8000; ✳) A family affair, this lovely guesthouse is a simple but proudly maintained establishment. You'll have to pay more for air-con (CFA500 to CFA1000 per night, depending on electricity consumption) but considering you get use of the kitchen, garden terrace and TV lounge, it's a great bargain.

ⓘ SET YOUR BUDGET

Budget
➡ Hotel room CFA10,000
➡ Sandwich CFA600
➡ Fruit juice CFA400
➡ *Moto-taxi* ride CFA300

Midrange
➡ Hotel room CFA20,000
➡ Two-course dinner CFA4000
➡ Drink in a bar CFA1000
➡ Intercity bus ride CFA7000

Top End
➡ Hotel room CFA40,000
➡ Two-course meal CFA10,000
➡ Cocktail CFA2000
➡ 4WD with driver, per day CFA50,000

Hôtel Belle-Vue   HOTEL $$
(☑ 22 20 22 40; www.hotel-togo-bellevue.com; Kodjoviakopé; s CFA29,000-35,000, d CFA31,000-40,000; P ✳ @ ☎) In the leafy district of Kodjoviakopé, the Belle-Vue is a stylish option that won't break the bank. Rooms are spotless and elegantly decorated with African print curtains and dark-wood furniture. It is also home to one of Lomé's best restaurants, La Belle Époque, and has a great *paillote* (shaded seats) bar in a lush garden. A cool retreat.

★ Côté Sud   GUESTHOUSE $$
(☑ 91 93 45 50, 23 36 12 70; www.hotelcotesud.com; Rue Nima; r CFA23,000-30,000; ✳ ☎) Seeking a relaxing cocoon in Lomé with homely qualities? This champ of a guesthouse run by a French guy who fell in love with Togo has all the key ingredients, with five spacious, light and spick-and-span rooms, prim bathrooms and a small garden. The on-site restaurant (mains CFA3500 to CFA6000) is a winner – your host will treat you to tasty French dishes with an African twist.

★ Hôtel Napoléon Lagune   HOTEL $$
(☑ 22 27 07 32; www.napotogo.com; Rte 20 Bé; d CFA24,000-33,000; P ✳ ☎ ≋) Yes, the Napoléon Lagune is not in the centre, but its perch on a lively stretch of the Bé lagoon is outstanding. It offers a range of well-equipped if unspectacular rooms at reasonable prices. Good service, satellite TV, a plant-filled garden, a small pool and

TOGO LOMÉ

Lomé

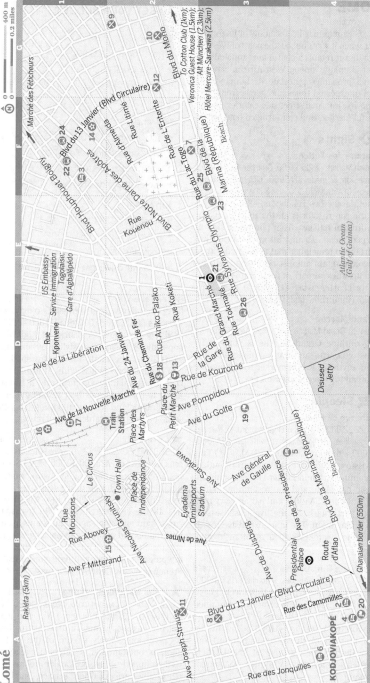

Lomé

an excellent restaurant (mains CFA2500 to CFA6000) are among the other highlights.

Veronica Guest House GUESTHOUSE $$$
(✆22 22 69 07; www.veronicatogo.com; Blvd du Mono; d CFA36,000-51,000; 🅿🛜❄) This charming 10-room hotel with professional staff, beautiful mahogany fittings and a pint-sized pool is a more Togolese alternative to the chain hotels. Although it is on the busy highway, the rooms have thick double glazing and views across the road to the beach. Meals are available (CFA10,000).

Hôtel Ibis-le Bénin HOTEL $$$
(✆22 21 24 85; www.ibishotel.com; Blvd de la Marina; d CFA56,000-60,000; 🅿❄🛜❄) Travellers love the swimming pool here, not to mention the expansive shady grounds. The rooms in the motel-like building lack character, but it's tidy enough and renovation plans are under way. Rooms on the top floors have lovely sea views.

Hôtel Mercure-Sarakawa RESORT $$$
(✆22 27 65 90; www.accorhotels.com; Blvd du Mono; r with city view CFA112,000-116,000, with sea view CFA124,000-128,000; 🅿❄❄) Despite its concrete-bunker exterior, this is one of West Africa's most exclusive hotels, 3km east of the centre on the coastal road to Benin. The 164 rooms are comfortable, but the Sarakawa's main drawcard is its stunning Olympic-size swimming pool set in acres of coconut grove. Rates include breakfast.

🍴 Eating

Nopégali Plage AFRICAN $
(✆222 80 62; Blvd du 13 Janvier; mains CFA1500-2000; ⊙8am-10pm daily) You'll find no cheaper place for a sit-down meal in the centre. It's very much a canteen, but a good one, with friendly service and copious African dishes prepared grandma-style.

Bena Grill STEAKHOUSE $$
(Marox; ✆22 21 50 87; Rue du Lac Togo; mains CFA2000-7000; ⊙breakfast, lunch & dinner daily) A nirvana for carnivores, this cheery restaurant in the market area is lauded for its top-quality meat dishes, including a sensational *côte porc grillée* (grilled pork rib). Also serves sandwiches, burgers and salads. It's next to the Marox supermarket.

Greenfield PIZZERIA, INTERNATIONAL $$
(✆22 21 21 55; Rue Akati; mains CFA2500-4400; ⊙lunch & dinner daily) It's a bit out of the action, but this great garden bar-restaurant, with a French owner, has an original décor, with colourful lanterns and funky colonial seats with retro faux-leather cushions. Food-wise, it features wood-fired pizzas (evenings only), meat grills, salads and pastas.

Lomé La Belle AFRICAN $$
(✆22 22 88 23; Blvd du 13 Janvier; mains CFA3000-5000; ⊙lunch & dinner daily) You'll find all the usual Togolese favourites served in hearty portions at this informal joint right in the centre. It has outdoor seating.

Big Metro AFRICAN **$$**
(Blvd du 13 Janvier; mains CFA1000-4500; ⊙lunch & dinner daily) This little eatery with a pavement terrace is a great spot to catch local vibes and nosh on unpretentious yet tasty African staples. The braised fish (CFA4000) is superb. Unfortunately, it's set on a busy thoroughfare.

★**Côté Jardin** INTERNATIONAL **$$$**
(Rue d'Assoli; mains CFA3000-7000; ⊙lunch & dinner Tue-Sun) Hands-down the most atmospheric eatery in Lomé, Côté Jardin has an exotic pleasure garden replete with tropical plants and woodcarvings. The supremely relaxing surrounds and eclectic menu make this a winner. Dim lighting contributes to romantic dining.

Le Pêcheur SEAFOOD **$$$**
(☑91 59 63 50; Blvd du Mono; mains CFA4500-8000; ⊙lunch Mon-Fri & dinner Mon-Sat) The name gives it away: this is a fantastic seafood place where you'll enjoy fish fillet *a la plancha* (cooked on a griddle) and skewered gambas. Well worth the splurge – if only it had an outdoor terrace!

★**La Belle Époque** FRENCH **$$$**
(☑22 20 22 40; Hôtel Belle-Vue, Kodjoviakopé; mains CFA4500-14,000; ⊙lunch & dinner daily) One of Lomé's finest tables, La Belle Époque, all crisp white table cloths and dimmed lighting, serves a refined French-inspired cuisine. You can also enjoy your meal in a verdant courtyard. Budget tip: ask for the 'Côté Paillotte' menu, with simpler dishes costing less than CFA5000.

Alt München FRENCH, GERMAN **$$$**
(☑22 27 63 21; Rte d'Aného; mains CFA5000-10,000; ⊙lunch & dinner Thu-Tue) A well-regarded restaurant just east of Hôtel Mercure-Sarakawa, offering a good selection of French and Bavarian specialities, including *jarret de porc* (pork knuckle) and *fondue bourguignonne* (meat fondue). Fish dishes are also available.

🍷 Drinking & Entertainment

Cotton Club MUSIC
(☑90 04 45 70; Ave Augustino de Souza; ⊙6pm-late Tue-Sun) This jazz and blues lounge bar is polished, homely and welcoming. Snacks are available.

Domino BAR
(665 Rue de la Gare; ⊙from 6pm) Den-like but cool and very popular, Domino houses Lomé's biggest selection of beers (50 or so) as well as a dozen whiskies.

Le Rézo JAZZ
(☑22 20 15 13; 21 Ave de la Nouvelle Marche; ⊙10am-1am) Inside, it's like a 1980s disco with its blacked-out windows, but Le Rézo is more contemporary than it looks, with giant screens showing Champions League football games, karaoke nights and live jazz on Thursday.

Byblos CLUB
(Blvd du 13 Janvier; admission around CFA5000; ⊙from 10pm Wed-Sun) This trendy nightclub is a favourite haunt of rich young Togolese.

Le 54 BAR
(☑22 20 62 20; Blvd du 13 Janvier; ⊙10am-midnight Thu-Sun) A nice blend of exhibition space, affordable craft and jewellery, and a vibrant restaurant-bar. There's great live music Thursday to Sunday, catering for all musical tastes.

🛍 Shopping

Village Artisanal SOUVENIRS
(☑221 68 07; Ave de la Nouvelle Marche; ⊙8am-5.30pm Mon-Sat) At this easy-going centre you'll see Togolese artisans weaving cloth, carving statues, making baskets and lampshades, sewing leather shoes and constructing cane chairs and tables – all for sale at reasonable fixed prices.

ℹ Information

INTERNET ACCESS
There are numerous internet cafes in Lomé. Expect to pay CFA300 per hour.

MONEY
All banks change cash. Banks with ATMs are easy to find in the centre; they accept Visa cards.
Banque Atlantique (☑22 20 88 92; Place du Petit Marché; ⊙8am-4pm Mon-Fri, 9am-2pm Sat) This is the only place that accepts MasterCard in Togo; also accepts Visa and has an ATM.

SAFE TRAVEL
There are pickpockets around the Rue de Grand Marché and along Rue du Commerce. Avoid walking on the beach alone, especially at night.

There is a very strong undertow along coastal waters, so if you'd like a swim, head for a pool, such as the ones available to nonguests at Hôtel Mercure-Sarakawa or Hôtel Ibis-le Bénin.

TELEPHONE

Local and international calls can be made from any of the multitude of private telephone agencies around the city.

ⓘ Getting There & Away

BUS & BUSH TAXI

Rakiéta (✆ 90 29 88 04) runs a daily bus service between Lomé and Kara (CFA5600, 6½ hours). It leaves at 7.30am from its depot in Atikoumé. Book ahead or arrive early (6am) on the day. This service is a better option than bush taxis.

Bush taxis and minibuses travelling east to Aného (CFA1000, one hour), Lac Togo/Agbodrafo (CFA800, 45 minutes) and to Cotonou (in Benin; CFA5000, three hours) leave from **Gare de Cotonou** (Blvd de la Marina), just west of the STIF bus station.

Gare d'Agbalépédo (Quartier Agbalépédo), 10km north of central Lomé, serves all northern destinations. Services include Atakpamé (CFA3500, two hours), Dapaong (CFA8500, 10 hours) and Kara (CFA6200, five hours).

Minibuses to Kpalimé (CFA2000, two hours) leave from **Gare de Kpalimé** (Rue Moyama), 1.5km north of the centre on Rte de Kpalimé.

There are also international services (see p379), including to/from Ghana.

ⓘ Getting Around

➤ To the airport (5km from central Lomé) the taxi fare is about CFA1500 (but count on CFA2000 from the airport into the city).

➤ Taxis are abundant and have no meters. Fares are CFA350 for a shared taxi (more after 6pm) and CFA1000 nonshared. A taxi by the hour should cost CFA2500 if you bargain well.

➤ Zippy little *taxi-motos* are also popular, if rather dangerous. You should be able to go anywhere in the centre for CFA300 to CFA500.

THE SOUTH

The area between Aného, Kpalimé and Atakpamé is one of the most alluring in West Africa, with a combination of superb beaches, a vast lake, forested hills and numerous waterfalls. If you could only see one place in Togo, this would surely be it.

Agbodrafo & Togoville

On the southern shores of **Lac Togo** (part of the inland lagoon that stretches all the way from Lomé to Aného), **Agbodrafo** is a popu-

---

COCO BEACH

Past the port and customs east of Lomé is another world – a mellow land of beachfront auberges where you can recharge the batteries. The best option on this part of the coast is **Hôtel Coco Beach** (✆ 22 71 49 37; www.hotel-togo-cocobeach.com; Coco Beach; s CFA31,000-39,000, d CFA33,000-62,000; P✷@☞☲), with boardwalks leading to a great restaurant (meals CFA5500 to CFA7000), a seafront bar, and a private beach with deckchairs and *paillotes* (shaded seats) for hire. It's also the safest beach to swim from, thanks to a reef that blocks the strong undertow. Rooms are bright and comfortable but devoid of character.

---

lar weekend getaway for frazzled Lomé residents. Swimming in the lake – croc and bug free – is blissful. It is also a good place to find a *pirogue* (traditional canoe) to **Togoville**, which was the former seat of the Mlapa dynasty and Togo's historical centre of voodoo.

🛏 Sleeping & Eating

Hôtel Le Lac   RESORT **$$$**
(✆ 90 36 28 58; www.hotellelactogo.com; r weekdays/weekends CFA44,000/35,000; P✷☲) East of Agbodrafo, this breezy resort-like venture on the shores of Lac Togo is a reliable choice. The renovated rooms are spacious, with private patios and sweeping lake views. There's a good restaurant (mains CFA2000 to CFA6000) overlooking the lake, a swimming pool and a small beach from where you can swim in the lake. *Pirogue* trips to Togoville (CFA3000) can easily be arranged.

ⓘ Getting There & Away

From the Gare de Cotonou in Lomé, bush taxis frequently travel along the coastal road to Aného (CFA1000) via Agbodrafo.

Aného

POP 49,000

All that remains of Aného's days as colonial capital in the late 19th century are crumbling pastel buildings. Voodoo is strong here and most obvious at **Vogan's Friday market**, one of the biggest and most colourful in Togo, about 20km northwest of Aného; taxis

---

DON'T MISS

HIKING IN THE KPALIMÉ AREA

The heartiest walk is up Togo's highest peak, **Mt Agou** (986m), 20km southeast of Kpalimé. The path climbs between backyards, through cocoa and coffee plantations and luxuriant forests bristling with life. Small terraced mountain villages pepper the slopes and provide fabulous views of the area. On a clear day, you can see Lake Volta in Ghana. The walk takes four hours' return from the village of Nyogbo. The track can be hard to find so it's best to take a guide. Alternatively, there is a road to the top so you could walk one way and arrange a taxi for your walk back.

The area around **Mt Klouto** (710m), 12km northwest of Kpalimé, is another walking heaven, with forested hills, waterfalls and a myriad butterflies. Early morning is the best time to search for them.

It's best to go with a local guide. As well as showing you the way, a good guide will show you cool plants, unusual fruit and veg, and fill you up on local culture and history. Contact Adetop (p379), which can arrange guided butterfly walks and village stays, as well as treks in the area.

from Aného (CFA800, 30 minutes) leave from the junction on route to Lomé.

🎉 Festivals & Events

Aného plays host to the **Festival des Divinités Noires** (Festival of Black Divinities), which has been held in December each year since 2006. It celebrates voodoo – expect singing, dancing, beating of drums and parades.

🛏 Sleeping & Eating

Hôtel Oasis　　　　　GUESTHOUSE $
(☑ 23 31 01 25; Rte de Lomé-Cotonou; d with fan/air-con CFA10,000/15,000; 🅿 ❄) An unbeatable location east of the bridge, looking across the lagoon and the beach to the sea. The terrace is a prime place for a sunset drink. Rooms are basic, though – you'll pay for the location.

La Becca Hôtel　　　　　HOTEL $$
(☑ 23 31 05 13; Route de Lomé-Cotonou; r with fan CFA11,000-13,000, with air-con CFA15,000-21,000; ❄) The cheap and cheerful La Becca is a good budget option, with smallish, yet well-scrubbed, rooms. The air-con rooms are significantly better than the fan-cooled units.

ℹ Getting There & Away

From the *gare routière* (bus station), bush taxis and minibuses head to Lomé (CFA1000, one hour), as well as to the Beninese border and Cotonou (CFA2500, 2½ hours).

Kpalimé

POP 101,000

Kpalimé is only 120km from Lomé, but feels like another world. Hidden among the forested hills of the cocoa and coffee region, it offers some of Togo's best scenery and hiking. It's also a busy place thanks to its proximity to the Ghanaian border and important market (Tuesday and Saturday), where local farmers sell their products along with the usual bric-a-brac of plasticware and clothes.

🛏 Sleeping & Eating

Auberge Vakpo Guest House　GUESTHOUSE $
(☑ 91 53 17 00, 24 42 56 64; www.vakpoguesthouse.com; Kpodzi; r with fan CFA8500-12,000, with air-con CFA9500-14,500; 🅿 ❄ 📶) A well-run little number with a quiet location near the Catholic church, Auberge Vakpo offers neat rooms with good bedding, meticulous bathrooms and a lovely pleasure garden complete with flower bushes, mural frescoes and sculptures. Meals are available for CFA3500.

Hôtel Chez Felicia　　　　HOTEL $
(☑ 90 10 97 77, 22 46 33 49; Rte de Missahoe; r with fan/air-con CFA7000/12,000; 🅿 ❄) Off the road to Klouto, the discreet Hôtel Chez Felicia is an excellent bargain. This low-slung building set in verdant surrounds shelters immaculate, bright rooms with back-friendly mattresses, crisply dressed beds and impeccable bathrooms. Meals are CFA2000 to CFA4000.

Le Geyser　　　　　　　HOTEL $$
(☑ 24 41 04 67; www.hotellegeyser.com; r CFA14,000-19,000; 🅿 ❄ 📶 🏊) You'll find the tranquil Hôtel Le Geyser 2km from the centre on the road to Klouto, in a balmy garden setting. Rooms are well-tended, functional and airy, and the restaurant (mains

CFA2000 to CFA5000) serves good African and European dishes. A real hit is the pool.

Chez Fanny INN $$
(☑24 41 00 99; hotelchezfanny@yahoo.fr; Rte de Lomé; r CFA18,000; P✻🤙) This jolly good villa 2km south of town is a homey retreat. The eight rooms are huge and the patio is a lovely spot to relax, despite the fact it overlooks the busy Rte de Lomé. The restaurant (mains CFA2000 to CFA6000) is the best in town.

Hotel Agbeviade HOTEL $$
(☑24 41 05 11; agbeviade2003@yahoo.fr; Rte de Missahoé; r with fan CFA8500, with air-con CFA16,500-19,500; ✻) Off the road to Klouto, the Agbeviade is a safe choice, although the smallish air-con rooms are a bit disappointing for the price. The short menu concentrates on European dishes.

★ Le Fermier AFRICAN, FRENCH $$
(☑90 02 98 30; mains CFA2000-4000; ⊙lunch & dinner daily) For excellent European and African food, try this low-roofed, intimate spot on the northwestern outskirts of town. You can't really go wrong – everything is pretty good – but if you want a recommendation, go for the *fufu* (pounded yam), served in a clay pot.

Chez Lazare FRENCH $$
(Rte de Missahoé; mains CFA1000-4000; ⊙lunch & dinner daily) Don't be put off by the unappealing concrete walls. Lazare cooks up excellent French specialities as well as pasta. How does a *côte de porc à la dijonnaise* (pork rib in mustard sauce) sound? The rooftop terrace is pleasant in the evening.

🍷 Drinking & Nightlife

Chez Fomen BAR
(Rue de Bakula; ⊙8am-late daily) This cheerful, easy-going bar is a fun place for a drink.

It also shows regular football games and serves food.

Bar Alokpa BAR
(⊙9am-late daily) A popular bar on the main road, north of the centre.

ℹ️ Information

Banks with ATMs and internet cafes can be found in the centre.

ℹ️ Getting There & Away

The *gare routière* is in the heart of town, two blocks east of the Shell petrol station. The road between Kpalimé and Atakpamé is the worst in the country, which means few taxis from Kpalimé travel further north than Atakpamé (CFA2000, four hours) and you'll have to change there for services to Sokodé or Kara.

You can get minibuses direct to Lomé (CFA2000, two hours), to the Ghanaian border (CFA1000, 30 minutes) and to Ho in Ghana (CFA1500, 1½ hours).

Atakpamé
POP 85,000

Once the favourite residence of the German colonial administrators, Atakpamé today is a commercial centre. There are no sights, but it makes a pleasant enough stopover on long journeys.

🛏️ Sleeping & Eating

Hôtel California HOTEL $
(☑23 35 85 44; Rte Internationale; r with fan & without bathroom CFA3000, r with air-con & bathroom CFA8000-10,000; ✻) Despite being at the back of the Total petrol station, this hotel-restaurant is a good surprise, with uncomplicated yet spotless rooms, salubrious bathrooms, excellent food (mains CFA1500 to CFA4000) and a friendly welcome. Opt

TOGO ATAKPAMÉ

WORTH A TRIP

CASCADE DE WOMÉ

One great attraction in the Kpalimé area is the **Cascade de Womé** (Womé Falls; ☑99 01 01 12; www.akatamanso-togo.comli.com; Womé; admission CFA1000; ⊙8am-5pm daily), 12km from Kpalimé. Access to the falls is at the village of Womé. You have to pay CFA1000 to the Association Akatamanso at the entrance to the village (ask for a receipt). It's a further 4km to the picnic area near the falls. From the picnic area, it's a short but steep descent to the waterfalls through lush vegetation. You can swim beneath the falls – bliss!

From Kpalimé, a *moto-taxi* ride to the falls should cost around CFA3500 return, including waiting time.

for the air-con rooms, which are noticeably better than the fan-cooled units.

Le Sahélien   AFRICAN $$

(☑ 440 12 44; Rte Internationale; mains CFA1500-4000; ☺ lunch & dinner daily) The downstairs *maquis* with its enormous grill and informal atmosphere does a brisk trade with the town's *moto-taxis*. Upstairs is more upmarket, and the roof terrace is a nice spot to catch the evening breeze. It also doubles as a hotel, but the rooms need a freshen-up.

ℹ Information

There are banks with ATMs as well as internet cafes in the centre.

ℹ Getting There & Away

Taxis and minibuses leave from the main *gare routière* south of the centre to Dapaong (CFA7500, eight hours), Kara (CFA4200, five hours), Kpalimé (CFA2000, four hours) and Lomé (CFA2800, two hours).

There's a secondary *gare routière* next to the market in the centre of town, from where taxis regularly go to Kpalimé (CFA2000).

THE NORTH

As you head north, Islam takes over from Christianity as the dominant religion. Most towns are short on sights, but for those with their own vehicle, or the determination to have a showdown with local bush taxis, fabulous highlights await in the castellated shapes of the Tamberma compounds in Koutammakou.

Kara

POP 109,000

Laid out by the Germans on a spacious scale, Kara is the relaxed capital of northern Togo and a good base for trips to Koutammakou. Because Eyadéma was from Pya, a Kabye village about 20km to the north, he pumped a lot of money into Kara and the region has remained a political stronghold of the Eyadéma clan.

✪✪ Festivals & Events

The area is famous for the **Evala** coming-of-age festival in July. The main event is *la lutte* (wrestling), in which greased-up young men try to topple each other in a series of bouts.

🛏 Sleeping & Eating

★ La Douceur   INN $

(☑ 660 11 64; douceurkara@yahoo.fr; off Rue de Chaminade; r with fan CFA6000, with air-con CFA8000-12,000; ❇ ☎) Down a dirt track in the stadium's neighbourhood you'll find this cosy bird's nest in a proudly maintained and flowered little compound. Rooms are spotless with simple decor, the well-stocked bar serves the coldest beer in town and the *paillote* restaurant (mains CFA1500 to CFA4000) does great food.

Marie-Antoinette   HOTEL, CAMPGROUND $

(☑ 26 60 16 07; http://ma.kara-tg.com; Rte Internationale; campsites per person CFA1500; s with fan CFA7500, d with fan CFA8500-9500, s with air-con CFA10,500-13,500, d with air-con 11,500-14,500; ℗ ❇ ☎) In a pretty house 3km south of Kara on Rte Internationale, Marie-Antoinette has rooms of varying size and shape. Opt for the dearer rooms, which are spacious and well organised, and come with bathrooms in good working order (hot water). Downside: the hotel is not shielded from the noise of the highway. The restaurant cooks up decent meals for CFA2500 and you can camp in the annexe across the street.

★ Centre Grill   AFRICAN, EUROPEAN $$

(Marox; ☑ 90 70 22 33; cnr Rte de Prison & Ave Eyadéma; mains CFA1300-3600; ☺ breakfast, lunch & dinner daily) An attractive place with its straw roof, wicker light shades and blackboard menus, Centre Grill serves divine Togolese food and good Western dishes. Try its *fufu sauce arachide* with grilled fish, or *pâte sorgho* (mashed sorghum), wash the lot down with a cold beer and polish it off with banana fritters. Great value.

WORTH A TRIP

PARC DE SARAKAWA

Unpretentious and relaxing, **Parc de Sarakawa** (☑ 90 55 49 21; hel228@hotmail.fr; adult/child CFA5000/2500; ☺ 8am-5pm daily) is easily accessed from Kara as a day trip. While its terrestrial wildlife-watching can't compare with that in the better-known parks in West Africa, it spreads out over 1500 acres and is home to various species of antelope, buffalo, ostrich and zebra. Game drives (CFA5000) can be arranged at the gate. There are plans to build a lodge within the park.

ⓘ Information

Banks with ATMs and internet cafes are easy to find in the centre.

ⓘ Getting There & Away

From the main *gare routière*, about 2km south of the town centre, minibuses regularly head south to Atakpamé (CFA4300, four hours), Kandé (CFA1200) and Lomé (CFA4800, seven hours). Taxis heading north to Dapaong (CFA3600, four hours) are scarce and it's not unusual to have to wait half a day for one to fill up.

For buses heading to Lomé, **Rakiéta** (Rue du 23 Septembre) has a daily departure at 7.30am (CFA5600, six hours) from its depot.

To get to the border with Benin via Kétao (CFA600, 30 minutes), get a minibus or bush taxi from **Station du Grand Marché** (Ave Eyadéma), next to the market.

Koutammakou

Also known as Tamberma Valley after the people who live here, Koutammakou has a unique collection of fortress-like mud houses, founded in the 17th century by people fleeing the slave-grabbing forays of Benin's Dahomeyan kings. Listed as a World Heritage Site by Unesco in 2004, the area is one of the most scenic in the country, with stunning mountain landscapes and intense light.

You can visit Koutammakou as a day trip from Kara. To get there, turn eastward off the Kara–Dapaong highway in Kandé and follow the track in the direction of Nadoba, the area's main village. About 2km down the road, you'll have to pay CFA1500 at the Accueil et Billetterie office to enter the site.

The *piste* is in good condition and crosses the valley all the way to Boukoumbé and Natitingou in Benin. If you don't have your own transport, chartering a taxi/*moto-taxi* for the day will cost around CFA20,000/5000.

In Nadoba, guides will be happy to show you the valley's highlights.

Dapaong

POP 31,800

This lively little town is a West African melting pot, with the Burkinabé and Ghanaian borders both within 30km. It sits in the middle of Togo's most arid landscape and

TAMBERMA COMPOUNDS

A typical Tamberma compound, called a *tata*, consists of a series of towers connected by a thick wall with a single entrance chamber, used to trap an enemy so he can be showered with arrows. The castle-like nature of these extraordinary structures helped ward off invasions by neighbouring tribes and, in the late 19th century, the Germans. As in the *tata somba* in nearby Benin, life in a *tata* revolves around an elevated terrace of clay-covered logs, where the inhabitants cook, dry their millet and corn, and spend most of their leisure time.

Skilled builders (that's what Tamberma means), the Tamberma only use clay, wood and straw – and no tools. There may be a fetish shrine in front of the compound.

gets the full force of the harmattan between November and February.

🛏 Sleeping & Eating

Hôtel Le Campement   HOTEL $

(☑ 90 01 81 06; Rte de la Station de Lomé; r with fan/air-con CFA9600/14,800; ᴘ ✳) Dapaong's only midrange hotel, but overpriced. However, rooms are pleasant and spacious, and the overgrown garden that is filled with oversized sculptures is a cool place to laze around. The French bar-restaurant is expensive (mains from CFA3500), but the food is very tasty and the desserts are amazing.

Auberge Idriss   GUESTHOUSE $

(☑ 27 70 83 49; off Rte Internationale; r with fan & without bathroom CFA4000, r with air-con & bathroom CFA13,000-15,000; ᴘ ✳) A tidy little guesthouse in a quiet neighbourhood 3km north of town. Rooms in the main building are spacious; those in the annexe have shared facilities but are cosier.

ⓘ Getting There & Away

Taxis leave the station on Rte de Nasablé for Sinkasse on the Burkinabé border (CFA1200), from where transport heads to Ouagadougou.

From Station de Lomé on Rte Internationale, 2km south of the centre, bush taxis head to Kara (CFA3800, four hours) and Lomé (CFA8000, 12 hours).

UNDERSTAND TOGO

Togo Today

In March 2010, president Faure Gnassingbé was re-elected for a second term. Unlike in 2005, the process was largely trouble free, but opposition parties claimed that these presidential elections – Faure won 60% of the vote – were marred by serious irregularities. Politically, the situation has barely evolved in 30 years.

Economically, there are better perspectives. Severely damaged by two decades of political unrest, the economy is now picking up. International business and aid donors are returning to Togo and Lomé's port infrastructure is expanding. Landlocked countries, such as Niger and Burkina Faso, increasingly use Lomé's port over that of Cotonou.

History

The country was once on the fringes of several great empires and, when the Europeans arrived in the 16th century, this power vacuum allowed the slave-traders to use Togo as a conduit.

Following the abolition of slavery, Germany signed a treaty in Togoville with local king Mlapa. Togoland, as the Germans called their colony, underwent considerable economic development, but the Togolese didn't appreciate the Germans' brutal 'pacification' campaigns. When the Germans surrendered at Kamina – the Allies' first victory in WWI – the Togolese welcomed the British forces.

However, the League of Nations split Togoland between France and Britain – a controversial move that divided the populous Ewe. Following a 1956 plebiscite, British Togoland was incorporated into the Gold Coast (now Ghana). French Togoland gained full independence in 1960 under the country's first president, Sylvanus Olympio. But his presidency was short-lived. Olympio, an Ewe from the south who appeared to disregard the interests of northerners, was killed by Kabye soldiers in 1963. His replacement was then deposed by Kabye sergeant Gnassingbé Eyadéma. The new leader established a cult personality and became increasingly irrational following a 1974 assassination attempt.

In 1990, France began pressuring Eyadéma to adopt a multiparty system, but he resisted. The following year, after riots, strikes and the deaths of pro-democracy protestors, 28 bodies were dragged from a lagoon and dumped in front of the US embassy, drawing attention to the repression in Togo.

Eyadéma finally agreed to a conference in 1991, where delegates stripped him of his powers and installed an interim government. However, Eyadéma-supporting troops later reinstalled Eyadéma. Back in power, the general retaliated by postponing planned elections, which prompted strikes in 1992. The strikes paralysed the economy and led to violence, during which 250,000 southerners fled the country.

Eyadéma triumphed his way through ensuing elections throughout the 1990s – elections typically marred by international criticism, opposition boycotts and the killing of rival politicians. Amnesty International made allegations of human rights violations, such as executions and torture, and pressure on the president increased at the same rate that aid from international donors decreased.

Eyadéma finally left office the way many suspected he would – in a coffin. Following his death in February 2005, his son, Faure Gnassingbé, seized power in a military coup, then relented and held presidential elections, which he won. Some 500 people were killed in riots in Lomé, amid allegations the elections were fixed.

Faure's Rally of the Togolese People (RPT) party won legislative elections in 2007, the first to be deemed reasonably free and fair by international observers. Opposition parties also won seats in parliament, a political first. Following this milestone, the EU resumed relations with Togo, which had been suspended for 14 years, and dealings with international agencies such as the IMF and the World Bank have restarted.

People

With about 40 ethnic groups in a population of over six million people, Togo has one of Africa's more heterogeneous populations. The three largest groups are the southern Ewe and Mina, and the northern Kabye; the latter counts President Gnassingbé among its population and is concentrated around Kara.

Religion

Christianity and Islam are the main religions in Togo – in the south and north respectively. However, a majority of the population have voodoo beliefs, which are strongest in the southeast.

The Arts

Batik and wax printing is popular throughout Togo, but the most well-known textile is the Ewe kente cloth, which is less brilliantly coloured than the Ashanti version.

Music and dance play an important part in Togolese daily life. Today, traditional music has fused with contemporary West African, Caribbean and South American sounds, creating a hybrid that includes highlife, reggae and soukous. Togo's most famous singing export was Bella Bellow, who, before her death in 1973, ruled the local music scene, toured internationally and released a recording, *Album Souvenir*. Nowadays, King Mensah is Togo's best-known artist, at home and abroad.

The fortified Tamberma compounds in Koutammakou are some of the most striking structures in West Africa.

Food & Drink

Togolese dishes, some of the best in West Africa, are typically based, as in much of the region, on a starch staple such as *pâte* (a dough-like substance made of corn, manioc or yam) accompanied by sauce. Some Togolese specialities are *fufu* (cooked and puréed yam served with vegetables and meat), *djenkoumé* (a *pâte* made with cornflour cooked with spices and served with fried chicken) and *pintade* (guinea fowl).

Common snacks include: *aloko* (fried plantain), *koliko* (yam chips), *gaou* (bean-flour fritters) and *wagasi* (a mild cheese fried in hot spice). You'll also find fresh fruit everywhere you go.

Togo has its fair share of generic (Flag, Castel, Lager) and local brews. *Tchoukoutou* (fermented millet) is the preferred tipple in the north. Elsewhere, beware of *sodabe*, a terrifyingly potent moonshine distilled from palm wine.

Environment

Togo's coastline measures only 56km, but the country stretches inland for over 600km. The coast is tropical; further inland are rolling hills covered with forest, yielding to savannah plains in the north.

Wildlife is disappointing because larger mammals have largely been killed or scared off. The country's remaining mammals (monkeys, buffaloes and antelopes) are limited to the north; crocodiles and hippos are found in some rivers.

The coastline faces serious erosion and pollution problems.

SURVIVAL GUIDE

 **Directory A–Z**

ACCOMMODATION

Togo has a fairly good range of accommodation options, from basic cubicle hotels to upmarket establishments with all mod cons. Unsurprisingly, Lomé has the widest range of hotels.

EMBASSIES & CONSULATES

British nationals should contact the **British High Commission** (✉ 302 213250; http://ukinghana. fco.gov.uk; 1 Osu Link) in Accra (Ghana).

French Embassy (✉ 22 23 46 00; www. ambafrance-tg.org; Ave du Golfe, Lagos)

German Embassy (✉ 22 23 32 32; www.lome. diplo.de; Blvd de la Marina, Lagos)

Ghanaian Embassy (✉ 22 21 31 94; Rue Moyama, Tokoin; ◷ 8am-2pm Mon-Fri)

US Embassy (✉ 22 61 54 70; http://togo. usembassy.gov; Blvd Eyadéma, Lagos)

INTERNET ACCESS

➡ In towns and cities, wi-fi is available at almost every midrange and top-end establishment.

➡ Internet cafes are easy to find in towns and cities but nonexistent in more remote areas.

MONEY

➡ The currency in Togo is the West African CFA franc.

➡ The best foreign currency to carry is euros, easily exchanged at any bank or hotel.

➡ Travellers cheques cannot be changed in Togo.

➡ You'll find Visa ATMs in major towns. Only Banque Atlantique in Lomé accepts MasterCard.

➡ Credit cards are accepted at a few upmarket hotels.

PRACTICALITIES

➜ **Electricity** Supply is 220V and plugs are of the European two-round-pin variety.

➜ **Languages** French, Ewé, Kabiyé.

OPENING HOURS

Administrative offices Open 7am to noon and 2.30pm to 5.30pm Monday to Friday.

Banks Open 7.45am to 4pm or 5pm Monday to Friday. Most banks are now open through lunchtime and on Saturday, too.

Restaurants Open for lunch and dinner daily, unless otherwise specified.

Shops Operate 7.30am to 12.30pm and 2.30pm to 6pm Monday to Saturday.

PUBLIC HOLIDAYS

Togo also celebrates Islamic holidays, which change dates every year.

New Year's Day 1 January

Meditation Day 13 January

Easter March/April

National Day 27 April

Labour Day 1 May

Ascension Day May

Pentecost May/June

Day of the Martyrs 21 June

Assumption Day 15 August

All Saints' Day 1 November

Christmas Day 25 December

SAFE TRAVEL

➜ Petty theft and muggings are common in Lomé, especially on the beach and near the Grand Marché. *Taxi-motos* in the city may be convenient, but they are dangerous.

➜ Driving in Togo is, to say the least, hair-raising: take care on the roads, particularly at night.

➜ The beaches along the coast are not safe for swimming because of strong currents.

TELEPHONE

Togo's country code is 228. Landline numbers start with 2, mobile numbers with 9. Make international calls at the private telephone agencies in every town.

Mobile phone coverage is excellent. Local networks include Togocel and Moov. Depending on which mobile network you use at home, your phone may or may not work in Togo – ask your mobile network provider. You can also bring your phone and buy a local SIM card. Top-up vouchers are easily available.

VISAS

Everyone except nationals of the Economic Community of West African States (Ecowas) countries needs a visa.

One-week extendable visas (CFA10,000) are issued at major border crossings with Ghana (Aflao/Lomé), Benin (Hilakondji) and Burkina Faso (Sinkasse), and upon arrival at the airport.

The **Service Immigration Togolaise** (☑250 78 56; Ave de la Chance, Service des Passeports; ☺8am-4pm Mon-Fri), near the GTA building 8km north of central Lomé, issues 30-day visa extensions in one or two days. They're free when you extend the seven-day visa. Four photos are required.

Visas for Onward Travel

The Visa des Pays de l'Entente, valid in Côte d'Ivoire, Niger, Benin and Burkina Faso, is available at the Service Immigration Togolaise. Bring two photos, your passport and CFA15,500. It takes 24 hours to process, but note that the office is closed on weekends.

If you're visiting only a single country, the following embassies deliver visas:

Benin A two-week/one-month single-entry visa costs CFA10,000/15,000. You need two photos and photocopies of your passport. It takes one day to process.

Burkina Faso Contact the French consulate in Lomé.

Ghana One-month single-entry visas are issued within three days for CFA20,000 and require four photos and a photocopy of your yellow-fever vaccination certificate.

WOMEN TRAVELLERS

The Togolese are rather conservative when it comes to marriage: it is therefore incomprehensible to them that women past their 20s might not be married. This will lead to many questions, but it is generally harmless. To avoid attracting any more attention, dress conservatively.

❶ Getting There & Away

AIR

Togo's international airport is 5km northeast of the centre of Lomé. A few major airlines operate in Togo and have offices in Lomé.

The main international carriers are Air France, Brussels Airlines, Royal Air Maroc and Ethiopian Airlines, which offer direct flights to France, Belgium, Morocco and Ethiopia respectively, and connecting flights to the rest of the world.

Other major airlines include Asky, which flies to major capitals in West and Central Africa, Air Burkina, with flights to Ouagadougou (Burkina Faso) and Air Côte d'Ivoire, which flies to Abidjan (Côte d'Ivoire).

➜ All airlines have offices in Lomé.

LAND
Benin

Bush taxis regularly ply the road between Gare de Cotonou in Lomé and Cotonou (Benin; CFA5000, three hours) via Hilakondji (CFA800, one hour), while **ABC** (☑ 90 07 69 56; Rue Olympos Sylvano) in Lomé has daily buses to Cotonou (CFA6000, three hours).

The main northern crossing is at Kétao (northeast of Kara). You can also cross at Tohoun (east of Notsé) or Nadoba (in Koutammakou country), arriving in Boukoumbé, but public transport is infrequent. Note that Beninese visas are not issued at the border.

Burkina Faso

The best way to get to Ouagadougou from Lomé is by bus, via Dapaong. **NTI** (☑ 90 19 80 92; Blvd du 13 Janvier), **CTS** (☑ 99 27 83 32; Blvd du 13 Janvier) and **TCV** (☑ 92 29 48 93; Ave Agustino de Souza) are reliable companies. NTI and CTS have three services weekly (CFA12,500) and TCV has two weekly (CFA15,000).

From Dapaong, you'll easily find a taxi to Sinkasse (CFA1500, 45 minutes), which straddles the border. From there it's CFA6000 to Ouagadougou by bus. The border is open from 6am to 6pm.

Ghana

From central Lomé it is only 2km – CFA500/1500 in a shared/chartered taxi or *taxi-moto* (CFA500) – to the chaotic border crossing (open 6am to 10pm) with Aflao in Ghana. From there, you can cross on foot to pick up minibuses to Accra.

STIF (☑ 99 42 72 72; off Blvd de la Marina) runs daily buses between Lomé and Abidjan via Accra (CFA6000, four hours), while **UTB** (☑ 99 45 46 34; Rue Sylvanus Olympo) offers three-weekly services between Lomé and Accra (CFA7000).

There are other crossings from Kpalimé to Ho and Klouto to Kpandu.

❶ Getting Around

BUS

➡ Buses are the most reliable way to get around, especially for long-distance trips.

➡ Rakiéta buses were more reliable than those of other companies at the time of writing.

➡ Buses almost always operate with guaranteed seating and fixed departure times.

BUSH TAXI

Togo has an extensive network of dilapidated bush taxis, which can be anything from an old pick-up truck to a normal sedan car or nine- or 15- seat people carriers. Travel is often agonisingly slow; unfortunately, these bush taxis are generally the only way to get around. Fares are fixed-ish.

CAR

➡ If you're driving, you will need an International Driving Permit (IDP). Police checkpoints are common throughout the country but rarely nasty or obstructive.

➡ Petrol stations are plentiful in major towns. A litre of petrol cost CFA610 at the time of research.

LOCAL TRANSPORT

➡ You'll find taxis in most cities. *Taxi-motos*, also called *zemi-johns*, are everywhere. A journey across town costs about CFA200, and more in Lomé. They are also a handy way to get to remote locations in the bush.

➡ Chartering a taxi will generally cost CFA2000 to CFA3000 per hour.

TOURS

1001 Pistes (1001 'sandy tracks'; ☑ 90 27 52 03; www.1001pistes.com) Run by a French couple, 1001 Pistes offers excellent excursions across the country. These range from easy day walks from Lomé to several-day hikes and 4WD adventures with bivouacs to whale-watching outings along the Atlantic coast. They also offer guided mountain-bike tours in Lomé and elsewhere in the country.

Adetop (☑ 90 08 88 54, 24 41 08 17; www.adetop-togo.com; Rte de Klouto) A small NGO promoting sustainable tourism, Adetop is based in Kpalimé but runs activities throughout the country. Its main activities are guided tours exploring the culture and heritage of Togo, as well as hiking.

Understand
West Africa

West Africa Today

Life is often difficult in this corner of the world. Drought, hunger and political instability continue to stalk the region, and much of the southern Sahara has become a no-go zone, the domain of bandits and Islamist rebels in no mood to compromise. At the same time, peace now reigns in countries previously wracked by seemingly intractable conflict, while democracy and prosperity are increasingly the norm elsewhere.

Best on Film

Moolaadé (Ousmane Sembene; 2005) An important film by one of West Africa's finest directors.
Kabala (Assana Kouyaté; 2002) Award-winning film about Malian village life.
Ezra (Newton Aduaka; 2007) A searing look at the abduction of child soldiers as seen from an African perspective.
Les Saignantes (Jean-Pierre Bekelo; 2005) Fascinating film from Cameroon with a female-dominated cast that sheds uncomfortable light on poor governance in Africa.

Best in Print

The Lost Kingdoms of Africa (Jeffrey Tayler; 2005) A modern journey through northern Nigeria, Niger and Mali.
The Shadow of the Sun (Ryszard Kapuściński; 2002) A masterpiece by one of Africa's most insightful observers.
Journey Without Maps (Graham Greene; 1936) One of the 20th century's best writers travels through Liberia and Sierra Leone.
Travels in the White Man's Grave (Donald MacIntosh; 2001) A little-known classic.

The Good News

Good news about Africa can be hard to find, but West Africa has much to be proud of. The one-time power-house of the region, Côte d'Ivoire, has emerged from a deeply troubled decade to find a peace that is fragile but somehow enduring. Liberia and Sierra Leone were for much of the 1990s among the most dangerous places on the continent, and yet both have made hugely impressive (and democratic) returns to peace. Sierra Leone, with its pristine beaches, fine ecotourism projects and abundant natural resources, is certainly one to watch.

Elsewhere, Guinea, Mauritania, Niger and Togo are all emerging from troubled periods and all face an uncertain future, but these shaky democracies were still holding on at the time of writing and may even go the distance.

But there are five undoubted stars of the West African political scene. Morocco has weathered the upheavals of the Arab Spring by inching towards greater freedoms while remaining stable and relatively prosperous; Morocco is where West Africa's inhabitants have the highest standard of living. Benin and Cape Verde rarely make the news, but continue to exhibit the stability, economic progress and good governance which are their trademark. The same could be said for Senegal – the 2012 elections proved the strength of the country's democratic institutions, although the subsequent dissolution of the parliament's upper house has caused disquiet in opposition circles.

And then there's Ghana, still the region's star performer with a series of successful elections under its belt at a time when its citizens are riding a wave of optimism thanks to the discovery of offshore oil.

The Bad News

Of course, it's not all good news. In Nigeria, the ongoing breach between north and south widens and narrows but never closes, while the far northeast, especially around Maiduguri, is experiencing one of the most difficult times in living memory. And on the economic front, Nigeria continues to disappoint. The country has received more than $325 billion in oil revenues over 30 years, yet the per capita income of its citizens is less than US$2 per day; the average Nigerian now earns less than in 1960, before oil was discovered. Even so, Nigeria's democracy is one of the most rambunctious on the continent even as it continues to lumber forwards, and the country's literary and musical output continues to be prodigious.

For more than a decade, Mali was the poster child for West Africa's democratic transition. But in 2012 the army seized power, and a potent cocktail of Tuareg and Islamist fighters seized vast swaths of the country's north; the Islamists won, and no one really disputes that al-Qaeda in the Islamic Maghreb now pulls the strings across the Malian Sahara. Elsewhere, Guinea-Bissau lurches from one crisis to the next, its political stability seriously compromised by the country's role as a reported hub of the global trade in illicit drugs. Cameroon, Burkina Faso and The Gambia are all stable but only because these are places where one-man rule has crowded out most opposition.

According to the UN's annual Human Development Index, which is based on economic and quality-of-life indicators, West Africa is the poorest region on earth. In the 187-country study, Niger was the second-worst place on earth in which to live. Also in the bottom 20 are Liberia, Burkina Faso, Sierra Leone, Guinea, Guinea-Bissau, Mali, Côte d'Ivoire and The Gambia. Rounding out the bottom five are Burkina Faso, Guinea-Bissau, Niger and Mali. Not one West African country appears in the 100 most developed countries in the world, with the highest-ranked countries being Morocco (130th) and Cape Verde (133rd).

Environmental degradation is another massive issue for the region, from the Sahel (one senior UN official described the region as the world's 'ground zero' for climate change) to deforestation in Cameroon and massive oil pollution in Nigeria's Niger Delta.

UNESCO WORLD HERITAGE–LISTED SITES: **40**

LONGEST/SHORTEST LIFE EXPECTANCY: **CAPE VERDE (76.11)/GUINEA-BISSAU (49.11)**

LONGEST RIVER: **NIGER (4100KM)**

if West Africa were 100 people

45 would be Nigerian
8 would be Moroccan
7 would be Ghanaian
6 would be Ivorian
34 would be Other

belief systems
(% of population)

60 Muslim
27 Christian
13 Animist

population per sq km

WEST AFRICA   MAURITANIA   NIGERIA

† ≈ 3 people

History

West Africa's story is one of history's grand epics. This is a place where the great issues and contradictions of Africa's past resonate through the present: from ancient empires of unrivalled extravagance to the ravages of slavery, from the region's fabulous natural resources to the destruction wrought by climate change, from proud independence and the colonial yoke to the more complicated sovereignty of the present. This is a tale that encompasses the stirring emptiness of the Sahara, the fluid interaction of trade and cultures along the Niger River and the clamour of the region's humid, tropical coasts. Above all, West African–style history is about an astonishing patchwork of peoples trying to write their own history against all the odds.

First Footprints on the Sahel

West Africa's earliest history is shrouded in mystery, its archaeological evidence either residing in the belly of a termite or consumed by tropical climates and the shifting sands of the Sahara.

The first meaningful signposts to West Africa's past appeared around 10,000 years ago in the Sahara, especially the Aïr Mountains of northern Niger and the Adrar des Ifôghas in Mali, where nomads roamed across a very different West Africa from the one you see today. Rivers, forests, vast lakes and savannah occupied much of what is now the Sahara, the human population was small and widely dispersed, and animals such as elephants, giraffes and the great cats were plentiful.

Around 5000 BC, domesticated cattle replaced elephants and giraffes in the carvings and finely rendered rock paintings left by hunter-gatherer peoples. This rock art, which serves as the Sahara's history books of the time, marks the moment when West Africans began to build sedentary settlements as water became scarcer.

The earliest signs of organised society in West Africa date from around 1500 BC, in present-day Mauritania and northern Nigeria, where the remains of stone villages and domestic animals have been found. As settlements spread, two dominant groups emerged, the first along the Niger River and the second around Lake Chad – both areas where soils were fertile and well suited to agriculture. These groups built large stone

> Opinion among historians is divided as to whether knowledge of ironworking was introduced to the region from Egypt or actually originated in West Africa.

TIMELINE	200,000 BC	From 5000 BC	450 BC
	Homo erectus, the predecessor of Homo sapiens, occupies much of West Africa, as suggested by the tools and other artefacts found in Senegal, Guinea, Mali, Mauritania and elsewhere.	The Sahara begins to become a desert. Most of West Africa's peoples forsake transient life and settle around water holes, begin to rely on agriculture, and start to move south.	The appearance of ironworking in central Nigeria enables the clearing of forests, which expands agricultural land and commences the process of denuding West Africa's landscape.

villages and even towns. The first urban settlement of note was Jenné-Jeno, in present-day Mali, which was established around 300 BC and is often considered the father of West African cities. By AD 500, towns and villages were dotted across the region.

West Africa's Golden Empires

Two-thirds of the world's gold once came from West Africa and the indigenous empires that controlled the West African interior, and hence the lucrative trans-Saharan trade routes were among the richest in the world.

Empire of Ghana

The Empire of Ghana was the first major state of its kind established in West Africa. It was founded in AD 300 with its capital at Koumbi Saleh, in present-day Mauritania, about 200km north of modern Bamako (Mali). By Ghana's 8th-century heyday, the empire covered much of present-day Mali and parts of eastern Senegal. Although smaller than the empires that followed it, Ghana was extremely wealthy and powerful, controlling not just trans-Saharan trade but also massive gold deposits; rumour had it that the streets were paved with gold and that the emperor of Ghana routinely tied his horse to a nugget of pure gold.

Islam was introduced by traders from the north, but it couldn't save Ghana – the empire was destroyed in the late 11th century by the better-armed Muslim Berbers of the Almoravid Empire from Mauritania and Morocco. The Almoravids justified their invasion by pointing to Ghana's half-hearted adoption of Islam, but many historians believe that it had more to do with the Almoravid desire for Ghana's gold and control of trade routes.

The Almoravids

In the 11th century the Sanhaja, the pious Saharan Berber tribe that founded the Almoravid dynasty, swept into southern Morocco from what is today Senegal and Mauritania. As they pushed north under Yahya ibn Umar and his brother Abu Bakr, they demolished brothels and musical instruments as well as their opponents. After Yahya was killed and Abu Bakr was recalled to the Sahara to settle Sanhaja disputes in 1061, their cousin Yusuf bin Tachfin was left to run military operations from a campsite that would become Marrakesh the magnificent. Almoravid power would range far beyond the city they founded, reaching deep into northern Iberia and south across the Sahara to destroy the Empire of Ghana, thereby making them one of ancient West Africa's most successful empires.

Wonders of the African World, by Henry Louis Gates Jr, is an at once scholarly and enthusiastic re-evaluation of African history before colonialism; its section on Timbuktu is fascinating.

African Rock Art, by David Coulson and Alec Campbell, is definitive and beautifully illustrated. It's one to keep on your coffee table, not carry in your backpack.

300 BC	AD 300	900	Around 1000
Jenné-Jeno is founded in what is now Mali and is recognised as West Africa's first-known urban settlement. By AD 800, Jenné-Jeno is home to an estimated 27,000 people.	The Empire of Ghana is founded in what is now the western Sahel. The first of the great West African empires, it holds sway over the region for 800 years.	Islam first reaches the Sahel, almost 250 years after it crossed the Sahara. It arrives as part of the trans-Saharan caravan trade and later becomes West Africa's predominant religion.	Timbuktu is founded, near where the Niger River enters the Sahara, as a seasonal encampment for Tuareg nomads. It later becomes a great centre of scholarship and wealth, home to 100,000 people.

Empire of Mali

The Empire of Mali, founded in the middle of the 13th century by Sundiata Keita, leader of the Malinké people, was perhaps the most legendary of West African empires. Such was its wealth and prestige that it, more than any other African empire, was to spark the outside world's interest in the continent.

Mali's heyday was the 14th century. Mali's kings controlled not only Saharan trade and the gold mines that had fuelled the prosperity of the Empire of Ghana, but also a swath of territory that stretched from modern-day Senegal in the west to Niger in the east. Their ambition was matched only by the extravagance of their rule.

One such monarch, King Abubakari II, sent an expedition across the Atlantic in an attempt to discover the Americas almost two centuries before Christopher Columbus. Only one ship returned, with stories of a great river running through the ocean's heart. Abubakari II himself led a second expedition of 200 ships. Not a single ship returned.

King Abubakari's anointed successor, King Kankan Musa (the grandnephew of Sundiata Keita), would prove to be one of the most extraordinary of all African kings. Like all of Mali's rulers, Musa was a devout Muslim and in 1324 he made his pilgrimage to Mecca, accompanied by an entourage of more than 60,000 people and needing 500 slaves to carry all the gold. Along the way he gave away so much of his gold as gifts that the world gold price did not recover for 12 years – some say for a generation. His actions attracted the attention of European merchants in Cairo and news spread quickly about a fabulously wealthy land in the desert's heart.

Under Malian sovereignty, trans-Saharan trade reached its peak, and the wealth created meant that Mali's main cities became major centres of finance and culture. The most notable was Timbuktu, where two Islamic universities were founded, and Arab architects from Granada (in modern-day Spain) were employed to design new mosques, such as Timbuktu's Dyingerey Ber mosque.

Empire of Songhaï

While Mali was at the height of its powers, the Songhaï people had established their own city-state to the east, around Gao in present-day Mali. As Mali descended into decadence and royal squabbles, Gao became powerful and well organised. At its height, the Songhaï Empire stretched from close to Lake Chad in the east to the hinterland of the Atlantic Coast in the west. Its emperors were reported to have travelled to Mecca with 300,000 gold pieces.

A hallmark of the Empire of Songhaï was the creation of a professional army and a civil service with provincial governors. The state even

CAPE BOJADOR

Until the Portuguese dispelled the myths, Cape Bojador was considered among sailors as the point of no return, beyond which lay monstrous sea creatures, whirlpools, boiling waters and waterless coastlines.

Late 11th century	1147	1240	1351
One of West Africa's empires of the Sahel is overthrown by armies crossing the Sahara as the Empire of Ghana is destroyed by the Berber armies of the Almoravid Empire.	The Almohads defeat the Almoravids and raze Marrakesh for good measure, only to later rebuild it as their capital under Yacoub al-Mansour.	Sundiata Keita founds the Empire of Mali with its capital at Niani. The empire rules the Sahel for two centuries and presides over West Africa's golden age.	Ibn Battuta leaves Fez to cross the Sahara, whereafter he travels extensively throughout the Empire of Mali. His later book is one of the earliest accounts of life in the region.

subsidised Muslim scholars, judges and doctors. By the mid-15th century, the Empire of Songhaï was at its most powerful and presided over most of West Africa, and by the 16th century, Timbuktu was an important commercial city with about 100,000 inhabitants and a great seat of learning, with its Sankore University home to 25,000 scholars.

But the Songhaï Empire would prove to be the last of West Africa's great empires. The golden period ended with an audacious invasion by Berber armies crossing the Sahara from Morocco in 1591.

Later States & Empires

As the Empire of Mali declined, the Wolof people established the Empire of Jolof (also spelt Yollof) in 1360 near the site of present-day Dakar in Senegal. Meanwhile, on the southeastern fringe of the Songhaï realm, the Hausa created several powerful city-states, such as Katsina, Kano and Zinder (still important trading towns today), but they never amalgamated into a single empire.

Further east again, on the shores of Lake Chad, the Kanem-Borno Empire was founded in the early 14th century. At its height it covered a vast area including parts of present-day Niger, Nigeria, Chad and Cameroon, before being loosely incorporated into the Songhaï sphere of influence; it nonetheless remained a powerful force until the 19th century.

To the south, between the 13th and 16th centuries, several smaller but locally powerful states arose in gold-producing areas: the kingdoms of Benin (in present-day Nigeria), Dahomey (Benin), Mossi (Burkina Faso) and Akan-Ashanti (Ghana).

Sundiata: An Epic of Old Mali, by DT Niane, is the most accessible English-language version of Mali's founding epic; it's like listening to the *griots* (praise singers attached to the royal court) during West Africa's glory days.

THE EPIC OF SUNDIATA

In the annals of West African history, few tales have endured quite like the story of Sundiata Keita. In the 13th century, a sacred hunter prophesied to a minor Malinké king known as 'Maghan the Handsome' that if he married an ugly woman she would one day bear him a son who would become a great and powerful king, known to all the world. Maghan followed the seer's advice, but when his son Sundiata was born, he was disabled and unable to walk. When Maghan's successors battled for the throne, Sundiata was bypassed and forced into exile, only to return one day as king. When he defeated his more powerful Sosso rivals in 1240, he was crowned 'Mansa', or 'King of Kings', whereafter he founded the Empire of Mali, with its capital at his village of Niani, close to the Guinea–Mali border. He drowned in 1255, but his legend lives on in the tales of *griots* and in songs that draw heavily on his story.

1375	1434	1482
Mali's King Kankan Musa is depicted on a 1375 European map of Africa holding a gold nugget. The caption reads: 'So abundant is the gold found in his country that he is the richest and most noble king in all the land'.	Portuguese ships become the first to round Cape Bojador in almost two millennia, beginning the era of European trade along West Africa's coast. Nine years later, they reach the Senegal River.	Portugal constructs the first European structure on West African soil, the warehouse-fortress of Sao Jorge de la Mina in what is now Ghana, symbolising increasingly prosperous trade between Portugal and West Africa.

BRIAN D CRUICKSHANK / GETTY IMAGES ©

➡ St George's Castle (p186)

Colonial West Africa

European Footholds

By the 13th century the financial stability of several major European powers depended largely on the supply of West African gold. With gold and intriguing tales of limitless wealth making their way across the Sahara and Mediterranean, European royalty became obsessed with West Africa. Thus it was that, at the precise moment when West Africa's empires went into decline and began to fragment, Europe began to turn its attention to the region.

Prince Henry of Portugal (Henry the Navigator, 1394–1460) was the first to act, encouraging explorers to sail down the coast of West Africa, which soon became known as Guinea. In 1434, a Portuguese ship rounded the infamous Cape Bojador (in present-day Morocco), the first seagoing vessel to do so since the Phoenicians in 613 BC. Prince Henry convinced his reluctant seamen with the words: 'You cannot find a peril so great that the hope of reward will not be greater'.

In 1443 Portuguese ships reached the mouth of the Senegal River. Later voyages reached Sierra Leone (1462) and Fernando Po (now Bioko in Equatorial Guinea, off the coast of Nigeria; 1472), while the first Portuguese settlers arrived on Cape Verde in 1462. As the Portuguese made contact with local chiefs and began to trade for gold and ivory, West Africa turned on its axis and the focus of its trade (and power) began shifting from the Sahara to the coast.

In 1482 the Portuguese built a fortified trading post at Elmina, on today's Ghanaian coast. It was the earliest European structure in sub-Saharan Africa. At around the same time, Portuguese traders and emissaries made their first contact with the Kingdom of Benin (in modern-day Nigeria), an advanced, stable state whose artisans had mastered highly skilled bronze and brass casting as early as the 13th century. The cordial relations and resulting trade between Portugal and Benin proved highly profitable.

By the early 16th century, with the Songhaï Empire still ruling much of the West African interior, French, British and Dutch ships had joined the Portuguese in making regular visits along the coast, building forts as they went. But with few large rivers that allowed access to the interior, the European presence in West Africa was confined to the coast and its immediate hinterland. The prolific gold mines that had first captured the attention of Europe remained in African hands.

Europe Ventures Inland

The inability to penetrate the West African interior haunted the great powers of Europe. In 1788, a group of influential Englishmen, led by Sir Joseph Banks, founded the Africa Association to promote African

Muqqadimah is the landmark account of early Moroccan and Berber history by Ibn Khuldun, renowned Arab historian at Kairaouine University in Fez. The man knew his history – six centuries later, scholars still reference his text.

Some historians believe that the Gambia River's name (and indeed the name of the country) derives from the Portuguese word *cambio*, meaning 'exchange' or 'trade'.

Late 15th century	1512	1591	1659
The Kingdom of Benin helps Portugal to capture and export slaves, transforming the slave trade from a small-scale African concern to a much larger global trade.	Leo Africanus writes that 'The rich king of Tombuto keeps a splendid and well-furnished court...a great store of doctors, judges, priests and other learned men, that are bountifully maintained at the king's expense.'	The Empire of Songhaï, the last and most extensive of the Sahel's empires, falls to al-Mansur, ruler of Marrakesh, who seizes the Songhaï political capital Gao, and its commercial and cultural capital Timbuktu.	The French establish their first permanent trading post at Saint-Louis in Senegal in 1638. Twenty-two years later, the British found a base at the mouth of the Gambia River.

SLAVERY IN WEST AFRICA

Slavery had existed in West Africa for centuries, but it gained momentum with the arrival of Islam, opening the region as it did to more far-reaching trade networks and to distant empires where slave-trading was widespread. The Moors, Tuareg and Soninke in particular were known as slave traders. Later, the Portuguese took the trade to a whole new level, transporting slaves en masse to work on the large sugar plantations in Portuguese colonies across the Atlantic (including present-day Brazil) between 1575 and 1600.

By the 17th and 18th centuries, other European nations (particularly England, Spain, France and Holland) had established colonies in the Americas, and were growing sugar, tobacco, cotton and other crops. Huge profits depended on slave labour and the demand for African slaves was insatiable, not least because conditions on the plantations were so bad that life expectancy after arriving in the Americas was often no more than a few years.

In most cases, European traders encouraged Africans on the coast to attack neighbouring tribes and take captives. These were brought to coastal slaving stations and exchanged for European goods such as cloth and guns. A triangular trans-Atlantic trade route developed – the slaves were loaded onto ships and transported to the Americas, the raw materials they produced were transported to Europe, and the finished goods were transported from Europe to Africa once again, to be exchanged for slaves and to keep the whole system moving. Exact figures are impossible to come by, but it is estimated that from the end of the 15th century until around 1870, when the slave trade was abolished, as many as 20 million Africans were captured. Up to half of these died, mostly while being transported in horribly overcrowded and unhealthy conditions.

But more than a century after the slave trade was abolished, slavery has yet to be consigned to history in West Africa, where people continue to be born into, and live their whole lives in, slavery. In Niger, the local anti-slavery NGO Timidria estimated in 2003 that 7% of Niger's population was living in conditions of forced labour, while **Anti-Slavery International** (www.antislavery.org) estimates that a significant number of Malians, and almost one-fifth of Mauritania's more than three million people, live in slavery; Mauritania finally criminalised slavery in August 2007.

In October 2008, Hadijatou Mani, an escaped slave, took Niger's government before the Court of Justice of the West African regional body Ecowas (Economic Community of West African States). The court upheld her argument that Niger's government had failed to protect her by not implementing Niger's own anti-slavery legislation and awarded her substantial compensation. The decision set a legal precedent which applies in all West African countries.

exploration. The French soon followed suit. Although questions of commerce and national prestige played an important role, the august men of the Africa Association and their French counterparts were driven by a burning desire to solve the great geographical questions of the age. In

1796	1828	1870	1884–85
The Scottish explorer Mungo Park arrives at the Niger River near Ségou and solves one of the great unanswered questions of African geography: the Niger flows east, not west.	Frenchman René Caillié becomes the first European to reach the fabled city of Timbuktu and return home alive. Two years earlier, the Scotsman Alexander Gordon Laing was murdered on the return journey.	The slave trade is officially abolished, but not before up to 20 million Africans were transported to the Americas, never to return. Around half died en route.	The Berlin Conference divides Africa. France is awarded one-third of the continent and 10 West African countries in what becomes known as Afrique Occidentale Française (French West Africa).

RECLAIMING WEST AFRICA'S HISTORY

West African history was, for centuries, assumed to be a solely oral tradition. Later, non-African historians interpreted the absence of written records as indicating an absence of civilisation; H Trevor Roper wrote in 1963 that 'Perhaps in the future there will be some African history to teach. But at present there is none. There is only the history of Europeans in Africa. The rest is darkness.'

That changed in the 1990s when an astonishing storehouse of manuscripts – up to five million across the Sahara by some estimates – was 'discovered' in Timbuktu and surrounding regions. The manuscripts, some of which dated to the 13th century, contained scholarly works of poetry, philosophy, astronomy, mathematics, geography, physics, optics and medicine.

The manuscripts also included detailed histories of the region written by Africans, as well as the first-known examples of local languages in their written form, thereby suggesting that Africans could read and write centuries before Europeans arrived. Timbuktu also had a book-making tradition far more advanced than anything that Europe could muster until the invention of movable type in the 15th century, and many books were printed on European-manufactured paper which had reached Timbuktu long before any explorers completed the journey.

According to Dr John Hunwick, a leading expert on Africa's written history: 'Africa has for too long been stereotyped as the continent of song and dance, where knowledge is only transmitted orally. We want to demonstrate that Africans think and write and have done so for centuries'. In short, the manuscripts could change forever the way we see West African history.

The oases of the Adrar region of Mauritania also have rich manuscript collections, especially Chinguetti and Ouadâne.

1796, more than 300 years after Europeans had first begun scouting the West African coast, Mungo Park finally determined that the Niger River flowed east, while it was not until 1828 that the Frenchman Réné Caillié became the first European to reach Timbuktu and return safely.

The legendary Sundiata Keita, founder of the Empire of Mali in the 13th century, included a clause prohibiting slavery in his Charter of Kurukanfuga.

West Africans were by no means passive bystanders, and local resistance was fierce. The most notable leader of the time was Omar Tall (also spelled Umar Taal), who led a major campaign against the French in the interior of Senegal from around 1850. After his death, the jihads known as the 'Marabout Wars' persisted in Senegal until the 1880s.

For all their progress, the European powers were largely confined to pockets of territory on the coast, among them the French enclave of Dakar (Senegal), and the British ports of Freetown (Sierra Leone) and Lagos (Nigeria). Portugal, no longer a major force, retained some territory, notably Bissau, capital of today's Guinea-Bissau. The relentless European

1912	1955–56	1957
France begins colonial rule over much of modern-day Morocco, with Spain controlling a small area in the north and what is now the Western Sahara. Berber opposition is constant.	Morocco becomes the first West African country to gain independence, with the exiled nationalist Mohammed V returning as king and ruler over the newly independent country.	Ghana gains independence after a long campaign entitled 'Self Government Now'. The campaign's leader, Kwame Nkrumah, becomes Ghana's post-independence leader and hero to millions of West Africans.

MAX MILLIGAN / GETTY IMAGES ©

➡ Kwame Nkrumah statue

pursuit of territory nonetheless continued, with brutal military expeditions into the interior increasingly the norm. Minor treaties were made with local chiefs, but the lives of ordinary West Africans were more often determined by unspoken understandings between European powers.

The Scramble for Africa

Europe's wholesale colonisation of Africa was triggered in 1879 by King Leopold of Belgium's claim to the Congo. The feeding frenzy that followed saw Africa parcelled out among the European powers. Africans had no say in the matter.

Togo and parts of Cameroon fell under German rule, Portugal held fast to Guinea-Bissau and Cape Verde, Britain staked its claim to The Gambia, Sierra Leone, the Gold Coast (Ghana) and Nigeria, while the Sahel (and Morocco and much of Cameroon) was the preserve of the French. These claims, at once military realities and colonial fantasies, as many Africans had not seen a European from the country to whom his or her land now supposedly belonged, were confirmed at the Berlin Conference of 1884–85. The final adjustments to the colonial map were made after Germany's defeat in WWI: Togo went to the French and Cameroon was divided between France and Britain.

Introducing 'civilisation' to the 'natives' officially replaced trade as the *raison d'être* of the colonial mission, but the primary aim of European governments was to exploit the colonies for raw materials. In West Africa, gem and gold mining was developed, but the once gold-rich region

Bury the Chains: The First International Human Rights Movement, by Adam Hochschild, is masterly in its treatment of the British campaign to abolish slavery in the 18th century.

EUROPEAN EXPLORERS IN WEST AFRICA

➠ *Travels in the Interior of Africa,* by Mungo Park, is an epic tale of exploration on the Niger River in the late 18th and early 19th centuries.

➠ *Difficult & Dangerous Roads,* by Hugh Clapperton, is a vivid portrait of the Sahara, Niger and Nigeria in the 1820s by this haughty but ever-observant traveller.

➠ *Travels Through Central Africa to Timbuktu,* by Réné Caillié, is the first account of Europe's first encounter with Timbuktu in 1828.

➠ *Travels & Discoveries in North and Central Africa 1849-1855,* by Heinrich Barth, is a fascinating insight into what is now Niger, Nigeria and Mali, from arguably West Africa's greatest explorer.

➠ *The Gates of Africa – Death, Discovery and the Search for Timbuktu,* by Anthony Sattin, is a stirring account of Europe's fascination with Timbuktu and West Africa.

➠ *The Race for Timbuktu – In Search of Africa's City of Gold,* by Frank T Kryza, covers similar terrain and is another great read.

1958	1973	1982	1983–87
Guinea opts to go it alone, rejecting ongoing French rule in favour of immediate independence. France takes revenge by withdrawing all assistance to the country.	Guinea-Bissau becomes the last West African country to achieve independence. Unlike former French and British colonies, Guinea-Bissau has to fight for its freedom in a bloody war that devastates the country.	Paul Biya takes power in Cameroon. At the time of writing, he is West Africa's longest-serving president, with Burkina Faso's Blaise Compaoré (1987) waiting to claim the title.	Thomas Sankara rules over Burkina Faso, a Ché Guevara–style figure who stamped out corruption and captured the imagination of a generation of West Africans.

disappointed the occupiers. Consequently, labour-intensive plantations were established, and cash crops such as coffee, cocoa, rubber, cotton and groundnuts (peanuts) came to dominate the economies of the fledgling colonies. Such infrastructure as was built in West Africa (the Dakar–Bamako rail line, for example) was designed primarily to benefit the colonial economy. Little or no attempt was made to improve living standards or expand education for West Africans, let alone build the institutions on which their future depended.

After the Berlin Conference, Britain's Lord Salisbury said: 'We have been giving away mountains and rivers and lakes to each other, only hindered by the small impediment that we never knew exactly where the mountains and rivers and lakes were.'

During the first half of the 20th century, France controlled its West African colonies with a firm hand, and through a policy of 'assimilation' allowed Africans to become French citizens if they virtually abandoned their African identity. Britain made no pretence of assimilation and was slightly more liberal in its approach towards its colonies. Portugal ruled its empire in Africa with a rod of iron.

Modern West Africa
The Road to Independence

Although nationalism and calls for independence grew in West Africa throughout the first half of the 20th century, it was not until after WWII that the winds of real change began to sweep the region.

In 1956, Morocco became the first country in West Africa to gain independence, followed a year later by Ghana, which did so with the reluctant blessing of Britain. In September 1958, the French government of Charles de Gaulle held a referendum in its African colonies in which Africans were asked to choose between immediate independence and remaining under French control. All chose the latter, except Guinea, which was to pay dearly for its independence. Affronted by Guinea's perceived lack of gratitude, the French, whose bureaucrats effectively ran Guinea and who had trained very few locals to a level capable of running the country, took revenge by removing its administrative staff and all financial assistance from Guinea, leaving its former colony to fend for itself. In 1960 Benin, Côte d'Ivoire, Nigeria, Togo, Senegal and several other countries won their independence. Most other countries in the region became independent in the following few years. Only recidivist Portugal held firm, not granting independence to Guinea-Bissau until 1973 and only then with great reluctance.

France encouraged its former colonies to remain closely tied in a trade-based 'community', and most did; Guinea was a notable exception, while Senegal and Côte d'Ivoire were the darlings of Franco–West African relations. In contrast, Britain reduced its power and influence in the region. The French maintained battalions of its own army in several former colonies, while the British preferred more discreet military assistance.

1997	2000	2005	2007
Sierra Leone erupts in a civil war in which hundreds of thousands are killed or maimed. Conflict in neighbouring Liberia and massive refugee camps in Guinea contribute to a regional humanitarian catastrophe.	Côte d'Ivoire begins its descent into anarchy. Within years, the country is divided in two and immigrants who helped build the country's economic miracle are made scapegoats.	Ellen Johnson-Sirleaf is elected president in Liberia, ending decades of civil war and in the process becoming Africa's first elected female president.	Tuareg rebels launch a rebellion in northern Niger and the conflict soon spills over into Mali. Much of the Sahara becomes the domain of rebels and government soldiers.

Independent West Africa

The period immediately following independence was a time of unbridled optimism in West Africa. For the first time in centuries, political power was in the hands of Africans themselves. Inspirational figures such as Kwame Nkrumah in Ghana and Léopold Senghor in Senegal spoke of a new African dawn, while Guinea's Sekou Touré was lauded for having thumbed his nose at the French.

Then reality set in. Without exception, the newly minted countries of West Africa were ill-equipped for independence. Colonialism had created fragile economies based on cash crops that were prone to huge price fluctuations, while artificial boundaries and divide-and-rule policies that had favoured some ethnic groups over others quickly created tensions. Education for Africans had never been a priority for the colonial administrators and few members of the new ruling class and bureaucrats had the necessary training or experience to tackle the massive challenges faced by the new states. The catch cry of Sekou Touré – who would prove to be a particularly nasty dictator – of preferring 'freedom in poverty to prosperity in chains' soon became horribly true. Poor governance, coups d'état and massive economic problems increasingly became the norm, with civil wars, border disputes and dictatorship often thrown in for good measure. When Côte d'Ivoire – for so long an exception and a byword for West Africa's post-independence progress and optimism – descended into civil war after 2000, it was a massive blow to the region's self-image.

The end of the Cold War led to dramatic changes throughout West Africa, as the popular demand for democracy gathered strength and multiparty elections were held in several countries. But even as democracy spread, West Africa's hopes of a new dawn were tempered by the scale of the challenges it faced, not least among them environmental degradation on a massive scale, widespread and worsening poverty across the region, and the ailing economic health of the two regional powerhouses, Nigeria and Côte d'Ivoire. And the fact remains that many West Africans have as little control over their own destinies and economic well being as they did at independence.

In the 8th century AD, Jenné-Jeno was a fortified town with walls 3.7m thick, home to 15,000 inhabitants and covering 33 hectares (just under half the size of modern Djenné), but around 1300 it was abandoned.

HISTORY MODERN WEST AFRICA

JENNÉ-JENO

2008	2011	2012	2012
Ghana wins plaudits for its peaceful democratic transition. With the discovery of offshore oil and a proven track record of democracy, Ghana is widely seen as West Africa's shining light.	In Côte d'Ivoire President Laurent Gbagbo refuses to accept the election victory of Alassane Outtara; Gbagbo is later captured and sent for trial in The Hague.	The Malian army seizes power, ending the country's democratic transition; Tuareg and Islamist rebels soon capture the north, including Timbuktu and Gao; the international community approves a regional military force.	Soon after being chosen as the NDC's candidate in upcoming elections, Ghanaian president Atta Mills dies; President John Mahama, his NDC successor, narrowly wins elections in December.

Culture & Daily Life

West Africa is one of the most intriguing gatherings of cultures on the planet. As a traveller, understanding even a little about the complicated issues that West Africans deal with on a daily basis – the role of traditional culture in modern life, the position of women in society and the complicated mosaic of multicultural relationships, for example – can go a long way towards gaining a foothold in the region. The region's cuisine, too, offers fascinating insights into one of Africa's least-known corners.

Cameroon alone has around 280 ethnic groups; tiny Togo counts 40 ethnic groups among its five million people; and Guinea-Bissau, a country of fewer than one million people, has 23.

Lifestyle

Family life is the bedrock for most West Africans. In traditional society, especially in villages, homes are arranged around a family compound and life is a communal affair – the family eats, takes important decisions, celebrates and mourns together in a space that is identifiably theirs and in a family group that spans generations. Such family structures remain strongly evident in many villages and rural areas, and family remains a critical source of support for many West Africans, not least because government welfare is largely nonexistent.

But things are changing. Vast numbers of Africans have migrated to cities, where ethnic identity takes on added significance, as recent arrivals in cities gravitate towards those with whom they share an ethnic tradition. Most (but by no means all) form friendships with people from their own ethnic groups. This is particularly true of minorities.

If family and ethnic identity are the fundamental foundations of a West African's existence, the nation to which they belong serves to announce who they are to the rest of the world. Most West Africans proudly identify themselves as being, for example, Malian or Nigerian, suggesting that one success of postcolonial West Africa has been the building of national identity in countries where borders often cut across longer-standing ethnic boundaries. That said, the tragic descent into conflict in Côte d'Ivoire suggests that ethnic origins remain hugely significant and a never-forgotten calling card.

In seven West African countries the female adult literacy rate is above 50%: Cape Verde (79.4%), Cameroon (67.8%), Ghana (61.2%), Liberia (56.8%), Mauritania (51.2%) and Nigeria (50.4%). Women fare worst in Niger (15.1%), Burkina Faso (15.2%), Mali (20.3%), Sierra Leone (24.4%) and Senegal (29.3%).

Traditional Culture

Before the arrival of colonialism, West African society was, in most cultures, organised along hierarchical lines: each person's place in society was determined by birth and the family's social status. At the top were traditional noble and warrior families, followed by farmers, traders and persons of lower caste, such as blacksmiths, leather workers, woodcarvers, weavers and musicians. Slaves were at the bottom of the social hierarchy. Difficult economic circumstances and urbanisation have reduced the importance of these traditional roles to some degree, but they remain important for many West Africans. For example, although slavery no longer officially exists, many descendants of former slaves still work as tenant farmers for the descendants of their former masters. Another surviving practice in traditional societies is that older people (especially men) are treated with deference, while teachers, doctors and other professionals (usually men) often receive similar treatment.

MATTHEW M. SCHOENFELDER / GETTY IMAGES ©

Women in Burkina Faso

But traditional culture is not just about immutable social roles and, as it most often manifests itself in public these days, it can often be a celebration of what binds communities together. Village festivals (*fêtes* in French), which are fundamental to traditional life, are held to honour dead ancestors and local traditional deities, and to celebrate the end of the harvest.

Multiculturalism

West Africans know a thing or two about living side by side with people from different cultures. For a start, West Africa as you see it today is the result of centuries of population shifts and mass migrations that have created a patchwork of diverse but largely cohabiting cultures. After the colonial period and independence, most groups found themselves being asked to share a new national identity with other cultures that were, in some cases, wholly different from their own. Later, widespread urbanisation produced polyglot West African cities that are among the most multicultural on earth. And then there are the twin issues of immigration and emigration – millions of West Africans live in Europe and elsewhere, creating new levels of multiculturalism in the Western countries they now inhabit.

The movement of people in search of opportunity within West Africa is less widely reported in the international media, but it operates on a much larger scale than emigration to Europe. Côte d'Ivoire's one-time economic miracle drew immigrants from across the region, providing much-needed labour for a booming economy and a livelihood for millions of citizens of neighbouring countries. However, after political instability began in 2000, the economy slumped and the country descended into a conflict that exposed the thin veneer of tolerance with which many Ivorians viewed the immigrants.

Despite rapid urbanisation, only in Cape Verde (62.6%), Gambia (57.7%), Morocco (57%), Cameroon (52.1%), Ghana (51.9%) and Côte d'Ivoire (51.3%) does more than half of the population live in cities. West Africa's least urbanised countries are Niger (17.8%), Burkina Faso (26.5%) and Mali (34.9%).

Women in West Africa

West African women face a formidable array of barriers to their participation in public life on an equal footing with men. In much of the region, social mores demand that a women is responsible for domestic work (cooking, pounding millet, child rearing, gathering firewood), while many women also work (often as market or street vendors) to supplement meagre family incomes. Indeed, it's a depressingly common sight to see women pounding millet or otherwise working hard while men lounge in the shade 'working' on their social relationships. Education of girls also lags significantly behind that of boys, as evidenced by often appalling female literacy rates. Little wonder, therefore, that West African women are greatly under-represented in most professions, let alone in government or at the upper levels of industry.

Monique and the Mango Rains: Two Years with a Midwife in Mali, by Kris Holloway, gives a human face to statistics about difficulties faced by women in traditional, rural West Africa. It's a great, sobering read.

Marriage & Polygamy

In traditional societies, marriages often took place between teenagers, but financial constraints and the growing demand for lavish weddings mean that many men cannot afford to get married until their late 20s or 30s.

Polygamy is reasonably widespread in West Africa. The practice, which pre-dates the arrival of Islam (the Quran allows up to four wives, provided the husband can provide for them all), is particularly strong in rural and predominantly Islamic areas; according to one study, half of all marriages in Senegal are polygamous. You will be told (by men) that women are not averse to polygamy, and that the wives become like sisters, helping each other with domestic and child-rearing duties. In reality, however, fighting and mistrust between wives is more common than marital bliss. However, as few if any countries in the region have outlawed polygamy, there's not much women can do. Leaving a marriage simply because a husband takes another wife can bring shame to the woman and her family. She might be cast out of the family home or even physically beaten as punishment by her own father or brothers.

Female Genital Mutilation

Female genital mutilation (FGM), often euphemistically termed 'female circumcision' or 'genital alteration', is widespread throughout West Africa. The term covers a wide range of procedures, but in West Africa the procedure usually involves removal of the entire clitoris (called infibulation).

Although outsiders often believe that FGM is associated with Islam, it actually pre-dates the religion (historical records of infibulation date back 6000 years) and has far more to do with longstanding cultural traditions than religious doctrine; in predominantly Muslim northern Mali, FGM prevalence rates are less than 10%. The procedure is usually performed by midwives on girls and young women. They sometimes use modern surgical instruments, but more often it's done with a razor blade or even a piece of glass. If the procedure is done in a traditional setting the girl will not be anaesthetised, although nowadays many families take their daughters to clinics to have the procedure performed by a trained doctor. Complications, especially in the traditional setting, include infection of the wound, leading to death, or scarring, which makes childbirth and urination difficult.

The Female Genital Cutting Education and Networking Project (www. fgmnetwork.org/ index.php) is an excellent resource on female genital mutilation (FMG), including statistics for many West African countries.

In West Africa, FGM is seen among traditionalists as important for maintaining traditional society. An unaltered woman would dishonour her family and lower its position in society, as well as ruining her own chances for marriage – a circumcised woman is thought to be a moral woman, and more likely a virgin. Many believe that if left, the clitoris can make a woman infertile, or damage and even kill her unborn children.

TIPS ON MEETING LOCALS

Greetings

There are few more important elements in person-to-person encounters in West Africa than greetings. In villages, highly ritualised greetings can seem to last an eternity. In cities, the traditional greetings may give way to shorter ones in French or English, but they're never forgotten. Muslims usually start with the traditional Islamic greetings, *Salaam aleikum* and *Aleikum asalaam* ('Peace be unto you', 'And peace be unto you'). This is followed by more questions, such as 'How are you?', 'How is the family?' and 'How are the people of your village?' The reply is usually *Al humdul'allah* (meaning 'Thanks be to God'). While language constraints may mean that your ability to greet West African–style is limited, launching straight into business is considered rude. Learning some greetings in the local language will smooth the way considerably in just about every circumstance.

Hand shaking is also an important part of greetings. Use a soft – rather than overly firm – handshake. Some Muslim men prefer not to shake hands with women, and West African women don't usually shake hands with their male counterparts.

Deference

Another consideration is eye contact, which is usually avoided, especially between men and women in the Sahel. If a West African doesn't look you in the eye during a conversation, remember that they're being polite, not cold. When visiting rural settlements it's a good idea to request to see the chief to announce your arrival and request permission before wandering through a village. You'll rarely be refused.

Conduct

Although West Africa is changing, social mores remain conservative, so please keep in mind the following guidelines:

➡ If you're in a frustrating situation, be patient, friendly and considerate. A confrontational attitude can easily inflame the situation (especially when dealing with police officers and immigration officials) and offend local sensibilities.

➡ Be respectful of Islamic traditions and don't wear revealing clothing; loose, lightweight clothing is preferable.

➡ Public displays of affection are usually inappropriate, especially in Muslim areas.

➡ Always ask permission to photograph people.

➡ Avoid vocal criticism of the government or country; the former could get your friends in trouble and many West Africans take the latter personally.

Some West African countries have enacted laws outlawing FGM, but poor enforcement means that, even where FGM is illegal, the practice continues as before. FGM is illegal in Guinea, for example, and punishable in some cases by life imprisonment with hard labour, yet an estimated 98.6% of women still undergo the procedure. Laws against FGM are also on the books in Burkina Faso, which nonetheless has a 76.6% prevalence rate, and in Côte d'Ivoire (44.5%). The practice is also extremely common in Mali (91.6%), Sierra Leone (80% to 90%), The Gambia (60% to 90%) and Nigeria (19%), none of which have laws outlawing FGM. FGM is a particularly common practice among the Fulani.

Gogo Mama: A Journey into the Lives of Twelve African Women, by Sally Sara, includes illuminating chapters on a Liberian former child soldier, a Ghanaian former slave and a Malian midwife.

Food & Drink

For most West Africans, food is a question of survival rather than enjoyment and, as a result, it's often monotonous. But for most travellers, the combination of unfamiliar tastes and the range of influences – including local, French and even Lebanese – results in some fine cuisine. The key is knowing where to find it (you won't find much variety outside larger cities), trying not to let the rather generous amounts of oil used in cooking bother you, and learning to appreciate the atmosphere – an essential ingredient in the region's cooking – as much as the food.

South of the Sahara: Traditional Cooking from the Lands of West Africa, by Elizabeth A Jackson, brings the flavours of West Africa to your kitchen; the writer lived in Africa for a time and loves her food.

COOKING

Staples & Specialities

Rice, rice and more rice is the West African staple that you'll eat again and again on your travels. Millet is also common, although this grain is usually pounded into flour before it's cooked. The millet flour is steamed then moistened with water until it thickens into a stiff porridge that can be eaten with the fingers. In the Sahel, couscous (semolina or millet grains) is always on the menu.

In coastal countries, staples may be root crops such as yam or cassava (also called manioc), which are pounded or grated before being cooked. They're served as a near-solid glob called *fufu* or *foufou* (which morphs into *foutou* further north) – kind of like mashed potatoes mixed with gelatin, and very sticky. You grab a portion (with your right hand), form a ball, dip it in the sauce and enjoy. In the coastal countries, plantain (green banana) is also common.

If all that sounds a little uninspiring, remember that the secret's often in the sauce, which usually goes by the name of *riz sauce*. In some Sahel countries, groundnuts (peanuts) are common, and a thick, brown groundnut sauce (usually called *arachide*) is often served, either on its own or with meat or vegetables mixed in with the nuts. When groundnut sauce is used in a stew, it's called *domodah* or *mafé*. Sometimes deep-orange palm oil is also added. Sauces are also made with vegetables or the leaves of staple food plants such as cassava. Stock cubes or sachets of flavouring are ubiquitous across the region (Maggi is the most common trade name) and are often thrown into the pot as well. Where it can be afforded, or on special occasions, meat or fish is added to the sauce, sometimes succulent slices, sometimes grimly unattractive heads, tails and bones.

Some of the most memorable regional specialties include the ubiquitous *jollof rice* (rice and vegetables with meat or fish and called *riz yollof* in Francophone countries) and *kedjenou* (Côte d'Ivoire's national dish of slowly simmered chicken or fish with peppers and tomatoes). *Poulet yassa* is a Senegalese dish consisting of grilled chicken in an onion-and-lemon sauce; the sauce is also used to make *poisson yassa* (fish), *viande yassa* (meat) and just plain old *yassa*. *Tiéboudienne* is Senegal's national dish of rice baked in a thick sauce of fish and vegetables.

Street Food

Street food tends to be absurdly cheap and is often delicious, especially the grilled fish.

MINDING YOUR MANNERS

If you're invited to share a meal with locals, there are a few customs to observe. You'll probably sit with your hosts on the floor and it's usually polite to take off your shoes. It may be impolite, however, to show the soles of your feet, so observe closely what your hosts do.

The food, normally eaten by hand (remember to use only the right hand and don't be embarrassed to ask for a spoon), is served in one or two large dishes. Beginners will just pick out manageable portions with their fingers, but experts dig deep, forming a ball of rice and sauce with the fingers. Everybody washes their hands before and after eating. As an honoured guest you might be passed choice morsels by your hosts, and it's usually polite to finish eating while there's still food in the bowl to show you've had enough.

CULTURE & DAILY LIFE FOOD & DRINK

Roadside bread vendor, Ouidah (p45), Benin

On street corners and around bus stations, especially in the morning, you'll see small booths selling pieces of bread with fillings or toppings of butter, chocolate spread, yoghurt, mayonnaise or sardines. In Francophone countries the bread is cut from fresh French-style loaves or baguettes, but in Anglophone countries the bread is often a less enticing soft, white loaf.

In the Sahel, usually around markets, women with large bowls covered with a wicker lid sell yogurt, often mixed with pounded millet and sugar. You can eat it on the spot or take it away in a plastic bag.

In the evenings you can buy *brochettes* (small pieces of beef, sheep or goat meat skewered and grilled over a fire) or lumps of roast meat sold by guys who walk around pushing a tin oven on wheels. Around markets and bus stations, women serve deep-fried chips of cassava or some other root crop.

In Francophone countries, grilled and roast meat, usually mixed with onions and spices, is sold in shacks. These are called *dibieteries* in some places, and you can eat on the spot or take away.

Another popular stand-by in the larger cities are Lebanese-style *shwarmas:* thin slices of lamb grilled on a spit, served with salad (optional) in Lebanese-style bread (pita) with a sauce made from chickpeas.

Literature & Cinema

West Africa punches above its weight when it comes to the arts. Nigeria's writers have been celebrated as some of Africa's finest throughout the English-speaking world, while names like Côte d'Ivoire's Ahmadou Kourouma have found an appreciative audience in Francophone circles. West Africa's world-renowned film festival has provided a vehicle for some of the most impressive cinematic output on the continent.

Literature

A particularly incisive account of the clash between modern and traditional views on polygamy is given in *So Long a Letter*, an especially fine novel written in the voice of a widow by Senegalese author Mariama Bâ.

Stories, usually in oral or musical form, have always played an important role in West African life. This is how cultural traditions and the great events of the day were chronicled and, in the frequent absence of written histories, such tales catalogued the collective memory of the region's peoples. The greatest and most famous historical tale is the *Epic of Sundiata*, the story of the founder of the Empire of Mali, which is still recounted by modern *griots* (praise singers), musicians and writers.

Modern-day West African writers have adapted this tradition, weaving compelling tales around the great issues facing modern West Africa, most notably the arrival and legacy of colonial powers, and the role of women within traditional society.

Nigeria dominates West Africa's Anglophone literary scene, while some of the best novels in Francophone West African literature have also been translated into English. A number of major West African authors have achieved international renown.

Anglophone West Africa

Names to watch out for include Aminatta Forna (Sierra Leone; *Ancestor Stones* and the memoir *The Devil that Danced on the Water*); Ghana's foremost writer, Ayi Kwei Armah (*The Beautiful Ones Are Not Yet Born*); Ama Ata Aidoo (Ghana; *Changes: A Love Story* and *Our Sister Killjoy*); Kojo Laing (Ghana; *Woman of the Aeroplanes*, *Search Sweet Country* and

---

TOP 10 WEST AFRICAN NOVELS

- Chinua Achebe, *Things Fall Apart*
- Ben Okri, *The Famished Road*
- Chimamanda Ngozi Adichie, *Half of a Yellow Sun*
- Helon Habila, *Measuring Time*
- Aminatta Forna, *Ancestor Stones*
- Ahmadou Kourouma, *Waiting for the Wild Beasts to Vote*
- Ousmane Sembène, *God's Bits of Wood*
- Amadou Hampaté Bâ, *The Fortunes of Wangrin*
- Mongo Beti, *The Poor Christ of Bomba*
- Ayi Kwei Armah, *The Beautiful Ones Are Not Yet Born*

Major Gentl and the Achimota Wars); and William Conton (The Gambia), whose 1960s classic *The African* is a semi-autobiographical tale of an African student in Britain who later returns to his homeland and becomes president.

Nigeria

Nigeria is credited with producing the first African novels of international quality. With *The Palm-Wine Drunkard*, about an insatiable drunkard who seeks his palm-wine tapster in the world of the dead, Amos Tutuola was the first African writer to catch the world's attention by providing a link between traditional storytelling and the modern novel. If Tutuola made the world sit up and take notice, Chinua Achebe won for African literature the international acclaim it still enjoys to this day. His classic work, *Things Fall Apart* (1958), has sold over eight million copies in 30 languages, more than any other African work. Set in the mid-19th century, this novel charts the collision between pre-colonial Ibo society and European missionaries. Achebe's *Anthills of the Savannah* is a satirical study of political disorder and corruption. It was a finalist for the 1987 Booker Prize. His memoir of the Biafra war, *There Was a Country: A Personal History of Biafra* (2012) has caused waves in Nigeria but has been critically acclaimed.

Building on the work of these early pioneers, Wole Soyinka has built up an extraordinary body of work, which includes plays (*A Dance of the Forest, The Man Died, Opera Wonyosi* and *A Play of Giants*), poetry (including *Idane & Other Poems*), novels (including *The Interpreters*), political essays and the fantastical childhood memoir *Ake*. Praised for his complex writing style, Soyinka won the Nobel Prize for Literature in 1986; he was the first author from Africa to achieve this accolade.

The exceptionally talented Ben Okri is a thoughtful essayist (*A Way of Being Free*) and an accomplished poet (*An African Elegy*), but his magical realist novels have seen him labelled the Nigerian Gabriel García Márquez. His novel *The Famished Road*, which follows Azaro, a spirit-child, won the Booker Prize in 1991. When critics grumbled that to appreciate the book's style and symbolism the reader had to 'understand Africa', Okri recalled reading Victorian novelists such as Dickens as a schoolboy in Nigeria. His *Songs of Enchantment* (1993) and *Infinite Riches* (1998) completed his Azaro trilogy. He continues to fuse modern style with traditional mythological themes in his later novels *Dangerous Love, Astonishing the Gods* and, most recently, *Starbook*.

Buchi Emecheta is one of Africa's most successful female authors. Her novels include *Slave Girl, The Joys of Motherhood, Rape of Shavi* and *Kehinde,* and they focus with humour and irrepressible irony on the struggles of African women to overcome their second-class treatment by society.

Two young Nigerian writers – Chimamanda Ngozi Adichie and Helon Habila – have successfully made the leap from promising talents to skilled novelists with a growing international following. Adichie in particular followed up her impressive first novel *Purple Hibiscus* (2004) with the exceptional *Half of a Yellow Sun* (2006), which is set in Nigeria during the Biafra war. Helon Habila, too, managed to build on the success of his first novel, *Waiting for an Angel* (2004), with an acclaimed follow-up, *Measuring Time* (2007), the stirring story of twins in a Nigerian village. His most recent offering is *Oil on Water* (2010).

Other young Nigerian novelists to watch out for include Helen Oyeyemi (*The Icarus Girl* and *White is for Witching*) and Uzodinma Iweala (*Beasts of No Nation*).

In 1952, Dylan Thomas described Amos Tutuola's *The Palm-Wine Drunkard* as 'brief, thronged, grisly and bewitching' and a 'nightmare of indescribable adventures'.

LITERATURE & CINEMA LITERATURE

Francophone West Africa

Until recently, Francophone West African writers were little known beyond France, but a flurry of translations into English has brought them the international readership they richly deserve.

Until his death in 1991, Amadou Hampaté Bâ, Mali's most prolific novelist, was one of the most significant figures in West African literature, as well as a leading linguist, ethnographer and religious scholar. It was Bâ who, in 1960, first said 'In Africa, when an old man dies, it's a library burning'. Three of his books – *The Fortunes of Wangrin* (which won the 1976 'Grand Prix litéraire de l'Afrique noire'), *Kaidara* and *Radiance of the Great Star* – are available in English.

The late Ousmane Sembène, from Senegal, better known as an acclaimed movie director, has also published short-story collections and *God's Bits of Wood*, an accomplished novel set in colonial Mali and Senegal. Two female Senegalese writers worth tracking down are Mariama Bâ, whose novel *So Long a Letter* won the Noma Award for publishing in Africa, and Fatou Diome, whose 2003 novel *The Belly of the Atlantic* was a bestseller in France. Nafissatou Dia Diouf is also attracting attention, although her *Retour d'Un Long Exil et Autres Nouvelles* (2001) and *Sables Mouvants* (2000) are still available only in French. The late Leopold Senghor, former Senegalese president and a literary figure of international note, is the author of several collections of poetry and writings.

Côte d'Ivoire's finest novelist, Ahmadou Kourouma, is widely available in English. His *Waiting for the Wild Beasts to Vote* is a masterpiece that evocatively captures both the transition to colonial rule and the subsequent corruption of power by Africa's leaders. *The Suns of Independence*, *Monnew* and *Allah Is Not Obliged* are also great reads.

Cameroon's best-known literary figure is the late Mongo Beti. *The Poor Christ of Bomba* is Beti's cynical recounting of the failure of a missionary to convert the people of a small village. Other works by Beti include *Mission to Kala* and *Remember Ruben*.

Camara Laye (Guinea) wrote *The African Child* (also called *The Dark Child*), which was first published in 1954 and is one of the most widely printed works by an African.

Morocco

The international spotlight first turned on Morocco's literary scene in the 1950s and '60s, when Beat Generation authors Paul and Jane Bowles took up residence in Tangier and began recording the stories of Moroccans they knew. From these efforts came Larb Layachi's *A Life Full of Holes* and Mohammed Mrabet's *Love with a Few Hairs*, and eventually Mohammed Choukri's *For Bread Alone*. Not surprisingly, these books are packed with sex, drugs and unexpected poetry, like a lot of Beat literature – but if anything, they're more streetwise, humorous and heartbreaking.

Numerous daring and distinctive Moroccan voices have found their way into print over the past two decades, both at home and abroad. Among the most famous works to be published by Moroccans living in Morocco are *Dreams of Trespass: Tales of a Harem Girlhood* and *The Veil and the Male Elite: A Feminist Interpretation of Islam*, both by Fatima Mernissi, an outspoken feminist and professor at the University of Rabat. In Rabati Leila Abouzeid's *The Year of the Elephant*, one woman's search for life after divorce becomes a metaphor for Morocco's search for true independence after colonialism. Fez-born expatriate author Tahar ben Jelloun combined poetic devices and his training as a psychotherapist in his celebrated novel *The Sand Child*, about a girl raised as a boy by her father in Marrakesh, and won France's Prix Goncourt for his book *The Sacred Night*.

The annual Caine Prize for African Writing (www.caineprize.com), which is awarded for the best published short story by an African writer, is one of Africa's most prestigious literary awards. Recent West African winners include Helon Habila (2001), SA Afolabi (2005), EC Osundu (2009) and Rotimi Babatunde (2012).

California Newsreel (www.newsreel.org) is a terrific resource on African film with extensive reviews and a Library of African Cinema, where you can order many of the best West African films, especially Fespaco prize winners.

Several recent Moroccan novels have explored the promise and trauma of emigration, notably Mahi Binebine's harrowing *Welcome to Paradise* and Laila Lalami's celebrated *Hope and Other Dangerous Pursuits*.

Cinema

West Africa rarely makes an appearance in cinemas beyond the region – *Blood Diamond*, set (but not filmed) in 1990s Sierra Leone, is a rare exception – and most West African films can be difficult for travellers to track down. But, despite limited resources, West African film is high quality, a regular presence at the world's best film festivals and has, for decades, been quietly gathering plaudits from critics. West Africa also has a respected film festival of its own, Fespaco, which takes place biannually in Ouagadougou in Burkina Faso and has placed quality film-making at the centre of modern West African cultural life.

The 1970s was the zenith of African filmmaking, and many films from this era still inspire the new generation of directors working today. From the 1980s onwards, however, directors have found it increasingly difficult to find the necessary finance, production facilities and – most crucially – distribution that would give West African directors the wider recognition they deserve.

A handful of themes resonate through postcolonial West African cinema: the exploitation of the masses by colonialists; corrupt and inefficient independent governments; the clash between tradition and modernity; and traditional African values (usually in a rural setting) portrayed as suffering from Western cultural influence. As such, the region's films act as a mirror to West African society and history.

Other West African films to look out for include *Dakan*, by Mohamed Camara of Guinea, which uses homosexuality to challenge prevailing social and religious taboos; *Clando*, by Cameroonian director Jean-Marie Teno, which depicts Africans choosing between fighting corrupt regimes at home and seeking a better life in Europe; and *The Blue Eyes of Yonta*, by Flora Gomes, one of few feature films ever made in Guinea-Bissau – it captures the disillusionment of young Africans who've grown up in the post-independence era.

Senegal, Mali & Burkina Faso

West African film is dominated by Senegal, Mali and Burkina Faso.

Ousmane Sembène (1923–2007) from Senegal was arguably West Africa's best-known director. His body of work includes *Borom Sarret* (1963), the first commercial film to be made in post-independence Africa, *Xala*, *Camp Thiaroye* and the critically acclaimed *Moolade*.

Mali's leading director is Souleymane Cissé, whose 1970s films include *Baara* and *Cinq Jours d'Une Vie*. Later films include the wonderful *Yeelen*, a prize winner at the 1987 Cannes festival, a lavish generational tale set in 13th-century Mali, and *Waati*. Cheick Oumar Sissoko has won prizes at Cannes and his *Guimba, un Tyran, une Epoque Guimba*, won the Étalon d'Or de Yennega, Africa's 'Oscar', at the 1995 Fespaco.

From Burkina Faso, Idrissa Ouédraogo won the 1990 Grand Prix at Cannes for *Tilä*, an exceptional cinematic portrayal of life in a traditional African village. He is one of very few West African film-makers to find genuine commercial success in the West. His other movies include *Yaaba*, *Samba Traoré*, *Kini* and *Adams*. Gaston Kaboré is another fine director whose film *Buud Yam*, a tale of childhood identity, superstition and a 19th-century African world about to change forever, was the 1997 winner of the Étalon d'Or de Yennenga.

Nigerian director Chico Ejiro (widely known as 'Mr Prolific') is famous for having directed more than 80 films in just eight years. He has been quoted as saying that he can complete a film in just three days. For a fascinating insight into the industry, track down the 2007 documentary *Welcome to Nollywood* by director Jamie Meltzer.

FESPACO

Burkina Faso may, as one of the world's poorest countries, be an unlikely venue for a world-renowned festival of film, but the biennial nine-day Pan-African Film Festival, Fespaco (Festival Pan-Africain du Cinema; www.fespaco.bf), goes from strength to strength.

Fespaco began in 1969, when it was little more than a few African filmmakers getting together to show their short films to interested audiences. Hundreds of films from Africa and the diaspora in the Americas and the Caribbean are now viewed every year, with 20 selected to compete for the prestigious Étalon D'Or de Yennenga – Fespaco's equivalent of the Oscar – as well as prizes in other categories (including TV).

Fespaco is held in Ouagadougou every odd year, in the second half of February or early March, and has become an essential pillar of Burkina Faso's cultural life. Since its early days, it has also helped stimulate film production throughout Africa and has become such a major African cultural event that it attracts celebrities from around the world.

Recent West African award-winners include Nigeria's Newton Aduaka, who received the Étalon d'Or de Yennenga for *Ezra* (which also appeared at the Sundance Film Festival) in 2007, while the runner-up award the same year went to *Les Saignantes* by Cameroonian director Jean Pierre Bekolo. In 2011, the top prize was won by Moroccan director Mohamed Mouftakir for his film *Pegasus*.

Nigeria

The international availability of works by African novelists owes much to the Heinemann African Writers Series, which publishes 273 novels that would otherwise be out of print or hard to find.

Nigeria is home to the world's second-largest film industry (behind India, but ahead of the USA, and worth US$250 million a year). Going by the name of 'Nollywood', it turns out massive numbers of low-budget, high-energy films (up to 200 a month) that are wildly popular on DVD, but which won't win any critics' awards.

Most industry watchers trace the birth of Nollywood to *Living in Bondage* (1992) by NEK Video Links, owned by Kenneth Nnebue in the eastern city of Onitsha. The wide reach of Igbo networks, aggressive marketing campaigns and the use of English as a primary language quickly broadened the industry's appeal. The staple of Nollywood films (and another secret of success) is their focus on the daily issues and dilemmas faced by ordinary Africans.

Thousands of films later, the industry is well established, and in recognition of the growing importance of the industry to Nigeria's economy, in 2010 president Goodluck Jonathon announced the creation of a $200 million loan fund to help finance local movie-making.

Morocco

Moolade, the powerful 2004 film by the Senegalese director Ousmane Sembène, is one of the few mass-release artistic endeavours to tackle head-on the taboo issue of female genital mutilation.

Until recently Morocco has been seen mostly as a stunning movie backdrop, easily upstaging the actors in such dubious cinematic achievements as *Alexandar, Ishtar, The Four Feathers, The Mummy, Troy* and *Sahara*. The country also had more golden moments on the silver screen in Hitchcock's *The Man Who Knew Too Much*, Orson Welles' *Othello, Gladiator*, and David Lean's *Lawrence of Arabia*. It has certainly proved its versatility with some big-name directors: it stunt-doubled for Somalia in Ridley Scott's *Black Hawk Down*, stood in for Tibet in Martin Scorcese's *Kundun*, and stole the show right out from under John Malkovich by playing itself in Bernardo Bertolucci's *The Sheltering Sky*. It also serves as the location for more than 1000 French, German and Italian productions each year.

French-backed independent Moroccan films are also now showing in select cinemas and on satellite television, and Franco-Moroccan films are now serious festival contenders. Franco-Moroccan director Leila Marrakchi was awarded 'Un Certain Regard' at the 2005 Cannes Film Festival for her first feature, *Marock*. In 2011 Mohamed Mouftakir won the prestigious Étalon d'Or in the Fespaco film festival.

Religion

Over half of all West Africans are Muslim and it's very much a north–south divide: the countries of Morocco, the Sahel and Sahara are predominantly Muslim, while Christianity is more widespread in the southern coastal countries. That said, in almost every country of the region, traditional or animist beliefs retain a significant hold over the population.

Traditional Religions

Before the arrival of Islam and Christianity, every race, tribe or clan in West Africa practised its own traditional religion. While many in the Sahel converted to Islam, and those in the south converted to Christianity, traditional religions remained strong and still retain a powerful hold over the consciousness of West Africans, even coexisting with established aspects of Islam or Christianity. When discussing traditional beliefs, terms such as 'juju', 'voodoo' and 'witchcraft' are frequently employed. In certain specific contexts these may be correct, but these are much misunderstood terms.

There are hundreds of traditional religions in West Africa, with considerable areas of overlap. What you won't find are any great temples (more modest local shrines often served the same purpose) or written scriptures (in keeping with West Africa's largely oral tradition). Beliefs and traditions can be complex and difficult to understand, but several common factors are found again and again. The following description provides an overview only, and is necessarily very simplified.

The Way of the Elders: West African Spirituality & Tradition, by Adama and Naomi Doumbia, is one of surprisingly few books to provide an overview of the foundations of traditional West African religions.

The Role of the Natural World

Almost all traditional religions are animist, meaning that they are based on the attribution of life or consciousness to natural objects or phenomena. Thus a certain tree, mountain, river or stone may be sacred (such as among the Lobi of southwestern Burkina Faso) because it represents, is home to, or simply is, a spirit or deity. The number of deities of each religion varies, as does the phenomena that represents them. The Ewe of Togo and Ghana, for example, have more than 600 deities, including one that represents the disease smallpox.

Totems, fetishes (talismans) and charms are also important features of traditional religions. Among the Senoufo, for example, the dead take on the form of the clan's animal totem. Masks also play a significant role, and often serve as mediums of intercession between the human and natural worlds.

The Role of Ancestors

In many African religions, ancestors play a particularly strong role; two powerful examples of this are found among the Igbo and Yoruba of Nigeria. The principal function of ancestors is usually to protect the tribe or family, and they may on occasion show their ancestral pleasure or displeasure (eg in the form of bad weather, a bad harvest, or when a living member of the family becomes sick). There are almost as many variations

Calligraphed Quran, Chinguetti (p247), Mauritania

on the theme as there are distinct cultural groups in West Africa. The Baoulé people of Côte d'Ivoire, for example, believe in a parallel world to our own where parallel relatives can have an important influence over the 'real' world. Many traditional religions also hold that the ancestors are the real owners of the land and, while it can be enjoyed and used during the lifetime of their descendants, it cannot be sold and must be cared for.

Communication with ancestors or deities may take the form of prayer, offerings (possibly with the assistance of a holy man, or occasionally a holy woman) or sacrifice. Requests may include good health, bountiful harvests and numerous children. Many village celebrations are held to ask for help from, or in honour of, ancestors and deities. The Dogon people in Mali, for instance, have celebrations before planting (to ensure good crops) and after harvest (to give thanks).

A Central Deity?

Several traditional religions accept the existence of a supreme being or creator, alongside spirits and deities. This being usually figures in creation myths and is considered too exalted to be concerned with humans – see, for example, the Bobo people of Burkina Faso and Mali. In many cultures, communication with the creator is possible only through lesser deities or through the intercession of ancestors.

Muslims form a majority in The Gambia, Guinea, Mali, Mauritania, Morocco, Niger, Senegal and Sierra Leone, and comprise 50% of the inhabitants of Burkina Faso and Nigeria. Only Cape Verde and Ghana have Christian majorities.

Islam

Islam's Origins

Abdul Qasim Mohammed ibn Abdullah ibn Abdal-Muttalib ibn Hashim (the Prophet Mohammed) was born in 570. Mohammed's family belonged to the Quraysh tribe, a trading family with links to Syria and Yemen. By the age of six, Mohammed's parents had both died and he came into the care of his grandfather, the custodian of the Kaaba in Mecca in Saudi Arabia.

At the age of 40, in 610, the Prophet Mohammed retreated into the desert and began to receive divine revelations from Allah via the voice of the archangel Gabriel; the revelations would continue throughout Mohammed's life. Three years later, Mohammed began imparting Allah's message to Meccans. He called on Meccans to turn away from pagan worship and submit to Allah, the one true god.

As such, Islam provided a simpler alternative to the established faiths, which had become complicated by hierarchical orders, sects and complex rituals, offering instead a direct relationship with God based only on the believer's submission to God (Islam means 'submission'). Not surprisingly, the Prophet's message and movement appealed especially to the poorer, disenfranchised sections of society.

The Spread of Islam

When Mohammed died in 632, the Arab tribes spread quickly across the Middle East, in very little time conquering what now constitutes Jordan, Syria, Iraq, Lebanon and Israel and the Palestinian Territories. To the west, the unrelenting conquest swept across North Africa. By the end of the 7th century, the Muslims had reached and conquered what is now Morocco. In 710, they marched on Spain.

The natural barrier formed by the Sahara meant that Islam took longer to trickle down into West Africa than elsewhere. It first reached the Sahel around 900, via trans-Saharan traders from present-day Morocco and Algeria. Islam cemented its position as the dominant religion in the Sahel in the 17th and 18th centuries, filling the vacuum left by the then-defunct Sahelian empires. Spiritual power was fused with political and economic hegemony, and Islamic jihads (holy wars) were declared on nonbelievers and backed by the powers of the state. In time, several Muslim states were established, including Futa Toro (in northern Senegal), Futa Djalon (Guinea), Masina (Mali) and the Sokoto state of Hausaland (Niger and Nigeria).

Although ordinary people in many regions preferred to retain their traditional beliefs, Islam quickly became the state religion in many West African kingdoms and empires, where rulers skilfully combined aspects of Islam with traditional religions in the administration of the state. The result was a fusion of beliefs that remains a feature of West African life today.

The Quran

For Muslims the Quran is the word of God, directly communicated to Mohammed. It comprises 114 suras, or chapters, which govern all aspects of a Muslim's life.

TIPS FOR TRAVELLERS IN ISLAMIC AREAS

When you visit a mosque, take off your shoes; women should cover their heads and shoulders with scarves. In some mosques, women are not allowed to enter if prayers are in progress or if the imam (prayer leader) is present; in others, there may be separate entrances for men and women. In others still, non-Muslims are not allowed to enter at all.

If you've hired a guide or taxi driver for the day, remember that he'll want to say his prayers at the right times, so look out for signs that he wants a few moments off, particularly around noon, late afternoon and sunset. Travellers on buses and bush taxis should also be prepared for prayer stops at these times.

Despite the Islamic proscription against alcohol, some Muslims may enjoy a quiet drink. Even so, it's impolite to drink alcohol in their presence unless they show approval.

During Islamic holidays, shops and offices may close. Even if the offices are officially open, during the Ramadan period of fasting, people become soporific (especially when Ramadan falls in the hot season) and very little gets done.

SONY & THE QURAN

West African Islam is generally regarded as more liberal than the Islam espoused by purists in Cairo or Mecca. In October 2008, that diversity of opinion was thrust into the international spotlight. A Sony video game, 'LittleBigPlanet', was withdrawn from sale after a Muslim playing a trial version of the game alerted Sony that a piece of background music included two phrases from the Quran. It could, he said, be considered blasphemous by Muslims for its combination of music and sacred words from Islam's holy book. Fearful of alienating Muslim gamers, Sony recalled the game and removed the song in question before releasing it back onto the market.

But the decision was viewed somewhat differently in West Africa. The offending song was 'Tapha Niang', recorded by Mali's master *kora* (harp-like instrument) player Toumani Diabaté, which had appeared on his acclaimed 2006 album *Boulevard de l'Independence*. Diabaté, a devout Muslim whose favourite live-music venue in Bamako was recently transformed into an Islamic cultural centre, denied that the song was in any way blasphemous. 'In my family there are only two things we know', he told the BBC, 'the Quran and the *kora*'. Expressing his disappointment, he went on to say that it was entirely acceptable in Mali for Islamic tenets to be put to music as a way of glorifying Islam.

It's not known whether the revelations were written down during Mohammed's lifetime, although Muslims believe the Quran to be the direct word of Allah as told to Mohammed. The third caliph, Uthman (644–56), gathered together everything written by the scribes (parchments, stone tablets, the memories of Mohammed's followers) and gave them to a panel of editors under the caliph's aegis. A Quran printed today is identical to that agreed upon by Uthman's compilers 14 centuries ago.

The Five Pillars of Islam

The five pillars of Islam (the basic tenets that guide Muslims in their daily lives) are as follows:

Shahada (the profession of faith): 'There is no god but Allah, and Mohammed is his Prophet' is the fundamental tenet of Islam.

Salat (prayer): Muslims must face Mecca and pray at dawn, noon, mid-afternoon, sunset and nightfall. Prayer times are marked by the call to prayer, which rings out across the towns and villages of the Sahel.

Zakat (alms): Muslims must give a portion of their income to the poor and needy.

Sawm (fasting): Ramadan commemorates Mohammed's first revelation, and is the month when all Muslims fast from dawn to dusk.

Haj (pilgrimage, usually written *hadj* in West Africa): Every Muslim capable of affording it should perform the *haj*, or pilgrimage, to the holiest of cities, Mecca, at least once in his or her lifetime. The reward is considerable: the forgiving of all past sins. This can involve a lifetime of saving money, and it's not unusual for families to save up and send one member. Before the advent of air travel, the pilgrimage often involved an overland journey of a year or more. In West Africa, those who complete the pilgrimage receive the honorific title of Hadj for men, and Hadjia for women.

Islamic Customs

In everyday life, Muslims are prohibited from drinking alcohol, eating carrion, blood products or pork (which are considered unclean), eating the meat of animals not killed in the prescribed manner, and eating food over which the name of Allah has not been said. Adultery, theft and gambling are also prohibited.

Islam is not just about prohibitions but also marks the important events of a Muslim's life. When a baby is born, the first words uttered to

Some Muslims believe that the Quran must be studied in its original classical Arabic form ('an Arabic Quran, wherein there is no crookedness'; sura 39:25) and that translations dilute the holiness of its sacred texts. For Muslims, the language of the Quran is known as *sihr halal* (lawful magic).

it are, in many places, the call to prayer. A week later there is a ceremony in which the baby's head is shaved and an animal sacrificed in remembrance of Abraham's willingness to sacrifice his son to Allah. The major event of a boy's childhood is circumcision, which normally takes place between the ages of seven and 12. When a person dies, a burial service is held at the mosque and the body is buried with the feet facing Mecca.

Islam in Morocco

As in many Muslim countries, most Moroccans follow the orthodox Sunni (as opposed to Shia) strain of Islam. There are four main schools of thought among the Sunnis emphasising different aspects of doctrine, and today the one most commonly followed in Morocco is the Maliki school. Historically this school has been less strict than others, with Maliki *qaids* (judges) applying the sharia law, or religious code, according to local custom rather than the absolute letter of the law.

One local tradition to emerge over centuries of Islamic practice in Morocco is the custom of venerating *marabouts*, or saints. *Marabouts* are devout Muslims whose acts of devotion and professions of faith were so profound that their very presence is considered to confer *baraka*, or grace, even after their death. Moroccans go out of their way to visit *marabouts'* tombs and *zaouias* (shrines) – and many claim that like a spa for the soul, the right *zaouia* can fix anything from a broken heart to arthritis.

This practice of honouring *marabouts* is more in line with ancient Berber beliefs and Sufi mysticism than orthodox Islam, which generally discourages anything resembling idol worship. But visits to *zaouias* are side trips for the many devout Moroccans who spend a lifetime preparing and planning for the haj. Moroccans do not necessarily see a conflict between *baraka* and belief, or between local customs and universal understanding.

Islam South of the Sahara

Islamic practice in sub-Saharan West Africa is extremely varied and perhaps more than anywhere else in the Islamic world, traditional animist beliefs are often fused with more orthodox doctrinal tenets.

In some countries, especially Senegal, *marabouts* wield considerable political power. Sufism, which emphasises mystical and spiritual attributes, was one of the more popular Islamic forms in West Africa; some scholars speculate that the importance that Sufis ascribe to religious teachers may have found favour in West Africa as it mirrored existing hierarchical social structures.

Quranic schools play an important role both socially and educationally in many Sahelian countries. In recent years, Islamic clerics (sometimes with the support of clerics and funds from Saudi Arabia) have begun to preach a stricter doctrinal line. This has particularly been the case in predominantly Muslim northern Nigeria where sharia law has been imposed. In its most extreme form, the shift has seen the rise of fundamentalist groups such as Boko Haram (with its roots in northeastern Nigeria) and Al-Qaeda in the Islamic Maghreb (AQIM); AQIM has been widely reported to have been a powerful force in the rebel occupation of northern Mali in 2012 and their foot soldiers were responsible for destroying numerous *marabout* tombs, including some in Timbuktu.

Christianity

Christianity arrived in West Africa later than Islam, during the age of colonial exploration; after the first wave of explorers, missionaries were among the first colonial settlers in West Africa. In general their success was limited in Sahelian countries where Islam had been established centuries before, but they found more fertile ground further south where traditional religions held sway. This story is reflected in the current

The schism between Sunnis and Shiites dates back to the first Islamic century and to a dispute over who should rule over the Muslim world as caliph. Beyond this early dynastic rivalry, there is little doctrinal difference between Shiite Islam and Sunni Islam. Sunnis comprise some 90% of the world's Muslims.

The *Lost Kingdoms of Africa*, by Jeffrey Tayler, is an engagingly told journey through the stories and terrain of the ancient Islamic kingdoms of West Africa's Sahel and southern Sahara.

distribution of Christian strongholds: Christianity is the majority religion in Cameroon, Cape Verde, Ghana and Liberia, and the largest religion in Benin and Togo. There are also significant Christian minorities in Nigeria and Côte d'Ivoire.

As with Islam, many West African Christians have held on to their traditional beliefs, and these are often practised side by side with Christianity. More often, the use of stories from traditional religions were inserted into Bible stories so as to make them more relevant to a West African audience, meaning that some liturgical and even some belief systems may appear different to the way that Christianity is practised in the West. There has, however, been something of a backlash against such doctrinal fusions, resulting in the rise of sometimes quite conservative evangelical churches that are becoming increasingly influential in some areas, particularly in Nigeria.

Islam: A Short History, by Karen Armstrong, is a first-rate primer on the world's fastest-growing religion; it's distinguished by a fair-minded approach and clear language.

Music

Music put West Africa on the map. Years ago, even if no one knew exactly where Senegal was, they knew that Youssou N'Dour lived there, and the great Baaba Maal. They could tell you that Salif Keita came from Mali, and Mory Kanté from Guinea. That Nigeria was home to Fela Kuti and juju music emperor King Sunny Ade. Reggae star Alpha Blondy defined Côte d'Ivoire. Saxophonist Manu Dibango was Cameroon, just as Cesária Evora was Cape Verde and Angélique Kidjo, Benin. All of these West African stars fuelled the global Afropop boom. Once filed under 'A' for Africa, they lent the world-music genre much-needed individuality, commerciality and cred.

Music of West Africa

The international success of these West African elders has paved the way for an apparently bottomless pot of talent. Desert rebels Tinariwen; dreadlocked Senegalese mystic Cheikh Lo; and his hotly tipped compatriot, Carlou D. The fresh prince of Côte d'Ivoire, Tiken Jah Fakoly, and its fresh princess, Dobet Gnahoré. Golden-voiced Mauritanian Daby Touré, and afrobeating politicos such as Nigeria's Femi and Sean Kuti (in looks, sound and sentiment, very much their father's sons). Mayra Andrade from Cape Verde, with her multicultural jazz, and Malians including ethereal songbird Rokia Traore, *kora* maestro Toumani Diabaté and husband-and-wife team Amadou and Mariam, whose eighth album, 2012's *Folila*, features such special guests as Santigold and Jake Shears from Scissor Sisters.

Mentioning these names is only scratching the surface. Music is everywhere in West Africa, coming at you in thunderous, drum-fuelled polyrhythms, through the swooping, soaring voices of *griots* (traditional musicians or minstrels; praise singers) and via socially-aware reggae, rap and hip-hop. From Afrobeat to pygmy fusion, highlife to *makossa*, *gumbe* to Nigerian gospel, genres are as entrenched as they are evolving, fusing and reforming. Little wonder that here – in this vast, diverse region, with its deserts, jungles, skyscrapers and urban sprawl – myriad ethnic groups play out their lives to music. Here are traditional songs that celebrate weddings, offer solace at funerals, keep work rhythms steady in the fields. Here are songs and rhythms that travelled out on slave ships to Cuba and Brazil. Songs that retell history and, in doing so, foster inter-clan and inter-religious respect.

In West Africa, too, are the roots of Western music (along with guitars, keyboards, Latin influences and other legacies of colonialism).

Not for nothing did Senegalese rap crew Daara J title their 2003 international debut *Boomerang*. 'Born in Africa, raised in America', says member Faada Freddy, 'rap has come full circle'. As has the blues. A host of American blues musicians – Ry Cooder, Corey Harris, Taj Mahal, Bonnie Raitt – have found inspiration in West Africa, in Mali in particular. 'The sound of our blues is dry like the Sahara, but it's the vast open space that shapes the desert blues,' says Vieux Farka Touré, guitar-toting son of the late great bluesman Ali Farka Touré. 'For me it will always be the music of openness'. Mali, however, is currently in crisis. A coup in Bamako on 22 March 2012 has sent the country into a tailspin, kickstarting the biggest humanitarian crisis the

Life is Hard, Music is Good is a feature-length documentary on the music and musicians of Mali. The result of over five years' worth of research by Kanaga System Krush, an indie label that focuses primarily on West African music, it mixes interviews with the likes of Toumani Diabaté, Djelimady Tounkara and honorary Malian Damon Albarn with footage of life across this increasingly strife-torn country.

Sahel has ever known. Radical Islamists holding the northern part of the country have banned all secular music. Ali Farka Touré's music has been outlawed in his hometown, Niafunké, where it once echoed joyously. That Mali – any part of Mali – should be without music is unthinkable, a travesty. An international protest movement is gathering pace.

The great bluesman Ali Farke Touré, who passed away in March 2006, was the mayor of his hometown, Niafunké, a village on the Niger River in Timbuktu (Tombouctou) province. In 2012 Islamist militants took over the town, imposing a strict social code that included the banning of all forms of music. 'I am happy he is not alive to see this because it would break his heart,' says his guitarist son Vieux. 'It is probably breaking his heart now, though, where he is.'

A Potted History of West African Music

The musical history of West Africa is closely linked to its diverse and long-established empires, such as Ghana's (6th to 11th centuries), where court music was played for chiefs, music accompanied ceremonies and chores, and music was played for pleasure at the end of the day. In the vast Mali Empire (13th to 15th centuries), music was the province of one social caste, the *jelis,* who still perform their folk styles today. Correspondingly in Senegal, *griots* – Wolof culture's *kora*-strumming, praise-singing caste – trace genealogies, recount epics and span generations. There are myriad musical styles in West Africa, courtesy of its hundreds of ethnic groups and various Islamic and European influences, but the *jeli/griot* tradition is arguably the best known.

Senegal, The Gambia, Guinea, Mali, Mauritania, Burkina Faso and Côte d'Ivoire all share the same *jeli* tradition, though each linguistic group calls it something different and each has its own subtly different sound. They are acknowledged as oral historians – nearly all children know the epic of Sundiata Keita, the warrior who founded the Mali Empire – and often as soothsayers but, although they top the bill at weddings and naming ceremonies, *griots* occupy a lowly rank in their hierarchical societies. Many big West African stars faced parental objections to their choice of career. Others, such as Salif Keita – a direct descendent of Sundiata and, as such, not a *jeli* – made their reputations in exile.

Oral tradition is equally strong in Nigeria, where stories of ancient Yoruba, Ashanti, Hausa and other kingdoms flourish. Like many a West African style, Yoruba music has its roots in percussion. Indeed, if there is any element common to the huge, diverse region that is West Africa, it is drumming. From the Ewe ensembles of Ghana – similar in style to those of Benin and Togo – to Senegal's *sabar* drummers, beating their giant instruments with sticks, drumming kick-started West Africa's musical heart. Often accompanied by ululation, vocal repetition, call-and-response vocals and polyrhythms, drums beat out a sound that immediately says 'Africa'.

As West African music travelled out on the slave ships (and brought other influences back with it later), so the music of the colonisers travelled in. The Portuguese presence in Cape Verde created *morna,* music of separation, and *saudade* and creole-style *gumbe* in Guinea-Bissau.

MUST-HAVE WEST AFRICAN ALBUMS

→ *Dimanche á Bamako* (Because) by Amadou and Mariam

→ *M'Bemba* (Universal Jazz France) by Salif Keita

→ *In the Heart of the Moon* (World Circuit) by Ali Farke Touré and Toumani Diabaté

→ *Worotan* (World Circuit) by Oumou Sangare

→ *Zombie* (Barclay/Universal) by Fela Kuti

→ *Specialist in All Styles* (World Circuit) by Orchestra Baobab

→ *Highlife Roots Revival* (World Music Network) by Koo Nimo

→ *Radio Salone* (Cumbancha) by Sierra Leone Refugee All Stars

→ *Segu Blue* (Outhere) by Bassekou Kouyaté and Ngoni Ba

DANITA DELIMONT / GETTY IMAGES ©

African drummers in Accra (p171), Ghana

Western-style dance orchestras had the colonial elite fox-trotting on the Gold Coast. Francophone Africa fell in love with Cuban dance music, a genre, in rhythm and structure, remarkably close to Mande music. Cuban music (and guitar-based Congolese rumba) introduced modern instruments to the region, creating a swath of dance bands such as Guinea's legendary Bembeya Jazz (a signifier of modern music, 'jazz' was commonly tagged on a band's name), who played local styles with Latin arrangements.

Post-independence, the philosophy of 'negritude' – or cultural rediscovery – arose among some 1960s-era West African governments. Popular Latin sounds were discouraged in favour of folkloric material. Electric Afropop began to incorporate traditional rhythms and instruments, such as the *kora* (a harp-like musical instrument with over 20 strings), *balafon* (xylophone) and *ngoni* (a stringed instrument). State-sponsored dance bands won big audiences and spawned even bigger stars. The first president of Senegal (poet Leopold Senghor) fostered the young Orchestra Baobab band, which made a phenomenal 21st-century comeback. Mali's Le Rail Band du Bamako (sponsored by the Malian Railway Company) became an African institution that launched the careers of two of Africa's greatest singers: Salif Keita and Mory Kanté.

When the young Salif Keita defected to the band's foreign-style rivals, Les Ambassedeurs du Motel, there was uproar. Fierce competition ensued throughout the 1970s, making Bamako the dance-music capital of West Africa. Meanwhile, in Nigeria, the poppy highlife sound of the 1940s, '50s and '60s gave way to genres with a strong percussive element, such as *juju* and *fuji*. The West's popular music genres – rock, soul, jazz, funk, pop – made their mark, each spawning its own 'Afro' equivalent. Today the likes of 1960s Sierra-Leonean Afro-soul king Geraldo Pino and Beninoise voodoo heroes Orchestre Poly Rythmo de Cotonou are being rediscovered by a new generation of Western hipsters.

Stephen Feld's *Jazz Cosmopolitanism in Accra: Five Musical Years in Ghana* (2012, Duke University Press) combines memoir, biography, ethnography and history in a compelling and accessible look at Ghana's coolest cats.

Based in Conakry, Radio Kankan (www.radio-kankan.com) is a French-language station devoted to news and music from the region.

The recording studios of Lagos offered commercial opportunities for Nigerian performers, as did those of 1980s Abidjan in Cotê d'Ivoire – a musical Mecca for artists from across the continent. But by the mid-1980s all eyes were on Paris, the city where Mory Kanté recorded his seminal club-floor anthem 'Yeke Yeke' (check out Kanté's excellent 2012 album *La Guinnéenne*) and where innumerable West African musicians lived.

Big names moved back and forth between Paris, London and West Africa, recording cassettes for the local market and albums for the international one, as remains the case today. With the 1990s world-music boom, many stars – Youssou N'Dour, Salif Keita, Cesária Evora, King Sunny Ade – established their own record companies and signed up local talent.

Some savvy Western record labels pre-empted mainstream interest in West African music. London-based World Circuit signed the likes of Oumou Sangaré, Orchestra Baobab and the late Ali Farka Touré – and more recently, Malian songbird Fatoumata Diawara – arguably doing for West Africa what it did for Cuba with the Buena Vista Social Club. West African artists are now staples of international festivals including Womad and Glastonbury. Club producers have remixed Femi Kuti and Rokia Traoré. West African albums make it into mainstream charts, West African musicians sell out Western venues and Western musicians look to West Africa for inspiration.

In West Africa, big-name artists attract hordes of followers wherever they go. The politicians who try to hijack such popularity are usually shrugged off. Mory Kanté and Baaba Maal are respectively United Nations and Oxfam Goodwill Ambassadors, using their stardom to campaign against poverty, disease and illiteracy. The great Youssou N'Dour – once described by *Rolling Stone* as 'perhaps the most famous singer alive' in much of Africa – has been Senegal's Minister of Tourism and Culture since April 2012.

Sierra Leone's Refugee All Stars is a band formed by a group of refugees displaced to Guinea by the Sierra Leone Civil War, and who tour extensively to raise awareness of humanitarian causes. Fatoumata Diawara and Oumou Sangaré sing, however obliquely, about women's rights. The rap movement in Senegal promotes peace and love. But freedom of expression is still curtailed; both Sean and Femi Kuti's pro-democracy narratives are censored in Nigeria, just as their father's were.

Guitar-based highlife is still a staple of Ghana, where hip-life – the country's very own hip-hop – is also huge. Nigerian music isn't as popular in the West as it was; Mali and Senegal are ahead in the popularity stakes, but the demand for the back catalogue of the late great Nigerian Fela Anikulapo Kuti continues apace. After revisiting their roots with traditional acoustic albums both Salif Keita and Baaba Maal have gone on to re-embrace electronica; Keita's 2013 album *Talé* is produced by Phillipe Cohen Solal of Paris-based experimentalist Gotan Project.

Everywhere, musicians are creating, collaborating, experimenting. New, exciting performers are constantly emerging. Traditional styles are proudly upheld and passed down. West Africa's musical heritage is rich and ever present. It's in the DNA of its people.

West African Instruments

West Africa's traditional instruments tend to be found in its rural areas and are generally fashioned from local materials – everything from gourds, stalks and shells to goat skin, cow horns and horse hair. Discarded objects and nature also have multiple musical uses; in Sierra Leone, empty Milo tins filled with stones were the core instrument for the genre called Milojazz. Hausa children in Nigeria beat rhythms on the inflated belly of a live pufferfish. The Pygmies of Cameroon beat rhythms on river water.

There are bells made of bronze in the Islamic orchestras of northern Nigeria, and scrapers made of iron in the south. In Cape Verde women

Sterns Music (www.sternsmusic.com) is the Amazon.com of the world-music scene, allowing you to search and buy from a large range of West African and other CDs and DVDs.

Akwaaba Music (www.akwaabamusic.com) is a Ghana-generated site dedicated to African music and pop culture: to finding new sounds and trends, sharing them, selling them, putting them out there.

SEUN KUTI

'We've got to get up and think, not get up and fight,' declares Seun (Shayoon) Kuti, on stage in flares and bodyshirt, an alto saxophone hanging around his neck. 'We have to start using our minds.'

There's no doubting that the thirtysomething is his father's son. 'Fela created Afrobeat to fight injustice,' he says over a trademark blend of jazz, funk and African high-life rhythms. 'What started in Nigeria is now a global movement. The message is beating louder than ever.'

Seun Kuti was 14 when his father, Fela Anikulapo Kuti, aka the Black President, died of AIDS in 1997. More than one million people lined the streets of Lagos, Nigeria's capital, to watch the funeral procession, mourning a rebel who took on the country's autocratic and corrupt leaders and was regularly beaten and incarcerated as a result.

Fela Kuti was a fearless voice of the masses, delivering politically charged songs with the self-same dance orchestra that backs Seun Kuti today.

'These guys are the real deal,' says Kuti, whose 2011 album *From Africa With Fury: Rise* was co-produced by Brian Eno. 'Some of them went through arrests and beatings with my dad. They are all activists. They all have strong political views.'

Seun's half-brother Femi, 20 years his senior, has been channelling the fury and passion of Afrobeat with his own band, Positive Force, for decades.

'Afrobeat is on the rise across the world. There are at least 20 places in New York where you can see Afrobeat live. There are Afrobeat bands in Australia.'

As a child Kuti was his father's orchestra's mascot, travelling everywhere with them as his mother sang and danced in the chorus. It was while watching Egypt 80's legendary concert at the Apollo Theatre in Harlem, New York, at the age of eight that he decided to become a singer ('My father laughed, then said, "Why not?"'). He joined the orchestra and often did an opening set at Fela's infamous Shrine nightclub in Lagos.

"Fela taught me that I am a member of the band," he says, "and that the band are the most important thing ever. When he died I knew I had to keep them going."

The young band leader took time out to study music in England, just as his father had done. After which, armed with an arsenal of Fela Kuti standards, Seun Kuti started performing and touring in earnest.

So does it bother him to be continually assessed in terms of what his father did? 'Being in my dad's shadow is a good place to be,' he says with a shrug. 'He was a very great man.'

'I'm an artist in my own right, of course, but ultimately it's Afrobeat that matters. Afrobeat is the truth.'

place a rolled-up cloth between their legs and beat it as part of their *batuco* music (the singer Lura does this live, with silver lamé). Everywhere, there is men's music and women's music, men's instruments and women's instruments: in Mauritania, men play the *tidinit,* a four-stringed lute, and women the *ardin,* a sort of back-to-front *kora.* Accordingly, there are men's dances and women's dances. And most of these, like most instrumental ensembles, are fuelled by drums.

West Africa has a phenomenal variety of drums. Kettle, slit and talking drums; water, frame and hourglass-shaped drums; log, goblet and double-headed barrel drums. Drums used for ritual purposes, like the *dundun* drums of the Yoruba, which communicate with the *orishas;* drums made from tree trunks and used for long-distance messages; drums that mark the major events of one's life – baptism, marriage, death – and drums for entertainment. 'Talking' drums, such as the Wolof *tama,* a small, high-pitched instrument clamped under the armpit and beaten fast with a hooked stick, or the *djembe,* the chalice-shaped drum ubiquitous from Ghana to Senegal, and in the West's endorphin-inducing African drum circles.

There's a diverse array of string instruments too, from the one-stringed viol of the Niger Tuareg and the 13-string *obo* zither of the Igbo in Nigeria,

Martin Scorsese presents the Blues: Feels Like Going Home (Martin Scorsese; 2003) follows musician Corey Harris' travels through Mississippi and West Africa, exploring the roots of blues music. Includes performances by Salif Keita, Habib Kolté, Taj Mahal and Ali Farka Touré.

to the 21-string *kora* – the harp-lute of the *griots* and one of the most sophisticated instruments in sub-Saharan Africa. *Kora* players are usually virtuosos, having studied their craft from childhood. Mory Kanté's amplified rock-style *kora* helped establish its reputation as a formidable solo instrument, while *kora* master Toumani Diabaté, son of the virtuoso Sidiki Diabaté, displayed its crossover potential by collaborating with everyone from flamenco musicians to African American bluesman Taj Mahal.

Regarded by some as the precursor to the banjo, the *ngoni* (*xalam* in Wolof, *hoddu* in Fula, *konting* in Mandinka) is also popular with *griots*. A feature in the 14th-century courts of Mali, it has between three and five strings that are plucked, and is tricky to play. Another well-known *griot* instrument is the *balafon,* a wooden xylophone with between 18 and 21 keys, suspended over a row of gourds to amplify the sound. The *balafon* is often played in pairs, with each musician – one improvising, one not – striking the keys with wooden mallets. The Susu people of Guinea are renowned *balafon* experts.

There are other xylophones with different names in West Africa, xylophones fashioned from huge logs, or xylophones amplified by boxes and pits. There are wind instruments (Fula shepherds play melodies on reed flutes) and brass instruments (the Niger Tuareg favour the *alghaita shawm* trumpet) and voices used as instruments – such as the timeless vocals of the *griots,* the polyphonic singing of the Pygmies and the sung poetry of the Tuareg.

Across the region, percussion vies and blends with brass, wood and wind instruments. In urban areas, traditional instruments complement and ground modern instruments. West Africa is, indeed, a hive of musical activity, thrumming to its own collective orchestra.

West African Musical Styles

While many of West Africa's mega-successful artists might be classified as 'Afro-pop', thanks to commercial sales at home and/or in the West, the region boasts a gamut of distinctive musical styles. The following are just a few of them.

Afrobeat

Co-created by the late, great Fela Kuti, Afrobeat is a hybrid of Nigerian highlife, Yoruba percussion, jazz, funk and soul. Fela, a singer, saxophonist and band leader, and one of the most influential 20th-century African figures, used Afrobeat to give voice to the oppressed. His onstage rants, tree-trunk-sized spliff in hand, were legendary. A succession of governments tried to shut him up. When he died of AIDS in 1997, a million people joined his funeral procession through Lagos. His eldest son, Femi, has picked up the baton, releasing fine albums such as *Africa for Africa* and reopening his father's Lagos nightclub, the Shrine. A host of Nigerian creatives – percussionist and singer Tony Allen, rapper Weird MC, Fela's youngest son, Seun – keep the flame alight. Afrobeat continues to cross over into dance mixes and hip-hop and reggae projects.

Cape Verdean Music

Cape Verdean music came late to the West. The undisputed star of the bluesy, melancholy songs (known as *morna*) was the 'barefoot diva' Cesária Evora, a barefoot, ciggie-puffing grandmother who passed away in December 2011. European influences are obvious in *morna,* the equivalent of Portugal's *fado,* while Africa is at the fore in other genres such as the dance-oriented *coladeira,* accordion-led *funana* and percussive women's music, *batuco.* Look out for the 2013 international debut album by 60-year-old *morna* balladeer Zé Luis, the Lisbon-based Lura and

Cassette piracy is a huge problem in West Africa and many high-profile names have devoted themselves to the task of its eradication. Dakar-based singer-songwriter Carlou D only sells his new CD *Audio Visa* (which is yet to be snapped up by an international label) at his live gigs for this very reason.

Just 4U, in Dakar (Senegal), is a cosy outdoor bar restaurant with tables and chairs arranged under canvas awnings. Nightly live music includes gigs by some of the capital's best musicians: Cheikh Lo, Carlou D, Orchestra Baobab.

Africanhiphop. com (www.africanhiphop.com) has been mapping the development of African hip-hop culture since the '90s; it features links, new productions and contributions from the artists themselves.

SALIF KEITA

Salif Keita stands on a floating stage on the Niger River in Segou, south-central Mali, and unleashes his powerful voice on an adoring 10,000-strong crowd. An attacking band on instruments modern and traditional – electric guitars, the long-necked *kamale ngoni* lute – back the pale, self-contained man known variously as the White Horse, the Malian Caruso and the Golden Voice of Africa. A fleet of pirogue boats, having drifted up as close as possible, sways on the water.

'I am black/my skin is white,' sings Keita, as a tall albino dancer with yellow braids throws shapes. 'The difference is on purpose/for us to complete each other.'

The song is the title track of Keita's award-winning 2010 album *La Difference*, a work that references his remarkable background: born a despised albino to a family descended from Sundiata Keita, the popular warrior chief who founded the Mali empire in the 13th century, Keita was subject to ancestral rules that forbade nobles from making music.

'It was easier for me to rebel since I was an albino,' says the musician, whose Malian-American wife, Coumba Makalou, heads the US-based Salif Keita Global Foundation, which is dedicated to highlighting the plight of people with albinism.

'I was already an outcast,' Keita adds. 'I left my family village and went to live on the streets of Bamako. I met homosexuals' – other outcasts – 'who helped me, who gave me clothes and shoes and then sent me to sing in bars.'

We're backstage at the eighth annual Festival on the Niger. It's February 2011, the month before a military coup in Mali's capital, Bamako, will overthrow the elected government of president Amadou Toumani Touré. Before the decades-long rebellion by ethnic Tuareg rebels in the north of the country will be hijacked by radical Islamists with links to al-Qaeda.

It's hard to imagine that within months hotels and bars will close, livelihoods will be taken away, and the application of a strict form of sharia law in northern Mali will almost silence the music.

However, down in Segou – a three-hour drive from Bamako – about 35,000 West Africans and Western tourists throng the dusty streets and banks of the Niger across the festival's four days. Most have come to see Keita.

'Of all Mali's many musicians, Salif is the most admired by Malians,' says Mamou Daffe, director of Festival on the Niger. 'Not only is he proof that anyone can succeed in life, he was the first artist to bring the music of Mali to international acclaim.'

When world music became a popular genre in the West in the late 1980s, Keita was at its vanguard. He moved to Paris, worked with Carlos Santana and jazz musicians Wayne Shorter and Joe Zawinul. In 1987 he released *Soro*, a hi-tech hybrid he calls his visiting card. In the late 90s he began spending increasing amounts of time in Mali, and in 2001 went back for good.

'For me to go forward I needed to remember where I came from,' says Keita, who owns a recording studio in Bamako and whose 2013 album *Talé* is fuelled by optimism.

Where he comes from is now a country in crisis: 'I am Muslim, but I am against – 1000 times against – fundamentalism', a prescient Keita told Freemuse.org in 2002.

'Let's fight to build our happiness,' he says now.

Tcheka, a singer-songwriter and guitarist who plays beats that are normally played on percussion.

Gumbe

Closely associated with Guinea-Bissau, *gumbe* is an uptempo, polyrhythmic genre that fuses about 10 of the country's folk-music traditions. Lyrics, sung in Portuguese creole, are topical and witty; instruments include guitars and the water drum, an upturned calabash floating in a bucket. *Gumbe* is sometimes used as an umbrella term for any folk music in Guinea-Bissau but should not be confused with *kizomba*, the popular dance and music originating from Angola. In Sierra Leone, *gumbe* evolved from the breezy, calypso-style guitar music called palm-wine or

REDFERNS VIA GETTY IMAGES / GETTY IMAGES ©

Senegalese artist Baaba Maal performs at Royal Festival Hall in London

maringa. The late SE Rogie and the Ghana-based elder statesman Koo Nimo, who also play highlife, are probably the best-known exponents.

Highlife

Ghana's urban, upbeat highlife, which started off in the dancehalls of the colonial Gold Coast, has had a ripple effect throughout West Africa. Trumpeter and band leader ET Mensah was the postwar, pan-African king of this sound, a blend of everything from Trinidadian calypso, brass-band music and Cuban son, to swing, jazz and older African song forms. Osibisa were *the* 'Afro-rock' pop-highlife group of the 1970s. Today's hybrids include gospel, hip-hop (hip-life) and the ever-popular guitar highlife. Amekye Dede and Jewel Ackah are popular highlife artists; Tic Tac, Sarkodie and FOKN Bois are living it large in hiplife. Highlife is also a staple of Sierra Leone, Liberia and (with a Congolese influence) Nigeria. Check out early recordings by Dr Victor Olaiya, Nigerian highlife's 'evil genius' and his band, Cool Cats.

Penned by Cuban ethnologist Carlos Moore, *Fela: This Bitch of a Life: The Authorised Biography of Africa's Musical Genius* (2010, Omnibus Press) is as it says. Based on many hours of conversation with Kuti himself, and re-issued to coincide with *FELA: The Musical*, which took London and Broadway by storm.

Juju

Juju music evolved from a mix of traditional Yoruba talking drums and folklore, and popular palm-wine guitar music. Its best known ambassador, King Sunny Ade, has been deploying his relentless blend of ringing guitar lines, multilayered percussion, tight harmonies and booty shaking for four decades now. In Nigeria he's known as KSA, the Minister for Enjoyment. Competition with his rival Sir Shina Peters continues. *Juju* is not to be confused with the Arabesque percussion frenzy that is *fuji*: main players include King Wasiu Ayinde Marshal (KWAM1) and King Saheed Osupa, who uses his songs to advise and educate his fans.

Makossa

A fusion of highlife and soul, influenced by Congolese rumba and characterised by electric guitars, Cameroon's distinctive pop-*makossa* music remains one of West Africa's most vibrant dance genres. Its biggest star is still the jazz-minded octogenarian sax player and singer Manu Dibango (track down his 1973 release, *Soul Makossa*), who has worked in related genres such as *mangambe*, *assiko* and *bikutsi*, and still sells out London venues such as Ronnie Scott's. The 1980s saw Sam Fan Thomas popularise *makassi*, a sort of *makossa*-lite. Other *makossa* names to look out for include Petit Pays, Sam Fan Thomas, Guy Lobe and the guitarist Vincent Nguini.

Mbalax

Taken from the Wolof word for rhythm, *mbalax* is Senegal's primary musical genre, an intensely polyrhythmic sound that evolved in the 1970s from Afro-Cuban dance bands such as the Star Band and Orchestra Baobab, and then fiercely reclaimed its African roots. Youssou N'Dour was the first to introduce more traditional elements, including *tassou* (a form of rap), *bakou* (a kind of trilling) and instruments such as the *tama* and *sabar* drums. Popular *mbalax* artists include Alloune Mbaye Nder, Fatou Gewel, Coumba Gawlo Seck and N'Dour's sister-in-law, Vivianne.

Reggae, Rap & Hip-Hop

Afro-reggae, rap and hip-hop are huge throughout West Africa. Elder Ivorian statesman Alpha Blondy has enjoyed a 20-year career, spawning hits like the classic 'Jerusalem', recorded in Jamaica with the Wailers. His younger, equally political, compatriots include Serge Kassy and Tiken Jah Fakoly. Ivorian hip-hop (think outfits such as 2431 and All Mighty) includes the gangsta-style rap dogba, which contrasts with the socially aware, antibling Wolof rap of Senegalese outfits such as Daara J and Positive Black Soul. In strife-torn Mali, rap music is now at the vanguard of messaging the population through music, including clarifying the political situation in the North and in Bamako. Rappers Amkoullel, Mylmoand Les Sofas de la Republique have much to say. Daddy Showkey is a well-known Nigerian reggae artist, and Nigerian hip-hop musicians include the duo P-Square along with Ice Prince and JJC aka Skillz. Rap Nigerien is a melange of different languages spoken in Niger – as deployed by groups such as Kamikaz and Metaphor – and covers such topics as forced marriages, child labour and corruption. The Gambia is the self-styled reggae capital of Africa; well-known artists include Horicane, Stalwart and Rebellion the Recaller.

Wassoulou

Wassoulou music is named after the region of the same name, south of Bamako in Mali, and the Fula people who inhabit it. Wassoulou is not *jeli* music – they have no castes – but is based on hunting songs. The women usually sing, and the men dance. The music is based on the *kamalengoni* (youth's harp) – a sort of funky, jittery bass guitar invented in the 1950s – and is augmented by the thwack and slap of the *fle*, a calabash strung with cowrie shells and thrown and spun in the air. Prominent artists include Oumou Sangare, Fatoumata Diawara and Coumbla Sidibei having shot to fame with her 1989 release, *Moussoulou*, Oumou Sangare is still the biggest Wassoulou star, singing in her native Bambara about injustices of life in West Africa – polygamy, the price of a bride – and is actively involved in Mali's burgeoning peace movement.

Afropop (www.afropop.org) aims to be the premier destination for web denizens interested in the contemporary music of Africa and the African diaspora; highlights include streaming audio and a searchable database.

Directed by Cheikhj Sene, better known as the rapper Keyti, *100% Galsen* is a 25-minute documentary about hip-hop in Senegal and a sort of grassroots versionof the multi-award-winning *Democracy in Dakar*, a 2007 film that presents a model for hip-hop as a force for social change.

MUSIC WEST AFRICAN MUSICAL STYLES

Arts & Craftwork

West Africa's artistic heritage, which encompasses traditional sculptures, masks, striking textiles and jewellery, is tied very much to the land and its people. Most such works were, in their original form, representations of the natural and spirit worlds. The creation of these arts and crafts is often the preserve of distinct castes of blacksmiths and weavers who rely on locally found or produced materials and many pieces still carry powerful meaning for West Africa's diverse peoples.

Masks

Some art historians believe that one of Picasso's most famous paintings, *Les Demoiselles d'Avignion*, depicts women wearing ceremonial Dogon masks.

In West Africa masks were rarely produced for purely decorative purposes. Rather, they were highly active signifiers of the spirit world and traditionally played a central role in ceremonies that served both to accompany important rites of passage and to entertain. There is a staggering range of shapes and styles of masks, all of which are invariably rich in meaning; they range from the tiny 'passport' mask of the Dan (Côte d'Ivoire) to the Dogon *imina-tiou* mask (Mali), which can tower up to 10m in height.

Masks, which are usually created by professional artisans, can be made of wood, brass, tin, leather, cloth, glass beads, natural fibres and even (in the case of the Ashanti) gold. They come in numerous forms, including face masks, helmet masks (which cover the whole head), headdresses (which are secured to the top of the head), the massive *nimba* masks of the Baga people in Guinea (which are carried on the dancer's shoulders) and the famous ivory hip masks from the Kingdom of Benin (present-day Nigeria), which are worn around the waist.

West African masks are usually classified as anthropomorphic (resembling the human form) and zoomorphic (the representation of deities in the form of animals). Anthropomorphic masks are often carefully carved and very realistic. Many groups use masks representing beautiful maidens, whose features reflect the aesthetic ideal of the people. The zoomorphic masks mostly represent dangerous and powerful nature spirits, and can be an abstract and terrifying combination of gaping jaws, popping eyes and massive horns. Some masks combine human and animal features. These convey the links between humans and animals, in particular the ability to gain and control the powers of animals and the spirits they represent.

African Elegance, by Ettagale Blauer, is a magnificently photographed chronicle of African art forms and their role in modern Africa. The sections on masks and jewellery are of particular interest.

The mask is only part of a complex costume that often covers the dancer's entire body. Made of plant fibre or cloth, often with elaborate appliqué, the costume is usually completed with a mane of raffia surrounding the mask. Most masks are associated with dance, although some are used as prestige symbols and are worn as amulets.

Textiles

Few places in the world can match West Africa for the beauty, vitality, colour and range of its textiles. Contrary to what many travellers expect, men are the main producers of textiles (the *bogolan* cloth of Mali is an exception), weaving wool, cotton, nylon, rayon and silk on a variety of looms. Most of West Africa's textiles follow the strip-cloth technique, whereby cloth is woven in narrow strips that are then sewn together. As many West Africans now wear Western clothes and traditional textiles are largely reserved for ceremonial occasions, the skills required to produce the finer textiles are disappearing, a trend that sales to collectors and tourists only partly ameliorates.

Kente Cloth

Clothing is one of the most important marks of distinction in Ashanti society, and the colourful kente cloth is the most famous expression of Ashanti exuberance. The basic traditional garment for men is a long rectangular piece of *ntoma* (cloth) passed over the left shoulder and brought around the body like a toga. The earliest kente cloth was cotton, but from the 18th century Ashanti weavers began incorporating designs using unravelled, imported Dutch silk. Silk has since gone on to be the fabric of prestige and the most expensive kente cloths contain silk (or imported rayon).

The weaving is done exclusively by men (usually working outdoors), who weave narrow, brightly coloured strips with complex patterns and rich hues. Kente cloth is worn only in the southern half of Ghana and is reserved for prestigious events. Although you'll find kente cloth on sale across Ghana, your best bet is to head to the Ashanti heartland, especially at Kumasi's Kejetia Market or the surrounding craft villages.

The Ewe also weave kente cloth, but their designs are somewhat different and include motifs of geometric figures. Every design has a meaning and some designs are reserved exclusively for royal families.

Adinkra Cloth

Just as impressive as the better-known kente cloth, adinkra cloth (a colourful cotton material with black geometric designs or stylised figures stamped on it) is also from Ghana. The word adinkra means 'farewell', and Ghanaians consider this fabric most appropriate for funerals.

Kente Cloth; Introduction to History, by Ernest Asamoah-Yaw, is a fascinating journey through the history of Ghana's most famous textile with good coverage of pattern and name origins.

African Textiles, by John Gillow, is at once visually eye-catching and a reasonably comprehensive study, including sections on Côte d'Ivoire, Mali, Sierra Leone, Cape Verde and the Niger Delta.

ARTS & CRAFTWORK TEXTILES

THE MASK COMES ALIVE

Behind almost every West African mask lies a story, often known only to members of a particular ethnic group. When masks and costumes are worn for a dance, which is accompanied by percussive music and song, they come alive and convey their meaning to the audience. Masked dances are used in initiation and coming-of-age ceremonies; in burial rituals, when dancing and celebrations assist the spirit of the dead to forsake the earth and reside with ancestors; in fertility rituals, which are associated with agriculture and the appeasement of spirits to ensure a successful harvest; and in the rituals surrounding childbirth. Masks fulfil the function of entertainment, with community-based dances and theatrical plays being created for social education and enjoyment.

The role of the mask is, however, changing. Christianity, Islam and the 20th century have all had a major impact on the animist masked dances of West Africa. Many dances are no longer performed, and others have transformed from sacred rituals to forms of entertainment. Since the arrival in Africa of tourists and collectors, artisans have begun to produce masks for widespread sale. Although this is a departure from the mask's role in traditional society, tourism can serve to keep artisans employed in their traditional art – evidence, perhaps, that masking traditions are never static and continue to transmute over time.

It's still possible to see masked dances in West Africa, although they may be specially arranged 'tourist performances'. Getting to see the real thing is often a matter of being in the right place at the right time.

ANGELA SEVIN PHOTOGRAPHY / GETTY IMAGES ©

Senegalese girls dressed in traditional African fabrics

Originally the printing was done on cotton pieces laid on the ground. Today, the cotton fabric is cut into long pieces, spread on a raised padded board and held in place by nails. The symbolic designs are cut on calabash stamps, and the dye is made from the bark of a local tree called *badie*. The printer dips the calabash into the hot dye and presses it onto the fabric. The rich colours are about far more than aesthetics: each colour has a special significance: vermilion (red) symbolises the earth, blue signifies love, and yellow represents success and wealth.

The village of Ntonso, close to Kumasi in central Ghana, is famous for its adinkra cloth.

Bogolan Cloth

Bogolan: Shaping Culture Through Cloth in Contemporary Mali, by Victoria L Rovine, is splendidly photographed and is a fine study of Mali's most recognisable textile art.

From the Sahel region of Mali comes *bogolan* cloth (called *bokolanfini* in Bambara, and often simply referred to as 'mud cloth'). This textile can be found in markets throughout West Africa, but its true home is in Djenné and Ségou, both in Mali.

The cloth is woven in plain cotton strips, sewn together and dyed yellow using a solution made from the leaves of a local tree. If you thought mud was mud, think again – after weaving, the cloth is covered in designs using various types of mud from different sources: mud from sandstone outcrops is used for reds and oranges; mud from riverbeds is used for blacks and greys. The cloth is left to dry in the sun, and the mud designs are then removed, leaving their imprint – the effect is very striking.

Designs are traditionally geometric and abstract, but *bogolan* cloth made specifically for tourists is more representational, showing animals, markets or village scenes. Some designs are very complex and involve many hours of work by the artists, who are all women.

Indigo Cloth

Another classic West African fabric is the indigo-dyed cotton worn primarily by the Tuareg as robes and headdresses. The indigo colour comes from the indigofera plant and the indigo vine; the plant is crushed and fermented, then mixed with an alkaline solution to produce the dye. The dyed cloth is often beaten with a mallet to produce a sheen. Among the Tuareg, cheaper dyed cotton from Nigeria or even China has begun to replace true indigo cloth, which can be outrageously expensive. Other West African peoples noted for their use of indigo include the Hausa, Dogon, Baoulé, Yoruba and Soninké, while it is also characteristic of Guinea's Fouta Djalon region.

The Yoruba produce an indigo-dyed cloth, *aderi,* which has designs that are applied using the tie-dye technique, or by painting motifs with a dye-resistant starch. The Dogon also produce an indigo cloth, which has geometric patterns.

Other Textiles

The Fula have a caste of weavers, called Maboub, who produce blankets known as *khasa*. These are usually made from camel hair, although the term is sometimes used to describe cotton blankets as well. The Maboub also make rare and expensive wedding blankets. These large and elaborately detailed textiles are traditionally displayed around the marriage bed.

The Fon and the Fanti are known for their appliqué banners and flags. Shapes of people and animals are cut from colourful material and are carefully sewn onto a cloth panel.

The Hausa are famous for their embroidery, which was once hand-stitched onto their robes and caps. Although they are now machine-stitched, the designs remain unchanged. In keeping with Islam, Hausa designs are nonfigurative.

Northern Côte d'Ivoire is famous for its Korhogo cloth, a coarse, cream-coloured cotton adorned with geometrical designs or fantastical animals.

In Morocco, 'Cactus silk' (or *soie végétale*) is made from cactus fibres typically woven with cotton (or synthetic) threads in another colour to produce cloth with a spectacular sheen and a starchy crispness. Moroccan embroidery ranges from simple Berber designs to minutely detailed terz fezzi, the elaborate nature-inspired patterns in blue on white linen that women in Fez traditionally spent years mastering for their dowries.

Jewellery

Jewellery is a West African tradition of extraordinary variety and, like all West African art forms, jewellery traditionally serves a purpose beyond the purely decorative.

Few jewellery items carry a wealth of associations quite like the humble bead, which is elevated to high art in this part of the world. Beads are often used as objects representing spiritual values and can play a major role in community rituals such as birth, circumcision, marriage and death. The availability of European products, which arrived via trans-Saharan trade caravans long before Europeans themselves, accelerated during the colonial period, altering the bead-making tradition significantly. Beads are now more likely to be made of glass, after local jewellers started copying the highly decorative *millefiori* trading beads from Venice, which featured flowers, stripes and mosaic designs. Discarded bottles and medicine jars were pulverised into a fine powder to be remade into glass beads, and the Krobo in Ghana

Africa Adorned, by Angela Fisher, is an extravagantly beautiful coffee-table book that could just be the finest of its kind, with some exceptional and detailed sections on African jewellery.

The use of crosses in Tuareg culture (in jewellery and the shape of pommels on their camel saddles) led early European explorers to speculate that they were once Christians.

RELIGIOUS IMAGES / UIG / GETTY IMAGES ©

Ghanaian jewellery

still melt powdered glass in terracotta moulds. In a slight variation, the Nupe in central Nigeria wind molten glass on long iron rods to make beads and bracelets. Referred to as *bakim-mutum* by bead traders (most of whom sell glass beads by weight, hence their other name, 'pound beads'), beads are commonly worn by village chiefs and elders as a sign of power and wealth.

A variety of other materials are used in Africa for making beads, including coral, shell, copal, amazonite, silver, gold and brass. In Mali you'll see large amber beads and ornate gold earrings worn by Fula women. The Dogon also treasure amber, and use it in their necklaces, bracelets and pendants. They also use beads made of stone and terracotta incised with geometric patterns.

> Iron is no longer smelted in the Dogon Country; many Dogon blacksmiths now use iron taken from abandoned motor vehicles, which withstands heating and shaping better than new iron.

Rings in West Africa can be stunning. In Burkina Faso, look for Bobo bronze rings, which often have intricate designs, including a tick bird, a warrior on horseback or a chameleon. In Mali, older Dogon men wear large bronze rings as a sign of status. Cowrie shells are often used to decorate jewellery; for a long time these shells were used as money in many areas of Africa.

In most areas of the region, the preferred metal for jewellery is gold; the Ashanti are famous for their goldwork in jewellery, ornaments and staffs. In and near the Sahara, however, the Tuareg and Moors prefer silver. The Tuareg are renowned for their intricate filigree silverwork in jewellery and in the decoration on the handles of their daggers. Tuareg men and women often wear silver crosses as pendants around their necks; in Niger, Mali and neighbouring Algeria these crosses differ from place to place, the most famous being the *croix d'Agadez,* while most are characterised by protective symbolism. Some incorporate circle and phallus designs, or fertility symbols; those representing a camel's eye or jackal tracks are symbolic of power and cunning.

Totems & Talismans

An important feature of traditional religions is the totem, an object (usually representing an animal) that serves as an emblem for a particular ethnic group, and is usually connected with the original ancestor of that group. It is taboo for a member of the clan whose totem is, for example, a snake, to harm any snake, as this would be harming the ancestor. Other common totems include lions, crocodiles and birds, although many of the animals themselves have disappeared from the West African wild.

Talismans (sometimes called fetishes) are another important feature in animism. These are objects (or charms) that are believed to embody a spirit, and can take many forms. For example, bird skulls and other animal parts may be used as charms by a learned elder for helping

---

WEST AFRICAN ARCHITECTURE – TOP PICKS

Mudbrick Mosques
➡ Djenné Mosque (Mali)
➡ Dyingerey Ber Mosque and Sankoré Mosque, Timbuktu (Mali)
➡ Grande Mosquée, Bobo-Dioulasso (Burkina Faso)
➡ The seven mosques of Bani (Burkina Faso)
➡ Grande Mosquée, Agadez (Niger)

Fortified Villages
➡ Dogon Country (Mali)
➡ Tamberma Valley (Togo)
➡ Lobi family compounds (Burkina Faso)

Painted Facades
➡ Gourounsi homes, Tiébélé (Burkina Faso)
➡ Tichit (Mauritania)
➡ Oualâta (Mauritania)

Saharan Architecture
➡ Ouadâne (Mauritania)
➡ Chinguetti (Mauritania)
➡ Timbuktu (Mali)
➡ Agadez (Mali)

Traditional Palaces & Forts
➡ Foumban (Cameroon)
➡ Bafut (Cameroon)
➡ Bafoussam (Cameroon)
➡ Abomey (Benin)
➡ Ashanti buildings, Kumasi (Ghana)
➡ Ghana's colonial-era forts

Stilt Villages
➡ Ganvié (Benin)
➡ Nzulezu (Ghana)

THE BLACKSMITH – MASTER OF THE BLACK ARTS

In many West African societies, an almost mystical aura surrounds the blacksmith who, perhaps more than any other artisan caste, occupies a special place in community life. Feared due to their strange communion with fire and iron, which is believed to render them immune to evil spirits and give them special powers, and respected for the pivotal role they play in ritual and daily life, blacksmiths provide an unbroken connection to West Africa's past. They are the makers of all manner of tools, weapons and household implements, but they also serve as intermediaries (between social groups and between the human and spirit worlds) and operate at the heart of many traditional ceremonies.

Despite their pivotal role in traditional life, blacksmiths often live on the margins of the community with whom they work. Among the Dogon people of Mali, for example, blacksmiths may not marry outside the blacksmith caste, but the blacksmith's anvil is considered the foundation of the village; if the anvil is moved, it is believed that the village may drift. Within Tuareg society, blacksmiths (known as *inaden*) are customarily viewed with suspicion by other Tuareg, and the blacksmiths traditionally lived on the periphery of towns and villages, even though Tuareg life would be impossible without them. Blacksmiths produce weapons and jewellery, and they're also healers, herbalists, poets, singers, skilled sacrificers of animals, advisers in matters of tradition and the custodians of oral traditions. Noble Tuareg women even confide in the *inaden,* using them as go-betweens in marriage negotiations and as mediators in love affairs. So important are they that no Tuareg festival could be complete without *inaden* participation, and anyone who tries to prevent them from attending is shunned by the whole community.

Other communities in which blacksmiths play a special role include the Bambara, Senoufo and Wolof.

people communicate with their ancestors. The elders (usually men) responsible for these sacred objects are sometimes called fetish priests or *féticheurs*.

The most common charms found throughout West Africa are the small leather or metal amulets, often containing a sacred object, which are worn by people around the neck, arm or waist. These are called *grigri* and are usually worn to ward off evil or bring good luck. Many West African Muslims (including the Tuareg) also wear *grigri*, which are called *t'awiz* in other Islamic countries; there is often a small verse from the Quran inside and they are only considered effective if made by a *marabout* (saint).

Starbook, by Ben Okri, is a stirring fictional fable that takes place among a mystical group of artists and artisans in West Africa in the lead-up to the colonial era.

Figurative Sculpture

African sculpture is now considered one of the most dynamic and influential art forms around. Once relegated to curio cabinets and dusty museum storerooms, and labelled as crude, barbaric and primitive, African carving finally gained credibility in the early 20th century when Picasso, Matisse and others found inspiration in its radical approach to the human form.

Most West African sculpture is carved in wood, but superb bronze and iron figures are also produced, while some funerary figures are created in terracotta and mud. The strange and uncompromising forms found in West African sculpture are rarely the unique creations of an inspired artist – the sculptures have always been made to fulfil specific functions, using centuries-old designs redolent with meaning.

In West Africa, sculpture is mostly used in connection with ancestor or spirit worship. Many groups believe that the spirits of the dead can have a major impact, both positive and negative, on a person's life. Ancestral figures are carved and placed in shrines and altars where they receive libations and sacrificial blood. Some groups carve figures that are cared for by women to ensure fertility and in the hope that the resulting child will inherit the fine looks represented in the sculpture. The famous *akuaba* 'doll' of the Ashanti is the best-known example of this. Prestige objects are also carved, such as figurative staffs of office, commemorative statues and other regalia used by kings, chiefs, traditional healers and diviners as emblems of power.

West African sculpture is usually created by a professional artist, who is almost always male and who has learned his craft through an apprenticeship. It's mostly a family- or caste-specific occupation, and the forms and skills are passed down from generation to generation, resulting in highly refined styles.

Across the many styles produced in West Africa, some common characteristics exist. The figure is usually symmetrical and faces forward, the features are impassive and the arms are held to the side with the legs slightly bent at the knees. Certain features may be exaggerated, and the head is almost always large in proportion to the body.

The surface of the carving will often have tribal marks carved or burnt into the blackened face and torso. Sometimes the carving is highly polished, or painted with ochre or imported enamel paint.

Bronze & Brass Casting

West Africa's best-known castings were created for the Kingdom of Benin in present-day Nigeria. Plaques, statues and masks were produced to decorate the palaces and compounds of the kings and chiefs, and their discovery (and plundering) by Western governments and collectors did at least serve to challenge the prevailing view that African cultures were primitive.

West African brass and bronze is often cast using the *cire perdue* (lost wax) technique. The casting process involves creating a sculpture out of wax, which is then dipped in a silt-and-mud solution. When the sculpture is dry, clay is built around the form to create a strong mould. The mould is heated and the wax is melted out. Molten bronze is then poured into the empty mould and, when cool, the mould is broken away to reveal the bronze sculpture. Each cast is therefore unique. This process is thought to have produced the 1000-year-old beautifully intricate statues of the Ibo-Ikwu, which can be seen today in the National Museum in Lagos. Today, latex is often used instead of wax, which creates even finer detail.

The Yoruba cast ritual staffs called *edan*. These comprise male and female figures in bronze, surmounting an iron tip and joined together by a chain. Figurative weights for weighing gold were cast by the Ashanti, and often symbolised the colourful proverbs for which they are known.

Visual Arts

Calligraphy

Calligraphy is the standout visual art form in Morocco, practised and perfected in Moroccan *medersa* (Quranic schools) over the last thousand years. The Quran praises lines written with the *qalam*, or reed-handled pen, and it's easy to see why: it takes a steady hand and a light touch to use this fine-tipped brushpen, but it does make a glorious impression. Sometimes the elegant letters are so cleverly intertwined they're hard to read, even for very learned Moroccans – but most form an *aya*, or Quranic verse.

The style most commonly used for Qurans is Naskh, a slanting cursive script introduced by the Ummayads. Cursive letters ingeniously interlaced to form a shape or dense design are hallmarks of the Thuluth style, while high-impact graphic lettering is the Kufic style from Iraq.

West Africa: African Art and the Colonial Encounter, by Sidney Littlefield Kasfir, can be a little academic, but the influence of colonialism on African art forms is a fascinating subject.

PLAQUES

Among the British Museum's fine collection of Benin statues are 16th-century plaques depicting the Portuguese in knee breeches and boots, feathered hats, matchlocks, cross-hilt daggers and accompanied by dogs.

Zellij

Zellij is the art of Moroccan-style mosaics. Each *zellij* tile is individually sculpted in a precise geometric shape with a small hammer and screw-driver-sized chisel. Each tile must be exactly the right colour and shape, so that it fits together perfectly with hundreds or thousands of others to create a consistent pattern that covers an entire wall, floor or fountain. The best *zellij* is cut in small pieces that fit together so perfectly that the mortar is barely visible between pieces, and the surface appears smooth and almost unbroken. *Zellij* artisans can create 360 different shapes, and each one can take weeks or even months to master.

Zellij maâlems (master artisans) from Fez are generally considered the Nobel Prize winners of Moroccan mosaics, although those from Marrakesh and Meknès are not far behind.

Butabu: Adobe Architecture of West Africa, by James Morris, is a stunning photographic study of West Africa's traditional architecture with informative text; a great reminder of your visit.

Peoples of West Africa

Perhaps more than anything else, it's West Africa's people and the richness of their cultural traditions that lure travellers to the region. Beyond the French-speaking world this is Africa's least-known corner, and the diversity of distinct languages, histories and customs you'll encounter in West Africa is astounding.

Ashanti

Inhabiting the now-thinning forest of south-central Ghana, the Ashanti, an Akan-speaking people, are among West Africa's best-known peoples. Their fame derives in part from their artefacts and symbols (among them kente and *adinkra* cloth), which have become prized among collectors in the West. But it's the Ashanti affinity with gold, with its echoes of West Africa's great empires of antiquity, which gives them their greatest resonance.

In the 18th century, the Ashanti king, the Asantehene, united the fractured feudal states of what is now Ghana and, ruling from his capital at Kumasi, brought peace and prosperity to the country; Ashanti political administration was among the most sophisticated in West Africa prior to the colonial period. Everything about the Ashanti kingdom glittered with gold: the Asantehene controlled the region's most prolific gold mines, the goldsmiths of the royal court were among West Africa's most practised artisans and the kingdom's trading reach extended across the world. The Asantehene's sacred golden stool, which may only be shown in public four times each century, became the ongoing symbol of Ashanti extravagance.

Ashanti power waned with the arrival of British colonial forces and, later, was subsumed into the multi-ethnic modern state of Ghana. But Ashanti culture maintains a strong hold over Ghana, and modern Ghanaian leaders ignore the traditional Ashanti rulers at their peril.

The 1995 silver jubilee of the then-Asantehene Otumfuo Opoku Ware II became one of the most lavish traditional ceremonies in West Africa in modern times, attended by 75,000 people and showcasing an incredible collection of golden royal regalia.

Bambara

The Bambara (also known as Bamana) are the largest ethnic group in Mali. Concentrated in the south and centre of the country, they comprise around one-third of the population.

Although the Bambara are a predominantly Muslim people, their belief systems are laced with traditional beliefs and customs. Bambara men, for example, must pass through six secret societies during a seven-year coming-of-age initiation rite, a process that culminates in a symbolic death and rebirth. Masks play a spiritually charged role in traditional Bambara culture.

Bambara tradition decrees a highly regulated occupational caste system, among whose ranks are farmers, leather-workers, poets and blacksmiths. Each occupational group or caste has its own initiation rituals, for which particular masks are required, and only blacksmiths inherit the capacity to tap into the spiritual power, or *nyama*, that enables them to transform wood and iron into masks and other religious objects. Because *nyama* is inherited, blacksmiths must marry within their own occupational group. Blacksmiths also make hoes, door locks and guns, all of which are furnished with spiritual power as well as utility. Door locks often have a water-lizard symbol to protect the house from thieves, or a long-eared creature similar to a bat that is said to hear every sound, thus protecting the household.

Baoulé

The Baoulé of eastern and central Côte d'Ivoire, like the Ashanti of Ghana, are an Akan-speaking farming people. Their origins lie in Ghana, which they fled in the 16th century as Ashanti power grew. As they fled west, so the story goes, they came up against a river which they were unable to cross. With their pursuers close behind, they threw their most prized possessions into the river, among them the son of their ruler, Queen Pokou, whereupon hippopotami rose up to provide a bridge, allowing them to cross the river. The queen's lament of *baouli* (which means 'the child is dead') became the sorrowful name of a people.

The Baoulé claim to have resisted French colonial power longer than any other West African group. The Baoulé are distinguished by their belief in the *blolo* (meaning 'elsewhere' or 'the beyond'), another world, parallel to our own. A man may even have a *blolo bla,* a wife from beyond, and a woman a *blolo bian,* or other husband. Both can influence a partner's wellbeing, marital stability and sex life, usually negatively. Soothsayers play an important role in Baoulé culture; they're often used to 'call in' or 'bring down' the *blolo* partner to prevent further havoc. This can be done either by moulding a cone of fine kaolin clay mixed with secret herbs, or by fashioning a clay or wooden statue of the *blolo* partner, thus controlling the parallel-world partner.

> Baoulé society is considered to be one of West Africa's most egalitarian: everyone, from village elders to slaves, traditionally had a voice in the important decisions of Baoulé life.

Berber

For at least 5000 years, Morocco has been inhabited by a people with Saharan, Mediterranean and Sub-Saharan African roots collectively known as the Amazigh, or 'free people'. True to their name, they successfully ousted the many armies who swaggered into Amazigh territory with a mind to claiming it for themselves. The Romans certainly tried – for 250 years – and when they couldn't defeat their foes they badmouthed them, calling them 'Berbers', or Barbarians.

More than 60% of Moroccans now call themselves Amazigh or Berber, and Berber languages are currently spoken by upwards of 12 to 15 million Moroccans. Tashelhit is the most common Berber language, and is widely spoken in central Morocco. You'll also hear Tarifit along the Rif and Tamazight in the Middle Atlas.

With the backing of King Mohammed VI – who is part Berber himself – the ancient written Tifinagh alphabet has been recently revived as a national language, and is now being taught in some schools. Within the next decade, Berber will be taught in public schools across Morocco, along with the new lingua franca of trade and tourism: English.

Bobo

The ancestors of the 100,000 Bobo people arrived in West Africa almost 1200 years ago and the Bobo now occupy western Burkina Faso, around Bobo-Dioulasso, and southern Mali. The Bobo traditionally showed little interest in conquest. As a result, they made few enemies and thereby managed to escape subjugation by the powerful Mossi who ruled from Ouagadougou.

> The form of a butterfly is used in Bobo masks because butterflies appear in great swarms immediately after the first rains and are thus associated with the planting season.

The Bobo cosmology revolves around the creator god Wuro, who creates balance in the world by dividing everything into pairs. In the Bobo world view, human disruption to this natural order can only be rectified by Wuro, but as Wuro may neither be addressed nor spoken of nor depicted in any form, the Bobo communicate with Wuro through a mediating deity, Do. That effort to commune with Do gives the Bobo

Nigerian Fula (p432) girl

their most recognisable cultural forms, the renowned Bobo mask tradition, especially the famous butterfly and helmet masks. They are worn during funeral rites, and when invoking Do in planting-time ceremonies asking for rain and a good harvest. Other animals represented in Bobo masks include owls, buffaloes, antelopes, crocodiles and scorpions.

Dan

The animist Dan (also known as the Yacouba) inhabit the mountainous area around Man in Côte d'Ivoire, spilling over the border into Liberia. Although part of the wider Mande tradition, they are set apart by their Dan language, of which there are more than 320,000 speakers. Until recently Dan society lacked any overarching social organisation, with each village looking after its own affairs, although the secret leopard society (known as *go*) has become an important unifying vehicle for peacemaking between Dan communities. In Dan tradition, lavish giftgiving is considered an essential means of advancing socially.

Masks are an important element of Dan culture and the Dan mask tradition is one of Africa's most highly developed. Each village has several great masks that represent its collective memory and which are glorified during times of happiness and abundance. Masks are regarded both as divinities and repositories of knowledge. They dictate the community's values that give the clan cohesiveness and help preserve its customs. For example, harvest-time yields, or whether a woman will give birth to a son or a daughter, are believed to depend on masks, and no important action is undertaken without first addressing a mask to request its assistance.

Dogon: People of the Cliffs, by Agnes Pateaux, combines beautiful photography with text that gets to the heart of Dogon society, from the aura of blacksmiths to the changes assailing Dogon ways.

Dogon

The Dogon, who live along Mali's Falaise de Bandiagara (Bandiagara Escarpment), are among the region's most intriguing people, having unusual belief systems, masks and ceremonies.

TRADITIONAL CULTURE

Chances to experience and access traditional culture include the following:

⇒ The Moro-Naba ceremony is held every Friday in **Ouagadougou** (p60)

⇒ **Musée de Poni** (p69) in Gaoua is an excellent introduction to Lobi culture

⇒ **Kumasi** (p189) has monuments and museums dedicated to Ashanti traditions

⇒ **Ikeji** is the annual new yam festival; the most important Ikeji festival takes place in September at Arochukwu in southeastern Nigeria

The Dogon are traditionally farmers, and work for both men and women is a central feature of Dogon society. Crops such as millet and onions are planted in the fields below and atop the escarpment and on terraces created on the lower slopes. Unsurprisingly, many Dogon now choose to farm down on the plains where water is more plentiful.

Although Islam and Christianity have taken hold among many Dogon, traditional belief systems remain at the centre of Dogon life. Rituals surrounding masks, ceremonies, sacred spaces and the Dogon relationship with the natural world are among the most intricate in Africa.

Ewe

The Ewe people live in Ghana and are the most important ethnic group in southern Togo. The Ewe, who inhabit forests and fertile riverine soils, are accomplished agriculturalists and their cultivation of yams (a staple of the Ewe diet) has taken on a near-mythical status. The annual Ewe Yam Festival, called Hogbetsotso, is the highlight of the Ewe year and involves farmers presenting their crops to the ancestors and purifying ceremonial stools where, the Ewe believe, ancestral spirits reside. Funeral rites are another intricate Ewe ceremony.

Ewe chiefs, who are elected by consensus, must keep their heads covered in public and must never be seen to be drinking. More generally, the Ewe are known for their hard work, tidy villages, their love of education, their spirituality, and the power of their traditional shrines and priests.

The arts play an important role in Ewe life, with their subtly coloured kente cloth (which they learned from Ashanti weavers taken as prisoners by the Ewe) and for their *vu gbe* (talking drums) taking centre stage. The tonality of the Ewe spoken language and the rhythm of particular phrases and proverbs are combined in drumming to produce messages that range from the commonplace, which everyone understands, to a specialised repertoire known only to the master drummers. Drum language is used for communication, especially in times of crisis, and is an integral part of religious song and dance.

More than half of the almost 280 million West Africans are Nigerians. The numbers of Yoruba, Hausa or Igbo alone each exceed the national population of every other national country.

Fula

One of the most widespread of West African peoples, the Fula (also called Fulani, Peulh or Foulbé in French-speaking countries) are tall, lightly-built people who have been settling across the West African savannah and Sahel for centuries. They number more than 12 million, and are found from Senegal to Cameroon, and sometimes beyond. The Tukulor (Toucouleur) and the Wolof of Senegal, as well as the Fulbe Jeeri of Mauritania, are all of Fula origin.

Cattle occupy a central position in society and the Fula are traditionally nomadic cattle herders, following their herds in search of pasture and living in seasonal grass huts resembling large beehives; they're famous for putting the welfare of their animals above their own. Islam also plays a central role: town-dwelling Fula (Fulani Gida in some areas) adopted Islam as early as the 12th century and were major catalysts in its spread. Fula resistance to colonial rule was fierce, usually coalescing around a inspirational Islamic leader.

The nomadic Fula, or Wodaabé, are known for their public initiation ceremony in which young boys are lashed with long rods to the accelerating rhythm of drums, as part of their passage into manhood. There are many onlookers, including potential brides, and the boys must show no fear, though their ordeal leaves them scarred. At the annual Gerewol festival, where the young Wodaabé meet prospective marriage partners, men pay great attention to their appearance, adorning themselves with shining jewellery, feathers, sunglasses and elaborate make-up – anything to create an impression, and to look their best for the women.

Hausa

The dominant cultural group in northern Nigeria (Hausaland), the Hausa (with 27 million in Nigeria and almost six million in Niger) have played an important role in West African history. From their bases in Kano, Katsina, Sokoto and Zaria, the Hausa developed a reputation as a fiercely independent mercantile people, with Islam the dominant force. This mix of spiritual devotion and worldliness means that you'll likely see Quranic script alongside symbols of modern technology, such as bicycles and aeroplanes, in the mud-relief patterns on house walls in the old quarters of Nigerian towns such as Kano and Zaria.

The emirs of the Hausa states are known for the pomp with which they live and travel. Their bodyguards traditionally wear chain mail, carry spears and ride strikingly caparisoned horses, while attendants on foot wear red turbans, and brilliant red-and-green robes. Except on ceremonial occasions, especially during the Islamic festivals of Eid al-Kebir (Tabaski) and Eid al-Fitr, these days you'll more likely see an emir riding through town in a large American car, with the horn sounding – very Nigeria.

Although the city states, caliphates and trappings of power of Hausaland are what brought the group its renown, rural communities are the bedrock of Hausa society. Many rural Hausa farm grains, cotton and groundnuts; sacks of groundnuts stacked in pyramids are one of the distinctive sights of many Hausa markets.

Igbo

The Igbo (also known as Ibo) occupy densely settled farming areas in southeastern Nigeria. They form Nigeria's third-largest ethnic group with around 25 million Igbos in Nigeria alone. Their proximity to the Gulf of Guinea saw them devastated by slavery, while more than one million Igbo died during the Biafran War (1967–70). The Igbo have a reputation for hard work, ambition and a love of education.

Although predominantly Christian, many Igbo still practise the traditional religion of Odinani. An Igbo receives his destiny or *chi* directly from Chukwu, the benign god or 'great spirit' of creation. At death, a person returns his *chi* and joins the world of ancestors and spirits. From this spirit world, the deceased watches over living descendants, perhaps returning one day with a different *chi*. A traditionalist's daily preoccupation is to please and appease the *alusa,* the lesser spirits, who can blight a person's life if offended and bestow rewards if pleased.

Lobi

Tucked away in southwestern Burkina Faso, northern Côte d'Ivoire and northern Ghana, the Lobi have held fast to their traditions and ancestor-based belief systems more than most groups in the region. The Lobi are also distinguished by their architecture (they live in distinctive

Genii of the River Niger, by Jean-Marie Gibbal, is a fascinating study of the river peoples of eastern Mali, in particular their struggles to hold fast to traditional mythology in the face of Islam's march.

Women dancing in a Lobi (p433) village, Burkina Faso

mud-brick compounds resembling small fortresse) and by the fact that they don't use masks. Their name means 'Children of the Forest'.

Most Lobi woodcarvings are of human figures, typically 35cm to 65cm high, which represent deities and ancestors. The woodcarvings are used for ancestral shrines, and traditionally occupied every home. The Lobi also carve staffs and three-legged stools with human or animal heads, as well as combs with human figures or geometric decorations. Lobi carvings are distinguished by their rigid appearance, and for their realistic and detailed renderings of certain body parts, particularly the navel, eyes and hair.

Many Lobi ceremonies take place on or near the banks of the Mouhoun (or Black Volta) River which divides Ghana and Burkina Faso and, in Lobi tradition, separates this world from the afterlife. Fish and animals in the river are believed to be sacred, while fetishes, the spirit world and village priests still play an important role in daily Lobi life.

Lobi tradition, backed by the accounts of some Christian missionaries, holds that a Lobi man once converted to Christianity and threw his fetishes in a nearby lake, whereupon the fetishes leapt from the water to reclaim him.

Malinké

The Malinké (in some areas synonymous with, or closely related to, the Mandinka or Mandingo) are part of the larger Mande group, which also includes the Bambara and Soninké and is believed to have originated as early as 4000 years ago when agricultural peoples of the southern Sahara merged with the indigenous hunter-gatherers of the Niger River basin. Today, the Malinké are known as prolific traders and live in southern Mali as well as northern Guinea, Côte d'Ivoire, Senegal and The Gambia. Historically, they were famed hunters and warriors, and were prominent converts to Islam from the 11th century. In the mid-13th century the Malinké founded the powerful Empire of Mali.

Originally the Malinké were divided into 12 clans, each with its own king and highly stratified castes. The heads of these 12 clans formed a royal council, which elected a single leader, known as a *mansa*. The traditional hunter societies of the Malinké, with their secret initiation rites, still thrive today.

Music also accompanies almost all of the important events in Malinké life and its tradition of *jelis* or *griots* (praise singers) dates back to the days of the Empire of Mali. *Griots* were traditionally the custodians of West Africa's oral traditions and many born into the *griot* caste now rank among Mali's most famous musicians.

Mossi

When the empires of Mali and Songhaï reigned over West Africa from the 13th to 16th centuries, one group remained outside their orbit: the Mossi, now the largest ethnic group in Burkina Faso. In the 14th century they established powerful kingdoms in this area after leaving their original homeland around the Niger River, and they held off the larger empires of the time through a fierce army of feared warriors. The Mossi are known for their rigid social hierarchies and elaborate rituals, and many Mossi continue to follow traditional beliefs. They also exert considerable political influence in Burkina Faso today and the Mossi ruler, the 37th Moro-Naba, is regularly consulted on important issues by the government.

Artistically, the Mossi are best known for their tall wooden antelope masks, often more than 2m high and painted red and white. The masks were worn primarily at funerals.

Half of a Yellow Sun, by Nigerian novelist Chimanda Ngozi Adichie, is a stirring tale of the Biafra War with a nuanced look at the often fraught relations between Nigeria's main ethnic groups.

Senoufo

The Senoufo, a farming people who live in Côte d'Ivoire, western Burkina Faso and southern Mali, are, like the Lobi, renowned for having maintained their traditions in the face of assaults by colonialism, Islam and Christianity. The northern Côte d'Ivoire town of Korhogo is considered the Senoufo capital.

Animals are held in high regard in Senoufo culture, and when someone dies it is believed that they are transformed into the clan's animal totem. As a result, many Senoufo dances are associated with animals. One of these is the dance of the leopard men, which is performed in Natiokabadara, near Korhogo, as well as in other Senoufo areas when young boys return from their Poro (part of the secret Lô society) initiation-training sessions. In this and other dances, spirit masks (often of animal heads) are instrumental in making contact with the gods and driving away bad spirits.

When someone dies in traditional Senoufo society, the corpse is carried through the village in a procession, while men in grotesque masks chase away the soul of the deceased to ensure it leaves the village in peace and departs for the afterlife.

African Ceremonies, by Carol Beckwith and Angela Fisher, is a masterpiece, a stunning two-volume coffee-table book of photos of different rites and festivals from across Africa.

Songhaï

The Songhaï, heirs to the Empire of Songhaï, live predominantly in Niger and in northern Mali, between Timbuktu and Gao. They trace their roots back to a 7th- or 8th-century exodus from Mandinke lands, while other theories claim that the Tuareg founded the original Songhaï state; yet another hypothesis states that the ancestors of the Songhaï were the original inhabitants of the Upper Niger.

Songhaï villages are divided into neighbourhoods, each of which elects a head. These heads then come together to elect a village chief, who typically is of noble descent. Most Songhaï consider themselves Muslim, although their religious practices are often mixed with strong traditional elements, including ancestor worship and witchcraft. Large communities often have both a mosque and a troupe that specialises in mediums for spirit intervention.

Tuareg

The Tuareg are a nomadic people who traditionally roamed the Sahara from Mauritania to western Sudan; they now live in Niger, Mali, Libya and Algeria, with smaller communities in Burkina Faso and Nigeria. Tuareg origins lie with the Berbers of North Africa (their language, Tamashek, has Berber roots). Droughts and political conflict have ensured that few Tuareg remain purely nomadic.

The Tuareg traditionally follow a rigid status system, with nobles, blacksmiths and slaves all occupying strictly delineated hierarchical positions. The veils, or *taguelmoust,* that are the symbols of a Tuareg's identity serve as protection against the desert sand and wind-borne spirits, and as a social requirement; it is considered improper for a Tuareg man to show his face to a man of higher status.

Tuareg women – who are not veiled and who enjoy an unusual degree of independence – weave artificial strands into their plaits to which they attach cowrie shells. They also can be recognised by their large pieces of silver jewellery.

The Pastoral Tuareg: Ecology, Culture, and Society, by Johannes and Ida Nicolaisen, is a comprehensive two-volume study of the Tuareg with good photographs.

Wolof

The Wolof heartland is in Senegal, where they comprise about 43% of the population. They also live in Gambia (16%) and Mauritania (7%).

Although Islam has been an influence in Wolof areas since the 11th century, and Sufi Muslim Brotherhoods form the backbone of Wolof society, traditional beliefs persist. For example, there is a belief in a snake monster so terrible that to look upon it causes death. In order to guard against witches and other forms of evil, many Wolof wear leather-bound amulets containing written verses of the Quran.

Wolof society is hierarchical, with hereditary castes determining traditional occupations such as blacksmiths and *griots* (praise singers) and status. The Wolof, who are of Fula origin, tend to be tall and striking in their traditional flowing robes of white, dark blue or black.

Famous members of the Senegalese Wolof community include musician Youssou N'Dour, the late filmmaker Ousmane Sembène, and the former president of Senegal, Abdoulaye Wade.

Yoruba

The Yoruba, almost 30-million strong, are perhaps the largest ethnic group in West Africa, with their homeland extending from southwestern Nigeria into neighbouring Benin. It was here that the powerful Yoruba Kingdom of Ife (12th to 16th centuries) and Oyo Empire (17th to early 20th centuries) held sway over one of the region's most populous corners.

Yoruba traditionally live in towns, migrating seasonally to their more distant farmlands; the Nigerian cities of Lagos and Ibadan are considered important centres of Yoruban life. The urban culture of the Yoruba has facilitated the development of trade and elaborate arts, including the famous Benin bronzes. Every Yoruba town has an *oba* (crowned chief). The traditional head of all Yorubas is the *alafin,* who lives at Oyo, in Nigeria, while the *oni* (chief priest) lives at Ife. Formality, ceremony and hierarchy govern Yoruba social relations, and ostentation in dress and jewellery is a social requirement for women at traditional functions.

Many Yoruba are now Christian, although traditional practices persist, among them the belief that ancestor spirits, which reside in an afterworld known as Kutome, hold powers of protection over the living. During the annual Egungun Festival, these ancestors are summoned by members of the secret Egungun masking society to return, so as to restore the cosmic balance upset by human failings, and to advise their descendants.

The Yoruba have the highest ratio of twin births of any group in the world and twins occupy an important role in Yoruba mythology.

Environment

West Africa's numerous environmental woes – and the precarious subsistence conditions in which many West Africans live – exist alongside some stunning success stories, such as the greening of central Niger and the survival of Mali's desert elephants. It is also, according to one UN official, the world's 'ground zero' for vulnerable communities when it comes to climate change. It's as simple and as complicated as that: West Africa faces some of the most pressing environmental issues of our time.

The Land

West Africa spans some of the great landscapes of the African continent. Its geography is the story of three horizontal lines: a northern band of desert, a southern band of woodland and forest, and a semidesert zone in between known as the Sahel. Through it all snakes the region's lifeblood, the Niger River.

Although West Africa largely consists of a gently undulating plateau, there are some important highland areas: the borderlands between Nigeria and Cameroon rising to Chappal Wadi (2418m); the Jos Plateau (1781m) and Shebsi Mountains (2418m) in Nigeria; Mt Bintumani (1945m) in Sierra Leone; the rocky Aïr Mountains in Niger, rising to Mt Bagzane (2022m); Mt Nimba (1752m) in the border area between Guinea, Côte d'Ivoire and Liberia; and the Fouta Djalon in western Guinea (1538m). The peaks of the volcanic Cape Verde islands are also notable, with the highest being Mt Fogo (2829m). Mt Cameroon (4095m) is the highest point in West Africa.

West Africa's highlands create headwaters for several rivers, including the Niger. Other major rivers include the Senegal River, which forms the border with Mauritania; the Gambia River, again giving its name to the country it flows through; the Casamance River in southern Senegal; the Volta River in Ghana and Burkina Faso; and the Benue River (a major tributary of the Niger) in Nigeria and Cameroon.

If West Africa is overshadowed by the looming Sahara to the north, it is barricaded by the equally formidable Atlantic Ocean to the south. Many major cities (including 12 out of 17 West African capitals) are strung out along the coast like beads in a chain, in some areas forming an almost constant linear urban sprawl, cut only by national frontiers.

The Sahara

The Sahara is a notoriously unwieldy beast to quantify, but most estimates put its size at over nine million sq km, comparable in size to the continental United States. The Sahara occupies more than half of Mali, 75% of Mauritania and 80% of Niger.

The Sahara may be the world's largest desert, but it is also the youngest. Thousands of years ago the Sahara was a fertile land, alternating between savannah grasslands, forests and lakes watered by relatively frequent rainfall. It was home to abundant wildlife – elephants, giraffes, hippos, lions and other African mega-fauna – as depicted in the rock art

The UNEP's *Africa: Atlas of Our Changing Environment* (2008) is the definitive study of Africa's environment, with a detailed continental overview, country-by-country statistics and before-and-after satellite photos. It's available from www.earthprint.com.

Sahara: A Natural History, by Marq de Villiers and Sheila Hirtle, covers the natural and human history of the Sahara like no other recent book, and the lively text makes it a pleasure to read.

FRANS LANTING / GETTY IMAGES ©

A bushbuck in the Mole National Park (p195), Ghana

TOGO

found across the Sahara, especially in Niger's Aïr Mountains and Mali's Adrar des Ifôghas. The change began around 7000 years ago, when rains became less frequent and the land more arid. It was a gradual process that took 4000 years. As the Sahara became a desert, its people and wildlife retreated south. By 400 BC, the Sahara was the desert we know today, albeit on a smaller scale.

Contrary to popular misconceptions, sand covers just 20% of the Sahara's surface and just one-ninth of the Sahara rises as sand dunes. More typical of the Sahara are the vast gravel plains and plateaus such as the Tanezrouft of northwestern Mali. The Sahara's other signature landform is the desert massif, barren mountain ranges of sandstone, basalt and granite such as the Aïr Mountains (Niger) and Adrar des Ifôrhas (Mali).

By one estimate, the Sahara is home to 1400 plant species, 50 species of mammal and 18 species of bird.

The Sahel

Nearly half of Togo's land is considered arable, making it one of only two countries in Africa with more than 40% of its land suitable for farming. Just 0.2% of Mauritania can support agriculture.

The Sahel – a horizontal band stretching from the Atlantic coast to the Nile – is the transition zone between the forested lands of the south and the Sahara to the north. The Sahel is one of the direst stretches of inhabited geography on earth, beset by drought, erosion, creeping desertification, periodic locust invasions and increasingly infertile land.

That said, within its boundaries are many different subregions. Among these are zones that are variously described as semidesert savannah, Guinea savannah, Sudanese savannah, dry savannah or dry woodland savannah. In the north, near the true desert, the Sahel is dry, dusty, sparsely vegetated and barely distinguishable from the Sahara, but in the south, nearer the forests, it is greener and contains areas of light woodland fed by more plentiful rains.

Although the Sahel's boundaries are not fixed, the countries of West Africa that are considered to be all or partly in the Sahel are Senegal,

The Gambia, Guinea, Mali, Burkina Faso, Niger and Nigeria. The northern parts of the coastal countries of Côte d'Ivoire, Ghana, Togo, Benin and Cameroon are relatively dry and sometimes described as having a Sahelian climate or vegetation.

Wildlife

Human beings rule in West Africa, and it's possible that, no matter how long you spend here, you may never see more than the occasional reptile or hear more than a troop of monkeys, caterwauling through the trees but out of view. The once-plentiful wildlife of the region has been reduced by deforestation, encroaching deserts, ever-expanding human populations and drought to small, isolated pockets. As a result, West African animals are wild, wary and unaccustomed to large-scale safari tourism.

But, for all the doom and gloom, West Africa is the continent's most underrated wildlife-watching region. Its excellent national parks are home to many of Africa's classic mammal species. Yes, you have to travel further to see the animals than elsewhere on the continent, and these animals may retreat into the canopy at the first sign of human beings. For wildlife-watching purists, however, this is how wildlife safaris used to be: a place where the sense of a real quest survives without carloads of camera-toting tourists outnumbering the animals.

West Africa is also a world-class birding destination.

Mammals

First, some good news. Two of West Africa's most emblematic and endangered herds – the giraffes at Kouré in Niger and Mali's desert elephants – are holding their own in the most difficult of circumstances.

African Silences, by Peter Matthiessen, is a classic on African wildlife; the passages on Senegal, The Gambia and Côte d'Ivoire are so beautifully written that you'll return to them again and again.

SOS Sahel International (www.sossahel.org) is an NGO dedicated to the Sahel environment. It can be a good source of information on grassroots projects in the region.

ENVIRONMENT WILDLIFE

THE NIGER RIVER

Africa's third-longest river (4100km), the Niger owes its name to the Tuareg phrase *gher-n-gheren,* which means 'river among rivers', and its curious course has fascinated travellers for centuries.

The Niger begins its journey just over 200km from the Atlantic, at a spring in the Fouta Djalon highlands, on the Guinea–Sierra Leone border. Gathering strength and volume from countless mountain streams, the Niger flows deep into West Africa's heart, through the vast Niger Inland Delta of central Mali. From there, the Niger narrows and comes within touching distance of Timbuktu before it comes up against the impenetrable barrier of the Sahara and performs a long, laborious curve (known as the Niger Bend or Boucle du Niger). Thereafter, it courses down into Niger and crosses a slice of Benin before emptying into the Atlantic via a maze of swamps and channels (in Nigeria, west of Port Harcourt) called the Niger Delta.

Apart from its initial descent from the western highlands, the Niger flows on an extremely low gradient and is fed by highly variable rainfall. As such, its high and low points can vary by an extraordinary 10.7m and the river is highly susceptible to drought: in 1972 and again in 1984, the river almost dried up completely. Even more serious than the vagaries of seasonal fluctuations are the threats posed by human activity: by one estimate, the Niger's volume has fallen by 55% since the 1980s due to climate change, drought, pollution and population growth. Fish stocks have fallen, water hyacinth is a recurring problem, and the formation of sand bars has made navigation increasingly difficult. Given that an estimated 110 million people live in the Niger's basin, problems for the Niger could cause a catastrophic ripple well beyond the river's shoreline.

It may be almost 20 years old, but *The Strong Brown God,* by Sanche de Gramont, remains the most comprehensive geographical and human history of the Niger.

THE BAOBAB: KING OF THE AFRICAN BUSH

There's nothing quite like the baobab *(Adansonia digitata)*; its thick, sturdy trunk and stunted root-like branches are an instantly recognisable symbol of Africa. Thanks to its unusual form, many traditional cultures believe that the tree displeased a deity who promptly plucked it in anger and thrust it back into the ground upside down. Or as that great writer on Africa, Ryszard Kapuściński, wrote: 'Like elephants among other animals, so are baobabs among trees: they have no equals'.

Despite the apparent misdemeanours of its ancestor, today's baobab is revered by local people. Its wizened appearance, combined with an ability to survive great droughts and live for many hundreds of years, ensures that the baobab is believed to possess magical powers. Old trees often develop cavities, which are sometimes used to inter a revered *griot* (praise singer).

The baobab is found in most parts of West Africa and serves a variety of practical, often essential, purposes. The hollow trunk sometimes holds rainwater, making it a useful reservoir in times of drought. The tree's large pods (which resemble pendulous Christmas decorations and are sometimes called 'monkey bread') contain seeds encased in a sherbet-like substance that can be eaten or made into a juice-like drink. The pods themselves are used to make cups or bowls (often for drinking palm wine) and as fuel; they burn slowly and are especially good for smoking fish. The leaves of the baobab can be eaten when chopped, boiled and made into a sauce; they can also be dried and ground into a paste to use as a poultice for skin infections and joint complaints. Even the flowers are used as decoration at ceremonies.

Forty million metric tonnes of Saharan sand reaches the Amazon annually, replenishing mineral nutrients depleted by tropical rains. Half of this dust comes from the Bodele Depression on the Niger–Chad border, although the depression covers just 0.2% of the Sahara.

From 1976 to 1996, there were almost 5000 oil spills (equivalent to three million barrels of oil) in Nigeria's Niger Delta, where there are 66 gas fields and 500 oil wells.

In most cases, West Africa's elephants exist in small, isolated herds and are considered endangered. In Côte d'Ivoire, for example, the vast herds that gave the country its name have been reduced to around 300. Apart from Mali, the best places to see elephants include Ghana's Mole National Park, Burkina Faso's Ranch de Nazinga and Cameroon's Parc National de Waza.

Possibly the best-known and most easily observed mammals of West Africa are monkeys. These include several types of colobus and green or vervet monkeys. Other primates include mangabeys, baboons and galagos (bushbabies), as well as chimpanzees and the rare and endangered drill. Cameroon also hosts an endangered population of western lowland gorillas.

Mammals more readily seen include several beautiful antelope species, such as bushbucks, reedbucks, waterbucks, kobs, roans, elands, oribis and various gazelles and duikers; the sitatunga is more shy. The Sahel-dwelling dama gazelle is the largest gazelle species in Africa, but it is now close to extinction as its grazing lands have been taken over by cattle and reduced by desertification. The red-fronted gazelle may still survive in Mali's remote far east. Wild pig species include giant hogs and bush pigs (the West African species is often called the red river hog), which inhabit forest areas, and warthogs, frequently seen in drier savannah areas. Buffaloes in West Africa inhabit forest regions; they are smaller and redder than the East African version.

In the rivers, including the upper reaches of the Niger and Gambia Rivers, hippos can sometimes be seen, but numbers are low. Some hippos have adapted to live in salt water and exist in coastal areas such as the Orango Islands National Park in the Arquipélago dos Bijagós in Guinea-Bissau. A few forest areas, including Liberia's Sapo National Park and Sierra Leone's Tiwai Island Wildlife Sanctuary, are home to very small populations of elusive pygmy hippos, which are less aquatic than their larger cousins. Other marine mammals found in the region include dolphins, especially where the region's rivers meet the ocean, and humpback whales, which can be seen off Freetown Peninsula in Sierra Leone, especially in September and January.

Back on land, other highly endangered species that have somehow survived the human and climatic onslaught include the following:

➡ manatees (sea cows, a giant seal-like relative of the elephant) in Mali's Réserve d'Ansongo-Ménaka, in Senegal's Parc National du Niokolo-Koba, or in mangrove and delta areas along the coast, including the Parque Nacional do Catanhez in Guinea-Bissau

➡ one of the world's last colonies of monk seals along Mauritania's remote Atlantic coast

➡ olive baboons

➡ the Sahara's only amphibian, the spurred tortoise, in the remote Aïr Mountains of northern Niger

Birds

West Africa lies along one of the busiest bird migratory routes between Europe and Africa, and more than 1000 species have been recorded. Many of the species are endemic, while others are passing migrants, flying down the Atlantic coast to and from their wintering grounds, and some are African nomads moving within the continent in pursuit of seasons of plenty. Among those you're likely to see are flamingos, storks and pelicans (around waterways), beautiful gannets and fish-eating cormorants (in coastal areas), turacos – including the striking violet turaco – and African grey and red-billed hornbills.

It is estimated that 5000 million birds from Europe and Asia migrate to tropical Africa every year, a journey of up to 11,000km – less than half make it home, either dying en route or preferring to remain in Africa.

ENVIRONMENT WILDLIFE

BIRDS

BIODIVERSITY HOTSPOT: GUINEAN FORESTS OF WEST AFRICA

Of 34 internationally recognised 'biodiversity hotspots', eight are in Africa. In order to qualify as a biodiversity hotspot, a region must contain at least 1500 species of vascular plants (ie more than 0.5% of the world's total) and have lost at least 70% of its original habitat. Although only one of these – the Guinean forests of West Africa – is in West Africa, it is so vast that it passes through nine out of the 17 West African countries. This hotspot covers the heavily populated coastal belt and its hinterland, and includes Guinea, Sierra Leone, Liberia, Côte d'Ivoire, Ghana, Benin, Togo, Nigeria and southwestern Cameroon, as well as Equatorial Guinea and São Tomé & Príncipe. As such, it's a hugely significant indicator of the state of West Africa's environment.

The original extent of West Africa's Guinean forests was 620,314 sq km, of which only 93,047 sq km remain. It is also home to 31 endemic threatened birds, 35 endemic threatened mammals and 45 endemic threatened amphibians. The most prominent of the threatened mammals are pygmy hippos, Liberian mongooses, 12 primate species (including chimpanzees and gorillas), the African golden cat and the elephant. It also has what is easily the highest population density of any of the world's hotspots – 137 people per sq km.

The Guinean forests are home to 320 mammal species (more than 25% of Africa's mammals and including more than 20 primate species), 785 bird species, 210 reptile species, 221 amphibian species and over 9000 plant species, of which 1800 are endemic. Despite being such an important storehouse for Africa's biodiversity, less than 20% of the territory is adequately protected. The hotspot's landmark conservation parks – Sapo National Park (Liberia), Kakum National Park (Ghana), Korup National Park (Cameroon) and Takamanda National Park (Cameroon) – provide an example of what can be done, but many more such protected areas are needed, as is the development of conservation corridors, agro-forestry projects and a greater emphasis on ecotourism. Major threats include unregulated logging, mining, hunting (especially the trade in bushmeat) and human encroachment.

One of West Africa's best birdwatching destinations is tiny Gambia, with more than 560 species recorded and several easily accessed bird-watching sites, among them Abuko Nature Reserve, Tanji River Bird Reserve, Kiang West National Park and Baobalong Wetland Reserve.

Senegal also offers excellent birding, particularly in Parc National de la Langue de Barbarie and Parc National des Oiseaux du Djoudj. Both are famous for vast pelican and flamingo flocks. Parc National du Niokolo-Koba and the Siné-Saloum Delta region are some other terrific sites, and there are several other good sites in northern Casamance near Kafountine.

Sierra Leone's Tiwai Island Wildlife Sanctuary hosts hornbills, king-fishers and the rare white-breasted guinea fowl. Around Mt Bintumani, the endangered rufous fishing-owl has been sighted, while Outamba-Kilimi National Park supports kingfishers, waders, raptors and the spectacular great blue turaco. The rainforest-rich Gola Forest Reserve is another fine birding destination, home at last count to 333 bird species, including the Gola malimbe, while the Kambui Hills Forest Reserve is home to the white-necked rockfowl. Liberia's Sapo National Park and Côte d'Ivoire's Comoé National Park each host in excess of 500 species.

Further afield, other destinations that draw birders include Ghana's Mole National Park, Nigeria's Yankari National Park, Cameroon's Korup National Park and Mauritania's Parc National du Banc d'Arguin.

Reptiles & Amphibians

West Africa's most notable reptile is the Nile crocodile, which was once abundant all over the region; few remain, due to hunting and habitat destruction. Your best chance to see them is along the larger rivers such

Up to 90% of natural gas from the Niger Delta oil fields is burned as waste, releasing massive amounts of carbon dioxide into the atmosphere and causing acid rain.

According to the UNEP, Mt Nlonako in southwestern Cameroon is the richest single locality in the world for snake species – 63 different species.

GREENING NIGER: A SUCCESS STORY

When droughts struck Niger (and the rest of the Sahel) in 1968–74 and 1980–84, the country seemed destined for environmental oblivion. The desperate search for fire-wood and animal fodder denuded the landscape, accelerating the southward march of the Sahara, which left sandy wastelands where it went. Fast forward to 2009 and something remarkable has happened. Satellite images show that three of Niger's southern provinces (especially around Tahoua) now have between 10 and 20 times more trees than they did in the 1970s. According to the United Nations Environment Program (UNEP), this is 'a human and environmental success story at a scale not seen before in the Sahel'.

The secret to the success has been giving farmers the primary role in regenerating the land. Faced with arid soil where agriculture was almost impossible, farmers constructed terraces and rock bunds to stem soil erosion, trap rainfall and enable the planting of trees. Trees planted by the farmers now serve as windbreaks against the desert and, for the first time in a generation, agriculture (millet, sorghum and vegetables) is possible almost year round, even in the dry season, thanks to improved water catchment and soil quality. Farmers no longer uproot trees to plant crops, ploughing around them instead, with the result that crop yields have increased.

In what has become known as 'farmer-managed natural regeneration', the flow-on effects have been extraordinary: not only has agriculture become possible, subsistence levels have risen and the local economy is improving, and the region's groundwater table has also risen, in some places from a depth of 20m to 3m. In some areas, pockets of desert now resemble agricultural parklands, with more than 200 trees per hectare. Even in years of drought when crops fail, the trees, a small proportion of which can be sold for cash, serve as a last bastion against starvation; in the 2005 food crisis, death rates from hunger in the three southern provinces were much lower than elsewhere in the country.

AMAR GROVER / GETTY IMAGES ©

Gambia River, The Gambia (p152)

as the Gambia, Senegal and Niger, although an unlikely population also survives in Mauritania's Saharan oasis of Matmata. Two lesser-known species, the dwarf crocodile and the slender-nosed crocodile, also occur.

Turtles survive along the coast of West Africa and on some of the offshore islands. The females come to the beaches to lay eggs in the sand, sometimes several hundred at a time. The threats faced by turtles are considerable, and include damage by humans to nesting areas, hunting, and the effects of water pollution – turtles often mistake floating plastic bags for food. The best places to see sea turtles are at the conservation project at Ebodje in Cameroon, on the Cape Verdean island of Boa Vista in July and August, the João Vieira-Poilão National Marine Park in Guinea-Bissau, or in Ghana at Akwidaa Beach and Beyin.

West Africa has a full complement of both venomous and harmless snakes, but most fear humans and you'd be 'lucky' to even see one. The largest snake is the non-venomous python, which grows to more than 5m in length. It kills by coiling around and suffocating its prey – not the nicest way to go, but fortunately it doesn't usually fancy humans. The venomous puff adder, which reaches about 1m in length and enjoys sunning itself, isn't aggressive but, being very slow, it's sometimes stepped on by unwary people before it has had time to wake up. When stepped on, it bites. Take special care when hiking in bush areas, especially in the early morning, when this snake is at its most lethargic. The Sahara is home to the venomous horned viper.

Benin has the highest ratio (23%) of protected areas to total territory, followed by Côte d'Ivoire (16.4%), Burkina Faso (15.4%) and Ghana (14.7%). Lagging behind are Cape Verde (0.56%), Mauritania (1.7%), Mali (2.1%) and Nigeria (2.1%).

National Parks & Wildlife Reserves

West Africa has some outstanding national parks and reserves that provide the last refuge for the region's wildlife, protected areas amid a growing sea of humanity. Others exist in name only.

Whatever their status, few West African parks are set up for tourism – national-park offices are rare and trails are often poorly maintained. Visiting these parks usually requires arranging a visit through a private agency, preferably one from the park's hinterland and with a local guide to ensure that the proceeds of your visit benefit the local community.

Environmental Issues

There are many environmental issues confronting West Africa, all of them serious. Deforestation and desertification are perhaps the most widespread and urgent of the challenges, but soil erosion, air and water pollution, wildlife destruction, water scarcity, threats to coastal and marine ecosystems, overfishing, drought and the impact of cash crops such as cashews and rubber all pose significant threats to the West African environment.

MAJOR NATIONAL PARKS & WILDLIFE RESERVES

NATIONAL PARK	COUNTRY	WILDLIFE	BEST TIME TO VISIT
Parc National de la Pendjari	Benin	elephants, leopards, buffaloes, hippos, lions	Mar-May
* Parc Regional du W	Benin/Niger/ Burkina Faso	leopards, lions, cheetahs, elephants, baboons, Nile crocodiles, hyenas, over 300 bird species, 500 plant species	Mar-May; open mid-Dec–mid-Jun
Ranch de Nazinga	Burkina Faso	elephants, monkeys, crocodiles	Jan-Mar
Parc National de Waza	Cameroon	elephants, giraffes, lions, hippos	Mar & Apr
Parc National de Campo-Ma'an	Cameroon	rainforest, buffaloes, elephants, mandrills	Dec-Apr
Korup National Park	Cameroon	oldest rainforest in Africa; 50 large mammal species, over 300 bird species	Nov-May
Limbe Wildlife Centre	Cameroon	rescued gorillas, chimpanzees, drills	year round
* Réserve de Biosphere du Dja	Cameroon	rainforest; buffaloes, grey-necked rockfowl	Dec-Apr
Takamanda National Park	Cameroon	Cross River gorillas	Dec-Apr
* Parc National de Taï	Côte d'Ivoire	rainforest; chimpanzees	Dec-Feb
Kiang West National Park	The Gambia	baboons, colobus monkeys, hyenas, dolphins, crocodiles, over 300 bird species	Nov-May
Tanji River Bird Reserve	The Gambia	over 300 bird species	Nov-May
Ankasa Nature Reserve	Ghana	rainforest; forest elephants, leopards, bongos	Jan-Mar
Kakum National Park	Ghana	rainforest; elephants, colobus monkeys, antelopes, 300 bird species, 600 butterfly species	Jan-Mar
Mole National Park	Ghana	94 mammal species (incl elephants), over 300 bird species	Jan-Mar
Wechiau Community Hippo Sanctuary	Ghana	hippos	Nov-Jun
Parc National du Haut Niger	Guinea	dry rainforest; hippos, chimpanzees	Nov-Apr
Poilão National Marine Park	Guinea-Bissau	sea turtles	Oct & Nov

Deforestation

West Africa was once covered in forests, but only a tiny fraction of the original forest cover remains and even that is under threat. In 1990, for example, forests covered 42.1% of Liberian territory; 15 years later, the figure had dropped to just 32.7%. Other alarming falls were recorded during the same period in Benin (30% to 21.3%) and Togo (12.6% to 7.1%). Deforestation is similarly acute in Côte d'Ivoire.

The extent of the problem is evident from the causes – increased population growth, commercial logging, the clearing of trees for farming and slash-and-burn farming techniques – the effects of most of which are either irreversible or require massive investment from often impoverished governments. Potential earnings in global timber markets, for example,

NATIONAL PARK	COUNTRY	WILDLIFE	BEST TIME TO VISIT
Orango Islands National Park	Guinea-Bissau	saltwater hippos, crocodiles	Nov-Apr
Parque Natural dos Tarrafes do Rio Cacheu	Guinea-Bissau	hippos, manatees, panthers, gazelles, hyenas, over 200 bird species	Nov-Apr
Parque Nacional do Catanhez	Guinea-Bissau	chimpanzees, elephants, colobus monkeys, baboons, manatees	Nov-Apr
Sapo National Park	Liberia	forest elephants, pygmy hippos, chimpanzees, over 500 bird species	Nov-Apr
Réserve de Douentza	Mali	elephants	Jan-Jun
* Parc National du Banc d'Arguin	Mauritania	migratory birds	Dec & Jan
Afi Mountain Drill Ranch	Nigeria	rescued drills, chimpanzees	Oct-Feb
Gashaka-Gumti National Park	Nigeria	chimpanzees, lions, elephants, hippos	Nov-May
Yankari National Park	Nigeria	elephants, baboons, hyenas, lions, over 600 bird species	Nov-Mar
Parc National de la Langue de Barbarie	Senegal	hundreds of bird species	Nov-Apr
* Parc National des Oiseaux du Djoudj	Senegal	pelicans, flamingos, over 350 bird species	Nov-Apr
* Parc National de Niokolo-Koba	Senegal	lions, 80 mammal species, 350 bird species	Dec-May
Parc National du Delta du Saloum	Senegal	red colobus & patas monkeys, hyenas, sea turtles, dolphins	Nov-May
Gola Forest Reserve	Sierra Leone	rainforest; 333 bird species, elephants, leopards, zebras, duikers	Nov-Apr
Tiwai Island Wildlife Sanctuary	Sierra Leone	pygmy hippos, chimpanzees, 120 bird species	Nov-Apr
Outamba-Kilimi National Park	Sierra Leone	elephants, primates, hippos,	Nov-Apr
Parc National de Fazao-Malfakassa	Togo	elephants, monkeys, antelopes, over 200 bird species	Dec-May

* appears on Unesco's World Heritage list

GREENSHOOTS COMMUNICATIONS / ALAMY ©

Elephants in the Mole National Park (p195), Ghana

are infinitely more attractive (and lucrative) than preserving wildlife for the trickle of tourists who come to see it.

Conflict and refugee movement can also have important flow-on effects for local forest coverage. During the conflicts in Sierra Leone and Liberia, neighbouring Guinea played host to one of the world's largest refugee populations, especially in the Parrot's Beak region, wedged between its two neighbours. Satellite images from 1974 show that forests completely covered the Parrot's Beak wedge of Guinean territory; by 2002, satellite images showed that none of it had survived the massive human influx.

> A citizen of urban Britain, Australia or the USA consumes more than 50 times more of the earth's resources than a rural inhabitant of Niger or Guinea-Bissau.

Desertification

As forest cover diminishes, all too often the desert moves in. Desertification is one of the most serious forms of land degradation, and it's one to which the countries of the Sahel are particularly vulnerable. Some areas of the Sahel are losing over 50 metric tonnes of soil per hectare per year, and the desertification that results has reached critical levels in Niger, Mali and Mauritania, each of which could be entirely consumed by the Sahara within a generation. But desertification is also a problem for countries beyond the Sahelian danger zone: a high-to-moderate risk of desertification exists in Sierra Leone, Liberia, Guinea, Ghana, Nigeria and Senegal, which all suffer from serious erosion.

The major causes are desertification are easy to identify – drought, deforestation and the over-exploitation of fragile soils on the desert margin – and are the result of both human activity and climatic variation. But one of the most significant causes in West Africa is the use of deliberately started fires. Such fires are sometimes necessary for maintaining soil quality, regenerating savannah grasslands and ecosystems, enabling livestock production and as a form of pest control. But all too often the interval between fires is insufficient to allow the land to recover, thereby

> *Seeds of Famine,* by Richard Franke and Barbara Chasin, is as dry as the Sahel dust but essential reading for anyone keen to learn more about the connection between colonial policies and the droughts that still face the region.

exposing the soil to wind and heavy rains, and degrading the soil beyond the point of recovery.

West Africans are often blamed for the destruction of their own environment, but the reality is far more complex and there are other causes that date back even further. Many of the problems began in colonial times, when farmers were encouraged to plant thirsty cash crops (such as the peanut) that require intensive farming – traditional methods involved fallow periods, which allowed the soil to regenerate. Thus deprived of essential nutrients, the soil required fertilisers to recover, but these were often too expensive for poor farmers to afford. The soil began to unravel.

This process was exacerbated by well-intentioned animal-husbandry and well-building schemes funded by the EU in the 1960s and '70s. Herd sizes increased without any accompanying growth in pasturelands. In the absence of fodder, the additional cattle and goats ate the grasses and thorns that bound the soil together. Patches of desert began to appear around villages that once lay many kilometres south of the desert's southern boundary. As populations increased and enticements by Western seed companies prompted more farmers to increase the land under cultivation, the few remaining trees and forests were cut down, thereby accelerating a process that began centuries ago.

Community-Based Conservation

Sustainable environmental protection usually works only by involving local communities and providing them with the material benefits (tourism, sustainability of resources for future generations) that derive from preserving pristine environments.

The Gambia is the star performer among West African countries when it comes to ecotourism, with a host of community projects, ecolodges and wildlife parks. In addition to these, several forestry projects in The Gambia recognise this delicate balance, fusing environmental protection with traditional sources of livelihood. Natural woodland areas are not simply fenced off, but rather used in a sustainable way for the benefit of local communities, with the emphasis on sustainable resource management. In The Gambia's Kiang West National Park, limited cattle grazing and (more controversially) rice cultivation is permitted. Dead wood can be used for timber, fruits and edible leaves can be collected, and grasses can be harvested for thatch. These products can be used or sold, but all activities take place without destroying the growing trees. In this way, local people view the forest as a source of produce, income or employment, and have a real incentive to protect it in the

Until the intrepid Mungo Park reached the Niger River close to Ségou on 21 July 1796, European map-makers were convinced that the river flowed east–west and originated in the Nile or Lake Chad.

The West African countries with the most expansive forest cover are Guinea-Bissau (73.7%), Cameroon (45.6%), Senegal (45%), The Gambia (41.7%) and Sierra Leone (38.5%). Mauritania (0.3%) and Niger (1%) have almost no forests left.

ENVIRONMENT ENVIRONMENTAL ISSUES

PURIFY YOUR WATER & SAVE THE ENVIRONMENT

When confronted by West Africa's often overwhelming environmental issues, it's easy to feel helpless. But there is one small but very significant thing you can do to minimise your impact on the environment: don't buy bottled water. Instead, purify tap water for your drinking needs. Plastic water bottles and plastic bags are one of the most visible scourges across the West African landscape; you'll find plastic water bottles (and half-litre bags of mineral water) everywhere for sale when they're full, and then again littering the streets, fields and roadsides once empty. Water purification has come a long way since the days of unappealing iodine treatments, and one purification system we've trialled on the road in West Africa are Micropur tablets, although there are plenty of other brands on offer. The impact of travelling this way is easily calculated: if you drink 150L of purified water, you'll keep around 100 plastic water bottles off the streets, not to mention save a considerable amount of money (in the UK Micropur costs UK£6 per 100 tablets, enough to purify 100L).

Sahara Conservation Fund (www.saharaconservation.org) is one of few sources of information on the wildlife of the Sahara, and the efforts being undertaken to protect it. Its work was instrumental in convincing Niger's government to create Africa's largest protected area, the Termit & Tin Toumma National Nature and Cultural Reserve (97,000 sq km).

long term. Local inhabitants also take a leading role in environmental planning – at Niumi National Park, also in The Gambia, community groups have been established to give local people a formal voice in the park's management structure.

In Burkina Faso, small-scale NGO projects encourage farmers to return to traditional methods of cultivation, in particular the laying of *diguettes* or stone lines along field contours, which slow water run-off, maximise water penetration and reduce erosion. And in Niger, putting land conservation in the hands of local farmers has proved to be a stunning success.

Wildlife conservation is another area where involving local communities is beginning to reap rewards. Apart from several locally run sanctuaries in Ghana – such as the Boabeng-Fiema Monkey Sanctuary and Wechiau Community Hippo Sanctuary – some of the best results are to be seen in protecting Mali's desert elephants. Another excellent example is the Tabala Conservation Zone spanning the Guinea–Sierra Leone border.

Local community projects around Toubab Dialao and the Réserve de Popenguine in Senegal are a fine example of community-driven conservation. In Côte d'Ivoire, a village tourism project reduced forest clearing and poaching in one of West Africa's largest stands of rainforest in Parc National de Taï prior to the conflict; many such projects are yet to restart now that peace has returned to the country, however.

Survival Guide

Safe Travel

It's difficult to make generalisations about the personal-safety situation in West Africa. While there may be considerable risk in some areas, most places are completely safe. It's always important to be aware of potential problems and to keep your wits about you, but don't be paranoid, and do remember that most travellers experience no problems.

COMMON DANGERS

Beaches

Although you should be careful of thieves and hustlers on West Africa's beaches, a potentially greater risk awaits you in the water. In many places along the coast, the beaches can slope steeply and the waves can create a vicious undertow. Never plunge into the ocean without first seeking reliable local advice.

Cities

The danger of robbery with violence is much more prevalent in cities and towns than in rural or wilderness areas, where it's relatively rare. Most cities have their dangerous streets and beaches, but towns can differ; there's more of a danger in places frequented by wealthy foreigners than in those off the usual tourist track. Major cities with questionable reputations include Abidjan, Dakar, Douala, Lagos and Yaoundé. Muggings do occur, although pickpocketing and bagsnatching are more frequent.

Road Safety

Perhaps the greatest danger faced by travellers to West Africa is that caused by road accidents. Road conditions outside capitals are bad and, apart from potholes and the inevitable chickens, dangers include people as well as camels, cows and other animals moving into your path. Keep in mind that many locals

---

LATEST TRAVEL ADVICE

Lonely Planet's website (www.lonelyplanet.com) contains information on what's new, and any new safety reports, as well as reports from other travellers recounting their experiences while on the road. For Saharan travel, try the forum on www.sahara-overland.com.

Most governments have travel-advisory services detailing terrorism updates, potential pitfalls and areas to avoid. Remember, however, that some government travel advisories overstate the risks somewhat and you should read carefully through the reports to see when actual incidents occurred.

Australian Department of Foreign Affairs & Trade (☎1300 139 281; www.smartraveller.gov.au)

Canadian Department of Foreign Affairs & International Trade (☎1-800-267-6788; www.voyage.gc.ca)

French Ministere des Affaires Etrangeres Europeennes (www.diplomatie.gouv.fr/fr/conseils-aux-voyageurs_909/index.html)

New Zealand Ministry of Foreign Affairs & Trade (☎04-439 8000; www.mft.govt.nz/travel)

UK Foreign & Commonwealth Office (☎845 0850 2829; www.fco.gov.uk)

US Department of State (☎202-647-4000; www.travel.state.gov)

have not driven themselves, and are thus not aware of braking distances and similar concepts. One of the biggest hazards is overtaking blind or on curves. Throughout the region, travelling by road at night is unsafe; avoid doing so wherever possible.

Scams

The main annoyances you'll come across in West Africa are the hustlers, touts and con artists who prey on tourists. Scams are only likely to be tried in tourist areas; on most occasions, especially in remote or rural areas, you're more likely to come across genuine hospitality. Some examples of scams:

➡ You may be invited to stay in someone's house in exchange for a meal and drinks, but your new friend's appetite for food and beer may make this an expensive deal. More seriously, someone else might be back at the house going through your bag.

➡ Street sellers offering boxes of cassettes by local musicians frequently sell duds – try to listen to tapes before buying them.

➡ If you're unwise enough to sample local narcotics, or spend time with those who are taking drugs, don't be surprised if the dealers are in cahoots with the local police.

➡ Local lads may approach you in the street pretending to be a hotel employee or 'son of the owner'. Can you lend him some money? Don't be fooled, no matter how much he seems to know about you.

➡ Sock sellers bend down to show you how well the socks would go with your outfit while a friend relieves you of your wallet. Why socks? We have no idea...

➡ Don't accept drinks from newly found acquaintances on buses or trains, or you may soon find yourself asleep while your new friend runs off with your wallet.

SAFETY TIPS

➡ Avoid conspicuous displays of wealth, including expensive watches, mobile phones and bulging wallets.

➡ Walk purposefully and confidently and be discreet about consulting maps and guidebooks.

➡ Always take a taxi at night in city areas.

➡ Consider hiring somebody locally to accompany you when walking around a risky area – ask at your hotel for a reliable recommendation.

➡ Keep your backpack or suitcase locked whenever you leave it anywhere, whether it's on the roof of a bush taxi or in your hotel room.

REGION BY REGION

The Sahel & Sahara

The major concern at present is the Sahara. Much of Mali remains off-limits, with the north (including Timbuktu and Gao) under the control of Islamist rebels; in the past two years, foreigners have been kidnapped in Timbuktu and Hombori and there is growing evidence that al-Qaeda in the Islamic Maghreb (AQIM) now controls much of Mali's north. Neighbouring Niger is considered a little safer, but we still recommend against travel to Niger (its Saharan regions in particular) for the same reasons. Burkina Faso, on the other hand, neighbours both countries but is considered to be one of West Africa's safest countries. Our author visited Chinguetti and Ouadâne and other towns in the Mauritanian Sahara and these are generally considered to be safe, but always check the prevailing security situation before setting out.

The Coast

Most coastal countries in West Africa are considered safe for travel, including Cameroon, Benin, Togo, The Gambia, Ghana, Liberia, Morocco and Sierra Leone; this includes inland regions of these countries. Offshore, Cape Verde could just be the region's safest destination.

Senegal is considered safe, but check the prevailing security situation if you're travelling to the Casamance region.

The security situation in Côte d'Ivoire is improving with each passing year, but the fragile nature of the peace means that you should exercise great caution, especially in the north and west of the country. Safe travel is possible in Guinea and Guinea-Bissau, but the ongoing potential for instability there makes most travellers think twice.

Nigeria

As with most things in West Africa, Nigeria deserves special mention. This perennially complicated country has one of the highest road accident rates in the world, the extremist group Boko Haram poses a growing threat across the country, crime is endemic in Lagos and outbreaks of violence from the north to the Niger Delta are always possible. And yet, for all its challenges and potential pitfalls, we don't recommend against travelling to Nigeria. Just be careful...

Directory A–Z

Accommodation

There's almost always some sort of accommodation available in midsized and larger towns in West Africa, although quality and price vary widely.

All prices we give here are for rooms with a bathroom; exceptions are noted in specific listings.

Mali and Senegal tend to be the most expensive countries, with neither Nigeria nor Niger offering outstanding value for money when it comes to accommodation. Togo is one of the region's cheapest countries. In some countries, including Guinea, Mali, Burkina Faso and Nigeria, establishments charge a government tourist tax on top of the price they'll quote you. Sometimes (such as in Burkina Faso) this is a one-off payment regardless of the number of nights you stay, while in Nigeria or Mali it's a nightly surcharge added on to the quoted price.

In many parts of West Africa, particularly in the Sahel during the hot season, people often sleep outside their hut or on the flat roof of their house as it's much cooler. In some hotels this is also possible, and carrying a mattress onto the roof – where you'll have some breeze and views of the stars – is usually allowed if you ask.

One other thing to note is that in Guinea, Sierra Leone and some other countries, a man and a woman may share a room with no questions asked, but a same-sex couple, regardless of whether they are a couple, usually cannot.

B&Bs

Burkina Faso is leading the way in smaller, more intimate alternatives to hotels with a range of excellent B&Bs. Prices are usually cheaper than hotels, and the warmth and personality of the owners (often a French-Burkinabé couple) is a big drawcard. They're also known as *chambres d'hôtes* or *maisons d'hôtes*. A handful of similar places is appearing in Mali and Mauritania.

Campements

Most towns and many villages in Francophone countries have a *campement* whose primary purpose is not as a campground in the traditional sense (ie a place for tents), although some do provide areas where you can pitch a tent and have access to shower facilities. *Campements* offer cheap and simple accommodation that is far less elaborate than at a hotel, containing the bare necessities, shared facilities and little else, but some are very good quality, with prices on a par with midrange hotels. Either way, they're often the best (and sometimes only) option in small towns. Here, 4WDs fill the compound, and overlanders mingle with backpackers who've just arrived on the latest bush taxi.

In trekking areas such as Mali's Dogon Country, it is established practice for visitors to sleep on the roof of the *campements* in each village, as this is usually preferable to the stifling rooms.

Camping

There are few dedicated campgrounds in West Africa, and those that do exist cater mainly for overlanders in their own vehicle. Some hotels and *campements* allow camping or provide an area where tents can be pitched. Grassy knolls on which to pitch your tent are rare – you often have to force pegs through hard-packed gravel. Camping in the wild is risky in most countries as theft can be a problem; if you do decide to camp, always seek permission from the local village chief before setting up.

Hotels

Most hotels charge for a bed only, with all meals costing extra. If breakfast is included it's usually on a par with the standard of accommodation: a full buffet in more expensive places, instant coffee and bread further down the scale. Hotels are often called *auberges*.

Independent travellers on tight budgets are fairly well catered for, although there are almost no backpacker lodges. Although you will come across some gems, most of what's on offer is basic, devoid of any discernible character, and ranges from the recently swept to the downright grubby. The showers and toilets are usually shared and often of the squat variety. Some hotels in this price range double as brothels.

Midrange hotels tend to be at their best in the capitals or major towns, where you're likely to find at least one place with lovingly maintained rooms, private bathrooms, splashes of local colour, satellite TV and even a swimming pool. Most midrange places, though fine, fall somewhat short of this ideal. Most offer a choice between a fan and air-con.

West Africa has very few top-end hotels outside the capitals and offers little in the way of exclusive wildlife lodges or tented camps as found in East or Southern Africa.

Missions

If you're travelling on a tight budget, mission accommodation can be a good alternative to budget hotels, although rooms are usually reserved for mission or aid workers and are open to others only on a space-available basis. Usually called *missions catholique,* they're invariably clean, safe and good value, although these are not places to stagger home drunk at 4am – at many missions travellers are only allowed to stay if they respect the rules.

Resorts

You'll find European-style resorts all along the West African coast, but the best facilities are at those that cater to Europeans looking for a comfortable two-week beach holiday. These are especially popular in Senegal, The Gambia and Cape Verde, where you'll find all-inclusive packages of meals, accommodation and airport transfers. Although it's occasionally possible to get a room by simply walking in off the street, most rooms (and the best deals) are reserved for those who book the whole package through a travel agency in Europe.

Activities

If the region's natural beauty stirs not just your soul but also your body into action, West Africa has some world-class activities to get involved in. Desert expeditions, diving and snorkelling, deep-sea fishing, hiking, rock climbing, surfing and windsurfing are all possible. Adding to the allure is the fact that, unlike elsewhere in the world, you may be the only traveller taking part. Remember, however, that infrastructure can be rudimentary, so be prepared to be self-sufficient. West Africa is home to some outstanding guides, and young men ready to drop everything and take you out into the wilderness or on a limb: choose carefully.

Cycling

In several parts of West Africa, bicycles can be hired by the hour, day or week, and can be a good way to tour a town or area. Your choice may range from a new, imported mountain bike (*vélo tout terrain* in French, or VTT) to ancient, single-gear, steel roadsters.

Away from tourist areas, it's almost always possible to find locals willing to rent their bicycles for the day; good places to enquire include the market or your hotel. Costs range from US$1 to US$10 per day, depending on the bicycle and the area. Remember to always check the roadworthiness of your bicycle, especially if you're heading off-road.

The flat roads of Burkina Faso are particularly good for cycling, especially around Banfora in the country's southwest; cycling tours are possible around the otherworldly Sindou Peaks.

Desert Expeditions

For many travellers, West Africa means the Sahara, and deep desert expeditions used to be among the region's most rewarding activities. The security situation means that most such expeditions were not possible at the time of research. One exception is the Moroccan south around Merzouga, Erg Chebbi and Erg Chigaga.

The following information is included for when the situation stabilises sufficiently in northern Mali, Mauritania and Niger.

The main gateway towns to the Sahara, and hence the best places to organise Saharan expeditions, are Timbuktu and Gao (Mali), Atâr (Mauritania) and Agadez (Niger). In Mauritania, the remote outposts of Chinguetti, Ouadâne, Tidjikja and Tichit exist in splendid Saharan isolation, while the crater of Guelb er Richat, near Ouadâne, is stunning. In Niger, home to perhaps West Africa's best desert scenery, the Aïr Mountains and Ténéré Desert are simply extraordinary.

The main choice you'll have to make for your expedition is whether to travel by camel or 4WD. You'll cover far more territory if you rent a 4WD, but costs can be prohibitive (up to CFA65,000 per day, plus petrol). Travelling by camel is more economical and environmentally friendly and allows you to experience the desert at a more leisurely pace, although you'll cover less territory.

Diving & Snorkelling

Cape Verde is the best place in West Africa to go diving and snorkelling amid the dolphins, sharks and even whales, especially off the islands of Boa Vista and Sal. It's possible to take open-water PADI dive courses at both places, although remember that Cape Verde has no decompression chambers. March to November are the best months.

Other places where diving and/or snorkelling are possible include off Busua in Ghana, and Dakar and Saly in Senegal.

Fishing

The Atlantic waters off West Africa are some of the world's richest fishing grounds. Sierra Leone in particular is one of the world's most underrated deep-sea fishing destinations, especially off Freetown and Sherbro Island where many individual line-class records were set.

Other deep-sea fishing possibilities exist off the island of Sal in Cape Verde, in The Gambia, Guinea-Bissau's Arquipélago dos Bijagós, and Dakar and Saly in Senegal.

Less serious anglers could try a fishing course in Cape Coast in Ghana, while Lake Ahémé in Benin offers a fascinating insight into traditional fishing techniques.

Hiking

There are many spectacular hiking trails in West Africa. Morocco is arguably the region's premier hiking destination with a range of fine and reasonably well-marked

hiking trails throughout the Atlas Mountains. Most of these are accessible year-round and the network of maps and guides is sparse by European standards but easily the best in the region.

The set-up in this region is very different from that in East or Southern Africa and the experience is often less wilderness than a stirring combination of cultural and natural landscapes. There's little in the way of good walking infrastructure, such as detailed maps, marked trails or trail accommodation, and much of the hiking is through populated areas. All of which means that, as long as you don't mind roughing it, hiking can be a great way to interact with the locals: on foot you can meet on more equal terms than staring at each other through the windows of a bush taxi.

As there's very little formal organisation, expect to arrange everything yourself (eg bring a good water filter/purifier). Hiring a local guide (either for the entire expedition or to lead you from village to village) is usually a good idea. In some places,

because of the distances involved, it may also be necessary to use donkeys, hitching or public transport to get around.

Rock Climbing

West Africa has one world-class climbing destination, but it remained off limits at the time of writing: the area around Hombori in Mali, where some spectacular rock formations rise above the Sahel and attract a small but growing number of serious rock climbers from Europe. Another area with rock-climbing potential is Mali's Falaise de Bandiagara.

Otherwise, well-known 'climbing' destinations such as Mt Cameroon, Cape Verde's Mt Fogo and Sierra Leone's Mt Bintumani are actually strenuous hikes that involve no technical climbing.

Surfing, Windsurfing & Kitesurfing

West Africa may not be the world's most famous surfing destination, but discerning surfers are rapidly discovering the region's Atlantic coastline, partly for its waves

WEST AFRICA'S TOP HIKING TRAILS

- ⇒ Sindou Peaks, southwestern Burkina Faso
- ⇒ Mt Cameroon, Cameroon
- ⇒ Mandara Mountains, northern Cameroon
- ⇒ Santo Antão, Cape Verde
- ⇒ Mt Fogo, Cape Verde
- ⇒ Parque Natural Serra Malagueta, Cape Verde
- ⇒ Tongo Hills, Ghana
- ⇒ Around Ho, Ghana
- ⇒ Jebel Toubkal, Morocco
- ⇒ Rif Mountains, Morocco
- ⇒ Dadès & Todra Gorges, Morocco
- ⇒ Bassari country, Senegal
- ⇒ Gola Forest Reserve, Sierra Leone
- ⇒ Mt Bintumani, Sierra Leone
- ⇒ Kpalimé, Togo

and partly because you may just have the breaks to yourself.

In general terms, the waves off Mauritania, Morocco, Cape Verde, Senegal and The Gambia are best during the European winter, while the coast from Sierra Leone to Cameroon offers the best conditions during the European summer.

Ghana has at least two beaches that surfers rave about: Busua and Cape Three Points, while the Cape Verdean island of Sal is also popular. Even less-known, Bureh Beach, close to Freetown in Sierra Leone, has a fine right-handed break during the rainy season, while Robertsport in Liberia has that unmistakeable call of the remote that hard-core surfers love; *Sliding Liberia*, an award-winning documentary on surfing in Liberia, is definitely worth tracking down. Côte d'Ivoire, Morocco's Atlantic Coast and Dakar in Senegal are other options.

For wider coverage of surfing in the region, check out **Low Pressure** (www.low pressure.co.uk).

Cape Verde is rightly famous for offering some of the best windsurfing in the world. Most of the buzz surrounds the island of Sal, but Boa Vista is also fantastic. Kitesurfing is possible at both places. Other windsurfing possibilities exist in Senegal and at Essaouira in Morocco.

Swimming & Water Sports

You could head to a beach resort in Senegal, The Gambia or Cape Verde, but West Africa's beaches can be much more appealing than this. In fact, the West African coast has everything you dream of in a tropical beach, with pristine sand, swaying palm trees and, in some cases, not another tourist in sight. You just need to know where to look. Stay informed about the potential dangers of swimming at many West African beaches; locals are usually the best source of information.

There are plenty of waterborne activities (including sailing and other boat hire) in tourist areas such as The Gambia's Atlantic Coast, Senegal's Petite Côte or Morocco's Atlantic Coast. For a less-touristy feel, Busua, in Ghana, offers both jet-skiing and sea-kayaking, while jet-skiing can also be arranged on the more placid waters of Lake Bosumtwi.

Children

Having yet to acquire the stereotypes about Africa to which the rest of us are exposed, children's first impressions of the continent are likely to be the warmth and friendliness of the people. Indeed, many West Africans have grown up in large families and children help open doors to closer contact with local people, who are generally friendly, helpful and protective towards children. In short, travelling with children in West Africa adds a whole new dimension to your journey.

Practicalities

In West African countries with a mainstream tourism industry (eg Senegal and The Gambia), some package-tour hotels cater for families with children and, in large cities, top-end hotels usually have rooms with three or four beds for only slightly more than a double. Alternatively, arranging an extra bed or mattress is generally easy and inexpensive. You'll almost certainly want something with a private bathroom and hot water, thereby precluding most budget accommodation.

Despite such exceptions, there are very few child-oriented facilities in the region. In most hotels there are generally no discounts for children. Likewise, on

WEST AFRICA'S TOP BEACHES

- Ebodje, Cameroon
- Kribi, Cameroon
- Maio, Cape Verde
- Praia da Santa Mónica, Cape Verde
- Santa Maria, Cape Verde
- Tarrafal, Cape Verde
- Niega, Côte d'Ivoire
- Sanyang, The Gambia
- Akwidaa Beach, Ghana
- Anomabu, Ghana
- Busua, Ghana
- Kokrobite Beach, Ghana
- Arquipélago dos Bijagós, Guinea-Bissau
- Varela, Guinea-Bissau
- Robertsport, Liberia
- Essaouira, Morocco
- Cap Skiring, Senegal
- Bureh Beach, Sierra Leone

TEN WEST AFRICA BOOKS FOR KIDS

Start searching for children's books on West Africa and you'll quickly discover a whole library of everything from folk tales to simply told histories that you never knew existed. Aimed at children learning about the diverse peoples of the region, the *Heritage Library of African Peoples: West Africa* is an excellent series. Otherwise, here are some of our favourites:

➡ *The Adventures of Spider: West African Folktales* by Joyce Cooper Arkhurst (suitable for four to eight years)

➡ *The Fire Children: A West African Folk Tale* by Eric Maddern (four to eight years)

➡ *Why Mosquitoes Buzz in People's Ears: A West African Tale* by Verna Aardema (four to eight years)

➡ *The Hatseller and the Monkeys* by Baba Wague Diakite (four to eight years)

➡ *Sundiata: The Lion King of Mali* by David Wisniewski (four to eight years)

➡ *Traditional Stories from West Africa* by Robert Hull (seven to 11 years)

➡ *The Cow-Tail Switch and Other West African Stories* by Harold Courlander (nine to 12 years)

➡ *Indigenous Peoples of Africa – West Africa* by Tony Zurlo (nine to 12 years)

➡ *Ancient West African Kingdoms: Ghana, Mali and Songhai* by Mary Quigley (10 to 14 years)

➡ *Tales from West Africa* by Martin Bennett (mixed ages)

public transport, if you want a seat it has to be paid for. Most local children travel for free on buses but spend the whole journey on their parent's lap.

In addition to the length and discomfort involved in road journeys, possible concerns include the scarcity of medical facilities, especially outside major cities, and the difficulty of finding clean, decent bathrooms outside of midrange and top-end hotels. Canned baby food, powdered milk and sometimes also baby cereal (usually with sugar in it), disposable nappies, wipes and other items are available in most capitals, but not everywhere, and they are expensive. It's best to avoid feeding your children street food.

There are other factors to bear in mind when travelling with kids. The rainy season may mean that temperatures are lower, but the risks of malaria and other mosquito-borne diseases are higher. At all times, bring mosquito nets along for your children and ensure they sleep under them. Bring child-friendly mosquito repellent and long-sleeved shirts and trousers.

For more information and hints on travelling with children, Lonely Planet's *Travel with Children* is highly recommended.

Customs Regulations

Except in CFA (Communauté Financière Africaine)–zone countries, the import and export of local currency is either prohibited or severely restricted to negligible amounts, although enforcement of this regulation is fairly lax. As part of their fiscal control, some countries use currency declaration forms. More commonly, control consists simply of asking how much currency you have. Or, you may occasionally be asked to open your wallet or show the contents of your pockets – a wallet bulging with cash is likely to prompt underpaid and ever-hopeful airport agents (ie police and customs officials) to suddenly discover (ie invent) fictitious currency regulations that you've just violated by a sizeable proportion of the amount you have in your wallet.

It's worth doing a bit of advance planning to avoid a scenario like this. Divide your money and store it in several places so it's not all in one lump, and try to look as savvy as possible when going through customs checks. Responding creatively to questions is also helpful, for example explaining that you rely on a credit card for the majority of your expenses (be prepared to show a card), or (if it's true) explaining that you're just in transit and thus don't have much money with you.

Electricity

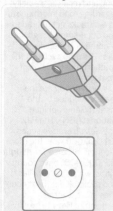

220V/230V/50Hz

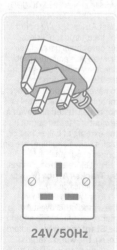

24V/50Hz

Embassies & Consulates

It's important to realise what your own embassy can and can't do to help if you get into trouble. Remember that you are bound by the laws of the country you are in and this is very much the approach your embassy will take. Your embassy will not be sympathetic if you end up in jail after committing a crime locally, even if such actions are legal in your own country.

In genuine emergencies you might get some assistance, but only if other channels have been exhausted. For example, if you need to get home urgently, a free ticket home is extremely unlikely – the embassy would expect you to have insurance. If you have all your money and documents stolen, it might assist with getting a new passport, but a loan for onward travel will be out of the question.

Some embassies used to keep letters for travellers or have a small reading room with newspapers and magazines from home, but few provide these services any more.

Note that in some parts of Africa, countries are represented by an 'honorary consul' who is not a full-time diplomat but usually an expatriate with limited (and rarely visa- or passport-issuing) duties. If your country does not have an embassy in a particular country, another embassy will likely be designated to look after your interests (eg Canadian embassies often have an 'Australian interests' section).

Gay & Lesbian Travellers

Homosexuality is explicitly illegal in 12 out of West Africa's 18 countries; the exceptions are Burkina Faso, Cape Verde, Côte d'Ivoire, Guinea-Bissau, Mali and Niger, although remember that even in these countries laws relating to 'offending public morals' may serve a similar purpose. Maximum legal penalties for homo-

sexual acts range from the death penalty in Mauritania and possibly Nigeria, to 14 years' imprisonment in The Gambia. In 2009, nine gay men in Senegal were sentenced to eight years each in prison for 'indecent conduct and unnatural acts', although these convictions were later overturned on appeal.

Regardless of the legality, however, all countries in West Africa are conservative in their attitudes towards gays and lesbians, and gay sexual relationships are taboo and are either extremely rare or conducted in the utmost secrecy. In most places, discretion is key and public displays of affection should be avoided as a means of showing sensitivity to local feelings, advice that applies to homosexual and heterosexual couples.

In the hotels of some countries (eg Guinea and Sierra Leone), same-sex couples, regardless of whether they are indeed a 'couple', will most likely be refused permission to share a room.

An excellent website to get the low-down on local laws and attitudes to homosexuality is **Global Gayz** (www.globalgayz.com), which has links to information about the situation for gays and lesbians in most West African countries. **ILGA** (www.ilga.org) is another good resource with information for many West African countries. **Afriboyz** (www.afriboyz.com/Homosexuality-in-Africa.html) is also worth checking out.

A US-based tour company offering specialist tours for gay men and women, including to West Africa, is **David Travel** (www.davidtravel.com).

Insurance

A travel insurance policy to cover theft and loss is recommended, and some sort of medical insurance is essential. Always check the small print when shopping around. Some policies specifically exclude 'dangerous activities', which can include scuba diving, off-road driving, motorcycling and even trekking, and a locally acquired motorcycle licence may not be valid under some policies. Also, some policies offer lower and higher medical-expense options, with the higher ones chiefly for countries such as the USA, which have extremely high medical costs.

Hospitals in Africa are not free, and the good ones are not cheap. If your policy requires you to pay on the spot and claim later, make sure you keep all documentation. Some policies ask you to call collect (reverse charges) to a centre in your home country where an immediate assessment of your problem is made.

Check in particular that the policy covers an emergency flight home, as emergency air evacuations can be extremely expensive. Worldwide cover to travellers from many countries is available online at www.lonelyplanet.com/travel_services. You can buy, extend and claim online anytime – even if you're already on the road.

Internet Access

Internet cafes are found throughout West Africa and there's usually at least one in every large or medium-sized town. Rates vary but you'll rarely pay more than €1 or US$1 for an hour online. Connection speeds are generally better in larger towns; some places still use dial-up connections, but services are improving all the time. For things like burning photo CDs, you're better off using internet cafes in capital and other large cities. If you'll be primarily using internet cafes, consider setting up a trip-specific email address as viruses and keystroke-capturing software are small but significant risks.

High-speed wireless access, or wi-fi, is increasingly the norm in top-end and many midrange hotels across the region; expect the number of places offering this service to grow rapidly over the next few years. Wi-fi access in such places is sometimes (but not always) free. In some countries, it may also be possible to obtain internet access through your mobile.

Maps

The regularly updated Michelin map *Africa: North and West* (sheet No 741, formerly No 153, then 953, then 971; scale 1:4,000,000) is one of the best and most detailed, and something of a classic. It's lent its name to the **153 Club** (www.the153club.org), whose members have travelled the regions covered by this map. Whether you join the club or not, the map is something no overland traveller should be without. Even so, if you're driving don't rely solely on the Michelin map as its scale makes it insufficiently detailed for most desert navigation; expect a few discrepancies between the map and reality, especially regarding road information, as old tracks get upgraded and once-smooth highways become potholed disasters. The map excludes the southernmost portion of Cameroon.

Worth noting are the maps produced by the Institut Géographique National (IGN). The *Pays et Villes du Monde* series (1:1,000,000) and the more recent IGN *Carte Touristique* (1:2,000,000) have country maps, which are excellent and available for most countries in West Africa.

If you're likely to be driving off-road (or simply love maps), you really must get hold of as many of the IGN-produced sheets as part of the *Carte Internationale du Monde* series (1:1,000,000) as possible. Devoted to West Africa, they're noted for their almost peerless topographical detail. Their drawback is an important one: they were surveyed in the 1960s and don't seem to have been updated since, meaning that road detail is not to be trusted and even a few natural features (such as the extents of Lake Chad or Mali's Lake Faguibine) are no longer accurate.

For GPS electronic maps, try **Tracks4Africa** (www.tracks4africa.co.za).

To try and track down these and other West Africa maps, your first stop should be **Stanfords** (www.stanfords.co.uk), the world's largest supplier of maps. They have stores in London, Manchester and Bristol in the UK.

In France, **IGN** (www.ign.fr) sells its sheet maps at stores in Paris and Dijon.

Money

Although ATMs are changing things a little, cash remains king in West Africa. And not just any cash: don't bring anything except euros in

---

FRENCH KEYBOARDS *AMY KARAFIN*

Many internet cafes in Francophone West Africa have 'French' keyboards, which can slow you down when typing if you're not used to them. Happily, though, some are loaded with English-language settings. To 'Anglicise' a keyboard, look for a 'Fr' icon on the bottom right of the screen, and scroll up to click on 'En'.

EXCHANGE RATES

COUNTRY	US$1	C$1	A$1	NZ$1	€1	UK£1	¥100
Benin (CFA)	497.5	501.4	515.6	408.2	655.96	802.5	585.1
Burkina Faso (CFA)	497.5	501.4	515.6	408.2	655.96	802.5	585.1
Cameroon (CFA)	497.5	501.4	515.6	408.2	655.96	802.5	585.1
Cape Verde (escudo; CVE)	82.4	83.1	85.4	67.6	110.3	132.9	96.9
Côte d'Ivoire (CFA)	497.5	501.4	515.6	408.2	655.96	802.5	585.1
The Gambia (dalasi; D)	30.8	31.1	31.9	25.3	40.7	49.7	36.3
Ghana (cedi; C)	1.9	1.9	1.9	1.5	2.5	3	2.2
Guinea (Guinean franc; GF)	6.9	7	7.2	5.7	9.2	11.2	8.2
Guinea-Bissau (CFA)	497.5	501.4	515.6	408.2	655.96	802.5	585.1
Liberia (Liberian dollar; L$)	72	72.6	74.6	59 95	116.4	84.7	
Mali (CFA)	497.5	501.4	515.6	408.2	655.96	802.5	585.1
Mauritania (ouguiya; UM)	294.7	297.1	305.4	241.8	389	475.4	346.6
Niger (CFA)	497.5	501.4	515.6	408.2	655.96	802.5	585.1
Nigeria (naira; N)	155.7	156.9	161.3	127.7	205.5	251.1	183.1
Senegal (CFA)	497.5	501.4	515.6	408.2	655.96	802.5	585.1
Sierra Leone (Leone; Le)	4300	4334.1	4456.5	527.8	5675.1	6936.3	5056.81
Togo (CFA)	497.5	501.4	515.6	408.2	655.96	802.5	585.1

For current exchange rates see www.xe.com

former French or Portuguese colonies, while US dollars and, to a lesser extent, UK pounds are preferred in Anglophone countries. Using a credit/debit card to withdraw from ATMs is increasingly possible, thereby allowing you to rely on this in combination with cash; Visa remains more widely accepted than MasterCard.

ATMs

ATMs are found in most major West African towns and cities. In theory they accept credit and debit cards from banks with reciprocal agreements. In almost all cases, Visa is the most widely accepted credit/debit card at most ATMs, with MasterCard increasingly (but far from universally) possible.

For security reasons, we advise against withdrawing money from an international account from a Nigerian ATM, while ATMs in Guinea-Bissau are yet to be integrated into international networks.

Whenever you do use an ATM, expect to be slugged with prohibitive bank fees from your bank back home (€15 to €20 is not unusual for a CFA200,000 transaction). For this reason, always take out the maximum the ATM allows.

Black Market

It can sometimes be best to change your money through unofficial sources such as money changers, supermarkets and other businesses, either for convenience (they keep longer hours than banks) or to get a better-than-official exchange rate. In CFA-zone countries, exchange-rate considerations rarely apply because local currency is easily converted and the rate is pegged to the euro, although Abidjan in Côte d'Ivoire has a thriving US-dollar black market. Unofficial money changers are also tolerated by the

authorities in some border areas, where there are rarely banks.

Although you may have no choice at a border crossing, the general rule throughout West Africa is to only change money on the street when absolutely necessary. The chances of getting ripped off are high, and even if the money changer is honest, you don't know who's watching from the other side of the street. Even at borders, be alert, as changers are notorious for pulling all sorts of stunts with bad rates and folded notes.

In countries with a real black market (eg Guinea and Nigeria), where you can get considerably more for your money, don't forget that this is against the law. What's more, dealers often work with corrupt police officers and can trap you in a set-up where you may be 'arrested', shaken down and eventually lose all your money.

18 COUNTRIES, 11 CURRENCIES

The difficulties of juggling the currencies of the 18 countries in West Africa is ameliorated by the fact that eight countries (Benin, Burkina Faso, Côte d'Ivoire, Guinea-Bissau, Mali, Niger, Senegal and Togo) use the West African CFA (Communauté Financière Africaine) franc, which can be used (or exchanged for local currency) in some other countries, such as The Gambia and Ghana. Many people will also accept it as valid currency, especially in taxis or at market stalls, in The Gambia and Guinea.

The CFA is fixed against (and supported by) the euro at a rate of 655.967:1, making it a 'hard' currency. One result of this arrangement is that most banks change euros into CFA without charging a fee or commission. That said, at hotels and foreign exchange bureaus, expect rates of 650 or lower, and plan on paying commissions when changing euro (or any other currency) travellers cheques into CFA.

In recent years, the political leaders of The Gambia, Ghana, Guinea, Nigeria and Sierra Leone – the majority of West Africa's non-CFA block – have spoken of moving towards their own common currency, to be known as the 'eco', which would later merge with the CFA and thereby create a single currency throughout most of West Africa. In the meantime, countries outside the CFA zone each have their own individual currencies.

Cameroon, as well as neighbouring Central African countries, uses the Central African CFA franc, which is linked to the euro at the same rate as the West African CFA franc. However, you can't make payments with Central African CFA in the West African CFA zone or vice versa.

Cash & Travellers Cheques

Cash is easily the most convenient way to carry your money as it's always the easiest to change. Remember, however, that it cannot be replaced if lost or stolen, even by insurance companies.

In CFA-zone countries, the best currency to travel with is definitely the euro. Other major international currencies such as the US dollar and the UK pound can be changed in capital cities and tourist areas, but at less-favourable rates. In the non-CFA countries, the best currency to travel with is US dollars, with euros and UK pounds sometimes accepted in larger cities.

Travellers cheques are refundable if lost or stolen, but they're usually difficult to change (sometimes only one bank will do it and sometimes only in capital cities) and almost always attract high commissions. As a result, few travellers use them in West Africa. The best countries for travellers cheques are Cape Verde and Ghana; they're not worth the paper they're printed on in Nigeria, Liberia, Guinea and Guinea-Bissau.

Well-known brands of travellers cheques are better as they're more likely to be recognised by bank staff. Amex, followed by Visa and Thomas Cook/MasterCard, are the most widely accepted, and some banks will take only one of these three. Most banks require you to show your original purchase receipts in order to change travellers cheques, so it's essential to bring these. Carry them with you (separately from your cheques), but also leave a copy at home, as well as elsewhere in your luggage, in case the original receipts or the cheques themselves are stolen.

For both cash and travellers cheques, take a mixture of high and low denominations. Rates are better for high denominations (ie €50, €100, US$50 or US$100). Note that the USA changed the design of the US$100 bill in the mid-1990s and old-style US$100 notes are not accepted at some places, especially those that don't have a light machine for checking watermarks.

You may also need some small amounts if you're about to leave the region, or a certain country, and only need to change a small amount. Also, a supply of small-denomination cash notes (eg US$1 and US$5 or the euro equivalent) can come in handy for cases when change is unavailable.

In addition to your main travel funds, carry an additional stash of cash with you, preferably kept separate from the rest of your cash and travellers cheques. This will serve as a contingency fund for emergencies.

Unless you're relying on ATMs, try to anticipate your needs and change enough in advance to cover yourself on weekends and during non-banking hours. If you do get stuck outside banking hours, you can try changing money at top-end hotels or tour companies, although rates are likely to be poor. Another option, and much better than changing on the street, is to ask discreetly at a shop selling imported items. 'The banks are closed, do you know anyone who can help me...?' is a better approach than 'Do you want to change money?'.

Credit Cards

You can rarely use a credit card to pay for items, and such occasions are limited to top-end hotels and restaurants, car-rental companies and air tickets; an extra commission is often attached, usually ranging from 3% to 15%. Visa is the most widely accepted card, followed a distant second by MasterCard; credit cards are useless in Sierra Leone, Guinea-Bissau and Liberia, and we advise against using them in Nigeria. Cape Verde and Morocco probably offer the widest choice of paying by credit card.

Watching a person put your card through the electronic credit-card machine (as opposed to letting them do it out of sight) is a good idea to ensure you don't receive unwanted bills back home.

International Transfers

Western Union Money Transfer has representatives in just about every West African country, usually as part of local banks or post offices.

International bank-to-bank money transfers may save you from carrying large amounts of money but are best used only as a last resort. Transfers can take three to four days, and sometimes several weeks, to clear. If you do need to transfer money, ask your forwarding bank to send you separate confirmation with full details, including the routing or transfer number, account and branch numbers, and address and telephone contacts. With this, you can then go to the recipient bank with proof that your money has been sent. Most countries will only give you cash in local currency.

Money Changers

The main places to change money are banks and forex bureaus. Where they exist, forex bureaus are often more efficient than banks, usually offer slightly higher rates and are open longer hours, though many don't accept travellers cheques. Charges and commissions vary, with some banks and forex bureaus charging a flat fee, and others a percentage commission; some charge both a fee and a commission. The bank or forex bureau with the higher commission may also offer a higher exchange rate, though, so you could still be better off.

Apart from export restrictions, exchanging CFA francs in countries outside the region is nearly impossible, except in France. In most countries in the CFA zone, it's relatively easy to change remaining CFA francs into euros but difficult to change CFA francs to dollars. On leaving non-CFA countries, it's usually not possible to reconvert local currency into foreign currency; you can usually change back to CFA francs in The Gambia and Guinea, where it's relatively straightforward, although rates are low. Try come to an arrangement with other travellers if you think you're going to be caught with a surfeit of local cash.

Also, note that if you're travelling between the West African and Central African CFA zones (eg from Niger to Cameroon), it's easy to change CFA notes of one zone for those of the other at banks, but more difficult to change coins.

Tipping

There are few clear rules on tipping in West Africa. In general, only the wealthy (ie well-to-do locals and nearly all foreign visitors) are expected to tip. Anyone staying in a fancy hotel would be expected to tip porters and other staff, but there would not be the same expectation from a backpacker in a cheap hotel.

Everyone – locals and foreigners – is expected to tip 10% at the better restaurants, although check whether service is included in the bill. At more basic restaurants and eating houses no tips are expected. There's a grey area between these two classes of restaurants, where tipping is rarely expected from locals but may be expected of foreigners. Even wealthier West Africans will sometimes tip at smaller restaurants – not so much because it's expected, but as a show of status.

Locals seldom tip in privately hired taxis, but some drivers expect well-heeled travellers to tip about 10%, especially if you have hired the vehicle for a lengthy trip. On most short trips, however, loose change is normally appreciated. In shared taxis around cities tipping is almost unheard of. If you rent a car with driver, a tip is always expected, usually about 10% of the total rental cost, and more if it is a multiday rental or if your driver has been exceptionally good. The same applies to guides.

Photography

If photography is a primary reason for your visit try to avoid the harmattan season, which is at its height in many areas of the region from January through to May. The region's extremes of climate, such as heat, humidity and very fine sand, can also take their toll on your camera, so always take appropriate precautions; changing lenses in a dust-laden wind is, for example, a recipe for disaster.

For more advice, Lonely Planet's *Travel Photography: A Guide to Taking Better Pictures* by Richard I'Anson is an excellent resource, full of helpful tips for photography while on the road.

Equipment

Memory cards are available in major cities of most West African countries, although you won't have much choice when it comes to the brand. Expect prices to be broadly similar to what you'd pay back home. The situation for batteries is similar, although for more professional cameras you're better off bringing your own supply. Most (but not all) internet cafes in major cities will let you burn photos onto CDs, although the equipment may not be up to scratch in more out-of-the-way places.

For charging batteries, remember to bring the necessary charger, plugs and transformer for the country you are visiting.

Lens paper and cleaners can be difficult to find in some countries, so bring your own. A dust brush is also useful.

Photographing People

As a matter of courtesy, don't photograph (or film) people without first asking their permission. Digital cameras have the advantage of being able to show people their photo immediately after you've taken it, which is usually temptation enough for most people to say yes. That said, while some West Africans may like being photographed, many don't. They may be superstitious about your camera, suspicious of your motives, or simply interested in whatever economic advantage they can gain from your desire to photograph them and demand a fee. In more conservative areas, including in many rural areas, men should never photograph women and in most circumstances should never even ask.

Restrictions

Avoid taking pictures of bridges, dams, airports, military equipment, government buildings, border crossings

---

TABASKI

Two weeks before Tabaski, sheep prices steeply rise, as every family is expected to provide one during the celebrations. Those who cannot afford a sheep are socially embarrassed and most will do anything to scrape together the money. One-third of the slaughtered animal is supposed to be given to the poor, one-third to friends, and one-third is left for the family. If you are invited to a Tabaski meal (it usually takes place after prayers at the mosque), you'll be participating in Muslim West Africa's most important and festive day of the year. It's celebrated with particular colour (and cavalry processions) in Kano (Nigeria), but is also a festive time in Senegal, Niger, Cameroon and Mali. Here and elsewhere during Tabaski (and during Eid al-Fitr and the other Islamic holidays), you'll see entire families dressed in their finest clothes, strolling in the streets or visiting the mosque.

---

and anything else that could be considered strategic. You may be arrested or have your camera and/or memory card confiscated. The definition of what is 'strategic' differs from one country to the next, and signs are rarely posted, so err on the side of caution and ask your friendly neighbourhood police officer for permission if in doubt.

Photography is usually allowed inside religious and archaeological sites, unless there are signs indicating otherwise. As a rule, however, do not photograph inside mosques during a service. You should also exercise caution around sacred sites.

Many West Africans are sensitive about the negative aspects of their country, so exercise discretion when taking photos in poorer areas.

Post

Postal services are moderately reliable in most West African capitals and cities. In rural areas, though, service can range from slow to non-existent.

Letters sent from a major capital take about a week to 10 days to reach most of Europe, and at least two weeks to reach North America or

Australasia, although it's sometimes much longer. For more speed and certainty, a few countries have 'express' services, but the main alternative (though expensive) is a courier service. **DHL** (www.dhl.com), for example, has offices in most West African capitals.

Public Holidays

You should always keep an eye out for the timing of local holidays – these can be wonderful occasions with countrywide parties or a day when everything grinds to a halt. One highlight of any trip to West Africa is witnessing one of the many ceremonies that are an integral part of traditional culture in the region.

Islamic Holidays

Important Islamic holidays, when much of West Africa's commercial life grinds to a halt, include the following:

Tabaski Also called Eid al-Kebir; it commemorates Abraham's readiness to sacrifice his son on God's command, and the last-minute substitution of a ram. It also coincides with the end of the pilgrimage to Mecca, and is the most important Muslim event, marked in most countries by great feasts with roasted sheep and a two-day public holiday.

Eid al-Fitr The second major Islamic holiday; it marks the end of Ramadan, the annual fasting month when Muslims do not eat or drink during daylight hours, but break their fast after sundown. Offices usually grind to a halt in the afternoon throughout Ramadan.

Eid al-Moulid Celebrates the birthday of the Prophet Mohammed. It occurs about three months after Tabaski.

Other Holidays

In addition to the Islamic ceremonies, there are many public holidays – either government or religious – when businesses and government offices are closed. Public holidays vary from country to country, but some – including Christmas and New Year's Day – are observed throughout the region. Government holidays are often marked with parades, dancing and other such events, while the Christian religious holidays invariably centre on beautiful church services and singing.

Telephone

Telephone and fax connections to places outside West Africa are reasonably good, as the transmission is usually via satellite. Calls between African countries, however, are often relayed on landlines or through Europe, which means the reception is frequently bad – assuming you can get a call through in the first place. Things are improving, but slowly.

The best places to make international calls (unless you have a fast internet connection and telephone through Skype or other software from your laptop or, less privately, at an internet cafe) are at government telephone offices or private telecentres, which you'll find in most towns. International calls using local mobile SIM cards can also work out cheaper than landlines.

Costs for international calls and faxes to Europe, the USA or Australasia start at about US$1 per minute, with a few countries offering reduced rates at night and on weekends.

Dial-direct or 'home-direct' numbers are available from a few countries. With these, you dial an operator in your home country who can reverse the charges, or charge the call to a phone-company charge card or your home number. These home-direct numbers are toll free, but if you are using a phone booth you may need a coin or phonecard to connect. Check with your phone company for access numbers and a list of countries where they have home-direct numbers.

Fax

Most cities and large towns have public telephone offices at the post office where you can make international calls and send faxes. There are also private telecommunications centres in major towns and cities throughout the region. Sending a fax from a hotel is much more expensive.

Mobile Phones

Mobile (cell) phones are everywhere in West Africa, to such an extent that many privately run telephone offices have closed down. In most countries, local SIM cards are readily available from street vendors in any town reached by mobile coverage; top-up cards are similarly widely available. If you prefer not to use your own phone, or your mobile hasn't been 'unlocked' as is the case with many US mobile phones, cheap mobile phones (as little as €15) can be purchased in capital cities and most larger towns. International calls using a local SIM card often work out cheaper than calling from landlines. Although mobile coverage is usually restricted to urban settlements, coverage is expanding all the time.

A European or North American mobile phone will probably have reception in most West African countries, whereby your carrier's local partner will allow you to receive and send text messages, as well as phone calls, although making calls can be extremely expensive. Remember that if someone

ISLAMIC HOLIDAY DATES

Since the Islamic calendar is based on 12 lunar months totalling 354 or 355 days, holidays are always about 11 days earlier than the previous year. The exact dates depend on the moon and are announced for certain only about a day in advance. Estimated dates for these events are:

EVENT	2013	2014	2015	2016	2017
Ramadan begins	9 Jul	29 Jun	18 Jun	7 Jun	28 May
Eid al-Fitr	8 Aug	29 Jul	18 Jul	7 Jul	27 Jun
Tabaski	15 Oct	4 Oct	24 Sep	13 Sep	2 Sep
Eid al-Moulid	25 Jan	14 Jan	3 Jan	Dec	Dec

calls your mobile phone while you're in West Africa, you may pay the bulk of the charge. In some cases, a local SIM card purchased in one country may also work in other West African countries where that carrier operates; Orange is one carrier that operates in a number of countries in the region and may offer such a service.

Time

Burkina Faso, Côte d'Ivoire, The Gambia, Ghana, Guinea, Guinea-Bissau, Liberia, Mali, Mauritania, Morocco, Senegal, Sierra Leone and Togo are on GMT/UTC. Cape Verde is one hour behind. Benin, Cameroon, Niger and Nigeria are one hour ahead.

Morocco is the only country covered in this book to observe daylight-saving time in summer – Moroccan clocks are turned forwards one hour on the last Sunday in April, then back again on the last Sunday in September.

Toilets

There are two main types of toilet: Western sit-down, with a bowl and seat; and African squat, with a hole in the ground. Standards vary tremendously, from pristine to those that leave little to the imagination as to the health or otherwise of the previous occupant.

In rural areas, squat toilets are built over a deep hole in the ground. These are called 'long drops', and the waste matter just fades away naturally, as long as the hole isn't filled with too much other rubbish (such as paper or synthetic materials, including tampons). Even some Western toilets aren't plumbed in, but just balanced over a long drop. In our experience, a noncontact hole in the ground is better than a filthy bowl to hover over any day.

Tourist Information

With just a handful of exceptions, West Africa's tourism authorities are not geared up for tourism, and there are few tourist offices abroad. Some countries run small tourist offices at their embassies, which may be helpful for getting moderately useful brochures or general travel information.

Once in West Africa, some countries have Ministry of Tourism information offices but, apart from offering a few old brochures, they're unlikely to be of much assistance. Otherwise, you'll usually have more success enquiring with staff at tour companies or hotels.

Travellers with Disabilities

West Africa has very few facilities for the disabled. This, combined with weak infrastructure in the region, can make travel difficult, although it's not impossible. Few hotels have lifts (and those that do are generally expensive hotels), streets may be either badly potholed or else unpaved, footpaths are few and far between, and ramps and other things to ease access are often non-existent. While accommodation at many budget hotels is on the ground floor, bathroom access can be difficult, and doors are not always wide enough for wheelchairs. Such difficulties are only partly counterbalanced by the fact that West Africans are usually very accommodating and willing to offer whatever assistance they can, as long as they understand what you need.

As for transport, most taxis in the region are small sedans, and buses are not wheelchair equipped. Minibuses and larger 4WD vehicles can usually be arranged

through car-rental agencies in major towns and cities, although this will be pricey.

In general, travel and access will probably be easiest in places with relatively good tourism infrastructure, such as Morocco or some of the coastal areas of Senegal and The Gambia. As far as we are aware, there are no facilities in the region specifically aimed at blind travellers.

Before setting out for West Africa, travellers with disabilities should consider contacting one of the recommended organisations that may be able to help with advice and assistance.

Access-able Travel Source (☑303-232 2979; www.access-able.com; PO Box 1796, Wheatridge, CO, USA) Has lists of tour operators offering tours for travellers with disabilities.

Royal Association for Disability & Rehabilitation (RADAR;☑020-7250 3222; www.radar.org.uk; 250 City Rd, 12 City Forum, London, UK, EC1V 8AF)

Tourism for All (☑0303-303 0146; www.tourismforall.org.uk; UK) Advice for disabled and less-mobile senior travellers.

Visas

This section contains general information about visas. See also the country chapters for specific information about each country.

The general rule for West Africa is to get your visas before leaving home. They are rarely issued at land borders and only occasionally at airports. Also, if you're flying from outside Africa, many airlines won't let you on board without a visa.

Visa agencies are worth considering if you need visas to several countries before you leave or if there's no relevant embassy in your country. For longer trips or more flexibility, it's possible to obtain most of your visas in the region as you go, although this requires some advance planning and careful checking of the location of embassies for the countries in question – most West African countries have insufficient resources to maintain expensive embassies in many countries.

Visa fees average between US$20 and US$50, with prices depending on where you apply, your nationality and whether you're asking for multiple- or single-entry visas. Always check the visa's validity length and its start date when deciding where to make your application. When applying for a visa, you may have to show proof that you intend to leave the country (eg an air ticket) or that you have enough funds to support yourself during your visit.

Most visa applications require between two and four identical passport photos, either black and white or colour. Inexpensive photo shops are found throughout the region, and rural areas sometimes have a village photographer who can do the job for you.

Visa des Pays de l'Entente

The Visa des Pays de l'Entente is a multi-country visa that covers travel in Benin, Burkina Faso, Côte d'Ivoire, Niger and Togo. If you've never heard of it, don't be surprised – it's so poorly publicised that most travellers never learn of its existence. Implementation of this relatively new visa is also still patchy, which significantly diminishes its appeal – the relevant authorities in Benin were, at the time of research, only issuing the visa to residents of Benin. In remote border crossings there is also the danger that officials won't recognise the visa and will force travellers to purchase a new individual country visa.

Before you go rushing off to your nearest West African embassy to ask for this visa, you need to learn how it works. For a start, it is only obtainable *within* these five West African countries, which means that first you must obtain a visa for the first of these countries and, once there, apply at the immigration or visa extension office in the capital city. To get the Visa des Pays de l'Entente, which is valid for two months, you'll need to take along CFA15,500 to CFA25,000 depending on the country, and up to two passport photos. It usually takes 24 to 72 hours for the visa to be issued.

Although the Visa des Pays de l'Entente may work out to be more convenient in some cases, it's worth remembering that it's only valid for one entry into each country: ideal for overlanders, less so for those who plan to visit countries more than once.

Volunteering

There are quite a large number of volunteers in West Africa, and it's a great way to reduce the ecological footprint of your trip and even make a contribution to local communities. It's also an amazing forum for self-exploration, especially if you touch a few lives and make friends along the way.

Keep in mind that there is no such thing as a perfect volunteer placement. Generally speaking, you'll get as much out of a program as you're willing to put into it; the vast majority of volunteers in West Africa walk away all the better for the experience.

Ghana in particular has numerous volunteering possibilities.

Organisations

The following international organisations are good places to start gathering information on volunteering, although they won't necessarily always have projects on the go in West Africa.

Coordinating Committee for International Voluntary Service (ccivs.org)

Earthwatch (www.earthwatch.org)

Frontier Conservation Expeditions (www.frontier.ac.uk)

Idealist.org (www.idealist.org)

International Volunteer-Programs Association (www.volunteerinternational.org)

Peace Corps (www.peacecorps.gov)

Voluntary Service Overseas (VSO; www.vso.org.uk)

Worldwide Experience (www.worldwideexperience.com)

Worldwide Volunteering (www.wwv.org.uk)

Women Travellers

When travelling in West Africa – solo or with other women – you're unlikely to encounter any more difficulties than you would elsewhere in the world. The female authors of *West Africa* have travelled for extended periods (including solo travel) and/or lived in West Africa, usually without incident, and most did their research travelling alone.

Hints

Although women will undoubtedly attract more attention than men, more often than not you'll meet only warmth and hospitality, and find that you receive kindness and special treatment that you wouldn't be shown if you were a man. While you're likely to hear some horror stories from expats who may be appalled at the idea of solo female travel, it's worth remembering that the incidence of rape or other real harm is extremely rare.

It's important to not let these concerns ruin your trip. Remember that some sections of the region, such

'C'EST MADAME? OU BIEN, MADEMOISELLE?'

Women travelling on their own through Francophone West Africa will undoubtedly hear these words ad nauseam: translated, the phrase means 'are you married or not?' Sometimes, for example when you're filling out forms or registering at a hotel, it's not ill-intentioned. But, all too often, it's a leering soldier or border official who's a little too eager for company. Although there's not much you can do to prevent the question, having at least a fictitious husband – ideally one who will be arriving imminently at that very place – can help in avoiding further advances. If you're travelling with a male companion, a good way to avoid unwanted interest is to introduce him as your husband. If you're questioned as to why your husband/children aren't with you, explain that you'll be meeting them later.

as parts of the Sahel, are wonderfully hassle free. You'll also have the opportunity to meet local women, something that few male travellers have the chance to do on the same terms. Good places to try include tourist offices, government departments or even your hotel, where at least some of the staff are likely to be formally educated young to middle-aged women. In rural areas, starting points include female teachers at a local school, or staff at a health centre where language barriers are less likely to be a problem.

That said, it's inevitable that you'll attract some unwanted attention. Here are a few tips:

➡ Dress modestly. This is the most successful strategy for minimising unasked-for male attention. Wear trousers or a long skirt, and a conservative top with sleeves. Tucking your hair under a cap or tying it back, especially if it's blonde, sometimes helps. Exposing your midriff is rarely a good idea.

➡ Use common sense. Trust your instincts and take the usual precautions when out. For example, if possible, avoid going out alone in the evenings, particularly on foot. Avoid isolated areas, roadways and beaches during both day and evening hours, and be cautious on beaches, many of which can become deserted very quickly. Throughout the region, hitching alone is not recommended.

➡ Don't worry about being rude, and don't feel the need to explain yourself. If you try to start explaining why you don't want to meet for a drink/go to a nightclub/get married on the spot, it may be interpreted as flirting.

➡ Ignore hissing, calls of 'chérie', or whatever. If you respond, it may be interpreted as a lead on.

➡ Wear a wedding ring or carry photos of 'your' children, which will make you appear less 'available'.

➡ Avoid direct eye contact with local men; dark sunglasses help. There are, however, times when a cold glare is an effective riposte to an unwanted suitor.

➡ On public transport, sit next to a woman if possible.

➡ If you need help (eg directions), ask a woman first, although local women are less likely than men to have had an education that included learning English.

➡ Go to the nearest public place, such as the lobby of a hotel, to get rid of any hangers-on. If they persist, asking the receptionist to call the police usually frightens them off.

Tampons & Sanitary Pads

Tampons (imported from Europe) are available from pharmacies or large supermarkets in capital cities throughout West Africa, and occasionally in other large towns. Elsewhere, the only choice is likely to be sanitary pads so you may want to bring an emergency supply.

Transport

GETTING THERE & AWAY

This section tells you how to reach West Africa by air, land and sea from other parts of the world and outlines the routes for onward travel from the region. Flights, tours and rail tickets can be booked online at www.lonelyplanet.com/travel_services.

Entering West Africa

Entering West Africa varies from country to country but is generally hassle free, provided you have all your documents in order. In order to smooth your entry, there are a few things .you must have when you arrive at your first West African border:

➡ Valid entry visa, unless you are entering a country where the visa is available on arrival.

➡ Your up-to-date international vaccination booklet (livre jeune), which contains proof of yellow-fever vaccination.

➡ Enough empty pages in your passport for visas, entry and exit stamps, and registration with police within some countries – make sure you have at least two pages per country.

➡ A passport that expires at least six months after your trip ends – it's not mandatory in all cases but some officials will cause problems if your passport is about to expire.

➡ The patience of a saint: bureaucracy can be epic in its obsession with minutiae.

➡ An awareness that some officials will assure you that your perfectly valid visa has expired – unless it has, they're just asking for a bribe.

Air

There are direct flights from Europe into every West Af-

rican capital, although very few airlines fly into Bissau (Guinea-Bissau), Freetown (Sierra Leone) and Monrovia (Liberia). Most of the best connections between Europe and sub-Saharan West Africa are via Casablanca with Royal Air Maroc. It's also relatively easy to fly into West Africa from North Africa and the Middle East, with a handful of airlines offering services from elsewhere in Africa. If you're travelling from Australia, Canada or the USA, you'll usually need to connect to a flight from Europe, the Middle East or South Africa.

Airports

International airports with the greatest number of incoming flights (and the best onward connections) include:

➡ Abidjan (Côte d'Ivoire)

➡ Accra (Ghana)

➡ Casablanca (Morocco)

➡ Dakar (Senegal)

➡ Douala (Cameroon)

➡ Lagos (Nigeria)

CLIMATE CHANGE & TRAVEL

Every form of transport that relies on carbon-based fuel generates CO_2, the main cause of human-induced climate change. Modern travel is dependent on aeroplanes, which might use less fuel per kilometre per person than most cars but travel much greater distances. The altitude at which aircraft emit gases (including CO_2) and particles also contributes to their climate change impact. Many websites offer 'carbon calculators' that allow people to estimate the carbon emissions generated by their journey and, for those who wish to do so, to offset the impact of the greenhouse gases emitted with contributions to portfolios of climate-friendly initiatives throughout the world. Lonely Planet offsets the carbon footprint of all staff and author travel.

CARNETS

A *carnet de passage* is like a passport for your car, a booklet that is stamped on arrival and departure from a country to ensure that you export the vehicle again after you've imported it. It's usually issued by an automobile association in the country where the vehicle is registered. Most countries of West Africa require a carnet although rules change frequently.

The sting in the tail with a carnet is that you usually have to lodge a deposit to secure it. If you default on the carnet – that is, you don't have an export stamp to match the import one – then the country in question can claim your deposit, which can be up to 300% of the new value of the vehicle. You can get around this problem with bank guarantees or carnet insurance, but you still have to fork out in the end if you default.

Should the worst occur and your vehicle is irretrievably damaged in an accident or catastrophic breakdown, you'll have to argue it out with customs officials. Having a vehicle stolen can be even worse, as you may be suspected of having sold it.

The carnet may need to specify any pricey spare parts that you're planning to carry, such as a gearbox, which is designed to prevent any spare-part importation rackets. Contact your local automobile association for details about necessary documentation at least three months in advance.

There are also international airports at:

➡ Bamako, Mopti and Gao (Mali)

➡ Banjul (The Gambia)

➡ Bissau (Guinea-Bissau)

➡ Conakry (Guinea)

➡ Cotonou (Benin)

➡ Freetown (Sierra Leone)

➡ Kano and Port Harcourt (Nigeria)

➡ Monrovia (Liberia)

➡ Niamey (Niger)

➡ Nouakchott, Nouâdhibou and Atâr (Mauritania)

➡ Ouagadougou and Bobo-Dioulasso (Burkina Faso)

➡ Praia and Sal (Cape Verde)

➡ Yaoundé and Garoua (Cameroon)

Airlines

Dozens of airlines fly into West Africa from elsewhere in Africa, as well as the Middle East and Europe. The most important ones include:

Air Burkina (www.air-burkina. com)

Air France (www.airfrance. com)

British Airways (www. britishairways.com)

Brussels Airlines (www. brusselsairlines.com)

EgyptAir (www.egyptair.com)

Emirates (www.emirates.com)

Ethiopian Airlines (www. ethiopianairlines.com)

Iberia (www.iberia.com)

Interair (www.interair.co.za)

Kenya Airways (www.kenya-airways.com)

KLM Royal Dutch Airlines (www.klm.com)

Lufthansa (www.lufthansa. com)

Middle East Airlines (www. mea.com.lb)

Royal Air Maroc (www. royalairmaroc.com)

South African Airways (www.flysaa.com)

TACV (www.flytacv.com)

TAP Air Portugal (www. flytap.com)

Virgin Atlantic (www.virgin-atlantic.com)

Tickets

Buying cheap air tickets in West Africa is a challenge. Usually the best deal you can get is an airline's official excursion fare, and there's no discount on single tickets unless you qualify for a 'youth' (under 26, sometimes 23) or 'student' rate. In cities that handle plenty of international traffic, such as Dakar or Abidjan, cheaper tickets are easier to come by from travel agents; in Bissau or Monrovia you won't have much choice about fares or airlines.

Charter flights are worth considering as they're generally direct and cheaper than scheduled flights. Some charter flights come as part of a package that includes accommodation and other services, but most charter companies sell 'flight only' tickets.

Land

Border Crossings

If you're travelling independently overland to West Africa – whether cycling, driving your own car or taking public transport – you can approach the region from three main directions: from the north, across the Sahara; from the south and southeast, through the countries bordering southern and eastern Cameroon; or from the east, through Chad. There is no regular, scheduled public transport along any of these routes.

If you're coming from the north, the main border-crossing point into sub-Saharan West Africa from Morocco and the Western Sahara is just north of Nouâdhibou. In theory, there are also crossings at Bordj Mokhtar (Algeria/Mali), Assamakka (Algeria/Niger) and Tumu (Libya/Niger) but these were either closed or not recommended at the time of writing.

If you come into West Africa from the south or east, the border-crossing points are at Garoua-Boulaï or Kenzou (for the Central African Republic); at Kousséri, Bongor or Léré (for Chad); Moloundou, in Cameroon's far southeastern corner (for Congo); Kye Ossi (for Gabon); and Ebebiyin or Campo (for Equatorial Guinea). Another option is to take the 'long way around', crossing the border on the northern side of Lake Chad on the route to Nguigmi (Niger). Remember that very few travellers use these routes.

Car & Motorcycle

Anyone planning to take their own vehicle to West Africa should check in advance what spare parts and petrol are likely to be available.

A number of documents are also required:

Carnet A *carnet de passage* is like a passport for your car, a booklet that is stamped on arrival and departure from a country to ensure that you export the vehicle again after you've imported it.

Green card Issued by insurers. Insurance for some countries is only obtainable at the border. Check with your insurance company or automobile association before leaving home.

International Driving Permit (IDP) Although most foreign licences are accept-

able in West African countries, an IDP issued by your local automobile association is highly recommended.

Vehicle registration documents Carrying all ownership papers is a must.

BRING YOUR OWN VEHICLE

If you want to travel in West Africa using your own car or motorbike, but don't fancy the Saharan crossing, another option is to ship it. The usual way of doing this is to load the car onto a ship in Europe and take it off again at either Dakar or Banjul (Abidjan and Tema, in Ghana, are other options).

Costs vary depending on the size of the vehicle and the final destination, but generally start from around US$1000. Apart from cost, your biggest problem is likely to be security – many drivers report theft of items from the inside and outside (such as lights and mirrors) of their car. Vehicles are usually left unlocked for the crossing and when in storage at the destination port, so chain or lock all equipment into fixed boxes inside the vehicle. Getting a vehicle out of port is frequently a nightmare, requiring visits to several different offices where stamps must be obtained and mysterious fees paid at every turn. You could consider using an official handling agent or an unofficial 'fixer' to take your vehicle through all this.

From Chad

Between Cameroon and Chad, the main border crossing is between Maroua (Cameroon) and Kousséri, although the actual border is at Nguelé. Corrupt officials abound here. For more adventure, try the crossings further south to the towns of Bongor or Léré; the former requires a *pirogue* (traditional canoe) across the Logone River.

For hard-core travellers, a more arduous (and adventurous) route into West Africa from Chad runs around the top of what's left of Lake Chad between Nguigmi in Niger and the Chadian capital N'Djaména.

From the North – Crossing the Sahara

With rebellion and banditry plaguing northern Mali and northern Niger at the time of writing, most trans-Saharan routes have fallen quiet. Apart from entering Mauritania via Morocco and Western Sahara, we are unable to recommend any of the other routes across the Sahara into West Africa; we have covered these routes below in case the situation changes in the next few years. There is no public transport along any of the routes covered here.

Whichever route you take, you'll need to get a thorough update on the security situation before setting off. Anybody planning to travel in the Sahara should check out the excellent website

---

DRIVING TO WEST AFRICA – FURTHER READING

Driving your own car or motorbike to West Africa, and driving off-road within the region, are vast subjects. Two specialist guides that we recommend:

➡ *Adventure Motorcycling Handbook*, by Chris Scott, covers all parts of the world where tar roads end. It contains stacks of good information on the Sahara and West Africa, all combined with humour and personal insights.

➡ *Sahara Overland (2nd Edition)*, by Chris Scott, is the best, most recent and most comprehensive book on all aspects of Saharan travel by two or four wheels, with information on established and newer Saharan routes, and more than 100 maps. Chris Scott's highly recommended website, www.sahara-overland.com, has updates of the book, as well as a useful forum.

put together by **Chris Scott** (www.sahara-overland.com); its forum is particularly useful on which routes are open. Be sure to bring sufficient food, water and warm clothes for the journey.

WESTERN SAHARA ROUTE

About 500km south of Agadir you enter the disputed territory of Western Sahara, where the main road continues along the coast to Dakhla, from where it's another 425km to Nouâdhibou in Mauritania. The road is now entirely sealed from Dakhla to Nouakchott, except for the 3km no man's land that separates the two border crossings. The border area is littered with landmines, so don't stray from the road.

A *grand taxi* (shared taxi) from Dakhla to the Mauritanian border costs Dh250 to Dh400, although make sure that you ask the driver to ferry you across no man's land to the Mauritanian border crossing – otherwise, it's a hot, 3km walk along a road lined with minefields unless you can hitch with lurking money-changers (for a fee). From the Mauritanian border post to Nouâdhibou costs UM1800 in a *grand taxi*. Going the other way, there are taxis most days from Nouâdhibou to Dakhla (UM11,500, eight hours).

If you're hitching, Hôtel Sahara in Dakhla is where most of the overlanders stay and is a good place to find other travellers to team up with or to look for a lift. There's a thriving trade in secondhand cars being driven from Europe to sell in West Africa and plenty of vacationing French travellers in campervans; remember that sharing costs is expected.

If you're driving your own car, fill your tank up in Western Sahara (the last petrol station is 80km before the border) as petrol is much cheaper here than in Mauritania.

Moneychangers will flag you down as you cross no man's land; their rates for ouguiya are poor. At the Mauritanian border post, you can buy a Mauritanian visa (€20), while those with their own vehicles will need to buy a temporary import form (*engagement sur honneur;* €10) and Mauritanian insurance (around €30 for two weeks). Expect searches for alcohol by Mauritanian customs. After Mauritanian border formalities it's approximately 45km further to Nouâdhibou.

In whichever direction you travel, expect to take a minimum of eight hours between Dakhla and Nouâdhibou, including two hours completing border formalities.

ROUTE DU HOGGAR

Although only for hard-core Saharan travellers in these troubled times, the Route du Hoggar, through Algeria and Niger, remains open provided you stick to the main highway and don't stray into the Aïr Mountains. The border crossing is between Assamakka (Niger) and In Guezzem (Algeria); make sure you have your visa and other paperwork in order in advance. If you're entering Niger here, you'll need a licensed desert guide and *feuille de route* (official itinerary). From Assamakka to Agadez, you must travel as part of an infrequent military convoy. If you are entering Algeria here, you'll need to be met by an official guide on the Algerian side of the border.

The Route du Hoggar is sealed, except for the 600km section between Tamanrasset ('Tam') and Arlit, although the road is in poor condition on many sections. Unless you have your own vehicle, you'll need to hitch a ride in trucks between Tamanrasset and Agadez. Very few travellers head south, but even fewer make the journey in reverse, due in large part to the difficulty of getting an Algerian visa in Niger.

OTHER ROUTES

The Route du Tanezrouft – which runs through Algeria and Mali, via Adrar and the border at Bordj-Mokhtar, ending in Gao – has always been one of the most romantic (for its sheer remoteness) and most dangerous trans-Saharan routes. Although it's technically easier than the Route du Hoggar, with a sand section more than 1300km long, northern Mali is currently a no-go area, the domain of a shadowy crowd of bandits, rebels and Islamic militants. In short, it has become one of the Sahara's most dangerous corners.

The other trans-Saharan route into West Africa – from Libya into northeastern Niger, via Bilma – was not an option at the time of writing. The Libya-Niger border has been closed to independent travellers for years.

From Central Africa

There are two main crossing points between Cameroon and the Central African Republic, but roads that are dire at the best of times are catastrophic in the rainy season. The standard route is via Garoua-Boulaï, which straddles the border. Buses and trucks go to Bangui, taking two days with an overnight in Bouar. An equally rough alternative is to go to Batouri further south and cross via Kenzou to Berbérati.

The overland route to Congo is an epic journey traversing long, rutted tracks (which are probably impassable in the rainy season) through dense rainforest. The route goes via Yokadouma, Moloundou and on to the border crossing at Sokambo on the Ngoko River. After crossing the river, there's onward transport to Pokola, where you must register with the Congolese police, and Brazzaville.

The main border crossings into Equatorial Guinea and Gabon are a few kilometres from each other, accessible from the Cameroonian town of Amban. In Amban the road splits, the easterly route heading for Bitam and Libreville (Gabon) and the westerly route heading for Ebebiyin and Bata (Equatorial Guinea). There's also a border crossing into Equatorial Guinea on the coast near Campo but it's frequently closed and should not be relied on.

From Algeria

Although there are frequent promises that it will reopen, the Morocco–Algeria border has been closed since 1994 and is likely to remain so for the foreseeable future.

Sea

Ferries run to Morocco from mainland Spain. Most services are run by the Spanish national ferry company, **Acciona Trasmediterránea** (☑902 454645; www.tras mediterranea.es). You can take vehicles on most routes.

A useful website for comparing routes and finding links to the relevant ferry companies is www.ferrylines.com.

Popular routes include:

➡ Algeciras to Tangier (1½ hours, up to eight daily). Buses from several Moroccan cities converge on Tangier to make the ferry crossing to Algeciras, then fan out to the main Spanish centres, and vice versa

➡ Barcelona to Tangier (24 to 35 hours, weekly)

➡ Tarifa to Tangier (35 minutes, up to eight daily)

➡ Almería to Nador (five to eight hours, up to three daily)

Tours

First-time travellers to West Africa may want to consider taking a tour – what you sacrifice in the freedom to go when and where you want, you gain in having someone else take care of all the logistics (such as visas, dealing with officialdom, organising transport and accommodation) that can drive independent travellers to distraction.

Two main options are available: inclusive tours (where you fly to your destination and spend two to three weeks in one or more countries) and overland tours (two- to six-month tours that begin in Europe and travel by land to and around West Africa). Some overland tours allow you to join for a short section (usually three to five weeks), flying out and back at either end. In addition to the recommended tours, some specialist travel agents also organise tours, as do numerous West African–based agencies, although with the latter you'll usually need to arrange your own flight into and out of the region.

Inclusive Tours

FRANCE

Explorator (www.explorator.fr)

Nouvelles Frontières (www.nouvelles-frontieres.fr) Mainstream French agency with tours to Senegal and Morocco.

Terres d'Aventure (www.ter dav.com) Adventurous trips to nine West African countries.

ITALY

Antichi Splendori Viaggi (www.antichisplendori.it) Trips to Morocco, Senegal, Ghana, Togo, Burkina Faso and Benin.

Harmattan Tours (www. harmattan.it) Experienced Africa hand covering eight West African countries.

NETHERLANDS

Sawadee Reizen (☑020-420 22 20; www.sawadee.nl) Covers Benin, The Gambia, Ghana, Senegal, Morocco and Togo.

SPAIN

Viajes Taranna (www. taranna.com) Tours to five West African countries.

Viatges Tuareg (☑932 652 391; www.tuareg.com) Respected Barcelona agency with tours to seven countries.

UK

Birdfinders (www.birdfinders. co.uk) Birdwatching tours

to Cape Verde, The Gambia, Ghana and Morocco.

Explore Worldwide (www.explore.co.uk) Well-established company offering a wide range of adventurous tours and treks in six West African countries.

From Here 2 Timbuktu (www.fromhere2timbuktu.com) Wonderful tours to Senegal, Morocco, Mauritania and Cameroon, with a focus on wildlife, music, culture and getting away from the tourist hordes.

Fulani Travel (www.fulani-travel.co.uk) Excellent African specialist agency with tours to eight countries.

Hidden Gambia (www.hiddengambia.com) The Gambia-specialist that avoids the package-tour resorts and heads upcountry.

Imaginative Traveller (www.imaginative-traveller. com) Adventure tours to 11 countries including Guinea-Bissau and Sierra Leone.

Limosa Holidays (www. limosaholidays.co.uk) Specialist birding trips, including The Gambia, Ghana and Morocco.

Naturetrek (www.nature trek.co.uk) Bird and wildlife specialists offering tours in Ghana and The Gambia.

Peregrine Adventures (www.peregrineadventures. com) Six-country tour of West Africa.

Rainbow Tours (www. rainbow tours.co.uk) Goes to Sierra Leone.

Responsible Travel (www. responsibletravel.com) Serves as a clearing house for eco-tours and sustainable travel operators with 12 West African countries covered.

Songlines Music Travel (www.songlines.co.uk/music-travel) Music-centred tours to Mali, Senegal, Cape Verde and Morocco.

Undiscovered Destinations (www.undiscov ered-destinations.com) Off-the-beaten-track agency that goes to Sierra Leone and Nigeria.

USA

Access Africa (www.acces
safrica.com) Tours to six West
African countries including a
Fespaco special.

Adventure Center (www.ad
venturecenter.com) Adventure
tours and activity-focused
trips to most West African
countries.

Adventures Abroad (www.
adventures-abroad.com)
Small-group tours to a handful of West African countries.

Born Free Safaris (www.
bornfreesafaris.com) Tours to
Ghana, Senegal, The Gam-
bia, Mali and Benin.

Elder Treks (www.eldertreks.
com) Tours for the over-50s
to Morocco, Burkina Faso,
Niger, Togo, Ghana and Benin.

Journeys International
(www.journeys-intl.com)
Small-group or customised
tours to a handful of West
African countries.

Palace Travel (www.pal
acetravel.com) West Africa
specialist with tours to most
countries in the region.

Spector Travel (www.spec
tortravel.com) An Africa specialist with tours to Senegal,
Ghana and elsewhere.

Wilderness Travel (www.
wildernesstravel.com) Trips to
Benin, Cape Verde, Ghana,
Morocco, Senegal, Sierra
Leone and Togo.

Overland Tours

For these trips, you travel
in an 'overland truck' with
about 15 to 28 other people,
a couple of drivers/leaders,
plus tents and other equipment. Food is bought along
the way and the group cooks
and eats together. Most of
the hassles (such as border
crossings) are taken care of
by the leader. Disadvantages
include a fixed itinerary and
the possibility of spending a
long time with other people
in relatively close confines.
That said, overland truck
tours are extremely popular.

The overland-tour market
is dominated by British companies, although passengers
come from many parts of

the world. Most tours start in
London and travel to West Africa via Europe and Morocco.
For those with plenty of time,
there's also the option to do
the West Africa trip as part of
a longer trans-Africa trip.

African Trails (www.african
trails.co.uk)

Dragoman (www.dragoman.
com)

Keystone Journeys (www.
keystonejourneys.com)

GETTING AROUND

Air

Travelling by bus, bush taxi
and even train are essential
parts of the West African experience, but so vast are the
distances that a few flights
around the region can widen
your options considerably if
your time is limited. The region has a reasonable network
of air routes, with the best
connections generally be-
tween Francophone countries.

Air safety is a major
concern in West Africa and
a spate of accidents (especially in Nigeria) means that
you should always be wary
of the region's local airlines,
particularly smaller operators. For more details on the
air safety record of individual
airlines, visit www.airsafe.
com/index.html.

Although the airports in
some capital cities are large
and cavernous, some smaller
West African airports are
little more than single-shed
terminals. Regardless of the
size, don't be surprised if you
spend half a day at check-in.

Airlines in West Africa

West African airlines come
and go with disturbing
regularity. **Royal Air Maroc**
(www.royalairmaroc.com) has
the most extensive regional
network, while **Air Burkina**
(www.air-burkina.com) has a
reasonably extensive West
African service as well as a domestic Ouagadougou–Bobo-

Dioulasso service, while **TACV**
(www.flytacv.com) connects
Praia (Cape Verde) to Dakar
(Senegal) on the mainland,
from where they also operate
a small range of services to
neighbouring countries. Some
Nigerian airlines also fly between Nigeria and other West
African countries.

Reputable travel agents
throughout the region can
also sometimes find tickets
for international airlines
as they hop between West
African cities as part of their
intercontinental routes.

Elysian Airlines (www.
elysianairlines.com) Domestic
Liberian, Cameroonian and
some wider West African
routes.

Mali Air Express (MAE;
www.mae-mali.com) Private
Malian airline with some
regional flights.

Tickets

Long distances, high fuel
costs and a state of budg-
etary crisis among most
regional airlines ensure that
fares within West Africa don't
come cheap. Flying from
Dakar (Senegal) to Abidjan
(Côte d'Ivoire), for example,
can cost the equivalent to
flying halfway across the USA.
Return fares are usually double the one-way fares, though
less expensive excursion fares
are occasionally available, as
are youth or student fares.

Once you've bought
your ticket, reconfirm your
reservation several times at
least, especially if the airline
you're flying with has a less-
than-stellar reputation for
reliability. After the flight, if
you checked-in luggage, hold
on to your baggage claim
ticket until you've exited the
baggage claim area at your
destination, as you'll often be
required to show it.

Bicycle

A small but growing number
of travellers visit West Africa on bicycle. As long as
you have sufficient time, a
sturdy bike, are ready to be

CHECKING IN

In some West African cities, check-in procedures are as much of an adventure as the flight itself. Conakry and Lagos win our vote as the airports with the most disorganised and chaotic check-in procedures, but every traveller probably has their own 'favourites'. The fun starts from the moment you enter the airport building. Underpaid security personnel, in an effort to subsidise their meagre incomes, may view the baggage check procedures as a chance to elicit bribes from tourists. After searching your bag, they might ask what you have for them or, alternatively, try to convince you that you've violated some regulation. Be compliant with requests to open your baggage, be friendly and respectful, smile a lot, and you should soon be on your way. Also remember that, in some cases, officials may search your bag out of genuine curiosity, so put your dirty underwear on top and watch their interest evaporate.

After getting past the initial baggage check, wade into the fray by the check-in counter. While some places have lines, many don't – just a sweaty mass of people, all waving their tickets and talking loudly to a rather beleaguered-looking check-in clerk.

The West African answer to this situation is the 'fixer' – enterprising locals who make their living by getting people smoothly checked in and through other formalities such as customs and airport tax, all for fees ranging from a dollar or two up to about US$10. Without the services of a fixer, the best strategy for avoiding the chaotic scene is to arrive early at the airport.

Once you have your boarding pass in hand, there's usually a second luggage inspection as you pass from the check-in terminal to the waiting area. Then it's just a matter of waiting, and often waiting far longer than you planned.

There is one exception to the general chaos of checking in, at least if you're flying Air France. In most West African capitals where Air France has late-night departures for Paris, the airline allows a morning check-in (either at a central Air France office or, less conveniently, at the airport itself).

---

self-sufficient and possess a willingness to rough it, cycling is an excellent way to get to know the region. You'll end up staying in small towns and villages, interact more with the local people without vehicle windows and other barriers between you, and eat West African food more frequently.

Wherever you go, you'll be met with great local curiosity (as well as much goodwill). As in most places in the world, don't leave your bike unattended for any lengthy period of time unless it's locked, and try to secure the main removable pieces. Taking your bike into your hotel room, should you decide to take a break from camping, is generally no problem. If you're camping near settlements in rural areas, ask the village headman each night where you can stay. Even if you don't have a tent, he'll find you somewhere to sleep.

Where to Cycle

Because of the distances involved, you'll need to plan your food and water needs in advance, and pay careful attention to choosing a route in order to avoid long stretches of semidesert, areas with no villages or heavily travelled roads. In general, cycling is best well away from urban areas, and in the early morning and late afternoon hours. When calculating your daily distances, plan on taking a break during the hottest, midday period, and don't count on covering as much territory each day as you might in a northern European climate.

The most popular long-haul cycling routes are:

➜ Burkina Faso to Ghana, Benin and Togo
➜ Within Senegal
➜ Benin to Côte d'Ivoire

When to Cycle

The best time to cycle is in the cooler, dry period from mid-October to February. Even so, you'll need to work out a way to carry at least 4L of water, and you'll also need to carry a water filter and purifier. If you get tired, or simply want to cut out the boring bits, bikes can easily be carried on bush taxis, though you'll want to carry some rags to wrap around the gearing for protection. You'll need to pay a luggage fee for this, but it shouldn't be more than one-third to one-half the price of the passenger fare.

Equipment

Mountain bikes are most suitable for cycling in West Africa and will give you the greatest flexibility in setting your route. While heavy, single-speed bicycles can be rented in many towns (and occasionally mountain bikes), they're not good for anything other than short, local rides, so you should bring your own bicycle into the country if you plan on riding extended distances. To rent a bike locally, ask staff at hotels, or enquire at bicycle-repair stands (every town market has one).

Apart from water, your main concern will be motorists. Cyclists are regarded as third-class citizens in West Africa, so make sure you know what's coming up behind you and be prepared to take evasive action, as local cyclists are often forced to do. A small rear-view mirror is well worth considering.

You'll need to carry sufficient spare parts and be proficient at repairs; punctures, in particular, will be frequent. Take at least four spare inner tubes, some tyre repair material and a spare tyre. Consider the number of tube patches you might need, square it, and pack those too. Some people don't like them but we've found inner-tube protectors indispensable for minimising punctures.

Transporting Your Bicycle

If you're planning to bring your bike with you on the plane to West Africa, some airlines ask that you partially dismantle it and put the pieces in a large bag or box. Bike boxes are available at some airports. Otherwise, you can arrange one in advance with your local bicycle shop. To fit it in the box, you'll usually need to take off (or turn) the handlebars, pedals and seat, and will need to deflate the tyres. Some airlines don't charge, while others (including many charter airlines) levy an extra fee – usually around US$50 to US$100 – because bike boxes are not standard size. Some airlines are willing to take your bike 'as is' – you can just wheel it to the check-in desk – although you'll still need to partially deflate the tyres and tie the handlebars into the frame. Check with the

airline in advance about their regulations.

Useful Resources

A highly recommended contact is **Bicycle Africa** (www.ibike.org/bikeafrica), which is part of the International Bicycle Fund, a low-budget, socially conscious organisation that arranges tours in some West African countries, provides fact sheets and posts letters from travellers who've travelled by bike in the area. Another useful resource is the **Cyclists' Touring Club** (CTC; ☎ 01483-238337; www.ctc.org.uk), a UK-based organisation which offers tips and information sheets on cycling in different parts of the world.

Boat

At several points along the West African coast you can travel by boat, either on a large passenger vessel or by local canoe. Some of the local canoe trips are definitely of the informal variety, and many are dangerous. Countries where ferries provide an important means of coastal transport include Cape Verde, Senegal, Sierra Leone, Liberia and Guinea-Bissau.

There are two ferries a week between Limbe (Cameroon) and Calabar (Nigeria). Unsafe speed boats also make the trip. Other places where you can cross international borders by boat are by barge from Guinea to Mali and, possibly, by ferry between Conakry (Guinea) and Freetown (Sierra Leone).

On most major rivers in the region, *pirogues, pinasses* (larger motorised boats, carrying cargo and anything from 10 to 100 passengers) and/or public ferries serve towns and villages along the way, and can be an excellent way to see the country. Some involve a simple river crossing, others can be a longer expedition where you sleep by the riverbank. Riverboat options include those along the Gambia and Senegal Rivers.

Remember that many such journeys are only possible at certain times of the year (usually August to December) when water levels are still high enough after the rains.

Whether you're renting a *pirogue* or *pinasse*, or taking a public ferry, check what food and water is included in the price you pay; it's always worth taking more just in case. On some journeys you'll be able to buy snacks and fruit along the way. Also, bring something to protect yourself from the sun, as few boats have any shade, and something to waterproof your gear. Avoid getting on boats that are overloaded, or setting off when the weather is bad, especially on sea routes in coastal areas.

Bus & Bush Taxi

The most common forms of public transport in West Africa are bus (*car* in some Francophone countries) and bush taxi (*taxi brousse*). Buses may be run by state-owned or private companies; bush taxis are always private, although the driver is rarely the owner of the vehicle. Vehicles are usually located at a bus and bush taxi park, called *gare routière* or sometimes *autogare* in Francophone countries, 'garage', 'lorry park' or 'motor park' in English-speaking countries, and *paragem* in Portuguese-speaking countries. Most large cities have several *gares routières*, one for each main direction or destination, often located on the road out of town headed in that direction.

In some countries, buses are common for intercity routes and bush taxis are hard to find; in other countries it's the reverse. Either way, travel generally costs between US$1.50 and US$2.50 per 100km. On routes between countries, fares can be higher because drivers have to pay additional fees (official and unofficial) to cross the border. You can save a bit of money by taking one vehicle to the border and then another on the other side, but this prolongs the trip considerably.

In many countries, transport fares are fixed by the government, so the only way the bush taxi drivers can earn a bit more is to charge for luggage. Local people accept this, so travellers should too, unless of course it's unreasonable. The fee for a medium-sized rucksack is around 10% of the fare. Small bags will be less and are often not charged at all. If you think you're being overcharged, ask other passengers, out of earshot of the driver. Once you know the proper rate, bargaining will be easy and the price should soon fall.

Bus

Long-distance buses (sometimes called a 'big bus' or *grand car,* to distinguish it from a minibus) vary in size – from 35 to 70 seats – and services vary between countries and areas. On the main routes buses are good quality, with a reliable service and fixed departure times (although arrival times may be more fluid depending on anything from checkpoints and breakdowns to the number of towns they stop in along the way).

On quiet roads in rural areas, buses may be decrepit, and may frequently break down, and stop regularly. These buses have no timetable and usually go when full or when the driver feels like it. They are usually overcrowded, in contrast with some of the better lines on major routes, where the one-person-per-seat rule is usually respected. Generally, bus fares are cheaper than bush taxi fares for a comparable route and are usually quicker.

You may arrange a long ride by bus (or bush taxi) and find yourself transferring to another vehicle somewhere along the way. There's no need to pay more – your driver pays your fare directly to the driver of the next

vehicle – but it can mean long waits while the arrangements are made.

RESERVATIONS

You can reserve in advance on some main-route buses, which is advisable. In some countries you book a place but not a specific seat. Just before the bus leaves, names are called out in the order that tickets were bought, and you get on and choose the seat you want. Seats to the front tend to be better ventilated and more comfortable. If you suffer from motion sickness, try to get a seat towards the front or in the middle. Whichever end of the bus you sit in, it's worth trying to get a seat on the side that will be away from direct sunlight for most of the journey.

Bush Taxi

A bush taxi (known as a *tro-tro* in Ghana) is effectively a small bus. Almost without exception, bush taxis leave when full, not according to any recognisable timetable. As soon as one car leaves, the next one starts to fill. Depending on the popularity of the route, the car may take half an hour or several days to fill. Either way, drivers jealously guard their car's place in the queue.

There are three main types of bush taxi in West Africa; minibus, Peugeot taxi and pick-up.

MINIBUS

Some routes are served by minibuses *(minicars)* – usually seating about 12 to 20 passengers. They're typically about 25% cheaper than Peugeot 504s, and sometimes more comfortable, depending on how full they are. They're also slower, take longer to fill, tend to stop more, and police checks at roadblocks take longer because there are more passengers to search.

PEUGEOT TAXI

Peugeot 504s, assembled in Nigeria or imported from Europe, are used all over West Africa and are also called *cinq-cent-quatre,* Peugeot taxi, *sept place* and *brake.* With three rows of seats, they're built to take the driver plus seven passengers. In some countries this limit is observed, in others it's flagrantly flaunted. All 504s in Mali, for example, take the driver plus nine passengers. In Guinea you might be jammed in with at least a dozen adults, plus children, the odd goat and bags, with more luggage and a couple of extra passengers riding on the roof.

BUSH TAXI TRICKS

Early customers can choose where to sit. Latecomers get no choice and are assigned to the least comfortable seats – usually at the back, where the seating is cramped and stuffy, seat springs work their way into any orifice and window-winders jam into knees. If you have a choice, the best seats are those in the front, near the window. Some travellers prefer the very front, though you're first in line if there's a collision. Better is the row behind the driver, near a window (ideally one that works), and preferably on the side with more shade during the journey.

If a group of passengers has been waiting a long time, and there are only two or three seats to fill, they may club together and pay extra so as to get moving. If you do this, don't expect a discount because you're saving the driver the hassle of looking for other passengers – time ain't money in Africa. If you pick up someone along the way, however, the fare they pay goes to the passengers who bought the seats, not to the driver.

By far the best time to catch bush taxis is early in the morning; after that, you may have difficulty finding vehicles on many routes. Sometimes, however, departures are determined by market days, in which case afternoon may be best.

If a bush taxi looks like it's going to get uncomfortably full, you can always buy two seats for yourself – it's simply double the price. Likewise, if you want to charter the whole car, take the price of one seat and multiply it by the number available. You can either hire a city taxi or a bush taxi (although in most places, city taxis won't have the necessary paperwork for long-distance routes), or ask around at your hotel and arrange something privately.

The price you pay will have to be worth the driver taking it out of public service for the day. If you want a deal including petrol, he'll reduce the speed to a slow trot and complain every time you take a detour. A fixed daily rate for the car, while you pay extra for fuel, is easier to arrange. Finding a car with a working petrol gauge may be tricky, but you can work on the theory that the tank will be empty when you start and, if you allow for 10km per litre on reasonable roads (more on bad roads), you should be OK.

That these cars do hundreds of thousands of kilometres on some of the worst roads in the world is a credit to the manufacturer and the ingenuity of local mechanics.

While some drivers are safe and considerate, others verge on insanity. Some cars are relatively new (there are quite a few Peugeot 505s, the later model, around these days) and well maintained, with comfortable seats. Others are very old, reduced to nothing more than chassis, body and engine: there's more weld than original metal, the tyres are bald, most of the upholstery is missing and little extras like windows, door handles and even exhaust pipes fell by the roadside long ago.

PICK-UP

With wooden seats down the sides, covered pick-ups (*bâchés*) are definitely 2nd class, but are sometimes the only kind of bush taxi available. They take around 16 passengers but are invariably stuffed with people and baggage, plus a few chickens, and your feet may be higher than your waist from resting on a sack of millet. Up on the roof go more bags, bunches of bananas, extra passengers and goats (also live). *Bâché* rides are often very slow, and police checks at roadblocks are interminable as drivers or passengers frequently lack vital papers. The ride is guaranteed to be unpleasant unless you adopt an African attitude, which means each time your head hits the roof as the vehicle descends into yet another big pothole, you roar with laughter. There's nothing like local humour to change an otherwise miserable trip into a tolerable, even enjoyable, experience.

Car & Motorcycle

Hire

There are car-rental agencies in most capital cities and tourist areas. Most international companies (Hertz, Avis, etc) are represented, plus smaller independent operators, but renting is invariably expensive – you can easily spend in one day what you'd pay for a week's rental in Europe or the USA. If the small operators charge less, it's usually because the vehicles are older and sometimes not well maintained, and corners can be cut on insurance, but it can also simply be because their costs are lower and they can do a better deal. If you have the time, check around for bargains. You will need to put down a large deposit (credit cards are usually, but not always, good for this). Prices in Morocco tend to be a little cheaper than elsewhere in the region.

It's very unlikely you'll be allowed to take a rental car across a border but, if you are (for example, from The Gambia into Senegal), make sure the paperwork is valid. If you're uncertain about driving, most companies provide a chauffeur at very little extra cost and, with many, a chauffeur is mandatory. In many cases it's cheaper to go with a chauffeur as you will pay less for insurance. It's also prudent, as getting stuck on your own is no fun and chauffeurs generally know the intricacies of checkpoint etiquette.

In tourist areas, such as The Gambia, Morocco and Senegal, and in some parts of Burkina Faso, it's possible to hire mopeds and motorbikes. In most other countries there is no formal rental available, but if you want to hire a motorbike (and know how to ride one) you can arrange something by asking at an auto-parts shop or repair yard, or by asking at the reception of your hotel. You can often be put in touch with someone who doesn't mind earning some extra cash by renting out their wheels for a day or two. Remember, though, that matters such as insurance will be easily overlooked, which is fine until you have an accident and find yourself liable for all bills. Also, if you do this, be sure to check out the motorbike in advance to ensure it's in acceptable mechanical condition.

Driving Licence

To drive a car or ride a motorbike in West Africa you'll need a driving licence and, ideally, an International Driving Permit (IDP). If you intend to hire a car, you will usually need both. IDPs are easy and cheap to get in your home country – they're usually issued by major motoring associations, such as the AA in Britain – and are useful if you're driving in countries where your own licence may not be recognised (officially or unofficially). They have the added advantage of being written in several languages, with a photo and many stamps, and so look more impressive when presented to car-rental clerks or policemen at road blocks.

Fuel & Spare Parts

The quality, availability and price of fuel (petrol and diesel – called *essence* and *gasoil*, respectively, in the Francophone countries, *gasolina* and *diesel*, or sometimes *gasóleo*, in former Portuguese colonies) varies greatly throughout the region. Where taxation, subsidies or currency rates make petrol cheaper in one country than its neighbour, you'll inevitably find traders who've carried large drums across the border to sell 'black market' fuel at the roadside. However, watch out for fuel sold in plastic bags

ROAD DISTANCES (KM)

	Abidjan (Côte d'Ivoire)	Accra (Ghana)	Bamako (Mali)	Banjul (The Gambia)	Bissau (Guinea-Bissau)	Conakry (Guinea)	Cotonou (Benin)	Dakar (Senegal)	Freetown (Sierra Leone)	Lagos (Nigeria)	Lomé (Togo)	Monrovia (Liberia)	Niamey (Niger)	Nouakchott (Mauritania)
Accra (Ghana)	560													
Bamako (Mali)	1160	1710												
Banjul (The Gambia)	2490	3210	1340											
Bissau (Guinea-Bissau)	2180	2900	1460	310										
Conakry (Guinea)	1700	2260	920	1230	980									
Cotonou (Benin)	910	360	2020	3360	3110	2610								
Dakar (Senegal)	2790	3350	1420	300	585	1530	3360							
Freetown (Sierra Leone)	1590	2090	1210	1440	1190	320	2440	1740						
Lagos (Nigeria)	1030	480	2140	3480	3230	2730	120	3560	2560					
Lomé (Togo)	760	200	1870	3220	2970	2460	160	3290	2290	280				
Monrovia (Liberia)	1020	1520	1040	1860	1610	740	1870	2160	570	1990	1720			
Niamey (Niger)	1570	1390	1410	2750	2880	2320	1040	2740	2900	1160	1190	2330		
Nouakchott (Mauritania)	2800	3360	1650	870	1180	2100	3670	570	2320	3790	3560	2730	3050	
Ouagadougou (Burkina Faso)	1070	970	900	2240	2360	1820	1120	2240	2400	1240	1240	1830	500	2550
Yaoundé (Cameroon)	2650	2100	3760	4410	4160	4350	1740	4670	4120	1620	1620	3610	2090	5240

(Ouagadougou (Burkina Faso) column value for Yaoundé: 2860)

ROAD SAFETY

Road safety is probably your biggest safety risk in West Africa. Bush taxi drivers, in particular, race along at hair-raising speeds and overtake blind to reach their destination before another car can get in front of them in the queue for the return journey. Drivers can be sleepy from a long day, and drink-driving is a problem. Travelling early in the morning is one step you can take to cut the risk, as drivers are fresher and roads less travelled. Avoid night travel at all costs. If you are in a vehicle and feel unsafe, and if it's a heavily travelled route, you can take your chances and get out at a major station to switch to another car (though don't expect a refund, and the second vehicle may not be much better). You can complain about dangerous driving, but this usually doesn't have any effect and, unless things are really out of control, you'll seldom get support from other passengers. Saying that you're feeling sick seems to get better results. Drivers are often quite considerate to ill or infirm passengers and, in any case, seem to care more about keeping vomit off their seats than about dying under the wheels of an oncoming lorry. You might be able to rally other passengers to your side this way as well. Most locals take a stoic approach to the situation, with many viewing accidents as a matter of the will of God or Allah. Drivers seem to discredit the idea that accidents are in any way related to vehicle speed or condition, or to wild driving practices.

or small containers along the roadside. While sometimes it's fine, it's often diluted with water or kerosene. Don't expect to find unleaded petrol beyond major cities and even there it may be scarce.

African mechanics are masters of ingenuity, using endlessly recycled parts to coax life out of ageing machines that would have long ago been consigned to the scrap heap in the West. That said, they're often unable to help with newer-model vehicles – for these, either bring your own spare parts, or check with your manufacturer for a list of accredited parts suppliers in West Africa. Be warned, however, there may be very few (or none at all) of the latter.

Insurance

Insurance is compulsory in most West African countries. Given the large number of minor accidents, not to mention major ones, fully comprehensive insurance is strongly advised, both for your own and any rental vehicle. Always check with your insurer whether you're covered for the countries you intend to visit and whether third-party cover is included. Car-hire companies customarily supply insurance, but check the cover and conditions carefully.

Make certain that you're covered for off-piste travel, as well as travel between countries (if you're planning cross-border excursions). A locally acquired motorcycle licence is not valid under some policies.

In the event of an accident, make sure you submit the accident report as soon as possible to the insurance company or, if hiring, the car-hire company.

Road Rules

Traffic drives on the right throughout West Africa (as in continental Europe and the USA), even in countries that have a British colonial heritage (such as The Gambia).

Hitching

As in any other part of the world, hitching or accepting lifts in West Africa is never entirely safe, and we don't recommend it. Travellers who decide to hitch should understand that they are taking a small but potentially serious risk. If you're planning to travel this way, take advice from other hitchers (locals or travellers) first. Hitching in pairs is obviously safer, while hitching through less-salubrious suburbs, especially at night, is asking for trouble. Throughout most of the region, women should avoid hitching alone.

In many countries, as you venture further into rural areas, however, the frequency of buses or bush taxis drops, sometimes to nothing. Then the only way around is to ride on local trucks, as the locals do. A 'fare' is payable to the driver, so in cases like this the line between hitching and public transport is blurred – but if it's the only way to get around, you don't have a choice anyway. Usually you'll be riding on top of the cargo – it may be cotton or rice in sacks, which are quite comfy, but it might be logs or oil drums, which aren't.

If you want to hitch because there's no public transport leaving imminently from the *gare routière,* you'll normally have to go well beyond the town limits, as bush taxi drivers may take umbrage at other vehicles 'stealing' their customers. Even so, you'll probably still have to pay for your lift – but at least you'll get moving more quickly.

Hitching in the Western sense (ie because you don't want to get the bus or, more specifically, because you don't want to pay) is also possible but may take a long time. The only people giving free lifts are likely to be foreign expatriates or the occasional well-off local (very few West Africans own a car). Remember, however, that most people with space in their car want payment – usually on a par with what a bus would have cost.

Local Transport

For getting around cities and larger towns, you'll generally have a choice of bus (capital cities only) and a range of taxis.

Bus

Within some capital cities, you may find well-developed city bus and minibus networks connecting the city centre and suburbs. In most other cities, it's minibuses only. In general, city buses travel along set routes, while minibuses may detour a little more.

Taxi

MOTORCYCLE TAXI

In many countries, motorcycle taxis (moto-taxis or motos) are used. While they're often cheaper than shared taxis and handy for zipping around, safety can be an issue. If you have a choice, it's usually better to pay slightly more and go with a regular shared taxi.

PRIVATE TAXI

Only in the bigger cities, such as Dakar, Abidjan and Ouagadougou, do taxis have meters (compteurs). Otherwise, bargaining is required or you'll be given the legally fixed rate. In any case, determine the fare before getting into the taxi. The fare from most airports into town is fixed, but some drivers (in Dakar, for example) will try to charge at least double this. In places like Bamako, it costs up to 50% more to go into town from the airport than it does to go the other way. The price always includes luggage unless you have a particularly bulky item. Also, fares invariably go up at night, and sometimes even in rainy weather.

If the city you're exploring is spread out and you've limited time, or if you're likely to be jumping in and out of taxis, consider renting a taxi by the hour or day. It will probably cost you less (anywhere from about US$20 to US$50 per day), and if the car breaks down it will be the driver's problem.

SHARED TAXI

Many cities have shared taxis that will stop and pick up more passengers even if they already have somebody inside; you pay just for one seat. Some run on fixed routes and are effectively a bus, only quicker and more comfortable. Others go wherever the first passenger wants to go, and other people will only be picked up if they're going in the same direction. They normally shout the name of the suburb or a landmark they're heading for as the taxi goes past. In some places, it's common for the waiting passengers to call out the name of their destination or point in the desired direction as the taxi passes by. Once you've got the hang of the shared taxi system, it's quick and inexpensive, and an excellent way to get around cities – and also a good way to experience local life. It's also one of West Africa's great bargains, as fares seldom exceed US$0.50. It's always worth checking the fare before you get in the car though, as they're not always fixed, and meters don't apply to shared trips. If you're the first person in the taxi, make it clear that you're expecting the driver to pick up others and that you don't want a private taxi (déplacement, depo, 'charter' or 'town trip') all to yourself.

WEST AFRICA'S TOP TRAIN RIDES

Taking a long-distance West African train is the ultimate road movie with all the region's colours, smells and improbabilities of life writ large. More than a form of transport, West African trains are like moving cities, a stage for street performers, marketplaces and prayer halls. And, like most forms of transport in West Africa, you'll have plenty of time to contemplate the experience, whether waiting on a platform for your train to appear a mere 12 hours late or stopped on remote rails in the middle of nowhere for no apparent reason. But for all their faults (and there are many) the trains work and are an essential part of the West African experience. Our three favourites:

➡ Zouérat to Nouâdhibou, Mauritania – one of the great train experiences of the world on the longest train in the world.

➡ Dakar to Bamako – another of Africa's great epics, at once endlessly fascinating and interminable (up to 40 hours).

➡ Yaoundé to N'Gaoundéré, Cameroon – like crossing a continent, from the arid north to the steamy south, with glorious rainforests en route.

Tours

Compared with most areas of the world, West Africa has few tour operators. Those that do exist are usually based in the capital cities and typically offer excursions for groups (rather than individuals) from one-day to one-week trips, or longer. Many good West African companies organise tours beyond the borders of their own country.

Benin

⇒ **Bénin Aventure** (www.beninaventure.com)

⇒ **Eco-Bénin** (www.ecobenin.org)

Burkina Faso

⇒ **Couleurs d'Afrique** (www.couleurs-afrique.com; Ave de l'Olympisme, Gounghin)

⇒ **L'Agence Tourisme** (Map p62; www.agence-tourisme.com; Rue Joseph Badoua, Hôtel les Palmiers, Burkina Faso)

Cameroon

⇒ **Safar Tours** (Map p82; www.safartours.com)

The Gambia

⇒ **Gambia Experience** (Map p158; ☑ 4461104; www.gambia.co.uk; Senegambia Beach Hotel, Kololi)

Mali

⇒ **Continent Tours** (www.continenttours.com)

⇒ **Geo Tours** (www.geotours.org)

⇒ **Tara Africa Tours** (www.tara-africatours.com)

⇒ **Toguna Adventure Tours** (www.togunaadventuretours.com)

Senegal

⇒ **Sahel Découverte Bassari** (Map p326; www.saheldecouverte.com)

⇒ **Senegal Experience** (www.senegal.co.uk)

Train

There are railways in Mauritania, Senegal, Mali, Côte d'Ivoire, Ghana, Burkina Faso, Togo, Nigeria and Cameroon. Most services run only within the country of operation, but there are international services, notably between Dakar and Bamako, and, depending on the security situation in Côte d'Ivoire, between Ouagadougou and Abidjan.

Some trains are relatively comfortable, with 1st-class coaches that may have air-conditioning. Some also have sleeping compartments with two or four bunks. Other services are 2nd or 3rd class only and conditions can be uncomfortable, with no lights, no toilets and no glass in the windows (equals no fun on long night journeys). Some trains have a restaurant on board, but you can usually buy things to eat and drink at stations along the way.

Health

As long as you stay up to date with your vaccinations and take basic preventive measures, you'd have to be pretty unlucky to succumb to most of the health hazards mentioned here. Africa certainly has an impressive selection of tropical diseases on offer, but you're more likely to get a bout of diarrhoea (in fact, you should bank on it), a cold or an infected mosquito bite than an exotic disease such as sleeping sickness. When it comes to injuries (as opposed to illness), the most likely reason for needing medical help in Africa is as a result of road accidents – vehicles are rarely well maintained, the roads are potholed and poorly lit, and drink-driving is common.

BEFORE YOU GO

A little planning before departure, particularly for pre-existing illnesses, will save you a lot of trouble later. Before a long trip get a check-up from your dentist and from your doctor if you take any regular medication or have a chronic illness, such as high blood pressure or asthma. You should also organise spare contact lenses and glasses (and take your optical prescription with you), get a first aid and medical kit together, and arrange necessary vaccinations.

It's tempting to leave it all to the last minute – don't!

Many vaccines don't take effect until two weeks after you've been immunised, so visit a doctor four to eight weeks before departure. Ask your doctor for an International Certificate of Vaccination (otherwise known as the yellow booklet or *livre jeune*), which will list all the vaccinations you've received. This is mandatory for the African countries that require proof of yellow-fever vaccination upon entry, but it's a good idea to carry it wherever you travel in case you require medical treatment or encounter troublesome border officials.

Travellers can register with the **International Association for Medical Advice to Travellers** (IAMAT; www. iamat.org). Its website can help travellers find a doctor who has recognised training. Those heading off to very remote areas might like to do a first-aid course (contact the Red Cross or St John Ambulance) or attend a remote medicine first-aid course, such as that offered by the **Royal Geographical Society** (www.wildernessmedicaltraining.co.uk).

If you are bringing medications with you, carry them in their original containers, clearly labelled. A signed and dated letter from your physician describing all medical conditions and medications, including generic names, is also a good idea. If carrying syringes or needles, be sure

to have a physician's letter documenting their medical necessity.

Insurance

Find out in advance whether your insurance plan will make payments to providers or will reimburse you later for overseas health expenditures (in many countries doctors expect payment in cash). It's vital to ensure that your travel insurance will cover the emergency transport required to get you to a hospital in a major city, to better facilities elsewhere in Africa, or all the way home by air and with a medical attendant if necessary. Not all insurance covers this, so check the contract carefully. If you need medical help, your insurance company might be able to help locate the nearest hospital or clinic, or you can ask at your hotel. In an emergency, contact your embassy or consulate.

The **African Medical and Research Foundation** (Amref; www.amref.org) provides an air-evacuation service in medical emergencies in some African countries, as well as air-ambulance transfers between medical facilities. Money paid by members to their flying doctor service entitles you to air-ambulance evacuation and the funds go into providing grassroots medical assistance for local people.

MANDATORY YELLOW-FEVER VACCINATION

➡ **North Africa** Not mandatory for any of North Africa, but Algeria, Libya and Tunisia require evidence of yellow-fever vaccination if entering from an infected country. It is recommended for travellers to Sudan and might be given to unvaccinated travellers leaving the country.

➡ **Central Africa** Mandatory in Central African Republic (CAR), Congo, Democratic Republic of Congo, Equatorial Guinea and Gabon, and recommended in Chad.

➡ **West Africa** Mandatory in Benin, Burkina Faso, Cameroon, Côte d'Ivoire, Ghana, Liberia, Mali, Niger, São Tomé and Príncipe and Togo, and recommended for The Gambia, Guinea, Guinea- Bissau, Mauritania, Nigeria, Senegal and Sierra Leone.

➡ **East Africa** Mandatory in Rwanda; it is advised for Burundi, Ethiopia, Kenya, Somalia, Tanzania and Uganda.

➡ **Southern Africa** Not mandatory for entry into any countries of Southern Africa, although it is necessary if entering from an infected country.

Recommended Vaccinations

The **World Health Organization** (WHO; www.who.int/en/) recommends that all travellers be covered for diphtheria, tetanus, measles, mumps, rubella and polio, as well as for hepatitis B, regardless of their destination. Planning to travel is a great time to ensure that all routine vaccination cover is complete. The consequences of these diseases can be severe and outbreaks do occur.

According to the **Centers for Disease Control and Prevention** (www.cdc.gov/travel), the following vaccinations are recommended for all parts of Africa: hepatitis A, hepatitis B, meningococcal meningitis, rabies and typhoid, and boosters for tetanus, diphtheria and measles. Yellow-fever vaccination is not necessarily recommended for all parts of West Africa, although the certificate is an entry requirement for many countries.

Medical Checklist

It is a very good idea to carry a medical and first-aid kit with you, so you can help yourself in the case of minor illness or injury. Following is a list of items you should consider packing:

➡ Acetaminophen (paracetamol) or aspirin

➡ Acetazolamide (Diamox) for altitude sickness (prescription only)

➡ Adhesive or paper tape

➡ Antibacterial ointment (prescription only) for cuts and abrasions (eg Bactroban)

➡ Antibiotics (prescription only), eg ciprofloxacin (Ciproxin) or norfloxacin (Utinor)

➡ Anti-diarrhoeal drugs (eg loperamide)

➡ Antihistamines (for hay fever and allergic reactions)

➡ Anti-inflammatory drugs (eg ibuprofen)

➡ Anti-malaria pills

➡ Bandages, gauze, gauze rolls

➡ Digital thermometer

➡ Insect repellent containing DEET for the skin

➡ Insect spray containing Permethrin for clothing, tents and bed nets

➡ Iodine tablets (for water purification)

➡ Oral rehydration salts

➡ Pocket knife

➡ Prickly-heat powder for heat rashes

➡ Scissors, safety pins, tweezers

➡ Sterile needles, syringes and fluids if travelling to remote areas

➡ Steroid cream or hydrocortisone cream (for allergic rashes)

➡ Sun block
If you are travelling through a malarial area – particularly an area where falciparum malaria predominates – consider taking a self-diagnostic kit that can identify malaria in the blood from a finger prick.

Websites

There is a wealth of travel-health advice available online. For further information, the **Lonely Planet website** (www.lonelyplanet.com) is a good place to start. The WHO publishes a superb book called *International Travel and Health,* which is revised annually and is available online at no cost. Other websites of general interest in this area are **MD Travel Health** (www.mdtravelhealth.com), which provides complete travel-health recommendations for every country, is updated daily and is also available at no cost; the **Centers for Disease Control and Prevention** (www.cdc.gov/travel); and **Fit for Travel** (www.fitfortravel. scot.nhs.uk), which has up-to-date information about outbreaks and is very user-friendly.

It's also a good idea to consult your government's travel-health website before departure, if one is available:

Australia (www.smartraveller. gov.au/tips/health.html)

Canada (www.hc-sc.gc.ca/index-eng.php)

UK (www.nhs.uk)

USA (www.cdc.gov/travel)

Further Reading

➜ *A Comprehensive Guide to Wilderness and Travel Medicine* (1998) by Eric A Weiss

➜ *Healthy Travel* (1999) by Jane Wilson-Howarth

➜ *Healthy Travel Africa* (2000) by Isabelle Young

➜ *How to Stay Healthy Abroad* (2002) by Richard Dawood

➜ *Travel in Health* (1994) by Graham Fry

➜ *Travel with Children* (2009) by Brigitte Barta

IN TRANSIT

Deep Vein Thrombosis

Blood clots can form in the legs during flights, chiefly because of prolonged immobility. This formation of clots is known as deep vein thrombosis (DVT), and the longer the flight, the greater the risk. Although most blood clots are reabsorbed uneventfully, some might break off and travel through the blood vessels to the lungs, where they could cause life-threatening complications.

The chief symptom of DVT is swelling or pain of the foot, ankle or calf, usually but not always on just one side. When a blood clot travels to the lungs, it could cause chest pain and breathing difficulty.

Travellers with any of these symptoms should immediately seek medical attention.

To prevent the development of DVT on flights you should walk about the cabin, perform isometric compressions of the leg muscles (ie contract the leg muscles while sitting), drink plenty of fluids and avoid alcohol.

Jet Lag & Motion Sickness

If you're crossing more than five time zones you could suffer jet lag, resulting in insomnia, fatigue, malaise or nausea. To avoid jet lag drink plenty of (nonalcoholic) fluids and eat light meals. Upon arrival, get exposure to natural sunlight and readjust your schedule (for meals, sleep, etc) as soon as possible.

Antihistamines such as dimenhydrinate (Dramamine) and meclizine (Antivert, Bonine) are usually the first choice for treating motion sickness. The main side effect of these drugs is drowsiness. A herbal alternative is ginger (in the form of ginger tea, ginger biscuits or crystallised ginger), which works like a charm for some people.

IN WEST AFRICA

Availability & Cost of Health Care

Health care in West Africa is varied: it can be excellent in the major cities, which generally have well-trained doctors and nurses, but it is often patchy off the beaten track. Medicine and even sterile dressings and intravenous fluids might need to be purchased from a local pharmacy by patients or their relatives. The standard of dental care is equally variable and there is an increased risk of hepatitis B and HIV transmission via poorly sterilised equipment. By and large, public hospitals in Africa of-

fer the cheapest service, but will have the least up-to-date equipment and medications; mission hospitals (where donations are the usual form of payment) often have more reasonable facilities; and private hospitals and clinics are more expensive but tend to have more advanced drugs and equipment and better-trained medical staff.

Most drugs can be purchased over the counter in West Africa, without a prescription. Many drugs for sale in West Africa might be ineffective: they might be counterfeit or might not have been stored under the right conditions. The most common examples of counterfeit drugs are malaria tablets and expensive antibiotics, such as ciprofloxacin. Most drugs are available in capital cities, but remote villages will be lucky to have a couple of paracetamol tablets. It is recommended that all drugs for chronic diseases be brought from home. Also, the availability and efficacy of condoms cannot be relied on – bring contraception. Condoms bought in West Africa might not be of the same quality as in Europe or Australia, and they might not have been correctly stored.

There is a high risk of contracting HIV from infected blood if you receive a blood transfusion in West Africa. To minimise this, seek out treatment in reputable clinics. If you have any doubts, the **Blood Care Foundation** (www.bloodcare.org.uk) is a useful source of safe, screened blood, which can be transported to any part of the world within 24 hours.

The cost of health care might seem cheap compared with its cost in first-world countries, but good care and drugs might not be available. Evacuation to good medical care (within West Africa or to your own country) can be very expensive. Unfortunately, adequate health care is available to very few West Africans.

Infectious Diseases

It's a formidable list but, as we say, a few precautions go a long way...

Cholera

Although small outbreaks can occur, cholera is usually only a problem during natural or human-made disasters. Travellers are rarely affected. It is caused by a bacteria and spread via contaminated drinking water. The main symptom is profuse, watery diarrhoea, which causes debilitation if fluids are not replaced quickly. An oral cholera vaccine is available, but it is not particularly effective. Most cases of cholera could be avoided by making sure you drink clean water and by avoiding potentially contaminated food. Treatment is by fluid replacement (orally or via a drip), but sometimes antibiotics are needed. Self-treatment is not advised.

Dengue Fever

Found in Senegal, Burkina Faso and Guinea, dengue fever (also called 'breakbone fever') is spread by mosquito bites. It causes a feverish illness with headache and muscle pains similar to those experienced with a bad, prolonged attack of influenza. There might be a rash. Self-treatment: paracetamol and rest. In rare cases in Africa this becomes severe dengue fever, with worsening symptoms including vomiting, rapid breathing and abdominal pain. Seek medical help as this can be fatal.

Diphtheria

Spread through close respiratory contact, diphtheria is found in all of Africa. It usually causes a temperature and a severe sore throat. Sometimes a membrane forms across the throat and a tracheostomy is needed to prevent suffocation. Vaccination is recommended for those likely to be in close contact with the local population in infected areas. More important for long stays than for short-term trips, the vaccine is given as an injection alone or with tetanus and lasts 10 years.

Filariasis

Tiny worms migrating in the lymphatic system cause filariasis. It is found in most of West Africa. A bite from an infected mosquito spreads the infection. Symptoms include itching and swelling of the legs and/or genitalia. Treatment is available.

Hepatitis A

Found in all of Africa, Hepatitis A is spread through contaminated food (particularly shellfish) and water. It causes jaundice and is rarely fatal, but can cause prolonged lethargy and delayed recovery. If you've had hepatitis A, you shouldn't drink alcohol for up to six months after, but once you've recovered, there won't be any long-term problems. The first symptoms include dark urine and a yellow colour to the whites of the eyes. Sometimes a fever and abdominal pain might occur. Hepatitis A vaccine (Avaxim, VAQTA, Havrix) is given as an injection: a single dose will give protection for a year and a booster after a year gives 10-year protection. Hepatitis A and typhoid vaccines can also be given as a single-dose vaccine (Hepatyrix or Viatim).

Hepatitis B

Spread through infected blood, contaminated needles and sexual intercourse, Hepatitis B is found in Africa. It can be spread from an infected mother to the baby in childbirth. It affects the liver, causing jaundice and occasionally liver failure. Most people recover completely, but some might be chronic carriers of the virus, which can lead eventually to cirrhosis or liver cancer. Those visiting high-risk areas for long periods or with increased social or occupational risk should be immunised. Many countries now give Hepatitis B as part of the routine childhood vaccination. It is given singly or can be given at the same time as Hepatitis A (Hepatyrix).

A course of vaccinations will give protection for at least five years. It can be given over four weeks or six months.

HIV

Human immunodeficiency virus (HIV), the virus that causes acquired immune deficiency syndrome (AIDS), is a huge problem in Africa but is most acutely felt in sub-Saharan Africa. The virus is spread through infected blood and blood products, by sexual intercourse with an infected partner and from an infected mother to her baby during childbirth and breastfeeding. It can be spread through 'blood to blood' contacts, such as with contaminated instruments during medical, dental, acupuncture and other body-piercing procedures, and through sharing intravenous needles. At present there is no cure; medication that might keep the disease under control is available, but these drugs are too expensive for the overwhelming majority of Africans and are not readily available for travellers either. If you think you might have been infected with HIV, a blood test is necessary; a three-month gap after exposure and before testing is required to allow antibodies to appear in the blood.

Leptospirosis

This is found in West Africa, including Morocco. It is spread through the excreta of infected rodents, especially rats. It can cause hepatitis and renal failure, which might be fatal. It is unusual for travellers to be affected unless they're living in poor sanitary conditions. It causes a fever and sometimes jaundice.

Malaria

One million children die annually from malaria in Africa. The risk of malarial transmission at altitudes higher than 2000m is rare. The disease is caused by a parasite in the bloodstream spread via the bite of the female Anopheles mosquito. There are several types of malaria, falciparum malaria being the most dangerous and the predominant form in Africa. Infection rates vary with season and climate, so check out the situation before departure. Unlike most other diseases regularly encountered by travellers, there is no vaccination against malaria (yet). However, several different drugs are used to prevent malaria and new ones are in the pipeline. Up-to-date advice from a travel-health clinic is essential, as some medication is more suitable for some travellers than for others. The pattern of drug-resistant malaria is changing rapidly, so what was advised several years ago might no longer be the case.

Malaria can present in several ways. The early stages include headache, fever, general aches and pains, and malaise, which could be mistaken for the flu. Other symptoms include abdominal pain, diarrhoea and a cough. Anyone who gets a fever in a malarial area should assume infection until a blood test proves negative, even if you have been taking antimalarial medication. If not treated, the next stage could develop within 24 hours, particularly if falciparum malaria is the parasite. The chain of events is jaundice, then reduced consciousness and coma (known as cerebral malaria), followed by death. Treatment in hospital is essential and the death rate can still be as high as 10% even in the best intensive-care facilities.

Many travellers are under the impression that malaria is a mild illness, that treatment

Malarial Risk in Africa

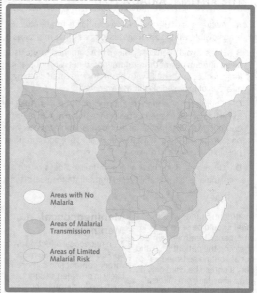

Areas with No Malaria

Areas of Malarial Transmission

Areas of Limited Malarial Risk

is always easy and successful and that taking antimalarial drugs causes more illness through side effects than actually getting malaria. In Africa, this is unfortunately not true. Side effects of the medication depend on the drug being taken. Doxycycline can cause heartburn and indigestion; mefloquine (Larium) can cause anxiety attacks, insomnia, nightmares and (rarely) severe psychiatric disorders; chloroquine can cause nausea and hair loss; and proguanil can cause mouth ulcers. These side effects are not universal and can be minimised by taking medication correctly, eg with food. Also, some people should not take a particular antimalarial drug, eg people with epilepsy should avoid mefloquine, and doxycycline should not be taken by pregnant women or children younger than 12.

If you decide that you really do not wish to take antimalarial drugs, you must understand the risks and be obsessive about avoiding mosquito bites. Use nets and insect repellent and report

any fever or flulike symptoms to a doctor as soon as possible. Some people advocate homeopathic preparations against malaria, such as Demal200, but there is no evidence that this is effective and doctors and even many homeopaths do not recommend their use.

People of all ages can contract malaria and falciparum causes the most severe illness. Repeated infections might result eventually in less-serious illness. Malaria in pregnancy frequently results in miscarriage or premature labour. Adults who have survived childhood malaria have developed immunity and usually only develop mild cases of malaria; most Western travellers have no immunity at all. Immunity wanes after 18 months of nonexposure, so even if you've had malaria in the past and used to live in a malaria-prone area, you might no longer be immune.

If you are planning a journey in a malarial area, particularly where falciparum malaria predominates, consider taking standby

THE ANTIMALARIAL A TO D

A – Awareness of the risk. No medication is totally effective, but protection of up to 95% is achievable with most drugs, as long as other measures have been taken.

B – Bites: avoid at all costs. Sleep in a screened room, use a mosquito spray or coils and sleep under a permethrin-impregnated net. Cover up at night with long trousers and long sleeves, preferably with permethrin-treated clothing. Apply appropriate repellent to all areas of exposed skin in the evenings.

C – Chemical prevention (ie antimalarial drugs) is usually needed in malarial areas. Expert advice is needed as resistance patterns can change, and new drugs are in development. Not all antimalarial drugs are suitable for everyone. Most antimalarial drugs need to be started at least a week in advance and continued for four weeks after the last possible exposure to malaria.

D – Diagnosis. If you have a fever or flulike illness within a year of travel to a malarial area, malaria is a possibility and immediate medical attention is necessary.

treatment. Standby treatment should be seen as emergency treatment aimed at saving the patient's life and not as routine self-medication. It should be used only if you will be far from medical facilities and have been advised about the symptoms of malaria and how to use the medication. Medical advice should be sought as soon as possible to confirm whether the treatment has been successful. The type of standby treatment used will depend on local conditions, such as drug resistance, and on what antimalarial drugs were being used before standby treatment. This is worthwhile, because you want to avoid contracting a particularly serious form such as cerebral malaria, which affects the brain and central nervous system and can be fatal in 24 hours. Self-diagnostic kits, which can identify malaria in the blood from a finger prick, are also available in the West.

The risks from malaria to both mother and foetus during pregnancy are considerable. Unless good medical care can be guaranteed, travel throughout Africa when pregnant – particularly to malarial areas – should be discouraged unless essential.

Meningococcal Meningitis

Meningococcal infection is spread through close respiratory contact and is more likely in crowded situations, such as dormitories, buses and clubs. Infection is uncommon in travellers. Vaccination is recommended for long stays and is especially important towards the end of the dry season, which varies across the continent. Symptoms include a fever, severe headache, neck stiffness and a red rash. Immediate medical treatment is necessary.

The ACWY vaccine is recommended for all travellers in sub-Saharan Africa. This vaccine is different from the meningococcal meningitis C vaccine given to children and adolescents in some countries; it is safe to give both types of vaccine.

Onchocerciasis

Also known as 'river blindness', this is caused by the larvae of a tiny worm, which is spread by the bite of a small fly. The earliest sign of infection is intensely itchy, red, sore eyes. Travellers are rarely severely affected. Treatment in a specialised clinic is curative.

Poliomyelitis

Polio is generally spread through contaminated food and water. The vaccine is one of those given in childhood and should be boosted every 10 years, either orally (a drop on the tongue) or as an injection. Polio can be carried asymptomatically (ie showing no symptoms) and could cause a transient fever. In rare cases it causes weakness or paralysis of one or more muscles, which might be permanent. The WHO states that Nigeria and Niger are polio hotspots following recent outbreaks.

Rabies

Rabies is spread by receiving the bites or licks of an infected animal on broken skin. It's fatal once the clinical symptoms start (which might be up to several months after the injury), so post-bite vaccination should be given as soon as possible. Post-bite vaccination (whether or not you've been vaccinated before the bite) prevents the virus from spreading to the central nervous system. Animal handlers should be vaccinated, as should those travelling to remote areas where a source of post-bite vaccine is not available within 24 hours. Three preventative injections are needed in a month. If you have not been vaccinated you will need a course of five injections starting within 24 hours or as soon as possible after the injury. If you have been vaccinated, you will need fewer post-bite injections and will have more time to seek medical aid.

Schistosomiasis

Also called bilharzia, this disease is spread by flukes that are carried by a species of freshwater snail. The flukes are carried inside the snail, which then sheds them into slow-moving or still water. The parasites penetrate human skin during paddling or swimming and then migrate to the bladder or bowel. They are passed out via stools or urine and can contaminate fresh water, where the cycle starts again. Avoid paddling or swimming in suspect freshwater lakes or slow-running rivers. There may be no symptoms or there may be a transient fever and rash, and advanced cases can have blood in the stool or in the urine. A blood test can detect antibodies if you have been exposed, and treatment is then possible in travel- or infectious-disease clinics. If not treated, the infection can cause kidney failure or permanent bowel damage. It isn't possible for you to infect others.

Tuberculosis (TB)

TB is spread through close respiratory contact and occasionally through infected milk or milk products. BCG (Bacille Calmette-Guérin) vaccination is recommended for those likely to be mixing closely with the local population, although it gives only moderate protection against TB. It is more important for long stays than for short-term stays. Inoculation with the BCG vaccine is not available in all countries. It is given routinely to many children in developing countries. The vaccination causes a small, permanent scar at the injection site and is usually given in a specialised chest clinic. It is a live vaccine and should not be given to pregnant women or immunocompromised individuals.

TB can be asymptomatic, only being picked up on a routine chest X-ray. Alternatively, it can cause a cough, weight loss or fever, sometimes months or even years after exposure.

Typhoid

This is spread through food or water contaminated by infected human faeces. The first symptom is usually a fever or a pink rash on the abdomen. Sometimes septicaemia (blood poisoning) can occur. A typhoid vaccine (typhim Vi, typherix) will give protection for three years. In some countries, the oral vaccine Vivotif is also available. Antibiotics are usually given as treatment and death is rare unless septicaemia occurs.

Trypanosomiasis

Spread via the bite of the tsetse fly, trypanosomiasis, also called 'sleeping sickness', causes a headache, fever and eventually coma. There is an effective treatment.

Yellow Fever

Travellers should carry a certificate as evidence of vaccination if they have recently been in an infected country, to avoid any possible difficulties with immigration. For a full list of these countries visit the **WHO website** (www.who. int/en) or the **Centers for Disease Control and Prevention website** (www.cdc. gov/travel). There is always the possibility that a traveller without a legally required, up-to-date certificate will be vaccinated and detained in isolation at the port of arrival for up to 10 days, or possibly repatriated.

Yellow fever is spread by infected mosquitoes. Symptoms range from a flulike illness to severe hepatitis (liver inflammation), jaundice and death. The yellow-fever vaccination must be given at a designated clinic and is valid for 10 years. It is a live vaccine and must not be given to immunocompromised or pregnant travellers.

Yellow Fever Risk in Africa

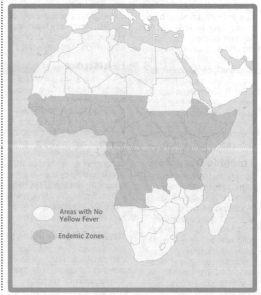

Areas with No Yellow Fever

Endemic Zones

Traveller's Diarrhoea

It's not inevitable that you will get diarrhoea while travelling in Africa, but it's certainly likely. Diarrhoea is the most common travel-related illness – figures suggest that at least half of all travellers to Africa will get diarrhoea at some stage. Sometimes dietary changes, such as increased spices or oils, are the cause. To help prevent diarrhoea, avoid tap water unless you're sure it's safe to drink. You should only eat cooked or peeled fresh fruits or vegetables, and be wary of dairy products that might contain unpasteurised milk. Although freshly cooked food can often be a safe option, plates or serving utensils might be dirty, so you should be very selective when eating food from street vendors (make sure that cooked food is piping hot all the way through). If you develop diarrhoea, be sure to drink plenty of fluids, preferably an oral rehydration solution containing water, and some salt and sugar. A few loose stools don't require treatment, but if you start having more than four or five a day you should start taking an antibiotic (often a quinoline drug, such as ciprofloxacin or norfloxacin) and an antidiarrhoeal agent (such as loperamide) if you are not within easy reach of a toilet. If diarrhoea is bloody, persists for more than 72 hours or is accompanied by a fever, shaking, chills or severe abdominal pain, you should seek medical attention.

Amoebic Dysentery

Contracted by eating contaminated food and water, amoebic dysentery causes blood and mucus in the faeces. It can be relatively mild and tends to come on gradually, but seek medical advice if you think you have the illness, as it won't clear up without treatment (which is with specific antibiotics).

Giardiasis

Like amoebic dysentery, this is caused by ingesting contaminated food or water. The illness appears a week or more after you have been exposed to the parasite. Giardiasis might cause only a short-lived bout of traveller's diarrhoea, but it can cause persistent diarrhoea. Seek medical advice if you suspect you have giardiasis, but if you are in a remote area you could start a course of antibiotics.

Environmental Hazards

Heat Exhaustion

This condition occurs following heavy sweating and excessive fluid loss with inadequate replacement of fluids and salt, and is common in hot climates when taking exercise before full acclimatisation. Symptoms include headache, dizziness and tiredness. Dehydration is happening by the time you feel thirsty – aim to drink sufficient water to produce pale, diluted urine. Treatment: fluid replacement with water and/or fruit juice, and cooling by cold water and fans. The treatment of the salt-loss component consists of consuming salty fluids, as in soup, and adding a bit more salt to food than usual.

Heatstroke

Heat exhaustion is a precursor to the much more serious heatstroke. In this case there is damage to the sweating mechanism, with an excessive rise in body temperature; irrational and hyperactive behaviour; and eventually loss of consciousness and death. Rapid cooling by spraying the body with water and fanning is best. Emergency fluid and electrolyte replacement is required by intravenous drip.

Insect Bites & Stings

Mosquitoes might not always carry malaria or dengue fever, but they (and other insects) can cause irritation and infected bites. To avoid these, take the same precautions as you would for avoiding malaria. Use DEET-based insect repellents. Excellent clothing treatments are also available; mosquitos that land on treated clothing will die.

Bee and wasp stings cause real problems only to those who have a severe allergy to the stings (anaphylaxis). If you are one of these people, carry an EpiPen – an adrenaline (epinephrine) injection, which you can give yourself. This could save your life.

Sandflies are found around the beaches. They usually only cause a nasty, itchy bite but can carry a rare skin disorder called cutaneous leishmaniasis. Prevention of bites with DEET-based repellent is sensible.

Scorpions are frequently found in arid or dry climates. They have a painful sting that is sometimes life-threatening. If stung by a scorpion, seek immediate medical assistance.

Bed bugs are found in hostels and cheap hotels and lead to itchy, lumpy bites. Spraying the mattress with crawling-insect killer after changing bedding will get rid of them.

Scabies are also found in cheap accommodation. These tiny mites live in the skin, often between the fingers, and they cause an intensely itchy rash. The itch is easily treated with malathion and permethrin lotion from a pharmacy; other members of the household also need treating to avoid spreading scabies, even if they do not show any symptoms.

Snake Bites

Avoid getting bitten! Don't walk barefoot or stick your hand into holes or cracks. Half of those bitten by venomous snakes are not actually injected with poison. If bitten by a snake, do not panic. Immobilise the bitten limb with a splint (such as a stick) and apply a bandage over the site, with firm pressure (similar to bandaging a sprain). Do not apply a tourniquet, or cut or suck the bite. Get medical help as soon as possible so antivenom can be given if needed. It will help get you the correct antivenom if you can identify the snake, so try to take note of its appearance.

Water

Never drink tap water unless it has been boiled, filtered or chemically disinfected (eg with iodine tablets). Never drink from streams, rivers or lakes. It's best to avoid drinking from pumps and wells – some do bring pure water to the surface, but the presence of animals can contaminate supplies.

Traditional Medicine

At least 80% of the African population relies on traditional medicine, often because conventional West-

ern-style medicine is too expensive, because of prevailing cultural attitudes and beliefs, or simply because in some cases it works. It might also be because there's no other choice: a WHO survey found that although there was only one medical doctor for every 50,000 people in Mozambique, there was a traditional healer for every 200 people.

Although some African remedies seem to work on malaria, sickle cell anaemia, high blood pressure and some AIDS symptoms, most African healers learn their art by apprenticeship, so education (and consequently application of knowledge) is inconsistent and unregulated. Conventionally trained physicians in South Africa, for example, angrily describe how their AIDS patients die of kidney failure because a *sangoma* (traditional healer) has given them an enema containing an essence made

from powerful roots. Likewise, when traditional healers administer 'injections' with porcupine quills, knives or dirty razor blades, diseases are often spread or created rather than cured.

Rather than attempting to stamp out traditional practices, or pretend they aren't happening, a positive step taken by some African countries is the regulation of traditional medicine by creating healers' associations and offering courses on topics such as sanitary practices. It remains unlikely in the short term that even a basic level of conventional Western-style medicine will be made available to all the people of Africa (even though the cost of doing so is less than the annual military budget of some Western countries). Traditional medicine, on the other hand, will almost certainly continue to be practised widely throughout the continent.

Language

West Africa's myriad ethnic groups speak several hundred local languages, many subdivided into numerous distinct dialects. The people of Nigeria – West Africa's most populous country – speak at least 350 languages and dialects, while even tiny Guinea-Bissau (population just over one million) has around 20 languages.

Consequently, common languages are essential, and several are used. These may be the language of the largest group in a particular area. For example, Hausa has spread out from its northern Nigerian heartland to become widely understood as a trading language in the eastern parts of West Africa. Two other regional lingua francas are Wolof and Yoruba, and we've included the basics of all three in this chapter. In some areas, the lingua franca is a creole – a combination of native African and imported European languages.

All of the countries covered in this book have one of the following languages as official language: English (Cameroon, the Gambia, Ghana, Liberia, Nigeria and Sierra Leone), French (Benin, Burkina Faso, Cameroon, Côte d'Ivoire, Guinea, Mali, Niger, Senegal and Togo), Portuguese (Cape Verde and Guinea-Bissau) or Arabic (Mauritania and Morocco). These languages are also included in this chapter, so you'll be able to get by and be understood across West Africa. See the relevant destination chapter for a list of African languages also spoken in each country.

WANT MORE?

For in-depth language information and handy phrases, check out Lonely Planet's *Africa Phrasebook*, *French Phrasebook*, *Moroccan Arabic Phrasebook* and *Portuguese Phrasebook*. You'll find them at **shop.lonelyplanet.com**, or you can buy Lonely Planet's iPhone phrasebooks at the Apple App Store.

ARABIC

The following phrases are in MSA (Modern Standard Arabic), which is the official language of the Arab world, used in schools, administration and the media. Note, though, that there are significant differences between MSA and the colloquial Arabic varieties, which are spoken in different countries but have no official written form: the Moroccan Arabic variety is known as Darija, and the dialect spoken in Mauritania is called Hassaniyya.

Arabic script is written from right to left. Read our coloured pronunciation guides as if they were English and you should be understood. Note that a is pronounced as in 'act', aa as the 'a' in 'father', aw as in 'law', ay as in 'say', ee as in 'see', i as in 'hit', oo as in 'zoo', u as in 'put', gh is a throaty sound, r is rolled, dh is pronounced as in 'that', th as in 'thin' and kh as the 'ch' in the Scottish *loch*. The apostrophe (') indicates the glottal stop (like the pause in the middle of 'uh-oh'). The stressed syllables are indicated with italics. Masculine and feminine options are indicated with 'm' and 'f' respectively.

Basics

Hello.	السلام عليكم.	as·sa·*laa*·mu 'a·*lay*·kum
Goodbye.	إلى اللقاء.	'i·laa al·li·*kaa*'
Yes.	نعم.	na·'am
No.	لا.	laa
Excuse me.	عفواً.	'af·wan
Sorry.	آسف.	'aa·sif (m)
	آسفة.	'aa·si·fa (f)
Please.	لو سمحتَ.	law sa·*mah*·ta (m)
	لو سمحتِ.	law sa·*mah*·ti (f)
Thank you.	شكراً.	*shuk*·ran

How are you?

| كيف حالك؟ | *kay*·fa haa·lu·ka (m) |
| كيف حالك؟ | *kay*·fa haa·lu·ki (f) |

Fine, thanks. And you?

بخيرٍ شكراً.   bi·*khay*·rin *shuk*·ran
وأنتَ/وأنتِ؟   wa·'*an*·ta/wa·'*an*·ti (m/f)

What's your name?

ما اسمكَ؟   maa '*is*·mu·ka (m)
ما اسمكِ؟   maa '*is*·mu·ki (f)

My name is ...

اسمي ...   '*is*·mee ...

Do you speak English?

هل تتكلّم/   hal ta·ta·*kal*·la·mu/
تتكلّمين   ta·ta·kal·la·*mee*·na
الإنجليزية؟   al·'inj·lee·*zee*·ya (m/f)

I don't understand.

أنا لا أفهم.   '*a*·naa laa '*af*·ham

Accommodation

Where's a ...?   أين أجدُ ...؟   '*ay*·na 'a·*ji*·du ...
  campsite   مخيم   mu·*khay*·yam
  guesthouse   بيت للضيوف   bayt li·du·*yoof*
  hotel   فندق   *fun*·duk
  youth hostel   فندق شباب   *fun*·duk sha·*baab*

Do you have   هل عندكم   hal '*in*·da·kum
a ... room?   غرفةٌ ...؟   *ghur*·fa·tun ...
  single   بسرير   bi·sa·*ree*·rin
   منفردٌ   *mun*·fa·rid
  double   بسرير   bi·sa·*ree*·rin
   مزدوّج   muz·*daw*·waj

How much is   كم ثمنه   kam *tha*·ma·nu·hu
it per ...?   لِـ ...؟   li ...
  night   ليلة واحدة   *lay*·la·tin *waa*·hid
  person   شخصٍ واحدة   *shakh*·sin *waa*·hid

Eating & Drinking

Can you   هل يمكنكَ أن   hal yum·*ki*·nu·ka 'an
recommend   توصي ...؟   too·*see*·ya ... (m)
a ...?   هل يمكنكِ أن   hal yum·*ki*·nu·ki 'an
   توصي ...؟   too·*see* ... (f)
  cafe   مقهىً   mak·*han*
  restaurant   مطعمٌ   mat·'*am*

What would you recommend?

ماذا توصي؟   maa·dhaa too·*see* (m)
ماذا توصين؟   maa·dhaa too·*see*·na (f)

What's the local speciality?

ما الوجبة الخاصّة   maa al·*waj*·ba·tul *khaa*·sa
لهذه المنطقة؟   li·*haa*·dhi·hil *man*·ta·ka

Do you have vegetarian food?

هل لديكم   hal la·*day*·ku·mu
طعامٌ نباتيّ؟   ta·'aa·mun na·*baa*·tee

I'd like the   أريد ... .   'u·*ree*·du ...
..., please.   لو سمحتَ.   law sa·*mah*·ta
  bill   الحساب   hi·*saab*
  menu   قائمة   kaa·'*i*·ma·tu
   الطعام   at·ta·'*aam*

beer   بيرة   *bee*·ra
bottle   زجاجة   zu·*jaa*·ja
breakfast   فطور   fu·*toor*
coffee   قهوة   *kah*·wa
cold   بارد/باردة   *baa*·rid/*baa*·ri·da (m/f)
cup   فنجان   fin·*jaan*
dinner   عشاء   'a·*shaa*'
drink   مشروب   mash·*roob*
fish   سمك   *sa*·mak
food   طعام   ta·'*aam*
fork   شوكة   *shaw*·ka
fruit   فاكهة   *faa*·ki·ha
glass   كأس   ka's
hot   حار/حارة   *haar*/*haa*·ra (m/f)
(orange) juice   عصير   'a·*see*·ru
   (برتقال)   (bur·tu·*kaal*)
knife   سكين   sik·*keen*
lunch   غداء   gha·*daa*'
market   سوق   sook
meat   لحم   lahm
milk   حليب   ha·*leeb*
mineral water   مياه معدنية   mi·*yaah* ma'·da·*nee*·ya
plate   صحن   sahn
spoon   ملعقة   *mal*·'a·ka
vegetable   خضراوات   khud·raa·*waat*
water   ماء   maa'
wine   نبيذ   na·*beedh*
with   مع   *ma*·a
without   بدون   bi·*doo*·ni

Emergencies

Help!   ساعدني!   saa·'*i*·du·nee (m)
   ساعديني!   *saa*·i·*dee*·nee (f)
Go away!   اتركني!   '*it*·ruk·nee (m)
   اتركيني!   'it·ru·*kee*·nee (f)

Call ...!   اتّصلْ بـ ...!   '*it*·ta·sil bi ... (m)
   اتّصلي بـ ...!   'it·ta·si·*lee* bi ... (f)
  a doctor   طبيب   ta·*beeb*
  the police   الشرطة   ash·*shur*·ta

Where are the toilets?

أين دورات المياه؟   '*ay*·na daw·*raa*·tul mee·*yaah*

Numbers – Arabic

1	١	واحد	waa·hid
2	٢	اثنان	'ith·naan
3	٣	ثلاثة	tha·laa·tha
4	٤	أربعة	'ar·ba·a
5	٥	خمسة	kham·sa
6	٦	ستة	sit·ta
7	٧	سبعة	sab·'a
8	٨	ثمانية	tha·maa·ni·ya
9	٩	تسعة	tis·'a
10	١٠	عشرة	'a·sha·ra
20	٢٠	عشرون	'ish·roon
30	٣٠	ثلاثون	tha·laa·thoon
40	٤٠	أربعون	'ar·ba·oon
50	٥٠	خمسون	kham·soon
60	٦٠	ستون	sit·toon
70	٧٠	سبعون	sab·'oon
80	٨٠	ثمانون	tha·maa·noon
90	٩٠	تسعون	tis·'oon
100	١٠٠	مائة	mi·'a
1000	١٠٠٠	ألف	'alf

Note that Arabic numerals, unlike letters, are written from left to right.

I'm lost.

أنا ضائع.   'a·naa daa·'i' (m)

أنا ضائعة.   'a·naa daa·'i·'a (f)

I'm sick.

أنا مريض.   'a·naa ma·reed

Shopping & Services

I'm looking for ...

أبحث عن ...   'ab·ha·thu 'an ...

Can I look at it?

هل يمكنني أن   hal yum·ki·nu·nee 'an
أراه؟   'a·raa·hu

Do you have any others?

هل عندك غيره؟   hal 'in·da·kum ghay·ru·hu

How much is it?

كم سعره؟   kam si'·ru·hu

That's too expensive.

هذا غالٍ جداً.   haa·dhaa ghaa·lin jid·dan

There's a mistake in the bill.

في خطأ في الحساب.   fee kha·ta' feel hi·saab

Where's an ATM?

أين جهاز الصرافة؟   'ay·na ji·haaz as·sar·raa·fa

Time & Dates

What time is it?

كم الساعة الآن؟   kam as·saa·'a·tul 'aan

It's (two) o'clock.

الساعة(الثانية).   as·saa·'a tu (ath·thaa·nee·ya)

Half past (two).

(الثانية)   (ath·thaa·nee·ya·tu)
والنصف.   wan·nus·fu

morning	صباح	sa·baah
afternoon	بعد الظهر	ba'·da adh·dhuh·ri
evening	مساء	ma·saa'
yesterday	أمس	'am·si
today	اليوم	al·yawm
tomorrow	غداً	gha·dan

Monday	يوم الاثنين	yawm al·'ith·nayn
Tuesday	يوم الثلاثاء	yawm ath·thu·laa·thaa'
Wednesday	يوم الأربعاء	yawm al·'ar·bi·aa
Thursday	يوم الخميس	yawm al·kha·mees
Friday	يوم الجمعة	yawm al·jum·'a
Saturday	يوم السبت	yawm as·sabt
Sunday	يوم الأحد	yawm al·'a·had

Transport & Directions

Is this the ...

هل هذا الـ ...   hal haa·dhaa al ...

to (...)?

إلى (...)؟   'i·laa (...)

boat	سفينة	sa·fee·na
bus	باص	baas
plane	طائرة	taa·'i·ra
train	قطار	ki·taar

What time's the ... bus?

في أيّ ساعةٍ   fee 'ay·yee saa·'a·tin
يغادرُ الباص   yu·ghaa·di·ru al·baas
الـ ...؟   al ...

first	أوّل	'aw·wal
last	آخر	'aa·khir

One ... ticket, please.

تذكرة ...   tadh·ka·ra·tu ...
واحدة، لو سمحت.   waa·hi·da law sa·mah·ta

one-way	ذهاب فقط	dha·haa·bu fa·kat
return	ذهاب	dha·haa·bu
	وإياب	wa·'ee·yaab

How much is it to ...?

كم الأجرة إلى ...؟   kam al·'uj·ra·ti 'i·laa ...

Please take me to (this address).

أوصلني عند   'aw·sal·nee 'ind
(هذا العنوان)   (haa·dhaa al·'un·waan)
لو سمحت.   law sa·mah·ta

Where's the (market)?

أين الـ(سوق)؟   'ay·na al (sook)

Can you show me (on the map)?

هل يمكنك أن   hal yum·ki·nu·ka 'an
توضح لي   tu·wad·da·ha lee
(على الخريطة)؟   ('a·laa al·kha·ree·ta) (m)

هل يمكنك أن   hal yum·ki·nu·ki 'an
توضحي لي   tu·wad·da·hee lee
(على الخريطة)؟   ('a·laa al·kha·ree·ta) (f)

What's the address?

ما هو العنوان؟   maa hu·wa al·'un·waan

FRENCH

The sounds used in spoken French can almost all be found in English. There are a couple of exceptions: nasal vowels (represented in our pronunciation guides by o or u followed by an almost inaudible nasal consonant sound m, n or ng), the 'funny' u (ew in our guides) and the deep-in-the-throat r. Bearing these few points in mind and reading our pronunciation guides below as if they were English, you won't have problems being understood. Note that syllables are for the most part equally stressed in French.

Masculine and feminine forms of words are provided in the following phrases where relevant, indicated with 'm' and 'f' respectively.

Basics

Hello.	*Bonjour.*	bon·zhoor
Goodbye.	*Au revoir.*	o·rer·vwa
Excuse me.	*Excusez-moi.*	ek·skew·zay·mwa
Sorry.	*Pardon.*	par·don
Yes.	*Oui.*	wee
No.	*Non.*	non
Please.	*S'il vous plaît.*	seel voo play
Thank you.	*Merci.*	mair·see
You're welcome.	*De rien.*	der ree·en

How are you?
Comment allez-vous?   ko·mon ta·lay·voo

Fine, and you?
Bien, merci. Et vous?   byun mair·see ay voo

My name is ...
Je m'appelle ...   zher ma·pel ...

What's your name?
Comment vous   ko·mon voo
appelez-vous?   za·play voo

Do you speak English?
Parlez-vous anglais?   par·lay·voo ong·glay

I don't understand.
Je ne comprends pas.   zher ner kom·pron pa

Accommodation

campsite	*camping*	kom·peeng
guesthouse	*pension*	pon·syon
hotel	*hôtel*	o·tel
youth hostel	*auberge de jeunesse*	o·berzh der zher·nes
a ... room	*une chambre ...*	ewn shom·brer ...
double	*avec un grand lit*	a·vek un gron lee
single	*à un lit*	a un lee

How much is it per night/person?
Quel est le prix   kel ay ler pree
par nuit/personne?   par nwee/per·son

Is breakfast included?
Est-ce que le petit   es·ker ler per·tee
déjeuner est inclus?   day·zher·nay ayt en·klew

Eating & Drinking

Can I see the menu, please?
Est-ce que je peux voir   es·ker zher per vwar
la carte, s'il vous plaît.   la kart seel voo play

What would you recommend?
Qu'est-ce que vous   kes·ker voo
conseillez?   kon·say·yay

I'm a vegetarian.
Je suis végétarien/   zher swee vay·zhay·ta·ryun/
végétarienne. (m/f)   vay·zhay·ta·ryen

I don't eat ...
Je ne mange pas ...   zher ner monzh pa ...

Cheers!
Santé!   son·tay

Please bring the bill.
Apportez-moi   a·por·tay·mwa
l'addition,   la·dee·syon
s'il vous plaît.   seel voo play

beer	*bière*	bee·yair
bottle	*bouteille*	boo·tay
bread	*pain*	pun
breakfast	*petit déjeuner*	per·tee day·zher·nay
cheese	*fromage*	fro·mazh
coffee	*café*	ka·fay
cold	*froid*	frwa
dinner	*dîner*	dee·nay
dish	*plat*	pla
egg	*œuf*	erf
food	*nourriture*	noo·ree·tewr
fork	*fourchette*	foor·shet

glass	verre	vair
grocery store	épicerie	ay·pees·ree
hot	chaud	sho
(orange) juice	jus (d'orange)	zhew (do·ronzh)
knife	couteau	koo·to
local speciality	spécialité locale	spay·sya·lee·tay lo·kal
lunch	déjeuner	day·zher·nay
main course	plat principal	pla prun·see·pal
market	marché	mar·shay
milk	lait	lay
plate	assiette	a·syet
red wine	vin rouge	vun roozh
rice	riz	ree
salt	sel	sel
spoon	cuillère	kwee·yair
sugar	sucre	sew·krer
tea	thé	tay
vegetable	légume	lay·gewm
(mineral) water	eau (minérale)	o (mee·nay·ral)
white wine	vin blanc	vun blong
with/without	avec/sans	a·vek/son

Emergencies

Help!
Au secours! — o skoor

I'm lost.
Je suis perdu/perdue. — zhe swee·pair·dew (m/f)

Leave me alone!
Fichez-moi la paix! — fee·shay·mwa la pay

Call a doctor.
Appelez un médecin. — a·play un mayd·sun

Call the police.
Appelez la police. — a·play la po·lees

I'm ill.
Je suis malade. — zher swee ma·lad

I'm allergic to ...
Je suis allergique à ... — zher swee za·lair·zheek a ...

Where are the toilets?
Où sont les toilettes? — oo son lay twa·let

Shopping & Services

I'd like to buy ...
Je voudrais acheter ... — zher voo·dray ash·tay ...

Can I look at it?
Est-ce que je peux le voir? — es·ker zher per ler vwar

Numbers – French

1	un	un
2	deux	der
3	trois	trwa
4	quatre	ka·trer
5	cinq	sungk
6	six	sees
7	sept	set
8	huit	weet
9	neuf	nerf
10	dix	dees
20	vingt	vung
30	trente	tront
40	quarante	ka·ront
50	cinquante	sung·kont
60	soixante	swa·sont
70	soixante-dix	swa·son·dees
80	quatre-vingts	ka·trer·vung
90	quatre-vingt-dix	ka·trer·vung·dees
100	cent	son
1000	mille	meel

How much is it?
C'est combien? — say kom·byun

It's too expensive.
C'est trop cher. — say tro shair

Can you lower the price?
Vous pouvez baisser le prix? — voo poo·vay bay·say ler pree

ATM	guichet automatique de banque	gee·shay o·to·ma·teek der bonk
internet cafe	cybercafé	see·bair·ka·fay
post office	bureau de poste	bew·ro der post
tourist office	office de tourisme	o·fees der too·rees·mer

Time & Dates

What time is it?
Quelle heure est-il? — kel er ay til

It's (eight) o'clock.
Il est (huit) heures. — il ay (weet) er

It's half past (10).
Il est (dix) heures et demie. — il ay (deez) er ay day·mee

morning	matin	ma·tun
afternoon	après-midi	a·pray·mee·dee
evening	soir	swar

yesterday	*hier*	yair
today	*aujourd'hui*	o·zhoor·dwee
tomorrow	*demain*	der·mun
Monday	*lundi*	lun·dee
Tuesday	*mardi*	mar·dee
Wednesday	*mercredi*	mair·krer·dee
Thursday	*jeudi*	zher·dee
Friday	*vendredi*	von·drer·dee
Saturday	*samedi*	sam·dee
Sunday	*dimanche*	dee·monsh

Transport & Directions

boat	*bateau*	ba·to
bus	*bus*	bews
plane	*avion*	a·vyon
train	*train*	trun
a ... ticket	*un billet ...*	un bee·yay ...
one-way	*simple*	sum·pler
return	*aller et retour*	a·lay ay rer·toor

I want to go to ...
Je voudrais aller à ...   zher voo·dray a·lay a ...

At what time does it leave/arrive?
À quelle heure est-ce qu'il part/arrive?   a kel er es kil par/a·reev

Does it stop at ...?
Est-ce qu'il s'arrête à ...?   es·kil sa·ret a ...

Can you tell me when we get to ...?
Pouvez-vous me dire quand nous arrivons à ...?   poo·vay·voo mer deer kon noo za·ree·von a ...

I want to get off here.
Je veux descendre ici.   zher ver day·son·drer ee·see

Where's ...?
Où est ...?   oo ay ...

What's the address?
Quelle est l'adresse?   kel ay la·dres

Can you show me (on the map)?
Pouvez-vous m'indiquer (sur la carte)?   poo·vay·voo mun·dee·kay (sewr la kart)

PORTUGUESE

Most sounds in Portuguese are also found in English. The exceptions are the nasal vowels (represented in our pronunciation guides by ng after the vowel), which are pronounced as if you're trying to make the sound through your nose; and the strongly rolled r (repre-sented by rr in our pronunciation guides). Also note that the symbol zh sounds like the 's' in 'pleasure'. The stressed syllables are indicated with italics.

Masculine and feminine forms of words are provided in the following phrases where relevant, indicated with 'm' and 'f' respectively.

Basics

Hello.	*Olá.*	o·laa
Goodbye.	*Adeus.*	a·de·oosh
Excuse me.	*Faz favor.*	faash fa·vor
Sorry.	*Desculpe.*	desh·kool·pe
Yes.	*Sim.*	seeng
No.	*Não.*	nowng
Please.	*Por favor.*	poor fa·vor
Thank you.	*Obrigado.*	o·bree·gaa·doo (m)
	Obrigada.	o·bree·gaa·da (f)
You're welcome.	*De nada.*	de naa·da

How are you?
Como está?   ko·moo shtaa

Fine, and you?
Bem, e você?   beng e vo·se

What's your name?
Qual é o seu nome?   kwaal e oo se·oo no·me

My name is ...
O meu nome é ...   oo me·oo no·me e ...

Do you speak English?
Fala inglês?   faa·la eeng·glesh

I don't understand.
Não entendo.   nowng eng·teng·doo

Accommodation

campsite	*parque de campismo*	paar·ke de kang·peezh·moo
guesthouse	*casa de hóspedes*	kaa·za de osh·pe·desh
hotel	*hotel*	o·tel
youth hostel	*pousada de juventude*	poh·zaa da do zhoo·veng·too·de

Do you have a single/double room?
Tem um quarto de solteiro/casal?   teng oong kwaar·too de sol·tay·roo/ka·zal

How much is it per night/person?
Quanto custa por noite/pessoa?   kwang·too koosh·ta poor noy·te/pe·so·a

Is breakfast included?
Inclui o pequeno almoço?   eeng·kloo·ee oo pe·ke·noo aal·mo·soo

Eating & Drinking

I'd like (the menu).
Queria (um menu).   ke·*ree*·a (oong me·*noo*)

What would you recommend?
O que é que   oo ke e ke
recomenda?   rre·koo·*meng*·da

I don't eat ...
Eu não como ...   e·oo nowng ko·moo ...

Cheers!
Saúde!   sa·*oo*·de

Please bring the bill.
Pode-me trazer a conta.   po·de·me tra·*zer* a *kong*·ta

beer	*cerveja*	ser·ve·zha
bottle	*garrafa*	ga·*rraa*·fa
bread	*pão*	powng
breakfast	*pequeno almoço*	pe·*ke*·noo aal·*mo*·soo
cheese	*queijo*	*kay*·zhoo
coffee	*café*	ka·*fe*
cold	*frio*	*free*·oo
dinner	*jantar*	zhang·*taar*
egg	*ovo*	o·voo
food	*comida*	koo·*mee*·da
fork	*garfo*	gar·foo
fruit	*fruta*	*froo*·ta
glass	*copo*	ko·poo
hot (warm)	*quente*	keng·te
juice	*sumo*	*soo*·moo
knife	*faca*	*faa*·ka
lunch	*almoço*	aal·*mo*·soo
main course	*prato principal*	*praa*·too preeng·see·*paal*
market	*mercado*	mer·*kaa*·doo
milk	*leite*	*lay*·te
plate	*prato*	*praa*·too
red wine	*vinho tinto*	vee·nyoo *teeng*·too
restaurant	*restaurante*	rresh·tow·*rang*·te
rice	*arroz*	a·*rrosh*
salt	*sal*	saal
spicy	*picante*	pee·*kang*·te
spoon	*colher*	koo·*lyer*
sugar	*açúcar*	a·*soo*·kar
tea	*chá*	shaa
vegetable	*hortaliça*	or·ta·*lee*·sa
vegetarian food	*comida vegetariana*	koo·*mee*·da ve·zhe·ta·ree·*aa*·na
(mineral) water	*água (mineral)*	*aa*·gwa (mee·ne·*raal*)

white wine	*vinho branco*	vee·nyoo *brang*·koo
with	*com*	kong
without	*sem*	seng

Emergencies

Help!   *Socorro!*   soo·*ko*·rroo
Go away!   *Vá-se embora!*   vaa·se eng·*bo*·ra

Call ...!   *Chame ...!*   *shaa*·me ...
   a doctor   *um médico*   oong me·dee·koo
   the police   *a polícia*   a poo·*lee*·sya

I'm lost.
Estou perdido.   shtoh per·*dee*·doo (m)
Estou perdida.   shtoh per·*dee*·da (f)

I'm ill.
Estou doente.   shtoh doo·*eng*·te

Where is the toilet?
Onde é a casa de   ong·de e a *kaa*·za de
banho?   ba·nyoo

Shopping & Services

I'd like to buy ...
Queria comprar ...   ke·*ree*·a kong·*praar* ...

Can I look at it?
Posso ver?   po·soo ver

How much is it?
Quanto custa?   kwang·too koosh·ta

It's too expensive.
Está muito caro.   shtaa mweeng·too kaa·roo

Can you lower the price?
Pode baixar o preço?   po·de bai·*shaar* oo pre·soo

ATM	*caixa automático*	*kai*·sha ow·too·*maa*·tee·koo
internet cafe	*café da internet*	ka·fe da eeng·ter·*ne*·te
post office	*correio*	koo·*rray*·oo
tourist office	*escritório de turismo*	shkree·*to*·ryo de too·*reezh*·moo

Time & Dates

What time is it?
Que horas são?   kee o·rash sowng

It's (10) o'clock.
São (dez) horas.   sowng (desh) o·rash

Half past (10).
(Dez) e meia.   (desh) e *may*·a

Numbers – Portuguese		
1	um	oong
2	dois	doysh
3	três	tresh
4	quatro	kwaa·troo
5	cinco	seeng·koo
6	seis	saysh
7	sete	se·te
8	oito	oy·too
9	nove	no·ve
10	dez	desh
20	vinte	veeng·te
30	trinta	treeng·ta
40	quarenta	kwa·reng·ta
50	cinquenta	seeng·kweng·ta
60	sessenta	se·seng·ta
70	setenta	se·teng·ta
80	oitenta	oy·teng·ta
90	noventa	no·veng·ta
100	cem	seng
1000	mil	meel

morning	manhã	ma·nyang
afternoon	tarde	taar·de
evening	noite	noy·te
yesterday	ontem	ong·teng
today	hoje	o·zhe
tomorrow	amanhã	aa·ma·nyang

Monday	segunda-feira	se·goong·da·fay·ra
Tuesday	terça-feira	ter·sa·fay·ra
Wednesday	quarta-feira	kwaar·ta·fay·ra
Thursday	quinta-feira	keeng·ta·fay·ra
Friday	sexta-feira	saysh·ta·fay·ra
Saturday	sábado	saa·ba·doo
Sunday	domingo	doo·meeng·goo

Transport & Directions

boat	barco	baar·koo
bus	autocarro	ow·to·kaa·roo
plane	avião	a·vee·owng
train	comboio	kong·boy·oo

... ticket	um bilhete de ...	oong bee·lye·te de ...
one-way	ida	ee·da
return	ida e volta	ee·da ee vol·ta

I want to go to ...
Queria ir a ...   ke·ree·a eer a ...

What time does it leave/arrive?
A que horas sai/chega?   a ke o·rash sai/she·ga

Does it stop at ...?
Pára em ...?   paa·ra eng ...

Please tell me when we get to ...
Por favor avise-me   poor fa·vor a·vee·ze·me
quando chegarmos   kwang·doo she·gaar·moosh
a ...   a ...

Please stop here.
Por favor pare aqui.   poor fa·vor paa·re a·kee

Where's (the station)?
Onde é (a estação)?   ong·de e (a shta·sowng)

What's the address?
Qual é o endereço?   kwaal e oo eng·de·re·soo

Can you show me (on the map)?
Pode-me mostrar   po·de·me moosh·traar
(no mapa)?   (noo maa·pa)

HAUSA

As one of the lingua francas of West Africa, Hausa is spoken by around 40 million people. For over half of these, Hausa is their first language. Most native speakers live in northern Nigeria and southern Niger, where Hausa is one of the national languages. It's also spoken in parts of Benin, Burkina Faso, Cameroon, Côte d'Ivoire and Ghana. In the past Hausa was written in a modified form of Arabic script, but since the early 19th century a slightly modified Roman alphabet is its official written form.

Hausa's glottalised consonants, represented in our pronunciation guides by an apostrophe after the letter (b', d', k', ts' and y'), are produced by tightening and releasing the space between the vocal cords; note that the sounds b' and d' have an extra twist – instead of breathing out, you breathe in. The apostrophe before a vowel (as in a'a) indicates a glottal stop (like the pause in 'uh-oh').

Hello.	Sannu.	san·nu
Goodbye.	Sai wani lokaci.	say wa·ni law·ka·chee
Yes.	I.	ee
No.	A'a.	a'a
Please.	Don Allah.	don al·laa
Thank you.	Na gode.	naa gaw·dey
Sorry.	Yi hak'uri.	yi ha·k'u·ree
Help!	Taimake ni!	tai·ma·kyey ni

Do you speak English?
Kana/Kina jin   ka·naa/ki·naa jin
turanci? (m/f)   too·ran·chee

I don't understand.		
Ban gane ba.	ban gaa·ney ba	
How much is it?		
Kud'insa nawa ne?	ku·d'in·sa na·wa ney	
Where are the toilets?		
Ina ban d'aki yake?	i·naa ban d'aa·kee yak·yey	

1	d'aya	d'a·ya
2	biyu	bi·yu
3	uku	u·ku
4	hud'u	hu·d'u
5	biyar	bi·yar
6	shida	shi·da
7	bakwai	bak·wai
8	takwas	tak·was
9	tara	ta·ra
10	goma	gaw·ma

WOLOF

Wolof is the lingua franca of Senegal (particularly the area north and east of Dakar and along the coast) and Gambia (the western regions), where it's spoken by about 80 percent of the population (eight million people) as a first or second language. It's also spoken on a smaller scale in the neighbouring countries of Mauritania, Mali and Guinea.

Note that in our pronunciation guides, the stressed syllables are in italics. Also, uh is pronounced as the 'a' in 'ago', kh is pronounced as the 'ch' in the Scottish loch and r is trilled.

Hello.	Salaam aleekum.	sa·laam a·ley·kum
Goodbye.	Mangi dem.	maan·gee dem
Yes.	Waaw.	waaw
No.	Déedéet.	dey·deyt
Please.	Bu la neexee.	boo la ney·khey
Thank you.	Jërejëf.	je·re·jef
Sorry.	Baal ma.	baal ma
Help!	Wóoy!	wohy

Do you speak English?		
Ndax dégg nga angale?	ndakh deg nguh an·ga·ley	
I don't understand.		
Dégguma.	deg·goo·ma	
How much is it?		
Ñaata lay jar?	nyaa·ta lai jar	
Where are the toilets?		
Ana wanag wi?	a·na wa·nak wee	

1	benn	ben
2	ñaar	nyaar
3	ñett	nyet
4	ñeent	nyeynt
5	juróom	joo·rohm
6	juróom benn	joo·rohm ben
7	juróom ñaar	joo·rohm nyaar
8	juróom ñett	joo·rohm nyet
9	juróom ñeent	joo·rohm nyeynt
10	fukk	fuk

YORUBA

Yoruba is one of the main lingua francas in the eastern part of West Africa and is spoken by around 25 million people. It is primarily used as a first language in southwestern Nigeria. There are also Yoruba speakers in Benin and eastern Togo, and a variety of the language is spoken in Sierra Leone.

Yoruba's nasal vowels, indicated in our pronunciation guides with ng after the vowel, are pronounced as if you're trying to force the sound through the nose.

Hello.	Pèlé o.	kpe·le o
Goodbye.	Ó dàbò.	oh da·bo
Yes.	Bééni.	be·e·ni
No.	Béékó.	be·e·ko
Please.	Jòwó.	jo·wo
Thank you.	Osé.	oh·shay
Sorry.	Má bìínú.	ma bi·i·nu
Help!	E ràn mí lówó o!	e rang mi lo·wo o

Do you speak English?		
Sé o ń so gèési?	shay o n so ge·e·si	
I don't understand.		
Èmi kò gbó.	ay·mi koh gbo	
How much is it?		
Èló ni?	ay·loh ni	
Where are the toilets?		
Ibo ni ilé igbònsè wà?	i·boh ni i·lay i·gbong·se wa	

1	òkan	o·kang
2	èjì	ay·ji
3	èta	e·ta
4	èrin	e·ring
5	àrun	a·rung
6	èfà	e·fa
7	èje	ay·jay
8	èjo	e·jo
9	èsan	e·sang
10	èwá	e·wa

GLOSSARY

The following is a list of words and acronyms used in this book that you are likely to come across in West Africa.

achaba – motorcycle taxi (northern Nigeria); see also *okada*

adinkra – handmade printed cloth from Ghana worn primarily by the Ashanti

Afrique Occidentale Française – see *French West Africa*

Afro-beat – a fusion of African music, jazz and soul originated and popularised by Fela Kuti of Nigeria; along with *juju* it's the most popular music in Nigeria

Akan – a major group of peoples along the south coast of West Africa; includes the Ashanti and Fanti peoples

akpeteshie – palm wine

akuaba – Ashanti carved figure

aluguer – for hire (sign in minibus)

animism – the base of virtually all traditional religions in Africa; the belief that there is a spirit in all natural things and that human spirits (ancestors) bestow protection

Asantehene – the king or supreme ruler of the Ashanti people

Ashanti – the largest tribal group in Ghana, concentrated around Kumasi

auberge – used in West Africa to mean any small hotel

autogare – see *gare routière*

bacalau – salted flakes of cod

bâché – covered pick-up ('ute') used as a basic bush taxi

balafon – xylophone

Bambara – Mali's major ethnic group found in the centre and south and famous for its wooden carvings

banco – bank; clay or mud used for building

Baoulé – an Akan-speaking people from Côte d'Ivoire with strong animist beliefs

Bobo – animist people of western Burkina Faso and southern Mali, famous for their mask traditions

bogolan cloth – often simply called mud-cloth, this is cotton cloth with designs painted on using various types of mud for colour; made by the Bambara of Mali but found throughout the region

boubou – the common name for the elaborate robe-like outfit worn by men and women

boukarous – open-sided, circular mud huts

brake – see *Peugeot taxi*

Bundu – Krio word for 'secret society'; used in Liberia and in certain parts of Sierra Leone and Côte d'Ivoire; includes the Poro society for men and the Sande for women; in Sierra Leone, the women's secret society is spelled Bondo

Burkinabé – adjective for Burkina Faso

bush taxi – along with buses, this is the most common form of public transport in West Africa; there are three main types of bush taxi: Peugeot taxi, minibus and pick-up (bâché)

buvette – refreshment stall

cadeau – gift, tip, bribe or handout, see also *dash*

campement – loosely translated as 'hostel', 'inn' or 'lodge', but it's not a camping ground (ie a place for tents, although some *campements* allow you to pitch tents); traditionally, *campements* offer simple accommodation

canoa – motor-canoe

car – large bus, see also *minicar*

carnet – document required if you are bringing a car into most countries of the region

car rapide – minibus, usually used in cities; often decrepit, may be fast or very slow

carrefour – literally 'crossroads', but also used to mean meeting place

carte jaune – vaccination certificate

case – hut

case à impluvium – huge round hut with a hole in the roof to collect rainwater

CFA – the West African franc (used in Benin, Burkina Faso, Côte d'Ivoire, Guinea-Bissau, Mali, Niger, Senegal and Togo) or Central African franc (Cameroon)

cidade – city

cinq-cent-quatre – 504; see *Peugeot taxi*

climatisée – air-conditioned; often shortened to 'clim'

coladeiras – old-style music; romantic, typically sentimental upbeat love songs

commissariat – police station

compteur – meter in taxi

correios – post office

couchette – sleeping berth on a train

croix d'Agadez – Tuareg talisman that protects its wearer from the 'evil eye'

Dan – an animist people living in western Côte d'Ivoire and Liberia with strong mask traditions

Dahomey – pre-independence name of Benin

dash – bribe or tip (noun); also used as a verb, 'You dash me something...'

déplacement – a taxi or boat that you 'charter' for yourself

djembe – type of drum

Dogon – people found in Mali, east of Mopti; famous for their cliff dwellings, cosmology and arts

durbar – ceremony or celebration, usually involving a cavalry parade, found, for example, in the Muslim northern Nigerian states

Ecowas – Economic Community of West African States

Eid al-Fitr – feast to celebrate the end of Ramadan

Eid al-Kabir – see *Tabaski*

Empire of Ghana – one of the great Sahel empires that flourished in the 8th to 11th centuries AD and covered much of present-day Mali and parts of Senegal

Empire of Mali – Islamic Sahel empire that was at its peak in the 14th century, covering the region between present-day Senegal and Niger

essence – petrol (gas) for car

Ewe – Forest-dwelling people of Ghana and Togo

fado – haunting melancholy blues-style Portuguese music

fanals – large lanterns; also the processions during which the lanterns are carried through the streets

Fanti – part of the Akan group of people based along the coast in southwest Ghana and Côte d'Ivoire; traditionally fishing people and farmers

fête – festival

fêtes des masques – ceremony with masks

fetish – sacred objects or talismans in traditional religions, sometimes called 'charms'

fiche – form (to complete)

Foulbé – see *Fula*

French West Africa – area of West and Central Africa acquired by France at the Berlin Conference in 1884–85 which divided Africa up between the European powers; 'Afrique Occidentale Française' in French

Fula – a people spread widely through West Africa, mostly nomadic cattle herders; also known as 'Fulani', 'Peul' or 'Foulbé'

fula-fula – converted truck or pick-up; rural public transport

funaná – distinctive fast-paced music with a Latin rhythm that's great for dancing; usually features players on the accordion and tapping with metal

gara – a thin cotton material, tie-dyed or stamp-printed, with bright colours and bold patterns

garage – bush taxi and bus park

gare lagunaire – lagoon ferry terminal

gare maritime – ferry terminal

gare routière – bus and bush-taxi station, also called 'gare voiture' or 'autogare'

gare voiture – see *gare routière*

gasoil – diesel fuel

gelli-gelli – minibus in The Gambia

gendarmerie – police station/post

gîte – used interchangeably in West Africa with *auberge* and *campement*

Gold Coast – pre-independence name for modern state of Ghana

Grain Coast – old name for Liberia

griot – traditional caste of musicians or praise singers; many of West Africa's music stars come from *griot* families

Hausa – people originally from northern Nigeria and southern Niger, mostly farmers and traders

highlife – a style of music, originating in Ghana, combining West African and Western influences

hôtel de ville – town hall

ibeji – Yoruba carved twin figures

IDP – International Driving Permit

Igbo – one of the three major peoples in Nigeria, concentrated predominantly in the southeast

IGN – Institut Géographique National

IMF – International Monetary Fund

immeuble – large building, for example, office block

impluvium – large round traditional house with roof constructed to collect rain water in central tank or bowl

insha'allah – God willing, ie hopefully (Arabic, but used by Muslims in Africa)

jardim – garden

jeli – see *griot*

juju – the music style characterised by tight vocal harmonies and sophisticated guitar work, backed by traditional drums and percussion; very popular in southern Nigeria, especially with the Yoruba; see also *voodoo*

kente cloth – made with finely woven cotton, and sometimes silk, by Ghana's Ashanti people

Kingdom of Benin – one of the great West African kingdoms (13th to 19th centuries); based in Nigeria around Benin City and famous for its bronze or brass

kora – harp-like musical instrument with over 20 strings

Lobi – people based in southwest Burkina Faso and northern Côte d'Ivoire, famous for their figurative sculpture and compounds known as *soukala*

lorry park – see *motor park*

luttes – traditional wrestling matches

macaco – monkey; a popular meat dish in upcountry Guinea-Bissau

mairie – town hall; mayor's office

maison d'hôte – small hotel or guesthouse

makossa – Cameroonian musical form that fuses Highlife and soul

malafa – crinkly voile material worn as a veil by women in Mauritania

Malinké – Guinea's major ethnic group, the people are also found in southern Mali, northwestern Côte d'Ivoire and eastern Senegal; closely related to the Bambara and famous for founding the Empire of Mali; also related to the Mandinka

Mandinka – people based in central and northern Gambia and Senegal; also the name of their language, which is closely related to Malinké; both Malinké and Mandinka are part of the wider Manding group

maquis – rustic open-air restaurant; traditionally open only at night

marché – market

mbalax – percussion-driven, Senegalese dance music

mercado – market

minicar – minibus

Moors – also called 'Maurs'; the predominant nomadic people of Mauritania, now also well known as merchants and found scattered over French-speaking West Africa

mornas – old-style music; mournful and sad, similar to the Portuguese *fado* style from whence they may have originated

Moro-Naba – the king of the Mossi people

Mossi – the people who occupy the central area of Burkina Faso and comprise about half the population of that country

motor park – bus and bush-taxi park (English-speaking countries); also called 'lorry park'

moto-taxi – motorcycle taxi

Mourides – the most powerful of the Islamic brotherhoods in Senegal

mud-cloth – see *bogolan cloth*

oba – a Yoruba chief or king

occasion – a lift or place in a car or bus (often shortened to 'occas')

okada – motorcycle taxi

oni – chief priest

orchestra – in West Africa, this means a group playing popular music

paillote – a thatched sun shelter (usually on a beach or around an open-air bar-restaurant)

palava – meeting place

paletuviers – mangroves

pam-pah – large cargo/passenger boats (Sierra Leone)

paragem – bus and bush-taxi park

patron – owner, boss

pensão – hotel or guesthouse

pension – simple hotel or hostel, or 'board'

Peugeot taxi – one of the main types of bush taxi; also called 'brake', 'cinq-cent-quatre', 'Peugeot 504' or *sept place*

Peul – see *Fula*

pinasse – large *pirogue*, usually used on rivers, for hauling people and cargo

pirogue – traditional canoe, either a small dugout or large,

narrow sea-going wooden fishing boat

pharmacie de garde – all-night pharmacy

piste – track or dirt road

poda-poda – minibus

posuban – ensemble of statues representing a proverb or event in Fanti culture

pousada – guesthouse

praça – park or square

praia – beach

préfecture – police headquarters

PTT – post (and often telephone) office in Francophone countries

Ramadan – Muslim month of fasting

residencial – guest house

rond-point – roundabout

rua – street

Sahel – dry semi-desert and savannah area south of the Sahara desert; most of Senegal, The Gambia, Mali, Burkina Faso and Niger; the name means 'coast' in Arabic

Scramble for Africa – term used for the land-grabbing frenzy in the 1880s by the European powers in which France, Britain and Germany laid claim to various parts of the continent

Senoufo – a strongly animist people straddling Côte d'Ivoire, Burkina Faso and Mali

sept place – Peugeot taxi seven-seater (usually carrying up to 12 people)

sharia – Muslim law

Songhaï – ethnic group located primarily in northeastern Mali and western Niger along the Niger River; also Empire of Songhaï which ruled the Sahel with its heyday in the 15th century

soukala – a castle-like housing compound of the Lobi tribe found in the Bouna area of southern Burkina Faso

spirale antimostique – mosquito coil

sûreté – police station

syndicat d'initiative – tourist information office

Tabaski – Eid al-Kabir; also known as the Great Feast, this is the most important celebration throughout West Africa

taguelmoust – shawl or scarf worn as headgear by Tuareg men

tama – hand-held drum

tata somba – a castle-like house of the Batammariba tribe who live in northwestern Benin and Togo

taxi brousse – bush taxi

taxi-course – shared taxi (in cities)

taxi-moto – see *moto-taxi*

télécentre – privately run telecommunications centres

tikit – traditional thatched stone hut used as accommodation in Mauritania

toca-toca – small minibus in Bissau

totem – used in traditional religions, similar to a fetish

town trip – private hire (taxi)

tro-tro – a minibus or pick-up

Tuareg – nomadic descendants of the North African Berbers; found all over the Sahara, especially in Mali, Niger and southern Algeria

voodoo – the worship of spirits with supernatural powers widely practised in southern Benin and Togo; also called *juju*

vu gbe – **talking drums**

wassoulou – singing style made famous by Mali's Oumou Sangaré

WHO – World Health Organization

Wolof – Senegal's major ethnic group; also found in The Gambia

woro-woro – minibus

Yoruba – a major ethnic group concentrated in southwestern Nigeria

zemi-john – motorcycle-taxi

Behind the Scenes

SEND US YOUR FEEDBACK

We love to hear from travellers – your comments keep us on our toes and help make our books better. Our well-travelled team reads every word on what you loved or loathed about this book. Although we cannot reply individually to postal submissions, we always guarantee that your feedback goes straight to the appropriate authors, in time for the next edition. Each person who sends us information is thanked in the next edition – the most useful submissions are rewarded with a selection of digital PDF chapters.

Visit **lonelyplanet.com/contact** to submit your updates and suggestions or to ask for help. Our award-winning website also features inspirational travel stories, news and discussions.

Note: We may edit, reproduce and incorporate your comments in Lonely Planet products such as guidebooks, websites and digital products, so let us know if you don't want your comments reproduced or your name acknowledged. For a copy of our privacy policy visit lonelyplanet.com/privacy.

OUR READERS

Many thanks to the travellers who used the last edition and wrote to us with helpful hints, useful advice and interesting anecdotes:

Tayo Akanni, Omar Alikaj, Dan Arenson, Bo Banks, Jack Beven, Iain Bisset, Suvi Brown, Jeroen Bruggeman, Lucky Burchett, Luke Cape, Lauren Carter, Vlaďka Chvátalová, Christine Cooper, Paul Costello, David Curran, Philippe De Roover, Grigorios Delichristos, Sumudu Dhanapala, Juergen Ditz, Lee Dobbs, Dagmar Dohr, Heinz Effertz, Lars Elle, Katy Ferrar, Kennet Fischer, Danny Fitzgerald, Kari Foley, Kelly Foster, Nicolas Fournier, Kathleen Fowler, Eddie Fox, Lucy Fulton, Anne-catherine Geerinckx, Marcin Grabiec, Persephone Harrington, Jonathan Harris, Steff Hazlehurst, Jessica Henry, Lauren Herwehe, Nakajima Hideaki, Frida Hoekman, Nynke Hofstra, Priska Jeuch, Timothy Johnston, Hannah Jones, Peter Kargaard, Erin Kieffer, Melissa Klar, Karen Kort, Ulrich Kröll, Rommert Kruithof, Anne Langdji, Stephany Laperriere, Mark Latchford, Rena Leore, Miguel Machado, Porshia Mack, Finn Mackenzie, Eythor Magnusson, Kian Marius Kottke, Guy Mccollum, Nicola Muehlig, Nicola Mühlig, Piers Newberry, René Olde Olthof, Dahlia Olinsky, Simon Paltere, Achim Pfriender, Bernard Pollack, Joshua Posen, Kate Rawlings, Anton Rijsdijk, Tina Röbel, David Roberts, Tim Rohe, Antti Saarela, Brigitte Schumann, Wanda Serkowska, Leticia Sevillano, Federica Seymandi, Kourtney Smienthree, Robert Sobotta, Lindsay Songstad, Pamela Spears, Monique Teggelove, Jonathan Thompson, Peter Tjallinks, Gregg Tully, Samantha Turay, Marc Van Der Stock, Michiel Van Agt, Liesbeth Vanzeir, Paul Vialard, Katrin Voelter, Julie Wang, Philipp Weckenbrock, Ryan Wilber, Craig Wirick, Emily Yost.

AUTHOR THANKS

Anthony Ham

Sincere thanks to all of those who have made West Africa such a special place for me to visit throughout the years. Special thanks to Jan and Ron, and to my three girls Marina, Carlota and Valentina: *Os quiero con todo mi corazon.* My work on this book is dedicated to Azima Ag Mohamed Ali – I hope you can return home soon, my friend.

Jean-Bernard Carillet

A huge thanks to everyone who made this trip a pure joy, including Arno, Gautier, Dominique, Julien, Myriam and all the travellers I met while on the road. I'm also grateful to my fellow author Émilie for her tips, and to Anthony Ham, coordinating author extraordinaire. And finally, once again a *gros bisou* to Christine and Eva.

Paul Clammer

There are always too many friends in Morocco to acknowledge everyone, but a particular thanks this time to Kerstin Brand in Marrakesh, Robert Johnstone in Fez and Alia Radman for being a hostess for Eid. In Mauritania, big thanks to Melissa Nielson Andersson and Natsuko Sawaya, Cora at Bab Sahara, and to my driver in the Adrar, Jid Moma.

Emilie Filou

Thanks to all the travellers, tourism professionals and friends who chipped in with recommendations, shared a meal or a *taxi-brousse* ride and were part of the journey – there are simply too many to name here. And thank you to my husband Adolfo for putting up with this crazy life.

Nana Luckham

Thanks to Patrick Smith, Reuben Swift and Yaa Yeboah.

Tom Masters

A huge debt of thanks to Rosemary Masters, who came to Africa for the first time in her 60s and proved to be an amazing travelling companion. She never lost her sense of humour despite illness, bad weather and lots of long journeys. Enormous thanks also to Niall Cowley, whose company and high spirits in Cameroon were unforgettable, whether driving down the worst roads I've ever been on, befriending the mayor of Kumba, or surviving a night in a hotel in Wum without first eating fish from a plastic bag. Grids!

Anja Mutić

Obrigada, Hoji, for coming along for the ride and making it more fun. A huge thanks to Samira and her crowd in Mindelo, who made me fall in love with the city. Special thanks go to Cristiano and Larissa on Boa Vista, Kate on Santo Antão and Patti for being a great connector. Finally, to my always-laughing mum and the inspiring memory of my father.

Caroline Sieg

Thanks to everyone who took the time to share their tips with me and for the countless friendly conversations at waterside bars across The Gambia and Senegal. And a very special *merci* to Gilles in Dakar for some sensational nights out on the town.

Kate Thomas

A big *obrigada* to everyone who helped out in the *terra sabi* (delicious land) of Guinea-Bissau, especially Matt Boslego, Holly Pickett (for her company on the tough road to Varela), Brian King, Ze Manel, Amelia 'Betty' Gomes, Aicha and Bassiro Djalo, the Mama Djombos and the extended Djalo-King clan. Thanks to Lassana Cassama, Gorka Gamarra and, on the island of Bolama, to Felipa and to Queba Dabo for such a warm welcome. In lovely Liberia, special thanks to Othello Garblah, Saad Karim (for his company and couch), Saki Golafale, taximan Alpha, Chawki Bsaibes and Jamal. In Sierra Leone, Fid Thompson's help was invaluable. Thank you Fid! Shout-outs also to Koumba Jalloh, Aminata Seye, Nelson Gbarpor and Faty Serif. On the road in Côte d'Ivoire, thanks to Hortense and Franck, Amie 'Rainbow', David Diallo and Tessa, for fun had on our foodie tours of

THIS BOOK

This 8th edition of Lonely Planet's *West Africa* guidebook was researched and written by Anthony Ham (coordinating author), Jean-Bernard Carillet, Paul Clammer, Emilie Filou, Nana Luckham, Tom Masters, Anja Mutić, Caroline Sieg, Kate Thomas and Vanessa Wruble, and Jane Cornwell wrote the Music chapter. The previous edition was also coordinated by Anthony Ham.

This guidebook was commissioned in Lonely Planet's Melbourne office, and produced by the following:

Commissioning Editors William Gourlay, Glenn van der Knijff

Coordinating Editors Briohny Hooper, Tasmin Waby

Senior Cartographer Jennifer Johnston

Coordinating Layout Designer Jacqui Saunders

Managing Editors Brigitte Ellemor, Bruce Evans, Angela Tinson

Managing Cartographer Adrian Persoglia

Managing Layout Designer Jane Hart

Assisting Editors Sarah Bailey, Penny Cordner, Victoria Harrison, Kate James, Shawn Low, Anne Mason, Anne Mulvaney, Ross Taylor, Jeanette Wall

Cartographers Valeska Cañas, Julie Dodkins, Xavier Di Toro

Assisting Layout Designer Adrian Blackburn

Cover Research Naomi Parker

Internal Image Research David Nelson

Language Content Branislava Vladisavljevic

Thanks to Shahara Ahmed, Laura Crawford, Ryan Evans, Larissa Frost, Genesys India, Jouve India, Annelies Mertens, Trent Paton, Dianne Schallmeiner, Kerrianne Southway, Gerard Walker

Abidjan. Thanks to all the wonderful people I've known in six years' worth of time and trips to a region that I consider home, West Africa.

Vanessa Wruble

Many thanks to my excellent research assistant David Idagu, the amazingly generous Lemi Ghariokwu, Rikki Stein (and Captain!), Yeni, Femi and Seun Kuti (and Osaro, Shigogo, Patches and Vibes), Obi Asika, Osahon Akpata, Azu Nwagbogu and AAF, Chike Nwagbogu Nike Davies-Okundaye, Robin Campbell, everyone at Pandrillus, Glenna Gordon, Ruth McDowall, Raphael Ayukotang, Vincent Taibi (in absentia), Lost In Lagos, and the dude who took me to the pharmacy.

ACKNOWLEDGMENTS

Climate map data adapted from Peel MC, Finlayson BL & McMahon TA (2007) 'Updated World Map of the Köppen-Geiger Climate Classification', *Hydrology and Earth System Sciences*, 11, 163344.

Cover photograph: Traditionally painted flat-roofed mud house, Ghana, Ariadne Van Zandbergen/Alamy.

Index

Map Legend

Sights
- Beach
- Bird Sanctuary
- Buddhist
- Castle/Palace
- Christian
- Confucian
- Hindu
- Islamic
- Jain
- Jewish
- Monument
- Museum/Gallery/Historic Building
- Ruin
- Sento Hot Baths/Onsen
- Shinto
- Sikh
- Taoist
- Winery/Vineyard
- Zoo/Wildlife Sanctuary
- Other Sight

Activities, Courses & Tours
- Bodysurfing
- Diving/Snorkelling
- Canoeing/Kayaking
- Course/Tour
- Skiing
- Snorkelling
- Surfing
- Swimming/Pool
- Walking
- Windsurfing
- Other Activity

Sleeping
- Sleeping
- Camping

Eating
- Eating

Drinking & Nightlife
- Drinking & Nightlife
- Cafe

Entertainment
- Entertainment

Shopping
- Shopping

Information
- Bank
- Embassy/Consulate
- Hospital/Medical
- Internet
- Police
- Post Office
- Telephone
- Toilet
- Tourist Information
- Other Information

Geographic
- Beach
- Hut/Shelter
- Lighthouse
- Lookout
- Mountain/Volcano
- Oasis
- Park
- Pass
- Picnic Area
- Waterfall

Population
- Capital (National)
- Capital (State/Province)
- City/Large Town
- Town/Village

Transport
- Airport
- Border crossing
- Bus
- Cable car/Funicular
- Cycling
- Ferry
- Metro station
- Monorail
- Parking
- Petrol station
- Subway station
- Taxi
- Train station/Railway
- Tram
- Underground station
- Other Transport

Note: Not all symbols displayed above appear on the maps in this book

Routes
- Tollway
- Freeway
- Primary
- Secondary
- Tertiary
- Lane
- Unsealed road
- Road under construction
- Plaza/Mall
- Steps
- Tunnel
- Pedestrian overpass
- Walking Tour
- Walking Tour detour
- Path/Walking Trail

Boundaries
- International
- State/Province
- Disputed
- Regional/Suburb
- Marine Park
- Cliff
- Wall

Hydrography
- River, Creek
- Intermittent River
- Canal
- Water
- Dry/Salt/Intermittent Lake
- Reef

Areas
- Airport/Runway
- Beach/Desert
- Cemetery (Christian)
- Cemetery (Other)
- Glacier
- Mudflat
- Park/Forest
- Sight (Building)
- Sportsground
- Swamp/Mangrove

Nana Luckham

Guinea, Niger Born in Tanzania to a Ghanaian mother and an English father, Nana started life criss-crossing Africa by plane and then bumping along the roughest of roads. After working as an editor in London and as a United Nations press officer in New York, she became a full-time travel writer. Since then she has hauled her backpack all over Africa researching guidebooks to destinations such as Algeria, Kenya, South Africa, Malawi, Ghana and Benin.

Read more about Nana at:
lonelyplanet.com/members/NanaLuckham

Tom Masters

Cameroon Tom is a Berlin-based writer and photographer whose work has taken him to some of the strangest and most challenging countries on earth. Having covered Liberia and Niger for the last edition of *West Africa*, Tom was very happy to head to the equator for the relative ease of Cameroon. This time round Limbe, the Ring Road villages and sticky Douala all worked their magic on him. Tom can be found online at www.tommasters.net.

Read more about Tom at:
lonelyplanet.com/members/TomMasters

Anja Mutić

Cape Verde Croatian-born, New York–based Anja swayed to the infectious rhythms of Cape Verdean music long before she ever visited the archipelago. For this book, she spent several weeks braving prop planes, scary volcano climbs and rough ocean crossings to find the islands' best-kept secrets. She left the country charmed with the *morabeza* (hospitality) of its people and finally understood *sodade*, the bittersweet longing that Cesária Évora sang about. Anja is online at www.everthenomad.com.

Read more about Anja at:
lonelyplanet.com/members/AnjaMutic

Caroline Sieg

Gambia, Senegal Caroline is a half-Swiss, half-American writer, editor and digital content manager based in Berlin. Her relationship with Africa began when she first visited Senegal years ago and fell in love with *mbalax* music and the architecture of Saint-Louis. She was delighted to return, wear her travel writer's cap and cover it for Lonely Planet.

Read more about Caroline at:
lonelyplanet.com/members/CarolineSieg

Kate Thomas

Cote d'Ivoire, Guinea-Bissau, Liberia, Mali, Sierra Leone After Kate's first trip to Liberia in 2007, she was so taken by the destination that she left her job and moved there for two years. Since then she's combined travel writing with reporting on Africa, covering the fallout of conflicts in Mali and Libya and exploring rainforests, cities and lonely islands. While researching this edition, she ate oysters on the beaches of Guinea-Bissau and experienced music, dancing, thirsty taxi rides, hungry political debate and popped tyres. After six years in the region, today Kate is mostly based in the seaside city of Dakar.

Vanessa Wruble

Nigeria When not writing for Lonely Planet, Vanessa runs Okayafrica, a website and lifestyle company started by the legendary hip-hop band The Roots, which showcases new African music, art and culture. She has previously been a freelance writer, a humanitarian aid worker, a TV correspondent/producer, an interactive artist and, of course, a world traveller. She holds two (somewhat useless) master's degrees (Psychology and Interactive Media), and dreams of living on a tropical beach. You'll currently find her in Brooklyn.

Contributing Authors

Jane Cornwell is an Australian-born, UK-based journalist, author and broadcaster, who wrote the African Music chapter. After graduating with a master's degree in anthropology, she left for London. She currently writes about arts, books and music – most notably world music – for a range of UK and antipodean publications, including the *Times*, *Evening Standard* and the *Australian* newspaper. She regularly travels about the planet interviewing world musicians.

OUR STORY

A beat-up old car, a few dollars in the pocket and a sense of adventure. In 1972 that's all Tony and Maureen Wheeler needed for the trip of a lifetime – across Europe and Asia overland to Australia. It took several months, and at the end – broke but inspired – they sat at their kitchen table writing and stapling together their first travel guide, *Across Asia on the Cheap*. Within a week they'd sold 1500 copies. Lonely Planet was born.

Today, Lonely Planet has offices in Melbourne, London and Oakland, with more than 600 staff and writers. We share Tony's belief that 'a great guidebook should do three things: inform, educate and amuse'.

OUR WRITERS

Anthony Ham

Coordinating Author Anthony has been travelling around Africa for more than a decade. A writer and photographer, his past Lonely Planet guidebooks include *Kenya*, *Botswana & Namibia*, *Africa*, *Libya* and three previous editions of *West Africa*. Anthony has written and photographed for magazines and newspapers around the world, among them *Travel Africa* and *Africa Geographic*. When he's not in Africa, Anthony divides his time between Madrid and Melbourne, where he lives with his wife and two daughters. Anthony wrote the Plan Your Trip, Understand and Survival Guide chapters.

Read more about Anthony at:
lonelyplanet.com/members/Anthony_Ham

Jean-Bernard Carillet

Benin, Togo A Paris-based journalist and photographer, Jean-Bernard has travelled the breadth and length of Africa for more than two decades and has been thoroughly enlightened by 23 of its amazing countries. Highlights while researching this edition include investigating voodoo culture in Ouidah and Abomey, learning fishing techniques on Lake Ahémé and looking for photogenic waterfalls near Kpalimé. Jean-Bernard's wanderlust has taken him to six continents and inspired numerous articles and his writing of some 30 guidebooks, including Lonely Planet's *Africa* and *Ethiopia, Djibouti & Somaliland*.

Paul Clammer

Mauritania, Morocco Paul has contributed to more than 25 Lonely Planet guidebooks, including several editions of *Morocco*, where he's also worked as a tour guide. He arrived in Nouakchott for his second stint as a Mauritanian author and was researching during the uncertain period after the accidental shooting of the president. Find him at www.paulclammer.com; he tweets at @paulclammer.

Read more about Paul at:
lonelyplanet.com/members/PaulClammer

Emilie Filou

Burkina Faso, Ghana Emilie first travelled to Africa at age eight to visit her grandparents who had taken up a late career opportunity in Mali. More visits ensued, including an epic family holiday in Togo and Benin, the highlight of which was the beautiful and amusingly named town of Grand Popo ('big poo' in French was simply hilarious when you were aged 10). Emilie is now a freelance journalist specialising in business and development issues in Africa. Her website is www.emiliefilou.com; she tweets at @EmilieFilou.

Read more about Emilie at:
lonelyplanet.com/members/EmilieFilou

OVER MORE
PAGE WRITERS

Published by Lonely Planet Publications Pty Ltd
ABN 36 005 607 983
8th edition – Sep 2013
ISBN 978 1 74179 797 8
© Lonely Planet 2013   Photographs © as indicated 2013
10 9 8 7 6 5 4 3 2 1
Printed in China

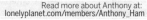